# A-Z LEEDS and BRADFORD

CW00531638

## CONTENTS

## REFERENCE

| | | | | |
|---|---|---|---|---|
| Motorway | **M1** | Map Continuation | **85** | Large Scale City Centre **4** |
| Proposed | | Car Park | | **P** |
| A Road | **A61** | Church or Chapel | | † |
| Under Construction | | Fire Station | | ■ |
| Proposed | | House Numbers — A & B Roads only | | 13 / 8 |
| B Road | **B6157** | Hospital | | **H** |
| Dual Carriageway | | Information Centre | | **i** |
| One Way Street — Traffic flow on A Roads is indicated by a heavy line on the driver's left. | | National Grid Reference | | $^4$30 |
| | | Police Station | | ▲ |
| Large Scale Pages Only | → | Post Office | | ★ |
| Pedestrianized Road | | Toilet | | ▽ |
| Restricted Access | | with facilities for the Disabled | | ♿ |
| City Centre Loop — Large Scale Pages Only | → ① → | Viewpoint | | ⁂ ※ |
| Residential Walkway | | Educational Establishment | | |
| Track / Footpath | | Hospital or Health Centre | | |
| Local Authority Boundary | | Industrial Building | | |
| Posttown Boundary | | Leisure or Recreational Facility | | |
| Postcode Boundary | | Place of Interest | | |
| Railway — Station, Private Sta., Level Crossing, Tunnel | | Public Building | | |
| | | Shopping Centre or Market | | |
| Built Up Area | ALMA ST. | Other Selected Buildings | | |

## SCALE

| Map Pages 8-145 | Map Pages 4-7 |
|---|---|
| 1:14908 (4¼ inches to 1 mile) 5.4cm to 1km | 1:7454 (8½ inches to 1 mile) 10.8cm to 1km |
| 0 — ¼ — ½ Mile | 0 — ⅛ — ¼ Mile |
| 0 250 500 750 Metres | 0 100 200 300 Metres |

## Geographers' A-Z Map Company Ltd.

Head Office:
Fairfield Road, Borough Green, Sevenoaks, Kent, TN15 8PP
Telephone 01732 781000

Showrooms:
44 Gray's Inn Road, London, WC1X 8HX
Telephone 0171 440 9500

Based upon the Ordnance Survey mapping with the permission of the Controller of Her Majesty's Stationery Office.

© Crown Copyright (399000).

Edition 1 1999
Copyright © Geographers' A-Z Map Co. Ltd. 1999

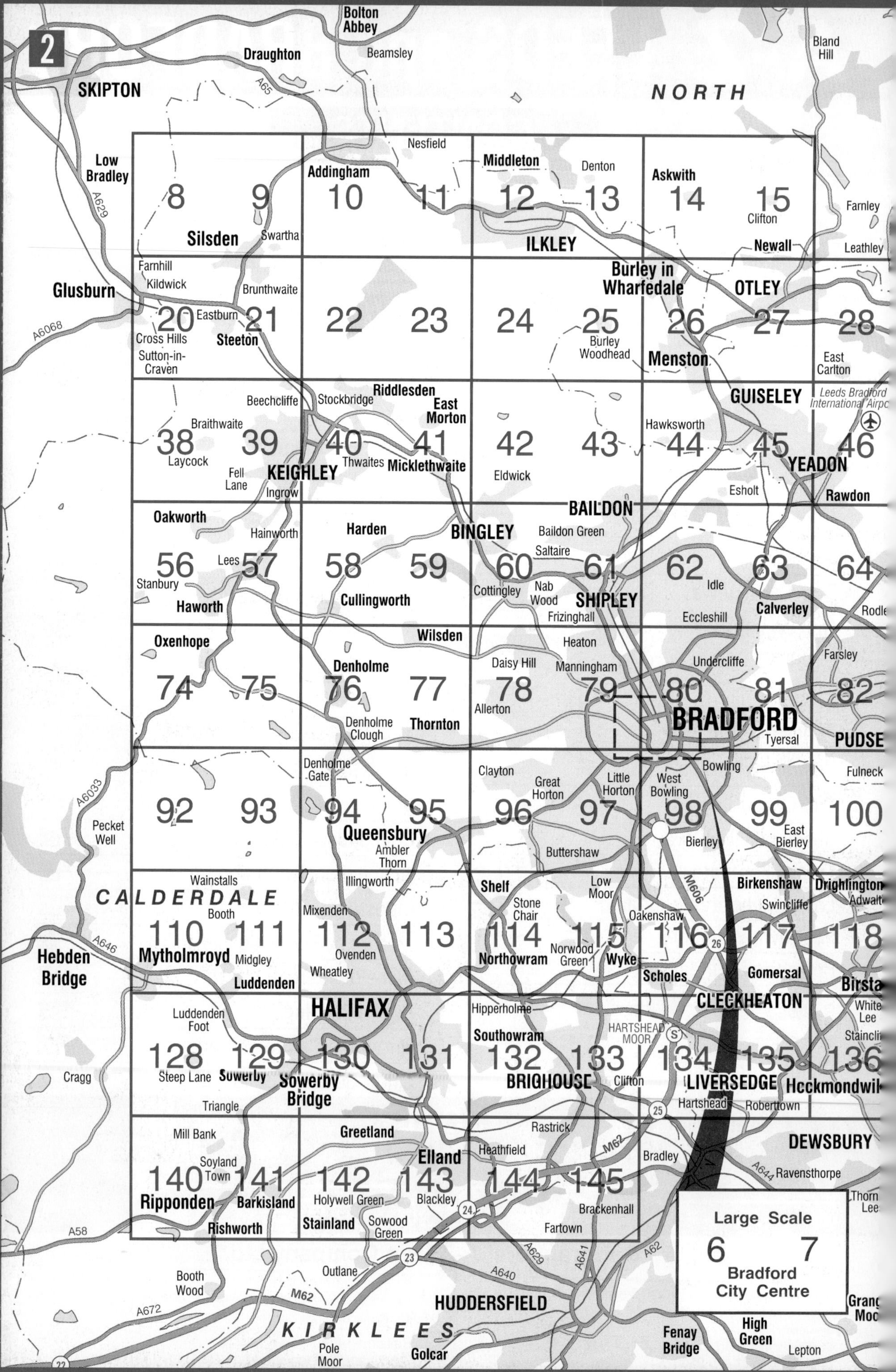

**2**

NORTH

SKIPTON

Draughton · Bolton Abbey · Beamsley · Bland Hill

Low Bradley **8** **9** Nesfield · Addingham **10** **11** Middleton **12** Denton **13** Askwith **14** **15** Farnley

Silsden · Swartha · ILKLEY · Clifton · Newall · Leathley

Glusburn · Farnhill · Kildwick · Brunthwaite · Burley in Wharfedale · OTLEY

**20** Eastburn **21** **22** **23** **24** **25** **26** **27** **28**

Cross Hills · Steeton · Sutton-in-Craven · Burley Woodhead · Menston · East Carlton

Beechcliffe · Stockbridge · Riddlesden · East Morton · GUISELEY · Leeds Bradford International Airport

Braithwaite **38** **39** **40** **41** **42** **43** Hawksworth **44** **45** **46**

Laycock · Fell Lane · KEIGHLEY · Thwaites · Micklethwaite · Eldwick · YEADON · Esholt · Rawdon

Ingrow · BAILDON

Oakworth · Hainworth · Harden · BINGLEY · Baildon Green

**56** Lees **57** **58** **59** **60** Saltaire **61** **62** **63** **64**

Stanbury · Cottingley · Nab Wood · SHIPLEY · Idle · Calverley · Rodle

Haworth · Cullingworth · Frizinghall · Eccleshill

Oxenhope · Wilsden · Heaton · Undercliffe · Farsley

**74** **75** Denholme **76** **77** Daisy Hill **78** **79** **80** **81** **82**

Manningham · BRADFORD · Tyersal · PUDSE

Allerton · Denholme Clough · Thornton · Fulneck

Denholme Gate · Clayton · Great Horton · Little Horton · West Bowling · Bowling

**92** **93** **94** **95** **96** **97** **98** **99** **100**

Pecket Well · Queensbury · Ambler Thorn · Buttershaw · Bierley · East Bierley

Wainstalls · Illingworth · Shelf · Low Moor · Birkenshaw · Drighlington

CALDERDALE · Booth · Mixenden · Stone Chair · Oakenshaw · Swincliffe · Adwalt

**110** **111** **112** **113** **114** **115** **116** **117** **118**

Hebden Bridge · Mytholmroyd · Midgley · Ovenden · Wheatley · Northowram · Norwood Green · Wyke · Scholes · Gomersal · CLECKHEATON · Birsta

Luddenden · Hipperholme · White Lee · Staincli

Luddenden Foot · HALIFAX · Southowram · HARTSHEAD MOOR

**128** **129** **130** **131** **132** **133** **134** **135** **136**

Cragg · Steep Lane · Sowerby · Sowerby Bridge · BRIGHOUSE · Clifton · LIVERSEDGE · Heckmondwi

Triangle · Hartshead · Roberttown · DEWSBURY

Mill Bank · Greetland · Rastrick · Heathfield · Bradley · Ravensthorpe

Soyland Town **140** **141** **142** **143** Elland **144** **145** · Thorn Lee

Ripponden · Barkisland · Holywell Green · Blackley · Brackenhall · Fartown

Rishworth · Stainland · Sowood Green · Grang Moo

Booth Wood · Outlane · HUDDERSFIELD · Fenay Bridge · High Green · Lepton

KIRKLEES · Pole Moor · Golcar

**Large Scale**
**6** **7**
**Bradford City Centre**

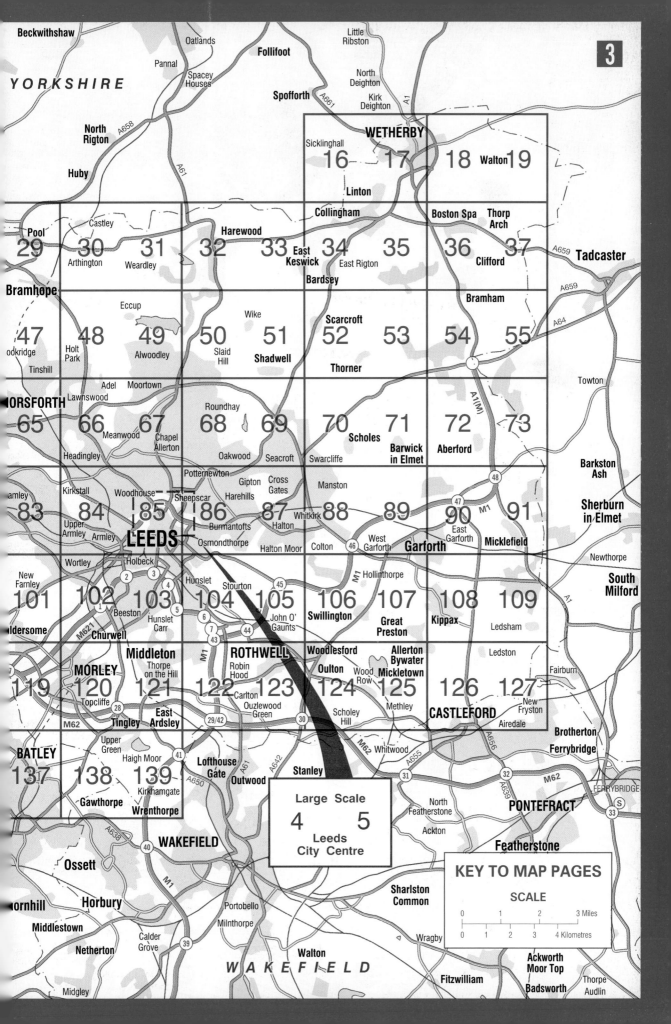

**3**

YORKSHIRE

Beckwithshaw
Oatlands
Pannal
Spacey Houses
Follifoot
Little Ribston
North Deighton
Kirk Deighton
Spofforth
A661
A1

**WETHERBY**

North Rigton
Huby
A658
A61

Sicklinghall
**16**  **17**  **18**  Walton **19**

Linton

Collingham
Boston Spa
Thorp Arch

Pool
**29**
Castley
**30**
Weardley
**31**
Arthington
Harewood
**32**
**33** East Keswick
**34** East Rigton
**35**
Boston Spa **36** Clifford
**37**
A659 Tadcaster

Bramhope

Bardsey

A659

A64

Bramham

Eccup
Wike
Scarcroft

ookridge
**47**
Holt Park
**48**
Alwoodley
**49**
**50** Slaid Hill
Shadwell **51**
**52**
**53**
Thorner
Bramham **54**  **55**

Tinshill

Adel  Moortown
Roundhay

A1(M)

Towton

ORSFORTH
Lawnswood
**65**
Meanwood **66**
Chapel Allerton **67**
**68**
**69**
Oakwood  Seacroft
**70**
Scholes
**71**
Barwick in Elmet
**72**
Aberford
**73**

Headingley

Swarcliffe

Barkston Ash

Potternewton
Gipton  Cross Gates
Manston

48

Sherburn in Elmet

amley
Kirkstall
Woodhouse
**83**  **84**
Upper Armley  Armley
Sheepscar
**85**  **86**
Burmantofts
Harehills
**87** Whitkirk
Halton
**88**
**89**
West Garforth
**90** East Garforth
**91**
Mickledfield

47

M1

**LEEDS**
Osmondthorpe
Halton Moor
Colton
46
Garforth

Newthorpe

New Farnley
**101**
Wortley
Holbeck
**102**
2
Beeston
**103**
3
4
Hunslet
**104**
5
Stourton
**105**
45
John O' Gaunts
**106**
Swillington
**107**
Hollinthorpe
**108**
Kippax
**109**
Ledsham

South Milford

A1

ldersome
M621
Churwell
1
Hunslet Carr
6
7
43
44

M1

Woodlesford

Ledston

Fairburn

Middleton
**119**
MORLEY
**120**
Thorpe on the Hill
**121**
**122**
Robin Hood
Carlton
Ouzlewood Green
**123**
**124**
Oulton
Wood Row
Allerton Bywater
Mickletown
**125**
Methley
**126**
Ledston
**127**
New Fryston

Topcliffe
28
M62
Tingley
East Ardsley
29/42
30
Scholey Hill
**CASTLEFORD**
Airedale

Brotherton
Ferrybridge

BATLEY
Upper Green
Haigh Moor
41
Lofthouse Gate
Outwood
A61
A650
A642
Stanley
31
Whitwood
A655
A656
M62
FERRYBRIDGE

**137**
**138** Gawthorpe
**139** Kirkhamgate
Wrenthorpe
A638

Large Scale
**4**  **5**
Leeds City Centre

North Featherstone
Ackton

**PONTEFRACT**
32
M62
S
33

WAKEFIELD
40
Ossett
M1

Portobello
Milnthorpe

Featherstone

**KEY TO MAP PAGES**

SCALE

ornhill
Horbury
Middlestown
Calder Grove
39
Walton
Sharlston Common
Wragby

0 ___ 1 ___ 2 ___ 3 Miles
0 _ 1 _ 2 _ 3 _ 4 Kilometres

Netherton
Midgley

WAKEFIELD

Ackworth Moor Top
Badsworth
Fitzwilliam
Thorpe Audlin

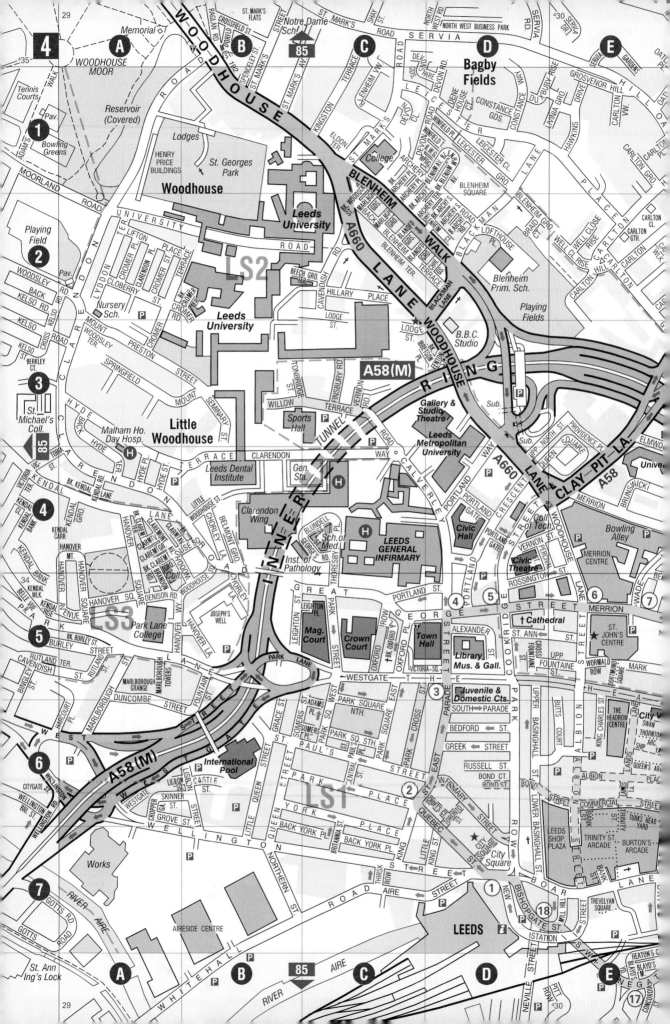

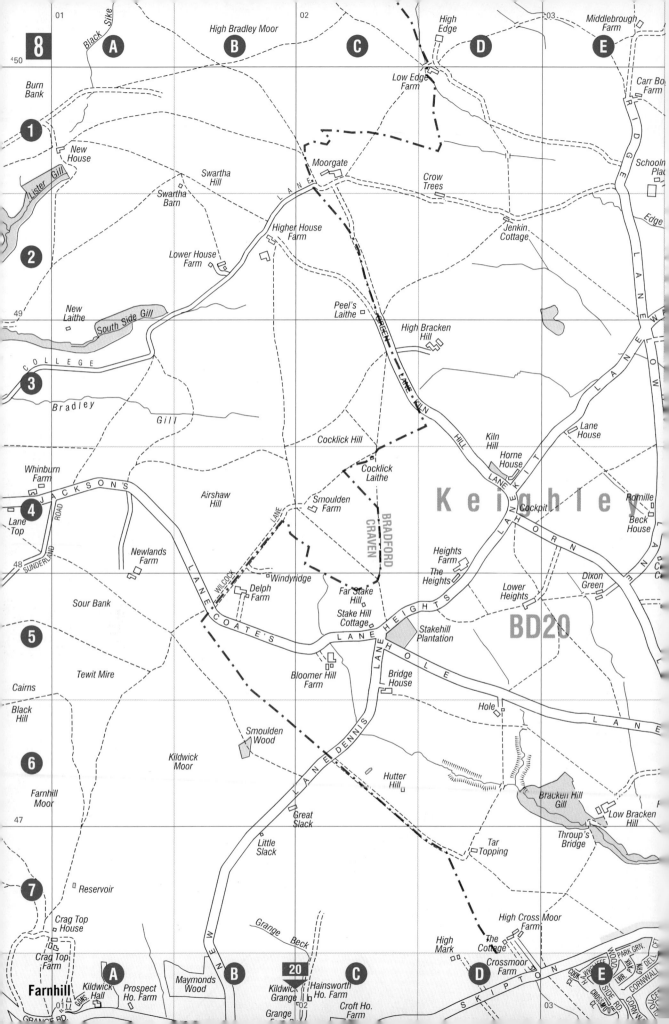

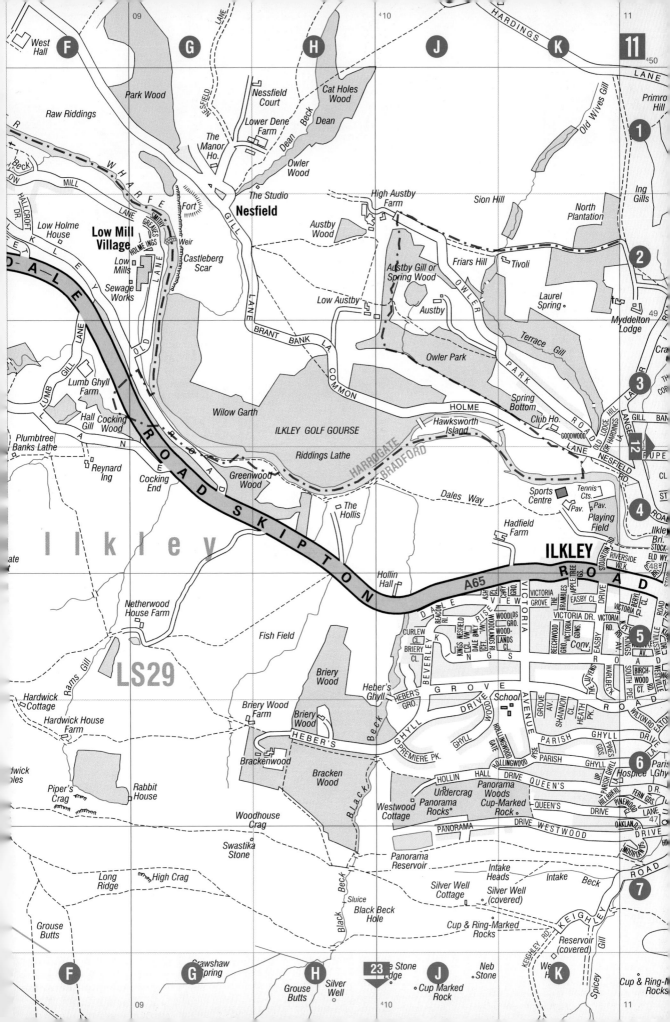

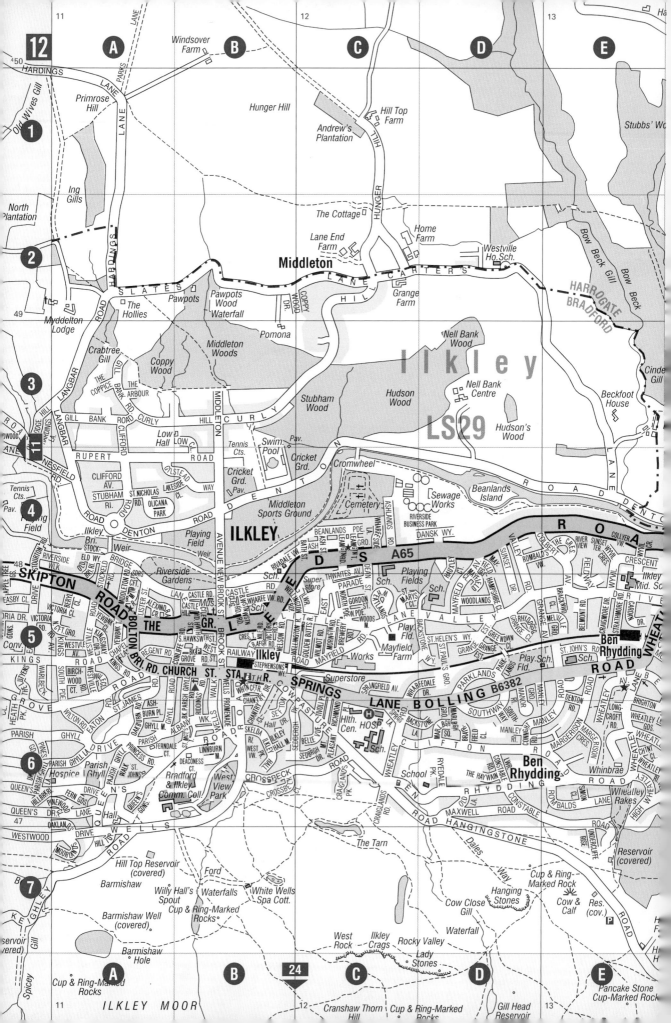

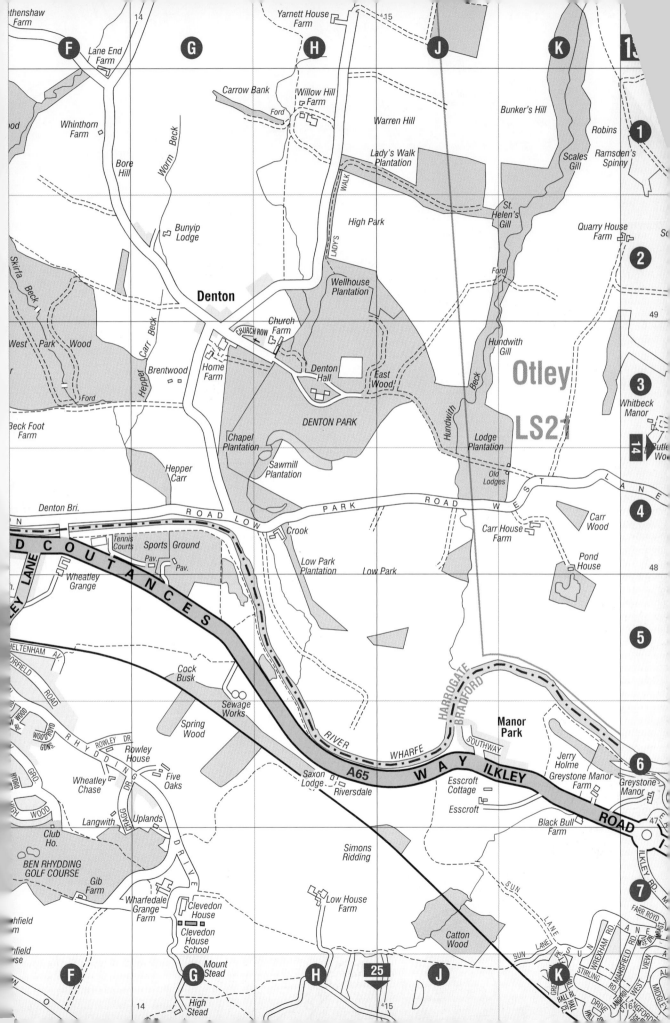

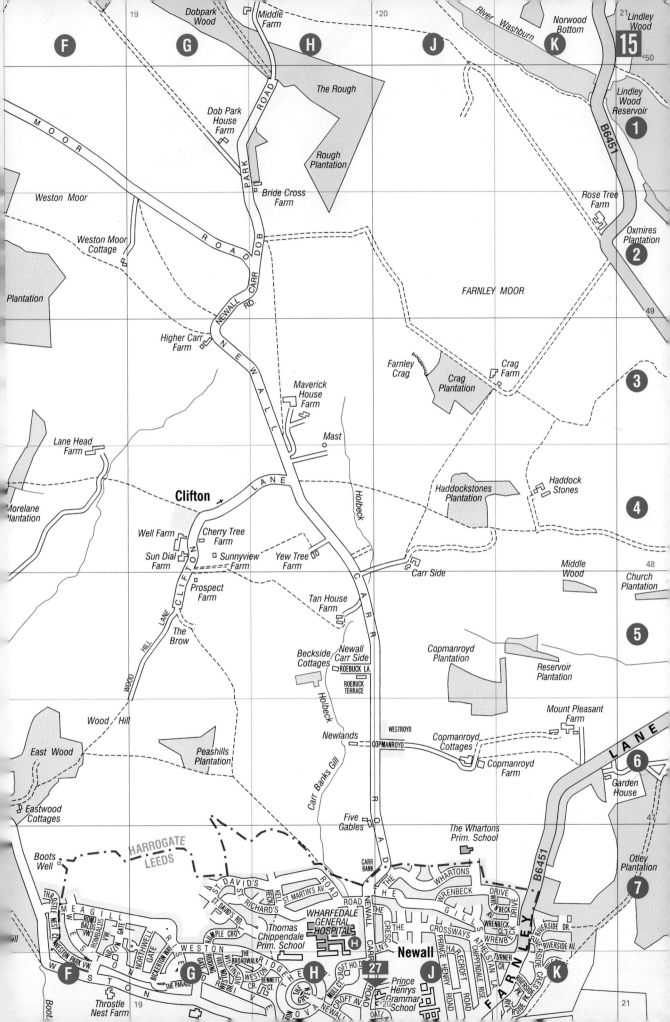

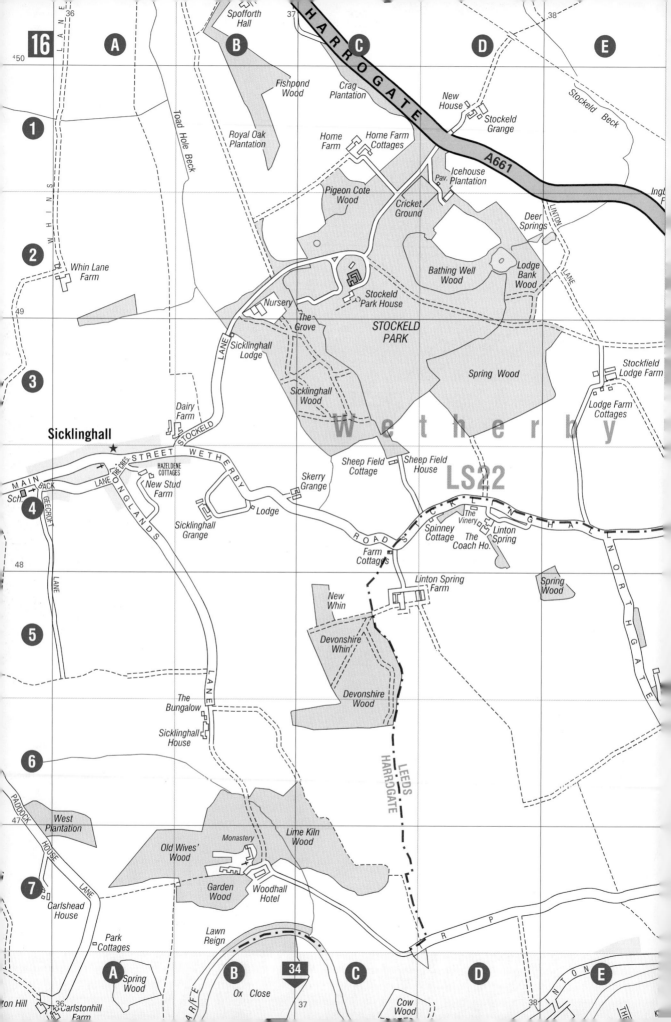

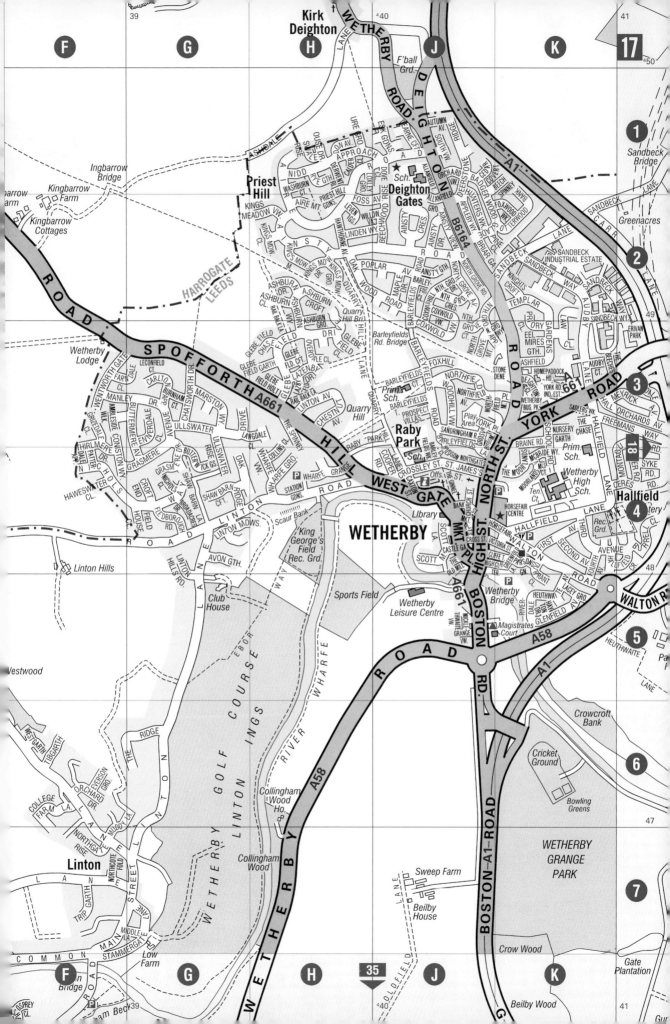

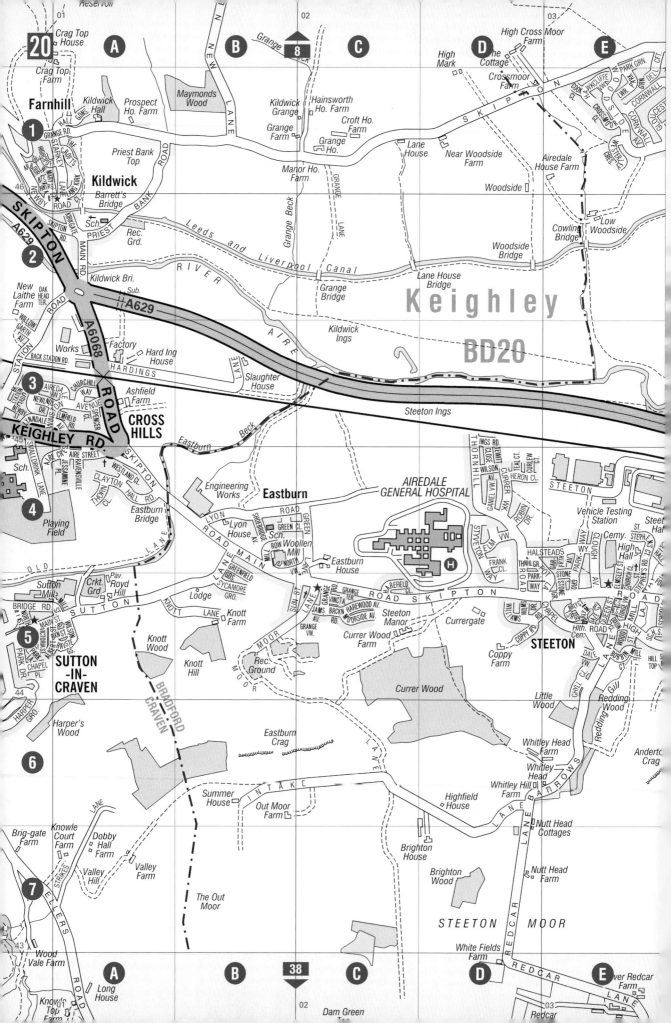

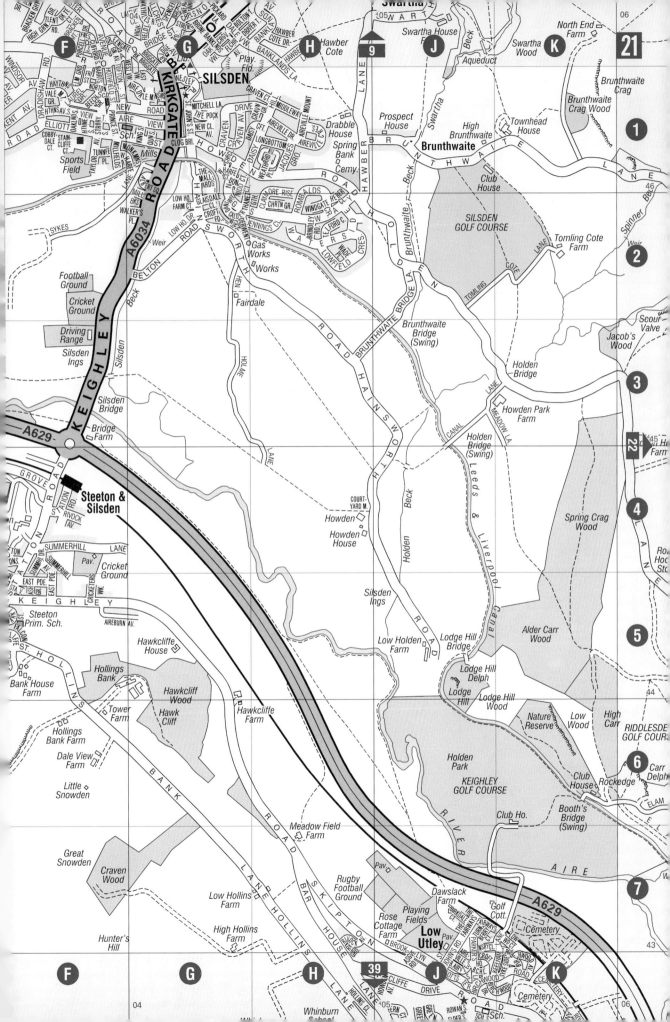

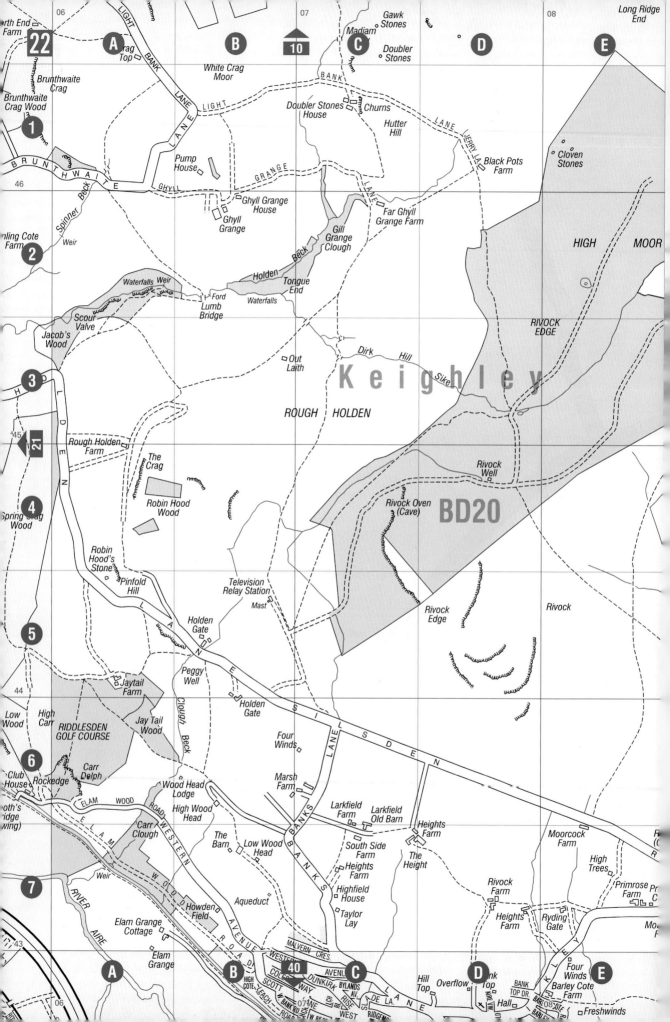

**F** **G** **H** **J** **K**

**25**

16 FARR ROYD

**1**

Low House Farm

415

13

Batton Wood

Whifedale Grange Farm

Clevedon House

Clevedon House School

Mount Stead

High Stead

Reservoir

**Stead**

Low Stead Farm

Kennels Farm

Stead Hall Farm

Stead Hall Wood

Rushy Beck

Scalebor Gill

Scalebor Park Farm

**BURLEY IN WHARFEDALE**

46 Smit

Dales Way

Rushy Beck

Low Cragg Farm

High Cragg Farm

Stead Crag

Rose Farm

Garden Centre

Robin Hole

Moor House

Weir

Colston House

Colston Lodge

Clinic

Sports Grd. Pav.

**2**

THE CRES

Wes Lodg

*DANGER AREA*

Lanshaw Delves

Woofa Bank

Little Skirtful of Stones

Coldstone House (Rock)

Coldstone Beck

Barks Crag

Plane Tree Farm

Woodhead

Ashburn

Reservoir (covered)

Hollin Nook

Moorlands

Coldstone Beck

**3**

Carr

445

26

Coldstone

Dales Way

Jubilee Trees

Moor La.

Ghylmoor

Rose Garth

Spring Acres

Far Bron

Hillside

Rough Hole

Carr Beck

**BURLEY MOOR**

Crag Top Farm

Crag Top

Highfield House

**Burley Woodhead**

Prospect Row

Redwalls

Hag Farm

**4**

Lower Lanshaw Dam

Carr Bottom Reservoir

York View Farm

High Meadows Farm

Field Head Farm

Jumb Beck Farm

Bleach Mill

*Butts*

Great Skirtful of Stones

Carr Bottom

Beestone Farm

Turnpike Farm

Bracken Hill

Stock Gate Farm

Almscliffe View

**5**

*BRADFORD LEEDS*

Black Beck

Craven Hall Hill

Stocks Hill

*DANGER AREA*

Rifle Range

Reservoir (covered)

Heather Bank

Gynesta

Hilltop Farm

Highf. Hou.

44

**6**

Wayside

Matthew

Middle Beck

Hawksworth Moor

Reva Hill

Dike

**7**

Horncliff Beck

Intake Gate Farm

43

Whin Hills

415

BINGLEY

ROAD

43

**F** **G** **H** **J** **K**

14 16

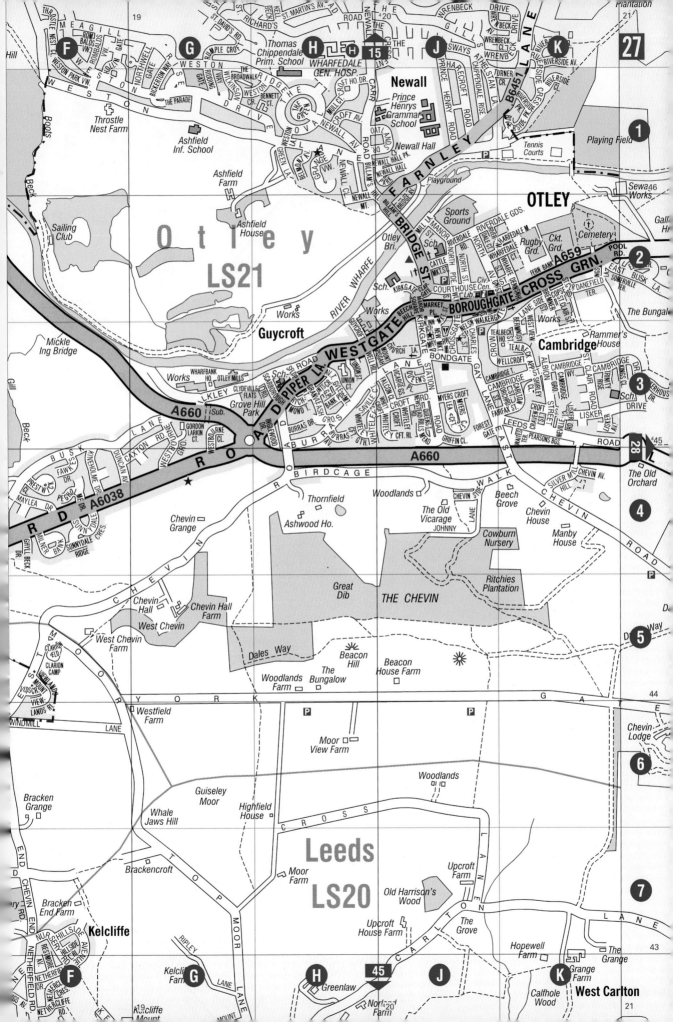

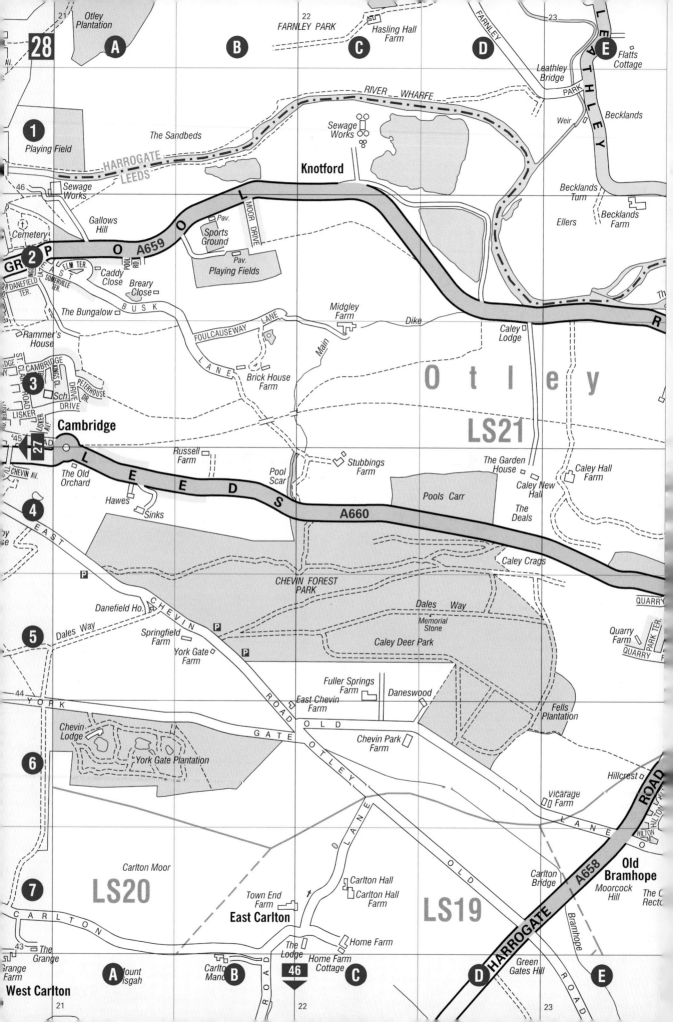

**28**

A · B · C · D · E

Otley Plantation

FARNLEY PARK

Hasling Hall Farm

Leathley Bridge

Flatts Cottage

**1** Playing Field

The Sandbeds

RIVER WHARFE

Sewage Works

Knotford

Weir

Becklands

PARK

Becklands Turn

Ellers

Becklands Farm

Sewage Works

Cemetery

Gallows Hill

Pav.

Sports Ground

MOOR DRIVE

**2** GR P O A659 POOL RD.

ELM TER.

SOMERVILLE TER.

Caddy Close

Breary Close

Pav.

Playing Fields

DANEFIELD TER.

The Bungalow

BUSK

FOULCAUSEWAY LANE

Midgley Farm

Dike

Caley Lodge

Rammer's House

LANE

Main

**3** CLARO ROAD CAMBRIDGE KINGS CL. PETERHOUSE DRIVE Sch. DRIVE

Brick House Farm

O t l e y

LS21

LISKER DR.

LISKER AV.

Cambridge

**27**

CHEVIN AV.

L E E D S

Russell Farm

Pool Scar

Stubbings Farm

The Garden House

Caley Hall Farm

The Old Orchard

Hawes

Sinks

Pools Carr

Caley New Hall

Caley Hall Farm

The Deals

**4** EAST

A660

Caley Crags

QUARRY

**5** Dales Way

Danefield Ho.

CHEVIN

Springfield Farm

York Gate Farm

P

P

CHEVIN FOREST PARK

Dales Way

Memorial Stone

Caley Deer Park

Quarry Farm

QUARRY PARK TER.

QUARRY

**6** YORK

Chevin Lodge

York Gate Plantation

ROAD

GATE

OLD

OTLEY

Fuller Springs Farm

East Chevin Farm

Daneswood

Chevin Park Farm

Fells Plantation

Hillcrest

Vicarage Farm

HILTON

ROAD

Carlton Moor

LS20

Carlton Bridge

A658

Old Bramhope

**7** CARLTON

Town End Farm

Carlton Hall

Carlton Hall Farm

LS19

HARROGATE

Moorcock Hill

The Rector

The Grange

Grange Farm

West Carlton

A · Mount Pisgah · B Carlton Manor · **46** Home Farm · C · D HARROGATE Green Gates Hill · E

East Carlton

The Lodge

Home Farm Cottage

ROAD

Bramhope

21 · 22 · 23

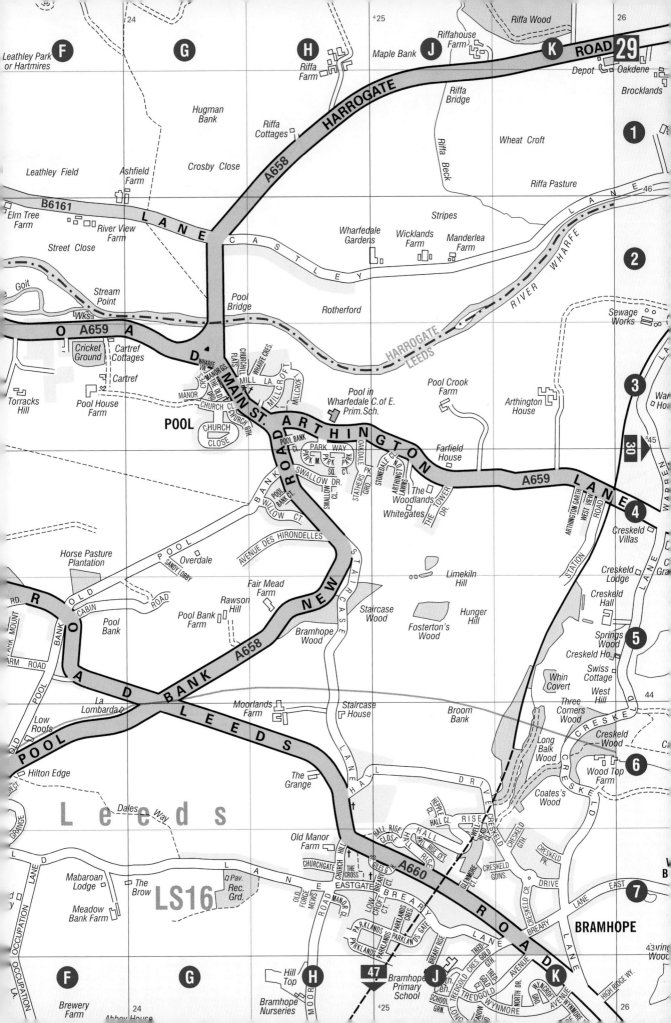

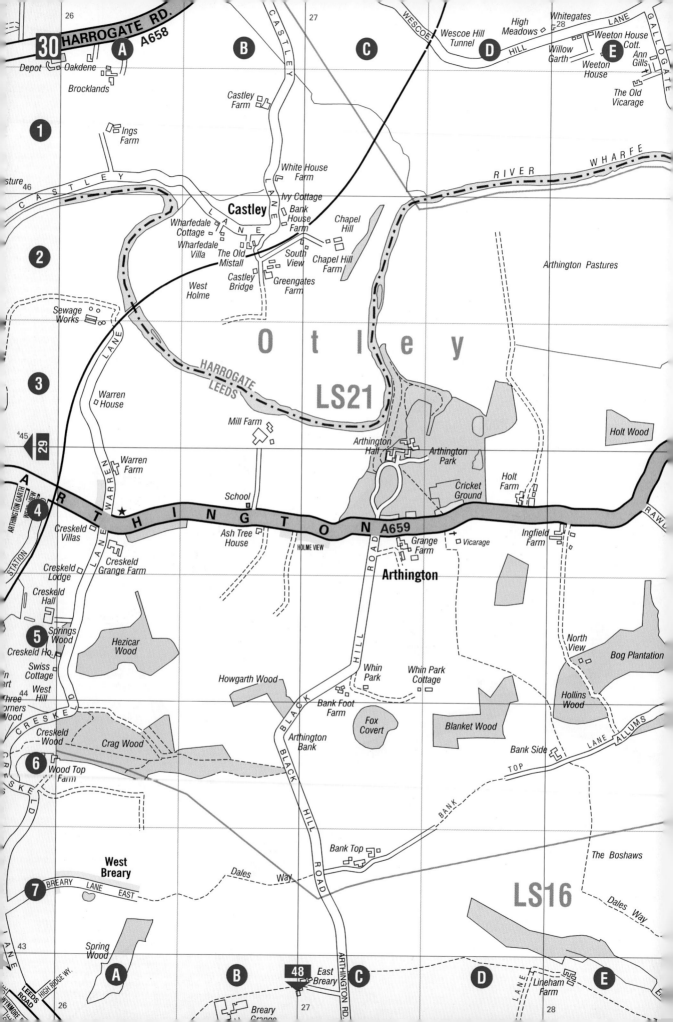

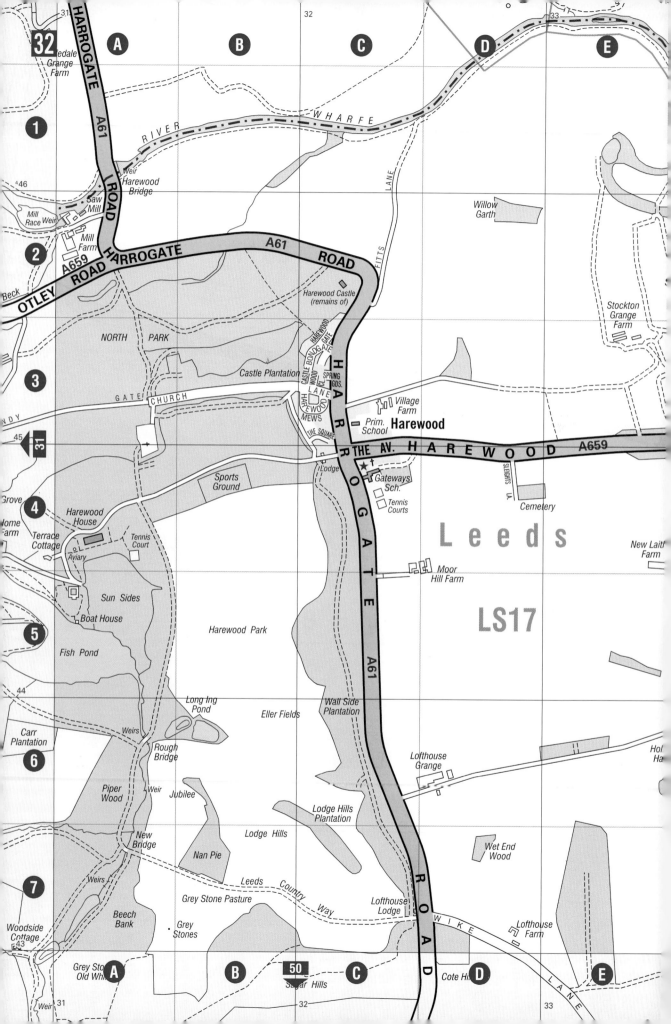

**32**

HARROGATE

A

B

C

D

E

1

2

3

4

5

6

7

Tedale Grange Farm

HARROGATE ROAD

A61

River

WHARFE

Weir
Harewood Bridge

Saw Mill

Mill Race Weir

Mill Farm

A659

OTLEY ROAD

HARROGATE

A61

ROAD

Beck

FITTS LANE

Willow Garth

Stockton Grange Farm

NORTH PARK

Harewood Castle (remains of)

Castle Plantation

CASTLE

HAREWOOD GATE

WOOD

SPRING GDS.

BOND GATE

GATE

CHURCH

LANE

HAREWOOD MEWS

Village Farm

Prim. School

**Harewood**

HAROGATE

THE SQUARE

THE AV.

HAREWOOD

A659

SLEIGHTS LA.

Lodge

Gateways Sch.

Tennis Courts

Cemetery

New Laith Farm

Grove

Sports Ground

Home Farm

Harewood House

Terrace Cottage

Tennis Court

Aviary

**L e e d s**

Moor Hill Farm

Sun Sides

Boat House

Harewood Park

**LS17**

Fish Pond

Long Ing Pond

Eller Fields

Wall Side Plantation

Carr Plantation

Weirs

Rough Bridge

Lofthouse Grange

Hol Ha

Piper Wood

Weir

Jubilee

Lodge Hills Plantation

New Bridge

Nan Pie

Lodge Hills

Wet End Wood

Weirs

Leeds

Country

Way

Lofthouse Lodge

Woodside Cottage

Beech Bank

Grey Stone Pasture

Grey Stones

Lofthouse Farm

Grey St Old Wh

Weir

A

B

**50**
Sugar Hills

C

WIKE

ROAD

D

Cote Hi

E

LANE

46

45

31

44

43

31

32

33

CHAPEL

34

Cliffe Ho.
Farm

Owl Head
Wood

435

CARLSHEAD
Carlshead
House

36

**F** Carthick House
Farm

**G** Chapel
Hill
Bank Hill

**H**

**J**

**K**

**33**

Wetherby LS22

Carlston Hill

**1** Carltonhill
Farm

HARROGATE

LEEDS

Carthick Wood

RIVER WHARFE

446

**2**

Stockton
Farm

Hill Climb
Course

Middlefield
Farm

Farfield
Farm

Moor End
Farm

Teal's
Wood

FITTS

LANE

HAREWOOD A659 ROAD

Stadthouse

**3**

AVENUE

MOOR

LUMBY

CLEAVESTY

**34** 45

Vicarage
Farm

Moorside
Farm

LANE

EAST
KESWICK

ROSE CROFT

WHITEGATE

**4**

SOUTH MT

THE GROVE

Manor House
Farm

Danetree

SOUTH
BANK

THE ARGYLE

PADDOCK

Vicar's Whin

LANE

MOOR

Old Hall
Farm

Moat
Field

Reighton
House

CHURCH
LANE

GARTH

PAINTERS
CT.

KESWICK
GRANGE

MEADOW
CROFT

STREET

**5**

Cut Whin
Wood

Burn's
Farm

44

Tevant
Cottage

Tevant
Farm

GATEON
HOUSE

LANE

KESW

**6** Rigt
Gran

Hollin Hall
Ponds

Spring
Wood

Gateon House
Farm

GATEON

Reservoirs
(covered)

Whin Hill
House

Rigton Moor

Well

**7** Quarry
Dene

Quarry
Hill F43n

Rigton Carr
Farm

SPEAR FIR

GILL BECK

School House
Whin

The Ho

Way

Leeds Country

**F**

**G** Biggin
Farm

**H**

**51**

Rigton Moor
Farm

**J**

SPEAR
Works

435

**K** Mowbray
House

HURCH

SMITHY

36

WETHERBY G

TRIP GARTH

MIDDLE LA
STAMMERGATE
MAIN
ROAD
39
WETHERBY GOLF COURSE
Low Farm
WETHERBY RD.
Beilby House
BOSTO
Crow Wood
40
41
Gate Plantation

MMON
Linton Bridge
P
Collingham Beck
A58
STREET
Beilby Wood
GREAT
1
Gu

COLLINGHAM
WETHERBY
STREET
WATTLESYKE
A659
NORTH
446
Grange Moor

D
ROAD
GFL
OSPREY
FL
BECK LN
BRIDGE
STATION LA
SMITHY
PADDOCK
CHURCH LANE
SCHOOL
MCGARTH WILLA
THE GARTH
GARTH AV
GARTH END
HOLLYBUS GREEN
MAIN
Lilac Farm
BIRDALE
Tree Tops
Collingham Fields
FIELD
OLDFIELD
A659
2
M

HASTINGS CT
ELIZABETH CT
BROOKSIDE
WAR CL
LANE
LANE
GREEN
LS22
Low Cow Moor Wood
Walk-a-bout

CRABTREE HILL
CRABTREE GRN
CRABTREE GREEN
Providence House
W e t h e r b y
Whinney Cow Moor Wood
Howcroft Wood
LANE
Collingham Moo
3

JEWITT
Cow Moor
MOOR
36
45

Comb Bank
COMPTON
LANE
Compton Cottages
Compton Grove
LANE
Quarry Plantation
CLI
4

Compton
COMPTON
Compton Grove
Waver Spring Pond
Dalton Parlours
CLI

LS23
Parlours Plantation
5

44

LANE
D
A
L
T
O
N
WEST WOODS
6

LADY WOOD
Lund Wood
Lund Wood Close
Dalton Hill
7

LANE
Old Pickhill Rash
Hope Hall
43

Stubbings
THORNE
LANE
DALTON LANE
39
440
LANE THORN
41
43
Hope Hall Cottages

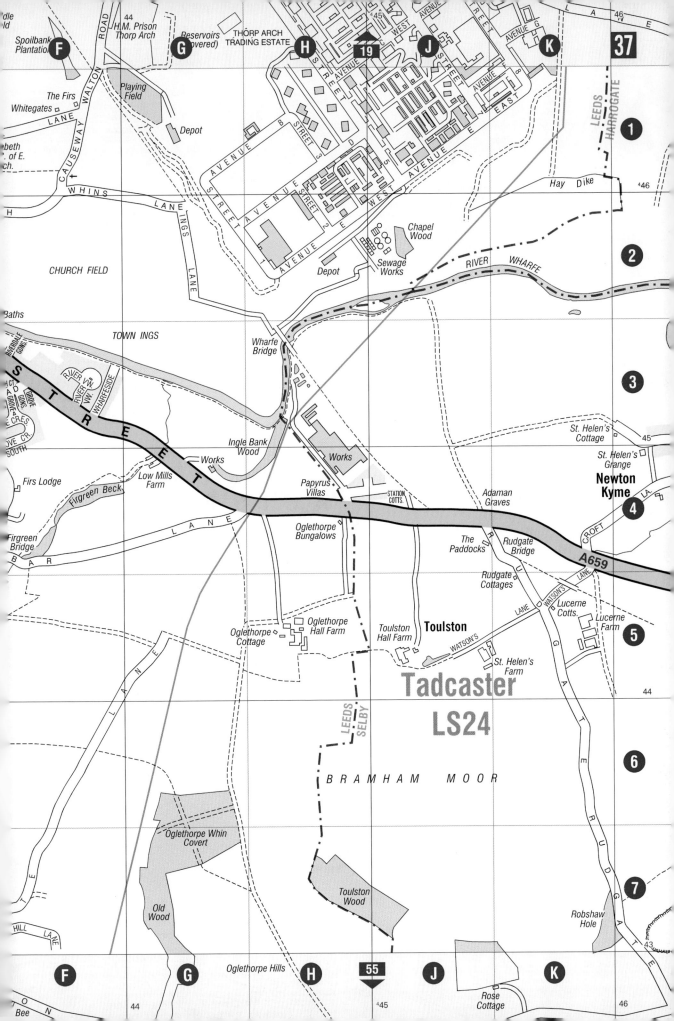

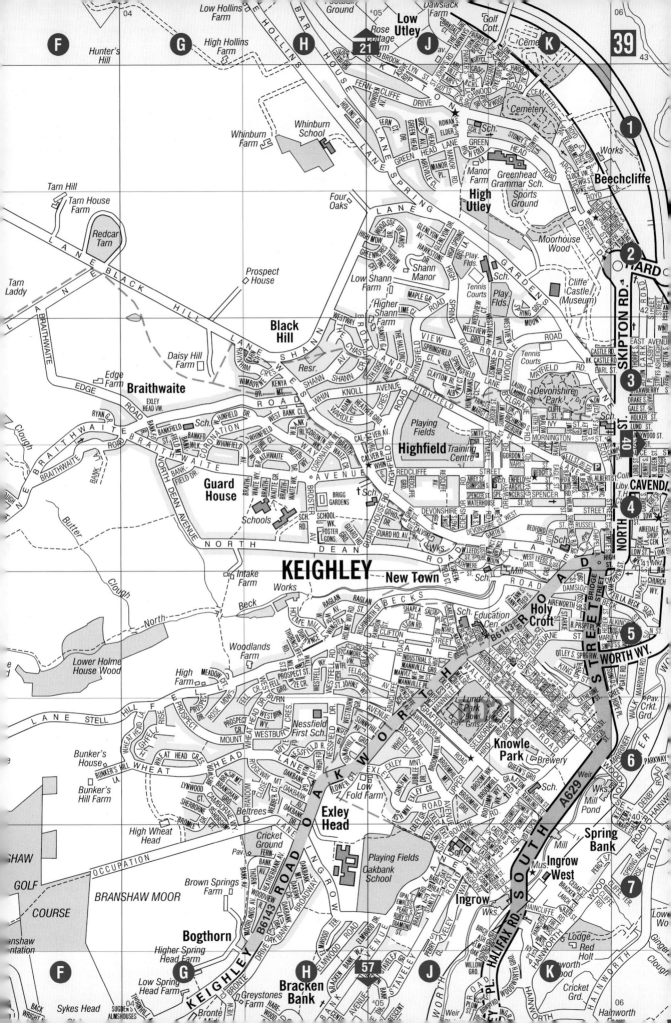

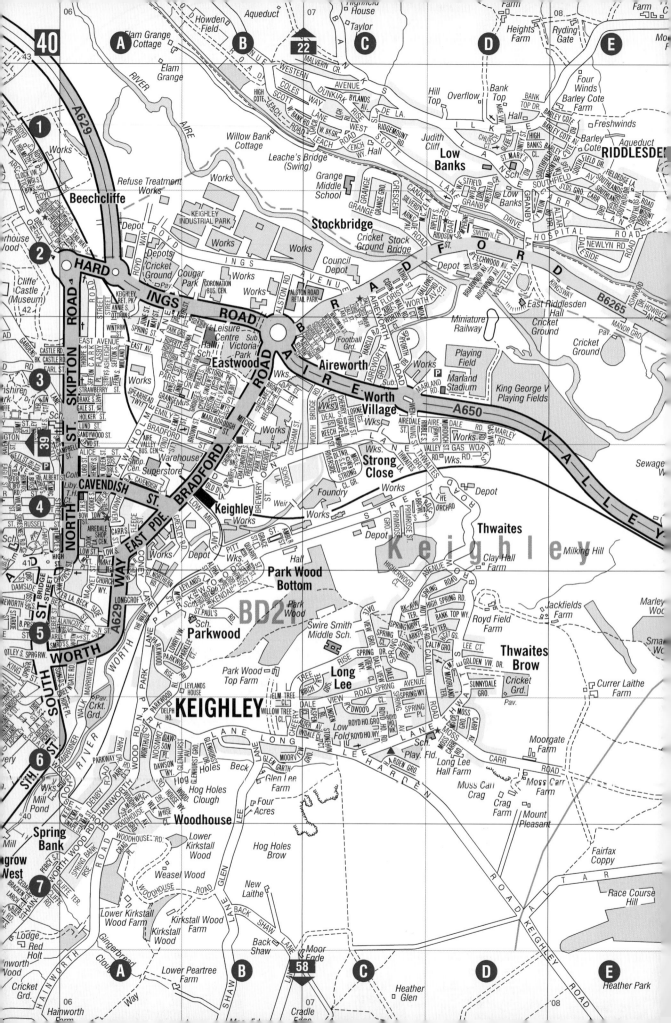

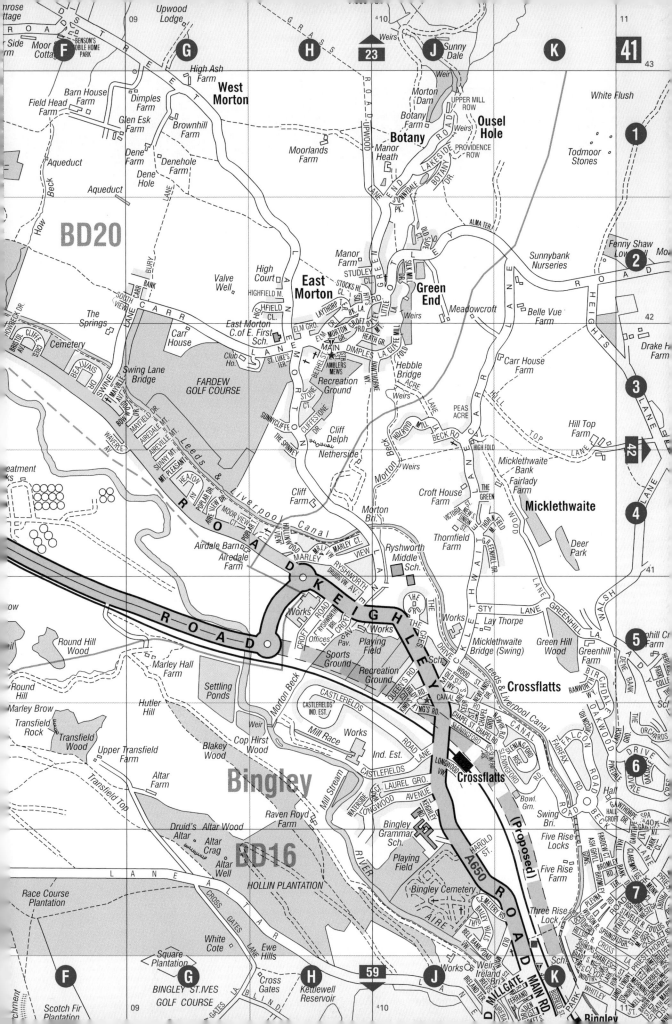

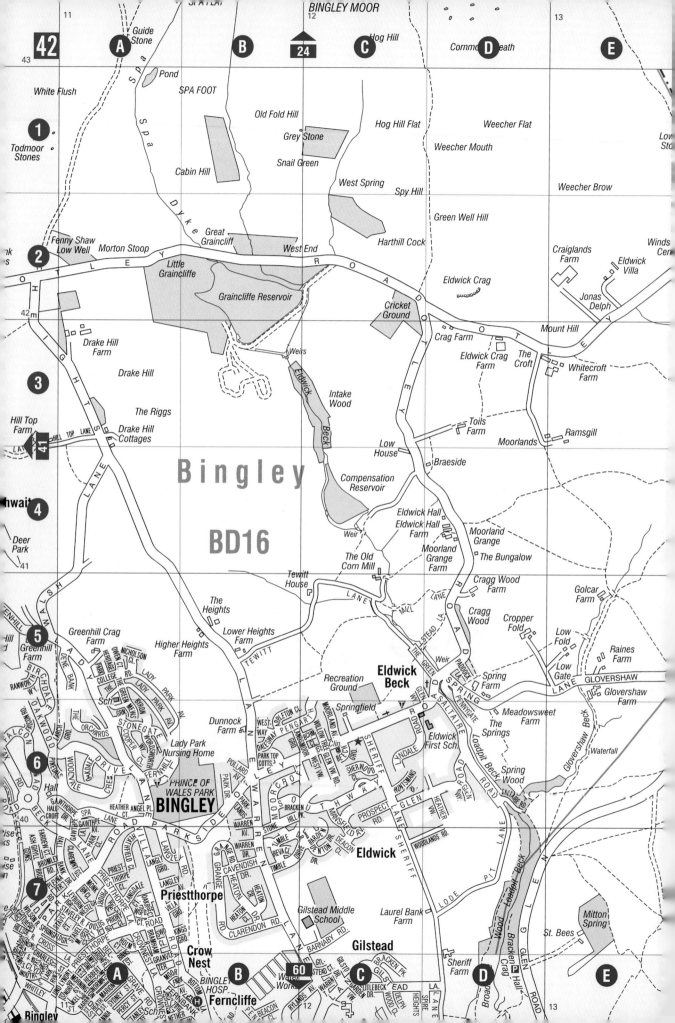

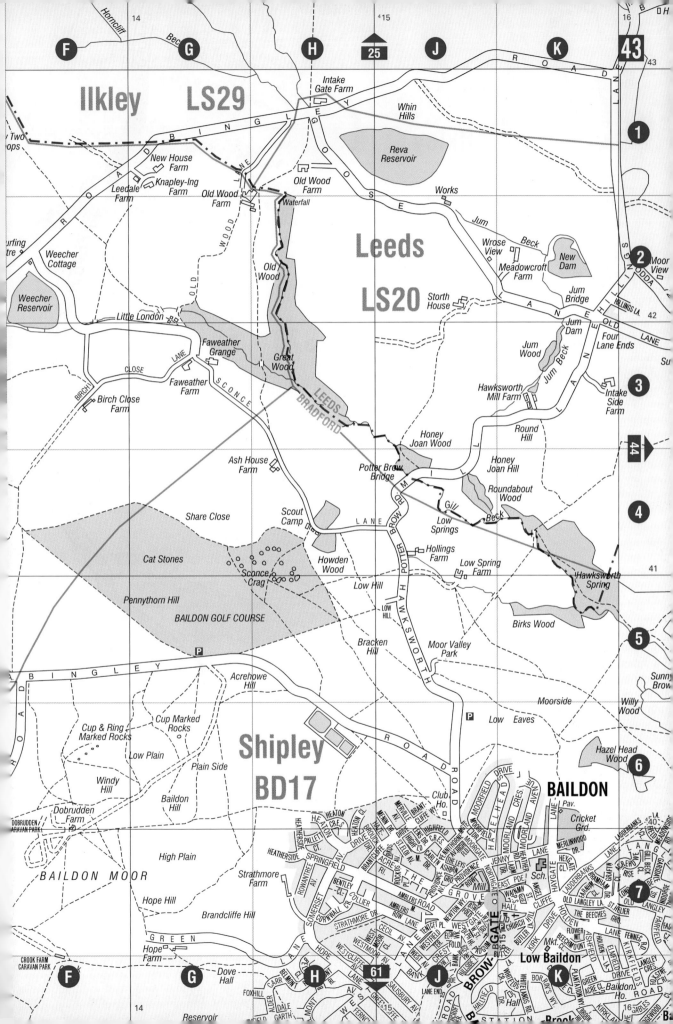

**F**  **G**  **H**  **31**  **J**  **K**  Woodside Cottage  **49**

29  Grove Farm  Waterhouse Whin  Langley Well  Swan Bushes  Grey Ston Old Whi.  31  43

Leeds Country Way  Hazelwood Leys  **1**

Brookland Farm  Thorn Bush Farm  Mount Pleasant Farm  Bank House Farm  Weir

Eccup Filtration Works  Weir

Village  Black Smith La.  Eccup  Road  Eccup Beck  Rookery Farm  Owlet Hall  Herd Farm  **2**

r-car-nook Beck  Conduit  42  Eccup Beck  Eccup  High Wood  **3**

Dales Way  ECCUP  RESERVOIR  Wigton Knowle  **50**

Goodrick Plantation  Alwoodley Old Hall  Wigton Knowle  **4**

**L e e d s**  Reservoir Lodge  Lane  SAND MOOR GOLF COURSE

Adel Head  Adel Brow  Lakeland Cr.  Lakeland Dr.  Goodrick  **LS17**  Club House  41  Wigton Gr.  Ercm Ct.

**Alwoodley Park**  Windermere Dr.  Woodley  Drive  The Avenue  Mount Gdns.  Mount Dr.  Hanmore Cl.  Mount Rise  FAIRWAY  Sandmoor Grn.  Sandmoor Lane  Sandmoor  Lane  **5**

Crescent Ct.  Crescent Vw.  The View  Quarry Gdns.  Edgbaston Ct.  Hillingdon Wlk.  The Mount Wy.  Meadow Way  Alwoodley Moss  Park Road  Sandmoor Chase  Brookside  Alwoodley Chase

The Valley  The Court  Lane End Ct.  Old Barn Cl.  The Close  Lib. & Comm. Cen.  Winding Way  Sandmoor Cl.  Fairfield  Pav.  **6**

Adel Brow  The Grove  Lane  Moss Gdns.  Far Moss  Moss Valley  Sports Ground  Pavilion  MOORTOWN  GOLF COURSE  Club House  Sandmoor Mews  Primrose View  Recre. Grou

Alwoodley ngs Plantation  Alwoodley Ct.  Alwoodley Gdns.  Alwoodley Lawns  Blackmoor Ct.  King Dr.  Sunningdale  **ALWOODLEY**  Grange Park Rd.  Holt Grange Ct.  Primley Pk. Rd.  Primley Pk. Ct.  Primley Pk. Wy.  Primley Park Grn.  Primley Pk. Cl.  Park  Burton  Sandmoor Ct.  The Nook  Sandhill Mt.  40  Sandhill

Buck Stone Rd.  Buck Stone Oval  Sunningdale  Silverdale  George Lyttleton Centre  St. Andrew's Cft.  St. Andrew's Wlk.  Primley Park Gro.  Hawk's Nest Gdns.  Hawk's Nest West  Primley Park Rise  Cavendish Mews  Primley Pk. Mt.  Belvedere Rd.  Belvedere Gro.

**Black Moor**  Buck Stone La.  Birkdale Gro.  Birkdale Mt.  **Camp Town**  Wentworth Av.  Turnbery Pl.  St. Andrew's Wy.  Wentworth Cres.  Primley Park Cres.  Primley Park Av.  Ten.  Cts.  Sandhill  Sandhill Gdns.  Belvedere Ct.

Seven Arches  Scotland Wood  Buck Stone Grn.  Deanswood  Prim. Sch.  Nursery Gro.  Birkdale Dr.  Birkdale Rise  Gleneagles Rd.  Turnbery Gro.  NURSERY  ROAD  Allerton High School  Fir Tree Gdns.  Hill  Primley Gdns.  Greystones Ct.  Nursery Res. (Cov.)  Synagogue  Ingledew  Sandringham Gdns.

29  30  Cranmer Bank  Deans  **F**  **G**  Bishop her Prim. Sch.  Park & Ride  **67**  **H**  Lingfield  Fir Tree Green  Fir Tree Cl.  Fir Tree Gro.  Fir Tree La.  Prim. Sch.  War Mem.  **J**  Pepper Hills  Princess  **K**  Sandringham Cres.  **HARROGATE — A61**  **ROAD**

Scotland Wood  LINGFIELD  APPROACH  30  Allerton

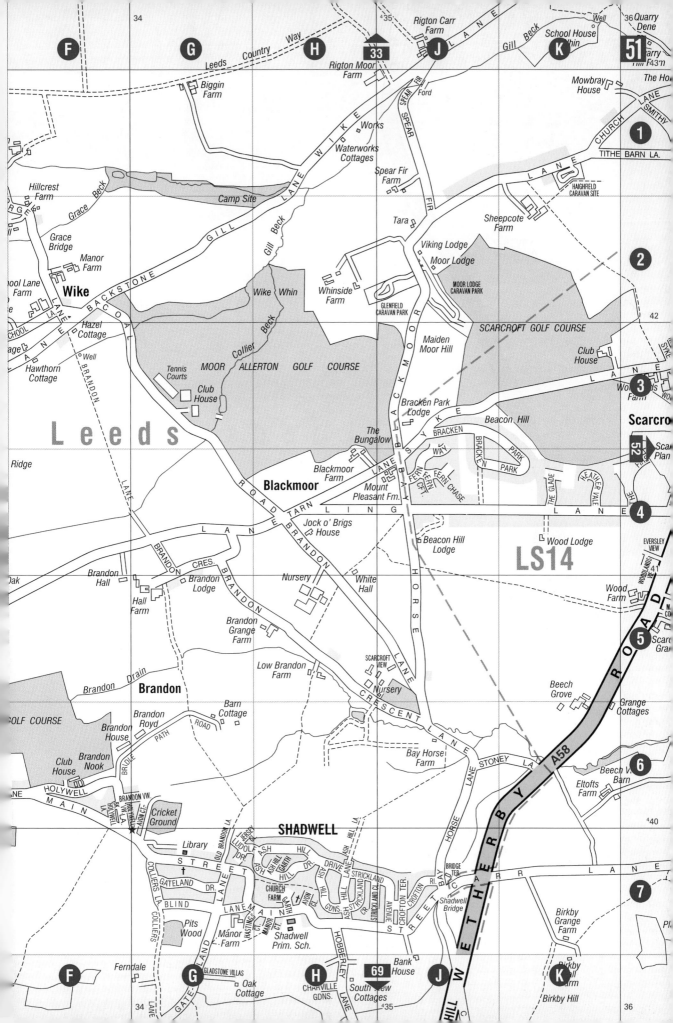

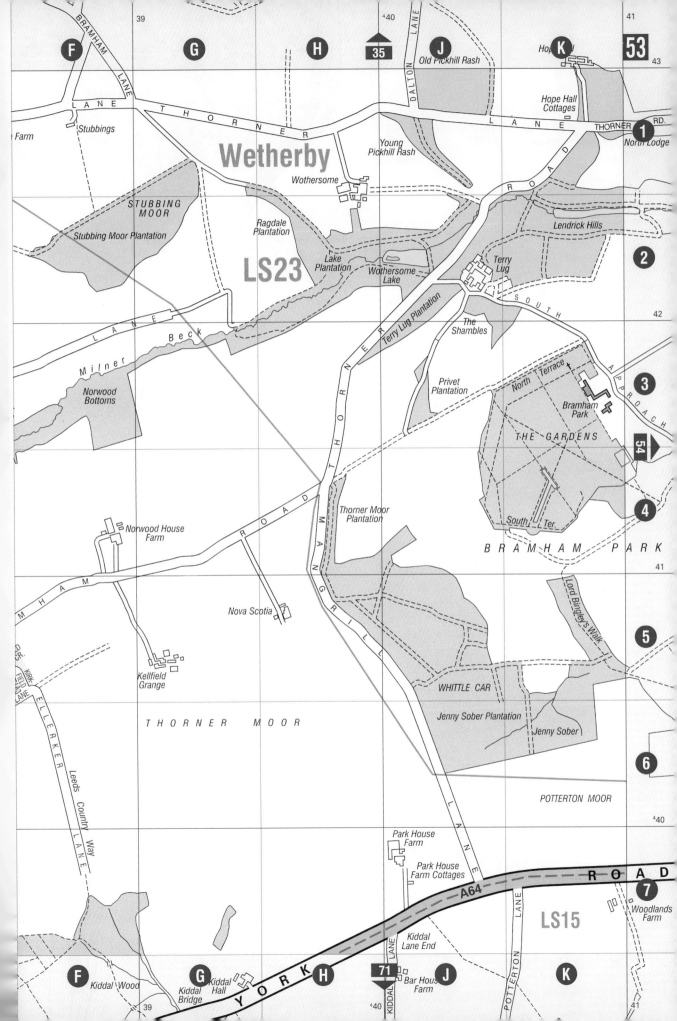

**F** **G** **H** ⬆ **35** **J** **K** **53**

39 ⁴40 41 43

DALTON LANE

BRAMHAM LANE

THORNER LANE

Farm

Stubbings

Old Pickhill Rash

Hope Hall

Hope Hall Cottages

THORNER RD.

**1** North Lodge

## Wetherby

Young Pickhill Rash

Wothersome

STUBBING MOOR

Stubbing Moor Plantation

Ragdale Plantation

Lendrick Hills

**LS23**

Lake Plantation

Wothersome Lake

Terry Lug

**2**

SOUTH

42

Milner Beck

LANE

Terry Lug Plantation

The Shambles

Norwood Bottoms

Privet Plantation

North Terrace

Bramham Park

**3**

THE GARDENS

APPROACH

**54** ◢

Norwood House Farm

Thorner Moor Plantation

South Ter.

**4**

ROAD

THORNER ROAD

BRAMHAM GRILL

B R A M H A M   P A R K

41

Nova Scotia

Lord Bingley's Walk

**5**

KIRK FIELD LANE

Kellfield Grange

WHITTLE CAR

Jenny Sober Plantation

Jenny Sober

**6**

ELLERKER LANE

T H O R N E R   M O O R

POTTERTON MOOR

⁴40

Leeds Country Way

Park House Farm

Park House Farm Cottages

R O A D

**7**

A64

LS15

Woodlands Farm

**F** Kiddal Wood

**G** Kiddal Hall

Kiddal Bridge

Y O R K H **H**

⬇ **71**

Kiddal Lane End

Bar House Farm

**J**

KIDDAL LANE

POTTERTON LANE

**K**

39 ⁴40 41

**Wetherby**

**LS23**

**BRAMHAM**

North Lodge Plantations

North Lodge

BIGGIN PARK

Lendrick Hills

Bramham Beck

College Farm

Bramham Biggin

Oldroad Plantation

East Lodge Cottages

Biggin Wood

Bowcliffe Hall

Bowcliffe Farm

Wellhill Plantation

Well Hill

Wellhill Farm

Pav. Playing Field

Bramham House

Bramham Lodge

RAKES WOOD

Paradise Farm

Dawsonfield Plantation

Open Rakes

Camp Hill

BRAMHAM PARK

Temple

BLACK FEN

Openrakes Brook

SPEN

Spen Farm

Obelisk

Temple

New Black Fen

Beccamoor Wood

Whitewells Bottom

Crossroads Farm

Blackfen Plantation

Whin Covert

Whitewells Wood

Becca Moor

LEEDS SELBY

POTTERTON MOOR

White Wells

Windsor Farm

Whitewell Farm

YORK RD. LEEDS A64

Bimbo Farm

Becca Lodge

Becca Moor

A1(M)

ROAD

A1(M) MOTORWAY

Woodlands Farm

Cowthwaite Plain

Greystone Plain

Beccamoor Plantation

Roughclose Wood

Brickpond Runner

THORNER ROAD TENTER HILL

ABERFORD HEADLEY

A1

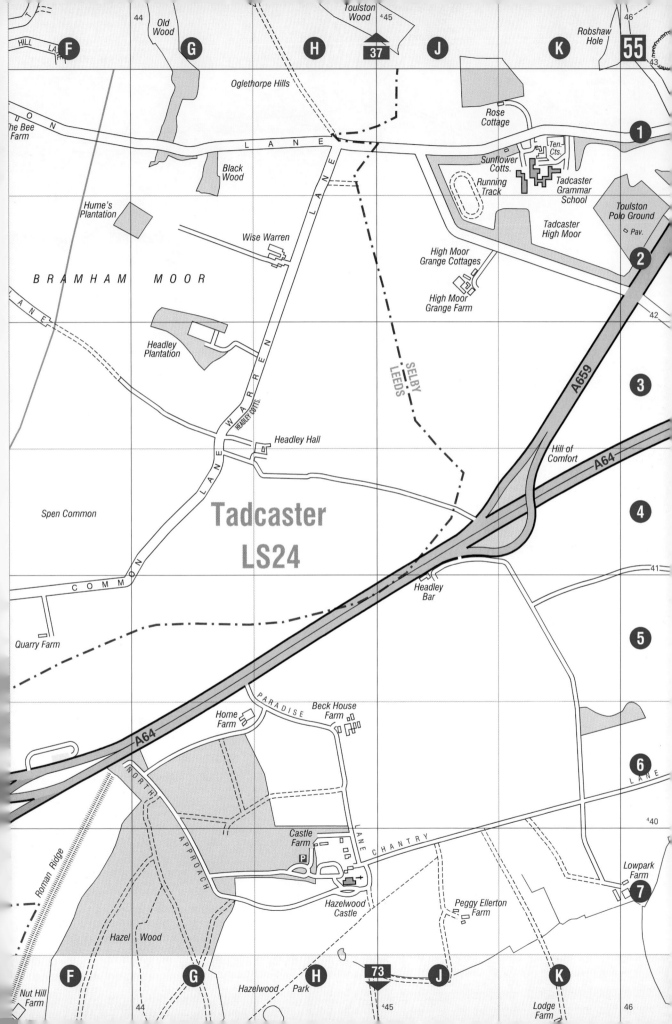

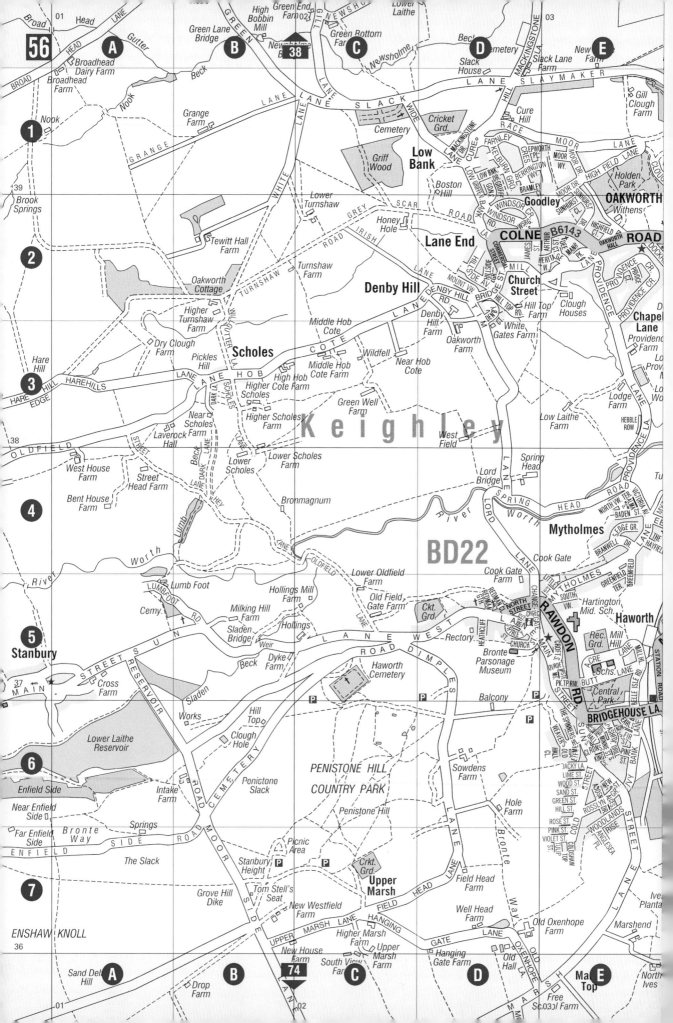

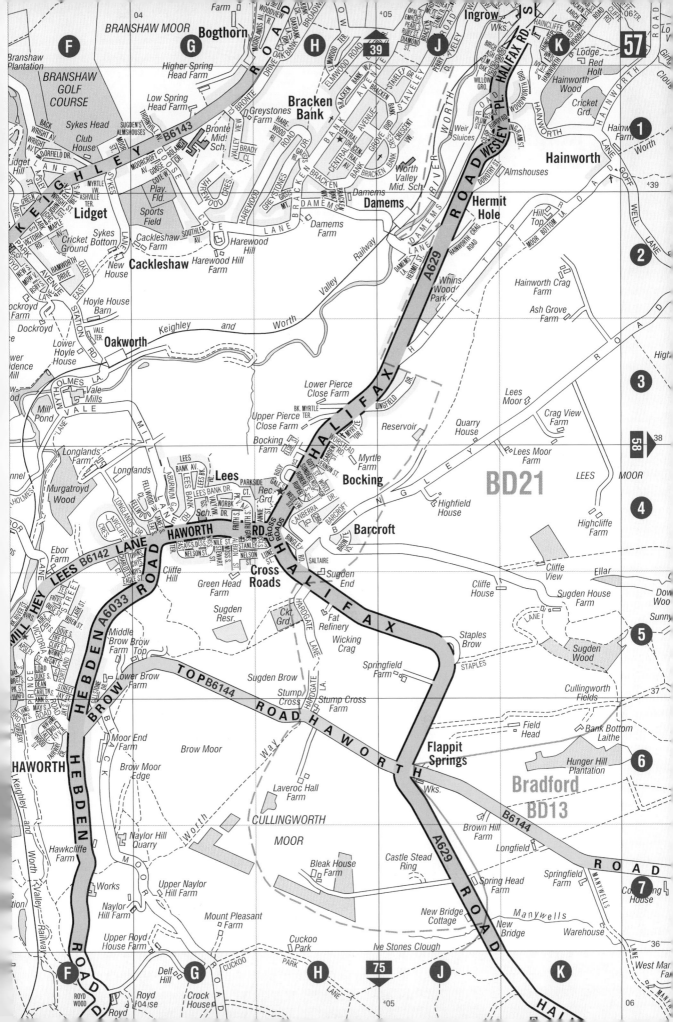

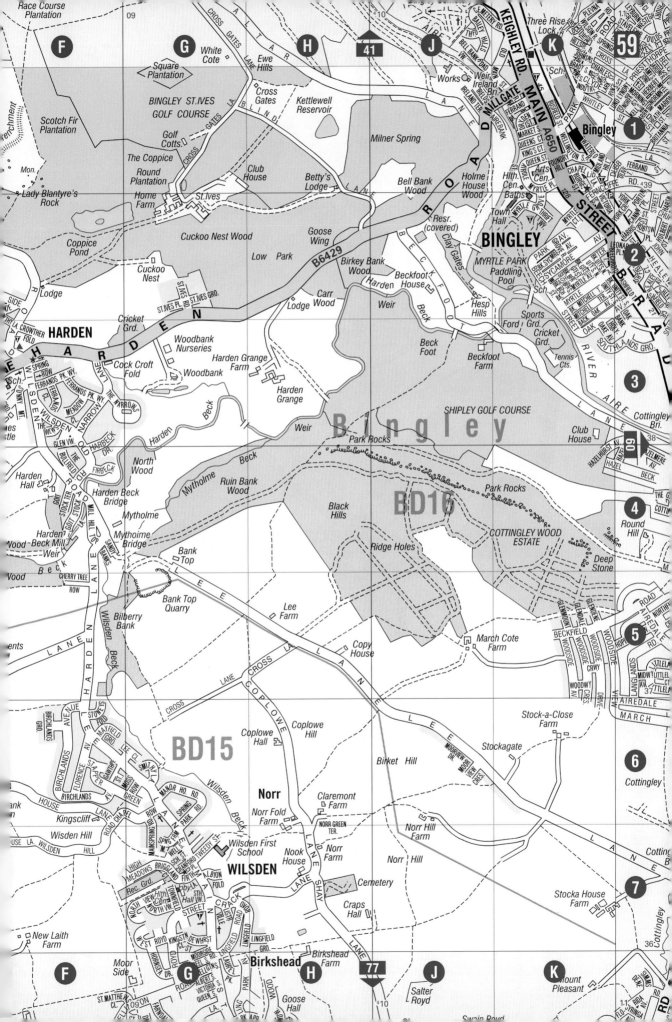

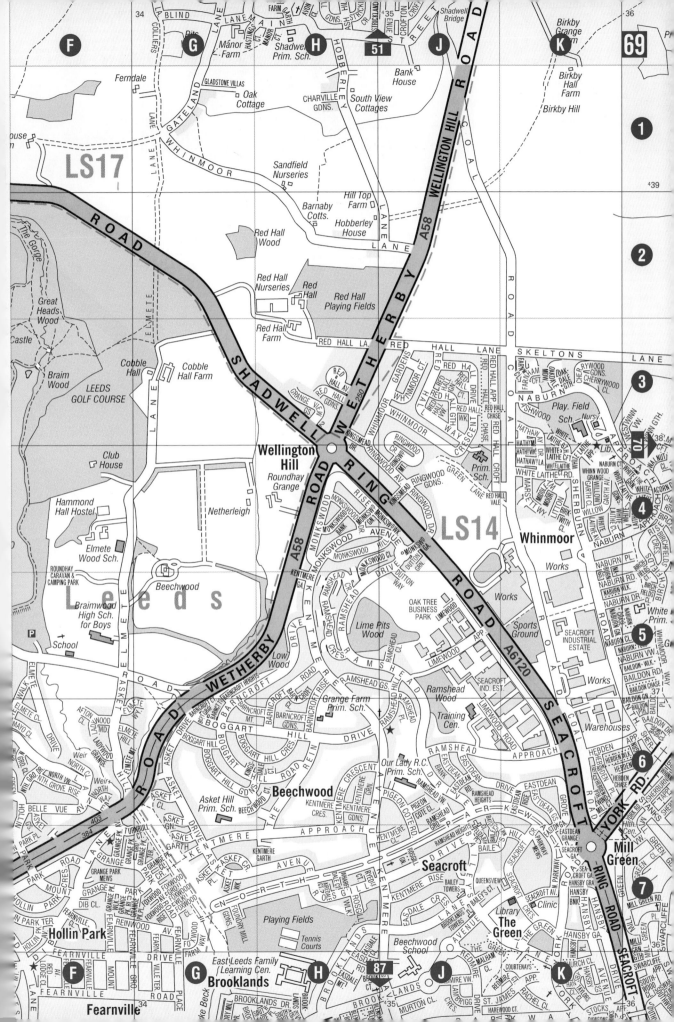

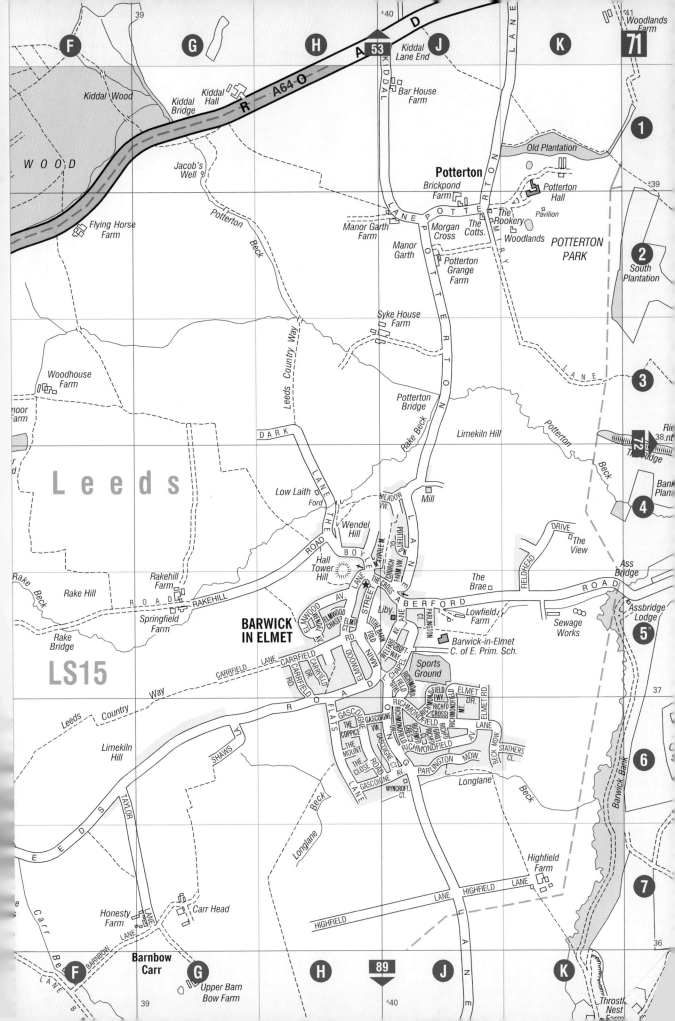

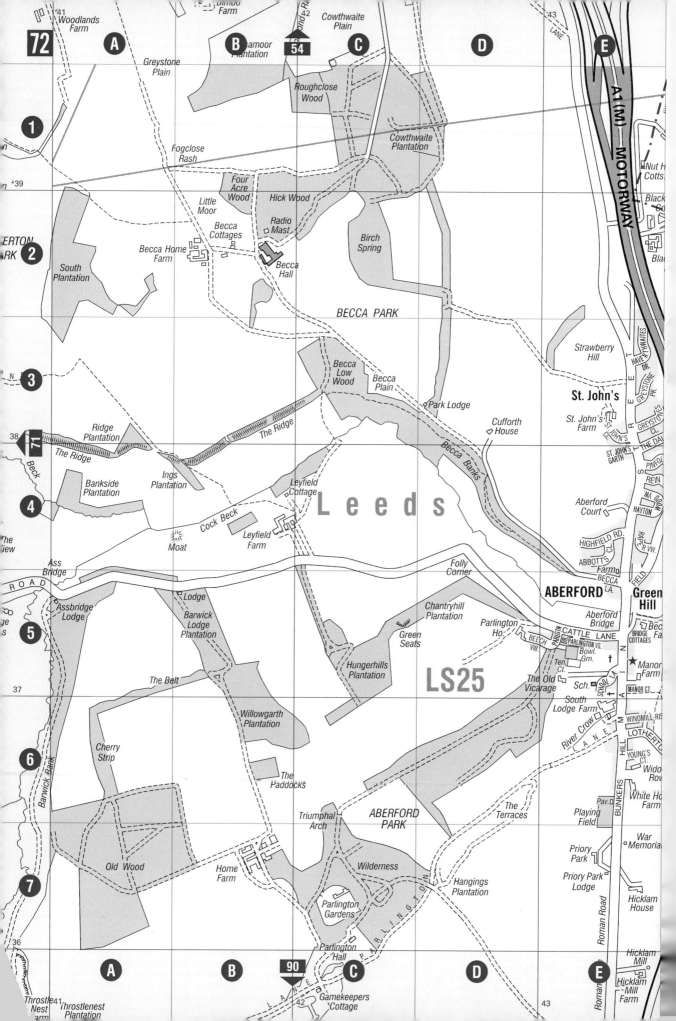

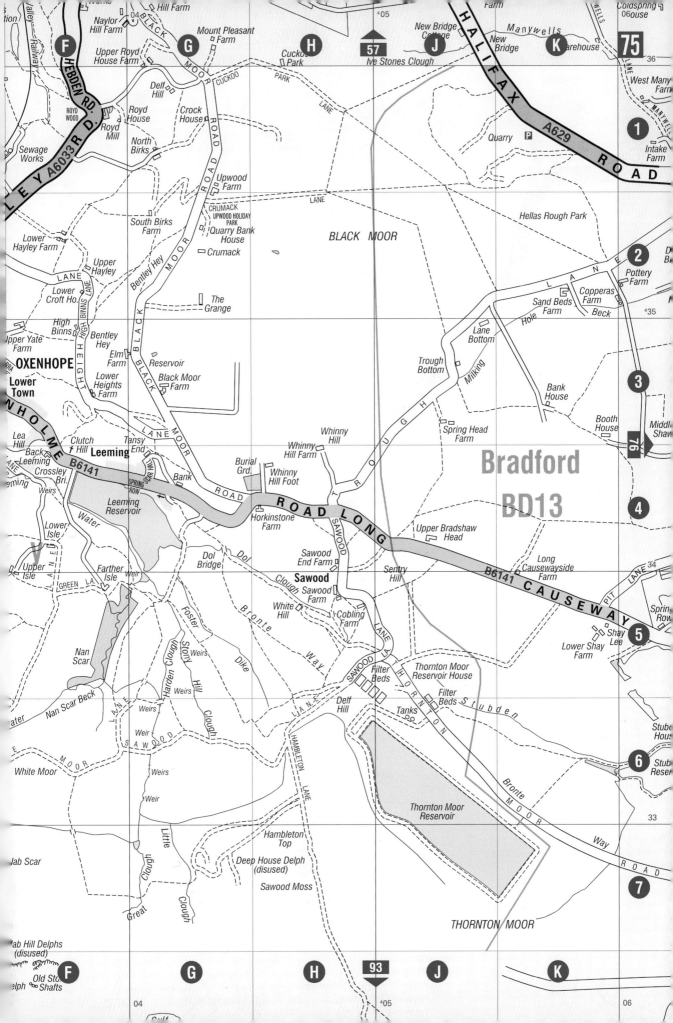

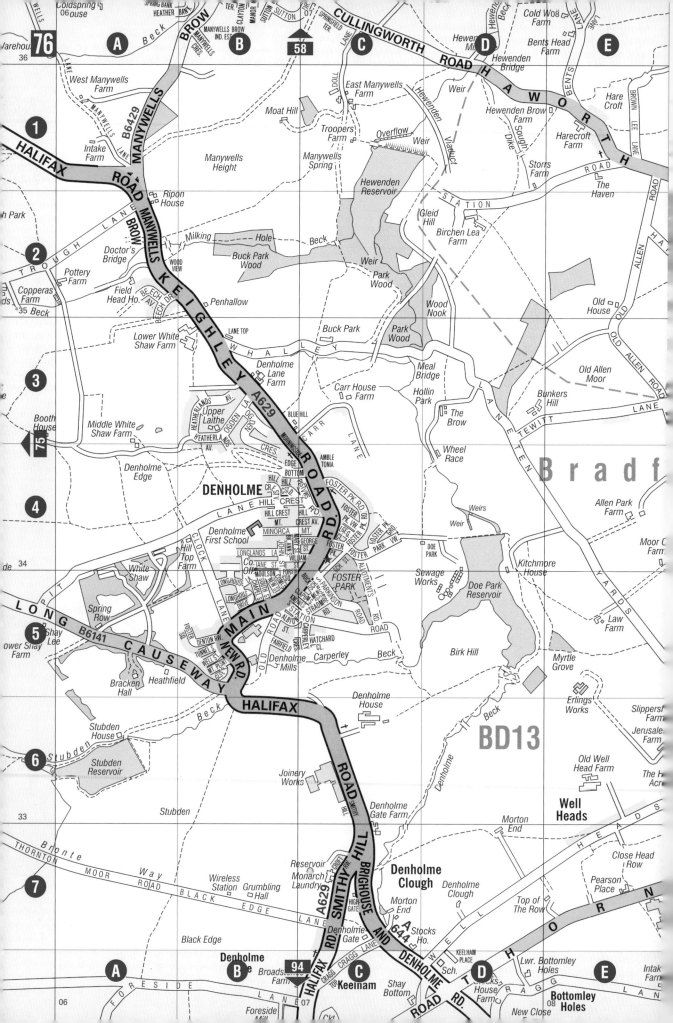

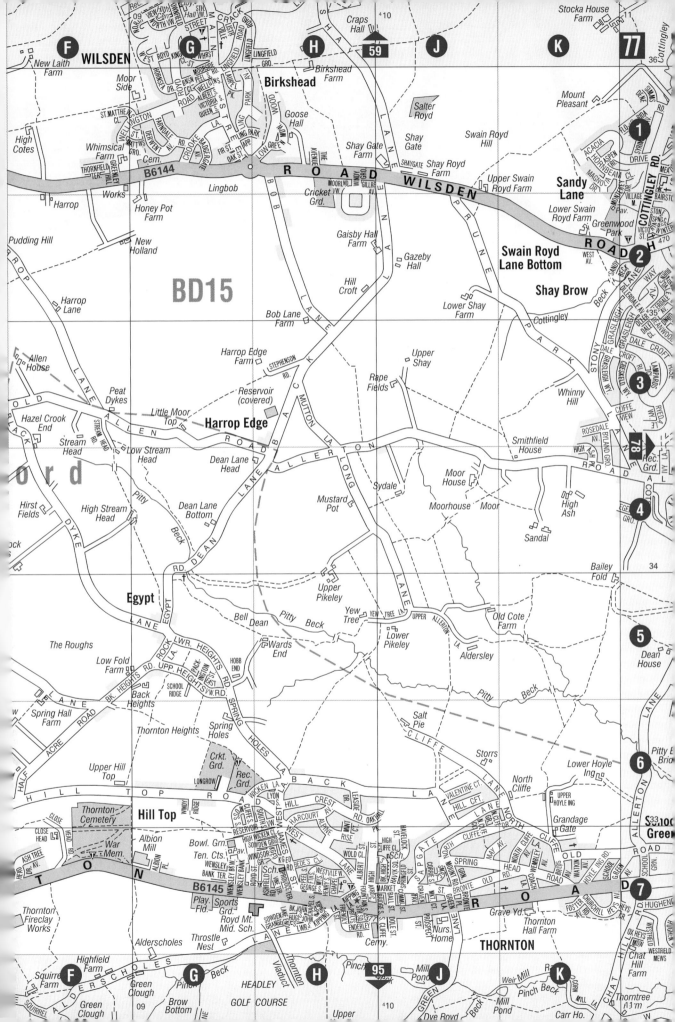

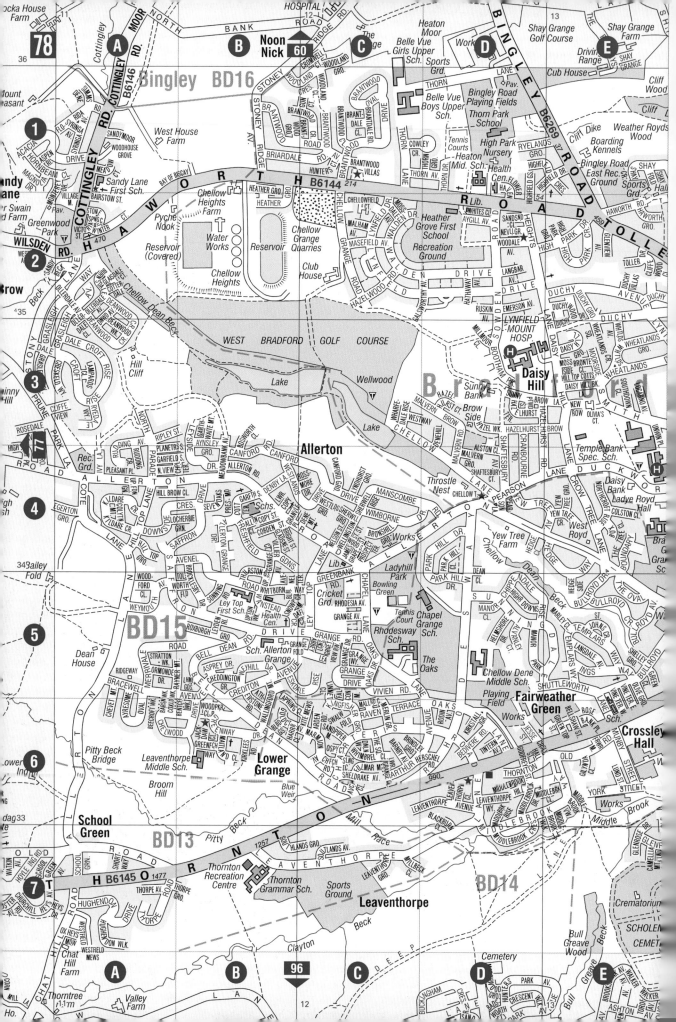

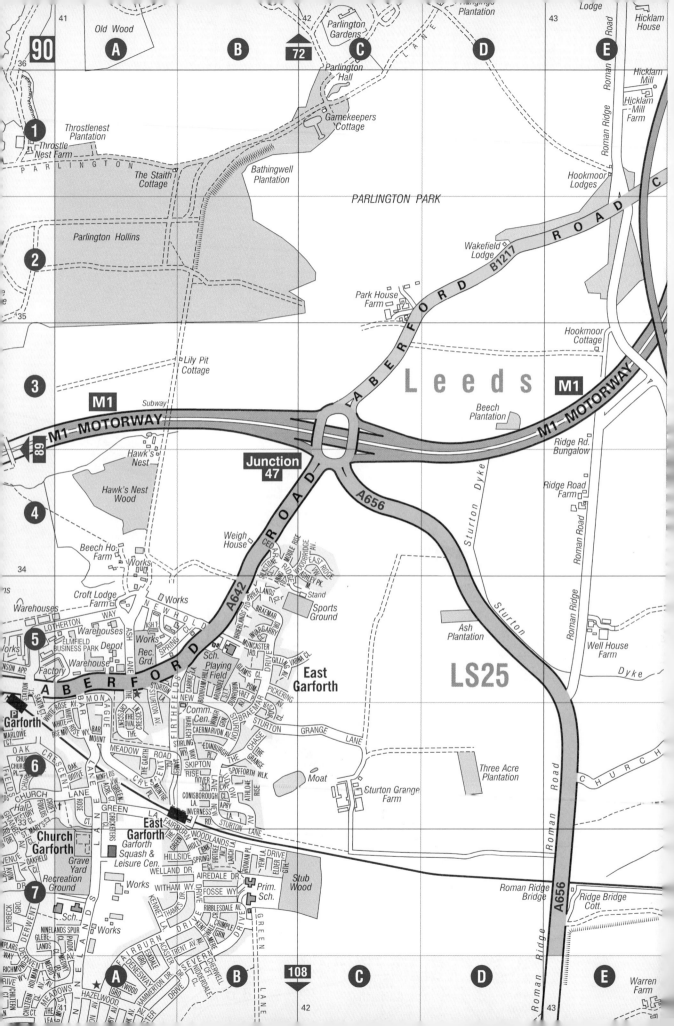

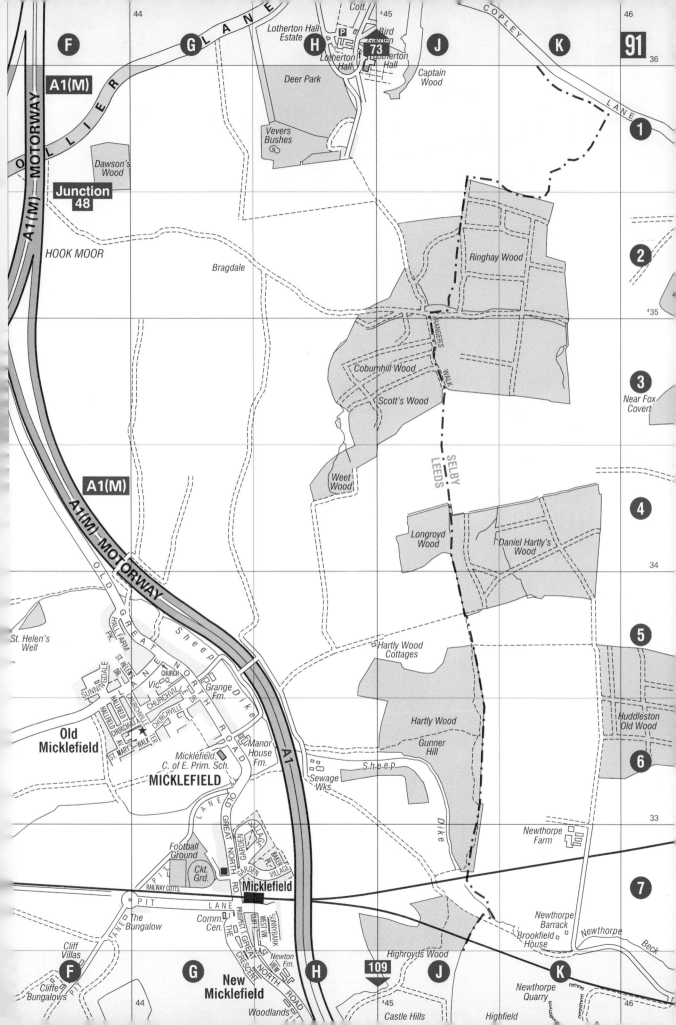

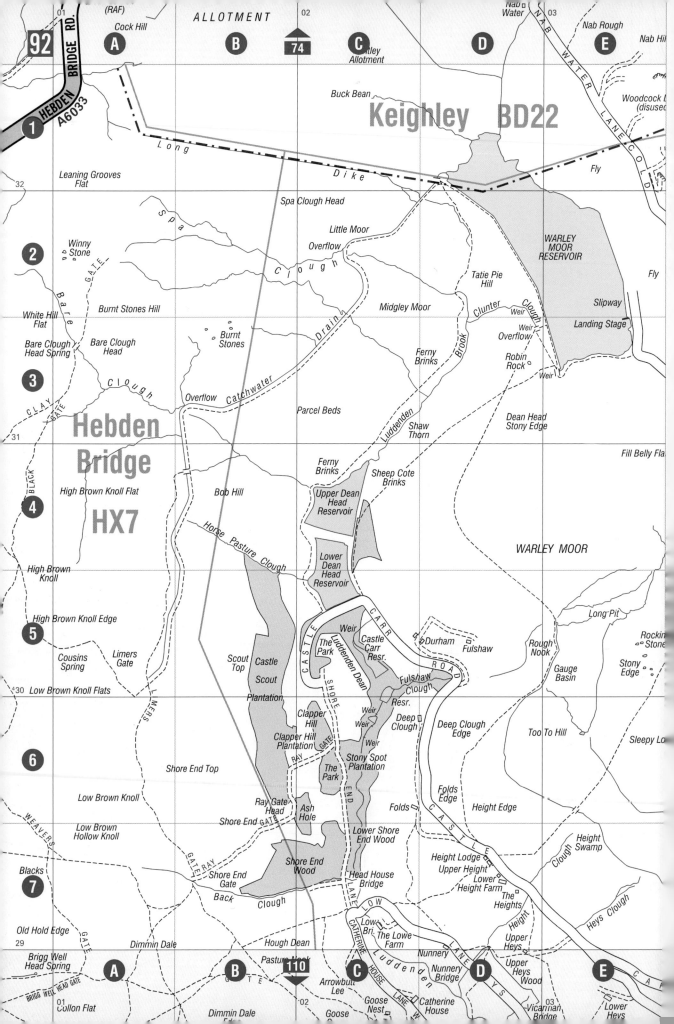

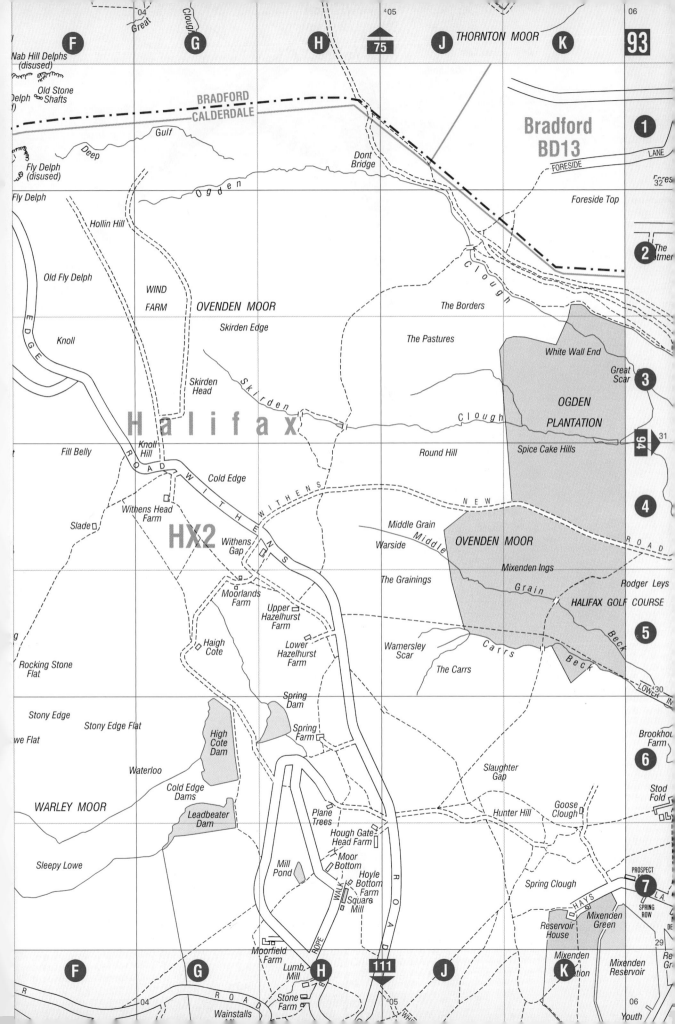

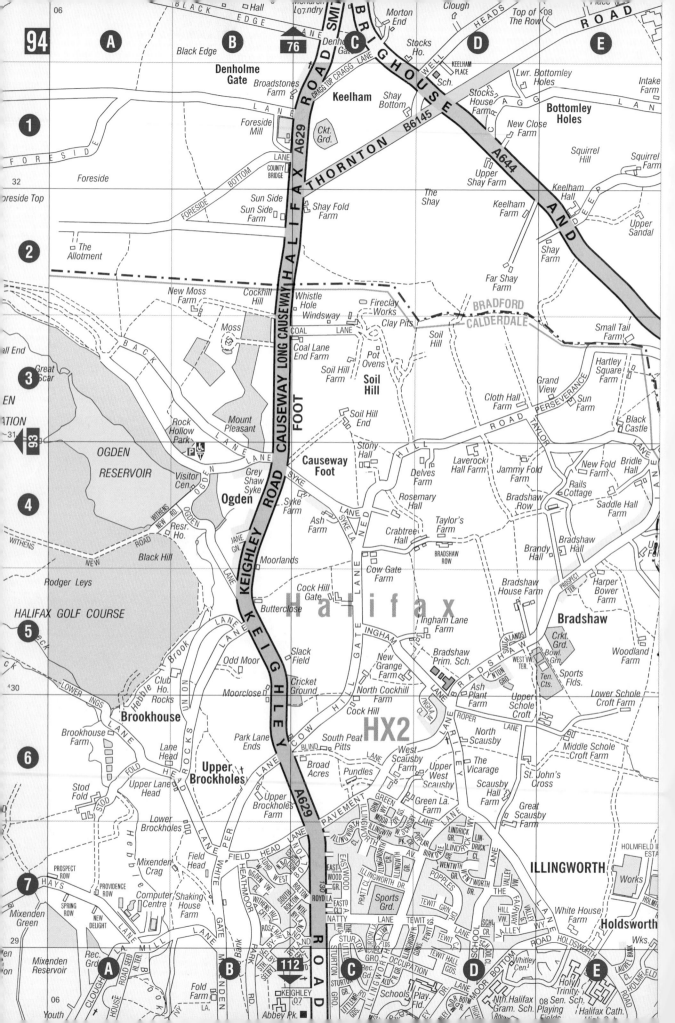

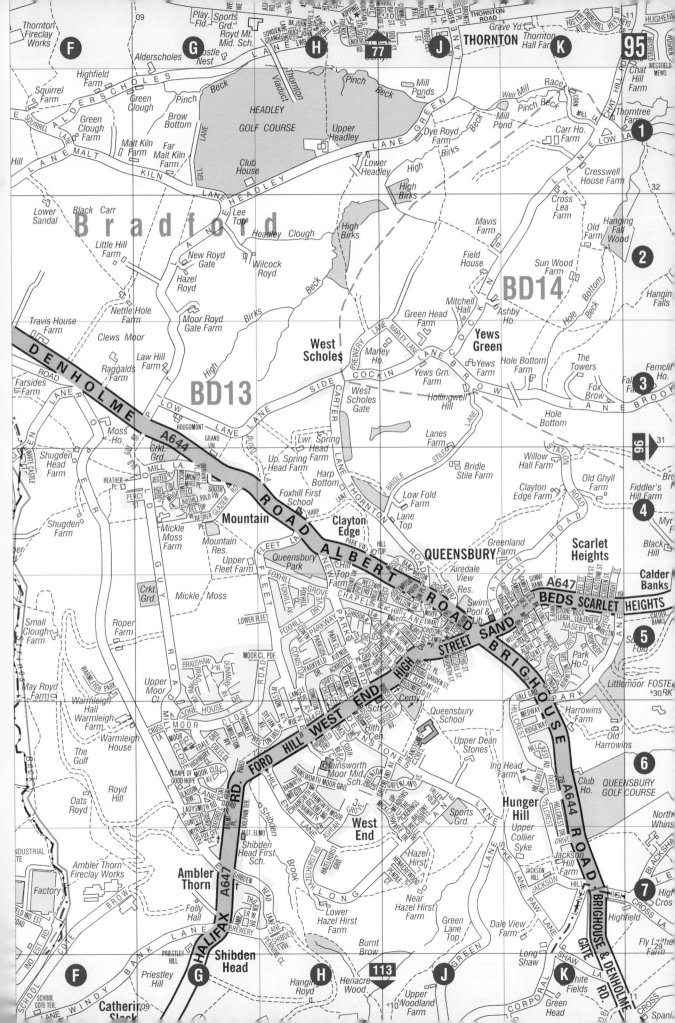

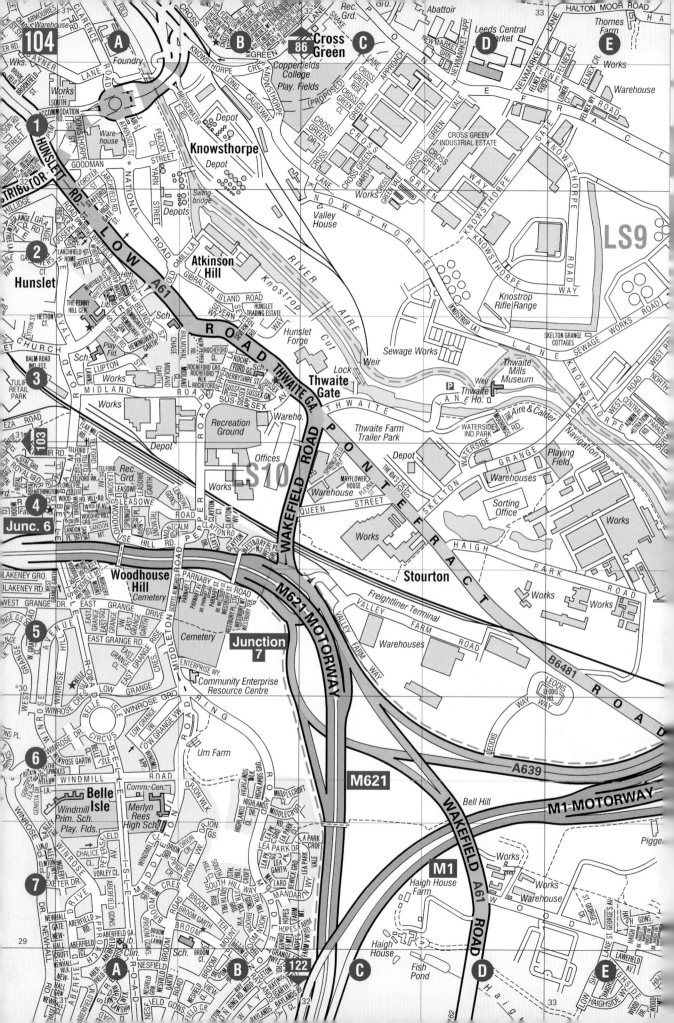

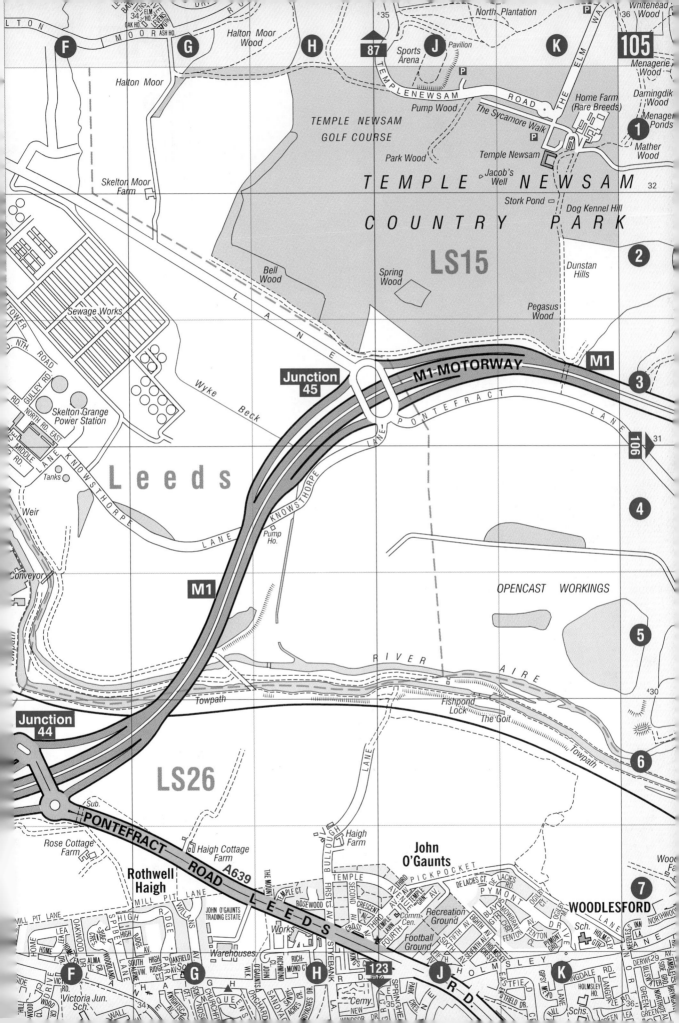

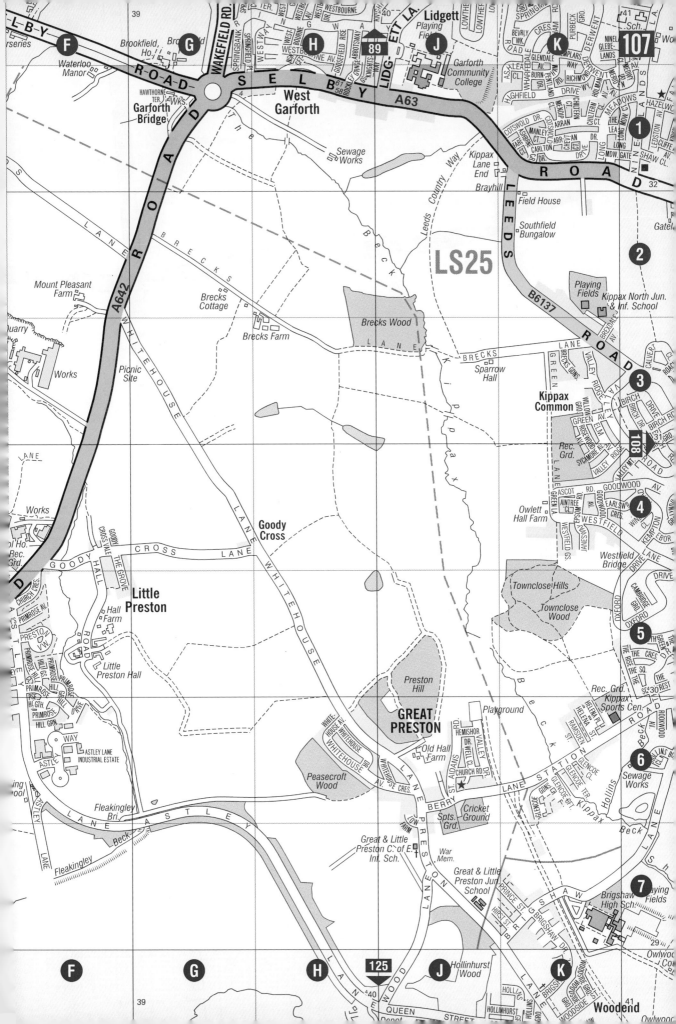

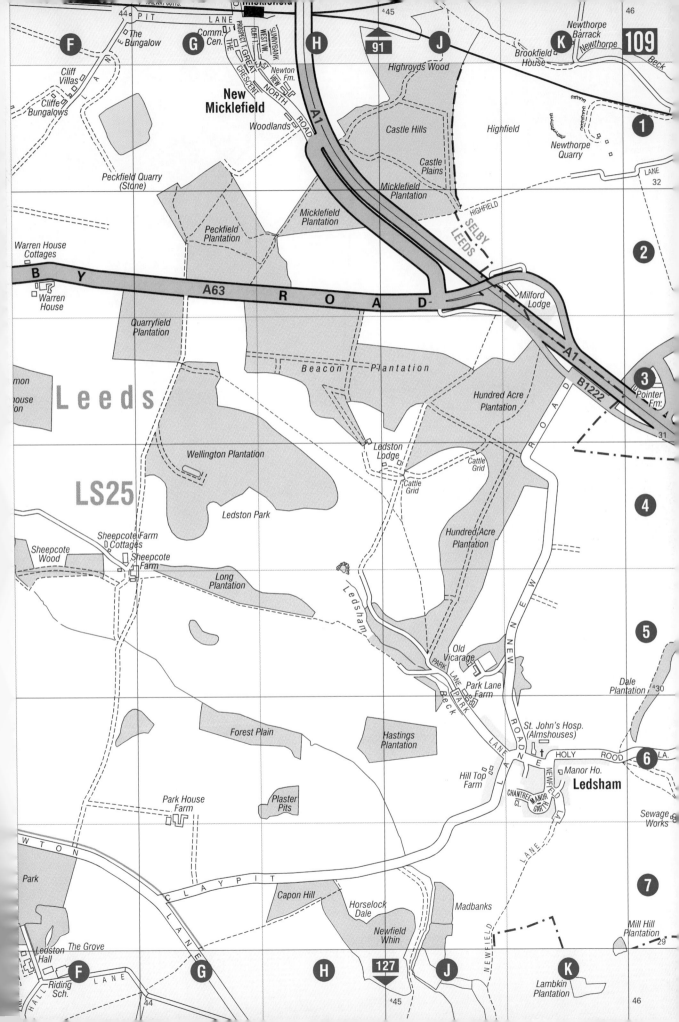

**F** **G** **H** **J** **K**

RAILWAY COTTS.
PIT LANE
44 45 46

The Bungalow
Comm. Cen.
Newthorpe Barrack
Newthorpe

Cliff Villas
PROSPECT
GREAT
SUNNYBANK
WEST VW.
CLIFF T.
Brookfield House
Newthorpe
Beck

Cliffe Bungalows
THE CRESCENT
NORTH ROAD
Newton Fm.
Newton Vw.
Highroyds Wood

**1**

**New Micklefield**
Woodlands
Castle Hills
Highfield
Newthorpe Quarry

LANE 32

Peckfield Quarry (Stone)
A1
Castle Plains

Mickliefield Plantation
Castle Plains
Mickliefield Plantation

Peckfield Plantation
Mickliefield Plantation
HIGHFIELD

**2**

Warren House Cottages
B Y
SELBY
LEEDS

Warren House
A63  R O A D
Milford Lodge

Quarryfield Plantation
A1

**Leeds**
B e a c o n   P l a n t a t i o n
Hundred Acre Plantation
B1222
Pointer Fm.

Ledston Lodge
Cattle Grid
31

**LS25**
Wellington Plantation
Cattle Grid
Hundred Acre Plantation

**4**

Ledston Park

Sheepcote Farm Cottages
Sheepcote Wood
Long Plantation
Ledsham Beck
Hundred Acre Plantation

Sheepcote Farm

**5**
Old Vicarage
Park Lane Farm
NEW ROAD

Dale Plantation
30

Forest Plain
Hastings Plantation
St. John's Hosp. (Almshouses)
HOLY ROOD LA.

**6**

Hill Top Farm
Manor Ho.
**Ledsham**

Park House Farm
Plaster Pits
CHANTREE CL.
MANOR GARTH
NEWFIELD LA.
Sewage Works

NWTON
Park
CLAYPIT LANE
Capon Hill
Horselock Dale
Madbanks

**7**

Ledston Hall
The Grove
Newfield Whin
NEWFIELD LANE
Mill Hill Plantation
29

Riding Sch.
HALL LANE
**F** **G** 44 **H** 127 45 **J** **K**
Lambkin Plantation
46

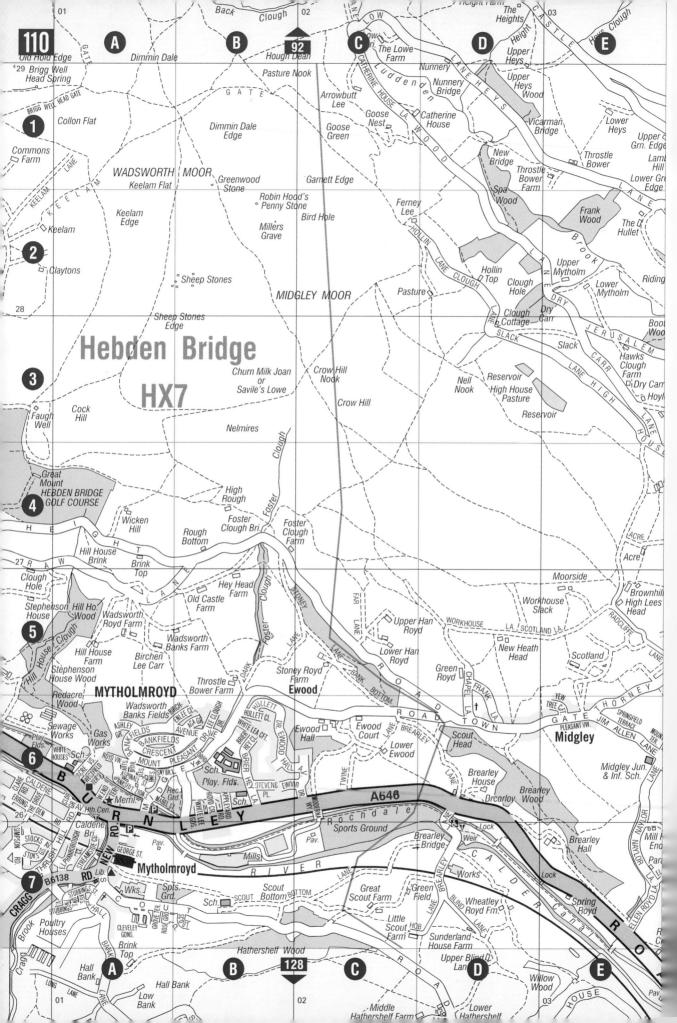

**92**

Old Hold Edge

A    Dimmin Dale    B    Hough Dean    C    The Lowe    D    Upper Heys    E

29 Brigg Well Head Spring    Pasture Nook    Low Bri    The Lowe Farm    Height Farm    The Heights    Hey's Clough

BRIGG WELL HEAD GATE    Nunnery    Upper Heys Wood    Lower Heys

1    Collon Flat    Dimmin Dale Edge    Arrowbutt Lee    Nunnery Bridge    Upper Grn. Edge

Commons Farm    Goose Nest    Catherine House    New Bridge    Vicarman Bridge    Throstle Bower    Lamb Hill

WADSWORTH MOOR    Greenwood Stone    Goose Green    Garnett Edge    Spa Wood    Throstle Bower Farm    Frank Wood    Lower Gr Edge

Keelam Flat    Robin Hood's Penny Stone    Bird Hole    Hollin Top    The Hullet

2    Keelam    Keelam Edge    Millers Grave    Ferney Lee    Clough Hole    Upper Mytholm    Riding

28    Claytons    Sheep Stones    Pasture    Clough Cottage    Dry Carr    Lower Mytholm    JERUSALEM

MIDGLEY MOOR    Nell Nook    High House Pasture    Clough Carr    Slack    Hawks Clough Farm    Boot Woo

Sheep Stones Edge    Churn Milk Joan or Savile's Lowe    Crow Hill Nook    Reservoir    Slack    Dry Carr    Hoyl

# Hebden Bridge
# HX7

3    Cock Hill    Crow Hill    Reservoir

Faugh Well    Nelmires    LANE HIGH HOUSE

Great Mount    High Rough    Foster Clough    Moorside    Acre    LACRE

4    HEBDEN BRIDGE GOLF COURSE    Wicken Hill    Rough Bottom    Foster Clough Bri.    Foster Clough Farm    Acre    Brownhill High Lees Head    RADCLIFFE

Hill House Brink    Brink Top    Hey Head Farm    Workhouse Slack    WORKHOUSE    Scotland

27    Clough Hole    Old Castle Farm    Upper Han Royd    SCOTLAND LA.    New Heath Head    Scotland

5    Stephenson Hill Ho. House    Wood    Wadsworth Royd Farm    Wadsworth Banks Farm    Stoney Royd Farm    Lower Han Royd    Green Royd    FRANK LA.    YEW TREE CFT.

Hill House Wood    Birchen Lee Carr    Throstle Bower Farm    Stoney Royd Farm    CHAPEL LA.    ROAD TOWN    Springfield Terrace    JIM ALLEN LA.    MOUN TER

Stephenson House Wood    **MYTHOLMROYD**    Ewood    GATE    Pleasant Vw.    **Midgley**    PLEASANT VW.

Redacre Wood    Wadsworth Banks Fields    Ewood Hall    Ewood Court    Lower Ewood    BREARLEY    Scout Head    THORNEY

Sewage Works    Gas Works    HULLETT DR.    Brearley House    Brearley Wood    Midgley Jun. & Inf. Sch.

6    WHITE HOUSES    Sch.    ASHLEY GRT.    BANKFIELDS CRESCENT    HULLETT CL.    WHITE LEA CFT.    Play. Flds.    Drcarloy

BURNLEY    MOUNT    PLEASANT    A646    Rochdale    Sports Ground    Brearley Bridge    Weir    Brearley Hall

26    CLARE RD    CALDENE    THE DENE    Caldene Bri.    Memll.    MABEL ST.    STEVENS PL.    Pav.    Pav.    Lock    Lock    Brearley Hall

7    B6138    RD    Lib    GEORGE ST.    **Mytholmroyd**    Mills    Great Scout Farm    Green Field    Works    Lock    Spring Royd

CRAGG    Poultry Houses    Wks.    Spts. Grd.    Sch.    Scout Bottom    RIVER    CALDER    Wheatley Royd Fm.    Sunderland House Farm    Ellen Royd La.

Brink Top    Sch.    Scout Bottom    Little Scout Farm    HOB    Mill

**128**

A    Hall Bank    B    Hatharshelf Wood    C    Upper Blind Lane    D    Lower Hathershelf    E

Low Bank    Long Lane    Middle Hathershelf Farm    Willow Wood

01    02    03

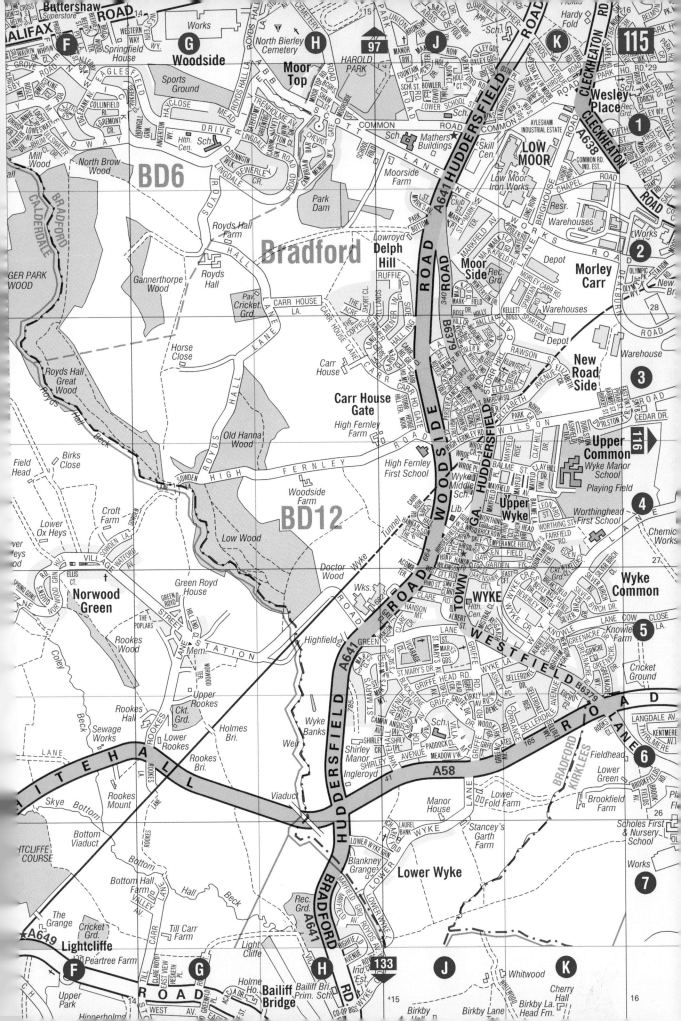

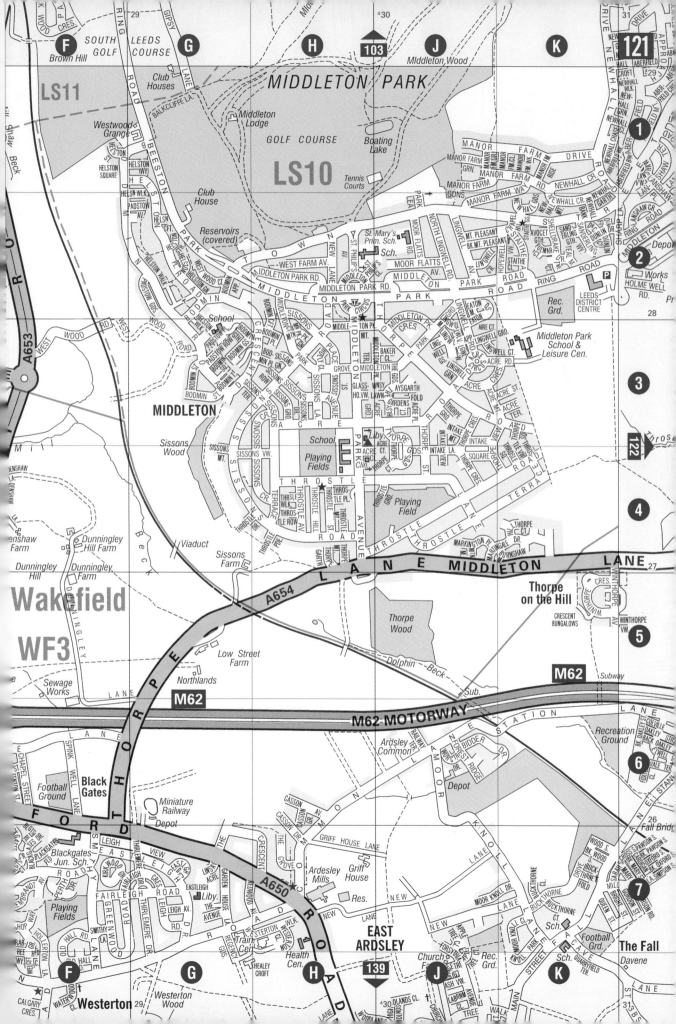

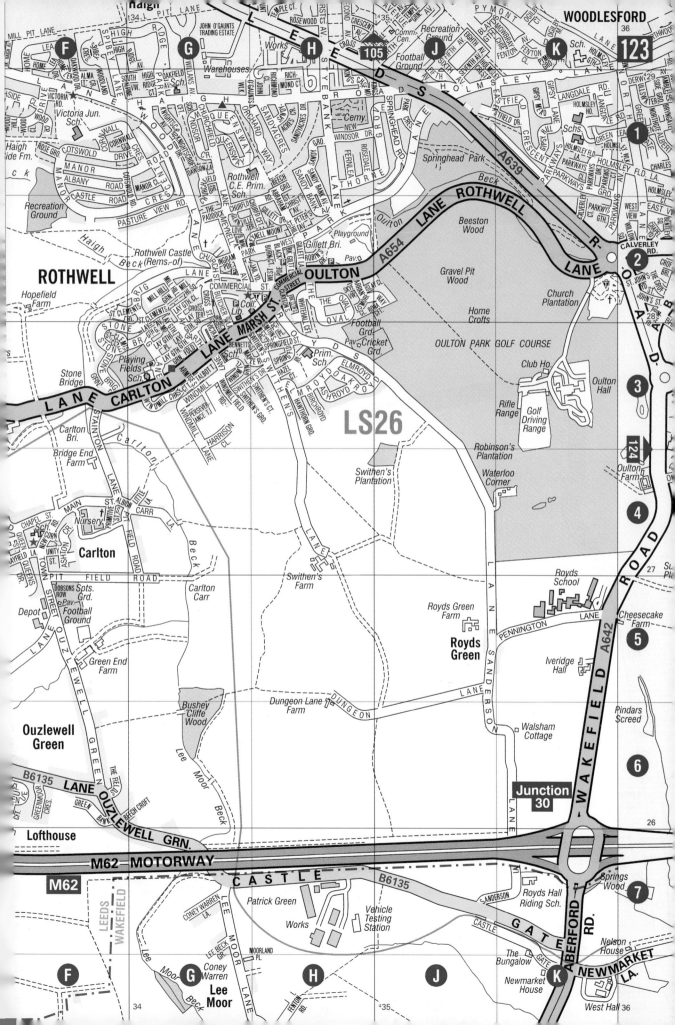

**A**  **B**  108  **C**  **D**  Seldon Hill  **E**

42  43

Brigshaw High Sch.  Playing Fields

Woodend

Owlwood Cotts.

Owl Wood

Owlwood Ho.

Owlwood Farm

Pit Plantation

Sewage Works

Kippax Park

Sheffield

Beck

Home Farm

Low Lodge

**A656 ROAD**

Roman Road

GREEN LANE

Elm Tree Farm

Lady Elizabeth Hastings C. of E. Prim. Sch.

**Ledston**

Manor Farm

Vicarage

Chestnut Farm

HIGHFIELD

Whin Covert

Little Plantation

Allerton Plantation

Park Lane Farm

Sheffield Beck

Sewage Wks.

LANE MAIN LEDSTONE STREET

**Playing Field**

**ALLERTON BYWATER**

MANOR PK. AV.

BLANDS CRES.

BLANDS TER.

BLANDS GRO.

BLANDS AV.

GRANGE PK. CL.

Allerton Bywater Prim. Sch.  Liby.

VICARS TER.

ST. MY'S. CT.

Spts. Grd.

PARK LANE

PARK AV.

PARK AVENUE

NEWTON

LEDSTON INGS

Depot

LEDSTONE LANE

DIKE

28

Sluices

STATION ROAD

ST. MAIN ST.

VICTORIA CL.

WHITE ST.

MOSS LEVEL ST.

ROBINSON ST.

Station Ter.

ROAD

Roman Ridge

Depot

ARROW LIN

**P**

**Leeds LS26**

125

Parlour Pit Wood

PROVIDENCE PL.

BOAT LA.

BACK

Sluice

Cricket Ground

ROAD

Roman Ridge

MICKLETOWN

CONEY MOOR GRO.

MOOR VIE 27

**Lower Mickletown**

LANE

BOAT

RIVER

Coney Moor

Willow Grove Farm

Quarry (sand)

AIRE

Allerton Ings

BARNSDALE

Ledston Ings

Bulholme Clough

Bulholme Lock

Coney Moor Common

Quarry (sand)

**THE OXBOW LAKES**

River Calder (Old Course)

River Calder (Old Course)

The Island

**LEEDS**

**WAKEFIELD**

Junction Houses

Aire & Calder Navigation

Castleford Cut

Works

Works

**Castleford Ings**

Works

RIVER

RYEBREAD

26

RIVER CALDER

The Island

River Calder (Old Course)

Recreation Ground

Works

Depot

Wharf

Works

Riverside Medical Cen.

Comm. Recreation Cen. Ground

Depot

WILLIAM STREET

WILLIAM ST.

GREEN ST.

JAMES ST.

HUNT ST.

MILL LANE

AIRE ST.

Weir

Castleford Bridge

Playing Fields

Depot

Factory

Wheldon Inf. Sch.

SCHOOL

QUEEN

WILLIAM ST.

THOMAS ST.

ELAND ST.

BRAZIL ST.

NEW

SWING

**A6032**

7

**LEEDS A639 ROAD**

Methley Bridge

Methley Bridge Farm

Rec. Grd. Playgrnd

JIN-WHIN HILL

RAGLAND ST.

GLAN CL.

WOOD VW.

Recreation Ground

**Whitwood Mere**

**METHLEY A6032 ROAD**

BRYANT

PHILLIPS ST.

HUNT ST.

TELFORD

DAVID ST.

**SAVILE RD.**

POTTER ST.

CALDER ST.

CINDER LA.

Works

MOSS ST.

CROSS ST.

SCHOOL

DUKES

WELLINGTON ST.

VICTORIA ST.

MILTON ST.

WOOD

LISTER ST.

WILSON ST.

Works

CARLTON ST.

FLORENCE ST.

STATION RD.

**A655 ROAD**

**ALBION ST.**

CHURCH STREET

MARY

BACK BANK

Lib & Mus.

Hlth Cen.

BRADLEY

WESLEY

WELBECK

CARLTON ST.

SAGAR

BRIDGE ST.

YORK

Lib. & P.O.

**Castleford**

CAMBRIDGE RD.

STANLEY ST.

DENTON TER.

**A656 PONTEFRACT RD.**

EASTFIELD

MEDLEY

MORRISON

Play.

**A**  Three Lane Ends Prim. Sch.

WOODVIEW BUNGALOWS

W. CR.

W. VW.

Cemy.

**B**  **CASTLEFORD**

RALWY ST.

PAULINE ST.

Foundry

Works

HIGH ST.

CHURCH

HIGH OXFORD ST.  MIDDLE OXFORD ST.

Dep.

42  43

**C**

Trading Est.

Enterprise

Bus. Sta.

Sub.

LWR. OXFORD ST.

**D**

GLEBE

OXFORD ST.

HUGH

AMBLER

**E**

SMAWTHORNE LA.

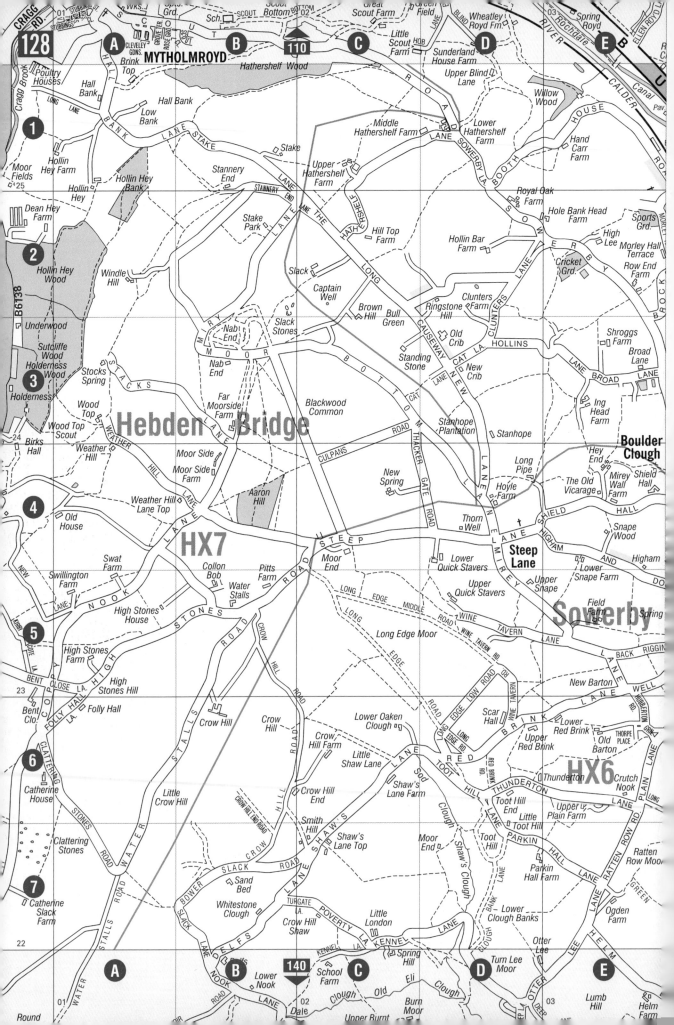

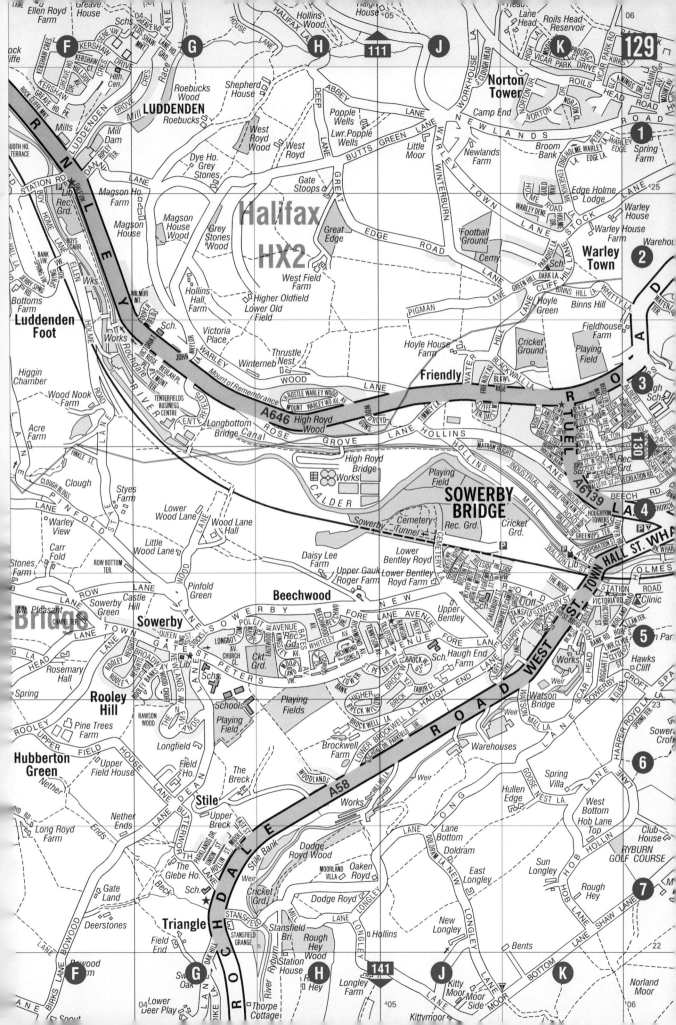

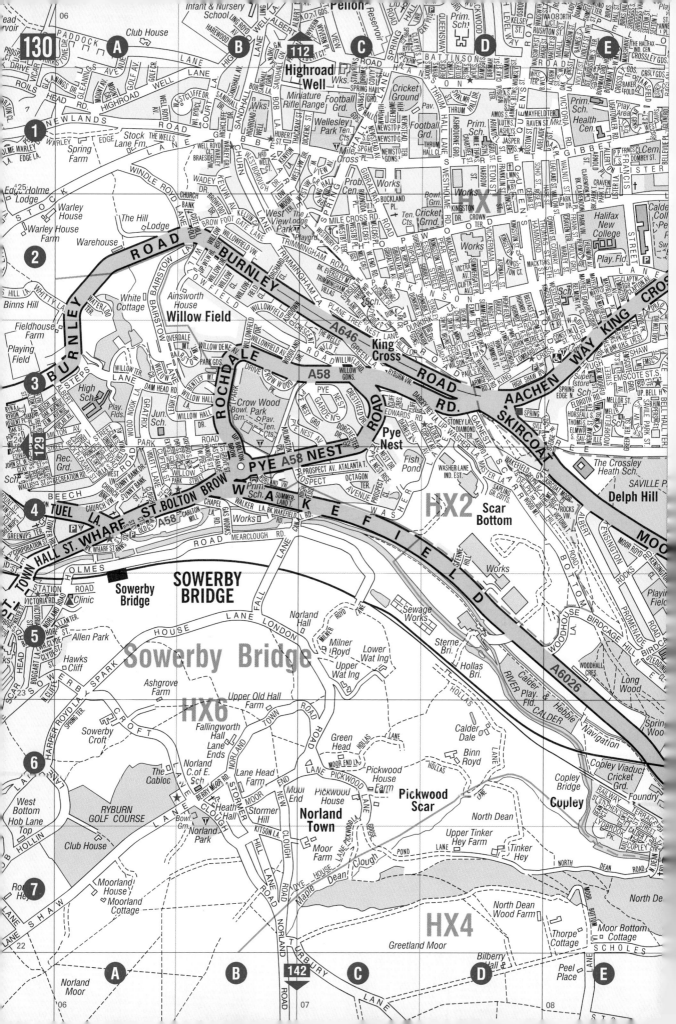

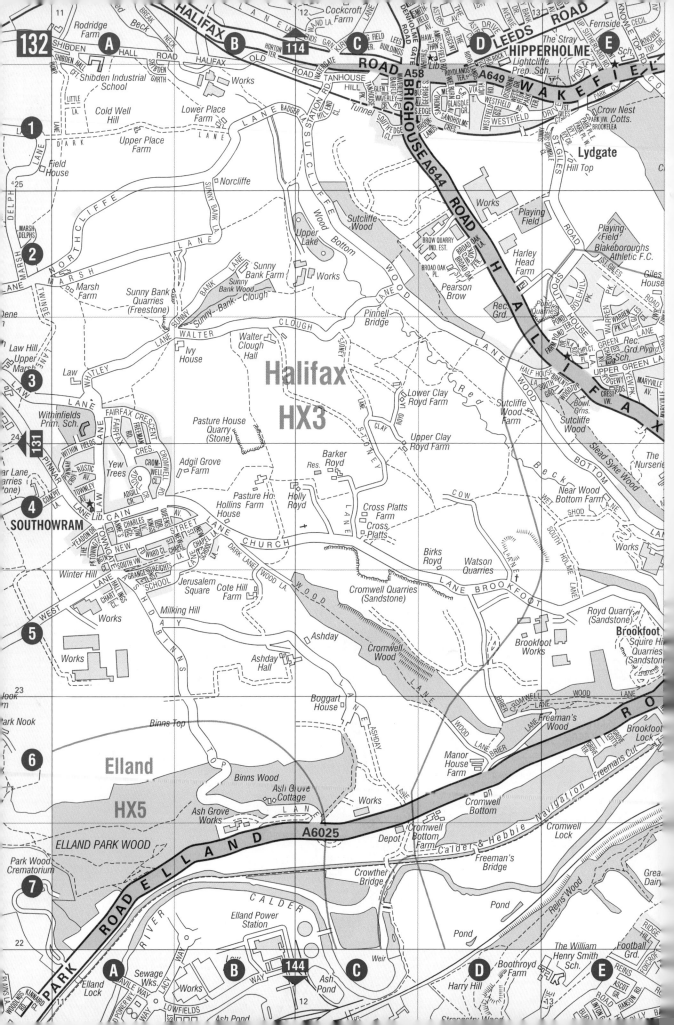

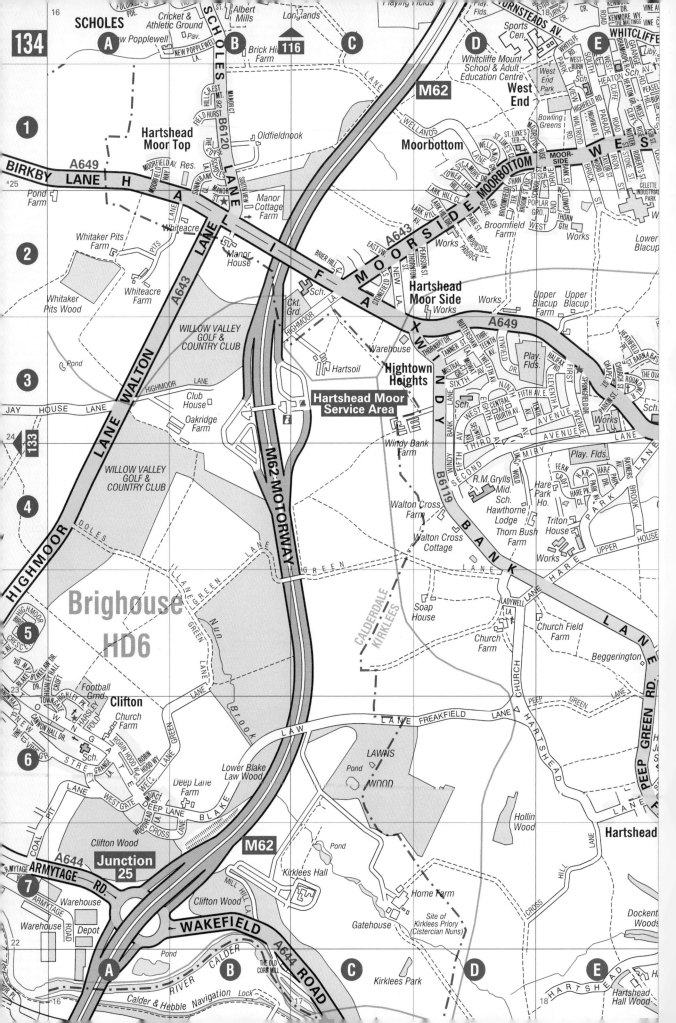

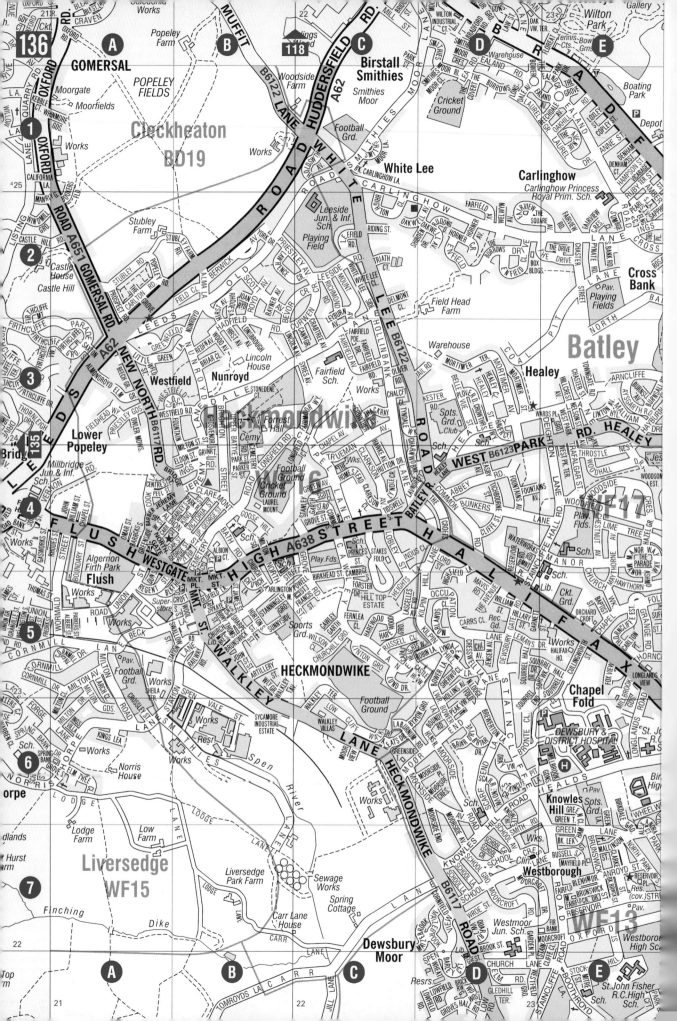

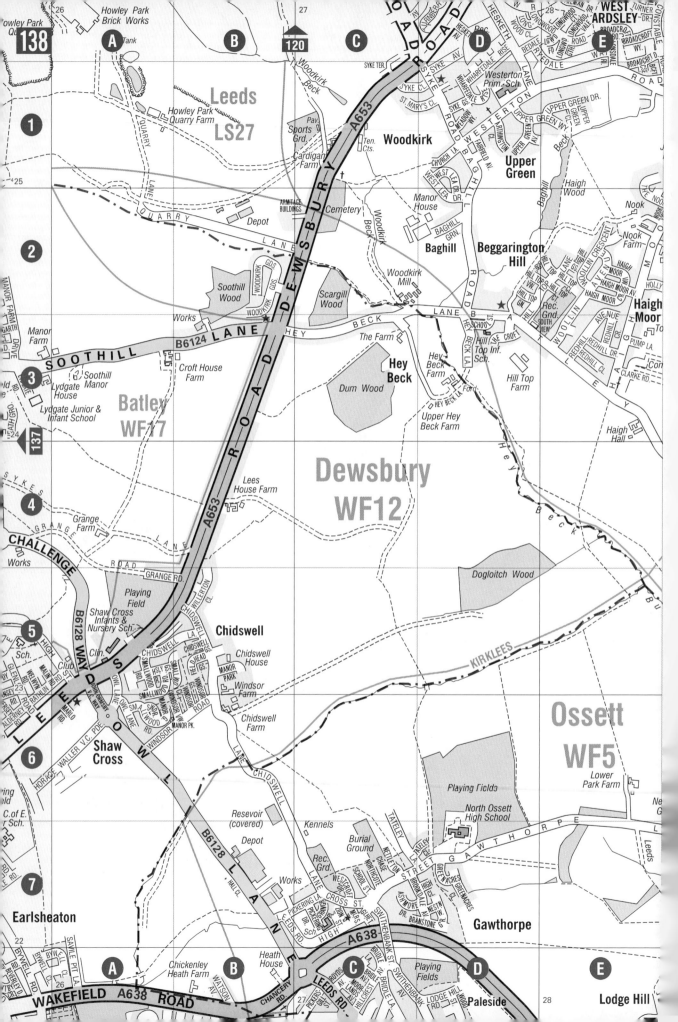

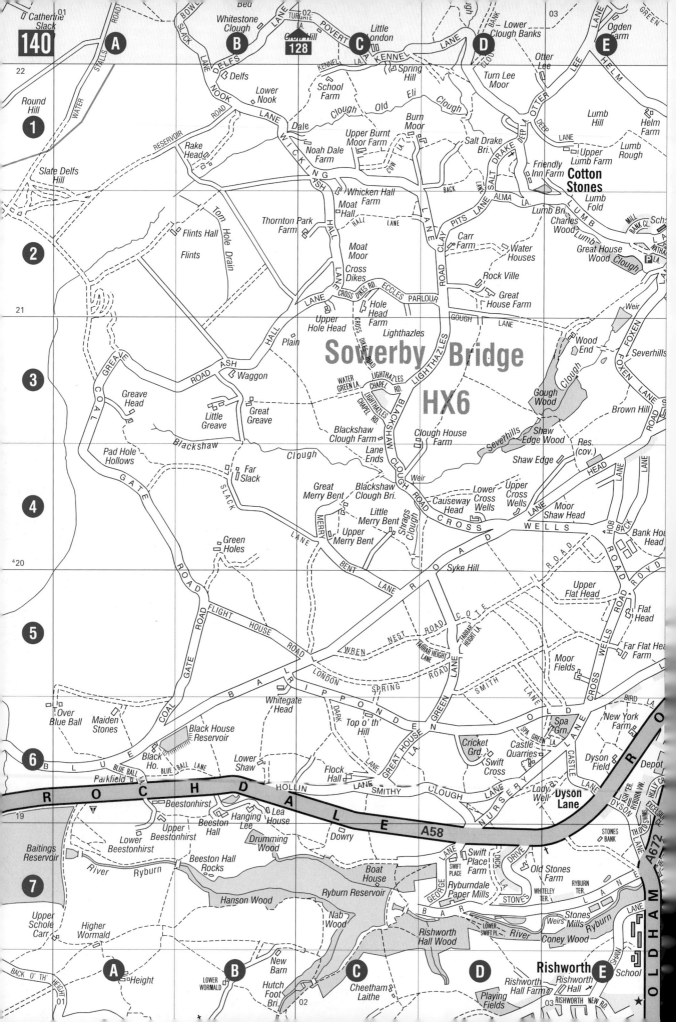

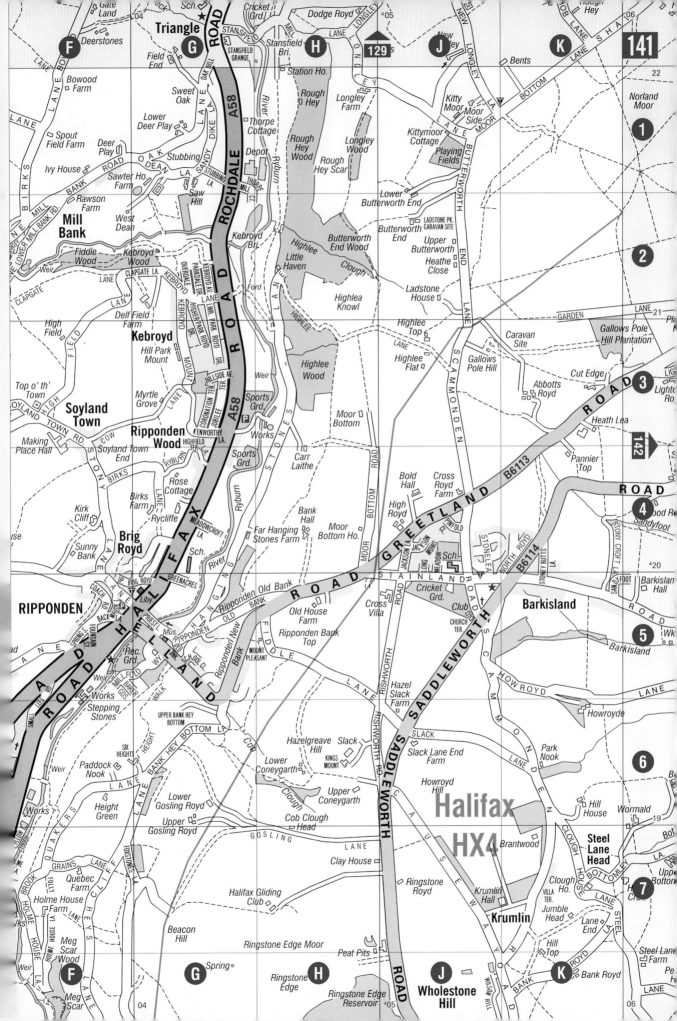

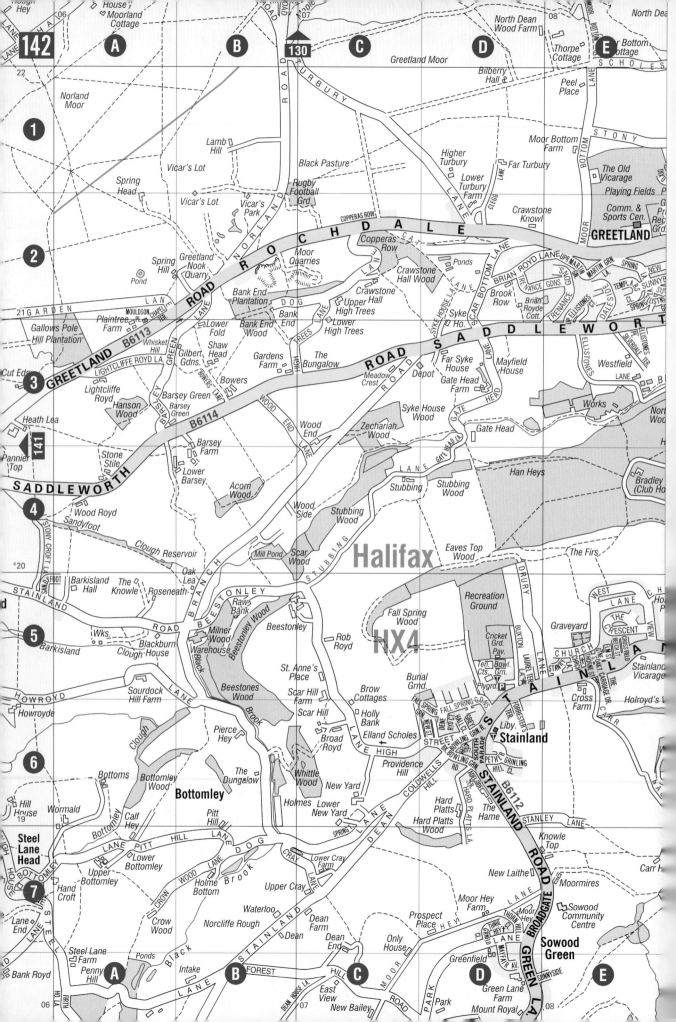

# INDEX

Including Streets, Places & Areas, Industrial Estates, Selected Junction Names,
Selected Subsidiary Addresses and Selected Tourist Information.

## HOW TO USE THIS INDEX

1. Each street name is followed by its Posttown or Postal Locality and then by its map reference; e.g. Aachen Way. *Hal* —3D **130** is in the Halifax Posttown and is to be found in square 3D on page **130**. The page number being shown in bold type.
   A strict alphabetical order is followed in which Av., Rd., St., etc. (though abbreviated) are read in full and as part of the street name; e.g. Adam St. appears after Adams Pk. but before Adam's Wlk.

2. Streets and a selection of Subsidiary names not shown on the Maps, appear in the index in *Italics* with the thoroughfare to which it is connected shown in brackets; e.g. *Abbey Gth. Yead* —5K **45** (off Well Hill)

3. Places and areas are shown in the index in **bold type**, the map reference referring to the actual map square in which the town or area is located and not to the place name; e.g. **Aberford.** —5E **72**

4. Map references shown in brackets; e.g. Aireside Cen. Leeds —6G **85** (7B **4**) refer to entries that also appear on the large scale pages 4-5 (Leeds) and 6-7 (Bradford).

5. With the now general usage of Postcodes for addressing mail, it is not recommended that this index is used for such a purpose.

## GENERAL ABBREVIATIONS

| | | | | |
|---|---|---|---|---|
| All : Alley | Clo : Close | Gth : Garth | M : Mews | VI : Sixth |
| App : Approach | Comn : Common | Ga : Gate | Mt : Mount | S : South |
| Arc : Arcade | Cotts : Cottages | Gt : Great | N : North | Sq : Square |
| Av : Avenue | Ct : Court | Grn : Green | Pal : Palace | Sta : Station |
| Bk : Back | Cres : Crescent | Gro : Grove | Pde : Parade | St : Street |
| Boulevd : Boulevard | Cft : Croft | Ho : House | Pk : Park | Ter : Terrace |
| Bri : Bridge | Dri : Drive | Ind : Industrial | Pas : Passage | III : Third |
| B'way : Broadway | E : East | Junct : Junction | Pl : Place | Trad : Trading |
| Bldgs : Buildings | VIII : Eighth | La : Lane | Quad : Quadrant | Up : Upper |
| Bus : Business | Embkmt : Embankment | Lit : Little | Res : Residential | Va : Vale |
| Cvn : Caravan | Est : Estate | Lwr : Lower | Ri : Rise | Vw : View |
| Cen : Centre | Fld : Field | Mc : Mac | Rd : Road | Vs : Villas |
| Chu : Church | V : Fifth | Mnr : Manor | St : Saint | Wlk : Walk |
| Chyd : Churchyard | I : First | Mans : Mansions | II : Second | W : West |
| Circ : Circle | IV : Fourth | Mkt : Market | VII : Seventh | Yd : Yard |
| Cir : Circus | Gdns : Gardens | Mdw : Meadow | Shop : Shopping | |

## POSTTOWN AND POSTAL LOCALITY ABBREVIATIONS

| | | | | |
|---|---|---|---|---|
| *Aber* : Aberford | *Crack* : Crackenedge | *Heck* : Heckmondwike | *M'end* : Moorend | *S Mil* : South Milford |
| *Add* : Addingham | *Cra V* : Cragg Vale | *H Eld* : High Eldwick | *Msde* : Moorside | *S'wram* : Southowram |
| *Adel* : Adel | *Cro H* : Cross Hills | *High* : Highfield | *Moort* : Moortown | *Sower* : Sowerby |
| *Ain T* : Ainley Top | *Cro R* : Cross Roads | *H'town* : Hightown | *Morl* : Morley | *Sower B* : Sowerby Bridge |
| *All* : Allerton | *Ctly* : Cottingley | *Hip* : Hipperholme | *Mt Tab* : Mount Tabor | *Sow* : Sowood |
| *All B* : Allerton Bywater | *Cull* : Cullingworth | *H'bck* : Holbeck | *Myth* : Mytholmroyd | *Stainc* : Staincliffe |
| *Alw* : Alwoodley | *Cut H* : Cutler Heights | *H Wd* : Holme Wood | *Nesf* : Nesfield | *Slnd* : Stainland |
| *App B* : Apperley Bridge | *D Hill* : Daisy Hill | *H'fld* : Holmfield | *N Clift* : Newall with Clifton | *Stain* : Stainton |
| *A'ley* : Armley | *Dean C* : Dean Clough Ind. Pk. | *Holy G* : Holywell Green | *N Bnk* : New Bank | *Stanb* : Stanbury |
| *Arth* : Arthington | *Denh* : Denholme | *H'fth* : Horsforth | *N Brig* : New Brighton | *Stan* : Stanley |
| *Askw* : Askwith | *Den* : Denton | *Hov E* : Hove Edge | *N Farn* : New Farnley | *S'ley* : Stanningley |
| *Bail* : Baildon | *Dew* : Dewsbury | *Hud* : Huddersfield | *Newt K* : Newton Kyme | *Steet* : Steeton |
| *Bail B* : Bailiff Bridge | *Dew M* : Dewsbury Moor | *H'let* : Hunslet | *N Wort* : New Wortley | *Stum X* : Stump Cross |
| *B Top* : Bank Top | *Dlgtn* : Drighlington | *Hun P* : Hunslet Bus. Pk. | *Norl* : Norland | *Sut Cr* : Sutton-in-Craven |
| *Bard* : Bardsey | *E Ard* : East Ardsley | *Huns* : Hunsworth | *Norr* : Norristhorpe | *Swil* : Swillington |
| *Bklnd* : Barkisland | *E Bier* : East Bierley | *Hyde P* : Hyde Park | *N'wram* : Northowram | *Swil C* : Swillington Common |
| *Bar E* : Barwick in Elmet | *Eastb* : Eastbourne | *Idle* : Idle | *Nor G* : Norwood Green | *Tad* : Tadcaster |
| *Bat* : Batley | *Ebrn* : Eastburn | *Idle M* : Idle Moor | *Oaken* : Oakenshaw | *Thack* : Thackley |
| *Bat C* : Batley Carr | *E Kes* : East Keswick | *I'ly* : Ilkley | *Oakw* : Oakworth | *Thornb* : Thornbury |
| *Bees* : Beeston | *E Mor* : East Morton | *I'wth* : Illingworth | *Ogden* : Ogden | *T'ner* : Thorner |
| *Ben R* : Ben Rhydding | *Eccl* : Eccleshill | *Int* : Intake | *Oldf* : Oldfield | *T'tn* : Thornton |
| *Bier* : Bierley | *Eccup* : Eccup | *Kear* : Kearby | *Oss* : Ossett | *Thor A* : Thorp Arch |
| *Bgly* : Bingley | *Eld* : Eldwick | *Kei* : Keighley | *Otley* : Otley | *Thpe* : Thorpe (nr. Ashbourne) |
| *Bkby* : Birkby | *Ell* : Elland | *Kild* : Kildwick | *Oult* : Oulton | *Thor* : Thorpe (nr. Wakefield) |
| *B'shaw* : Birkenshaw | *Esh* : Esholt | *Kip* : Kippax | *Oven* : Ovenden | *T Brow* : Thwaites Brow |
| *Birs* : Birstall | *Euro I* : Euroway Ind. Est. | *Kirk D* : Kirk Deighton | *Oven W* : Ovenden Wood | *Ting* : Tingley |
| *B'ley* : Blackley | *Fag* : Fagley | *K'gate* : Kirkhamgate | *Oxe* : Oxenhope | *Tong* : Tong |
| *B Spa* : Boston Spa | *Fair* : Fairburn | *Kirks* : Kirkstall | *Pel* : Pellon | *Tri* : Triangle |
| *B'twn* : Boothtown | *F'hll* : Farnhill | *Lais* : Laisterdyke | *Pen I* : Penraevon Ind. Est. | *Tyer* : Tyersal |
| *B'frd* : Bradford | *F'ley* : Farnley | *Lay* : Laycock | *Pool W* : Pool in Wharfedale | *Utley* : Utley |
| *Bdly* : Bradley | *Fars* : Farsley | *Leat* : Leathley | *Pott* : Potternewton | *Wadsw* : Wadsworth |
| *Bshw* : Bradshaw | *Far* : Fartown | *Led* : Ledsham | *Pot* : Potterton | *Wains* : Wainstalls |
| *B'ham* : Bramham | *F'stne* : Featherstone | *Leds* : Ledston | *Pud* : Pudsey | *Wake* : Wakefield |
| *B'hpe* : Bramhope | *Fern* : Ferncliffe | *Leeds* : Leeds | *Q'bry* : Queensbury | *Wltn* : Walton |
| *Bmly* : Bramley | *Field B* : Fieldhead Bus. Cen. | *Light* : Lightcliffe | *Ragg* : Raggalds | *Warley* : Warley |
| *Brigh* : Brighouse | *Five L* : Five Lane Ends | *Lind* : Lindley | *Ras* : Rastrick | *W Bowl* : West Bowling |
| *Broc* : Brockholes | *Fix* : Fixby | *Lntn* : Linton | *Rawd* : Rawdon | *Wgte* : Westgate |
| *Brun I* : Brunswick Ind. Est. | *Flush* : Flush | *List* : Listerhills | *Rawf* : Rawfolds | *Weston* : Weston |
| *Bur W* : Burley in Wharfedale | *Four E* : Four Lane Ends | *Lit T* : Little Town | *Raw* : Rawmarsh | *W Park* : West Park |
| *Bur W* : Burton on the Wolds | *Friz* : Frizinghall | *Liv* : Liversedge | *Riddl* : Riddlesden | *West I* : West 26 Ind. Est. |
| *Butt* : Buttershaw | *Fry* : Fryston | *Loft* : Lofthouse | *Ripp* : Ripponden | *Wee* : Weeton |
| *C'ley* : Calverley | *Gar* : Garforth | *Lwr W* : Lower Wortley | *Rbtwn* : Roberttown | *Weet* : Weetwood |
| *Carl* : Carlton | *Gild* : Gildersome | *L Wyke* : Lower Wyke | *Rob H* : Robin Hood | *Weth* : Wetherby |
| *Carr G* : Carr Gate | *Gil* : Gilstead | *Lfds B* : Lowfields Bus. Pk. | *Rod* : Rodley | *Wheat* : Wheatley |
| *C'frd* : Castleford | *Gom* : Gomersal | *Low M* : Low Moor | *Rothw* : Rothwell | *Wibs* : Wibsey |
| *Caus F* : Causeway Foot | *Gt Hor* : Great Horton | *Lowt* : Lowtown | *Round* : Roundhay | *Wike* : Wike |
| *C'gts* : Crossgates | *Gre* : Greengates | *Low U* : Low Utley | *Sandb* : Sandbeds | *Wilsd* : Wilsden |
| *C Grn* : Cross Green | *G'lnd* : Greetland | *Ludd* : Luddenden | *S'cft* : Scarcroft | *Windh* : Windhill |
| *Chap A* : Chapel Allerton | *Guis* : Guiseley | *L'ft* : Luddendenfoot | *Schol* : Scholes (nr. Cleckheaton) | *Whinm* : Whinmoor |
| *Chap* : Chapeltown | *Haig* : Haigh | *Mann* : Manningham | *Scholes* : Scholes (nr. Leeds) | *W'wood* : Whitwood |
| *Chur* : Churwell | *Hain* : Hainworth | *Mar* : Marsh | *Seac* : Seacroft | *W'wd M* : Whitwood Mere |
| *Cytn* : Clayton | *Hal* : Halifax | *Mean* : Meanwood | *Shad* : Shadwell | *W'ford* : Woodlesford |
| *Cleck* : Cleckheaton | *Halt* : Halton | *Men* : Menston | *Shaw B* : Shaw Cross Bus. Pk. | *Wort* : Wortley |
| *Cliff* : Clifford | *Hang H* : Hanging Heaton | *Meth* : Methley | *Sheep* : Sheepridge | *Woth* : Wothersome |
| *Clif* : Clifton | *H'den* : Harden | *M'fld* : Micklefield | *She* : Shelf | *Wren* : Wrenthorpe |
| *Clif C* : Clifton Common | *Hare* : Harewood | *M'wte* : Micklethwaite | *Sher E* : Sherburn in Elmet | *Wrose* : Wrose |
| *Coll* : Collingham | *Harts* : Hartshead | *Mick M* : Mickletown Methley | *Shib* : Shibden | *Wyke* : Wyke |
| *Colt* : Colton | *Haw* : Haworth | *Midd* : Middleton | *Shipl* : Shipley | *Wyth I* : Wyther Park Ind. Est. |
| *Cnly* : Cononley | *H'wd* : Hazlewood | *Midg* : Midgley | *Sick* : Sicklinghall | *Yead* : Yeadon |
| *Cook* : Cookridge | *Head* : Headingley | *Mill B* : Mill Bank | *Sid* : Siddal | |
| *Cop* : Copley | *H'tn* : Heaton | *Mir* : Mirfield | *Sils* : Silsden | |
| *Cowl* : Cowling | *H Bri* : Hebden Bridge | *Mix* : Mixenden | *Ski G* : Skircoat Green | |

# INDEX

Allenby Cres.—Ashford Grn.


Allenby Cres. Leeds —6G 103
Allenby Dri. Leeds —6G 103
Allenby Gdns. Leeds —6G 103
Allenby Gro. Leeds —6G 103
Allenby Pl. Leeds —6G 103
Allenby Rd. Leeds —6G 103
Allenby Vw. Leeds —5H 103
Allen Cft. B'shaw —2J 117
Allerby Grn. B'frd —7F 97
Allerton. —4B 78
Allerton Av. Leeds —2K 67
Allerton Bywater. —1K 125
Allerton Clo. All —4B 78
Allerton Ct. Leeds —2K 67
(off Harrogate Rd.)
Allerton Dri. E Kes —3A 34
Allerton Grange Av. Leeds —3A 68
Allerton Grange Clo. Leeds —4J 67
Allerton Grange Cres. Leeds —4K 67
Allerton Grange Cft. Leeds —4A 68
Allerton Grange Dri. All —4B 78
Allerton Grange Dri. Leeds —4K 67
Allerton Grange Gdns. Leeds —4K 67
Allerton Grange Ri. Leeds —4J 67
Allerton Grange Va. Leeds —4K 67
Allerton Grange Wlk. Leeds —4K 67
Allerton Grange Way. Leeds —4K 67
Allerton Gro. Leeds —2K 67
Allerton Hall. Leeds —5J 67
Allerton Hill. Chap A —5J 67
Allerton La. T'tn & All —6A 78
Allerton M. Leeds —3K 67
Allerton Pk. Leeds —5K 67
Allerton Pl. Hal —1E 130
Allerton Pl. Leeds —2K 67
Allerton Rd. All & B'frd —4H 77
(in two parts)
Allerton St. Leeds —3D 84
Allerton Ter. Leeds —4D 84
Alliance St. Leeds —6A 84
Allinson St. Leeds —7E 84
Allison Dri. Hud —7H 145
Allison La. B'frd —1K 79
Allison St. F'stne —5H 71
Allison Ter. K'gte —6H 139
Alloe Fld. Pl. Hal —1C 112
Alloe Fld. Vw. Hal —1C 112
Allotments Rd. Denh —4C 76
All Saint's Circ. W'ford —1B 124
All Saint's Dri. W'ford —1A 124
All Saints Rd. B'frd —1H 97
All Saint's Rd. W'ford —7B 106
All Saint's Vw. W'ford —7A 106
All Souls' Rd. Hal —6G 113
All Souls' St. Hal —6G 113
All Souls' Ter. Hal —6G 113
Allums La. Arth —6E 30
Alma Clo. Fars —2A 82
Alma Cotts. Leeds —7D 66
Alma Gro. Shipl —4K 61
Alma La. Heck —2B 136
Alma La. Sower B —2D 140
Alma Pl. Kei —7A 40
Alma Rd. Leeds —7D 66
Alma St. B'frd —1E 98
Alma St. Cut H —2F 99
Alma St. Haw —4E 56
Alma St. Kei —7A 40
Alma St. Leeds —4A 86 (3K 5)
Alma St. Q'bry —5H 95
Alma St. Shipl —4K 61
Alma St. W'ford —7A 106
Alma St. Yead —4A 46
Alma Ter. B'frd —5F 81
Alma Ter. E Mor —2J 41
Alma Ter. Kei —7A 40
Alma Ter. Rothw —1F 123
Almondroyd. Heck —3A 136
Almond St. B'frd —7E 80
Almond Way. Bat —6D 118
Almscliffe Av. Dew —7J 137
Almscliffe Pl. B'frd —1F 81
Almshouse Hill. B'ham —1D 54
Alpha St. Kei —4B 40
Alpine Clo. Bat —4F 137
Alpine Ri. T'tn —6H 77
Alpine Ter. Rothw —1F 123
Alston Clo. B'frd —4D 78
Alston La. Leeds —2J 87
Alston Rd. Kei —2B 40
Alston Rd. Retail Pk. Kei —2B 40
Altar Dri. B'frd —2G 79
Altar Dri. Riddl —2E 40
Altar La. Bgly —7D 40
Altar Vw. Bgly —6J 41
(off Sleningford Rd.)
Althorpe Gro. B'frd —6C 62
Alton Gro. B'frd —2F 79
Alton Gro. Shipl —7H 61
Alum Ct. B'frd —2G 79
Alum Dri. B'frd —2G 79
Alvanley Ct. B'frd —5D 78
Alva Ter. Shipl —6H 61
Alwen Av. Hud —7F 145
Alwoodley. —6J 49
Alwoodley Chase. Leeds —6A 50
Alwoodley Ct. Leeds —6F 49
Alwoodley Ct. Gdns. Leeds —5G 49
Alwoodley Gdns. Leeds —6G 49
Alwoodley Gates. —5A 50
Alwoodley La. Leeds —5F 49
Alwoodley Park. —5G 49
Amberley Ct. B'frd —7E 80
(off Amberley St.)
Amberley Gdns. Leeds —7D 84
Amberley Rd. Leeds —7C 84
Amberley St. B'frd —7E 80
(in two parts)
Amberley St. Leeds —7C 84
Amber St. Bat —1E 136
Amberton App. Leeds —1E 86
Amberton Clo. Leeds —7E 68
Amberton Cres. Leeds —1E 86
Amberton Gdns. Leeds —1E 86
Amberton Gth. Leeds —1E 86
Amberton Gro. Leeds —1E 86
Amberton La. Leeds —1E 86
Amberton Mt. Leeds —1E 86
Amberton Pl. Leeds —1D 86
Amberton Rd. Leeds —1D 86
Amberton St. Leeds —1E 86
Amberton Ter. Leeds —1E 86
Amblers Bldgs. Pud —7C 82
(off Amblers Ct.)
Amblers Ct. Pud —7C 82
Amblers Cft. B'frd —2D 62
Amblers M. Bail —7J 43
Amblers M. E Mor —3H 41
Amblers Row. Bail —7J 43
Amblers Ter. Hal —6G 113
Ambler St. B'frd —4J 79
Ambler St. C'frd —7D 126
Ambler St. Kei —4B 40
Ambler Thorn. —7G 95
Amblerthorne. B'shaw —2K 117
Ambler Way. Q'bry —7G 95
Ambleside Av. B'frd —3F 79
Ambleside Gdns. Pud —6A 82
Ambleside Gro. W'ford —1A 124
Ambleside Rd. C'frd —6K 127
Ambleside Wlk. Weth —3F 17
Amble Tonia. Denh —4C 76
Ambleton Way. Q'bry —6G 95
Amelia St. Shipl —3F 61
America La. Brigh —6J 133
America La. Sut Cr —3A 38
America Moor La. Morl —5D 66
Amisfield Rd. Hal —7D 114
Amos St. Hal —1D 130
Amport Clo. Brigh —7H 133
Amundsen Av. B'frd —7C 62
Amyroyce Dri. Shipl —5A 62
Amy St. Bgly —1A 60
Amy St. Hal —5E 112
Ancaster Cres. Leeds —5B 66
Ancaster Rd. Leeds —5B 66
Ancaster Vw. Leeds —5B 66
Anchorage, The. Bgly —7K 41
Anchor Ct. B'frd —2B 6
Anchor Pl. Brigh —1K 145
Anderson Av. Leeds —3A 86 (1K 5)
Anderson Ho. Bail —3H 61
(off Fairview Ct.)
Anderson Mt. Leeds —3A 86 (1K 5)
Anderson St. B'frd —4J 79
Anderton Fold. Hal —5A 114
Anderton St. Cro H —3A 20
(off Bk. Station Rd.)
Andover Grn. B'frd —2G 99
Andrew Clo. Hal —4A 132
Andrews Mnr. Yead —4K 45
(off Manor Sq.)
Andrew Sq. Far —2B 82
Andrew St. Fars —3B 82
Anerley St. B'frd —4D 98
Angel Ct. Leeds —4F 85
Angel Pl. Bgly —6A 42
Angel Row. Rothw —2C 122
Angel St. Bail —7K 43
Angel Way. B'frd —6K 79 (4B 6)
Angerton Way. B'frd —1G 115
Anglesea Pl. Haw —7E 56
Angus Av. Wyke —6J 115
Anlaby St. B'frd —1F 99
Anne Ga. B'frd —6B 80 (3G 7)
Anne's Ct. Hal —4A 132
Anne St. Bat —1E 136
Anne St. B'frd —3F 97
Annie St. Cro R —4H 57
Annie St. Kei —2A 40
Annie St. Morl —3B 120
Annie St. Shipl —6J 61
Annie St. Sower B —4K 129
Anning Fold. Gar —5B 90
Annison St. B'frd —6C 80 (4H 7)
Ann Pl. B'frd —1A 98 (7D 6)
Ann St. Haw —5F 57
Ann St. Kei —5K 39
Anroyd St. Dew —7E 136
Anson Gro. B'frd —4F 97
Anthony La. H'den —2F 59
Antler Complex. Morl —3H 119
Anvil Ct. B'frd —4H 79
(off Carlisle St.)
Anvil St. B'frd —4H 79
Anvil St. Brigh —5G 133
Apex Bus. Cen. Leeds —1J 103
Apex Way. Leeds —1J 103
Apperley Bridge. —4G 63
Apperley Gdns. B'frd —4G 63
Apperley La. B'frd & Yead —4G 63
Apperley Rd. B'frd —4E 62
Appleby La. Gar —6B 90
Appleby Pl. Leeds —5G 87
Appleby Wlk. Leeds —5G 87
Appleby Way. Morl —2B 120
Appleby Way. Weth —2J 17
Apple Clo. Birs —5E 118
Applegarth. W'ford —7A 106
Apple Ho. Ter. L'ft —6G 111
Apple St. Kei —1J 57
Apple St. Oxe —3E 74
Appleton Clo. Bgly —6B 42
Appleton Clo. Leeds —5B 86
Appleton Clo. Oaken —2B 116
Appleton Ct. Leeds —5B 86
Appleton Gro. Leeds —5D 86
Appleton Sq. Leeds —5B 86
Appleton Way. Leeds —5B 86
Apple Tree Clo. B Spa —3D 36
Apple Tree Clo. E Ard —7J 121
Apple Tree Ct. E Ard —1J 139
Apple Tree Gdns. I'ly —5K 11
Appleyard Rd. H Bri —6B 110
Approach, The. Scholes —5D 70
April Ct. Liv —6J 135
Aprilia Ct. Cytn —1D 96
Apsley Cres. B'frd —4J 79
Apsley St. Haw —5F 57
Apsley St. Kei —6K 39
Apsley St. Oakw —1F 57
Apsley Ter. Oakw —1F 57
(off Green La.)
Aquamarine Dri. Far —7J 145
Aquila Way. Liv —3F 135
Arbour, The. F'hll —1A 20
Arbour, The. I'ly —3A 12
Arcadia St. Kei —6K 39
Archbell Av. Brigh —1H 145
Archer Rd. Brigh —7K 133
Archery Pl. Leeds —3H 85 (1C 4)
Archery Rd. Leeds —3H 85 (1C 4)
Archery St. Leeds —3H 85 (2D 4)
Archery Ter. Leeds —3H 85 (2D 4)
Arches St. Hal —2F 131
Arches, The. Hal —6G 113
Archibald Ho. Rothw —3G 123
Archibald St. B'frd —6J 79
Arctic Pde. B'frd —2G 97
Arctic St. Cro R —4G 57
Arctic St. Kei —1K 39
Arden M. Hal —3F 131
Ardennes Clo. B'frd —1B 80
Arden Rd. B'frd —6C 78
Arden Rd. Hal —2F 131
Ardsley Clo. B'frd —4H 99
(in two parts)
Argent Way. B'frd —4H 99
Argie Av. Leeds —2B 84
Argie Gdns. Leeds —3C 84
Argie Rd. Leeds —3C 84
Argie Ter. Leeds —3C 84
Argyle M. E Kes —5A 34
Argyle Rd. Leeds —5K 85 (5H 5)
Argyle St. B'frd —3D 98
Argyle St. Kei —4K 39
Argyll Clo. Bail —2A 62
Argyll Clo. H'fth —7F 47
Arkendale M. B'frd —3E 96
Arksey Pl. Leeds —5C 84
Arksey Ter. Leeds —5C 84
Arkwright St. Cytn —2B 96
Arkwright St. Leeds —5E 84
Arkwright St. Tyer —7G 81
Arkwright Wlk. Morl —1A 120
Arlesford Rd. B'frd —4G 99
Arley Gro. Leeds —5C 84
Arley Pl. Leeds —5C 84
Arley St. Leeds —5C 84
Arley Ter. Leeds —5C 84
Arlington Bus. Cen. Leeds —6D 102
Arlington Cres. Hal —3B 130
Arlington Gro. C'frd —7F 127
Arlington Gro. Leeds —7D 68
Arlington M. Heck —5C 136
Arlington Rd. Leeds —1D 86
Arlington St. B'frd —7D 80 (5K 7)
Armadale Av. B'frd —6D 98
Armgill La. B'frd —1K 79
Armidale Way. B'frd —2B 80
Armitage Av. Brigh —1H 145
Armitage Rd. Bkby —7F 145
Armitage Rd. Hal —3D 130
Armitage Rd. Oaken —3B 116
Armitage Sq. Pud —7B 82
Armitage St. C'frd —7C 126
Armitage St. Rothw —3G 123
Armley Grange Av. Leeds —4K 83
Armley Grange Cres. Leeds —4K 83
Armley Grange Dri. Leeds —5K 83
Armley Grange Mt. Leeds —5K 83
Armley Grange Oval. Leeds —4K 83
Armley Grange Ri. Leeds —5K 83
Armley Grange Vw. Leeds —5A 84
Armley Grange Wlk. Leeds —5A 84
Armley Gro. Pl. Leeds —6D 84
Armley Lodge Rd. Leeds —4C 84
Armley Mills Museum. —4D 84
Armley Pk. Ct. Leeds —5C 84
(off Stanningley Rd.)
Armley Pk. Rd. Leeds —4C 84
Armley Ridge Clo. Leeds —5A 84
Armley Ridge Rd. Leeds —2K 83
(in two parts)
Armley Ridge Ter. Leeds —4A 84
Armley Rd. Leeds —5C 84
(in two parts)
Armouries Dri. Leeds —7K 85
Armstrong St. B'frd —7F 81
Armstrong St. Fars —3B 82
Armytage Rd. Brigh —6J 133
Armytage Way. Brigh —7K 133
Arncliffe Av. Kei —5J 39
Arncliffe Cres. Brigh —1E 144
Arncliffe Cres. Morl —5G 67
Arncliffe Gdns. Bat —3F 137
Arncliffe Gth. S'ley —4B 82
Arncliffe Grange. Leeds —2K 67
Arncliffe Gro. Kei —6J 39
Arncliffe Rd. Bat —3E 136
Arncliffe Rd. Kei —6J 39
Arncliffe Rd. Leeds —4A 66
Arncliffe St. S'ley —3B 82
Arncliffe Ter. B'frd —7H 79
Arndale Cen. Head —7D 66
Arndale Cen. Leeds —3A 88
Arndale Ho. B'frd —4E 6
Arndale Shop. Cen. Shipl —5H 61
(off Market St.)
Arne Clo. Sils —6H 9
Arnford Clo. B'frd —5B 80 (1G 7)
Arnold Av. Hud —7F 145
Arnold Pl. B'frd —5J 79
Arnold Royd. Brigh —2E 144
Arnold St. B'frd —4J 79
Arnold St. Hal —1E 130
Arnold St. Liv —4J 135
Arnold St. Sower B —4K 129
Arnside Av. Riddl —2C 40
Arnside Clo. C'frd —7K 127
Arnside Cres. C'frd —7K 127
Arnside Rd. B'frd —4A 98
Arran Ct. Gar —1K 107
Arran Dri. Gar —1K 107
Arran Dri. H'fth —7F 47
Arran Way. Rothw —2H 123
Arrow La. Leds —3E 126
Art Gallery (1853) & Salts Mill. —3F 61
Arthington. —4C 30
Arthington Av. Leeds —4K 103
Arthington Clo. Ting —1D 138
Arthington Ct. Leeds —4K 103
Arthington Gth. Arth —4K 29
Arthington Gro. Leeds —4K 103
Arthington La. Pool W —3H 29
Arthington Lawns Pool W —4J 29
Arthington Pl. Leeds —4K 103
Arthington Rd. Leeds —1C 48
Arthington St. B'frd —5J 79 (1A 6)
Arthington St. Leeds —4K 103
Arthington Ter. Leeds —4K 103
Arthington Vw. Leeds —4K 103
Arthur Av. B'frd —6C 78
Arthur Gro. Bat —7D 118
Arthursdale. —5D 70
Arthursdale Clo. Scholes —5D 70
Arthursdale Dri. Scholes —5D 70
Arthursdale Grange. Scholes —5D 70
Arthur St. Bgly —7K 41
Arthur St. Brigh —6J 133
Arthur St. Far —3B 82
Arthur St. Idle —6D 62
Arthur St. Oakw —2E 56
Arthur St. S'ley —3C 82
Arthur Ter. Fars —3B 82
(off Arthur St.)
Artillery St. Heck —5B 136
Artist St. A'ley —6F 85
Arum St. B'frd —3J 97
Arundel Clo. Bat —5F 119
Arundel St. Gar —5B 90
Arundel St. Hal —1D 130
Arundel Wlk. Bat —6F 119
Ascot Av. B'frd —4E 96
Ascot Dri. B'frd —4E 96
Ascot Gdns. B'frd —4E 96
Ascot Gro. Brigh —1E 144
Ascot Pde. B'frd —4E 96
Ascot Rd. Kip —4K 107
Ascot Ter. Leeds —6B 86
Ash Av. Leeds —7D 66
Ashbourne Av. B'frd —2B 80
Ashbourne Av. Cleck —2F 135
Ashbourne Bank. B'frd —2B 80
Ashbourne Clo. B'frd —2B 80
Ashbourne Cres. B'frd —2B 80
Ashbourne Cres. Gar —1K 107
Ashbourne Cres. Q'bry —5H 95
Ashbourne Cft. Cleck —2F 135
Ashbourne Dri. B'frd —2B 80
Ashbourne Dri. Cleck —2F 135
Ashbourne Gdns. B'frd —2B 80
Ashbourne Gdns. Cleck —2F 135
Ashbourne Gth. B'frd —1C 80
Ashbourne Gro. B'frd —2B 80
Ashbourne Gro. Hal —1D 130
Ashbourne Haven. B'frd —2B 80
Ashbourne Mt. B'frd —2B 80
Ashbourne Oval. B'frd —2B 80
Ashbourne Ri. B'frd —2B 80
Ashbourne Rd. B'frd —2B 80
Ashbourne Rd. Kei —7J 39
Ashbourne Vw. Cleck —2F 135
Ashbourne Way. B'frd —1B 80
Ashbourne Way. Cleck —2F 135
Ashbrooke Pk. Leeds —4J 103
Ash Brow Rd. Hud —6H 145
Ashburn Clo. Weth —2H 17
Ashburn Cft. Weth —2H 17
Ashburn Dri. Weth —2H 17
Ashburn Gro. Bail —7J 43
Ashburn Gro. Weth —2H 17
Ashburnham Gro. B'frd —2H 79
Ashburn Pl. I'ly —6A 12
Ashburn Way. Weth —2H 17
Ashby Av. Leeds —3H 83
Ashby Clo. Liv —7H 135
Ashby Cres. Leeds —4H 83
Ashby Mt. Leeds —3H 83
Ashby Sq. Leeds —3H 83
Ashby St. B'frd —2C 98
Ashby Ter. Leeds —3H 83
Ashby Vw. Leeds —3H 83
Ash Clo. Hal —7D 114
Ash Clo. I'ly —5J 11
Ash Ct. Schol —7B 116
Ash Cres. Leeds —7D 66
Ash Cft. B'frd —6G 97
Ashcroft Clo. Bat —5F 137
Ashdale La. Kirk D —1H 17
Ashday La. Hal —5A 132
Ashdene. Leeds —3H 101
Ashdene Clo. Pud —1C 100
Ashdene Ct. Cull —6B 58
Ashdene Cres. Pud —1C 100
Ashdown Clo. B'frd —5H 97
Ashdown Clo. Hal —2B 130
Ashdown Ct. Shipl —5G 61
Ashdown St. Leeds —4G 83
Ashfield. B'frd —5F 99
Ashfield. Leeds —2A 102
Ashfield. Weth —3K 17
Ashfield Av. B'frd & Shipl —7H 61
Ashfield Av. Morl —1G 85
Ashfield Clo. Hal —5D 112
Ashfield Clo. Leeds —2K 101
(LS12)
Ashfield Clo. Leeds —1B 88
(LS15)
Ashfield Ct. Bgly —2A 60
Ashfield Cres. Bgly —2A 60
Ashfield Cres. S'ley —4B 82
Ashfield Dri. Bail —7K 43
Ashfield Dri. B'frd —7H 61
Ashfield Dri. Hal —5D 112
Ashfield Gro. B'frd —7G 61
Ashfield Gro. S'ley —4B 82
Ashfield Pk. Leeds —7E 66
Ashfield Pl. Fag —3F 81
Ashfield Rd. Birs —5E 118
Ashfield Rd. B'frd —3D 62
Ashfield Rd. G'lnd —2F 143
Ashfield Rd. Morl —1G 85
Ashfield Rd. Shipl —5E 60
Ashfield Rd. S'ley —4B 82
Ashfield Rd. T'tn —7H 77
Ashfield St. Hud —7H 145
Ashfield St. Kei —5K 39
(off Minnie St.)
Ashfield Ter. Bgly —2A 60
Ashfield Ter. G'lnd —1F 143
Ashfield Ter. Haw —6E 56
Ashfield Ter. Leeds —1B 88
Ashfield Ter. Mar —1G 135
(off Pyenot Hall La.)
Ashfield Ter. Thpe —5B 122
Ashfield Ter. Wyke —3K 115
Ashfield Way. Leeds —2K 101
Ashford Dri. Pud —7D 82
Ashford Grn. B'frd —5F 97

Ash Gdns.—Bk. Burchett Gro.

Ash Gdns. Leeds —7D 66
Ash Ghyll Gdns. Bgly —7K 41
Ash Gro. Bgly —3A 60
Ash Gro. B'shaw —1J 117
Ashgrove. B'frd —7K 79 (6B 6)
Ash Gro. Cleck —2D 134
Ash Gro. Clif C —5J 133
Ash Gro. Eccl —2E 80
Ash Gro. Gom —6J 117
Ashgrove. Gre —5G 63
Ash Gro. H'fth —2G 65
Ash Gro. I'ly —4C 12
Ash Gro. Kei —7J 39
Ash Gro. Leeds —2F 85
Ash Gro. Otley —3H 27
Ash Gro. Pud —7C 82
Ash Gro. Steet —5F 21
Ashgrove Av. Hal —5H 131
Ashgrove Cres. Kip —3B 108
Ashgrove Cft. Kip —4B 108
Ashgrove M. Rod —1D 82
Ashgrove Mt. Kip —3A 108
Ashgrove Pl. Hal —5J 131
Ashgrove Rd. Kei —1J 39
Ash Gro. Ter. Brigh —7G 133
(off Thomas St.)
Ash Hall La. Ripp —3B 140
Ash Hill Dri. Leeds —7H 51
Ash Hill Gdns. Leeds —7H 51
Ash Hill Gth. Leeds —7H 51
Ash Hill La. Leeds —7H 51
Ash Hill Wlk. B'frd —2D 98
Ash Ho. Leeds —7G 87
Ashington Clo. B'frd —2F 81
Ashlands Rd. I'ly —4C 12
Ash La. Gar —5A 90
Ashlar Gro. Q'bry —7H 95
Ashlea Av. Brigh —1H 145
Ashlea Clo. Brigh —1H 145
Ashlea Clo. Gar —1K 107
Ashlea Ct. Leeds —2G 83
(off Ashlea Ga.)
Ashlea Dri. Brigh —1H 145
Ashlea Ga. Leeds —2G 83
Ashlea Grn. Leeds —2G 83
Ashleigh Dale. Hud —7D 144
Ashleigh Gdns. W'ford —1A 124
Ashleigh Rd. Leeds —4A 66
Ashleigh St. Kei —3A 40
Ashley Av. Leeds —3C 86
Ashley Clo. Gom —5J 117
Ashley Gro. H Bri —6A 110
Ashley La. Shipl —4H 61
Ashley Pk. M. Gar —4C 90
Ashley Rd. Bgly —2A 60
Ashley Rd. Leeds —3B 86
Ashley Rd. Lwr W —7B 84
Ashley Rd. Wyke —5J 115
Ashley St. Hal —1D 130
Ashley St. Shipl —4H 61
Ashley Ter. Leeds —3C 86
Ashmead. Bat —5E 136
Ashmead. Cliff —5D 36
Ash Mdw. Clo. Hud —6J 145
Ashmere Gro. Hud —7J 145
Ash M. B'frd —5G 63
Ashmore Dri. Oss —7C 138
Ash Mt. B'frd —1H 97
Ashmount. Cytn —2D 96
Ash Mt. Kei —6J 39
Ash Rd. Leeds —1C 84
Ashroyd. Rothw —3H 123
Ash St. Cleck —1E 134
Ash St. I'ly —4C 12
Ash St. Oxe —2E 74
Ash Ter. Bgly —2K 59
Ash Ter. Gar —5A 90
Ash Ter. Leeds —7D 66
Ash Ter. Sower B —6E 140
Ashtofts Mt. Guis —2G 45
Ashton Av. B'frd —1E 96
Ashton Av. Leeds —3B 86
Ashton Clough Rd. Liv —4J 135
Ashton Ct. Leeds —2C 86
(nr. Ashton Rd.)
Ashton Ct. Leeds —1B 86
(off Karnac Rd.)
Ashton Cres. Carl —4F 123
Ashton Gro. Leeds —3B 86
Ashton Ho. B'frd —7D 6
Ashton Mt. Leeds —3B 86
Ashton Pl. Leeds —3B 86
Ashton Rd. Leeds —2C 86
Ashton Rd. Ind. Est. Leeds —2C 86
Ashton St. B'frd —6K 79 (3B 6)
Ashton St. Leeds —2B 86
Ashton Ter. Leeds —3B 86
Ashton Ter. Rothw —3D 122
(off Wakefield Rd.)
Ashton Vw. Leeds —3B 86
Ashton Wlk. B'frd —5C 62
Ash Tree App. Leeds —1B 88
Ash Tree Av. T'tn —7F 77
Ash Tree Bank. Leeds —7B 70
Ash Tree Clo. Leeds —7B 70
Ash Tree Ct. Leeds —7B 70
Ash Tree Gdns. Hal —2A 112
Ash Tree Gdns. Leeds —7B 70
Ash Tree Grange. Leeds —7B 70
(off Ash Tree Bank)
Ashtree Gro. B'frd —4F 97
Ash Tree Gro. Kip —5B 108
Ash Tree Gro. Leeds —7B 70
Ash Tree Pk. Kip —5B 108
Ash Tree Rd. Hal —2A 112
Ash Tree Vw. Leeds —7B 70
(off Ash Tree Gdns.)
Ash Tree Wlk. Bur W —1A 26
Ash Tree Wlk. Chap —6A 68
Ash Tree Wlk. Leeds —7B 70
(off Ash Tree Clo.)
Ash Vw. E Ard —1J 139
Ash Vw. Leeds —7D 66
Ash Villa. Hal —2E 130
(off Lister La.)
Ash Vs. Leeds —1B 88
Ashville Av. Leeds —2D 84
Ashville Cft. Hal —7B 112
Ashville Gdns. Hal —7B 112
Ashville Gro. Hal —6B 112
Ashville Gro. Leeds —2D 84
Ashville Rd. Leeds —2D 84
Ashville St. Hal —6E 112
Ashville Ter. Fars —3B 82
(off New St.)
Ashville Ter. Leeds —2D 84
Ashville Ter. Oakw —1F 57
Ashville Vw. Leeds —3E 84
Ashwell La. B'frd —1G 79
Ashwell Rd. H'tn —1G 79
Ashwell Rd. Mann —4H 79
Ashwood. Leeds —3K 69
Ashwood Clo. Hud —6J 145
Ashwood Dri. Gild —7F 101
Ashwood Dri. Riddl —2E 40
Ashwood Gdns. Gild —7F 101
Ashwood Gro. Gild —7G 101
Ashwood Pde. Gild —7F 101
(off Ashwood Gdns.)
Ashwood St. B'frd —5F 99
Ashwood Ter. Leeds —1F 85
Ashwood Vs. Leeds —1F 85
Ashworth Clo. Dew —7G 137
Ashworth Gdns. Dew —7G 137
Ashworth Grn. Dew —7G 137
Ashworth Pl. B'frd —5K 97
Ashworth Rd. Dew —7G 137
Asket Av. Leeds —7G 69
Asket Clo. Leeds —6G 69
Asket Cres. Leeds —7G 69
Asket Dri. Leeds —6G 69
Asket Gdns. Leeds —6F 69
Asket Gth. Leeds —7G 69
Asket Grn. Leeds —6G 69
Asket Hill. Leeds —5F 69
Asket Pl. Leeds —7G 69
Asket Wlk. Leeds —7G 69
Askey Av. Morl —5H 67
Askey Cres. Morl —4H 67
Askham Rd. C'frd —6K 127
Askrigg Dri. B'frd —2D 80
Askwith. —4B 14
Askwith La. Askw —4B 14
Aspect Gdns. Pud —5A 82
Aspect Ter. Pud —5A 82
Aspen Clo. Kei —6C 40
Aspen Ct. Ting —6C 120
Aspen Gro. Dew —7F 137
Aspen Mt. Leeds —2J 65
Aspen Ri. All —1K 77
Aspinall St. Hal —2D 130
Aspinall St. H Bri —6A 110
Asprey Dri. All —5B 78
Asquith Av. Gild —1J 119
Asquith Clo. Morl —2K 119
Asquith Dri. Morl —2K 119
Asquith St. Birs —5F 119
Assembly St. Leeds —6J 85 (7F 5)
Astley Av. Swil —5E 106
Astley La. Swil —5F 107
Astley La. Ind. Est. Swil —6F 107
Astley Way. Swil —6F 107
Aston Av. Leeds —3H 83
Aston Clo. Liv —6H 135
Aston Cres. Leeds —3J 83
Aston Dri. Leeds —3J 83
Aston Gro. Leeds —3J 83
Aston Mt. Leeds —3J 83
Aston Pl. Leeds —3J 83
Aston Rd. B'frd —3A 98
Aston Rd. Leeds —3H 83
Aston St. Leeds —3H 83
Aston Ter. Leeds —3J 83
Aston Vw. Leeds —3H 83
Astor Gro. Leeds —3E 82
Astor St. Leeds —3E 82
Astra Bus. Pk. Leeds —4J 103
Astral Av. Hal —7D 114
Astral Clo. Hal —7D 114
Astral Vw. B'frd —4G 97
Astura Ct. Leeds —7H 67
Atalanta Ter. Hal —4C 130
Atamco Ho. Cleck —1G 135
(off Albion St.)
Atha Clo. Leeds —5G 103
Atha Cres. Leeds —5G 103
Atha St. Leeds —5G 103
Athelstan La. Otley —7J 15
Atherstone Rd. All —6B 78
Atherton La. Brigh —1H 145
Athlone Dri. Dew —6J 137
Athlone Gro. Leeds —6C 84
Athlone Ri. Gar —6B 90
Athlone St. Leeds —6C 84
Athlone Ter. Leeds —6C 84
Athol Clo. Hal —4E 112
Athol Cres. Hal —4E 112
Athol Gdns. Hal —4E 112
Athol Grn. Hal —4E 112
Athol Rd. B'frd —3H 79
Athol Rd. Hal —4E 112
Athol St. Hal —4E 112
Athol St. Kei —2C 40
Atkinson Hill. —2B 104
Atkinson's Ct. Hal —7G 113
Atkinson St. H'let —1A 104
Atkinson St. Shipl —4H 61
Atlanta St. Leeds —3E 82
Atlas Mill Rd. Brigh —6G 133
Atlas St. B'frd —4H 79
Auckland Rd. B'frd —5G 97
Audby Ct. Weth —3K 17
Audby La. Weth —2K 17
Aurelia Ho. B'frd —3J 79
Austell Ho. B'frd —2K 97
(off Park La.)
Austhorpe. —5C 88
Austhorpe Av. Leeds —6C 88
Austhorpe Ct. Leeds —6C 88
(off Austhorpe Dri.)
Austhorpe Dri. Leeds —6C 88
Austhorpe Gdns. Leeds —5D 88
Austhorpe Gro. Leeds —6C 88
Austhorpe La. Leeds —4B 88
Austhorpe Rd. Leeds —3A 88
Austhorpe Vw. Leeds —5B 88
Austin Av. Brigh —4F 133
Austin Rd. C'frd —7K 127
Austin St. Kei —3B 40
Authorpe Rd. Leeds —6F 67
Autumn Av. Leeds —3E 84
Autumn Av. Weth —1J 17
Autumn Cres. H'fth —5H 65
Autumn Gro. Leeds —3E 84
Autumn Pl. Leeds —3E 84
Autumn St. Hal —3D 130
Autumn St. Leeds —3E 84
Autumn Ter. Leeds —3E 84
Auty Sq. Morl —4B 120
Avenel Rd. All —4B 78
Avenel Ter. All —5B 78
Avenham Way. B'frd —5C 80 (2H 7)
Av. Des Hirondelles. Pool W —4G 29
Avenue A. Thor A —7H 19
Avenue B. Thor A —1G 37
Avenue C East. Thor A —7J 19
Avenue Cres. Leeds —1B 86
Avenue C West. Thor A —1H 37
Avenue D. Thor A —2H 37
Avenue E East. Thor A —1J 37
Avenue E West. Thor A —2H 37
Avenue F. Thor A —1J 37
Avenue G. Thor A —7K 19
Avenue Gdns. Leeds —6G 49
Avenue Hill. Leeds —1A 86
Avenue Lawns. Leeds —6F 49
Avenue No.1. Brigh —7G 133
Avenue No.2. Brigh —7G 133
Avenue Rd. B'frd —3B 98
Avenue St. B'frd —5F 99
Avenue Ter. Yead —4B 46
Avenue, The. Alw —6F 49
Avenue, The. Bat —1E 136
Avenue, The. Bgly —4B 60
Avenue, The. Birs —6C 118
(in two parts)
Avenue, The. Cytn —3A 96
Avenue, The. Coll —1E 34
Avenue, The. Dew —5D 136
Avenue, The. Hal —7D 114
Avenue, The. Hare —4C 32
Avenue, The. H'fth —3D 64
Avenue, The. Idle —1G 63
(in three parts)
Avenue, The. Leeds —6A 86 (7J 5)
(nr. Mill St.)
Avenue, The. Leeds —4B 106
(nr. Pontefract La.)
Avenue, The. Leeds —2B 88
(nr. Sandbed La.)
Avenue, The. Round —4C 68
Avenue, The. Scholes —4D 70
Avenue, The. Ting —7G 121
Avenue, The. Wilsd —1H 77
Av. Victoria. Leeds —4C 68
Averingcliffe Rd. B'frd —6F 63
Aviary Gro. Leeds —5C 84
Aviary Mt. Leeds —5C 84
Aviary Pl. Leeds —5C 84
Aviary Rd. Leeds —5C 84
Aviary Row. Leeds —5C 84
Aviary St. Leeds —5C 84
Aviary Ter. Leeds —5C 84
Aviary Vw. Leeds —5C 84
Avocet Clo. B'frd —6C 78
Avocet Gth. Leeds —2K 121
Avon Clo. Leeds —7H 51
Avon Ct. Leeds —6G 51
Avondale. Kei —3J 39
Avondale Ct. Leeds —1K 67
Avondale Cres. Shipl —5G 61
Avondale Gro. Shipl —5G 61
Avondale Mt. Shipl —5G 61
Avondale Pl. Hal —4F 131
Avondale Rd. Shipl —5E 60
Avondale St. Leeds —4G 83
Avondale Vs. T'ner —1C 70
Avon Dri. Gar —7K 89
Avon Gth. Weth —4G 17
Aydon Way. She —7E 96
Aygill Av. B'frd —2D 78
Aylesbury St. Kei —7J 39
Aylesford Mt. Leeds —2D 88
Aylesham Ind. Est. Low M —1K 115
Aynholme Clo. Add —1D 10
Aynholme Dri. Add —1D 10
Aynsley Gro. All —3B 78
Ayresome Av. Leeds —2C 68
Ayresome Oval. All —6A 78
Ayresome Ter. Leeds —2B 68
Ayreville Dri. Hal —1C 114
Ayrton Cres. Bgly —1A 60
Aysgarth Av. Hal —2G 133
Aysgarth Clo. Leeds —6B 86
Aysgarth Clo. Wyke —5J 115
Aysgarth Cres. Hal —4J 111
Aysgarth Dri. Leeds —6B 86
Aysgarth Fold. Midd —3J 121
Aysgarth Pl. Leeds —6B 86
Aysgarth Rd. Bat —3E 136
Aysgarth Wlk. Leeds —6B 86
Ayton Clo. B'frd —5C 80 (2J 7)
Ayton Ho. B'frd —5H 99
Azealea Ct. B'frd —5D 80 (2K 7)
(in two parts)

Bachelor La. H'fth —3G 65
Bk. Ada St. Kei —4J 39
(off Devonshire St.)
Bk. Aireview Ter. Kei —5C 40
Bk. Aireville St. Kei —1J 39
Bk. Airlie Av. Leeds —1B 86
(off Airlie Av.)
Bk. Airlie Pl. Leeds —1B 86
(off Airlie Pl.)
Bk. Albert Gro. Leeds —6D 66
Bk. Albert Ter. Leeds —3E 84
(off Burley Lodge Rd.)
Bk. Alcester Pl. Leeds —1B 86
(off Alcester Pl.)
Bk. Alcester Rd. Leeds —1B 86
(off Alcester Rd.)
Bk. Alcester Ter. Leeds —1B 86
(off Alcester Ter.)
Bk. Allerton Ter. Leeds —5K 67
Bk. Alma St. Yead —4A 46
(off Alma St.)
Bk. Ann St. Denh —4B 76
(off William St.)
Bk. Archery Pl. Leeds —1C 4
Bk. Archery Rd. Leeds —2D 4
Bk. Archery St. Leeds —2D 4
Bk. Archery Ter. Leeds —2C 4
Bk. Ash Gro. Leeds —2F 85
(in two parts)
Bk. Ashgrove W. B'frd —7K 79 (6B 6)
Bk. Ashley Av. Leeds —3C 86
(off Ashley Av.)
Bk. Ashley St. Leeds —3C 86
(off Ashley Rd.)
Bk. Ashville Av. Leeds —2E 84
(off Ashville Av.)
Bk. Ashville Gro. Leeds —2D 84
(off Ashville Gro.)
Bk. Ashville Rd. Leeds —2D 84
(off Ashville Rd.)
Bk. Ashville Ter. Leeds —2D 84
(off Ashville Ter.)
Bk. Ashwood Ter. Leeds —1F 85
Bk. Aston Pl. Leeds —3J 83
(off Aston Rd.)
Bk. Aston Rd. Leeds —3H 83
Bk. Aston St. Leeds —3H 83
Bk. Aston Ter. Leeds —3J 83
(off Aston Rd.)
Bk. Aston Vw. Leeds —3H 83
Bk. Athlone Av. Leeds —6C 84
Bk. Athlone Gro. Leeds —6C 84
(off Athlone St.)
Bk. Athlone Ter. Leeds —6C 84
(off Athlone St.)
Bk. Atlanta St. Leeds —3E 82
Bk. Austhorpe Rd. Leeds —3A 88
(off Austhorpe Rd., in two parts)
Bk. Autumn Rd. Leeds —3E 84
(off Autumn Ter.)
Bk. Autumn Ter. Leeds —3E 84
(off Autumn Ter.)
Bk. Aviary Rd. Leeds —5C 84
(off Aviary Gro.)
Bk. Aylesbury St. Kei —7J 39
(off Queen's Rd.)
Bk. Baker St. Shipl —4G 61
Bk. Baldovan Ter. Leeds —1B 86
(off Baldovan Ter.)
Bk. Balfour St. Bgly —2K 59
Bk. Balfour St. Kei —5K 39
Bk. Bank St. C'frd —7D 126
Bk. Bank Ter. Far —3C 82
Bk. Banstead St. Leeds —2B 86
(off Banstead Ter. E.)
Bk. Barden Pl. Leeds —6A 84
(off Whingate Rd.)
Bk. Barkly Gro. Leeds —4G 103
(off Barkly Gro.)
Bk. Barkly Pde. Leeds —5G 103
(off Barkly Pde.)
Bk. Barkly Ter. Leeds —4G 103
(off Barkly Ter.)
Bk. Barrowby Vw. Leeds —6C 88
Bk. Bath Rd. Leeds —3G 83
(off Cross Bath Rd.)
Bk. Beamsley Gro. Leeds —3E 84
(off Beamsley Gro.)
Bk. Beamsley Mt. Leeds —3E 84
(off Beamsley Mt.)
Bk. Beamsley Ter. Leeds —3E 84
(off Beamsley Ter.)
Bk. Beaumont St. Bat —5G 137
Bk. Beck La. Add —1D 10
Bk. Beech St. Bgly —2K 59
Bk. Beechwood Gro. Leeds —2D 84
Bk. Beechwood Rd. Leeds —2D 84
(off Beechwood Pl.)
Bk. Bellbrooke Gro. Leeds —3D 86
(off Bellbrooke Gro.)
Bk. Bellbrooke Pl. Leeds —3D 86
(off Bellbrooke Pl.)
Bk. Bellbrooke Ter. Leeds —3D 86
(off Bellbrooke St.)
Bk. Belvedere Av. Leeds —4H 103
(off Belvedere Av.)
Bk. Bentley Av. Leeds —6F 67
(off Bentley Gro.)
Bk. Bentley Gro. Leeds —6F 67
(off Bentley Gro.)
Bk. Berkeley Av. Leeds —2C 86
(off Berkeley Av.)
Bk. Berkeley Ter. Leeds —2C 86
(off Berkeley Ter.)
Bk. Beverley Ter. Leeds —3H 103
Bk. Blackwood Gro. Hal —7D 112
Bk. Blenheim Av. Leeds —3H 85 (1D 4)
Bk. Blenheim Mt. B'frd —3J 79
Bk. Blenheim Ter. Leeds —3H 85 (2C 4)
Bk. Boundary Ter. Leeds —4E 84
(off Burley Rd.)
Bk. Bower Rd. Ell —2A 144
Bk. Bowling Grn. Rd. Slnd —6D 142
Bk. Branch Pl. Leeds —2A 102
(off Branch Pl.)
Bk. Breary Av. H'fth —3H 65
Bk. Breary Ter. H'fth —3H 65
(off Breary Av.)
Bk. Briggate. Sils —7G 9
Bk. Broad La. Leeds —1H 83
Bk. Broomfield Cres. Leeds —1D 84
Bk. Broomfield Pl. Leeds —2D 84
(off Broomfield Pl.)
Bk. Broomfield Rd. Kei —4K 39
Bk. Broomfield Rd. Leeds —2D 84
(off Newport Rd.)
Bk. Broomfield St. Kei —4K 39
Bk. Broughton Av. Leeds —3C 86
(off Broughton Av.)
Bk. Broughton Ter. Leeds —3C 86
(off Broughton Ter.)
Bk. Brudenell Gro. Leeds —3F 85
(off Brudenell Gro.)
Bk. Brudenell Mt. Leeds —2E 84
(off Brudenell Mt.)
Bk. Brudenell Rd. Leeds —2E 84
(off Brudenell Rd.)
Bk. Brunswick St. Dew —7E 136
Bk. Brunswick St. Leeds —4J 85 (4F 5)
Bk. Burchett Gro. Leeds —1G 85
(off Burchett Gro.)

A-Z Leeds & Bradford 149

Bk. Burchett Pl. Leeds —1G 85 (off Burchett Pl.)
Bk. Burley Hill. Leeds —3C 84
Bk. Burley Lodge Rd. Leeds —3E 84 (off Burley Lodge Rd.)
Bk. Burley Lodge Ter. Leeds (off Burley Lodge Ter.) —4E 84
Bk. Burley St. Leeds —5A 4
Bk. Burlington Pl. Leeds —4H 103 (off Burlington Pl.)
Bk. Burlington Rd. Leeds —4H 103 (off Burlington Rd.)
Bk. Burton Cres. Leeds —6D 66
Bk. Burton Ter. Leeds —3J 103
Bk. Buxton St. Kei —4B 40 (off Buxton St.)
Bk. Byrl St. Kei —2A 40 (off Byrl St.)
Bk. Caister St. Kei —7K 39 (off Oakfield Rd.)
Bk. Caledonia Rd. Kei —3B 40 (off Caledonia Rd.)
Bk. Camberley St. Leeds —3H 103 (off Camberley St.)
Bk. Carberry Pl. Leeds —3E 84 (off Carberry Pl.)
Bk. Carberry Rd. Leeds —3E 84 (off Carberry Rd.)
Bk. Carberry Ter. Leeds —3E 84 (off Carberry Pl.)
Bk. Carlinghow La. Bat —1C 136
Bk. Carter Mt. Leeds —5A 88 (off Carter Mt.)
Bk. Cartmel Rd. Kei —4J 39 (off Devonshire Rd.)
Bk. Castle Rd. Kei —3K 39
Bk. Cavendish Rd. B'frd —5D 62
Bk. Cavendish St. Kei —4A 40
Bk. Cavendish Ter. Hal —1E 130
Bk. Chapel La. Leeds —1D 84 (off Broomfield Rd.)
Bk. Chapel St. B'frd —6B 80 (4G 7)
Bk. Charles St. Brigh —5G 133 (off Charles St.)
Bk. Charlton Rd. Leeds —6C 86
Bk. Chatsworth Rd. Leeds —2C 86 (off Chatsworth Rd.)
Bk. Chestnut Av. Leeds —3B 88 (off Chestnut Av.)
Bk. Chiswick Ter. Leeds —3E 84 (off Burley Lodge Rd.)
Bk. Christ Chu. Vw. Leeds —5B 84 (off Stanningley Rd.)
Bk. Church La. Kirks —1A 84 (off Hesketh Rd.)
Bk. Church La. Leeds —6D 48
Bk. Claremont Av. Leeds —4A 4
Bk. Claremont Gro. Leeds —4A 4
Bk. Claremont St. Rothw —1A 124
Bk. Claremont Ter. Leeds —4A 4
Bk. Claremount Ter. Hal —5G 113
Bk. Clarence Rd. H'fth —5F 65
Bk. Clarence St. Hal —1F 131
Bk. Clarendon Pl. Hal —1E 130
Bk. Clarkson Vw. Leeds —1G 85 (off Clarkson Vw.)
Bk. Clayton St. Rothw —2H 123
Bk. Cliff Mt. Leeds —1G 85 (off Cliff Mt.)
Bk. Clifton Ter. Leeds —3D 86 (off Clifton Ter.)
Bk. Clipston Av. Leeds —6F 67 (off Clipston Av.)
Bk. Clough. Hal —5A 114
Bk. Clovelly Pl. Leeds —3H 103 (off Clovelly Pl.)
Bk. Colenso Mt. Leeds —2F 103 (off Colenso Mt.)
Bk. Colenso Rd. Kei —2C 40 (off Aireworth Rd.)
Bk. Colenso Rd. Leeds —2F 103 (off Colenso Rd.)
Bk. Colton Rd. Leeds —6C 84
Bk. Colwyn Vw. Leeds —4H 103 (off Colwyn Vw.)
Bk. Commercial St. Hal —1G 131 (off Commercial St.)
Bk. Compton St. Kei —3B 40 (off Compton St.)
Bk. Conway St. Leeds —2B 86 (off Conway St.)
Bk. Cowper Gro. Leeds —2C 86 (off Cowper Gro.)
Bk. Cowper St. Leeds —2A 86 (off Cross Cowper St.)
Bk. Craggwood Rd. H'fth —5G 65
Bk. Cranbrook Av. Leeds —3G 103 (off Cranbrook Av.)
Bk. Cranbrook Ter. Leeds —3G 103 (off Cranbrook Av.)
Bk. Croft Ho. La. Kei —1J 39
Bk. Cromer Av. Kei —6K 39 (off Cromer Rd.)
Bk. Cromer Gro. Kei —7K 39 (off Cromer Rd.)
Bk. Cromer Ter. Leeds —3G 85 (2B 4)
Bk. Cromwell Ter. Hal —1F 131
Bk. Cross Flatts Av. Leeds —4G 103 (off Cross Flatts Av.)
Bk. Cross Flatts Cres. Leeds (off Cross Flatts Cres.) —4F 103
Bk. Cross Flatts Gro. Leeds (off Cross Flatts Gro.) —4G 103
Bk. Cross Flatts Mt. Leeds —4G 103 (off Cross Flatts Mt.)
Bk. Cross Flatts Pl. Leeds —4F 103 (off Cross Flatts Pl.)
Bk. Cross Flatts Row. Leeds (off Cross Flatts Row) —4F 103
Bk. Cross Grn. Cres. Leeds —7B 86 (off Cross Grn. Cres.)
Bk. Cross Grn. La. Leeds —7B 86 (off Cross Grn. La.)
Bk. Cross La. Ell —3J 143 (off Linden Rd.)
Bk. Dalton Gro. Leeds —4G 103 (off Dalton Gro.)
Bk. Dalton Rd. Leeds —4G 103
Bk. Dargai St. Leeds —2J 85
Bk. Dawlish Av. Leeds —5D 86 (off Dawlish Av.)
Bk. Dawlish Mt. Leeds —5D 86 (off Dawlish Mt.)
Bk. Dawlish Rd. Leeds —5D 86 (off Dawlish Rd.)
Bk. De Lacy Mt. Leeds —7A 66 (off Abbey Rd.)
Bk. Delph Mt. Leeds —1G 85 (off Delph Mt.)
Bk. Dent St. Leeds —6B 86 (off Dent St.)
Bk. Devonshire La. Leeds —2C 68
Bk. Dorset Mt. Leeds —1C 86 (off Dorset Mt.)
Bk. Dorset Rd. Leeds —1C 86 (off Dorset Rd.)
Bk. Dorset Ter. Leeds —2C 86 (off Dorset Ter.)
Bk. Dudley Hill Rd. B'frd —3D 80
Bk. East Pk. Rd. Leeds —6C 86 (off E. Park Rd.)
Bk. Eaton St. Kei —7J 39 (off Queen's Rd.)
Bk. Ecclesburn Gro. Leeds —6D 86 (off Ecclesburn Gro.)
Bk. Ecclesburn St. Leeds —6C 86 (off Ecclesburn St.)
Bk. Edensor Rd. Kei —4J 39 (off Devonshire Rd.)
Bk. Edinburgh Rd. Leeds —5A 84 (off Town St.)
Bk. Elford Pl. Leeds —2B 86 (off Elford Gro., in two parts)
Bk. Elizabeth St. B'frd —1A 98 (7D 6)
Bk. Ellers Gro. Leeds —1B 86 (off Ellers Gro.)
Bk. Ellers Rd. Leeds —1B 86 (off Ellers Rd.)
Bk. Elmfield Ter. Hal —3F 131
Bk. Elsworth St. Leeds —6D 84
Bk. Emily St. Kei —3A 40 (off Cross Emily St.)
Bk. Eric St. Kei —3A 40 (off Eric St.)
Bk. Eric St. Leeds —7G 65
Bk. Eshald Pl. Rothw —1B 124
Bk. Esmond Ter. Leeds —6C 84
Bk. Estcourt Av. Leeds —7C 66 (off Ash Rd.)
Bk. Eversley Mt. Hal —2C 130
Bk. Fairford Pl. Leeds —3J 103
Bk. Ferguson St. Hal —2G 131
Back Fld. T'tn —7J 77 (off Havelock Sq.)
Bk. Field Ct. T'tn —7J 77 (off Bk. High St.)
Bk. Florist St. Kei —2C 40 (off Florist St.)
Back Fold. Cytn —1B 96
Bk. Foster Rd. Kei —7K 39 (off Oakfield Rd.)
Bk. Garton Rd. Leeds —6C 86 (off Garton Rd.)
Bk. Garton Ter. Leeds —6C 86 (off Garton Ter.)
Bk. Gathorne St. Leeds —2A 86 (off Gathorne St.)
Bk. Gerard St. Hal —1F 131
Bk. Giles St. N. B'frd —1K 97 (7C 6)
Bk. Giles St. S. B'frd —1K 97 (7C 6)
Bk. Gillett La. Rothw —2H 123
Bk. Girlington Rd. B'frd —4F 79
Bk. Gladstone Rd. Hal —1F 131
Bk. Gladstone St. Bgly —2K 59
Bk. Glebe Ter. Leeds —6D 66 (off Glebe Ter.)
Bk. Glen Ter. Hal —3F 131
Bk. Glenthorpe Ter. Leeds —5C 86 (off Glenthorpe Ter.)
Bk. Glossop St. Leeds —1H 85 (off Glossop St.)
Bk. Gooder La. Brigh —7H 133
Bk. Gordon Ter. Leeds —6F 67 (off Gordon Ter.)
Bk. Graham Gro. Leeds —2D 84
Bk. Granby Gro. Leeds —1D 84 (off Granby Rd.)
Bk. Grange Av. Leeds —1K 85 (off Grange Av.)
Bk. Grange Cres. Leeds —1A 86 (off Grange Cres.)
Bk. Grange Ter. Leeds —1K 85 (off Grange Ter.)
Bk. Grange Vw. Leeds —1A 86 (off Grange Vw.)
Bk. Grant St. Kei —4J 39
Bk. Grassington Ter. Kei —3A 40 (off Lawkholme La.)
Bk. Gt. Russell St. B'frd —6J 79 (4A 6)
Bk. Greaves St. B'frd —3K 97 (off Greaves St.)
Back Grn. Chur —7C 102
Bk. Greenhow Wlk. Leeds —3D 84 (off Greenhow Rd.)
Bk. Greenmount Ter. Leeds (off Greenmount Ter.) —3H 103
Bk. Grosvenor Ter. Hal —1E 130
Bk. Grosvenor Ter. Leeds —1F 85 (off Grosvenor Ter.)
Bk. Grouse St. Kei —3B 40 (off Parson St.)
Bk. Grove Gdns. Leeds —6E 66 (off Grove Gdns.)
Bk. Grovehall Av. Leeds —5G 103
Bk. Grovehall Dri. Leeds —5G 103
Bk. Grove Rd. I'ly —5B 12
Bk. Haigh Av. Rothw —7F 105
Bk. Haigh St. Rothw —7E 104
Bk. Haigh Vw. Rothw —7E 104
Bk. Halliday Gro. Leeds —5A 84
Bk. Halliday Pl. Leeds —5A 84
Bk. Hamilton Av. Leeds —1A 86 (off Hamilton Av.)
Bk. Hamilton Vw. Leeds —1A 86 (off Hamilton Vw.)
Bk. Harehills Av. Leeds —1A 86 (off Harehills Av.)
Bk. Harehills Pk. Vw. Leeds —3D 86 (off Harehills Pk. Vw.)
Bk. Harehills Pl. Leeds —2B 86 (off Harehills Pl.)
Bk. Hares Av. Leeds —1B 86 (off Hares Av.)
Bk. Hares Mt. Leeds —1A 86 (off Hares Mt.)
Bk. Hares Ter. Leeds —1B 86 (off Hares Ter.)
Bk. Hares Vw. Leeds —1B 86 (off Hares Vw.)
Bk. Harold Gro. Leeds —3E 84 (off Harold Gro.)
Bk. Hartley Av. Leeds —1H 85 (off Hartley Av.)
Bk. Hartley Gro. Leeds —1G 85 (off Hartley Gro.)
Bk. Hartley St. Morl —4C 120
Bk. Hawksworth Gro. Leeds —6H 65
Bk. Headingley Av. Leeds —7C 66 (off Ash Rd.)
Bk. Headingley Mt. Leeds —7C 66 (off Ash Rd.)
Bk. Heathfield Ter. Leeds —6D 66 (off Heathfield Ter.)
Bk. Heddon St. Leeds —6E 66 (off Heddon St.)
Bk. Heights Rd. T'tn —6F 77
Bk. Henrietta St. Bat —3G 137
Bk. Hessle Av. Leeds —2E 84 (off Hessle Av.)
Bk. Hessle Mt. Leeds —2E 84 (off Hessle Mt.)
Bk. Hessle Ter. Leeds —2E 84 (off Hessle Ter.)
Bk. Hessle Vw. Leeds —2E 84 (off Hessle Vw.)
Bk. Highbury Ter. Leeds —6E 66 (off Highbury Ter.)
Bk. Highfield Rd. Leeds —3H 83
Bk. High St. T'tn —7J 77
Bk. Highthorne Gro. Leeds —5A 84
Bk. Hillcrest Av. Leeds —1A 86 (off Hillcrest Av.)
Bk. Hillcrest Vw. Leeds —1A 86 (off Hillcrest Vw.)
Bk. Hilltop Av. Leeds —1B 86 (off Hilltop Av.)
Bk. Hill Top Mt. Leeds —1B 86 (off Hill Top Mt.)
Bk. Hilton Pl. Leeds —1B 86 (off Hilton Pl.)
Bk. Hilton Rd. Leeds —1B 86 (off Hilton Rd.)
Bk. Hird St. Kei —5K 39
Backhold Av. Hal —6J 131
Backhold Dri. Hal —6H 131
Backhold Hall. Hal —5J 131
Backhold La. Hal —6H 131
Backhold Rd. Hal —6J 131
Bk. Hollyshaw Ter. Leeds —5A 88
Bk. Holywell La. Leeds —6F 51
Bk. Hope Hall Ter. Hal —2G 131
Bk. Hovingham Gro. Leeds —1C 86 (off Hovingham Gro.)
Bk. Hovingham Mt. Leeds —1C 86 (off Hovingham Mt.)
Bk. Hovingham Ter. Leeds —1C 86 (off Hovingham Ter.)
Bk. Hyde Gro. Kei —3B 40 (off Kirby St.)
Bk. Hyde Ter. Leeds —4G 85 (3A 4)
Bk. Ibbetson Pl. Leeds —3D 4
Bk. Ingledew Cres. Leeds —2D 68
Bk. Ivy Av. Leeds —5C 86 (off Ivy Av.)
Bk. Ivy Gro. Leeds —6D 86 (off Ivy Gro.)
Bk. Ivy Mt. Leeds —5C 86 (off Ivy Mt.)
Bk. Ivy St. Leeds —5C 86 (off Ivy St.)
Bk. John St. T'tn —7H 77
Bk. Karnac Rd. Leeds —1B 86 (off Karnac Rd.)
Bk. Kelso Rd. Leeds —3F 85 (2A 4)
Bk. Kendal La. Leeds —4A 4
Bk. Kennerleigh Wlk. Leeds —4A 88 (off Kennerleigh Wlk.)
Bk. Kensington St. B'frd —4G 79 (off Kensington St.)
Bk. Kensington Ter. Leeds —2F 85
Bk. Kings Av. Leeds —3E 84 (off Kings Av.)
Bk. Kirby St. Kei —3B 40 (off Kirby St.)
Bk. Kirkgate. Shipl —5G 61
Bk. Kitson St. Leeds —6B 86 (off Kitson St.)
Bk. Knowle Mt. Leeds —2D 84 (off Stanmore Hill)
Bk. Laisteridge La. B'frd —7J 79 (6A 6)
Bk. Lake St. Leeds —4K 103
Bk. Lambton Gro. Leeds —1B 86 (off Lambton Gro.)
Bk. Landseer Av. Leeds —2J 83 (off Raynville Rd.)
Bk. Landseer Gro. Leeds —2J 83 (off Raynville Rd.)
Bk. Landseer Ter. Leeds —2J 83 (off Raynville Rd.)
Back La. All —3H 77
Back La. All B —4B 126
Back La. Askw —5C 14
Back La. Bees —5F 103
Back La. B'ham —7D 36
Back La. Bmly —4H 83
Back La. Bur W —1B 26
Back La. Cytn —2C 96
Back La. Dlgtn —7D 100
Back La. E Mor —2H 41
Back La. Fars —2B 82
Back La. Guis —2E 44
Back La. Hal —2B 112
Back La. H'tn —1G 79
Back La. Heck —4B 136
Back La. H'fth —4F 65
Back La. Idle —4D 62
Back La. Leeds —4G 101
Back La. Loft —6E 122
Back La. Oakw —4D 38
Back La. Ogden —3A 94
Back La. Q'bry —4A 96
Back La. Ripp —5F 141 (nr. Halifax Rd.)
Back La. Ripp —4E 140 (nr. Hob La.)
Back La. Sick —4A 16
Back La. Sils —7G 9
Back La. Sower B —1D 140
Back La. T'tn —6H 77
Back La. Yead —5J 45
Bk. Langdale Gdns. Leeds —1C 84 (off Kirkstall La.)
Bk. Langdale Ter. Leeds —1C 84 (off Kirkstall La.)
Bk. Laurel Mt. Leeds —7K 67
Bk. Leatham St. Dew —7E 136
Bk. Lime St. Kei —1K 57 (off Ivy St. S.)
Bk. Linden Gro. Leeds —3J 103 (off Linden Gro.)
Bk. Lindum St. B'frd —3J 79 (off Manningham La.)
Bk. Lodge La. Leeds —4H 103 (off Lodge La.)
Bk. Lombard St. Yead —7J 45
Bk. Longroyd Ter. Leeds —3J 103 (off Longroyd Ter.)
Bk. Lord St. Hal —1F 131
Bk. Low La. H'fth —3H 65 (off Springfield Mt.)
Bk. Lucas St. Leeds —1G 85 (off Lucas St.)
Bk. Lunan Pl. Leeds —1B 86 (off Lunan Pl.)
Bk. Lunan Ter. Leeds —1B 86 (off Lunan Ter.)
Bk. Lyons St. Q'bry —5K 95
Bk. Lytton St. Hal —6G 113
Bk. Mafeking Av. Leeds —5G 103 (off Mafeking Av.)
Bk. Mafeking Mt. Leeds —5G 103
Bk. Malt St. Kei —7J 39 (off Bracken Rd.)
Bk. Mannville Rd. Kei —5J 39 (off Malsis Rd.)
Bk. Manor Dri. Leeds —1E 84 (off Manor Av.)
Bk. Manor Gro. Leeds —6K 67 (off Manor Gro.)
Bk. Manor St. B'frd —2D 80
Bk. Market St. B'frd —5J 97
Bk. Markham Av. Leeds —1B 86 (off Markham Av.)
Bk. Marriot St. Dew —7H 137
Bk. Marshall Av. Leeds —3B 88 (off Marshall Av.)
Bk. Marshall St. Leeds —3A 88 (off Marshall St.)
Bk. Marshall Ter. Leeds —3A 88 (off Marshall Ter.)
Bk. Mary St. Kild —2A 20 (off Mary St.)
Bk. Mary St. Wake —7A 122
Bk. Masham St. Leeds —6D 84 (off Bk. Middle Cross St.)
Bk. Mayville Av. Leeds —2E 84 (off Mayville Av.)
Bk. Mayville Pl. Leeds —2E 84 (off Mayville Pl.)
Bk. Mayville St. Leeds —2E 84 (off Mayville St.)
Bk. Mayville Ter. Leeds —2E 84 (off Mayville Ter.)
Bk. Meadow Vw. Leeds —2E 84 (off Meadow Vw.)
Bk. Methley Dri. Leeds —6K 67 (off Methley Dri.)
Bk. Mexborough Av. Leeds —1K 85 (off Mexborough Av.)
Bk. Mexborough Dri. Leeds —2K 85 (off Mexborough Dri.)
Bk. Mexborough Gro. Leeds (off Mexborough Gro.) —1K 85
Bk. Mexborough St. Leeds —1K 85 (off Mexborough St.)
Bk. Meynell Av. Rothw —2G 123
Bk. Middle Cross St. Leeds —6D 84
Bk. Middleton Rd. I'ly —5A 12
Bk. Middleton Vw. Leeds —3G 103
Bk. Midland Rd. Leeds —2F 85 (off Midland Rd.)
Bk. Milan Av. Leeds —2B 86 (off Karnac Rd.)
Bk. Milan Rd. Leeds —2B 86 (off Milan Rd.)
Bk. Milan St. Leeds —2C 86 (off Milan St.)
Bk. Milton Ter. Hal —1F 131
Bk. Mitchell Ter. Bgly —2K 59
Bk. Mitford Rd. Leeds —6D 84
Bk. Model Rd. Leeds —6D 84
Bk. Model Ter. Leeds —6D 84
Bk. Model Vw. Leeds —6D 84
Bk. Monk Bri. Dri. Leeds —6F 67 (off Monk Bri. Dri.)
Bk. Monk Bri. St. Leeds —6F 67 (off Monk Bri. St.)
Bk. Montpelier Ter. Leeds —1G 85 (off Montpelier Ter.)
Bk. Moorfield St. Hal —3E 130
Bk. Moorfield Ter. Leeds —5A 84
Bk. Morning St. Kei —7K 39 (off Morning St.)
Bk. Morritt Dri. Leeds —5H 87
Bk. Mount Av. Bat —5H 137
Bk. Mt. Pleasant. Leeds —2J 121
Bk. Mount Vw. Leeds —1F 85 (off Grosvenor Rd.)
Bk. Muff St. B'frd —1D 98 (7K 7)
Bk. Myrtle Av. Bgly —2K 59
Bk. Myrtle Ter. Cro R —3H 57
Bk. Nansen St. Leeds —3E 82
Bk. Newport Gdns. Leeds —2D 84 (off Newport Rd.)
Bk. Newport Mt. Leeds —2D 84 (off Newport Rd.)

Bk. Newport Pl.—Bank Holme Ct.


Bk. Newport Pl. Leeds —2D 84
(off Newport Rd.)
Bk. New St. Slnd —6D 142
(off High St. Stainland,)
Bk. Newton Gro. Leeds —1A 86
Bk. Newton La. Leds —6D 108
Bk. New York St. Leeds —6J 85 (7F 5)
Bk. Nice Vw. Leeds —1B 86
(off Nice Vw.)
Bk. Norman Pl. Leeds —2C 68
(off Norman Pl.)
Bk. Norman Ter. Leeds —2C 68
(off Norman Ter.)
Bk. Northbrook St. Leeds —5K 67
(off Northbrook St.)
Bk. North Pk. Av. Leeds —4B 68
Bk. North St. Oaken —3C 116
Bk. Norwood Gro. Leeds —2E 84
(off Norwood Gro.)
Bk. Norwood Pl. Leeds —2E 84
(off Norwood Pl.)
Bk. Norwood Rd. Leeds —2E 84
(off Norwood Rd.)
Bk. Norwood Ter. Leeds —2E 84
Bk. Nowell Cres. Leeds —4D 86
(off Nowell Cres.)
Bk. Nowell Mt. Leeds —4D 86
(off Nowell Mt.)
Bk. Nowell Pl. Leeds —4D 86
(off Nowell Pl.)
Bk. Nowell Ter. Leeds —4D 86
(off Nowell Ter.)
Bk. Nunington St. Leeds —5D 84
(off Armley Pk. Rd.)
Bk. Nunington Vw. Leeds —4C 84
(off Armley Pk. Rd.)
Bk. Nunroyd Rd. Leeds —3K 67
(off Nunroyd Rd.)
Bk. Oakfield Ter. Leeds —6E 66
(off Brookfield Rd.)
Bk. Oakley St. Wake —6A 122
Bk. Oakley Ter. Leeds —4J 103
(off Oakley Ter.)
Bk. Oak Rd. Leeds —7K 67
(off Chapel Rd.)
Bk. Oakwood Av. Leeds —6D 68
(off Oakwood Av.)
Bk. Oakwood Dri. Leeds —6D 68
(off Oakwood Dri.)
Bk. of the Mill. H'den —3E 58
Bk. Osmondthorpe La. Leeds
(off Osmondthorpe La.) —5E 86
Bk. Otterburn St. Kei —3A 40
(off Ashleigh St.)
Bk. Outwood La. H'fth —5G 65
Bk. Overdale Ter. Leeds —5J 87
(off Overdale Ter.)
Bk. Oxford Pl. Leeds —5C 4
Bk. Oxford St. Wake —7A 122
Bk. Paget St. Kei —4J 39
(off Devonshire St.)
Bk. Parish Ghyll Rd. I'ly —6B 12
Bk. Park Cres. Leeds —2D 68
Bk. Parkfield Pl. Leeds —3G 103
(off Parkfield Pl.)
Bk. Parkfield Rd. Leeds —3G 103
(off Parkfield Rd.)
Bk. Park Ter. Hal —2E 130
Bk. Park Vw. Leeds —3G 103
(off Park Vw.)
Bk. Park Vw. Av. Leeds —2D 84
Bk. Parkville Rd. Leeds —2G 83
Bk. Parnaby Av. Leeds —5B 104
(off Parnaby Av.)
Bk. Parnaby St. Leeds —5B 104
Bk. Parnaby Ter. Leeds —5B 104
(off Parnaby Ter.)
Bk. Pasture Gro. Leeds —5K 67
(off Pasture Gro.)
Bk. Pasture Rd. Leeds —1B 86
(off Pasture Rd.)
Bk. Pawson St. Wake —7A 122
Bk. Pelham Rd. B'frd —2D 80
Bk. Pleasant St. Sower B —4A 130
Bk. Pollard La. Leeds —7G 65
Bk. Poplar Av. Leeds —3B 88
(off Poplar Av.)
Bk. Potternewton La. Leeds —6J 67
Bk. Potters St. Leeds —6K 67
(off Potternewton La.)
Bk. Prospect Pl. Kei —5K 39
Bk. Providence Av. Leeds —1G 85
(off Delph La.)
Bk. Providence St. Bat —3G 137
Bk. Purlwell Hall Rd. Bat —5G 137
Bk. Purlwell La. Bat —4G 137
Bk. Quarry Mt. Ter. Leeds —1G 85
(off Quarry Mt. Ter.)
Bk. Queen St. G'lnd —3G 143
Bk. Ravenscar Av. Leeds —6C 68
(off Ravenscar Av.)
Bk. Raynville Mt. Leeds —2J 83
(off Raynville Rd.)
Bk. Regent Pk. Ter. Leeds —1F 85
(off Regent Pk. Ter.)
Bk. Regent Ter. Leeds —3F 85
Bk. Reginald Mt. Leeds —1K 85
(off Reginald Mt.)
Bk. Reginald Pl. Leeds —1K 85
(off Reginald Pl.)
Bk. Reginald Ter. Leeds —1K 85
(off Reginald St.)
Bk. Rhodes St. Hal —1F 131
Bk. Ribble St. Kei —3D 40
(off Ribble St.)
Bk. Richardson St. Oaken —3C 116
Bk. Richmond Mt. Leeds —1E 84
(off Manor Av.)
Bk. Ridge Mt. Ter. Leeds —1G 85
(off Cliff Rd.)
Bk. Ridge Vw. Leeds —7G 67
Bk. Rigging La. Sower B —5E 128
Bk. Ripley St. Riddl —2D 40
(off Ripley St.)
Bk. Ripon St. Hal —2C 130
Bk. Ripon Ter. Hal —6F 113
Bk. River St. Haw —5F 57
Back Rd. Wyke —3J 115
Bk. Roberts St. Rothw —1A 124
Bk. Rochester Ter. Leeds —1D 84
(off Broomfield Rd.)
Bk. Rokeby Gdns. Leeds —7C 66
(off Ash Rd.)
Bk. Roman Gro. Leeds —2C 68
Bk. Roman Pl. Leeds —2D 68
Bk. Roman St. Leeds —2D 68
Bk. Rose Av. H'fth —5F 65
(off Rose St.)
Bk. Rosebank Cres. Leeds —3F 85
(off Rosebank Cres.)
Bk. Rosemont Wlk. Leeds —3G 83
Bk. Rossall Rd. Leeds —1C 86
(off Rossall Rd.)
Bk. Rossington Rd. Leeds —1A 86
(off Spencer Pl.)
Bk. Roundhay Cres. Leeds —7B 68
(off Roundhay Cres.)
Bk. Roundhay Gro. Leeds —7B 68
(off Roundhay Gro.)
Bk. Roundhay Pl. Leeds —7B 68
(off Roundhay Pl.)
Bk. Roundhay Vw. Leeds —7B 68
(off Roundhay Vw.)
Back Row. Leeds —7H 85
Bk. Rowland Ter. Leeds —3J 103
(off Rowland Ter.)
Bk. Rowsley St. Kei —4B 40
(off Rowsley St.)
Bk. Roydwood Ter. Cull —6B 58
Bk. Rupert St. Kei —3A 40
(off Rupert St.)
Bk. Russell St. B'frd —1K 97 (7C 6)
Bk. Ruthven Vw. Leeds —2C 86
(off Ruthven Vw.)
Bk. Rydal St. Kei —5J 39
Bk. Rylstone St. Kei —3C 40
Bk. St Alban Cres. Leeds —4E 86
(off St Alban Cres.)
Bk. St Elmo Gro. Leeds —5C 86
(off St Elmo Gro.)
Bk. St Ives Mt. Leeds —5A 84
Bk. St Mary's Rd. Leeds —7K 67
Bk. St Paul's Rd. Shipl —5G 61
Bk. Salisbury Gro. Leeds —5C 84
Bk. Salisbury Ter. Hal —6F 113
Bk. Salisbury Ter. Leeds —5C 84
(off Armley Lodge Rd.)
Bk. Saltaire Rd. N. Shipl —4G 61
Bk. Sandhurst Gro. Leeds —2C 86
(off Sandhurst Gro.)
Bk. Sandhurst Pl. Leeds —2C 86
(off Sandhurst Pl.)
Bk. Sandhurst Rd. Leeds —2C 86
(off Sandhurst Rd.)
Bk. Savile Pde. Hal —3F 131
Bk. Savile Pl. Leeds —2K 85
(off Savile Pl.)
Bk. Savile Rd. Leeds —2K 85
(off Savile Rd.)
Bk. School St. Morl —3B 120
(off School St.)
Bk. School Vw. Leeds —2E 84
(off School Vw.)
Bk. Seaforth Av. Leeds —3D 86
(off Seaforth Av.)
Bk. Seaforth Pl. Leeds —2C 86
(off Seaforth Pl.)
Bk. Seaforth Ter. Leeds —2C 86
(off Seaforth Ter.)
Bk. Sefton Av. Leeds —3G 103
(off Sefton Av.)
Bk. Sefton Ter. Leeds —3G 103
(off Sefton Ter.)
Bk. Shaftesbury Av. Leeds —3C 68
Bk. Shaw La. Kei —7B 40
Bk. Shepherds. Leeds —1A 86
(off Shepherd's La.)
Bk. Shepherd's Pl. Leeds —1B 86
(off Shepherd's Pl.)
Bk. Sholebroke Av. Leeds —7K 67
Bk. Sholebroke Pl. Leeds —1K 85
(off Sholebroke Pl.)
Bk. Sholebroke Vw. Leeds —1K 85
(off Sholebroke Vw.)
Bk. Sidlaw Ter. Leeds —1B 86
(off Markham Av.)
Bk. Simpson St. Kei —4J 39
Bk. Sladen St. Kei —4J 39
Bk. Smith Row. B'frd —3J 97
Bk. S. End Gro. Leeds —3J 83
Bk. Southfield Sq. B'frd —4J 79
(off Southfield Sq.)
Bk. South Pde. Ell —4J 143
(in two parts)
Bk. Spencer Mt. Leeds —1A 86
(off Spencer Mt.)
Bk. Springfield Mt. Leeds —5A 84
Bk. Springfield Pl. B'frd —1C 6
Bk. Springfield Rd. Ell —2A 144
Bk. Spring Gro. Wlk. Leeds —3E 84
(off Spring Gro. Wlk.)
Bk. Stanley St. Leeds —3B 86
(off Stanley Av.)
Bk. Stanmore Pl. Leeds —2C 84
(off St Michaels La.)
Bk. Stanmore St. Leeds —2C 84
(off St Michaels La.)
Bk. Station Rd. Bat —4H 137
Bk. Station Rd. Cro H —3A 20
(in two parts)
Bk. Stonegate Rd. Leeds —5F 67
Backstone Gill La. Wike —2F 51
Bk. Stone Hall Rd. B'frd —1D 80
Backstone La. I'ly —6C 12
Backstone Way. I'ly —5D 12
Bk. Storey Pl. Leeds —4G 87
Bk. Stratford Av. Leeds —3G 103
(off Stratford Av.)
Bk. Stratford St. Leeds —3H 103
(off Stratford St.)
Bk. Stratford Ter. Leeds —3H 103
(off Stratford Ter.)
Bk. Strathmore Dri. Leeds —2C 86
(off Strathmore Dri.)
Back St. B'ham —1C 54
Bk. Sunnydene. Leeds —4H 87
Bk. Sutton App. Leeds —4G 87
Bk. Sycamore Av. Bgly —2K 59
Bk. Tamworth St. B'frd —7G 81
Bk. Tempest Rd. Leeds —3G 103
(off Tempest Rd.)
Bk. Temple Vw. Leeds —3G 103
Bk. Thornhill St. C'ley —6K 63
Bk. Thornville Row. Leeds —2E 84
(off Thornville Row)
Bk. Tower Gro. Leeds —5A 84
Bk. Trafford Av. Leeds —3D 86
(off Trafford Av.)
Bk. Trentham Pl. Leeds —4H 103
(off Trentham Pl.)
Bk. Trinity Ter. B'frd —1K 97 (7C 6)
Bk. Unity St. N. Bgly —2K 59
Bk. Unity St. S. Bgly —2K 59
Bk. Vicars Rd. Leeds —1B 86
(off Vicars Rd.)
Bk. Victoria Av. Leeds —5C 86
(off Victoria Av.)
Bk. Victoria Gro. Leeds —5D 86
(off Victoria Gro.)
Bk. Victoria St. Hal —1G 131
Bk. Victor Ter. Hal —7D 112
Bk. Violet Ter. Sower B —4A 130
(off Violet Ter.)
Bk. Wakefield Rd. Sower B —4B 130
Bk. Walmsley Rd. Leeds —2E 84
(off Walmsley Rd.)
Bk. Walnut St. Kei —7K 39
(off Walnut St.)
Bk. Warwick Ter. Bat —5H 137
Bk. Waverley Rd. Ell —4K 143
Bk. Welburn Av. Leeds —5B 66
Bk. Welton Av. Leeds —2E 84
(off Welton Rd.)
Bk. Welton Gro. Leeds —2E 84
(off Welton Gro.)
Bk. Welton Mt. Leeds —2E 84
(off Welton Mt.)
Bk. Welton Pl. Leeds —2E 84
(off Welton Pl.)
Bk. Wesley Rd. Leeds —6C 84
Bk. Wesley St. C'frd —7D 126
Bk. Westbourne Ter. Leeds —2A 4
(off Cromer Ter.)
Bk. Westbury St. Leeds —5B 104
Bk. Westfield Rd. Leeds —4F 85
(off Westfield Rd.)
Bk. Westlock Av. Leeds —4C 86
(off Westlock Av.)
Bk. Westmorland Mt. Leeds —1H 83
Bk. Weston Rd. I'ly —5B 12
Bk. Westover Rd. Leeds —2G 83
Bk. West St. Sower B —5K 129
Bk. Wetherby Gro. Leeds —3C 84
(off Argie Av.)
Bk. Wetherby Rd. Leeds —6D 68
(off Wetherby Rd.)
Bk. Wharf St. Sower B —4A 130
Bk. Wheat St. Kei —7J 39
(off Bracken Rd.)
Bk. Wickham St. Leeds —3G 103
(off Wickham St.)
Bk. William Av. Leeds —5G 87
(off William Av.)
Bk. William St. Brigh —7G 133
(off William St.)
Bk. Wilton Gro. Leeds —6E 66
(off Wilton Gro.)
Bk. Winfield Gro. Leeds —1D 4
Bk. Winston Gdns. Leeds —7C 66
(off Ash Rd.)
Bk. Winterburn St. Kei —3A 40
(off Ashleigh St.)
Bk. Wolseley Ter. Hal —1D 130
Bk. Woodbine Ter. Leeds —6E 66
Bk. Woodland Pk. Rd. Leeds
(off Woodland Pk. Rd.) —7E 66
Bk. Woodstock St. Leeds —2C 4
Bk. Wood St. Wake —7K 121
Bk. Wright Av. Oakw —1F 57
Bk. York Cres. Hal —3D 130
(off Up. Washer La.)
Bk. York Pl. Leeds —6G 85 (7B 4)
(in two parts)
Bk. York St. Leeds —6K 85 (7G 5)
Bacon St. Guis —3H 45
Baddeley Gdns. B'frd —3C 62
Baden St. Haw —4E 56
Baden Ter. Cleck —1F 135
(off Tofts Rd.)
Baden Ter. Leeds —5G 83
(off Pudsey Rd.)
Badgergate Av. Wilsd —1G 77
Badger Hill. Brigh —3E 144
Badger La. Hal —1B 132
Badgers Mt. Leeds —3D 88
Badgers Way. B'frd —1A 80
Badger Wood Glade. Weth —1J 17
Badsworth Ct. Cytn —1D 96
**Bagby Fields. —2H 85 (1D 4)**
**Baghill. —2D 138**
Baghill Grn. Ting —2D 138
Baghill Rd. Ting —2D 138
**Bagley. —1C 82**
Bagley La. Fars —1B 82
Bagley La. Rod —1C 82
Bagnall Ter. B'frd —5H 97
Bagshaw Museum & Art Gallery. —7E 118
**Baildon. —1J 61**
Baildon Av. Kip —3B 108
Baildon Chase. Leeds —5A 70
Baildon Clo. Leeds —6A 70
Baildon Dri. Leeds —6A 70
**Baildon Green. —2H 61**
Baildon Grn. Leeds —6A 70
**Baildon Holmes. —3J 61**
Baildon Holmes. Bail —3J 61
Baildon Mills. Bail —7J 43
(off Northgate)
Baildon Path. Leeds —6A 70
Baildon Pl. Leeds —6A 70
Baildon Rd. Bail —1J 61
Baildon Rd. Leeds —5A 70
Baildon Wlk. Leeds —5A 70
**Baildon Wood Bottom. —3H 61**
Baildon Wood Ct. Bail —3J 61
Bailes Rd. Leeds —7G 67
Bailey Hall Bank. Hal —1H 131
Bailey Hall Rd. Hal —2H 131
Bailey Hills Rd. Bgly —7J 41
Bailey Pl. Leeds —6D 66
Bailey's Clo. Leeds —6J 69
Bailey's Ct. Leeds —7J 69
Bailey's Hill. Leeds —7J 69
Bailey's La. Leeds —7J 69
Bailey's Lawn. Leeds —7J 69
Bailey St. B'frd —1B 98
Bailey Towers. Leeds —7J 69
Bailey Wells Av. B'frd —3J 97
**Bailiff Bridge. —1H 133**
Bainbrigge Rd. Leeds —1D 84
Baines St. Bat —4F 137
Baines St. Hal —7E 112
Baines St. Rothw —3G 123
Baird St. B'frd —2A 98
Bairstow La. Sower B —2A 130
Bairstow Mt. Sower B —3B 130
Bairstow's Bldgs. Hal —4D 112
Bairstow St. All —2A 78
Baker Av. Leeds —7B 50
Baker Cres. Morl —5K 67
Baker Dri. Leeds —6D 84
Baker Fold. Hal —1E 130
(off Lister's Clo.)
Baker M. T'tn —7H 77
Baker Pl. Leeds —7D 66
Baker Rd. Morl —5K 67
Baker Sq. Leeds —1D 66
Baker St. B'frd —3D 80
Baker St. Morl —5K 67
Baker St. Shipl —4G 61
Baker St. N. Hal —2E 112
Baker Vs. All —5B 78
Baker Yd. W'ford —1A 124
Bakes St. B'frd —2G 97
Balbec Av. Leeds —7E 66
Balbec St. Leeds —7E 66
Balcony Cotts. Q'bry —6J 95
Baldovan Mt. Leeds —1B 86
Baldovan Pl. Leeds —1B 86
Baldovan Ter. Leeds —1B 86
Baldwin La. Q'bry —4A 96
Balfour St. Bgly —2K 59
Balfour St. B'frd —2C 98
Balfour St. Kei —5K 39
Balkcliffe La. Leeds —1G 121
Balk La. B'frd —2H 97
Balkram Dri. Hal —2K 111
Balkram Edge. Hal —2H 111
Balkram Rd. Hal —2K 111
Balks. Liv —4H 135
Balk St. Bat —3F 137
Balk, The. Bat —1G 137
Ballantyne Rd. B'frd —2C 62
Ball Royd Rd. Hud —7H 145
Ball St. T'tn —7J 77
Balme La. B'frd —4K 115
Balme Rd. Cleck —7F 117
Balme St. B'frd —6B 80 (3F 7)
Balme St. Wyke —4J 115
Balmfield. Liv —6J 135
Balmfield Cres. Liv —6J 135
Balmoral Chase. Leeds —3B 104
Balmoral Pl. Hal —2G 131
Balmoral Pl. Q'bry —7G 95
Balmoral Ter. Leeds —6E 66
Balmoral Way. Yead —5B 46
Balm Pl. Leeds —1G 103
Balm Rd. Leeds —4A 104
Balm Rd. Ind. Est. Leeds —3K 103
Balm Wlk. Leeds —1F 103
Bamburgh Clo. Leeds —2C 88
Bamburgh Rd. Leeds —2C 88
Bamford Ho. B'frd —5G 99
(off Tong St.)
Bance Rd. H'fth —4F 65
Bangor Gro. Leeds —2A 102
Bangor Pl. Leeds —2A 102
Bangor St. Leeds —2A 102
Bangor Ter. Leeds —2A 102
Bangor Vw. Leeds —2A 102
**Bank. —6A 86**
Bank. B'frd —7E 62
Bank Av. H'fth —4F 65
Bank Av. Morl —2A 120
Bank Bottom. Hal —1H 131
Bank Bottom. H Bri —5C 110
Bank Bottom La. Hal —6H 111
Bank Clo. B'frd —7E 62
Bank Crest. Bail —1J 61
Bankcrest Ri. Shipl —5C 60
Bank Dri. B'frd —5K 97
Bank Edge Clo. Hal —2B 112
Bank Edge Gdns. Hal —4C 112
Bank Edge Rd. Hal —3C 112
Bank End. G'lnd —2B 142
Banker St. Leeds —4D 84
Bankfield. Bard —6B 34
Bankfield Av. Shipl —5D 60
Bankfield Dri. Kei —4G 39
Bankfield Dri. Shipl —5D 60
Bankfield Gdns. Hal —2K 131
Bankfield Gdns. Leeds —3C 84
Bankfield Grange. G'lnd —2G 143
Bankfield Gro. Leeds —2C 84
Bankfield Gro. Shipl —6D 60
Bankfield Mt. Kei —3G 39
Bankfield Museum & Duke of Wellington. —6G 113
Bank Fld. Rd. Bat —3G 137
Bankfield Rd. Kei —3G 39
Bankfield Rd. Leeds —3C 84
Bankfield Rd. Shipl —5D 60
Bankfields Av. H Bri —6A 110
Bankfields Cres. H Bri —6A 110
Bankfield St. Kei —3G 39
Bankfield Ter. Bail —2K 61
Bankfield Ter. Leeds —3C 84
Bankfield Vw. Hal —6F 113
Bankfield Wlk. Kei —3G 39
**Bank Foot. —3G 137**
**(nr. Batley)**
**Bank Foot. —5J 97**
**(nr. Truncliffe)**
Bank Foot Pl. Bat —3G 137
Bank Foot St. Bat —3G 137
Bank Gdns. H'fth —4F 65
Bank Hey Bottom La. Ripp —6G 141
Bank Holme Ct. B'frd —4H 99


A-Z Leeds & Bradford 151

Bankhouse—Beech Gro.


**Bankhouse. —1B 100**
Bank Ho. B'frd —3H 7
Bankhouse. Pud —1B 100
Bank Ho. Slnd —5B 142
**Bankhouse Bottom. —2B 100**
Bank Ho. Clo. Morl —2A 120
Bankhouse La. Hal —6H 131
Bank Ho. La. Mt Tab —3F 111
Bankhouse La. Pud —1B 100
Bank Ho. Ter. Hal —6H 131
Banklands. Sils —7G 9
Banklands Av. Sils —7H 9
Banklands La. Sils —7H 9
Bank La. Kei —4F 39
Bank La. Oakw —2D 56
Bank La. Oxe —3A 74
Bank La. Sils —1G 9
Bank Pde. Otley —3H 27
Bank Rd. Sower B —5K 129
(in two parts)
Bank Royd La. Bklnd —7K 141
Banks End. Ell —3C 144
Banks End Rd. Ell —3C 144
Banksfield Av. Yead —3K 45
Banksfield Clo. Yead —3K 45
Banksfield Cres. Yead —3K 45
Banksfield Gro. Yead —3K 45
Banksfield Mt. Yead —3K 45
Banksfield Ri. Yead —3K 45
Banksfield Rd. H Bri —6A 110
Banksfield Ter. H Bri —6A 110
Banksfield Ter. Yead —4K 45
Bank Side. Bail —1J 61
Bank Side St. Leeds —2B 86
Bankside Ter. Bail —2H 61
Banks La. Riddl —7C 22
Bank Sq. Morl —2A 120
Banks St. Bat —4G 137
Bank St. B'frd —6A 80 (4E 6)
(in two parts)
Bank St. Brigh —6G 133
Bank St. C'frd —7D 126
Bank St. Cleck —1E 134
Bank St. Dew —7H 137
*Bank St. Kei —4A 40*
*(off Airedale Shop. Cen.)*
Bank St. Leeds —6E 4
(in two parts)
Bank St. Liv —4K 135
Bank St. Morl —2A 120
Bank St. Shipl —5H 61
Bank St. Weth —4J 17
Bank St. Wibs —5J 97
Bank Ter. Morl —2B 120
Bank Top. S'wram —2J 131
**Bank Top. —7E 62**
**(nr. Eccleshill)**
**Bank Top. —3K 131**
**(nr. Halifax)**
Bank Top Dri. Riddl —1D 40
Bank Top La. Arth —6D 30
Bank Top Way. Kei —5D 40
Bank Vw. Bail —2H 61
Bank Vw. L'ft —2F 129
*Bank Vw. Mill B —2F 141*
*(off Lumb La.)*
*Bank Vw. Ho. Bail —2J 61*
*(off Bank Vw.)*
Bank Vw. Ter. Leeds —6H 67
Bank Wlk. Bail —1J 61
Bankwell Fold. B'frd —5K 97
Bankwood Way. Birs —3F 119
Bannerman St. B'frd —2C 116
Banner St. B'frd —7C 80 (5J 7)
Bannockburn Ct. B'frd —5D 98
Banstead St. E. Leeds —2B 86
Banstead St. W. Leeds —2B 86
Banstead Ter. E. Leeds —2B 86
Banstead Ter. W. Leeds —2B 86
Bantam Clo. Morl —3D 120
**Bantam Grove. —3D 120**
Bantam Gro. La. Morl —3D 120
Bantree Ct. B'frd —2C 62
*Baptist Fold. Q'bry —6H 95*
*(off Russell Rd.)*
Baptist Pl. B'frd —6K 79 (3C 6)
Baptist St. Bat —5E 136
Barberry Av. B'frd —5G 81
Barber Sq. Heck —4A 136
Barber St. Brigh —5H 133
*Barber Wlk. Dew —7G 137*
*(off Wellington Wlk.)*
Barbor Pk. Leeds —2D 68
Barclay Clo. Cull —6C 58
Barclay St. Leeds —3G 5
**Barcroft. —4H 57**
Barcroft. Cro R —4H 57
Barcroft Gro. Yead —5J 45
Barden Av. B'frd —5D 96
Barden Clo. Bat —3F 137
Barden Clo. Leeds —6A 84
Barden Dri. Bgly —7C 42
Barden Grn. Leeds —6A 84
Barden Gro. Leeds —6A 84
Barden Mt. Leeds —6A 84
Barden Pl. Leeds —6A 84
Barden St. B'frd —4H 79
Barden Ter. Leeds —6A 84
**Bardsey. —6B 34**
Bardsey Cres. B'frd —6C 80
*Bardsey Ho. B'frd —1F 99*
*(off Parsonage Rd.)*
Bardsley Cres. B'frd —4J 7
Bare Head La. Hal —2H 113
Barfield Av. Yead —5J 45
Barfield Cres. Leeds —6B 50
Barfield Dri. Yead —5J 45
Barfield Gro. Leeds —6C 50
Barfield Mt. Leeds —6C 50
Barfield Rd. Hal —1C 132
Bargess Ter. Kip —5B 108
Bargrange Av. Shipl —6H 61
Barham Gro. C'frd —7D 126
Barham Ter. B'frd —1F 81
Bar Ho. La. Kei —7H 21
Baring Av. B'frd —5F 81
Barker Clo. Hal —5J 131
Barker Ct. Bkby —7E 144
**Barkerend. —6C 80 (3J 7)**
Barkerend Rd. B'frd —6B 80 (3G 7)
Barker Hill. Leeds —5F 101
Barker Ho. Hal —5J 131
Barker Pl. Leeds —4H 83
Barker St. Liv —4K 135
Barkers Well Fold. Leeds —3H 101
Barkers Well Gth. Leeds —3J 101
Barkers Well Ga. Leeds —3J 101
Barkers Well Lawn. Leeds —3J 101
**Barkisland. —5K 141**
Bark La. Add —1E 10
Barkly Av. Leeds —5G 103
Barkly Dri. Leeds —5G 103
Barkly Gro. Leeds —4G 103
Barkly Pde. Leeds —5G 103
Barkly Pl. Leeds —5G 103
Barkly Rd. Bees —4F 103
Barkly St. Leeds —5G 103
Barkly Ter. Leeds —5G 103
Barkston Wlk. All —6A 78
Bar La. B Spa —4F 37
Bar La. Gar —6A 90
Bar La. H'fth —4C 64
Bar La. Riddl —2D 40
Bar La. Sower B —7D 140
Barlby Way. Leeds —6E 68
Barleycorn Yd. Leeds —6B 84
Barley Cote Av. Riddl —1D 40
Barley Cote Gro. Riddl —1E 40
Barley Cote Rd. Riddl —1E 40
Barley Cft. Dew —7D 136
Barley Fld. Ct. Halt —5J 87
Barleyfields Clo. Weth —2J 17
Barleyfields Ct. Weth —3J 17
Barleyfields La. Weth —3J 17
Barleyfields M. Weth —3J 17
Barleyfields Rd. Weth —3J 17
(in two parts)
Barleyfields Ter. Weth —3J 17
Barleyfields Wlk. Weth —4J 17
Barleyhill Cres. Gar —7J 89
Barleyhill La. Gar —6J 89
Barleyhill Rd. Gar —6H 89
Barley M. Rob H —4D 122
Barley St. Kei —7J 39
Barlow Rd. Kei —3K 39
Barlow St. B'frd —6D 80 (3K 7)
Barmby Pl. B'frd —4D 80
Barmby Rd. B'frd —4D 80
Barmby St. Wyke —3K 115
Bar Mt. Gar —6A 90
Barmouth Ter. B'frd —4B 80
Barnaby Rd. Bgly —7C 42
Barnard Clo. Leeds —2C 88
Barnard Rd. B'frd —1C 98 (7H 7)
Barnard Ter. B'frd —1C 98 (7H 7)
Barnard Way. Leeds —2C 88
**Barnbow Carr. —1F 89**
Barnbow La. Leeds —1F 89
(in two parts)
Barnbrough St. Leeds —3C 84
Barnby Av. B'frd —6C 78
Barn Clo. Men —6B 26
Barncroft Clo. Leeds —5H 69
Barncroft Ct. Leeds —6G 69
Barncroft Dri. Leeds —6G 69
Barncroft Gdns. Leeds —6H 69
Barncroft Grange. Leeds —6G 69
Barncroft Heights. Leeds —5G 69
Barncroft Mt. Leeds —6G 69
Barncroft Ri. Leeds —6H 69
Barncroft Rd. Leeds —6H 69
Barncroft Towers. Leeds —6G 69
Barnes Rd. B'frd —5F 79
Barnet Gro. Morl —2A 86
Barnet Rd. Leeds —6D 84
Barnsdale Rd. All B —5D 126
Barnsdale Rd. Meth —2B 68
Barnsley Beck Gro. Bail —1K 61
Barnstaple Wlk. B'frd —4F 99
Barn St. Oxe —3E 74
Barnswick Vw. Leeds —7J 47
Baron Clo. Leeds —2G 103
Baronscourt. Leeds —5B 88
Baronsmead. Leeds —5A 88
Baronsway. Leeds —5A 88
Barrack Rd. Leeds —2K 85 (1H 5)
Barracks St. Heck —4A 136
Barrack St. Leeds —3K 85 (1G 5)
Barraclough Bldgs. B'frd —5G 63
Barraclough Sq. B'frd —3J 115
Barraclough St. Low M —1H 115
Barran Ct. Leeds —2B 86
Barran St. Bgly —1A 60
Barras Gth. Pl. Leeds —7B 84
Barras Gth. Rd. Leeds —7B 84
Barras Pl. Leeds —7B 84
Barras St. Leeds —7B 84
Barras Ter. Leeds —7B 84
Barrett St. Sils —1F 21
Barrington Clo. Hal —4A 132
Barrington Pde. Gom —7J 117
**Barrowby. —5F 89**
Barrowby Av. Leeds —6C 88
Barrowby Clo. Men —6D 26
Barrowby Cres. Leeds —5C 88
Barrowby Dri. Leeds —6D 88
Barrowby La. Gar —5H 89
Barrowby La. Leeds —5C 88
(in two parts)
Barrowby Rd. Leeds —6D 88
Barrowclough La. Hal —1K 131
Barrows La. Steet —6D 20
Barry St. B'frd —6A 80 (4D 6)
Barsley Grn. La. Bklnd —1A 20
Bar St. Bat —4H 137
Barthorpe Av. Leeds —4H 67
Barthorpe Clo. B'frd —4H 99
Barthorpe Cres. Leeds —4J 67
Bartle Clo. B'frd —3F 97
Bartle Fold. B'frd —2G 97
Bartle Gill Dri. Bail —7A 44
Bartle Gill Ri. Bail —7A 44
Bartle Gill Vw. Bail —7A 44
Bartle Gro. B'frd —3F 97
Bartle La. B'frd —3F 97
Bartle Pl. B'frd —3F 97
Bartle Sq. B'frd —2G 97
Bartlett La. Morl —3B 120
Barton Ct. Leeds —6A 88
Barton Dri. Leeds —4F 103
Barton Gro. Leeds —2G 103
Barton Hill. Leeds —2G 103
Barton Mt. Leeds —2G 103
Barton Pl. Bat —4G 137
Barton Pl. Leeds —2G 103
Barton Rd. Leeds —2G 103
Barton St. B'frd —3H 97
*Barton St. Brigh —5G 133*
*(off Manley St.)*
Barton Ter. Leeds —2G 103
Barton Vw. Leeds —2G 103
Barum Top. Hal —1G 131
Barwick Grn. B'frd —5E 96
**Barwick in Elmet. —5H 71**
Barwick Rd. Gar —5J 89
Barwick Rd. Leeds —2K 87
Basil St. B'frd —3H 97
Baslow Gro. B'frd —3F 79
Batcliffe Dri. Leeds —6C 66
Batcliffe Mt. Leeds —7C 66
Bateman St. B'frd —4K 79
Bates Av. Sower B —5H 129
Bateson St. B'frd —5G 63
Bath Clo. Leeds —3G 83
Bath Gro. Leeds —3G 83
Bath La. Leeds —4G 83
Bath Pl. Cleck —1F 135
Bath Pl. Hal —6F 113
Bath Rd. Bmly —4G 83
Bath Rd. Cleck —1F 135
Bath Rd. Hal —4G 131
Bath Rd. Heck —4B 136
Bath Rd. Leeds —7G 85
Bath St. Bat —3H 137
Bath St. B'frd —6C 80 (4H 7)
Bath St. Dew —7G 137
Bath St. Ell —3K 143
Bath St. Hal —2H 131
Bath St. I'ly —4C 12
Bath St. Kei —4K 39
**Batley. —4H 137**
Batley Art Gallery. —3G 137
Batley Bus. Cen. Bat —2F 137
**Batley Carr. —5F 137**
Batley Enterprise Cen. Bat —2F 137
Batley Fld. Hill. Bat —2G 137
Batley Rd. Heck —4C 136
Batley Rd. Ting & K'gte —3D 138
Batley Rd. Wren —7J 139
Batley St. Hal —6E 112
Batter La. Rawd —7A 46
Battinson Rd. Hal —7D 112
Battinson's St. Hal —3J 131
Battye St. B'frd —7E 80
Battye St. Dew —7H 137
Bavaria Pl. B'frd —4H 79
Bawn App. Leeds —1J 101
Bawn Av. Leeds —7J 83
Bawn Chase. Leeds —7J 83
Bawn Dri. Leeds —7J 83
Bawn Gdns. Leeds —7J 83
Bawn La. Leeds —7J 83
*Bawn Path. Leeds —7K 83*
*(off Bawn Gdns.)*
*Bawn Va. Leeds —7J 83*
*(off Bawn Gdns.)*
*Bawn Wlk. Leeds —7K 83*
*(off Bawn Av.)*
Bawson Ct. Gom —6J 117
Baxandall St. B'frd —3K 97
Baxter La. Hal —4A 114
*Bay Horse Ct. Otley —2J 27*
*(off Courthouse St.)*
Bay Horse La. Leeds & S'cft —4J 51
Bay Horse Yd. Fars —2B 82
Bayldons Pl. Bat —3G 137
Bayne Dri. B'frd —6D 98
Bay of Biscay. All —1A 78
Bayswater Cres. Leeds —2B 86
Bayswater Gro. B'frd —3F 81
Bayswater Gro. Leeds —2B 86 (1K 5)
Bayswater Mt. Leeds —2B 86 (1K 5)
Bayswater Pl. Leeds —2B 86
Bayswater Rd. Leeds —2A 86 (1K 5)
Bayswater Row. Leeds —2B 86
Bayswater Ter. Hal —5G 131
Bayswater Ter. Leeds —2B 86
Bayswater Vw. Leeds —3B 86
Bayton La. Yead & H'fth —5B 46
Beacon Av. Morl —7B 68
Beacon Brow. B'frd —4D 96
Beacon Clo. Bgly —1B 60
Beacon Gro. B'frd —5F 97
Beacon Gro. Morl —7B 68
Beacon Hill Rd. Hal —7H 113
(in two parts)
Beacon Pl. B'frd —5E 96
Beacon Ri. I'ly —5J 11
Beacon Rd. B'frd —4D 96
Beaconsfield Ct. Gar —5K 89
Beaconsfield Rd. Cytn —2C 96
Beaconsfield St. Hal —2J 131
Beacon St. Add —1E 10
Beacon St. B Top —4E 96
Beacon St. Wibs —5G 97
Beamsley Gro. Gil —1B 60
Beamsley Gro. Leeds —3E 84
*Beamsley Ho. Shipl —7H 61*
*(off Bradford Rd.)*
Beamsley Mt. Leeds —3E 84
Beamsley Pl. Leeds —3E 84
Beamsley Rd. B'frd —3H 79
Beamsley Rd. Shipl —7H 61
Beamsley Ter. Leeds —3E 84
Beamsley Vw. I'ly —5J 11
Beamsley Wlk. B'frd —3G 79
Beancroft Rd. C'frd —7D 126
Beanlands Pde. I'ly —4C 12
Bean St. Ell —3C 144
Bearing Av. Leeds —4J 103
*Bear Pit Gdns. Leeds —2D 84*
*(off Chapel La.)*
Beatrice St. Cleck —7F 117
Beatrice St. Kei —2K 39
Beatrice St. Oxe —3E 74
Beaufort Gro. B'frd —2C 80
Beaumont Av. Leeds —2C 68
*Beaumont Ct. Bat —4G 137*
*(off Bank St.)*
Beaumont Pl. Bat —4D 136
Beaumont Rd. B'frd —4H 79
Beaumont Sq. Pud —7B 82
Beaumont St. Bat —4G 137
Beauvais Dri. Riddl —3F 41
Becca Hall. —2B 72
Becca La. Aber —6E 72
**Beck Bottom. —5J 139**
Beck Bottom. C'ley —2C 82
Beck Bottom. K'gte —5J 139
Beckbury Clo. Fars —3B 82
Beckbury St. Fars —3B 82
Beckenham Pl. Hal —7C 112
Becket La. Loft —5E 122
Beckett Ct. Colt —7B 88
**Beckett Park. —7C 66**
Beckett Rd. Dew —6F 137
(in two parts)
Beckett's Pk. Cres. Leeds —7C 66
Beckett's Pk. Dri. Leeds —7C 66
Beckett's Pk. Rd. Leeds —7D 66
Beckett St. Bat —5G 137
Beckett St. Leeds —5A 86 (5K 5)
Beckfield Rd. Bgly —5K 59
Beckfoot La. Bgly —2J 59
**Beck Hill. —1E 114**
Beck Hill. B'frd —7E 96
Beckhill App. Leeds —6G 67
Beckhill Av. Leeds —6G 67
Beckhill Chase. Leeds —6G 67
Beckhill Clo. Leeds —6G 67
Beckhill Dri. Leeds —5G 67
Beckhill Fold. Leeds —5G 67
Beckhill Gdns. Leeds —6G 67
Beckhill Gth. Leeds —6G 67
Beckhill Ga. Leeds —6G 67
Beckhill Grn. Leeds —6G 67
Beckhill Gro. Leeds —6G 67
Beckhill Lawn. Leeds —6G 67
Beckhill Pl. Leeds —5G 67
Beckhill Row. Leeds —5G 67
Beckhill Va. Leeds —5G 67
(in two parts)
Beckhill Vw. Leeds —6G 67
Beckhill Wlk. Leeds —5G 67
Beck La. Bgly —6K 41
Beck La. Coll —1F 35
Beck La. Heck —5A 136
Beck Mdw. Bar E —6J 71
Beck Rd. Bgly —3J 41
Beck Rd. Leeds —1B 86
Beck Side. Kei —5A 40
Beckside Clo. Add —1D 10
Beckside Clo. Bur W —1A 26
Beckside La. B'frd —2G 97
Beckside Rd. B'frd —1G 97
Beckside Vw. Morl —3C 120
Becks Rd. Kei —5J 39
Beck St. Kei —5K 39
Beckwith Dri. B'frd —7F 63
Bedale. Ting —7D 120
Bedale Av. Brigh —1E 144
Bedale Dri. B'frd —5E 96
Bede's Clo. T'tn —7H 77
Bedford Clo. Leeds —1J 65
Bedford Ct. Leeds —6E 68
Bedford Dri. Leeds —1J 65
Bedford Gdns. Leeds —1J 65
Bedford Gth. Leeds —1J 65
Bedford Grn. Leeds —1J 65
Bedford Gro. Leeds —2J 65
Bedford Mt. Leeds —2J 65
(in two parts)
Bedford Pl. Guis —3G 45
Bedford Row. Leeds —2K 103
Bedford St. B'frd —7B 80 (6F 7)
*Bedford St. Cleck —1E 134*
*(off Westgate)*
Bedford St. Ell —3K 143
Bedford St. Hal —1F 131
Bedford St. Kei —4K 39
Bedford St. Leeds —5H 85 (6D 4)
Bedford St. N. Hal —1F 131
Bedford Vw. Leeds —1J 65
Bedivere Rd. B'frd —6D 78
Bedlam La. Arth —5F 31
Beech Av. Denh —2A 76
Beech Av. H'fth —5G 65
Beech Av. Leeds —5C 84
Beech Av. Sower B —3K 129
**Beechcliffe. —2A 40**
Beech Clo. B'frd —2D 62
Beech Clo. Hal —1D 114
Beech Clo. Leeds —2F 87
Beech Clo. Men —4C 26
Beech Cres. Bail —3F 61
Beech Cres. B'frd —4D 80
Beech Cres. Leeds —2F 87
*Beech Cft. Bail —3H 61*
*(off Valley Vw.)*
Beech Cft. Loft —6F 123
Beechcroft Clo. Leeds —5D 102
Beechcroft Mead. Leeds —7C 50
Beechcroft Vw. Leeds —5D 102
Beechdale Av. Bat —1E 136
Beech Dri. Denh —2A 76
Beech Dri. H'fth —5F 65
Beech Dri. Leeds —5C 84
Beecher St. Hal —5F 113
Beecher St. Kei —3C 40
Beeches End. B Spa —3E 36
Beeches Rd. Kei —3C 40
Beeches, The. Bail —7K 43
Beeches, The. Guis —1G 45
Beeches, The. Pud —5K 81
*Beeches, The. Schol —7B 116*
*(off Field Hurst)*
*Beeches, The. Schol —1B 134*
*(off Scholes La.)*
Beeches, The. Weth —3K 17
Beechfield. Leeds —3H 101
*Beechfield Ter. Cleck —1G 135*
*(off Mayfield Ter.)*
Beech Gro. Bgly —6C 42
Beech Gro. B'frd —4D 80 (1K 7)
Beech Gro. Cytn —2C 96
Beech Gro. Gom —6J 117
Beech Gro. Hal —1G 133
Beech Gro. Heck —3A 136
Beech Gro. Morl —4K 119
Beech Gro. Rothw —1H 123
Beech Gro. Sils —1F 21


152 A-Z Leeds & Bradford

Beech Gro. Av.—Birks Hall Ter.


Beech Gro. Av. Gar —7J 89
Beech Gro. Ter. Gar —7J 89
Beech Gro. Ter. Leeds —3H 85 (2B 4)
Beech Hill. Otley —2J 27
Beech La. Leeds —2E 86
Beech Lees. Fars —1A 82
Beech Mt. Leeds —2F 87
Beechmount Clo. Bail —7K 43
Beech Rd. B Spa —2C 36
Beech Rd. B'frd —7J 97
Beech Rd. Sower B —4A 130
Beechroyd. Pud —7C 82
Beechroyd Ter. Bgly —2K 59
Beech Spinney. Weth —1K 17
Beech Sq. Cytn —2C 96
Beech St. Bgly —2K 59
Beech St. Ell —3K 143
Beech St. Hal —1F 131
Beech St. Holy G —5E 142
Beech St. Kei —3C 40
Beech St. Steet —5E 20
Beech St. Ting —6E 120
Beech Ter. B'frd —5D 80 (1K 7)
Beechtree Ct. Bail —2G 61
Beech Vw. Aber —5D 72
Beech Vw. Sower B —3K 129
Beech Wlk. Adel —2D 66
Beech Wlk. B'shaw —3K 117
Beech Wlk. Dew —7G 137
(off Swindon Rd.)
Beech Wlk. Leeds —2F 87
Beech Way. Birs —5E 118
**Beechwood. —1F 65**
**(nr. Horsforth)**
**Beechwood. —6H 69**
**(nr. Seacroft)**
**Beechwood. —5H 129**
**(nr. Sowerby Bridge)**
Beechwood. W'ford —7A 106
Beechwood Av. B'frd —4G 97
Beechwood Av. Dlgtn —7B 100
Beechwood Av. Hal —2E 112
Beechwood Av. Leeds —2D 84
Beechwood Av. Riddl —2D 40
Beechwood Av. She —2B 114
Beechwood Av. Shipl —5E 60
Beechwood Av. Sower B —5H 129
Beechwood Cen. Rothw —7A 106
(off Church St.)
Beechwood Clo. Hal —3D 112
Beechwood Clo. H'fth —1E 64
Beechwood Ct. Leeds —6B 48
(LS16)
Beechwood Ct. Leeds —2D 84
(off Bk. Beechwood Gro.)
Beechwood Ct. Seac —6G 69
Beechwood Cres. Leeds —2D 84
Beechwood Cres. Sower B —5H 129
Beechwood Dri. B'frd —4H 97
Beechwood Dri. Hal —2D 112
Beechwood Dri. Sower B —5H 129
Beechwood Gro. B'frd —4H 97
Beechwood Gro. Dlgtn —7B 100
Beechwood Gro. Fix —5G 145
Beechwood Gro. Hal —3D 112
Beechwood Gro. I'ly —5K 11
Beechwood Gro. Leeds —2D 84
Beechwood Gro. Shipl —5E 60
Beechwood Mt. Leeds —2D 84
Beechwood Pl. Leeds —2D 84
Beechwood Ri. Weth —2J 17
Beechwood Rd. B'frd —4G 97
Beechwood Rd. Hal —3D 112
Beechwood Rd. Leeds —2D 84
Beechwood Row. Leeds —2D 84
Beechwood St. Leeds —2D 84
Beechwood St. S'ley —4A 82
Beechwood Ter. Leeds —2D 84
Beechwood Vw. Leeds —2D 84
Beechwood Vs. Hal —3D 112
Beechwood Wlk. Leeds —2D 84
Beecroft Clo. Leeds —2E 82
Beecroft Cres. Leeds —2F 83
Beecroft Gdns. Leeds —2E 82
Beecroft Mt. Leeds —2E 82
Beecroft St. Kei —4B 40
Beecroft St. Leeds —2A 84
Beecroft Wlk. All —6A 78
Beehive St. B'frd —7F 97
Beehive Yd. B'frd —7F 97
**Beeston. —4E 102**
**Beeston Hill. —2G 103**
Beestonley La. Slnd —5B 142
Beeston Pk. Cft. Leeds —4E 102
Beeston Pk. Gth. Leeds —4E 102
Beeston Pk. Gro. Leeds —4E 102
Beeston Pk. Pl. Leeds —4E 102
**Beeston Park Side. —6H 103**
Beeston Pk. Ter. Leeds —4E 102
Beeston Rd. Leeds —4F 103
**Beeston Royds. —4B 102**
Beevers Ct. Leeds —2A 66
**Beggarington Hill. —2D 138**
Bela Av. B'frd —4E 98
**Beldon Hill. —4F 97**
Beldon La. B'frd —5F 97
Beldon Pk. Av. B'frd —4F 97
Beldon Pk. Clo. B'frd —4F 97
Beldon Pl. B'frd —3D 80
Beldon Rd. B'frd —3G 97
Belfast St. Hal —2D 130
Belford Clo. B'frd —3F 99
Belfry, The. Yead —5A 46
Belgrave Av. Hal —7H 113
Belgrave Clo. Hal —7H 113
Belgrave Cres. Hal —7H 113
Belgrave Dri. Hal —6J 113
Belgrave Gro. Hal —6H 113
Belgrave M. Rawd —7J 45
Belgrave Mt. Hal —6H 113
Belgrave Pk. Hal —6H 113
Belgrave Rd. Bgly —7A 42
Belgrave Rd. Kei —3K 39
Belgrave St. Leeds —5J 85 (5E 4)
Belgrave St. Sower B —4K 129
Belinda St. Leeds —2A 104
Bell Bank Vw. Bgly —7J 41
Bellbrooke Av. Leeds —3D 86
Bellbrooke Gro. Leeds —3D 86
Bellbrooke Pl. Leeds —3D 86
Bellbrooke St. Leeds —3C 86
Bellcross Dri. Hal —6H 113
Bell Dean Rd. All & B'frd —5B 78
**Belle Isle. —6A 104**
Belle Isle Cir. Leeds —6A 104
Belle Isle Clo. Leeds —6A 104
Belle Isle Pde. Leeds —5A 104
Belle Isle Rd. Haw —5E 56
Belle Isle Rd. Leeds —4A 104
Bellerby Brow. B'frd —5D 96
Belle Vw. Q'bry —7J 95
Belle Vue. Eccl —7E 62
Belle Vue. I'ly —6C 12
Belle Vue. Mann —4K 79
Belle Vue Av. Leeds —6F 69
Belle Vue Av. Scholes —5D 70
Belle Vue Ct. Leeds —4F 85
(off Consort Ter.)
Belle Vue Cres. Hal —2B 114
Belle Vue Cres. Hud —6J 145
Belle Vue Dri. Fars —2A 82
Belle Vue Est. Scholes —6D 70
Bellevue Pl. Hal —1E 130
Belle Vue Ri. Hal —2B 114
Belle Vue Rd. Hal —2B 114
Belle Vue Rd. Leeds —4F 85 (5A 4)
Belle Vue Rd. Scholes —6D 70
Belle Vue St. Bat —3D 136
Belle Vue Ter. Gild —1H 119
Belle Vue Ter. Guis —3G 45
Bellevue Ter. Hal —3J 131
Bellgrave Gdns. Hal —6H 113
Bell Gro. Leeds —2G 83
Bell Hall Mt. Hal —3E 130
Bell Hall Ter. Hal —3E 130
Bell Hall Vw. Hal —3F 131
Bell Ho. Av. B'frd —5D 98
Bellhouse Cres. B'frd —6D 98
Bell La. Leeds —2G 83
Bellmount Clo. Leeds —2H 83
Bellmount Gdns. Leeds —1G 83
Bellmount Grn. Leeds —2H 83
Bellmount Pl. Leeds —1G 83
Bellmount Vw. Leeds —2H 83
Belloe St. B'frd —2K 97
Bell Rd. Leeds —2G 83
Bellshaw St. B'frd —6E 78
Bell St. Hal —6H 113
Bell St. Leeds —5K 85 (5H 5)
Bell St. Wyke —3J 115
Bellwood Av. Cliff —4D 36
Belmont Av. Bail —1H 61
Belmont Av. Low M —7A 98
Belmont Av. Otley —1H 27
Belmont Clo. Bail —1H 61
Belmont Cres. Low M —7A 98
Belmont Cres. Shipl —4G 61
Belmont Gdns. Low M —7K 97
Belmont Grange. Liv —6J 135
(off Norristhorpe La.)
Belmont Gro. B'frd —7K 97
Belmont Gro. Leeds —4G 85 (4B 4)
Belmont Gro. Rawd —6A 46
Belmont Pl. Hal —2E 130
Belmont Ri. Bail —1H 61
Belmont Ri. Low M —7A 98
Belmont Rd. I'ly —5E 12
Belmont St. B'frd —7E 62
Belmont St. Hal —7J 113
Belmont St. Sower B —4A 130
Belmont Ter. L'ft —3G 129
Belmont Ter. Shipl —4G 61
Belmont Ter. Thpe —5B 122
Belton Clo. B'frd —3G 97
Belton Gro. Hud —7B 144
Belton Rd. Sils —2G 21
Belvedere Av. Alw —7K 49
Belvedere Av. Bees —4H 103
Belvedere Ct. Alw —7A 50
Belvedere Ct. Leeds —7A 68
(off Harehills La.)
Belvedere Gdns. Leeds —7A 50
Belvedere Gro. Leeds —7K 49
Belvedere Mt. Leeds —4H 103
Belvedere Rd. Bat —5F 137
Belvedere Rd. Leeds —7K 49
Belvedere St. B'frd —5H 79
Belvedere Ter. B'frd —5H 79
Belvedere Ter. Leeds —4H 103
Belvedere Vw. Leeds —7A 50
Belvoir Gdns. Hal —5G 131
Bempton Ct. B'frd —2H 97
Bempton Gro. Birs —5D 118
Bempton Ho. B'frd —6E 62
(off Savile Av.)
Bempton Pl. B'frd —2H 97
Benbow Av. B'frd —7G 63
Bendigo Rd. Dew —7K 137
Benjamin St. Liv —5K 135
Benn Av. B'frd —2F 97
Benn Cres. B'frd —2F 97
Bennett Ct. Leeds —5B 88
Bennett Ct. Otley —1H 27
Bennett La. Dew & Bat —5J 137
Bennett Rd. Leeds —7D 66
Bennett St. Hal —2J 131
Bennett St. Liv —4K 135
Bennetts Yd. Rothw —3G 123
Benns La. Hal —5G 111
Benny Parr Clo. Bat —3J 137
**Ben Rhydding. —6D 12**
Ben Rhydding Dri. I'ly —5E 12
Ben Rhydding Rd. I'ly —6C 12
Benroyd Ter. Holy G —6G 143
(in two parts)
Benson Gdns. Leeds —7B 84
Benson's Mobile Home Pk. Riddl —7F 23
Benson St. Leeds —3K 85 (2G 5)
Bentcliffe Av. Leeds —2K 67
Bentcliffe Clo. Leeds —3A 68
Bentcliffe Ct. Leeds —3A 68
Bentcliffe Dri. Leeds —2A 68
Bentcliffe Gdns. Leeds —3A 68
Bentcliffe Gro. Leeds —3A 68
Bentcliffe La. Leeds —3K 67
Bentcliffe Mt. Leeds —3A 68
Bentcliff Wlk. All —6B 78
Bent Clo. La. Cra V —5A 128
Bentfield Cotts. Cytn —1C 96
Bentley Av. Hal —1G 133
Bentley Clo. Bail —7H 43
Bentley Ct. Leeds —6F 67
Bentley Gro. Leeds —6F 67
Bentley La. Leeds —6F 67
Bentley Mt. Leeds —6F 67
Bentley Mt. Sower B —3B 130
Bentley Pde. Leeds —6F 67
Bentley Royd Clo. Sower B —5J 129
Bentley Sq. W'ford —2A 124
Bentley St. Wyke —4K 115
Benton Pk. Av. Rawd —6A 46
Benton Pk. Cres. Rawd —6A 46
Benton Pk. Dri. Rawd —6A 46
Benton Pk. Rd. Rawd —6A 46
Bents La. Wilsd —1E 76
Benyon Pk. Way. Leeds —2D 102
Beresford Rd. B'frd —7H 97
Beresford St. Oaken —2C 116
Berger Bldgs. Ell —2A 144
Berger Ho. B'frd —4J 79
Berkeley Av. Leeds —2C 86
Berkeley Cres. Leeds —2C 86
Berkeley Gro. Leeds —2C 86
Berkeley Ho. B'frd —3G 99
(off Stirling Cres.)
Berkeley Mt. Leeds —2C 86
Berkeley Rd. Leeds —2C 86
Berkeley St. Leeds —2C 86
Berkeley Ter. Leeds —2C 86
Berkeley Vw. Leeds —2C 86
Berking Av. Leeds —5B 86
Berking Row. Leeds —5B 86
Berkley Ct. Leeds —4F 85 (3A 4)
Bermondsey St. Otley —3K 27
Bernard St. Hud —6K 145
Bernard St. W'ford —1B 124
Berrington Way. Oakw —1D 56
Berry La. Hal —1H 131
Berry La. Kei —6K 39
Berry La. W'ford —6J 107
Berry Moor Rd. Norl —6B 130
Berry's Bldgs. Hal —3D 112
Berry St. Kei —4B 40
Bertha St. Fars —3B 82
Bertie St. B'frd —3E 98
Bertram Dri. Bail —3H 61
Bertram Rd. B'frd —3J 79
Bertrand St. Leeds —1G 103
Berwick Av. Heck —2B 136
Berwick St. Hal —1H 131
Beryl Dri. Kei —3B 40
Beryl Mt. Wyke —3J 115
Bescaby Gro. Bail —1A 62
Besha Av. Low M —1K 115
Besha Gro. Low M —1K 115
Bessbrook St. Leeds —3K 103
Bessingham Gdns. B'frd —6F 97
Best La. Oxe —3E 74
Beswick Clo. B'frd —6F 81
Bethel Rd. Shipl —4K 61
Bethel St. Brigh —6H 133
Bethel St. E Mor —3H 41
Bethel St. Hal —5E 112
Bethel Ter. Ludd —6F 111
Beulah Gro. Leeds —2H 85
Beulah Mt. Leeds —2H 85
Beulah Pl. L'ft —3G 129
Beulah St. Leeds —2H 85
Beulah Ter. Leeds —3A 88
(off Austhorpe Rd.)
Beulah Ter. Leeds —2H 85
(off Beulah St.)
Beulah Vw. Leeds —2H 85
Bevan Ct. B'frd —3F 97
Beverley Av. Leeds —3H 103
Beverley Av. Wyke —5K 115
Beverley Clo. Ell —2B 144
Beverley Ct. Hud —7H 145
Beverley Ct. Leeds —2K 67
Beverley Dri. Dew —7K 137
Beverley Dri. Wyke —5K 115
Beverley Gdns. Bat —5F 119
Beverley Ho. Far —3B 82
Beverley Mt. Leeds —3H 103
Beverley Pl. Hal —6F 113
Beverley Ri. I'ly —5J 11
Beverley St. B'frd —1F 99
Beverley Ter. Hal —6F 113
(in two parts)
Beverley Ter. Leeds —3H 103
Beverley Vw. Leeds —3H 103
Beverley Wlk. Gar —7K 89
Bevor Cres. Heck —2B 136
Bewerley Cres. B'frd —1G 115
Bewick Gro. Leeds —7B 104
Bexley Av. Leeds —3B 86
Bexley Gro. Leeds —3B 86
Bexley Mt. Leeds —3B 86
Bexley Pl. Leeds —3B 86
Bexley Rd. Leeds —3B 86
Bexley Ter. Leeds —3B 86
Bexley Vw. Leeds —3B 86
Beza Rd. Leeds —3K 103
Beza St. Leeds —3K 103
Bickerdike Pl. All B —3B 126
(off St Mary's Ct.)
Bickerdike Ter. Kip —5A 108
Bickerton Way. Otley —1G 27
Biddenden Rd. Leeds —3D 88
Bidder Dri. E Ard —6J 121
Bideford Av. Leeds —1B 68
Bideford Mt. B'frd —3G 99
**Bierley. —5D 98**
Bierley Hall Gro. B'frd —7D 98
Bierley Ho. Av. B'frd —5D 98
Bierley La. B'frd —7D 98
Bierley Vw. B'frd —5D 98
Big Mdw. Dri. Add —1B 10
Billam's Hill. Otley —1H 27
Billey La. Leeds —1J 101
(in two parts)
Billingbauk Dri. Leeds —4H 83
Billing Ct. Rawd —1B 64
Billing Dri. Rawd —1C 64
Billingsley Ter. B'frd —2D 98
Billing Vw. B'frd —5E 62
Billing Vw. Rawd —1B 64
Billingwood Dri. Rawd —1B 64
Billsdale Ho. B'frd —4E 62
(off Thorp Gth.)
Bilsdale Grange. B'frd —6F 97
Bilsdale Way. Bail —2G 61
Bilton Pl. B'frd —5J 79 (2A 6)
**Bingley. —2K 59**
Bingley Bank. Bard —1A 52
Bingley Rd. Bail —5F 43
Bingley Rd. B'frd —7D 60
Bingley Rd. Cro R & Kei —4H 57
Bingley Rd. Cull —6B 58
Bingley Rd. Men —1G 43
(in two parts)
Bingley Rd. Shipl —4D 60
Bingley St. B'frd —6G 79
Bingley St. Leeds —5F 85 (5A 4)
Binks Fold. Wyke —5K 115
Binnie St. B'frd —6D 80 (3K 7)
Binns Hill La. Sower B —2K 129
Binns La. B'frd —1F 97
Binns St. Bgly —1A 60
Binns Top La. Hal —5A 132
Binswell Fold. Bail —7J 43
Bircham Clo. Bgly —6C 42
Birch Av. B'frd —4B 98
Birch Av. Leeds —5J 87
Birch Cliff. Bail —2H 61
Birch Clo. B'frd —4B 98
Birch Clo. Brigh —5J 133
Birch Clo. La. Bgly —3F 43
Birch Ct. Morl —5B 120
Birch Cres. Leeds —5J 87
Birchdale. Bgly —5K 41
Birch Dri. Kip —3A 108
**Birchencliffe. —7B 144**
Birchencliffe Hill Rd. Hud —7B 144
Birchenlee Clo. Myth —6B 110
Birches, The. B'hpe —1K 47
Birches, The. Guis —1G 45
Birchfield Av. Gild —1G 119
Birchfields Av. Leeds —4A 70
Birchfields Clo. Leeds —5A 70
Birchfields Ct. Leeds —4A 70
Birchfields Cres. Leeds —4A 70
Birchfields Gth. Leeds —4A 70
Birchfields Ri. Leeds —5A 70
Birch Gro. Bat —7E 118
Birch Gro. B'frd —5A 98
Birch Gro. Kei —7K 39
Birch Gro. Kip —4A 108
Birch Hill Ri. H'fth —4J 65
Birchington Av. Hud —7A 144
Birchington Clo. Hud —7B 144
Birchington Dri. Hud —7A 144
Birchlands Av. Wilsd —6F 59
Birchlands Gro. Wilsd —6F 59
Birch La. B'frd —3A 98
(in five parts)
Birch La. Hal —7G 111
Birch M. Adel —2D 66
Birch Rd. Kip —3A 108
Birchroyd. Rothw —3H 123
Birch St. B'frd —5F 79
Birch St. Morl —5B 120
Birch Tree Gdns. Kei —5C 40
Birchtree Way. Leeds —2J 65
Birch Way. B'frd —4B 98
Birchwood Av. Birs —5D 118
Birchwood Av. Kei —1K 39
Birchwood Av. Leeds —1C 68
Birchwood Clo. Hud —7D 144
Birchwood Ct. I'ly —5A 12
Birchwood Ct. Liv —5K 135
Birchwood Dri. Kei —1J 39
Birchwood Hill. Leeds —7C 50
Birchwood Mt. Leeds —7C 50
Birchwood Rd. Kei —1J 39
**Birdacre. —6K 117**
Birdale Fld. La. Coll —2H 35
Birdcage. Hal —7H 113
Birdcage Hill. Hal —5E 130
Birdcage La. Hal —5E 130
Birdcage Wlk. Otley —4H 27
Bird Holme La. Hal —6B 114
Bird La. Ripp —6E 140
**Birds Royd. —7H 133**
Birds Royd La. Brigh —7H 133
Birdswell Av. Brigh —5K 133
Birfed Cres. Leeds —2B 84
Birkby Brow Cres. Bat —5F 119
Birkby Hall Rd. Hud —7F 145
Birkby Haven. B'frd —6E 96
Birkby La. Bail B —1H 133
Birkby Rd. Hud —7C 144
Birkby St. Wyke —3K 115
Birkdale Clo. Cull —6C 58
Birkdale Clo. Leeds —7H 49
Birkdale Ct. Low U —7J 21
Birkdale Dri. Leeds —7G 49
Birkdale Grn. Leeds —7H 49
Birkdale Gro. Dew —6E 136
Birkdale Gro. Hal —7D 94
Birkdale Gro. Leeds —7G 49
Birkdale Mt. Leeds —7H 49
Birkdale Pl. Leeds —7G 49
Birkdale Ri. Leeds —7G 49
Birkdale Rd. Dew —7F 137
Birkdale Wlk. Leeds —7G 49
Birkdale Way. Leeds —7H 49
**Birkenshaw. —1J 117**
**Birkenshaw Bottoms. —3A 118**
Birkenshaw La. B'shaw —2K 117
Birkett St. Cleck —7F 117
Birkhead St. Heck —5C 136
Birkhill. C'frd —7J 127
Birkhill Cres. B'shaw —2K 117
Birkhouse La. Brigh —2J 133
Birkhouse Rd. Brigh —1J 133
Birklands Rd. Hud —7F 145
Birklands Rd. Shipl —5H 61
Birklands Ter. Shipl —5H 61
Birk La. Morl —3J 119
Birk Lea St. B'frd —2B 98
**Birks. —7F 79**
**(nr. Bradford)**
**Birks. —5A 120**
**(nr. Morley)**
Birks Av. B'frd —1F 97
Birks Fold. B'frd —7F 79
Birkshall La. B'frd —7D 80 (6K 7)
Birks Hall La. Hal —7E 112
Birks Hall St. Hal —7E 112
Birks Hall Ter. Hal —7E 112


A-Z Leeds & Bradford 153

Birkshead—Bradford & Wakefield Rd.


**Birkshead. —1H 77**
Birksland Ind. Est. B'frd —1D 98 (7K 7)
Birksland Moor. B'shaw —4K 117
Birksland St. B'frd —1D 98 (7K 7)
Birks La. Sower B —2F 141 (nr. Mill Bank Rd.)
Birks La. Sower B —4F 141 (nr. Stony La.)
Birkwith Clo. Leeds —4K 69
Birnam Gro. B'frd —2C 98
Birr Rd. B'frd —2H 79
**Birstall. —6C 118**
Birstall La. Dlgtn —2C 118
**Birstall Smithies. —7D 118**
Bishopdale Dri. Coll —2E 34
Bishopdale Holme. B'frd —6E 96
Bishopgate St. Leeds —6H 85 (7D 4)
Bishop St. B'frd —2H 79
Bishop Way. Ting —7F 121
*Bismarck Ct. Leeds —2H 103 (off Bismarck St.)*
Bismarck Dri. Leeds —2H 103
Bismarck St. Leeds —2H 103
Bittern Ri. Morl —4C 120
Blackbird Gdns. B'frd —6B 78
Black Brook Way. G'lnd —3G 143
Black Bull St. Leeds —7K 85
*Black Bull Yd. Rothw —2H 123 (off Commercial St.)*
Blackburn Clo. B'frd —6D 78
Blackburn Clo. Oven —4D 112
Blackburn Ct. Rothw —2H 123
Blackburn Ho. Hal —4E 112
Blackburn Pl. Bat —3H 137
Blackburn Rd. Birs —6C 118
Blackburn Rd. Brigh —4F 133
Blackburn's Yd. C'frd —7D 126
Black Dyke La. T'tn —3F 77
Blackedge. Hal —1H 131
Black Edge La. Denh —7B 76
Blackett St. C'ley —5K 63
Black Ga. H Bri —4A 92
**Black Gates. —6F 121**
Blackgates Ct. Ting —7F 121
Blackgates Cres. Ting —7F 121
Blackgates Dri. Ting —7F 121
Blackgates Fold. Ting —7F 121
Blackgates Ri. Ting —7F 121
Blackgates Rd. Wake —7F 121
**Black Hill. —3H 39**
Black Hill La. Kei —2F 39
Black Hill La. Leeds —2C 48
Black Hill Rd. Arth —6B 30
Blackhouse Rd. Hud —7H 145
**Blackley. —5J 143**
Blackley Rd. Ell —4H 143
Blackman La. Leeds —3H 85 (2D 4)
Blackmires. Hal —2E 112
Black Moor. —7G 49 (nr. Alwoodley)
Blackmoor. —4H 51 (nr. Shadwell)
Blackmoor Ct. Leeds —6F 49
Blackmoor La. Bard —3J 51
Black Moor Rd. Leeds —1F 67
Black Moor Rd. Oxe —3G 75
Black Moor Top. Haw —6F 57
Blackpool Gro. Leeds —2A 102
Blackpool Pl. Leeds —2A 102
Blackpool St. Leeds —2A 102
Blackpool Ter. Leeds —2A 102
Blackpool Vw. Leeds —2A 102
Blackshaw Beck La. Q'bry —7A 96
Blackshaw Clough Rd. Sower B —3C 140
Blackshaw Dri. B'frd —6D 96
Blacksmith Fold. B'frd —2G 97
Blacksmith La. Leeds —2F 49
Blackstone Av. Wyke —5J 115
*Black Swan Ginnell. Hal —1G 131 (off Silver St.)*
Black Swan Pas. Hal —1G 131
Blackthorn Ct. Leeds —6K 103
Blackwall. Hal —2G 131
Blackwall La. Sower B —3J 129
Blackwall Ri. Sower B —3J 129
Blackwood Av. Leeds —1H 65 (in two parts)
Blackwood Gdns. Leeds —1H 65
Blackwood Gro. Hal —7D 112
Blackwood Gro. Leeds —1H 65
Blackwood Mt. Leeds —1H 65
Blackwood Ri. Leeds —1H 65
Blacup Moor Vw. Cleck —1F 135
Blairsville Gdns. Leeds —1F 83
Blairsville Gro. Leeds —1G 83
Blaithroyd La. Hal —2J 131
Blake Cres. Guis —3H 45
Blake Gro. Leeds —6K 67
Blake Hill. Hal —4J 113
Blakehill Av. B'frd —3E 80
Blake Hill End. Hal —2K 113
Blakehill Ter. B'frd —3E 80
Blake Law Dri. Clif —5K 133
Blake Law La. Brigh —6B 134
Blakeney Gro. Leeds —5K 103
Blakeney Rd. Leeds —5K 103
Blakeridge La. Bat —3F 137
Blamires Pl. B'frd —3F 97
Blamires St. B'frd —3F 97
Blanche St. B'frd —7F 81
Blandford Gdns. Leeds —3H 85 (2C 4)
Blandford Gro. Leeds —2C 4
Blands Av. All B —2A 126
Blands Cres. All B —2A 126
Blands Gro. All B —2A 126
Blands Ter. All B —2A 126
Bland St. Hal —1F 131
Blanket Hall St. Heck —5B 136
Blayds Gth. W'ford —7J 105
Blayd's M. Leeds —6J 85 (7E 4)
Blayds St. Leeds —6B 86
Blayd's Yd. Leeds —6J 85 (7E 4)
Bleach Mill La. Men —5K 25
Bleak St. Gom —7A 118
Bleak St. Lwr. Gom —7A 118
Bleasdale Av. Hud —7F 145
Blencarn Clo. Leeds —1H 87
Blencarn Gth. Leeds —1H 87
Blencarn Lawn. Leeds —1H 87
Blencarn Path. Leeds —1H 87
Blencarn Rd. Leeds —1H 87
Blencarn Vw. Leeds —1H 87
Blencarn Wlk. Leeds —1H 87
Blenheim Av. Leeds —3H 85 (1D 4)
*Blenheim Ct. Hal —7F 113 (off Dene Pl.)*
Blenheim Ct. Leeds —2D 4
Blenheim Cres. Leeds —1D 4
Blenheim Dri. Bat —2G 137
Blenheim Dri. Dew —7E 136
Blenheim Gro. Leeds —3H 85 (2D 4)
Blenheim Hill. Bat —1H 137
Blenheim Mt. B'frd —3J 79
Blenheim Pl. B'frd —3D 62
Blenheim Rd. B'frd —4J 79
Blenheim Sq. Bat —2G 137
Blenheim Sq. Leeds —3H 85 (2D 4)
*Blenheim St. Kei —6K 39 (off Victoria Rd.)*
Blenheim Ter. Bat —2G 137
Blenheim Ter. Leeds —2C 4
Blenheim Ter. Morl —1A 120
Blenheim Vw. Leeds —3H 85 (1C 4)
Blenheim Wlk. Leeds —3H 85 (1C 4)
*Blenkinsop Ct. Morl —5B 120 (off Britannia Rd.)*
Blind La. Bgly —1H 59
Blind La. Dlgtn —7D 100
Blind La. E Ard —3G 139
Blind La. Hal —6C 94
Blind La. Leeds —7G 51
Blind La. L'ft —7D 110
Blind La. Q'bry —3G 95
Blucher St. B'frd —7F 81
Blue Ball La. Sower B —6A 140 (in two parts)
Blue Ball Rd. Ripp —6A 140
Bluebell Clo. All —5B 78
Bluebell Ct. Birs —5C 118
Bluebell Wlk. Ludd —7G 111
Blue Hill. Denh —3B 76
Blue Hill Cres. Leeds —7A 84
Blue Hill Grange. Leeds —1A 102
Blue Hill Gro. Leeds —7A 84
Blue Hill La. Leeds —7A 84
Blundell St. Leeds —4H 85 (4C 4)
Blythe Av. B'frd —5G 79
Blythe St. B'frd —6J 79 (4A 6)
Boar La. Leeds —6J 85 (7D 4)
Boat La. All B —4B 126
Boat La. Meth —5A 126
*Bobbin Mill Clo. Steet —5E 20 (off Bobbin Mill Ct.)*
Bobbin Mill Ct. Steet —5E 20
Bob La. Hal —1B 130
Bob La. Wilsd —2H 77
**Bocking. —4H 57**
Bodiham Hill. Gar —5B 90
Bodkin La. Oxe —3A 74 (in two parts)
Bodley Ter. Leeds —4D 84
Bodmin App. Leeds —2G 121
Bodmin Av. Shipl —5B 62
Bodmin Cres. Leeds —2G 121
Bodmin Cft. Leeds —2H 121
Bodmin Gdns. Leeds —3G 121
Bodmin Gth. Leeds —3G 121
Bodmin Pl. Leeds —3H 121 (in two parts)
Bodmin Rd. Leeds —1F 121
Bodmin Sq. Leeds —3G 121
Bodmin St. Leeds —3G 121
Bodmin Ter. Leeds —3G 121
Bogart La. Hal —6D 114
Boggart Hill. Leeds —6G 69
Boggart Hill Cres. Leeds —6G 69
Boggart Hill Dri. Leeds —6G 69
Boggart Hill Gdns. Leeds —6G 69
Boggart Hill Rd. Leeds —6G 69
Bog La. Scholes —7E 70
**Bogthorn. —7G 39**
Boland Cres. Oakw —1G 57
Boldmere Rd. Leeds —6G 87
Boldron Holt. B'frd —6F 97
Boldshay St. B'frd —5D 80 (2K 7)
Bold St. B'frd —4J 79
Bolehill Pk. Hov E —2E 132
*Bolingbroke Ct. B'frd —7D 6 (off Elsdon Gro.)*
Bolingbroke St. B'frd —4K 97
Bolland Bldgs. Low M —2B 116
Bolland St. Low M —2A 116
Bolling Hall Museum. —3C 98
Bolling Rd. B'frd —7B 80 (6F 7)
Bolling Rd. I'ly —6D 12
Bolsover Clo. Gar —6B 90
Boltby La. B'frd —6E 96
**Bolton. —2C 80**
Bolton Bri. Rd. I'ly —5A 12
Bolton Brow. Sower B —4A 130
Bolton Ct. B'frd —3C 80
*Bolton Ct. I'ly —5A 12 (off Bolton Bri. Rd.)*
Bolton Cres. B'frd —1D 80
Bolton Dri. B'frd —7D 62
Bolton Grange. Yead —5A 46
Bolton Gro. B'frd —1D 80
Bolton Hall Rd. B'frd —1K 79
Bolton La. B'frd —3K 79
**Bolton Outlanes. —1C 80**
Bolton Rd. Add —1D 10
Bolton Rd. B'frd —3B 80 (1F 7)
Bolton Rd. Sils —1G 21
Bolton Rd. Yead —5A 46
Bolton St. B'frd —6C 80 (3F 7)
Bolton St. Low M —1J 115 (in two parts)
Bolton Ter. Sils —7G 9
Bolton Way. B Spa —3C 36
**Bolton Woods. —1A 80**
*Bonaccord Sq. Bat —4G 137 (off Purlwell La.)*
*Bonaccord Ter. Bat —4G 137 (off Greatwood St.)*
Bond Ct. Leeds —6D 4
*Bond Ct. Leeds —3E 84 (off Alexandra Rd.)*
Bondgate. Hare —3C 32
Bondgate. Otley —3J 27
Bond St. Bat —2G 137
Bond St. Birs —6C 118
Bond St. Brigh —5G 133
Bond St. Dew —7G 137
Bond St. Leeds —5H 85 (6D 4)
Bonegate Av. Brigh —5H 133
Bonegate Rd. Brigh —5G 133
Bonn Rd. B'frd —3G 79
Bonwick Mall. B'frd —7E 96
Bookers Fld. Gom —2A 136
**Booth. —4G 111**
Bootham Pk. D Hill —3D 78
Booth Ho. Rd. L'ft —1D 128
Booth Ho. Ter. L'ft —1F 129
Boothman Wlk. Kei —6J 39
**Boothroyd. —7E 136**
Booth Royd. B'frd —3D 62
Booth Royd Dri. B'frd —3D 62
Boothroyd Dri. Leeds —7F 67
Booth Royd La. Brigh —1D 144
Boothroyd La. Dew —7E 136
*Booth's Bldgs. Brigh —1H 133 (off Wyke Old La.)*
Booth St. B'frd —5D 62
Booth St. Bur W —1A 26
Booth St. C'frd —7D 126
Booth St. Cleck —7F 117
Booth St. Q'bry —5H 95
Booth St. Shipl —5K 61
Booth's Yd. Pud —6C 82
**Boothtown. —6F 113**
Booth Town Rd. Hal —4F 113
Border Clo. Hud —7K 143
Boroughgate. Otley —2J 27
*Borough Mkt. Hal —1G 131 (off Market St.)*
Borrin's Way. Bail —1K 61
Borrough Av. Leeds —4A 68
Borrough Vw. Leeds —4A 68
Borrowdale Clo. Leeds —3K 83
Borrowdale Cres. Leeds —3K 83
Borrowdale Cft. Yead —4K 45
Borrowdale Dri. C'frd —6K 127
Borrowdale Rd. Dew —6J 137
Borrowdale Ter. Leeds —2H 87
Boston Av. Leeds —2K 83
Boston M. B Spa —3E 36
Boston Rd. B Spa —3D 36
Boston Rd. Weth —5J 17
**Boston Spa. —2D 36**
Boston St. C'frd —7E 126
Boston St. Hal —1D 130
Boston St. Sower B —5J 129
Boston Towers. Leeds —4J 5
Boston Wlk. B'frd —6F 97
Bosworth Clo. All —3B 78
**Botany. —1J 41**
Botany Av. B'frd —1B 80
Botany Bay Rd. Leeds —5D 84
Botany Dri. E Mor —1J 41
Bottom Boat Rd. Stan —7C 124 (in two parts)
**Bottomley. —6B 142**
**Bottomley Holes. —1E 94**
Bottomley La. Bklnd —7K 141
Bottomley St. B'frd —2K 97
Bottomley St. Brigh —4G 133
Bottomley St. Butt —7F 97
Bottoms. Hal —5H 131
Bottoms La. B'shaw —3K 117
**Boulder Clough. —3E 128**
Boulevard, The. Fars —3B 82
*Boulevard, The. Hal —2F 131 (off Park Rd.)*
Boundary Clo. Colt —6C 88
Boundary Farm Rd. Leeds —1G 67
Boundary Pl. Leeds —3A 86 (1J 5)
Boundary Rd. Dew —6D 136
Boundary St. Heck —4A 136
Boundary St. Leeds —3A 86 (1J 5)
*Boundary Ter. M'end —5D 136 (off Halifax Rd.)*
Boundary, The. B'frd —4E 78
Bourbon Clo. B'frd —6H 97
Bourne St. Thack —3D 62
Bowater Ct. B'frd —4H 99
Bowbridge Rd. B'frd —2A 98
Bowcliffe Rd. B'ham —1C 54
Bower Grn. B'frd —6E 80
Bower La. Dew —5D 136
Bower Rd. Leeds —2C 88
Bower Slack Rd. Sower B —7B 128
Bowers La. Bklnd —1A 20
Bower St. B'frd —1A 98
Bower, The. Bat —1D 136
Bowes Nook. B'frd —7E 96
Bowfell Clo. Leeds —1J 87
Bow Grn. Cytn —2D 96
Bowland Av. Bail —3E 60
Bowland Clo. Leeds —6G 87
Bowland St. B'frd —5K 79 (1B 6)
Bowler Clo. Low M —1J 115
**Bowling. —1D 98**
Bowling All. Brigh —1G 145
Bowling All. Ter. Brigh —1G 145
Bowling Bk. La. B'frd —1C 98 (7J 7)
Bowling Ct. Brigh —5F 133
Bowling Ct. Ind. Est. B'frd —7E 80
Bowling Dyke. Hal —7G 113
*Bowling Grn. Ct. Holy G —6D 142 (off Bk. Bowling Grn. Rd.)*
Bowling Grn. Fold. Wyke —4J 115
Bowling Grn. Rd. Slnd —6D 142
Bowling Grn. Ter. Leeds —1H 103
Bowling Hall Rd. B'frd —2C 98
Bowling Old La. B'frd —4K 97 (in five parts)
Bowling Pk. Clo. B'frd —2B 98
Bowling Pk. Dri. B'frd —3B 98
Bowl Shaw La. Hal —1K 113
Bowman Av. B'frd —7H 97
Bowman Gro. Hal —1E 130
Bowman La. Leeds —6K 85
Bowman Pl. Hal —1E 130
Bowman Rd. B'frd —7H 97
Bowman St. Hal —1E 130
Bowman Ter. Hal —1E 130
Bownas Rd. B Spa —2C 36
Bowness Av. B'frd —1F 81
Bowness Av. C'frd —6K 127
Bowood Av. Leeds —5G 67
Bowood Cres. Leeds —5G 67
Bowood Gro. Leeds —5G 67
Bowood La. Sower B —7F 129
Bow St. Kei —4A 40
Bow St. Leeds —6A 86
Bowwood Dri. Sandb —3F 41
Box Bldgs. Bat —2D 136
Boxhill Rd. Ell —3K 143
Box Tree Clo. B'frd —4E 78
Box Trees La. Hal —4B 112
Boxwood Rd. Ell —4K 143
Boyd Av. B'frd —4G 81
Boy Home La. Hal —2F 129
Boy La. B'frd —7D 98
Boy La. Hal —5B 112
Boyle, The. Bar E —4H 71
Boyne St. Hal —1F 131
Boynton St. B'frd —3K 97 (in two parts)
Boynton Ter. B'frd —3A 98
Boys La. Hal —3H 131
Boys Scarr. L'ft —2F 129
Bracewell Av. All —5A 78
Bracewell Bank. Hal —5D 112
Bracewell Dri. Hal —5D 112
Bracewell Gro. Hal —6E 112
Bracewell Hill. Hal —5D 112
*Bracewell Mt. Hal —5D 112 (off Bracewell Hill)*
Bracewell St. Kei —4C 40
Bracken Av. Brigh —3G 133
**Bracken Bank. —1H 57**
Bracken Bank Av. Kei —2H 57
Bracken Bank Cres. Kei —1H 57
Bracken Bank Gro. Kei —1H 57
Bracken Bank Wlk. Oakw —2H 57
Bracken Bank Way. Kei —1H 57
Brackenbeck Rd. B'frd —2F 97
Brackenbed La. Hal —6D 112
*Brackenbed Ter. Hal —6D 112 (off Brackenbed La.)*
Bracken Clo. Brigh —3G 133
Bracken Ct. Leeds —3J 67
Bracken Ct. Lwr W —1E 102
Brackendale. B'frd —2B 62
Brackendale Av. B'frd —2C 62
Brackendale Dri. B'frd —2B 62
Brackendale Gro. B'frd —2B 62
Brackendale Pde. B'frd —2B 62
Bracken Dri. Sils —7F 9
Bracken Edge. B'frd —5E 62
Bracken Edge. Leeds —7B 68
Bracken Ghyll Dri. Sils —7F 9
Bracken Gro. Hud —5H 145
**Brackenhall. —5J 145**
Bracken Hall Countryside Centre. —1E 60
Brackenhall Ct. B'frd —2F 97
Bracken Hall Rd. Hud —6J 145
Bracken Hill. Hal —6C 112
Bracken Hill. Leeds —3J 67
Brackenhill Dri. B'frd —3F 97
Brackenholme Royd. B'frd —6E 96
Bracken Mt. Sils —7F 9
Bracken Pk. Bgly —1C 60
Bracken Pk. Eld —6B 42
Bracken Pk. S'cft —3J 51
Bracken Rd. Brigh —4G 133
Bracken Rd. Ebrn —5C 20
Bracken Rd. Kei —7J 39
Brackens La. Hal —7B 96
Bracken Sq. Hud —5J 145
Bracken St. Kei —7K 39
Brackenwood Clo. I'ly —5E 12
Brackenwood Clo. Leeds —5A 68
Brackenwood Dri. Leeds —4A 68
Brackenwood Grn. Leeds —4A 68
Bradbeck Rd. B'frd —6F 79
Bradburn Rd. Rob H —4C 122
Bradd Clo. Liv —3K 135
Bradfield Clo. Hud —4K 145
**Bradford. —6A 80 (4D 6)**
Bradford Bulls Rugby League Football. —6A 98
Bradford Bus. Pk. B'frd —4A 80
Bradford City Football Club. —4K 79
Bradford Industrial & Horses at Work Museum. —2F 81
Bradford La. B'frd —6F 81
**Bradford Moor. —5E 80**
Bradford Old Rd. Bgly —5B 60 (in two parts)
Bradford Old Rd. Hal —4G 113
Bradford Rd. Bail B —7H 115
Bradford Rd. Bgly —2A 60
Bradford Rd. Birs & Bat —5A 118
Bradford Rd. B'frd —7C 62
Bradford Rd. Brigh —4H 133
Bradford Rd. Bur W —2C 26
Bradford Rd. Cytn —1C 96
Bradford Rd. Cleck —3C 116
Bradford Rd. Dew —7G 137
Bradford Rd. Dlgtn —2F 119 (nr. Wakefield Rd.)
Bradford Rd. Dlgtn —7B 100 (nr. Whitehall Rd.)
Bradford Rd. Gom —6H 99
Bradford Rd. Hal —4A 114 (nr. Bk. Clough)
Bradford Rd. Hal —6A 114 (nr. Leeds Rd.)
Bradford Rd. Hud & Brigh —7H 145
Bradford Rd. Kei & Riddl —4B 40
Bradford Rd. Men & Guis —6D 26
Bradford Rd. Otley —4D 26
Bradford Rd. Raw & Liv —2H 135
Bradford Rd. Shipl —5G 61
Bradford Rd. Thornb & Pud —4H 81
Bradford Rd. Wake —6D 120
Bradford Rd. Wren & Wake —3K 139
Bradfords Clo. B'ham —7C 36
Bradford St. Dew —7H 137
Bradford St. Kei —3A 40
Bradford & Wakefield Rd. B'frd —7A 100


154 A-Z Leeds & Bradford

Bradlaugh Rd.—Bronte Clo.


Bradlaugh Rd. B'frd —5H 97
Bradlaugh Ter. B'frd —5J 97
Bradley Av. C'frd —7C 126
Bradley Av. Hal —6K 111
Bradley Av. Sils —7F 9
Bradley Boulevd. Hud —6J 145
Bradley Ct. G'Ind —3F 143
Bradley Dri. Sils —7F 9
Bradley Gro. Sils —7F 9
**Bradley Hill. —3E 82**
Bradley La. G'Ind —3F 143
Bradley La. Pud —6K 81
Bradley Ri. Sils —7F 9
Bradley Rd. Hud —4J 145
Bradley Rd. Sils —6F 9
Bradley St. Bgly —1K 59
Bradley St. B'frd —1J 79
Bradley St. C'frd —7D 126
Bradley Ter. Leeds —7C 50
Bradley Vw. Holy G —5F 143
**Bradshaw. —5D 94**
Bradshaw La. Hal —5D 94
Bradshaw Row. Hal —4D 94
*Bradshaw Vw. Hal —7C 94 (off Moor Top Gdns.)*
Bradshaw Vw. Q'bry —5G 95
Bradstock Gdns. Morl —1A 120
Brady Clo. Oakw —1G 57
Brae Av. B'frd —2B 80
Braemar Dri. Gar —5B 90
Braeside. Hal —1B 130
Brafferton Arbor. B'frd —6E 96
Braine Rd. Weth —3K 17
**Braithwaite. —3G 39**
Braithwaite Av. Kei —3G 39
Braithwaite Cres. Kei —4H 39
Braithwaite Dri. Kei —4H 39
Braithwaite Edge Rd. Kei —3F 39
Braithwaite Gro. Kei —4H 39
Braithwaite Rd. Kei —4F 39
Braithwaite Row. Leeds —4A 104
Braithwaite St. Leeds —7F 85
Braithwaite Wlk. Kei —4H 39
Braithwaite Way. Kei —4H 39
Bramble Av. B Spa —3B 36
Bramble Clo. Cytn —3C 96
Brambles, The. I'ly —5K 11
Bramble Wlk. Birs —6D 118
Brambling M. Morl —3C 120
**Bramham. —1D 54**
Bramham Dri. Bail —7K 43
Bramham La. Woth —6D 34
Bramham Park. —3K 53
Bramham Rd. Bgly —7A 42
Bramham Rd. Cliff —6D 36
Bramham Rd. T'ner —5E 52
**Bramhope. —1J 47**
Bramhope Rd. Cleck —7E 116
Bramleigh Dri. Morl —1A 120
Bramleigh Gro. Morl —1A 120
**Bramley. —3G 83**
Bramley Cen. Leeds —2H 83
Bramley Clo. Oakw —1D 56
Bramley Fold. Hal —7D 114
Bramley Gdns. Leeds —3A 70
Bramley La. Hal —7C 114
Bramley St. B'frd —1A 98 (in two parts)
Bramley Vw. Hal —7E 114
Bramstan Av. Leeds —2E 82
Bramstan Clo. Leeds —2E 82
Bramstan Gdns. Leeds —2E 82
Bramston Gdns. Ras —1G 145
Bramston St. Brigh —7G 133
Brancepeth Pl. Leeds —6E 84
Branch Clo. Leeds —2A 102
Branch End. Gild —7H 101
Branch La. Hud —6B 144
Branch Pl. Leeds —2A 102
Branch Rd. A'ley —5C 84
Branch Rd. Bklnd —5B 142
Branch Rd. Bat —3G 137
Branch Rd. Dew —7G 137
Branch Rd. Lwr W —2A 102
Branch Rd. Schol —6B 116
Branch St. Leeds —2A 102
Brander App. Leeds —4F 87
Brander Clo. Leeds —4F 87
Brander Dri. Leeds —4E 86
Brander Gro. Leeds —4E 86
Brander Mt. Leeds —3E 86 (in two parts)
Brander Rd. Leeds —3F 87
Brander St. Leeds —3F 87
Brandfort St. B'frd —1G 97
**Brandon. —5G 51**
Brandon Ct. Leeds —6E 50
Brandon Cres. Leeds —4G 51
Brandon La. Leeds —4H 51
Brandon La. Wike —3F 51
Brandon Rd. Leeds —5G 85 (5A 4)
Brandon St. Leeds —6F 85
Brandon Ter. Leeds —6D 50
Brandon Vw. Leeds —6F 51
Brandon Way. Leeds —7K 67
**Brandy Carr. —4K 139**
Brandy Carr Rd. K'gte —6H 139
Branksome Ct. B'frd —3F 79
Branksome Cres. B'frd —3F 79
Branksome Dri. Shipl —4C 60
Branksome Gdns. Shipl —4C 60
Branksome Gro. Shipl —4C 60
Branksome Pl. Leeds —3E 84 (LS6)
*Branksome Pl. Leeds —4A 4 (off Brandon Rd.)*
Bransby Clo. Fars —3C 82
Bransby Ct. Fars —3C 82
Bransby Ri. Fars —2C 82
Bransdale Av. Guis —3G 45
Bransdale Clo. Bail —2G 61
Bransdale Clo. Guis —3G 45
Bransdale Clough. B'frd —5E 96
Bransdale Gdns. Guis —3G 45
Bransdale Gth. Guis —3G 45
Branshaw Dri. Kei —6G 39
Branshaw Gro. Kei —6G 39
Branshaw Mt. Kei —6G 39
Branstone Gro. Oss —7C 138
Bran St. Kei —7K 39
Brant Av. Hal —3D 112
Brant Bank La. Nesf —3H 11
Brantcliffe Dri. Bail —7H 43
Brantcliffe Way. Bail —6J 43
Brantdale Clo. B'frd —1C 78
Brantdale Rd. B'frd —1C 78
Brantford St. Leeds —6K 67
Brantwood Av. B'frd —1C 78
Brantwood Clo. B'frd —1C 78
Brantwood Cres. B'frd —1B 78
Brantwood Dri. B'frd —1C 78
Brantwood Gro. B'frd —1B 78
Brantwood Oval. B'frd —1C 78
Brantwood Rd. B'frd —1B 78
Brantwood Vs. B'frd —1C 78
Branwell Av. Birs —4C 118
Branwell Dri. Haw —4E 56
Branwell Lodge. B'frd —3G 97
Brassey Rd. B'frd —2C 98
Brassey St. Hal —2F 131
Brassey Ter. B'frd —2C 98
Brathay Gdns. Leeds —2J 87
Braybrook Ct. B'frd —2J 79
Bray Clo. B'frd —4D 96
Brayshaw Dri. B'frd —4D 96
Brayshaw Fold. Low M —1A 116
Brayshaw Rd. E Ard —2J 139
Brayside Av. Hud —7F 145
Brayton App. Leeds —7A 70
Brayton Clo. Leeds —7A 70
Brayton Gth. Leeds —7B 70
Brayton Grange. Leeds —7B 70
Brayton Grn. Leeds —7B 70 (in two parts)
Brayton Gro. Leeds —7A 70
Brayton Pl. Leeds —7B 70
Brayton Ter. Leeds —7A 70
Brayton Wlk. Leeds —7A 70
Brazil St. C'frd —7E 126
Breakmoor Av. Sils —7G 9
Break Neck. Hal —7A 114
Breaks Fld. Wyke —5K 115
Breaks Rd. Low M —1A 116
Brearcliffe Clo. B'frd —7G 97
Brearcliffe Dri. B'frd —7G 97
Brearcliffe Gro. B'frd —7G 97
Brearcliffe Rd. B'frd —7H 97
Brearcliffe St. B'frd —7G 97
Brearley Gdns. Liv —6J 135
Brearley La. H Bri & L'ft —6C 110
*Brearley Pl. Bat —4G 137 (off Gt. Wood St.)*
Brearley St. Bat —4F 137
Brearton St. B'frd —5A 80 (1D 6)
Breary Av. H'fth —3H 65 (in two parts)
Breary Ct. B'hpe —7J 29
Breary La. B'hpe —7J 29
Breary La. E. B'hpe —7K 29
Breary Ri. B'hpe —7J 29
Breary Ter. H'fth —3H 65
Breary Wlk. H'fth —3H 65
Breck Lea. Sower B —6J 129
Brecks. Cytn —1D 96
Brecks Gdns. Kip —3K 107
Brecks La. Swil & Kip —2G 107
Brecks Rd. Cytn —1D 96
Breck Willows. Sower B —6H 129
Brecon App. Leeds —4F 87
Brecon Clo. B'frd —5D 62
Brecon Ct. Leeds —4F 87
Brecon Ri. Leeds —4F 87
Bredon Av. Shipl —5B 62
Breighton Adown. B'frd —6D 96
Bremit Vs. B'frd —6H 97
Bremit Wlk. B'frd —6H 97
Bremner St. Otley —2K 27
Brendon Ct. B'frd —3F 99
Brendon Dri. Hud —7D 144
*Brendon Ho. B'frd —4G 99 (off Landscove Av.)*
Brendon Wlk. B'frd —4F 99 (in two parts)
Brentford Rd. Low M —7J 97
Brentwood Clo. Bat —3J 137
Brentwood Ct. Leeds —4A 66
Brentwood Gdns. B'frd —6K 97
Brentwood Gro. Leeds —6C 84
Brentwood St. Leeds —6C 84
Brentwood Ter. Leeds —6C 84
Brett Gdns. Leeds —2H 103
Brewerton La. Dew —6D 136
Brewery La. Cytn —3H 95
Brewery La. Q'bry —7G 95
Brewery Rd. I'ly —5C 12
Brewery Rd. Kei —1J 57
Brewery St. Hal —5G 113
Brewery St. Heck —5B 136
Brewery St. Kei —4B 40
Brexdale Av. Kip —3K 107
Brian Cres. Leeds —3K 87
Brian Pl. Leeds —2K 87
Brian Royd La. G'Ind —2D 142
**Brianside. —2K 87**
Brian St. Hud —7B 144
Brian Vw. Leeds —2A 88
Briar Clo. Ell —4J 143
Briar Clo. Fars —3B 82
Briar Clo. Heck —3B 136
Briardale Rd. B'frd —1B 78
Briardene. Rothw —3A 124
Briar Dri. Dew —6D 136
Briarfield Av. B'frd —5C 62
Briarfield Clo. B'frd —5C 62
Briarfield Clo. I'ly —6D 12
Briarfield Gdns. Shipl —6H 61
Briarfield Gro. B'frd —5C 62
Briarfield Rd. Shipl —7J 61
Briar Ga. Weth —2J 17
Briar La. Hud —7B 144
Briarlea Clo. Yead —6H 45
Briarlyn Av. Hud —7A 144
Briarlyn Rd. Hud —7A 144
Briarmains Rd. Birs —5D 118
Briar Rhydding. Bail —2A 62
Briarsdale Ct. Leeds —2E 86
Briarsdale Cft. Leeds —2E 86
Briarsdale Gth. Leeds —2E 86
Briarsdale Heights. Leeds —2E 86
Briar Wood. Shipl —5A 62
Briarwood Av. B'frd —5H 97
Briarwood Av. Riddl —2D 40
Briarwood Cres. B'frd —5H 97
Briarwood Dri. B'frd —5H 97
Briarwood Gro. B'frd —4H 97
Brickfield Gro. Hal —2E 112
Brickfield La. Hal —2E 112
Brickfield Ter. Hal —2E 112
Brick Mill Rd. Pud —7D 82
Brick Row. Dew —7D 136
Brick Row. Wyke —4J 115
Brick St. Cleck —1E 134
Brick St. Leeds —6K 85 (7H 5)
Brick Ter. Brigh —7H 133
Brick & Tile Ter. Brigh —7G 133
Bridge Av. Otley —2J 27
Bridge Clo. B Spa —2E 36
Bridge Cotts. Aber —5E 72
Bridge Ct. Leeds —1G 103
Bridge Ct. Morl —4B 120
Bridge End. Brigh —7G 133
Bridge End. Leeds —6J 85 (7E 4) (in two parts)
Bridge Fold. Kirks —1K 83
Bridge Foot. Thor A —2E 36
Bridge Gth. Cliff —4D 36
Bridgegate Way. B'frd —7F 63
Bridgehouse La. Haw —6E 56
Bridge La. Hal —1A 114
Bridge La. I'ly —4A 12
Bridge Paddock. Coll —1F 35
Bridge Rd. B Spa —2E 36
Bridge Rd. Brigh —6G 133
Bridge Rd. Kirks —1K 83
Bridge Rd. Leeds —1G 103
Bridge Rd. Oxe —6A 74
Bridge Rd. Rod —7C 64
Bridge Rd. Sils —7G 9
Bridge Rd. Sut Cr —5A 20
Bridge St. Bat —3H 137
Bridge St. Birs —7C 118
Bridge St. B'frd —7A 80 (5E 6)
Bridge St. C'frd —7E 126
Bridge St. Heck —4A 136
Bridge St. Kei —5K 39
Bridge St. Leeds —5K 85 (5G 5)
Bridge St. Morl —4B 120
Bridge St. Oakw —2D 56
Bridge St. Otley —2J 27
Bridge St. Sils —7G 9
Bridge St. Sower B —5K 129
Bridge St. T'tn —7J 77
Bridge Ter. Leeds —7J 51
Bridge Vw. Leeds —7C 64
Bridgewater Ct. Leeds —6F 67
Bridgewater Rd. Leeds —1B 104
Bridgeway. B'frd —4F 99
Bri. Wood Clo. H'fth —3H 65
Bri. Wood Vw. H'fth —2H 65
Bridgland Av. Men —5C 26
Bridgwater Rd. B'frd —3G 79
Bridle Av. Oss —7C 138
Bridle Dene. Hal —2C 114
Bridle La. Oss —7C 138
Bridle Path Rd. Leeds —3J 87 (LS15)
Bridle Path Rd. Leeds —6F 51 (LS17)
Bridle Path Wlk. Leeds —3J 87
Bridle Stile. Hal —2C 114
Bridle Stile La. Q'bry —4J 95
Bridle St. Bat —3J 137
Bridport Ho. B'frd —2H 7
Brierdene. Sils —7G 9
Brierfield Gdns. Gild —1G 119
Brier Hey Clo. H Bri —6B 110
Brier Hey La. Myth —6B 110
Brier Hill Clo. Cleck —2C 134
Brier Hill Vw. Bdly —4K 145
Brierlands Clo. Gar —5B 90
Brierlands Fold. Gar —5B 90
Brier La. Brigh —6D 132
Brierley Clo. Shipl —6J 61
Brier St. Hal —5G 113
Brier St. Kei —7K 39
Briery Clo. I'ly —5J 11
Briery Fld. Shipl —7H 61
Briggate. Brigh —6G 133 (in two parts)
Briggate. Ell —2K 143
Briggate. Leeds —6J 85 (7E 4)
Briggate. Shipl —4H 61
Briggate. Sils —7G 9
Briggate. Windh —5H 61
Brigg Gdns. Kei —4H 39
Briggland Ct. Wilsd —7G 59
Briggs Av. B'frd —5G 97
*Briggs Bldgs. Morl —3B 120 (off Melbourne St.)*
Briggs Gro. B'frd —5G 97
Briggs Pl. B'frd —5G 97
Briggs St. Q'bry —5H 95
Brigg Well Head Ga. H Bri —1A 110
**Brighouse. —5H 133**
Brighouse & Denholme Rd. Denh & Q'bry —7C 76
Brighouse & Denholme Rd. Hal —7K 95
Brighouse Rd. Hip —1C 132
Brighouse Rd. Hud —6B 144
Brighouse Rd. Low M —2K 115
Brighouse Rd. Q'bry —5J 95
Brighouse Wood La. Brigh —5F 133
*Brighouse Wood Row. Brigh —5F 133 (off Brighouse Wood La.)*
Brighton Av. Morl —2K 119
Brighton Cliff. Leeds —3G 83
Brighton Clo. Bat —2C 136
Brighton Gro. Leeds —4H 83
Brighton Rd. I'ly —6E 12
Brighton St. B'frd —3C 62
Brighton St. Hal —6E 112
Brighton St. Heck —3B 136
Brighton St. Shipl —4H 61
Brighton Ter. Schol —7B 116
Bright St. All —4B 78
Bright St. B'frd —4E 98
Bright St. Cytn —2B 96
Bright St. Dew —7G 137
Bright St. E Ard —7K 121
Bright St. F'hll —1A 20
Bright St. Haw —5F 57
Bright St. Morl —3K 119
Bright St. Q'bry —5K 95
Bright St. Sower B —3K 129
Bright St. S'ley —3D 82
Brignall Cft. Leeds —4B 86
Brignall Gth. Leeds —4B 86
Brignall Way. Leeds —4B 86
**Brig Royd. —4F 141**
Brigshaw Dri. All B —7K 107
Brigshaw La. All B & Kip —7K 107
Brindley Gro. B'frd —6C 78
Brindley Rd. Sils —2H 21
Brisbane Av. B'frd —2A 80
Briscoe La. G'Ind —2F 143
Bristol Av. Riddl —3F 41
Bristol St. Hal —5H 131
Bristol St. Leeds —4K 85 (3H 5)
Britannia Bldgs. Morl —5K 119
Britannia Clo. S'ley —3D 82
Britannia Ct. Leeds —5E 82
Britannia Ho. B'frd —4E 6
Britannia Rd. Morl —5K 119
Britannia Sq. Morl —5K 119
Britannia St. Bgly —1A 60
Britannia St. B'frd —7B 80 (6F 7)
Britannia St. Leeds —6H 85 (7C 4)
Britannia St. S'ley —3D 82
Britannia Ter. Cleck —7F 117
Britton St. Gom —2H 135
Broadacres Dri. Weth —4G 17
Broad Carr La. Holy G —5G 143
Broad Carr Ter. Holy G —4H 143
Broadcroft Chase. Ting —1E 138
Broadcroft Dri. Ting —1E 138
Broadcroft Gro. Ting —7E 120
Broadcroft Way. Ting —7E 120
Broadfield Clo. B'frd —5G 99
Broadfields. H'fth —3H 65
Broadfield Way. Add —1B 10
**Broad Folds. —2C 96**
Broadfolds. Cytn —2C 96
Broadgate. Holy G —7D 142
Broadgate Av. H'fth —4H 65
Broadgate Ct. H'fth —4H 65
Broadgate Cres. H'fth —4G 65
Broadgate Dri. H'fth —3H 65
Broadgate La. H'fth —3G 65
Broadgate M. H'fth —4H 65
Broadgate Ri. H'fth —4H 65
Broadgate Wlk. H'fth —4G 65
Broad Head La. Oakw —1A 56
Broad Ings Way. She —2B 114
Broadlands. Kei —3H 39
Broadlands St. B'frd —2F 99
Broad La. B'frd —1F 99
Broad La. Leeds & S'ley —3E 82
Broad La. L'ft —3E 128
Broad La. Clo. Leeds —1J 83
Broadlea Av. Leeds —1J 83
Broadlea Clo. Leeds —1J 83
Broadlea Cres. B'frd —3B 98
Broadlea Cres. Leeds —1J 83
Broadlea Gdns. Leeds —1J 83
Broadlea Gro. Leeds —1J 83
Broadlea Hill. Leeds —1J 83
Broadlea Mt. Leeds —2K 83
Broadlea Oval. Leeds —1J 83
Broadlea Pl. Leeds —2J 83
Broadlea Rd. Leeds —1J 83
Broadlea St. Leeds —1J 83
Broadlea Ter. Leeds —1J 83
Broadlea Vw. Leeds —1H 83
Broadley Clo. Hal —6A 112
Broadley Cres. Hal —6K 111
Broadley Gro. Hal —6A 112
Broadley Laithe. Hal —5A 112
Broadley Rd. Hal —6K 111
Broadmead. C'frd —7F 127
Broad Oak La. Hal —2D 132
Broad Oak Pl. Hal —2D 132
Broad Oak St. Hal —2D 132
Broad Oak Ter. Hal —2D 132
Broad Royd. Holy G —6C 142
Broadstones Pk. Bgly —2D 60
Broadstone Way. B'frd —5G 99
Broad St. B'frd —6A 80 (3E 6)
Broad St. Fars —2A 82
Broad St. Hal —1G 131
Broad Tree Rd. Hal —5E 112
Broadwalk, The. Otley —1G 27
Broadwater Ho. B'frd —7D 6
Broadway. Bgly —1A 60
Broadway. B'frd —7A 80 (5E 6)
Broadway. Guis —3E 44
Broadway. Hal —3J 131
Broadway. H'fth —6C 64
Broadway. Kirks —5J 65
Broadway. Leeds —7H 87
Broadway. Sower B —5G 129
Broadway Av. B'frd —4K 97
Broadway Av. Leeds —3E 84
Broadway Clo. B'frd —4K 97
Broadway Ct. Sower B —5G 129
Broadway Dri. H'fth —4F 65
Broadwood Av. Hal —6A 112
Brocklesby Dri. All —5B 78
Brocks. Hal —3E 128
Brockwell Gdns. Sower B —5J 129
Brockwell La. Tri —6H 129
Brodrick Ct. Leeds —7D 66
*Broken Way. B'frd —4K 97 (off Manchester Rd.)*
Bromet Pl. B'frd —2D 80
Bromford Rd. B'frd —2D 98
Bromley Gro. Kei —6G 39
Bromley Rd. Bat —5J 137
Bromley Rd. Bgly —7K 41
Bromley Rd. Hud —7F 145
Bromley Rd. Shipl —4E 60
Bromley St. Bat —5H 137
Bromley St. B'frd —7D 6
Brompton Av. B'frd —3C 98
Brompton Gro. Leeds —4H 103
Brompton Mt. Leeds —4H 103
Brompton Rd. B'frd —2C 98
Brompton Row. Leeds —4H 103
Brompton Ter. B'frd —2C 98
Brompton Ter. Leeds —4H 103
Brompton Vw. Leeds —4H 103
Bronshill Gro. All —4C 78
Bronte Clo. B'frd —3E 78
Bronte Clo. Dew —6D 136
Bronte Clo. Gom —6K 117


A-Z Leeds & Bradford 155

Bronte Dri. Oakw —1G 57
Bronte Ho. B'frd —2G 99 (off Eversley Dri.)
Bronte Old Rd. T'tn —7J 77
Bronte Parsonage Museum. —5D 56
Bronte Pl. T'tn —7J 77
Bronte Rd. Birs —6C 118
Bronte St. Haw —5D 56
Bronte St. Kei —3B 40
Bronte Vs. Cro R —4H 57
Brookdale Av. Oss —7C 138
Brook Dri. Holy G —5G 143
Brooke St. Brigh —7G 133
Brooke St. Cleck —1G 135
Brooke St. Heck —5B 136
Brookeville Av. Hal —1C 132
Brookfield Av. Cleck —6G 117
Brookfield Av. Leeds —1B 86
Brookfield Av. Rod —6B 64
Brookfield Av. Shipl —4K 61
Brookfield Av. Wyke —6A 116
Brookfield Ct. Leeds —6B 64
Brookfield Dri. Wyke —6A 116
Brookfield Gdns. Leeds —7B 64
Brookfield Pl. Leeds —6E 66
Brookfield Rd. B'frd —5C 80 (2J 7)
Brookfield Rd. Leeds —6E 66
Brookfield Rd. Shipl —4K 61
Brookfield St. Leeds —1K 103
Brookfield Ter. Cleck —6G 117
Brookfield Ter. Leeds —1K 103 (LS10)
Brookfield Ter. Leeds —6E 66 (off Brookfield Rd.)
Brookfield Vw. Cleck —6G 117
Brookfoot. —5F 133
Brookfoot Av. B'shaw —2J 117
Brookfoot La. Hal & Brigh —5D 132
Brook Grain Hill. Brigh —1G 145
Brook Grains La. Ripp —7F 141
Brook Hill. —1K 61
Brook Hill. Bail —1K 61
Brookhill Av. Leeds —7A 50
Brookhill Clo. Leeds —7A 50
Brookhill Cres. Leeds —7A 50
Brookhill Dri. Leeds —7A 50
Brookhill Gro. Leeds —7A 50
Brookhouse. —6A 94
Brookhouse Gdns. B'frd —4H 63
Brooklands. —1G 87
Brooklands. E Kes —5A 34
Brooklands. Hal —1D 132
Brooklands Av. Holy G —5F 143
Brooklands Av. Leeds —1H 87
Brooklands Av. T'tn —7K 77
Brooklands Clo. Holy G —5F 143 (off Shaw La.)
Brooklands Clo. Leeds —1G 87
Brooklands Clo. Men —5D 26
Brooklands Ct. Leeds —1H 87
Brooklands Cres. Leeds —1G 87
Brooklands Cres. Yead —5K 45
Brooklands Dri. Leeds —1G 87
Brooklands Dri. Yead —5K 45
Brooklands Gth. Leeds —1H 87
Brooklands Gro. Men —5D 26
Brooklands La. Leeds —1H 87
Brooklands La. Men —5C 26
Brooklands Towers. Leeds —7J 69
Brooklands Vw. Leeds —1H 87 (in two parts)
Brooklands Wlk. Men —5D 26
Brooklands Way. Men —5C 26
Brook La. Cytn —3A 96
Brook La. Liv —4E 134
Brooklea. Hal —1E 132
Brookleigh. C'ley —6K 63
Brooklyn Av. Leeds —6C 84
Brooklyn Ct. Cleck —7F 117
Brooklyn Dri. Cleck —7F 117
Brooklyn Grange. Cleck —7G 117
Brooklyn Pl. Leeds —6C 84
Brooklyn Rd. Cleck —7F 117
Brooklyn St. Kei —7J 21
Brooklyn St. Leeds —6C 84
Brooklyn Ter. Brigh —3E 132
Brooklyn Ter. Leeds —6C 84
Brook Row. G'lnd —5G 143
Brookroyd. —7E 118
Brookroyd Av. Brigh —2H 133
Brookroyd Gdns. Bat —7D 118
Brookroyd La. Bat —6D 118
Brooksbank Av. B'frd —1E 96
Brooksbank Dri. Leeds —5J 87
Brooksbank Gdns. Ell —3K 143
Brookside. Coll —2F 35
Brookside. Leeds —6A 50
Brookside Fold. Oxe —3E 74
Brooks Ter. Q'bry —4B 96
Brook St. C'frd —4J 127
Brook St. Dew M —7D 136
Brook St. Ell —3A 144
Brook St. I'ly —5B 12
Brook St. Kei —6K 39
Brook Ter. L'ft —5G 111
Broombank. Hud —7D 144
Broom Clo. Brigh —2E 144
Broom Clo. Leeds —7B 104
Broom Ct. Leeds —1B 122
Broom Cres. Leeds —7A 104
Broom Cft. Cytn —2B 96
Broom Cross. Leeds —7A 104
Broome Av. B'frd —2A 80
Broomfield. Cleck —2E 134 (off W. End Dri.)
Broomfield. Ell —3H 143
Broomfield. Leeds —7B 40
Broomfield Av. Hal —5F 131
Broomfield Cres. Leeds —1D 84
Broomfield Pl. Cytn —3A 96
Broomfield Pl. Kei —4K 39
Broomfield Pl. Leeds —2D 84
Broomfield Rd. Fix —5G 145
Broomfield Rd. Kei —4K 39
Broomfield Rd. Leeds —1D 84
Broomfields. —1B 98 (7F 7)
Broomfield St. Kei —4K 39
Broomfield St. Leeds —2D 84
Broomfield St. Q'bry —5J 95
Broomfield Ter. Cleck —2D 134
Broomfield Ter. Leeds —2D 84
Broomfield Vw. Leeds —2D 84
Broom Gdns. Leeds —7A 104
Broom Gth. Leeds —7B 104
Broom Gro. Leeds —1B 122
Broomhill Av. Kei —6J 39
Broomhill Av. Leeds —2K 67
Broomhill Bottom. Holy G —7C 142
Broomhill Cres. Leeds —2K 67
Broomhill Dri. Kei —6J 39
Broomhill Dri. Leeds —3J 67
Broomhill Gro. Kei —6J 39
Broomhill Mt. Kei —6J 39
Broom Hill Rd. Leeds —4D 86
Broomhill St. Kei —7J 39
Broomhill Ter. Bat —5H 137
Broomhill Wlk. Kei —6J 39
Broomhill Way. Kei —6J 39
Broom Lawn. Leeds —7A 104
Broom Mt. Leeds —1B 122
Broom Nook. Leeds —7B 104
Broom Pl. Leeds —7B 104
Broom Rd. Leeds —1A 122
Broomsdale Rd. Bat —2J 137
Broom St. B'frd —7B 80 (6F 7)
Broom St. Cleck —2D 134
Broom Ter. Leeds —7B 104
Broom Vw. Leeds —7B 104
Broom Wlk. Bat —3J 137
Broom Wlk. Leeds —1B 122
Broster Av. Kei —4H 39
Brougham Rd. Hal —6G 113
Brougham St. Hal —6G 113
Brougham Ter. Hal —5G 113
Broughton Av. B'frd —5D 98
Broughton Av. Leeds —3C 86
Broughton Ho. B'frd —5H 99
Broughton Ter. Leeds —3C 86
Broughton Ter. S'ley —5C 82
Brow Bottom. —2K 111
Brow Bottom La. Hal —1J 111
Browcliff. Sils —7G 9
Browfield Ter. Sils —7H 9
Browfoot. Shipl —4K 61
Browfoot Dri. Hal —2B 130
Brow Foot Ga. Hal —2B 130 (off Brow Foot Ga. La.)
Brow Foot Ga. La. Hal —2B 130
Browgate. Bail —1J 61
Brow La. Cytn —3J 95
Brow La. Hal —1E 112
Brow La. She —1D 114
Brow La. Shib —3J 113
Brown Av. Leeds —2E 102
Brown Bank Cvn. Site. Sils —5K 9
Brown Bank La. Sils —7H 9
Brownberrie Av. H'fth —1G 65
Brownberrie Cres. H'fth —1F 65
Brownberrie Dri. H'fth —1G 65 (in two parts)
Brownberrie Gdns. H'fth —1F 65
Brownberrie La. H'fth —1D 64
Brownberrie Wlk. H'fth —1G 65
Brownberry Gro. Hal —7D 96
Brown Hill. —7D 118
Brown Hill Av. Leeds —3C 86
Brownhill Clo. Bat —6D 118
Brown Hill Clo. B'shaw —7J 99
Brown Hill Cres. Leeds —3C 86
Brown Hill Dri. B'shaw —1J 117
Brownhill End. —6D 118
Brownhill Gth. Bat —6D 118
Brownhill Rd. Bat —6D 118
Brown Hill Ter. Leeds —3C 86
Browning Av. Hal —5H 131
Browning Rd. Hud —6K 145
Browning St. B'frd —6D 80 (4K 7)
Brown La. E. Leeds —1F 103
Brown La. W. Leeds —1E 102
Brownlea Clo. Yead —6H 45
Brown Lee La. Wilsd —1E 76
Brown Pl. Leeds —2E 102
Brown Rd. Leeds —2E 102
Brown Royd. —5H 79
Brownroyd Hill. —5J 97
Brownroyd Hill Rd. B'frd —5H 97
Brownroyd St. B'frd —5H 79
Brownroyd Wlk. B'frd —4H 97
Brown's Pl. Bat —4F 137
Brown's St. Bat —4G 137
Brown's Ter. Bat —4F 137 (off Brown's Pl.)
Brown St. Kei —3B 40
Brow Quarry Ind. Est. Hal —2D 132
Brow Rd. Haw —6F 57
Browsfield Rd. Add —1B 10
Browsholme St. Kei —5A 40
Brow St. Kei —5B 40
Brow Top. Cytn —4A 96
Brow Top Rd. Cro R —6F 57
Brow Wood Cres. B'frd —2A 80
Brow Wood Ri. Hal —1D 114
Brow Wood Rd. Hal —1D 114
Brow Wood Ter. B'frd —7F 97
Bruce Gdns. Leeds —6E 84
Bruce Lawn. Leeds —6E 84
Bruce St. Hal —2D 130
Brudenell Av. Leeds —2F 85
Brudenell Gro. Leeds —2F 85
Brudenell Mt. Leeds —2E 84
Brudenell Rd. Leeds —2E 84
Brudenell St. Leeds —2F 85
Brudenell Vw. Leeds —2F 85
Brunel Clo. B'frd —3G 79
Brunel Ct. B'frd —3C 80
Brunel Ct. Hal —5F 113 (off See Mill La.)
Brunel Gdns. B'frd —3J 97 (off Ida St.)
Brunswick Arc. Kei —4A 40 (off Airedale Shop. Cen.)
Brunswick Ct. Leeds —4K 85 (4G 5)
Brunswick Dri. Dew —7E 136
Brunswick Gdns. Gar —6K 89
Brunswick Gdns. Hal —1F 131
Brunswick Ho. Bgly —2B 60
Brunswick Pl. B'frd —5F 63
Brunswick Pl. Morl —3B 120 (off Clough St.)
Brunswick Rd. B'frd —5F 63
Brunswick Rd. Pud —5C 82
Brunswick Row. Leeds —4K 85 (5G 5)
Brunswick St. Bat —3G 137
Brunswick St. Cull —6C 58
Brunswick St. Dew —7E 136
Brunswick St. Fern —1B 60
Brunswick St. Heck —5B 136
Brunswick St. Morl —2A 120
Brunswick St. Q'bry —5K 95
Brunswick Ter. Leeds —4J 85 (4E 4)
Brunswick Ter. Low M —7J 97
Brunswick Ter. Morl —3C 120
Bruntcliffe. —3J 119
Bruntcliffe Av. Morl —3J 119
Bruntcliffe Clo. Morl —3K 119
Bruntcliffe Dri. Morl —3K 119
Bruntcliffe La. Morl —3J 119
Bruntcliffe Rd. Morl —3H 119
Bruntcliffe Way. Morl —3J 119
Brunthwaite. —1J 21
Brunthwaite Bri. La. Sils —3H 21
Brunthwaite La. Sils —1J 21
Brussels St. Leeds —6K 85 (7H 5)
Bryan Clo. C'frd —7A 126
Bryan La. Hud —6C 144
Bryan Rd. Ell —3H 143
Bryanstone Rd. B'frd —1F 99
Bryan St. Brigh —7G 133
Bryan St. Fars —1B 82
Bryan St. N. Far —1B 82
Bryer St. Dew —7G 137
Bryngate. Oult —1A 124
Bryony Ct. Leeds —2B 122
Bubwith Gro. Hal —2C 130 (off Trimmingham Rd.)
Buchan Towers. B'frd —7D 6
Buckden Ct. Sils —7G 9
Buckfast Ct. B'frd —5D 62
Buckingham Av. Leeds —1E 84
Buckingham Cres. Cytn —1D 96
Buckingham Dri. Leeds —1E 84
Buckingham Gro. Leeds —1E 84
Buckingham Ho. Leeds —1E 84 (off Headingley La.)
Buckingham Mt. Leeds —2E 84
Buckingham Rd. Leeds —2E 84
Buckland Pl. Hal —2C 130
Buckland Rd. B'frd —5F 79
Buck La. Bail —1B 62
Buckle La. Men —7D 26
Buckley Av. Leeds —3H 103
Buckley La. Hal —5A 112 (in two parts)
Buck Mill La. B'frd —2C 62
Buck Stone Av. Leeds —7F 49
Buck Stone Clo. Leeds —7G 49
Buck Stone Cres. Leeds —7G 49
Buck Stone Dri. Leeds —7F 49
Buckstone Dri. Rawd —1J 63 (in two parts)
Buck Stone Gdns. Leeds —7G 49
Buck Stone Grn. Leeds —7F 49
Buck Stone Gro. Leeds —7F 49
Buck Stone Mt. Leeds —7F 49
Buck Stone Oval. Leeds —7G 49
Buck Stone Ri. Leeds —7F 49
Buck Stone Rd. Leeds —7F 49
Buck Stone Vw. Leeds —7F 49
Buck Stone Way. Leeds —7F 49
Buck St. B'frd —7C 80 (6H 7)
Buck St. Denh —5C 76
Buckthorne Clo. E Ard —7K 121
Buckthorne Ct. E Ard —7K 121
Buckthorne Dri. E Ard —7K 121
Buckthorne Fold. E Ard —7K 121
Buckton Clo. Leeds —2G 103
Buckton Mt. Leeds —2G 103
Buckton Vw. Leeds —2G 103
Bude Rd. B'frd —5B 98
Bude Rd. Leeds —3H 103
Bula Clo. Kip —4B 108
Bullace Trees La. Liv —5G 135
Bull Clo. La. Hal —2F 131
Buller Clo. Leeds —4E 86
Buller Ct. Leeds —4E 86
Buller Gro. Leeds —4D 86
Buller St. B'frd —1E 98
Buller St. Rothw —1A 124
Bullerthorpe La. Leeds —7D 88
Bullerthorpe La. W'ford —6C 106
Bullfield, The. H'den —4F 59
Bull Grn. Hal —1G 131
Bullough La. Rothw —7H 105
Bullroyd Av. B'frd —5E 78
Bullroyd Cres. B'frd —5E 78
Bullroyd Dri. B'frd —5E 78
Bullroyd La. B'frd —5E 78
Bungalows, The. Hal —6J 131 (nr. Backhold Av.)
Bungalows, The. Hal —4D 112 (nr. Grove Pk.)
Bungalows, The. Hal —6B 112 (nr. Ryecroft Cres.)
Bungalows, The. Hal —5D 112 (off Ovenden Grn.)
Bungalows, The. Leeds —2B 88 (off Church La.)
Bunkers Hill. Aber —6E 72
Bunkers Hill. Esh —6D 44
Bunker's Hill La. Kei —6F 39
Bunkers La. Bat —4D 136
Burberry Clo. B'frd —6E 98
Burchett Gro. Leeds —1G 85
Burchett Pl. Leeds —1G 85
Burchett Ter. Leeds —1H 85
Burdale Pl. B'frd —7H 79
Burdett Ter. Leeds —3C 84
Burdock Way. Hal —2F 131 (in two parts)
Burking Rd. Dew —7F 137
Burland Ter. Swil —4E 106
Burleigh St. Hal —3D 130
Burley. —4C 84
Burley Ct. Steet —5E 20
Burley Grange Rd. Leeds —3C 84
Burley Hill Cres. Leeds —2B 84
Burley Hill Dri. Leeds —2B 84
Burley in Wharfedale. —1A 26
Burley La. H'fth —5F 65
Burley La. Men —6B 26
Burley Lodge Pl. Leeds —4E 84 (off Burley Lodge Rd.)
Burley Lodge Rd. Leeds —3E 84
Burley Lodge St. Leeds —4E 84
Burley Lodge Ter. Leeds —4E 84
Burley M. Steet —5E 20
Burley Pl. Leeds —4D 84
Burley Rd. Leeds —2C 84
Burley Rd. Men —4C 26
Burley Rd. Trad. Est. Leeds —2C 84
Burley St. B'frd —1K 79
Burley St. Ell —3K 143
Burley St. Leeds —5F 85 (5A 4)
Burley Wlk. Bat —3F 137
Burley Wood Cres. Leeds —2B 84
Burley Woodhead. —4J 25
Burley Wood La. Leeds —2C 84
Burley Wood Mt. Leeds —2B 84
Burley Wood Vw. Leeds —2C 84
Burlington Av. B'frd —4G 81
Burlington Pl. Leeds —4H 103
Burlington Rd. Leeds —4H 103
Burlington St. B'frd —4K 79
Burlington St. Hal —1D 130
Burmah St. Hal —1D 130
Burmantofts. —4C 86
Burmantofts St. Leeds —5A 86 (5J 5)
Burned Gro. Hal —7C 96
Burned Rd. Hal —7C 96
Burneston Gdns. B'frd —6E 96
Burnett Av. B'frd —3K 97
Burnett Pl. B'frd —3K 97
Burnett Ri. Q'bry —6G 95
Burnett St. B'frd —6B 80 (4G 7)
Burnham Av. B'frd —4D 98
Burnham Ct. Weth —3G 17
Burnham Rd. Gar —1K 107
Burniston Clo. Wilsd —1G 77
Burnley Hill Ter. Hal —3B 114
Burnley Rd. H Bri —6A 110
Burnleys Ct. Meth —7H 125
Burnleys Dri. Meth —7H 125
Burnleys M. Meth —7H 125
Burnleys Vw. Meth —6H 125
Burnleyville. Gom —6K 117
Burn Rd. Hud —7C 144
Burnsall Av. Bat —3E 136
Burnsall Ct. Leeds —5B 84
Burnsall Cft. Leeds —5B 84
Burnsall Gdns. Leeds —5B 84
Burnsall Grange. Leeds —6B 84 (off Gelder Rd.)
Burnsall Ho. B'frd —6E 62 (off Rowantree Dri.)
Burnsall M. Sils —7G 9
Burnsall Rd. Bat —3E 136
Burnsall Rd. B'frd —6D 80 (in two parts)
Burnsall Rd. Brigh —1E 144
Burnsall Rd. Liv —4H 135
Burns Ct. Bat —5B 118
Burnsdale. All —2A 78
Burnshaw M. Leeds —4K 121
Burns Hill. Add —1C 10
Burnside Av. Hal —1D 114
Burnside Clo. Bat —6E 118
Burns St. Hal —3D 112
Burns Way. Cliff —4D 36
Burnt Side Rd. Leeds —4G 101
Burnup Gro. Cleck —1E 134
Burnwells. —2C 62
Burnwells. B'frd —2C 62
Burnwells Av. B'frd —2C 62
Burrage St. Bgly —1K 59
Burras Av. Otley —3H 27
Burras Dri. Otley —3H 27
Burras La. Otley —3H 27
Burras Rd. B'frd —4D 98
Burrell Clo. Weth —4A 18
Burrows, The. Bat —1D 136
Burrow St. B'frd —7A 80 (6D 6)
Burr Tree Dri. Leeds —6B 88
Burr Tree Gth. Leeds —6B 88
Burr Tree Va. Leeds —6B 88
Burrwood Ter. Holy G —4F 143
Burrwood Way. Holy G —4F 143
Burton Av. Leeds —3J 103
Burton Cres. Leeds —6D 66
Burton M. Leeds —6K 49
Burton Rd. Leeds —3J 103
Burton Row. Leeds —2J 103
Burton's Arc. Leeds —6J 85 (7E 4)
Burton St. B'frd —2C 98
Burton St. Fars —2B 82
Burton St. Hal —2E 112
Burton St. Kei —1K 39
Burton St. Leeds —2J 103
Burton Ter. Leeds —3J 103
Burton Way. Leeds —4C 86
Bury La. Sandb —2G 41
Busfield St. Bgly —1K 59
Busfield St. B'frd —3D 98
Bushill Fold. Q'bry —4G 95
Bus. & Innovation Cen. B'frd —4B 6 (off Angel Way)
Buslingthorpe. —1J 85
Buslingthorpe Grn. Leeds —2J 85
Buslingthorpe La. Leeds —1J 85
Buslingthorpe Va. Leeds —1J 85
Bussey Ct. Leeds —2G 85
Busy La. Shipl —3A 62
Butcher Hill. Leeds & H'fth —4J 65
Butcher La. Rothw —2G 123
Butchers Row. Leeds —6F 5
Butcher St. B'frd —7K 79 (4B 6)
Butcher St. Leeds —7H 85
Bute Av. Brigh —3G 133
Bute St. B'frd —1K 79
Butler La. Bail —1K 61 (in two parts)
Butler St. E. B'frd —5C 80 (2J 7)
Butler St. W. B'frd —5C 80 (2H 7)
Butterbowl Dri. Leeds —1J 101
Butterbowl Gdns. Leeds —1K 101
Butterbowl Gth. Leeds —1J 101
Butterbowl Gro. Leeds —1J 101
Butterbowl Lawn. Leeds —1J 101
Butterbowl Mt. Leeds —1K 101
Butterbowl Rd. Leeds —1K 101

Butterfield Ind. Est.—Castle Ga.


Butterfield Ind. Est. Bail —2A 62
Butterfield's Bldgs. Morl —2K 119
Butterfield St. Leeds —6B 86
Butterley St. Leeds —1J 103
Buttermere Av. Weth —3G 17
Buttermere Rd. B'frd —2C 80
**Buttershaw. —7F 97**
Buttershaw Dri. B'frd —6E 96
Buttershaw La. B'frd —7H 97
Buttershaw La. Liv —3D 134
Butterwick Gdns. Weth —4G 17
Butterworth End La. Norl —1J 141
Butterworth La. Sower B —6G 129
Butt Hill. Kip —5A 108
Buttholme Ga. B'frd —6F 97
Butt La. B'frd —4D 62
Butt La. Haw —5E 56
Butt La. Leeds —7H 83
Button Hill. Leeds —1K 85
Buttress La. Ludd —6G 111
Butts Ct. Leeds —5J 85 (6E 4)
Butts Gth. T'ner —6D 52
Butts Gth. Vw. T'ner —6D 52
Butts Gth. Wlk. T'ner —6D 52
Butts Grn. La. Hal —1H 129
Butts Hill. Gom —7K 117
Butts La. Guis —2G 45
Butts Mt. Leeds —6D 84
Butts Ter. Guis —2G 45
*Butts, The. E Mor —3H 41*
*(off Morton La.)*
Butts Yd. Cleck —1F 135
Buxton Av. B'frd —1J 79
Buxton La. B'frd —1J 79
Buxton La. Holy G —5D 142
Buxton St. B'frd —3H 79
Buxton St. Hal —6E 112
Buxton St. Kei —4B 40
Byeway. Guis —2E 44
Byland. Hal —7B 94
Byland Clo. B Spa —3C 36
Byland Gro. All —3K 77
Bylands Av. Riddl —1C 40
Byrl St. Kei —3B 40
Byron Av. Sower B —3K 129
Byron Gro. Dew —6C 136
Byron M. Bgly —6A 42
Byron St. B'frd —5D 80 (2K 7)
Byron St. Hal —1D 130
Byron St. Leeds —4K 85 (4G 5)
Byron St. Sower B —3K 129
Bywater Row. B'shaw —2K 117
Bywell Clo. Dew —7A 138
Bywell Rd. Dew —7K 137

Cabbage Hill. Leeds —7B 84
Cabin Rd. Pool W —5F 29
**Cackleshaw. —2G 57**
Cad Beeston. Leeds —3G 103
Cad Beeston M. Leeds —3G 103
**Caddy Field. —2J 131**
*Cadney Cft. Hal —2G 131*
*(off Harrison Rd.)*
Caenarvon Clo. Bat —6E 118
Caernarvon Av. Gar —6B 90
Cain Clo. Leeds —6B 86
Cain La. Hal —4A 132
Cairns Clo. B'frd —2B 80
Caister Clo. Bat —5E 118
*Caister Gro. Kei —7K 39*
*(off Caister Way.)*
Caister St. Kei —7K 39
Caister Way. Kei —7K 39
*Caistor Gth. B'frd —6E 62*
*(off Rowantree Dri.)*
Calde Ct. Low M —1A 116
Caldene Av. H Bri —6A 110
Caldene Av. Low M —1A 116
Calder Av. Hal —3D 130
**Calder Banks. —5A 96**
Calder Banks. Q'bry —5A 96
Calder Clo. C'frd —7H 127
*Calder Clo. G'lnd —2H 143*
*(off Calder St.)*
Calder Clo. Weth —1H 17
Caldercroft. Ell —3A 144
Calderdale Bus. Pk. Hal —4D 112
Calderdale Industrial Museum. —1H 131
Calderdale Way. G'lnd & Ell —2J 143
Calder Gro. H Bri —6A 110
*Calder Ho. Ell —2K 143*
*(off Southgate)*
Calderstone Av. B'frd —6D 96
Calder St. Brigh —7J 133
Calder St. C'frd —7C 126
Calder St. G'lnd —2H 143
Calder Ter. Hal —7E 130
Calder Trad. Est. Brigh —2H 133
Calder Vw. Ras —7F 133
Calder Way. Sils —2G 21
Caledonia Ct. K'gte —6H 139
Caledonia Rd. Bat —3H 137
Caledonia Rd. Kei —3B 40
Caledonia St. B'frd —1A 98 (7E 6)
Calgary Cres. Wake —1F 139
Calgary Pl. Leeds —6K 67
California La. Gom —1K 135
California M. Morl —1B 120
California St. Morl —3B 120
Call La. Leeds —6J 85 (7F 5)
Calls, The. Leeds —6J 85 (7F 5)
Calpin Clo. Idle —4D 62
Calton Gro. Kei —5D 40
Calton Rd. Kei —5D 40
Calton St. Kei —6K 39
(in two parts)
Calver Av. Kei —3H 39
Calver Gro. Kei —4J 39
**Calverley. —5K 63**
Calverley Av. B'frd —5F 81
Calverley Av. Leeds —2F 83
**Calverley Bridge. —6C 64**
Calverley Ct. Leeds —2F 83
Calverley Ct. W'ford —2K 123
Calverley Cutting. B'frd —4H 63
Calverley Dri. Leeds —2F 83
Calverley Gdns. Leeds —1E 82
Calverley Gth. Leeds —2F 83
Calverley Gro. Leeds —2F 83
Calverley La. C'ley —6A 64
(in two parts)
Calverley La. H'fth —5C 64
Calverley La. Leeds —1D 82
Calverley Moor Av. Pud —4J 81
Calverley Rd. W'ford —2A 124
Calverley St. Leeds —4H 85 (4C 4)
Calverley Ter. Leeds —2F 83
Calver Rd. Kei —4J 39
Calversyke St. Kei —4J 39
Calvert Clo. Kip —3A 108
Camargue Fold. B'frd —1B 80
Camberley Clo. Pud —7C 82
Camberley Mt. B'frd —2G 99
Camberley St. Leeds —3J 103
Camberley Way. Pud —7C 82
Camborne Dri. Hud —6F 145
Camborne Rd. Hud —6F 145
Camborne Way. Kei —6G 39
Cambrian Bar. Low M —1H 115
Cambrian St. Leeds —2G 103
Cambrian Ter. Leeds —2G 103
**Cambridge. —3K 27**
Cambridge Clo. Morl —2B 120
Cambridge Ct. Morl —3B 120
Cambridge Dri. Bmly —2F 83
Cambridge Dri. Otley —3K 27
Cambridge Gdns. Leeds —2F 83
Cambridge Gro. Kip —5A 108
Cambridge Gro. Otley —3K 27
Cambridge Pl. B'frd —5B 80 (1G 7)
Cambridge Pl. Q'bry —5J 95
Cambridge Pl. Sid —5J 131
Cambridge Rd. Birs —6B 118
Cambridge Rd. Leeds —2H 85
Cambridge St. Bat —3G 137
Cambridge St. B'frd —2H 97
Cambridge St. C'frd —7D 126
Cambridge St. Cytn —2B 96
Cambridge St. Guis —2G 45
Cambridge St. Heck —5C 136
Cambridge St. Otley —3J 27
Cambridge St. Q'bry —5K 95
Cambridge Ter. Otley —3J 27
*Cambridge Ter. Sid —5J 131*
*(off Cambridge Pl.)*
Cambridge Way. Otley —3K 27
Camden Rd. C'frd —7K 127
Camden St. Sower B —5K 129
Camden Ter. B'frd —4K 79
Camellia Mt. B'frd —7E 78
Cameron Av. Wyke —6H 115
Camerton Grn. B'frd —4B 98
Cam La. Brigh —4K 133
Camm St. Brigh —5H 133
Campbell St. Kei —4A 40
Campbell St. Q'bry —5K 95
Campbell St. S'ley —3B 82
**Camp Field. —7H 85**
Camp Rd. B'hpe —2H 47
Camp Sq. T'ner —6D 52
**Camp Town. —7H 49**
Campus Rd. B'frd —7J 79 (5A 6)
Camroyd St. Dew —7H 137
Canada Cres. Rawd —7A 46
Canada Dri. Rawd —6A 46
Canada Rd. Rawd —6A 46
Canada Ter. Rawd —7A 46
Canal La. Sils —3J 21
Canal Pl. Leeds —6F 85
Canal Rd. A'ley —5C 84
Canal Rd. Bgly —5J 41
Canal Rd. B'frd —7J 61 (1F 7)
Canal Rd. Leeds —7C 64
Canal Rd. Riddl —2C 40
Canal Rd. Sower B —4B 130
Canal St. Brigh —6H 133
Canal St. Hal —2H 131
Canal St. Leeds —6E 84
Canal Wharf. Kirks —2K 83
Canal Wharf. Leeds —6H 85
Canary St. Cleck —7F 117
Canberra Clo. Cro R —4H 57
Canberra Dri. Cro R —4H 57
Canford Dri. All —4B 78
Canford Gro. All —4C 78
Canford Rd. All —4B 78
Canker La. Hal —4E 112
Canker La. Hud —7J 145
Canning Av. Wake —7K 139
Canning St. B'frd —1C 98
Cannon Gro. Heck —3C 136
Cannon Hall Clo. Brigh —5K 133
Cannon Hall Dri. Brigh —6K 133
Cannon Mill La. B'frd —2G 97
Cannon St. Bgly —2A 60
Canon St. Hal —3D 130
Canterbury Av. B'frd —3J 97
Canterbury Cres. Hal —6F 113
Canterbury Dri. Leeds —1C 84
Canterbury Rd. Dew —7K 137
Canterbury Rd. Leeds —1C 84
Capas Heights Way. Heck —5C 136
Cape Ind. Est. Far —2C 82
Capel Ct. C'ley —6K 63
Capel St. Brigh —7G 133
Capel St. C'ley —6K 63
Cape of Good Hope. Q'bry —6G 95
Cape St. B'frd —5A 80 (1E 6)
Capitol Pde. Leeds —5F 67
Captain St. B'frd —6B 80 (2F 7)
Carberry Pl. Leeds —3E 84
Carberry Rd. Leeds —3E 84
*Carberry Ter. Leeds —3E 84*
*(off Carberry Pl.)*
Cardan Dri. I'ly —5E 12
Carden Av. Leeds —6G 87
Carden Rd. B'frd —1G 99
Cardigan Av. Morl —5A 120
Cardigan Clo. Bat —3J 137
Cardigan Ct. Leeds —1E 84
Cardigan Fields Rd. Leeds —4C 84
Cardigan La. Leeds —3D 84
(in three parts)
Cardigan Rd. Leeds —1D 84
Cardigan St. Q'bry —5K 95
Cardigan Ter. E Ard —7A 122
Cardigan Trad. Est. Leeds —4D 84
Cardinal Av. Leeds —6F 103
Cardinal Cres. Leeds —6F 103
Cardinal Gdns. Leeds —6E 102
Cardinal Gro. Leeds —6E 102
Cardinal Rd. Leeds —6E 102
Cardinal Sq. Leeds —5F 103
Cardinal Wlk. Leeds —5E 102
Carisbrooke Cres. B'frd —6H 97
Carisbrooke La. Gar —5B 90
Cark Rd. Kei —3A 40
*Carlby Gro. Kei —5J 39*
*(off Carlby St.)*
Carlby St. Kei —5J 39
*Carlecotes Ho. B'frd —2G 99*
*(off Ned La.)*
Carleton Clo. B Spa —2B 36
Carleton Dri. B Spa —3B 36
Carleton St. Kei —2K 39
Carling Clo. B'frd —3F 97
**Carlinghow. —1E 136**
*Carlinghow Ct. Dew —5D 136*
*(off Occupation La.)*
Carlinghow Hill. Bat —2F 137
Carlinghow La. Bat —1C 136
Carlisle Av. Yead —5A 46
Carlisle Clo. Dew —6G 137
Carlisle Dri. Pud —7B 82
Carlisle Gro. Pud —7B 82
Carlisle Pl. B'frd —4J 79
Carlisle Rd. B'frd —4H 79
Carlisle Rd. Leeds —7K 85
Carlisle Rd. Pud —7B 82
Carlisle St. B'frd —4J 79
Carlisle St. Far —4A 82
Carlisle St. Hal —7C 112
Carlisle St. Kei —4B 40
Carlisle Ter. B'frd —4J 79
Carlrayne La. Men —5C 26
**Carlton. —4F 123**
Carlton App. Weth —3G 17
Carlton Av. Bat —5F 137
Carlton Av. Pud —6C 82
Carlton Av. Shipl —4E 60
Carlton Carr. Leeds —3J 85 (2E 4)
Carlton Clo. Cleck —1F 135
Carlton Clo. Leeds —2E 4
Carlton Ct. Cleck —7F 117
Carlton Ct. Leeds —2E 102
Carlton Cft. Leeds —1F 5
Carlton Dri. Bail —7J 43
Carlton Dri. B'frd —1H 79
Carlton Dri. Gar —1K 107
Carlton Dri. Guis —1H 45
Carlton Dri. Shipl —7G 61
Carlton Gdns. Leeds —3J 85 (2F 5)
Carlton Gth. Leeds —2E 4
Carlton Gth. Shad —6C 50
Carlton Ga. Leeds —3J 85 (2E 4)
*Carlton Grange. Yead —4A 46*
*(off Cemetery Rd.)*
Carlton Gro. B'frd —3K 97
Carlton Gro. Ell —2B 144
Carlton Gro. Leeds —3J 85 (1E 4)
Carlton Gro. Shipl —7H 61
Carlton Hill. Leeds —3J 85 (2E 4)
Carlton Ho. Ter. Hal —3E 130
Carlton La. Guis & Yead —1H 45
Carlton La. Loft —6E 122
Carlton La. Rothw —3F 123
*Carlton Lanes Shop. Cen. C'frd*
*(off Carlton St.) —7D 126*
Carlton M. Guis —2H 45
Carlton Mill. Sower B —4B 130
Carlton Moor M. Leeds —2B 122
Carlton Mt. Yead —3A 46
Carlton Pde. Leeds —3J 85 (2F 5)
Carlton Pl. Hal —2G 131
Carlton Pl. Leeds —3J 85 (1E 4)
Carlton Ri. Leeds —3J 85 (2E 4)
Carlton Ri. Pud —6C 82
Carlton Rd. Dew —7G 137
Carlton Rd. Heck —2A 136
Carlton Rd. Liv —5J 135
Carlton Rd. Shipl —4E 60
Carlton Row. Leeds —6A 84
Carlton St. B'frd —7K 79 (5B 6)
Carlton St. C'frd —7D 126
(in three parts)
Carlton St. Hal —2G 131
Carlton St. Haw —5F 57
Carlton St. Otley —3K 27
Carlton Ter. Hal —2G 131
Carlton Ter. Pud —5C 82
Carlton Ter. Stainc —5E 136
Carlton Ter. Yead —4A 46
Carlton Towers. Leeds —3J 85 (2F 5)
Carlton Trad. Est. Leeds —5D 84
Carlton Vw. All B —1K 125
Carlton Vw. Leeds —3J 85 (1E 4)
Carlton Wlk. Leeds —3J 85 (2E 4)
Carlton Wlk. Shipl —4F 61
Carlton Way. Cleck —1F 135
Carlyle Cres. C'frd —7G 127
Carlyle Rd. C'frd —7G 127
Carmel Rd. Hal —5G 113
Carmona Av. Shipl —7H 61
Carmona Gdns. Shipl —7H 61
Carnaby Rd. B'frd —4E 96
Carnation St. B'frd —7E 80
Carnegie Dri. Shipl —5J 61
Carnoustie Gro. Bgly —5B 60
*Caroline St. Cleck —7F 117*
*(off Carver St.)*
Caroline St. Shipl —4F 61
Carperley Cres. Denh —5C 76
Carr Bank. E Mor —2G 41
Carr Bank Otley —7H 15
Carr Bottom Av. B'frd —4H 97
Carrbottom Fold. B'frd —5J 97
Carr Bottom Gro. B'frd —4H 97
Carr Bottom Rd. B'frd —4H 97
Carr Bottom Rd. Gre —5G 63
Carr Bri. Av. Leeds —1H 65
Carr Bri. Clo. Leeds —1H 65
Carr Bri. Dri. Leeds —1H 65
Carr Bri. Vw. Leeds —1H 65
Carr Clo. Rawd —1B 64
*Carr Ct. Bat —6G 137*
*(off Trinity St.)*
Carr Crofts. Leeds —6B 84
Carr Crofts Dri. Leeds —6B 84
Carr Croft's Ter. Leeds —6B 84
Carrfield Dri. Bar E —5H 71
Carr Fld. Dri. Ludd —7G 111
Carrfield La. Bar E —5G 71
Carrfield Rd. Bar E —5H 71
Carr Ga. Cres. Carr G —3K 139
Carr Ga. Dri. Carr G —3K 139
Carr Ga. Mt. Carr G —3K 139
Carr Grn. Av. Brigh —3F 145
Carr Grn. Clo. Brigh —3F 145
Carr Grn. Dri. Brigh —3F 145
Carr Grn. La. Brigh —2F 145
Carr Gro. Kei —2E 40
Carr Hall La. Holy G —6E 142
Carr Hall Rd. Wyke —4J 115
Carr Hill Av. C'ley —6J 63
Carr Hill Dri. C'ley —6J 63
Carr Hill Gro. C'ley —6J 63
Carr Hill Nook. C'ley —6J 63
Carr Hill Ri. C'ley —6J 63
Carr Hill Rd. C'ley —6J 63
Carrholm Cres. Leeds —5H 67
Carrholm Dri. Leeds —5H 67
Carrholm Grn. B'frd —1H 115
Carrholm Gro. Leeds —5H 67
Carrholm Mt. Leeds —5H 67
Carrholm Rd. Leeds —5H 67
Carrholm Vw. Leeds —5H 67
**Carr House Gate. —3J 115**
Carr Ho. Ga. Wyke —3J 115
Carr Ho. Gro. Wyke —3J 115
Carr Ho. La. Hal —7D 96
Carr Ho. La. Wyke —2H 115
(in three parts)
Carr Ho. Mt. Wyke —3J 115
Carr Ho. Rd. Hal —1D 114
Carr Houses. Meth —7J 125
Carriage Dri., The. G'lnd —1G 143
Carriage Dri., The. Holy G —5E 142
Carriage Dri., The. Leeds —3E 68
(in two parts)
Carricks Clo. Low M —1A 116
Carrier St. Hal —1G 131
Carrington St. B'frd —6E 80
(in two parts)
Carrington Ter. Guis —3F 45
Carr La. Bgly —3J 41
Carr La. Carl —4G 123
Carr La. Denh —3C 76
Carr La. Heck —7B 136
Carr La. Low M —3K 115
Carr La. Rawd —1B 64
Carr La. Riddl —2E 40
Carr La. Sandb —2G 41
Carr La. Shipl —4J 61
Carr La. T'ner —7J 51
Carr La. Weth —2K 17
(in two parts)
Carr Mnr. Av. Leeds —4H 67
Carr Mnr. Cres. Leeds —3H 67
Carr Mnr. Cft. Leeds —5H 67
Carr Mnr. Dri. Leeds —4H 67
Carr Mnr. Gdns. Leeds —4H 67
Carr Mnr. Gth. Leeds —3H 67
Carr Mnr. Gro. Leeds —4H 67
Carr Mnr. Mt. Leeds —4H 67
Carr Mnr. Pde. Leeds —4H 67
Carr Mnr. Pl. Leeds —4H 67
Carr Mnr. Rd. Leeds —5H 67
Carr Mnr. Vw. Leeds —3H 67
Carr Mnr. Wlk. Leeds —5H 67
Carr Moor Side. Leeds —3J 103
Carr Moor St. Leeds —4K 103
Carroll St. B'frd —7C 80 (5H 7)
Carr Rd. C'ley —5H 63
Carr Rd. Wyke —4J 115
Carr Row. Wyke —4J 115
Carrs Clo. Dew —5D 136
Carr Side Cres. Bat —5G 137
Carr St. Birs —6C 118
Carr St. B'frd —4K 97
Carr St. Brigh —4G 133
Carr St. Cleck —1F 135
Carr St. Dew —6G 137
Carr St. Heck —4A 136
Carr St. Kei —4A 40
Carr St. Liv —3J 135
Carr Top Clo. Bat —6F 137
Carr Wood Clo. C'ley —6J 63
Carr Wood Gdns. C'ley —6J 63
Carr Wood Way. C'ley —5J 63
Carter Av. Leeds —5A 88
Carter La. Leeds —4A 88
Carter La. Q'bry —3H 95
Carter Mt. Leeds —5A 88
Carter's La. Midd —2C 12
Carter Sq. B'frd —5F 63
Carter St. B'frd —7B 80 (6G 7)
Carter Ter. Leeds —4A 88
Cart Ga. B'frd —5K 97
Cartmell Dri. Leeds —6F 87
Cartmel Rd. Kei —3J 39
Cartwright Hall Art Gallery & Museum. —2J 79
Cartwright St. Rawf —2G 135
Carver St. Cleck —7F 117
Caryl Rd. B'frd —3C 98
Cashmere St. Kei —4J 39
Casson Av. E Ard —6H 121
Casson Dri. E Ard —6H 121
Casson Fold. Hal —5A 114
Casson Gro. E Ard —6H 121
Casterton Gdns. Leeds —2J 87
Castle Av. Brigh —1F 145
Castle Carr Rd. Hal —5C 92
Castle Clo. Bard —7B 34
Castle Clo. Birs —6E 118
Castle Cft. H'den —3E 58
Castlefield Ct. C'frd —7D 126
Castlefields. Rothw —2D 122
Castlefields Cres. Brigh —1F 145
Castlefields Dri. Brigh —1F 145
Castlefields Ind. Est. Bgly —6H 41
Castlefields La. Bgly —6H 41
Castlefields Rd. Bgly —5H 41
Castlefields Rd. Brigh —1F 145
**Castleford Ings. —6E 126**
*Castleford Mkt. Hall. C'frd —7D 126*
*(off Carlton St.)*
Castleford Museum. —7D 126
Castleford Tigers Rugby League Football. —6F 127
Castle Ga. I'ly —5B 12

Castle Ga.—Chestnut Ri.


Castle Ga. Stan —7J 123
Castle Ga. Weth —4J 17
Castle Ga. W'ford —7H 123
Castlegate Dri. B'frd —6E 62
Castlegate Ho. Ell —2K 143 (off Crown St.)
Castle Grange. Yead —5B 46
Castle Gro. Bard —7B 34
Castle Gro. H'den —3E 58
Castle Gro. Av. Leeds —5D 66
Castle Gro. Dri. Leeds —6D 66
Castle Head Clo. Loft —7F 122
Castle Head La. Loft —7B 122 (in two parts)
Castle Hill. Brigh —1F 145
Castle Hill. I'ly —5B 12
Castle Hill Rd. Gom —2K 135
Castle Hill Vw. Heck —5D 136
Castle Ings Clo. Leeds —3H 101
Castle Ings Dri. Leeds —3H 101
Castle Ings Gdns. Leeds —3H 101
Castle La. Ripp —6E 140
Castle M. Shipl —5H 61
Castlemore Rd. Bail —2K 61
Castle Pl. Brigh —1G 145 (off Thornhill Rd.)
Castlerigg Grn. B'frd —1F 115
Castle Rd. I'ly —5B 12 (in two parts)
Castle Rd. Kei —3K 39
Castle Rd. Rothw —2F 123
Castle Rd. Shipl —5H 61
Castle St. B'frd —1A 98 (7E 6)
Castle St. Leeds —5G 85 (6B 4)
Castle Ter. Brigh —1F 145 (off Castle Av.)
Castleton Clo. Leeds —6F 85
Castleton Rd. A'ley —5E 84
Castle Vw. Leeds —3H 67
Castle Wood Clo. Hare —3C 32
Castle Wood Clo. H'fth —4H 65
**Castley. —2B 30**
Castle Yd. I'ly —5B 12
Castley La. Leat —2H 29
Castlfields Dri. Brigh —1F 145
Cater St. B'frd —6B 80 (4G 7)
Cathcart St. Hal —6F 113
Cathcart St. Leeds —2G 85
Cathedral Clo. B'frd —6B 80 (3F 7)
Catherine Clo. Hud —7A 144
Catherine Cres. Ell —3K 143
Catherine Gro. Leeds —3H 103
Catherine Ho. La. Hal —7C 92
Catherine Rd. Hud —5H 145
**Catherine Slack. —1F 113**
Catherine Slack. Brigh —2F 133
Catherine St. Brigh —5G 133
Catherine St. Ell —3K 143
Catherine St. Kei —6K 39 (in two parts)
Cat La. Cra V —3C 128 (in two parts)
Cat La. G'lnd —2C 142
Catlow St. C'frd —7C 126
Cattle La. Aber —5E 72
Cattle Mkt. St. Otley —2J 27
Cauldwell Gdns. B'frd —2A 98
Caulms Wood Rd. Dew & Earl —7H 137
Causeway. Bklnd —6J 141
Causeway. Hal —1H 131
**Causeway Foot. —3B 94**
Causeway Foot. Hal —3B 94
Cautley Rd. Leeds —7B 86
Cavalier App. Leeds —7B 86
Cavalier Clo. Leeds —7B 86
Cavalier Ct. Leeds —7B 86
Cavalier Dri. App B —5G 63
Cavalier Gdns. Leeds —7B 86
Cavalier Ga. Leeds —7B 86
**Cavalier Hill. —6A 86**
Cave Hill. N'wram —3K 113
Cave La. E Ard —7K 121
Cavendish Ct. B'frd —7E 62 (off Cavendish Rd.)
Cavendish Ct. Shop. Cen. Kei —4A 40
Cavendish Dri. Bgly —7B 42
Cavendish Dri. Guis —3F 45
Cavendish Gro. Guis —3F 45
Cavendish M. Leeds —7K 49
Cavendish Pl. S'ley —4B 82
Cavendish Ri. Pud —6E 82
Cavendish Rd. B'frd & Eccl —7E 62
Cavendish Rd. Guis —3F 45
Cavendish Rd. Idle —5D 62
Cavendish Rd. Leeds —3H 85 (2C 4)
Cavendish Sq. S'ley —4C 82 (off Cavendish Pl.)
Cavendish St. Hal —1E 130
Cavendish St. Kei —4A 40
Cavendish St. Leeds —5F 85 (5A 4)
Cavendish St. Pud —6E 82
Cavendish St. Yead —4A 46
Cavendish Ter. Hal —1E 130
Cawcliffe Dri. Brigh —3G 133
Cawcliffe Rd. Brigh —4G 133
Cawley Gth. Heck —5C 136
Cawley La. Heck —4C 136
Cawood Haven. B'frd —6E 96
Cawthorne Av. Hud —7G 145
Caxton Rd. Otley —4G 27
Caxton St. Weth —4J 17
Caygill Ter. Hal —3G 131
Caythorpe Rd. Leeds —5B 66
Caythorpe Wlk. B'frd —7E 62
Cecil Av. Bail —7J 43
Cecil Av. B'frd —2H 97
Cecil Av. Hal —7E 114
Cecil Gro. Leeds —5C 84
Cecil Mt. Leeds —5C 84
Cecil Rd. Leeds —5C 84
Cecil St. Cro R —4H 57
Cecil St. Leeds —5C 84
Cedar Av. Leeds —6B 84
Cedar Clo. Leeds —6C 84
Cedar Ct. Leeds —2K 67 (off Harrogate Rd.)
Cedar Ct. Rothw —1C 124
Cedar Covert. Weth —1J 17
Cedar Dri. Wyke —3A 116
Cedar Gro. Bail —3E 60
Cedar Gro. Bat —6G 137
Cedar Gro. G'lnd —2F 143
Cedar Mt. Leeds —6B 84
Cedar Pl. Leeds —6B 84
Cedar Ridge. Gar —4B 90
Cedar Rd. Leeds —6C 84
Cedars, The. B'hpe —1K 47
Cedar St. Bgly —6J 41
Cedar St. Hal —2D 130
Cedar St. Kei —7K 39
Cedar St. Leeds —6B 84
Cedar Ter. Leeds —6B 84
Cedar Way. Gom —7J 117
Celette Ind. Pk. Cleck —1E 134
Cemetery La. Carl —6E 122
Cemetery La. Kei —1K 39
Cemetery La. Sower B —4J 129
Cemetery Rd. Bat —3F 137
Cemetery Rd. Bgly —7J 41
Cemetery Rd. Butt —7H 97
Cemetery Rd. Four E & L Grn —5F 79
Cemetery Rd. Heck —4B 136
Cemetery Rd. Leeds —2G 103
Cemetery Rd. Pud —5A 82
Cemetery Rd. Stanb —6B 56
Cemetery Rd. Yead —4A 46
Centenary Rd. Bail —7B 44
Centenary Sq. B'frd —7A 80 (5E 6)
Centenary Way. Bat —2F 137
Central Arc. Cleck —1G 135 (off Cheapside)
Central Av. Bail —2H 61
Central Av. B'frd —2J 97
Central Av. Hud —6H 145
Central Av. Kei —1H 57
Central Av. Liv —3D 134
Central Av. Shipl —5H 61
Central Clo. Hud —6H 145
Central Dri. C'frd —7K 125
Central Dri. Hud —7H 145
Central Dri. Kei —1H 57
Central Pde. Cleck —1G 135 (off Market St.)
Central Pde. Leeds —3E 104
Central Pk. Hal —3F 131
Central Rd. Leeds —6J 85 (7F 5)
Central St. Hal —1G 131
Central St. Leeds —5H 85 (6C 4)
Centre 27 Bus. Pk. Birs —4F 119
Centre St. B'frd —3J 97
Centre St. Heck —4A 136
Century Pl. B'frd —4J 79
Century Rd. Ell —2K 143
Century Way. Leeds —6D 88
Ceres Rd. Weth —4A 18
Chaddle Wood Clo. H'fth —3G 65
Chadwell Spring. Bgly —5A 60
Chadwick Cres. Dew —7F 137
Chadwick St. Leeds —7K 85 (in two parts)
Chadwick St. S. Leeds —7K 85
Chaffinch Rd. B'frd —6C 78
Chain St. B'frd —6K 79 (3C 6)
Chain St. C'frd —7C 126
Chalcroft Clo. Heck —3C 136
Chalfont Rd. Leeds —4B 66
Chalice Clo. Leeds —7A 104
Challenge Way. Bat —4K 137
Challis Gro. B'frd —3A 98
Chalner Av. Morl —5K 119
Chalner Clo. Morl —5K 119
Chancellor Ct. Leeds —6J 85 (7F 5)
Chancellor St. Leeds —2H 85
Chancery Rd. Oss —7B 138
Chancery Ter. Hal —6G 131
Chandler Clo. Birs —6C 118
Chandlers, The. Leeds —7G 5
Chandlers Wharf. Leeds —6C 64
Chandos Av. Leeds —4A 68
Chandos Fold. Leeds —4A 68
Chandos Gdns. Leeds —4A 68
Chandos Gth. Leeds —4A 68
Chandos Grn. Leeds —4A 68
Chandos Pl. Leeds —4B 68
Chandos St. B'frd —7B 80 (6F 7)
Chandos St. Kei —6K 39 (in two parts)
Chandos Ter. Leeds —4B 68
Chandos Wlk. Leeds —4A 68
Changegate. Haw —5D 56
Changegate Ct. Haw —5D 56
Change La. Hal —6J 131
Channing Way. B'frd —7A 80 (5E 6)
Chantree La. B'frd —7E 62
Chantree Mt. Leeds —7B 70
Chantree Vs. Hal —4H 131
Chantrell Ct. Leeds —6K 85 (7G 5)
Chantry Clo. I'ly —6B 12
Chantry Cft. Leeds —6B 88
Chantry Dri. I'ly —5B 12
Chantry Gth. Leeds —6B 88
Chantry La. H'wd —7J 55
**Chapel Allerton. —5J 67**
Chapel Av. Heck —3C 136
Chapel Clo. Gar —6J 89
Chapel Clo. Hal —1D 114
Chapel Clo. Holy G —5F 143
Chapel Ct. Brigh —3E 132
Chapel Ct. Halt —5J 87
Chapel Ct. Q'bry —4B 96 (off Chapel La.)
Chapel Cft. Brigh —2F 145
**Chapel Fold. —5E 136**
Chapel Fold. A'ley —6C 84 (off Wesley Rd.)
Chapel Fold. Bat —5E 136
Chapel Fold. Bees —4E 102
Chapel Fold. B'frd —5H 97
Chapel Fold. Halt —5J 87
Chapel Fold. L Wyke —7J 115
Chapel Fold. Pud —7C 82 (off Littlemoor Rd.)
**Chapel Green. —3K 97**
Chapel Grn. Pud —7B 82
Chapel Gro. Bgly —6J 41
**Chapel Hill. —1G 33**
Chapel Hill. Kear —1F 33
Chapel Hill. Leeds —2K 121
Chapel Hill. Morl —2A 120
Chapel Hill. Yead —4K 45
Chapel Ho. I'ly —5B 12 (off Burnside)
Chapel Ho. Rd. Low M —7K 97
**Chapel Lane. —2E 56**
Chapel La. Yead —4K 45
Chapel La. All —5C 78
Chapel La. A'ley & N Farn —6C 84
Chapel La. Bar E —5J 71
Chapel La. Bgly —1K 59
Chapel La. Birs —6C 118
Chapel La. Cliff —4D 36
Chapel La. Esh —6E 44
Chapel La. F'ley —1H 101
Chapel La. Gar —6J 89
Chapel La. Hal —5H 131
Chapel La. Heck —3C 136
Chapel La. I'ly —5A 12
Chapel La. Kei —4K 39
Chapel La. Kip —5B 108
Chapel La. Lay —4E 38
Chapel La. Leeds —1D 84 (in two parts)
Chapel La. L'ft —5D 110
Chapel La. Q'bry —4B 96 (nr. Highgate Rd.)
Chapel La. Q'bry —5H 95 (nr. New Pk. Rd.)
Chapel La. S'wram —4A 132
Chapel La. Sower B —4B 130
Chapel Pl. Leeds —7D 66
Chapel Rd. Bgly —6J 41
Chapel Rd. Leeds —7K 67
Chapel Rd. Low M —1K 115 (in two parts)
Chapel Rd. Steet —5E 20
Chapel Row. Wilsd —6F 59
Chapel Sq. Leeds —7D 66 (off Chapel St.)
Chapel St. Add —1D 10
Chapel St. Bgly —6J 41
Chapel St. B'frd —6B 80 (4G 7) (BD1)
Chapel St. B'frd —2K 97 (BD5)
Chapel St. C'ley —5K 63
Chapel St. Cleck —7G 117
Chapel St. Denh —5B 76
Chapel St. E Ard —1J 139
Chapel St. Eccl —1F 81
Chapel St. Halt —5J 87
Chapel St. Head —7D 66
Chapel St. H'town —3E 134
Chapel St. Holy G —5F 143
Chapel St. Liv —4A 136
Chapel St. L'ft —7C 112
Chapel St. Morl —4J 119
Chapel St. Q'bry —5J 95
Chapel St. Rawd —7K 45
Chapel St. Rod —7C 64
Chapel St. Sils —7G 9
Chapel St. S'ley —4C 82
Chapel St. T'tn —7H 77
Chapel St. Ting —6F 121
Chapel St. Wibs —5J 97
Chapel St. N. Hal —4D 112
Chapel Ter. Bklnd —1A 20
Chapel Ter. Leeds —7D 66 (off Chapel St.)
Chapel Ter. Sower B —5F 129
Chapel Ter. T'tn —7H 77
**Chapeltown. —5A 68**
Chapeltown. Hal —1G 131
Chapeltown. Pud —7B 82
Chapeltown Rd. Leeds —2K 85 (1G 5)
Chapel Wlk. B'frd —1F 81
Chapel Yd. Colt —7B 88 (off Meynell Rd.)
Chapel Yd. W'ford —2A 124
Chapman St. B'frd —7F 81
Charing Cross M. Leeds —2H 85
Charles Av. B'frd —6F 81
Charles Av. Hal —4A 132
Charles Av. Leeds —7B 86
Charles Gdns. Leeds —1G 103
Charles Gro. W'ford —1A 124
Charles Jones Ct. Bat —3F 137
Charles Sq. Rd. Hal —1H 131
Charles St. Bat —4G 137
Charles St. Bgly —1K 59
Charles St. B'frd —6A 80 (4E 6)
Charles St. Brigh —5G 133
Charles St. C'frd —7E 126
Charles St. Eastb —7J 137
Charles St. Ell —3K 143
Charles St. Fars —2B 82
Charles St. Gom —7K 117
Charles St. H'fth —4F 65
Charles St. Morl —3B 120
Charles St. Otley —3J 27
Charles St. Q'bry —5H 95
Charles St. Shipl —4H 61
Charles St. Sower B —4K 129
**Charlestown. —2A 62**
Charlestown Rd. Hal —7H 113
Charlesworth Gro. Hal —7C 112
Charlesworth Sq. Gom —7J 117
Charlesworth Ter. Hal —7C 112
Charlotte Clo. Birs —4D 118
Charlotte Ct. B'frd —3H 97
Charlotte Ct. Haw —4F 57
Charlotte Gro. Leeds —5K 87
Charlton Clo. B'frd —1D 80
Charlton Ct. Hal —7C 112
Charlton Gro. Leeds —6C 86
Charlton Gro. Sils —2H 21
Charlton Pl. Leeds —6C 86
Charlton Rd. Leeds —6C 86
Charlton St. Leeds —6C 86
Charnwood Bank. Bat —4C 136
Charnwood Clo. B'frd —3D 80
Charnwood Gro. B'frd —3E 80
Charnwood Rd. B'frd —3E 80
Chart Clo. Gar —6J 89
Charterhouse Rd. B'frd —3D 62
Charteris Rd. B'frd —6C 78
Chartist's Ct. Morl —4A 120 (off Gt. Northern St.)
Chartists Way. Morl —4A 120
Chartwell Ct. Leeds —6D 50
Charville Gdns. Leeds —1H 69
Chase, The. Bur W —3B 26
Chase, The. Gar —6B 90
Chase, The. Kei —3H 39
Chase, The. Rawd —7J 45
Chase, The. Weth —3K 17
Chase Way. B'frd —4A 98
Chassum Gro. B'frd —3G 79
Chaster St. Bat —2E 136 (in two parts)
Chatham St. B'frd —4B 80
Chatham St. Hal —1F 131
Chat Hill Rd. T'tn —1K 95
Chatswood Av. Leeds —6F 103
Chatswood Cres. Leeds —6F 103
Chatswood Dri. Leeds —5F 103
Chatsworth Av. Pud —5J 81
Chatsworth Clo. Leeds —2C 86
Chatsworth Ct. B'frd —5G 79 (off Girlington Rd.)
Chatsworth Cres. Pud —5J 81
Chatsworth Dri. Pud —5J 81
Chatsworth Dri. Weth —3G 17
Chatsworth Fall. Pud —5J 81
Chatsworth M. Morl —4C 120
Chatsworth Pl. B'frd —3H 79
Chatsworth Ri. Pud —5J 81
Chatsworth Rd. Leeds —2C 86
Chatsworth Rd. Pud —5J 81
Chatsworth St. Kei —4B 40
Chatts Wood Fold. Oaken —2D 116
Chaucer Av. Pud —7D 82
Chaucer Gdns. Pud —7D 82
Chaucer Gro. Pud —7D 82
Cheapside. Bat —3H 137
Cheapside. B'frd —6A 80 (3E 6)
Cheapside. Cleck —1G 135
Cheapside. Hal —1G 131
Cheapside. She —1C 114
Cheddington Gro. All —5B 78
Chel Bus. Cen. Leeds —3K 85 (1H 5)
Chellowfield Ct. B'frd —2C 78
Chellow Grange Rd. B'frd —2C 78
Chellow La. B'frd —3C 78
Chellow St. B'frd —4K 97
Chellow Ter. B'frd —4D 78
Chelmsford Rd. B'frd —5E 80
Chelmsford Ter. B'frd —6E 80
Chelsea Clo. Leeds —7C 84
Chelsea Mans. Hal —5A 114
Chelsea Rd. B'frd —2F 97
Chelsea St. Kei —5K 39
Chelsea Vw. Hal —6A 114 (off Bradford Rd.)
Chelsfield Ct. Leeds —2D 88
Chelsfield Way. Leeds —2D 88
Cheltenham Av. I'ly —5F 13
Cheltenham Ct. Hal —4H 131
Cheltenham Gdns. Hal —4H 131
Cheltenham Pl. Hal —4H 131
Cheltenham Rd. B'frd —7B 62
Cheltenham St. Leeds —7D 84
Chelwood Av. Leeds —1B 68
Chelwood Cres. Leeds —2B 68
Chelwood Dri. All —6A 78
Chelwood Dri. Leeds —1B 68
Chelwood Gro. Leeds —1B 68
Chelwood Mt. Leeds —1B 68
Chelwood Pl. Leeds —1A 68
Chenies Clo. Leeds —4G 87
Chepstow Clo. Gar —6B 90
Cheriton Dri. Q'bry —5K 95
Cherry Ct. Leeds —4J 5
Cherry Fields. B'frd —1A 80
Cherry Gro. I'ly —5K 11
Cherry Lea Ct. Rawd —6K 45
Cherry Pl. Leeds —4A 86 (4J 5)
Cherry Ri. Leeds —4A 70
Cherry Row. Leeds —4A 86 (4J 5)
Cherry St. Haw —4G 57
Cherry St. Kei —3C 40
Cherry Tree Av. B'frd —5F 63
Cherry Tree Ct. E Ard —1J 139
Cherry Tree Cres. Fars —2B 82
Cherry Tree Dri. Fars —2B 82
Cherry Tree Dri. G'lnd —2F 143
Cherry Tree Gdns. Thack —3B 62
Cherry Tree Ri. Kei —6B 40
Cherry Tree Row. H'den —5F 59
Cherry Tree Wlk. E Ard —1J 139
Cherrywood Clo. Leeds —3K 69
Cherrywood Gdns. Leeds —3K 69
Cherwell Cft. Gar —1B 108
Chesham St. Kei —4B 40
Chesney Av. Leeds —2K 103
Chesney Pk. Ind. Est. Leeds —2K 103
Chester Clo. Hal —6F 113
Chester Gro. Hal —6F 113
Chester Pl. Hal —6F 113
Chester Rd. B'twn —6F 113
Chester St. B'frd —7A 80 (5C 6)
Chester St. Hal —6F 113
Chester St. Leeds —5C 84
Chester St. Sower B —4K 129
Chester Ter. Hal —6F 113
Chesterton Ct. Colt —7B 88
Chestnut Av. Bat —4E 136
Chestnut Av. B Spa —2C 36
Chestnut Av. Head —2E 84
Chestnut Av. Leeds —3B 88
Chestnut Av. Weth —3H 17
Chestnut Clo. G'lnd —2F 143
Chestnut Clo. I'ly —6E 12
Chestnut Clo. Kei —5H 39
Chestnut Clo. Leeds —7A 68 (off Harehills La.)
Chestnut Ct. Ripp —5F 141 (off Halifax Rd.)
Chestnut Ct. Shipl —5F 61
Chestnut Dri. Leeds —6B 48
Chestnut End. B Spa —3E 36
Chestnut Gdns. Leeds —7C 84
Chestnut Gro. B Spa —2C 36
Chestnut Gro. B'frd —1A 80
Chestnut Gro. C'ley —6K 63
Chestnut Gro. Leeds —2E 84
Chestnut Gro. Rothw —1C 124
Chestnut Pl. Leeds —2E 84
Chestnut Ri. Leeds —7B 84


158 A-Z Leeds & Bradford

Chestnut St.—Clifton


Chestnut St. Hal —2D 130
Chestnut St. Hud —6J 145
Chestnut St. Leeds —2E 84
Chestnut Way. Leeds —6B 48
Chevet Mt. All —6A 78
Chevin Av. Men —5C 26
(in two parts)
Chevin Av. Men —5D 26
(nr. Bradford Rd.)
Chevin Av. Otley —4K 27
Chevin Ct. Otley —2J 27
(off Courthouse St.)
Chevinedge Cres. Hal —7H 131
Chevin End. Men —7D 26
Chevin End Rd. Men & Guis —7F 27
Chevin Forest Park. —5C 28
Chevington Ct. Rawd —1J 63
Chevins Clo. Bat —7D 118
Chevin Side Otley —4J 27
Cheviot Ct. Gar —1K 107
Cheviot Ga. Low M —1H 115
Cheyne Wlk. Kei —5J 39
Chichester St. Leeds —5C 84
**Chidswell. —5B 138**
Chidswell Gdns. Dew —5B 138
Chidswell La. Dew & Oss —5B 138
Child La. Liv —6H 135
Childs La. Shipl —6A 62
Childs Rd. Wake —7K 139
Chiltern Clo. Gar —1K 107
Chiltern Ct. Gar —1K 107
Chiltern Rd. Dew —7K 137
Chiltern Way. Liv —3F 135
Chinewood Av. Bat —2F 137
Chippendale Ct. Men —6D 26
Chippendale Ri. B'frd —5D 78
Chippendale Ri. Otley —1J 27
Chirton Gro. Leeds —7C 68
Chislehurst Pl. B'frd —3J 97
Chiswick St. Leeds —4E 84
Chiswick Ter. Leeds —3E 84
(off Chiswick Vw.)
Chorley La. Leeds —4G 85 (4B 4)
(in two parts)
Chrisharben Pk. Cytn —2C 96
Chrismoor. B'frd —5C 62
Christ Chu. Av. Leeds —5B 84
Christ Chu. Mt. Leeds —5B 84
Christ Chu. Pde. Leeds —5B 84
Christ Chu. Pl. Leeds —5B 84
Christ Chu. Rd. Leeds —5B 84
Christ Chu. Ter. Leeds —5B 84
Christ Chu. Vw. Leeds —5B 84
Christiana Ter. Morl —2B 120
Christopher Clo. Sils —1G 21
Christopher Rd. Leeds —2H 85
Christopher St. B'frd —3J 97
Christopher Ter. B'frd —3J 97
Church App. Gar —6K 89
Church Av. Gild —6G 101
Church Av. H'fth —3F 65
Church Av. Leeds —5F 67
Church Av. Swil —4E 106
Church Bank. B'frd —6B 80 (4F 7)
Church Bank. Hal —2B 130
Church Bank. Sower B —4A 130
Church Causeway. Thor A —2E 36
Church Clo. Hal —2B 112
Church Clo. Leeds —1K 87
Church Clo. M'fld —5G 91
Church Clo. Pool W —3G 29
Church Clo. Steet —5E 20
Church Clo. Swil —4E 106
Church Ct. B'frd —1F 97
Church Ct. Riddl —1D 40
Church Ct. Yead —5K 45
Church Cres. H'fth —3F 65
Church Cres. Leeds —1J 67
Church Cres. Swil —5F 107
Church Cres. Yead —5J 45
Church Dri. E Kes —5K 33
Church Farm. T'ner —5D 52
Church Farm Clo. Loft —7E 122
Church Farm Gth. Leeds —7H 51
Church Farm Vw. Bar E —5J 71
Churchfield Clo. Liv —4J 135
Churchfield Cft. Rothw —2H 123
Churchfield Gro. Rothw —1G 123
Churchfield La. C'frd —7F 127
Churchfield La. Rothw —1G 123
Churchfield Rd. Rothw —2G 123
Church Fields. B'frd —3F 81
Churchfields Rd. Brigh —5G 133
Churchfield St. Bat —3G 137
Churchfield Ter. Liv —4J 135
Church Gdns. Gar —6K 89
Church Gdns. Gild —7G 101
Church Gdns. Leeds —1K 67
**Church Garforth. —7K 89**
Church Gth. Pool W —3G 29
Churchgate. B'hpe —7H 29
Churchgate. Gild —7G 101
Church Ga. H'fth —3F 65
Church Grange. Cleck —1G 135
(off Church St.)
Church Grn. B'frd —4J 79
(off Conduit St.)
Church Grn. Hal —6C 112
Church Gro. H'fth —3F 65
Church Hill. Bail —7K 43
Church Hill. B'ham —1D 54
Church Hill. B'hpe —7H 29
Church Hill. Eastb —7H 137
Church Hill. L'ft —6G 111
Church Hill. T'ner —5E 52
Church Hill Gdns. S'ley —3D 82
Church Hill Grn. S'ley —3D 82
Church Hill Mt. S'ley —3D 82
Church Ho. Ell —2K 143
(off Church St.)
Churchill Flats. Pool W —3G 29
Churchill Gdns. Leeds —2D 4
Churchill Gro. Heck —5C 136
Churchill Rd. T'tn —7K 77
Churchill Way. Cro H —3A 20
Church La. Adel —7C 48
Church La. Bard —1K 51
Church La. B'frd —6H 97
Church La. Brigh —6G 133
(nr. Commercial St.)
Church La. Brigh —5G 133
(nr. Elland La.)
Church La. Chap A —6K 67
Church La. Coll —1F 35
Church La. C'gts —3A 88
Church La. Dew M —7D 136
Church La. E Ard —1J 139
Church La. Ell —2D 144
Church La. Esh —6E 44
Church La. Gar —6K 89
Church La. Gom & Birs —7A 118
Church La. Hal —6C 112
Church La. Hare —3A 32
Church La. Heck —5B 136
Church La. H'town —6D 134
Church La. H'fth —3F 65
Church La. Kip —5B 108
Church La. Leeds —6K 85 (7G 5)
Church La. Liv —3J 135
Church La. Mean —5F 67
Church La. Meth —5G 125
Church La. M'fld —6E 90
Church La. Otley —3J 27
Church La. Pud —6C 82
Church La. S'wram —4B 132
Church La. Slnd —5E 142
Church La. Swil —5D 106
Church La. Ting —1D 138
Church La. Weston —7D 14
Church Meadows. Birs —6B 118
Church Meadows. B'ham —7D 36
Church M. B Spa —2D 36
Church M. B'frd —7E 96
(off Church St.)
Church Mt. H'fth —3F 65
Church Pk. Liv —6G 135
Church Pl. Gar —6K 89
Church Pl. Hal —1F 131
Church Rd. Bat —7D 118
Church Rd. B'frd —6H 97
Church Rd. H'fth —4F 65
Church Rd. Leeds —6C 84
Church Rd. Liv —6F 135
Church Rd. W'ford —6J 107
Church Row. Den —3G 13
Church Row. Leeds —6K 85 (7G 5)
Church Side. Meth —5G 125
Church Side Clo. Hal —6G 113
Church Side Dri. Hal —6G 113
Churchside Vs. Meth —5G 125
Church Sq. Gar —6K 89
**Church Street. —2D 56**
Church St. Add —1E 10
Church St. Bgly —2A 60
Church St. Birs —6C 118
Church St. B Spa —3D 36
Church St. Brigh —1F 145
Church St. Butt —7E 96
Church St. C'frd —7D 126
Church St. Cleck —1G 135
Church St. Cull —6B 58
Church St. Ell —2K 143
Church St. Gild —7G 101
Church St. G'lnd —2H 143
Church St. Guis —2G 45
Church St. Hal —2H 131
Church St. Haw —5D 56
Church St. Heck —5B 136
Church St. H'town —3E 134
Church St. I'ly —5A 12
Church St. Kei —4B 40
Church St. Kirks —1A 84
Church St. Leeds —3K 103
Church St. Liv —3J 135
Church St. Mann —4H 79
Church St. Morl —2A 120
Church St. Rothw —2G 123
Church St. Shipl —4K 61
Church St. Weth —4J 17
Church St. W'ford —7A 106
Church St. Yead —5J 45
Church Ter. Bklnd —5J 141
Church Ter. Hal —2B 112
Church Vw. Adel —6C 48
Church Vw. C'frd —7B 126
Church Vw. Cleck —7D 116
Church Vw. Kip —4D 108
Church Vw. Leeds —1B 84
Church Vw. Sower B —4A 130
Church Vw. T'ner —5D 52
Church Vw. M. Cliff —5D 36
Churchville. M'fld —6G 91
Churchville Av. M'fld —6F 91
Churchville Dri. M'fld —6G 91
Churchville Ter. M'fld —6G 91
Church Wlk. Bat —5E 136
Church Wlk. Leeds —7G 5
Church Wlk. N'wram —5A 114
Church Way. Kei —5A 40
Church Way. Morl —2A 120
Chu. Wood Av. Leeds —6C 66
Chu. Wood Mt. Leeds —5C 66
Chu. Wood Rd. Leeds —6C 66
Churn La. Hal —1B 130
Churn Milk La. Hal —3E 112
**Churwell. —7C 102**
Churwell Av. Dew —5D 136
Cinderhills La. Hal —5J 131
Cinder La. C'frd —7C 126
Cinder La. Cliff —4E 36
**City. —3B 120**
Citygate. Leeds —5F 85
City La. Hal —6C 112
City Mills. Morl —3B 120
(off Peel St.)
City Pk. Ind. Est. Leeds —3C 102
City Rd. B'frd —2A 6
(in two parts)
City Rd. B'frd —5J 79 (2A 6)
(in two parts)
City Sq. Leeds —6H 85 (7D 4)
City Ter. Hal —5D 112
City Varieties. —5J 85 (6E 4)
Cityway Ind. Est. B'frd —1D 98 (7J 7)
Civic Theatre. —4H 85 (4D 4)
Clapgate. Otley —2J 27
Clapgate La. Leeds —2B 122
Clapgate La. Sower B —2F 141
(in two parts)
Clapham Dene Rd. Leeds —4K 87
Clapham St. Denh —5C 76
Clapton Av. Hal —2E 130
Clapton Gro. Hal —2E 130
Clapton Mt. Hal —2E 130
(off King Cross St.)
Clara Dri. C'ley —5H 63
Clara Rd. B'frd —7B 62
Clara St. Brigh —7G 133
Clara St. Fars —3B 82
Clare Cres. Wyke —5J 115
Clare Hall La. Hal —2G 131
Claremont. B'frd —7K 79
Claremont. Heck —4B 136
Claremont. Pud —6D 82
Claremont. Wyke —5J 115
Claremont Av. Leeds —4G 85 (4A 4)
Claremont Av. Shipl —6A 62
Claremont Ct. Leeds —6E 66
Claremont Cres. Leeds —7F 67
Claremont Cres. Shipl —6A 62
Claremont Dri. Leeds —6E 66
Claremont Gdns. Bgly —7A 42
Claremont Gdns. Fars —3B 82
Claremont Gro. Leeds —4G 85 (4A 4)
Claremont Gro. Pud —6C 82
Claremont Gro. Shipl —6B 62
Claremont Pl. Leeds —6A 84
Claremont Rd. Dew —7F 137
Claremont Rd. Leeds —6E 66
Claremont Rd. Shipl —6A 62
Claremont St. Cleck —7F 117
Claremont St. Leeds —6A 84
Claremont St. Sower B —3A 130
Claremont St. W'ford —1A 124
Claremont Ter. B'frd —6B 6
Claremont Ter. Leeds —6A 84
Claremont Vw. Leeds —4G 85 (4A 4)
Claremont Vw. W'ford —2A 124
**Claremount. —6J 113**
Claremount. Leeds —6E 66
Claremount Ho. Hal —7H 113
(off Claremont Rd.)
Claremount Rd. Hal —5F 113
Claremount Ter. Hal —5G 113
Clarence Dri. H'fth —5F 65
Clarence Dri. Men —4B 26
Clarence Gdns. H'fth —5F 65
Clarence Gro. H'fth —5F 65
Clarence M. H'fth —5F 65
Clarence Rd. H'fth —5F 65
Clarence Rd. Leeds —6K 85
(in two parts)
Clarence Rd. Shipl —4F 61
Clarence St. Bat —3H 137
Clarence St. Cleck —1F 135
Clarence St. Hal —1F 131
Clarence St. Leeds —4G 83
Clarence Ter. Pud —5C 82
Clarendon Pl. Hal —1E 130
Clarendon Pl. Leeds —2A 4
Clarendon Pl. Q'bry —6G 95
Clarendon Rd. Bgly —7B 42
Clarendon Rd. B Spa —3C 36
Clarendon Rd. Leeds —3G 85 (3A 4)
Clarendon St. Haw —6E 56
Clarendon St. Kei —6K 39
Clarendon St. Leeds —3G 85
Clarendon Ter. Pud —7C 82
Clarendon Way. Leeds —4G 85 (4B 4)
Clare Rd. Cleck —1F 135
Clare Rd. Hal —2G 131
Clare Rd. H Bri —6A 110
Clare Rd. Wyke —5J 115
Clare Rd. Flats. Hal —2G 131
Clare Royd. Light —1G 133
Clare St. Hal —2G 131
Clarges St. B'frd —3J 97
Clarion Camp. Men —5F 27
Clarion Fld. Men —5F 27
Clark Av. Leeds —6B 86
Clark Cres. Leeds —6B 86
Clarke Rd. Wake —3E 138
Clarke St. C'ley —6K 63
Clarke St. Dew —7E 136
Clark Gro. Leeds —7B 86
Clark La. Leeds —6B 86
(in two parts)
Clark Mt. Leeds —6B 86
Clark Rd. Leeds —7B 86
Clark Row. Leeds —7B 86
Clarkson Av. Heck —4C 136
Clarkson Clo. Heck —4C 136
Clarkson Ter. Chur —6C 102
Clarkson Vw. Leeds —1G 85
Clark Spring Clo. Morl —7A 102
Clark Spring Ri. Morl —7B 102
Clark Ter. Leeds —6B 86
Clark Vw. Leeds —7B 86
Clattering Stones Rd. Cra V —6A 128
Clayborn Vw. Cleck —2G 135
Clay Butts. Hud —7E 144
Clayfield Dri. B'frd —4G 97
Clay Ga. H Bri —3A 92
Clay Hill Dri. Wyke —4K 115
(in two parts)
Clay Ho. La. G'lnd —2G 143
Claymore Ri. Sils —2H 21
Clay Pit La. Leeds —4J 85 (4E 4)
Claypit La. S Mil —7G 109
Claypit La. T'ner —6D 52
Clay Pits La. Hal —7C 112
Clay Pits La. Sower B —2D 140
Clay Royd La. S'wram —3C 132
Clay St. Hal —1D 130
Clay St. Sower B —4K 129
(in two parts)
**Clayton. —2C 96**
Clayton Av. Kip —4B 108
Clayton Clo. Leeds —4B 104
Clayton Clo. H'let —4B 104
Clayton Ct. Leeds —4K 65
Clayton Dri. Leeds —4B 104
**Clayton Edge. —4H 95**
Clayton Grange. Leeds —4K 65
Clayton Gro. Yead —4K 45
Clayton Hall Rd. Cro H —4A 20
**Clayton Heights. —4C 96**
Clayton La. B'frd —2A 98
Clayton La. Cytn —3B 96
Clayton Ri. Kei —3J 39
Clayton Rd. B'frd —2E 96
Clayton Rd. Leeds —4B 104
Clayton St. Rothw —2H 123
Clayton Ter. Cull —7B 58
Clayton Way. Leeds —4B 104
Clayton Wood Bank. Leeds —3K 65
Clayton Wood Clo. Leeds —3K 65
Clayton Wood Ri. Leeds —3K 65
Clayton Wood Rd. Leeds —3J 65
Clearings, The. Leeds —6K 103
Cleasby Rd. Men —7C 26
Cleavesty La. E Kes —3K 33
**Cleckheaton. —1F 135**
Cleckheaton Rd. Low M & B'frd —1K 115
Cleeve Hill. Rawd —7K 45
Clegg La. G'lnd —2D 142
Clegg St. Wyke —5J 115
Clement St. B'frd —5F 79
Clement St. Sower B —4K 129
Clement Ter. Morl —3B 120
(off Ackroyd St.)
Clement Ter. Rothw —3G 123
**Clerk Green. —4F 137**
Clerk Grn. St. Bat —4F 137
Clervaux Ct. Cytn —1D 96
Cleveden Pl. Hal —5E 112
Cleveland Av. Hal —4H 131
Cleveland Rd. B'frd —2H 79
Cleveley Gdns. H Bri —7A 110
Cleveleys Av. Leeds —2F 103
Cleveleys Ct. Leeds —2F 103
(off Cleveleys Av.)
Cleveleys Mt. Leeds —2F 103
Cleveleys Rd. Leeds —2F 103
Cleveleys St. Leeds —2F 103
(off Cleveleys Rd.)
Cleveleys Ter. Leeds —2F 103
Cliff Ct. Leeds —1G 85
Cliff Ct. Liv —5J 135
Cliff Cres. Hal —3C 130
Cliff Cres. Kip —5C 108
Cliffdale Rd. Leeds —1H 85
Cliffe Av. Bail —2J 61
Cliffe Av. H'den —3E 58
Cliffe Av. Light —1G 133
Cliffe Castle Museum & Gallery. —2K 39
Cliffe Ct. Yead —4A 46
(off Harper La.)
Cliffe Cres. Riddl —3F 41
Cliffe Dri. Rawd —1J 63
(in two parts)
Cliffe Gdns. Shipl —6H 61
Cliffe Ho. Av. Gar —1A 108
Cliffe La. Bail —3J 61
Cliffe La. Cleck —6G 117
Cliffe La. Rawd —2A 64
(in two parts)
Cliffe La. T'tn —6J 77
Cliffe La. S. Bail —3J 61
Cliffe La. W. Bail —2J 61
Cliffe Mill Fold. E Mor —3J 41
Cliffe Mt. Gom —6J 117
Cliffe Pk. Chase. Leeds —7A 84
Cliffe Pk. Clo. Leeds —7A 84
Cliffe Pk. Cres. Leeds —7A 84
Cliffe Pk. Dri. Leeds —7A 84
Cliffe Pk. Mt. Leeds —7A 84
Cliffe Pk. Ri. Leeds —7A 84
Cliffe Rd. B'frd —3B 80
Cliffe Rd. Brigh —6G 133
Cliffe Rd. Kei —7K 39
Cliffestone Dri. E Mor —3H 41
Cliffe St. Bat —4D 136
Cliffe St. Dew —7H 137
Cliffe St. Kei —3K 39
Cliffe St. T'tn —6G 77
Cliffe Ter. Bail —3J 61
Cliffe Ter. B'frd —4K 79
Cliffe Ter. Denh —5C 76
(off Station Rd.)
Cliffe Ter. Kei —7A 40
Cliffe Ter. Rob H —4C 122
Cliffe Ter. Sower B —3J 129
Cliffe Ter. Weth —4J 17
Cliffe Vw. All —3A 78
Cliffe Vw. Morl —4H 119
Cliffe Vs. N Brig —7C 60
Cliffe Wood Av. Shipl —6H 61
Cliffe Wood Clo. B'frd —2E 78
Cliff Gdns. Hal —3C 130
Cliff Hill La. Warley —2K 129
Cliff Hollins La. Oaken & E Bier —3D 116
Cliff La. Leeds —1F 85
(in two parts)
Cliff La. Ripp —7F 141
Cliff Mt. Leeds —1G 85
Cliff Mt. Ter. Leeds —1G 85
**Clifford. —5D 36**
Clifford Av. I'ly —4A 12
Clifford Clo. B'frd —7K 61
Clifford Moor Rd. B Spa —2B 36
Clifford Pl. Chur —7B 102
Clifford Rd. Bail —2J 61
Clifford Rd. B Spa —3E 36
Clifford Rd. B'ham —7D 36
Clifford Rd. I'ly —3A 12
Clifford St. B'frd —1A 98 (7E 6)
Clifford St. Sils —7F 9
Cliff Rd. Leeds —1G 85
Cliff Rd. Gdns. Leeds —1G 85
Cliff Side Gdns. Leeds —1G 85
Cliff St. Haw —5F 57
Cliff Ter. Hal —6G 131
Cliff Ter. Leeds —1G 85
Cliff Ter. M'fld —7H 91
Cliff Top Pk. Cvn. Site. Gar —2B 108
Cliff Va. Rd. Shipl —7H 61
Clifton. —6K 133
(nr. Brighouse)
Clifton. —4G 15
(nr. Newall)


A-Z Leeds & Bradford 159

Cross Albert Pl. Leeds —7D 84
Cross Aston Gro. Leeds —3J 83
Cross Av. Rothw —7H 105
Cross Aysgarth Mt. Leeds —6B 86
**Cross Bank. —2E 136**
Cross Bank Rd. Add —1A 10
Cross Bank Rd. Bat —2E 136
Cross Banks. Shipl —5H 61
Cross Bank St. Dew —7H 137
Cross Banstead St. Leeds —2B 86
Cross Barstow St. Leeds —7J 85
Cross Bath Rd. Leeds —3G 83
Crossbeck Clo. I'ly —6B 12
Crossbeck Rd. I'ly —6B 12
Cross Belgrave St. Leeds —5J 85 (5F 5)
Cross Bellbrooke Av. Leeds —3D 86 (off Bellbrooke Av.)
Cross Bell St. Leeds —5H 5
Cross Bentley La. Leeds —6F 67
Cross Burley Lodge Rd. Leeds (off Burley Rd.) —3E 84
Cross Cardigan Ter. Leeds —4C 84
Cross Catherine St. Leeds —6A 86 (7K 5)
Cross Chancellor St. Leeds —2H 85
Cross Chapel St. Leeds —7D 66
Cross Chestnut Gro. Leeds —2E 84 (off Chestnut Av.)
Cross Chu. St. Cleck —1G 135
Cross Cliff Rd. Leeds —1F 85
Cross Conway Mt. Leeds —2B 86
Cross Cowper St. Leeds —2K 85
Cross Crown St. Cleck —1F 135
Crossdale Av. B'frd —6E 96
Cross Dawlish Gro. Leeds —5D 86
Cross Dykes Rd. Sower B —2C 140 (in two parts)
Cross Easy Rd. Leeds —7B 86
Cross Emily St. Kei —3A 40
Cross End Fold. Add —1E 10
Cross Farm Ct. Oxe —2E 74
Cross Fld. Holy G —5E 142
Crossfield Clo. Oxe —2D 74
Crossfield Rd. Oxe —2D 74
Crossfield St. Leeds —2G 85 (1B 4)
**Crossflatts. —5K 41**
Cross Flatts. Leeds —3G 103
Cross Flatts Av. Leeds —4G 103
Cross Flatts Cres. Leeds —4F 103
Cross Flatts Dri. Leeds —3F 103
Cross Flatts Gro. Leeds —4F 103
Cross Flatts Mt. Leeds —4G 103
Cross Flatts Pde. Leeds —4F 103
Cross Flatts Pl. Leeds —4F 103
Cross Flatts Rd. Leeds —4F 103
Cross Flatts Row. Leeds —4F 103
Cross Flatts St. Leeds —4F 103
Cross Flatts Ter. Leeds —4F 103
Cross Fountaine St. Leeds —5H 85 (5D 4)
Cross Francis St. Leeds —2K 85
Crossgate. Otley —3J 27
**Cross Gates. —3K 87**
Cross Gates Av. Leeds —2A 88
Cross Gates La. Bgly —7G 41
Cross Gates La. Leeds —2K 87
Cross Gates Rd. Leeds —3J 87 (in two parts)
Cross Glen Rd. Leeds —5C 66
Cross Granby Ter. Leeds —7D 66
Cross Grange Av. Leeds —2A 86
Cross Grasmere St. Leeds —6D 84
**Cross Green. —1C 104**
Cross Grn. B'frd —2G 99
Cross Grn. Otley —2K 27
Cross Grn. App. Leeds —1C 104
Cross Grn. Av. Leeds —7B 86
Cross Grn. Clo. Leeds —1C 104
Cross Grn. Ct. Leeds —1D 104
Cross Grn. Cres. Leeds —7B 86
Cross Grn. Dri. Leeds —1C 104
Cross Grn. Gth. Leeds —1C 104
Cross Grn. Gro. Leeds —7B 86
Cross Grn. Ind. Est. Leeds —1D 104
Cross Grn. La. C Grn —7A 86
Cross Grn. La. Halt —5J 87
Cross Grn. Ri. Leeds —1C 104
Cross Grn. Rd. Leeds —7B 86
Cross Grn. Row. Leeds —5E 66
Cross Grn. Va. Leeds —2C 104
Cross Grn. Way. Leeds —1C 104
Cross Greenwood Mt. Leeds —5E 66
Cross Hartley Av. Leeds —1G 85 (off Delph La.)
Cross Heath Gro. Leeds —3E 102
Cross Henley Rd. Leeds —3G 83
**Cross Hill. —2G 143**
Cross Hill. G'lnd —2G 143
Cross Hill. Leeds —5E 102
Cross Hill La. Harts —7E 134
**Cross Hills. —3A 20**
Cross Hills. Hal —7G 113
Cross Hills. Kip —5A 108
Cross Hills Ct. Kip —5A 108
Cross Hills Dri. Kip —5A 108
Cross Hills Gdns. Kip —5A 108
Crosshills Mt. G'lnd —2G 143
Cross Hilton Gro. Leeds —1B 86
Cross Ingledew Cres. Leeds —2D 68
Cross Ingram Rd. Leeds —1F 103
Crossings, The. Bat —7D 118
Cross Kelso Rd. Leeds —4F 85 (3A 4)
Crossland Rd. Chur —7B 102
Crossland St. Leeds —7G 85
Crossland Ter. Leeds —3J 103
Cross La. Bgly —7K 41
Cross La. B'shaw & B'frd —7K 99
Cross La. B'frd —2H 97 (in two parts)
Cross La. Brigh —7A 134
Cross La. Ell —3J 143
Cross La. F'ley —1J 101
Cross La. Guis —6H 27
Cross La. Hal —1A 114 (nr. Cock Hill La.)
Cross La. Hal —3B 114 (nr. West St.)
Cross La. Oxe —2E 74
Cross La. Q'bry —6G 95
Cross La. Wilsd —6G 59
Cross La. Wort —6B 84
Cross Lea Farm Rd. Leeds —5K 65
Cross Leeds St. Kei —4K 39 (nr. Leeds St.)
Cross Leeds St. Kei —4A 40 (off North St.)
**Crossley. —7J 135**
Crossley Almshouses. Hal —2F 131
Crossley Clo. Hal —1E 130 (off Crossley Gdns.)
Crossley Gdns. Hal —1E 130 (in three parts)
**Crossley Hall. —6E 78**
Crossley Hall St. B'frd —6D 78
Crossley Hill. Hal —5H 131
Crossley Hill La. Hal —5H 131 (off Crossley Hill)
Crossley La. Mir —7J 135
Crossley Retail Pk. Hal —7F 113
Crossley St. B'frd —1H 97
Crossley St. Brigh —7H 133
Crossley St. Hal —1G 131
Crossley St. Liv —6A 136
Crossley St. Q'bry —5K 95
Crossley St. Weth —4J 17
Crossley Ter. Bat —5G 137
Crossley Ter. N. Hal —3E 112
Crossley Ter. S. Hal —3E 112
Cross Lidgett Pl. Leeds —4B 68
Cross Louis St. Leeds —2K 85
Cross Maude St. Leeds —7G 5 (off Maude St.)
Cross Mitford Rd. Leeds —6D 84
Crossmoor Clo. Sils —1E 20
Crossmount St. Bat —5G 137
Cross Osmondthorpe La. Leeds —5E 86
Cross Pk. St. Bat —3H 137
Cross Pk. St. Leeds —5J 87
Cross Peel St. Morl —3B 120
Cross Pl. Brigh —4H 133 (off Bradford Rd.)
Cross Quarry St. Leeds —1G 85
Cross Reginald Mt. Leeds —1K 85
Cross Rink St. Bat —5H 137
Cross River St. Kei —2C 40
Cross Rd. B'frd —4H 79
Cross Rd. H'fth —4E 64
Cross Rd. Idle —4E 62
Cross Rd. Oaken —2B 116
**Cross Roads. —4H 57**
Cross Roads. Kei —4H 57
Cross Rosse St. Shipl —4H 61
Cross Roundhay Av. Leeds —7B 68
Cross Row. Leeds —7E 88
Cross Rydal St. Kei —5J 39
Cross St Michaels La. Leeds —1D 84
Cross Speedwell St. Leeds —2H 85
Cross Springwell St. Leeds —7F 85
Cross Stamford St. Leeds —4K 85 (3H 5)
Cross St. Bat —3H 137
Cross St. B'frd —7F 97
Cross St. Brigh —4G 133
Cross St. C'frd —7C 126
Cross St. Cytn —2C 96
Cross St. Dew —7H 137
Cross St. E Ard —7A 122
Cross St. G'lnd —2H 143
Cross St. Hal —2H 131
Cross St. Holy G —5F 143
Cross St. Leeds —5J 87
Cross St. Liv —6J 135
Cross St. Oaken —3C 116
Cross St. Oss —7C 138
Cross St. Rothw —2G 123
Cross St. W'wd M —7B 126
Cross St. Weth —4J 17
Cross St. W. Hal —7C 112
Cross Sun St. B'frd —5B 80 (2F 7)
Cross Ter. Rothw —2G 123
Cross, The. Bar E —5H 71
Cross, The. B'ley —5K 143
Cross, The. B'hpe —7H 29
Cross Valley Dri. Leeds —4J 87 (off Valley Dri.)
Crossway. Bgly —5K 59
Crossways, The. Otley —7J 15
Cross Wells Rd. Ripp —4D 140
Cross Westfield Rd. Leeds —4F 85 (off Westfield Rd.)
Cross Wingham St. Leeds —3K 85 (1H 5)
Cross Woodstock St. Leeds —1C 4 (off Blenheim Wlk.)
Cross Woodview St. Leeds (off Woodview St.) —4H 103
Cross York St. Leeds —6K 85 (7G 5)
Crowgill Rd. Shipl —4H 61
Crow Hill End Rd. Sower B —6B 128
Crow Hill Rd. Cra V —5B 128
Crow La. Otley —3J 27
Crown Ct. Leeds —6J 85 (7F 5)
Crown Dri. Wyke —3J 115
**Crow Nest. —1A 60**
Crownest La. Bgly —7A 42
Crow Nest La. Leeds —4D 102
Crownest Rd. Bgly —1A 60
Crown Flatt Way. Dew —7J 137
**Crown Point. —6K 85 (7H 5)**
Crown Point Retail Pk. Leeds —7J 85
Crown Point Rd. Leeds —7K 85 (7G 5)
Crown Rd. Hal —5F 113
Crown St. B'frd —6J 79 (3A 6)
Crown St. Brigh —5G 133
Crown St. Bur W —1B 26
Crown St. Cleck —1F 135
Crown St. Ell —2K 143
Crown St. Hal —1G 131
Crown St. Leeds —6J 85 (7F 5)
Crown St. Wyke —3J 115
Crown Ter. Hal —2D 130 (nr. Hopwood La.)
Crown Ter. Hal —2D 130 (off Queen's Rd.)
Crowther Av. C'ley —6H 63
Crowther Fold. H'den —3F 59
Crowther Pl. C'frd —7D 126
Crowther Pl. Leeds —2H 85
Crowther Rd. Heck —3C 136
Crowthers St. Wyke —3J 115
Crowther St. Bat —3D 136
Crowther St. B'frd —5F 63
Crowther St. Cleck —7F 117
Crowthers Yd. Pud —7C 82
Crow Tree Clo. Bail —1K 61
Crow Tree La. B'frd —4E 78
Crowtrees Ct. Rawd —1A 64
Crowtrees Cres. Brigh —2F 145
Crowtrees La. Ras —2F 145
Crowtrees Pde. Brigh —2F 145 (off Crowtrees La.)
Crowtrees Pk. Brigh —1F 145
Crow Trees Pk. Rawd —7K 45
Crow Wood La. Holy G —7A 142
Crow Wood Pk. Hal —3B 130
Croydon Rd. B'frd —2F 97
Croydon St. Leeds —7F 85
Croydon St. Q'bry —5J 95
Crumack La. Oxe —2G 75
Crystal Ct. Hal —1E 130 (off Hanson La.)
Crystal Ter. B'frd —3E 98
Cuckoo Pk. La. Oxe —1G 75
Cudbear St. Leeds —7K 85
**Cullingworth. —7B 58**
Cullingworth Rd. Cull —7B 58
Cullingworth St. Dew —5E 136
Culpans Rd. Cra V —4C 128
Culver St. Hal —1G 131
Cumberland Av. Hud —4G 145
Cumberland Clo. Hal —3C 112
Cumberland Ct. Leeds —2D 84
Cumberland Ho. B'frd —2H 7
Cumberland Rd. B'frd —1G 97
Cumberland Rd. C'frd —5K 127
Cumberland Rd. Leeds —1F 85
Cunliffe La. Esh —6D 44
Cunliffe Rd. B'frd —3J 79
Cunliffe Rd. I'ly —5B 12
Cunliffe Ter. B'frd —3K 79
Cunliffe Vs. B'frd —2K 79
Cure Hill. Oakw —1D 56
Curlew Clo. I'ly —5J 11
Curlew Ct. Steet —4D 20
Curlew Ri. Morl —4D 120
Curlew St. B'frd —3J 97
Curly Hill. I'ly —3A 12
Currer Av. B'frd —5D 98
Currer St. B'frd —6B 80 (4F 7)
Currer St. Oaken —3C 116
Currer Wlk. Steet —4D 20
Curwen Cres. Heck —3C 136
Curzon Rd. B'frd —6D 80
Cuthberts Clo. Q'bry —6H 95
Cut La. Hal —2K 113
**Cutler Heights. —2F 99**
Cutler Heights La. B'frd —3E 98
Cutler La. Meth —4J 125
Cutler Pl. B'frd —2F 99
Cyprus Av. B'frd —3B 62
Cyprus Dri. B'frd —3C 62
Cyprus Gro. Gar —6J 89
Cyprus Rd. Gar —6J 89
Cyprus Ter. Gar —6J 89
Czar St. Leeds —1G 103

Dacre Clo. Liv —3H 135
Dacre St. B'frd —5B 80
Daffels Wood Clo. Bier —6D 98
Daffil Av. Chur —7B 102
Daffil Grange M. Morl —7B 102
Daffil Grange Way. Morl —7B 102
Daffil Gro. Chur —7B 102
Daffil Rd. Chur —7B 102
Daffodil Ct. All —5B 78
Dagenham Rd. B'frd —3E 98
Daily Ct. B'frd —3H 97
Daisy Bank. Hal —3F 131
Daisy Clo. Birs —5C 118
Daisy Cft. Sils —1H 21
Daisyfield Grange. Leeds —4H 83 (off Rossefield App.)
Daisyfield Rd. Leeds —4H 83
**Daisy Hill. —3E 78 (nr. Allerton)**
**Daisy Hill. —2C 120 (nr. Morley)**
Daisy Hill. Morl —2C 120
Daisy Hill. Sils —1H 21
Daisy Hill. Wyke —4J 115
Daisy Hill Av. Morl —1C 120
Daisy Hill Bk. La. B'frd —3E 78
Daisy Hill Clo. Morl —1B 120
Daisy Hill Gro. B'frd —3E 78
Daisy Hill La. B'frd —3E 78
Daisy Mt. Sower B —3J 129
Daisy Pl. Shipl —4F 61 (off Saltaire Rd.)
Daisy Rd. Brigh —7H 133
Daisy Row. Leeds —4H 83
Daisy St. B'frd —3G 97
Daisy St. Brigh —6G 133
Daisy St. Hal —2F 131
Daisy St. Haw —5G 57
Daisy Va. Ter. Thor —6A 122
Dalby Av. B'frd —4E 80
Dalby St. B'frd —5E 80
Dalcross Gro. B'frd —2B 98
Dalcross St. B'frd —2A 98
Dale Clo. Bat —6G 137
Dale Clo. Guis —3D 44
Dale Cres. Steet —5E 20
Dale Cft. Gar —5J 89
Dale Cft. I'ly —5J 11
Dale Cft. Ri. All —3K 77
Dale Gth. Bail —1H 61
Dale Gro. B'frd —3A 62
Dale La. Heck —3B 136
Dale Pk. Av. Leeds —7H 47
Dale Pk. Clo. Leeds —7H 47
Dale Pk. Gdns. Leeds —7H 47
Dale Pk. Ri. Leeds —7H 47
Dale Pk. Vw. Leeds —7H 47
Dale Pk. Wlk. Leeds —7H 47
Dale Rd. Dlgtn —5E 100
Dales Bank Holiday Pk. Sils —4F 9
Dales Dri. Guis —3D 44
Daleside. G'lnd —2E 142
Daleside Av. Pud —5J 81
Daleside Clo. Pud —4H 81
Daleside Gro. Oaken —3B 116
Daleside Gro. Pud —5J 81
Dale Side Ho. B'frd —3K 79
Daleside Rd. Pud —4H 81
Daleside Rd. Riddl —2E 40
Daleside Rd. Shipl —3K 61
Daleside Wlk. B'frd —4B 98
Daleson Cres. Hal —4A 114
Dale St. B'frd —6A 80 (3E 6)
Dale St. Kei —2C 40
Dale St. Shipl —5H 61
Dale St. Sower B —4K 129
Dalesway. Bgly —6B 42
Dales Way. Guis —3D 44
Dale, The. Aber —3E 72
Dale Vw. I'ly —5J 11
Dale Vw. L'ft —1F 129
Dale Vw. Sils —7G 9
Dale Vw. Steet —5E 20
Dale Vw. Clo. Kei —5C 40
Daleview Ct. Bail —2G 61
Dale Vw. Gro. Kei —5C 40
Dale Vw. Rd. Kei —6C 40
Dale Vw. Way. Kei —5C 40
Dale Vs. H'fth —5H 65
Dallam Av. Shipl —4E 60
Dallam Gro. Shipl —3E 60
Dallam Rd. Shipl —4E 60
Dallam Wlk. Shipl —4F 61
Dalton Av. Leeds —4G 103
Dalton Gro. Leeds —4G 103
Dalton La. B'ham —1J 63 (in two parts)
Dalton La. Kei —4B 40
Dalton Rd. Kei —4C 40
Dalton Rd. Leeds —4G 103
Dalton St. Sower B —3K 129
Dalton Ter. B'frd —5H 79
Dalton Ter. Kei —3C 40 (off Surrey St.)
Damask St. Hal —7F 113
Damems La. Oakw —2H 57
Damems Rd. Kei —2J 57
**Dam Head. —3J 113**
Dam Head Rd. Sower B —3A 130
Dam La. Yead —4A 46
Damon Av. B'frd —1G 81
Damside. Kei —5K 39
Danby Av. B'frd —6D 98
Danby Wlk. Leeds —6B 86 (7K 5)
Danebury Rd. Brigh —7H 133
Dane Ct. Rd. B'frd —3G 99
Danefield Ter. Otley —2K 27
Dane Hill Dri. B'frd —2G 99
Daniel Ct. B'frd —4H 99
Daniel St. B'frd —6F 81
Danny La. L'ft —1F 129
Dansk Way. I'ly —4D 12
Danum Dri. Bail —2J 61
Darcey Hey La. Hal —3C 130
Darcy Ct. Leeds —5A 88
Darfield Av. Leeds —2C 86
Darfield Cres. Leeds —2C 86
Darfield Gro. Leeds —2B 86
Darfield Ho. B'frd —6E 62 (off Summerfield Rd.)
Darfield Pl. Leeds —2C 86
Darfield Rd. Leeds —2C 86
Darfield St. B'frd —5K 79 (2C 6)
Darfield St. Leeds —2C 86
Dark La. Bat —4F 137
Dark La. Birs —4D 118
Dark La. Hal —2K 129
Dark La. H Bri —5B 110
Dark La. Oxe —2E 74
Dark La. Pot —3H 71
Dark La. Schol —4B 56 (in two parts)
Dark La. S'wram —1A 132 (nr. Barrowclough La.)
Dark La. S'wram —4B 132 (nr. Cain La.)
Dark La. Sower B —6C 140
Darkwood Clo. Leeds —7C 50
Darkwood Way. Leeds —7C 50
Darley Av. Leeds —7K 103
Darley Rd. Liv —3H 135
Darley St. B'frd —6A 80 (3D 6) (in two parts)
Darley St. Heck —4B 136
Darley St. Kei —2K 39
Darnay La. B'frd —3A 98
Darnell Ter. Leeds —7J 85
Darnes Av. Hal —3C 130
Darnley La. Leeds —7A 88
Darnley Rd. Leeds —5B 66
Darren St. B'frd —7G 81
Dartmouth Av. Morl —5A 120
Dartmouth Ter. B'frd —3J 79
Dartmouth Way. Leeds —4J 103
Darwin St. B'frd —3J 97
Davenport Ho. B'frd —2H 7
David La. Dew —6G 137
David St. C'frd —7B 126
David St. Leeds —7H 85
Davies Av. Leeds —4B 68
Dawlish Av. Leeds —5D 86
Dawlish Cres. Leeds —5D 86
Dawlish Gro. Leeds —6D 86
Dawlish Mt. Leeds —5D 86
Dawlish Pl. Leeds —5D 86
Dawlish Rd. Leeds —5D 86
Dawlish Row. Leeds —5D 86
Dawlish St. Leeds —5D 86
Dawlish Ter. Leeds —5D 86
Dawlish Wlk. Leeds —6D 86
Dawnay Rd. B'frd —3H 97
Dawson Av. B'frd —6J 97
Dawson Gdns. Dew —7F 137 (off Halliley St.)
Dawson Hill. Morl —2A 120
Dawson La. B'frd —5E 98

Duke St.—Ellercroft Rd.


Duke St. C'frd —7B 126
Duke St. Ell —3K 143
Duke St. Haw —5F 57
Duke St. Kei —2K 39
Duke St. Leeds —6K 85 (7H 5)
Duke St. L'ft —6F 111
Dulverton Clo. Leeds —5D 102
Dulverton Ct. Leeds —5D 102
Dulverton Gdns. Leeds —4C 102
Dulverton Gth. Leeds —5C 102
Dulverton Grn. Ctly —5C 102
Dulverton Grn. Leeds —5D 102
Dulverton Gro. B'frd —3F 99
Dulverton Gro. Leeds —5C 102
Dulverton Pl. Leeds —5C 102
Dulverton Sq. Leeds —5D 102
Dunbar Cft. Q'bry —5K 95
Duncan Av. Otley —4F 27
Duncan St. B'frd —1A 98 (7E 6)
Duncan St. Leeds —6J 85 (7F 5)
Dunce Pk. Clo. Ell —4K 143
Duncombe Rd. B'frd —6F 79
Duncombe St. B'frd —6G 79
Duncombe St. Leeds —5G 85 (6A 4)
Duncombe Way. B'frd —6G 79
Dundas St. Hal —3D 130
Dundas St. Kei —5B 40
Dunderdale Cres. C'frd —6K 127
Dungeon La. Oult —6H 123
Dunhill Cres. Leeds —5G 87
Dunhill Ri. Leeds —5G 87
Dunkhill Cft. Idle —5D 62
**Dunkirk. —2J 113**
Dunkirk Cres. Hal —2C 130
Dunkirk Gdns. Hal —3C 130
Dunkirk La. Hal —3C 130
Dunkirk Ri. Riddl —1C 40
Dunkirk St. Hal —2C 130
Dunkirk Ter. Hal —2D 130
Dunlin Clo. Morl —4D 120
Dunlin Ct. Leeds —2K 121
Dunlin Cft. Leeds —2K 121
Dunlin Dri. Leeds —2K 121
Dunlin Fold. Leeds —2K 121
Dunlin Way. B'frd —6C 78
Dunmill Fld. Leeds —3G 83
Dunmill Pas. Otley —3H 27
Dunmill Ri. Leeds —4A 104
Dunmill Va. Leeds —5K 83
Dunmore Av. Q'bry —5G 95
Dunningley La. Ting —5F 121
Dunnington Wlk. B'frd —1G 115
Dunnock Cft. Morl —4D 120
Dunrobin Av. Gar —6B 90
Dunsford Av. B'frd —6D 98
Dunstarn Dri. Leeds —1D 66
Dunstarn Gdns. Leeds —1E 66
Dunstarn La. Leeds —2D 66
Durban Av. Leeds —4F 103
Durban Cres. Leeds —4F 103
Durham Ct. Fars —2B 82
Durham Rd. B'frd —4G 79
Durham St. Hal —1C 130
Durham Ter. B'frd —4G 79
Durley Av. B'frd —2G 79
Durling Dri. Wrose —5A 62
Durlston Gro. Wyke —3K 115
Durlston Ter. Wyke —3K 115
Durrance St. Kei —5H 39
Durrant Clo. Weth —4K 17
Dutton Grn. Leeds —4J 69
Dutton Way. Leeds —5J 69
Duxbury Ri. Leeds —3H 85 (1D 4)
Dyehouse Dri. West I —5E 116
Dyehouse Fold. Oaken —2C 116
Dyehouse La. Brigh —7H 133
Dye Ho. La. Norl —7C 130
Dyehouse La. Pud —2C 100
(in two parts)
Dye Ho. La. Wilsd —7E 58
Dyehouse Rd. Oaken —2B 116
Dyer La. Hal —6D 112
Dyers Ct. Leeds —1F 85
Dyer St. Leeds —5K 85 (6G 5)
Dyke Clo. Mir —7J 135
Dymond Gro. Liv —5J 135
Dymond Rd. Liv —5K 135
Dymond Vw. Liv —5J 135
Dyson Ho. Leeds —2B 84
**Dyson Lane. —6E 140**
Dyson La. Sower B —6E 140
*Dyson Pl. Hal —5J 131*
*(off Ashgrove Av.)*
Dyson Rd. Hal —7D 112
Dyson St. B'frd —6K 79 (3B 6)
(BD1)
Dyson St. B'frd —1G 79
(BD9)
Dyson St. Brigh —5G 133

**E**aglesfield Dri. B'frd —1F 115
Eagle St. Haw —5F 57
Eagle St. Kei —4K 39
Ealand Av. Bat —1E 136
Ealand Cres. Bat —1E 136
Ealand Rd. Bat —7D 118
(in two parts)
Ealing Ct. Bat —2E 136
**Earlsheaton. —7K 137**
Earlsmere Dri. Morl —2K 119
Earl St. Haw —6E 56
Earl St. Kei —3K 39
Earlswood Av. Leeds —2B 68
Earlswood Chase. Pud —7C 82
Earlswood Cres. Kip —4K 107
Earlswood Mead. Pud —7B 82
Earl Ter. Hal —5E 112
Easby Av. Bat —4D 136
Easby Clo. I'ly —5K 11
Easby Dri. I'ly —5K 11
Easby Rd. B'frd —1K 97 (7B 6)
Easdale Clo. Leeds —7H 69
Easdale Cres. Leeds —7J 69
Easdale Mt. Leeds —1H 87
Easdale Rd. Leeds —1H 87
**East Ardsley. —1G 139**
East Av. Kei —3A 40
(in two parts)
E. Bath St. Bat —3H 137
E. Beck Ct. Askw —4B 14
**East Bierley. —7H 99**
East Bolton. Hal —7C 94
**Eastborough. —7H 137**
Eastborough Cres. Dew —7H 137
Eastbourne Rd. B'frd —7H 61
**East Bowling. —4C 98**
**Eastbrook. —7B 80 (5G 7)**
Eastbrook Well. B'frd —6B 80 (4F 7)
**Eastburn. —4B 20**
Eastbury Av. B'frd —5D 96
E. Busk La. Otley —2A 28
East Byland. Hal —1C 112
**East Carlton. —7B 28**
E. Causeway. Leeds —6D 48
E. Causeway Clo. Leeds —6D 48
E. Causeway Cres. Leeds —7D 48
E. Causeway Va. Leeds —7E 48
E. Chevin Rd. Otley —4K 27
E. Church St. Hal —1H 131
East Clo. Hud —7H 145
*East Ct. Far —2B 82*
*(off Ebenezer St.)*
East Cft. Wyke —5K 115
Eastdean Bank. Leeds —6J 69
Eastdean Dri. Leeds —6J 69
Eastdean Gdns. Leeds —6K 69
Eastdean Ga. Leeds —7K 69
Eastdean Grange. Leeds —7K 69
Eastdean Gro. Leeds —6K 69
Eastdean Ri. Leeds —6K 69
Eastdean Rd. Leeds —6J 69
East Dene. Sils —7G 9
East Down. C'frd —7G 127
East Dri. Gar —2B 108
Easterly Av. Leeds —1C 86
Easterly Clo. Leeds —2D 86
Easterly Cres. Leeds —1C 86
Easterly Cross. Leeds —1D 86
Easterly Gth. Leeds —1D 86
Easterly Gro. Leeds —1C 86
Easterly Mt. Leeds —1D 86
Easterly Rd. Leeds —1C 86
Easterly Sq. Leeds —1D 86
Easterly Vw. Leeds —1D 86
Eastfield Cres. W'ford —1K 123
Eastfield Dri. W'ford —1K 123
Eastfield Gdns. B'frd —3G 99
Eastfield La. Bur W —2C 26
Eastfield La. C'frd —7E 126
E. Field St. Leeds —6A 86 (7K 5)
**East Garforth. —5B 90**
Eastgate. B'hpe —7H 29
Eastgate. Ell —2K 143
Eastgate. Leeds —5J 85 (6F 5)
E. Grange Clo. Leeds —5A 104
E. Grange Dri. Leeds —5A 104
E. Grange Gth. Leeds —5A 104
E. Grange Ri. Leeds —5A 104
E. Grange Rd. Leeds —5A 104
E. Grange Sq. Leeds —5A 104
E. Grange Vw. Leeds —5A 104
Easthorpe Ct. B'frd —1F 81
**East Keswick. —5A 34**
E. King St. Leeds —6A 86
Eastland Wlk. Leeds —4J 83
Eastleigh. Ting —7G 121
Eastleigh Ct. Ting —7G 121
Eastleigh Dri. Ting —7F 121
Eastleigh Gro. B'frd —3J 97
**East Moor. —7E 48**
E. Moor Av. Leeds —3B 68
E. Moor Clo. Leeds —3B 68
E. Moor Cres. Leeds —2B 68
E. Moor Dri. Leeds —3C 68
Eastmoor Ho. B'frd —4H 99
E. Moor La. Leeds —7D 48
E. Moor Rd. Leeds —2B 68
**East Morton. —2H 41**
East Mt. Brigh —5G 133
E. Mount Pl. Brigh —5G 133
East Pde. Bail —7K 43
East Pde. B'frd —6B 80 (4G 7)
East Pde. I'ly —5C 12
East Pde. Kei —4A 40
East Pde. Leeds —5H 85 (6D 4)
East Pde. Men —6C 26
East Pde. Sower B —4B 130
East Pde. Steet —5F 21
E. Park Dri. Leeds —6B 86
E. Park Gro. Leeds —6C 86
E. Park Mt. Leeds —6C 86
E. Park Pde. Leeds —6C 86
E. Park Pl. Leeds —6C 86
E. Park Rd. Hal —6E 112
E. Park Rd. Leeds —6B 86
E. Park St. Leeds —6C 86
E. Park St. Morl —4K 119
E. Park Ter. Leeds —6C 86
E. Park Vw. Leeds —6C 86
East Riddlesden Hall. —2D 40
E. Ridge Vw. Gar —4C 90
**East Rigton. —6C 34**
East Rd. Low M —1A 116
*East Royd. Hal —6C 114*
*(off Groveville)*
East Royd. Oakw —2F 57
E. Side Ct. Pud —1F 101
E. Squire La. B'frd —4J 79
East St. Bat —3G 137
East St. Brigh —7G 133
East St. Hal —1G 133
East St. Hud —7B 144
East St. Leeds —6K 85 (7G 5)
(in three parts)
East St. Sower B —6G 129
East Ter. Cro R —4G 57
East Vw. C'frd —7A 126
East Vw. Cleck —2C 134
East Vw. Gild —2G 119
East Vw. Kip —4B 108
*East Vw. Leeds —3A 88*
*(off Swillington La.)*
East Vw. Light —1G 133
East Vw. M'fld —1H 109
East Vw. Pud —1C 100
East Vw. Sils —1G 21
East Vw. T'tn —5G 77
East Vw. W'ford —2A 124
East Vw. Yead —5A 46
*E. View Cotts. Lowt —5D 82*
*(off Lane End)*
E. View Rd. Yead —5A 46
*E. View Ter. Otley —3K 27*
*(off Carlton St.)*
E. View Ter. Wyke —3A 116
**Eastwood. —3B 40**
Eastwood Av. Hal —7C 94
Eastwood Av. Sower B —5H 129
Eastwood Clo. Hal —7C 94
Eastwood Cres. Bgly —4B 60
Eastwood Cres. Leeds —1B 88
Eastwood Dri. Leeds —7B 70
Eastwood Gdns. Leeds —1A 88
Eastwood Gth. Leeds —1B 88
Eastwood Gro. Gar —1A 108
Eastwood Gro. Hal —7C 94
Eastwood La. Leeds —1B 88
Eastwood Nook. Leeds —1B 88
*Eastwood's Farm. Hal —7C 94*
*(off Causeway Foot)*
Eastwood St. B'frd —1B 98 (7G 7)
Eastwood St. Brigh —5H 133
Eastwood St. Hal —5E 112
Easy Rd. Leeds —7B 86
Eaton Hill. Leeds —1J 65
Eaton M. Leeds —2J 121
Eaton Rd. I'ly —6A 12
Eaton Sq. Leeds —3J 121
Eaton St. Kei —7J 39
Ebberston Gro. Leeds —2F 85
Ebberston Pl. Leeds —2F 85
Ebberston Ter. Leeds —2F 85
Ebenezer Pl. B'frd —2H 97
Ebenezer St. B'frd —7B 80 (5F 7)
Ebenezer St. Fars —2B 82
Ebenezer St. Rob H —4D 122
Ebor La. Haw —4E 56
Ebor Mt. Kip —4A 108
Ebor Mt. Leeds —3F 85
Ebor Pl. Leeds —3F 85
Ebor St. Leeds —3F 85
*Ebor Ter. Leeds —4A 104*
*(off Woodhouse Hill Rd.)*
Ebor Way. Weth —5G 17
(nr. Linton La.)
Ebor Way. Weth & B Spa —6B 18
(nr. Watersole La.)
*Ebridge Ct. Bgly —1A 60*
*(off Edward St.)*
Ebury Clo. Bat —2H 137
Ebury St. Bat —2H 137
Ecclesburn Av. Leeds —6C 86
Ecclesburn Rd. Leeds —6C 86
Ecclesburn St. Leeds —6C 86
Ecclesburn Ter. Leeds —6C 86
Eccles Ct. B'frd —1D 80
**Eccleshill. —7D 62**
Eccles Parlour. Sower B —2C 140
**Eccup. —2F 49**
Eccup La. Leeds —5D 48
Eccup Moor Rd. Leeds —3E 48
Echo St. Liv —6H 135
Edale Gro. Q'bry —6G 95
Edale Way. Leeds —1K 65
Eddercliff Cres. Liv —2J 135
Edderthorpe. B'frd —6J 7
Edderthorpe St. B'frd —7C 80
Eddison Clo. Leeds —6D 48
Eddison St. Fars —3B 82
Eddison Wlk. Leeds —6D 48
Eden Clo. Wyke —4K 115
Eden Cres. Leeds —1B 84
Edendale. C'frd —7F 127
Eden Dri. Leeds —2B 84
Eden Gdns. Leeds —2B 84
Eden Gro. Leeds —2B 84
Eden Mt. Leeds —2B 84
Eden Rd. Leeds —1B 84
Edensor Rd. Kei —4J 39
Eden Wlk. Leeds —2B 84
Eden Way. Leeds —2B 84
Ederoyd Av. S'ley —4K 81
Ederoyd Cres. S'ley —4J 81
Ederoyd Dri. S'ley —4K 81
Ederoyd Gro. S'ley —4K 81
Ederoyd Mt. S'ley —4K 81
Ederoyd Ri. S'ley —4J 81
Edgar St. Cytn —2D 96
Edgbaston Clo. Leeds —5G 49
Edgbaston Wlk. Leeds —5G 49
Edgebank Av. B'frd —1F 115
Edge Bottom. Denh —4B 76
Edge End Gdns. B'frd —7E 96
Edge End Rd. B'frd —6E 96
Edgehill Clo. Q'bry —5K 95
Edgeholme La. Hal —1K 129
Edgemoor Clo. Hal —4F 131
Edgerton Ho. Hud —7D 144
Edgerton Rd. Leeds —4B 66
Edgware Av. Leeds —3B 86
Edgware Gro. Leeds —3B 86 (1K 5)
Edgware Mt. Leeds —3B 86 (1K 5)
Edgware Pl. Leeds —3B 86 (1K 5)
Edgware Rd. Leeds —3B 86
Edgware St. Leeds —3B 86 (1K 5)
Edgware Ter. Leeds —3B 86
Edgware Vw. Leeds —3B 86 (1K 5)
Edinburgh Av. Leeds —5A 84
Edinburgh Gro. Leeds —5A 84
Edinburgh Pl. Gar —6B 90
Edinburgh Pl. Leeds —5A 84
Edinburgh Rd. Leeds —5A 84
Edinburgh Ter. Leeds —5A 84
Edlington Clo. B'frd —3G 99
Edmonton Pl. Leeds —6K 67
Edmund St. B'frd —7K 79 (6C 6)
Edrich Clo. Low M —1A 116
Edroyd Pl. Fars —2B 82
Edroyd St. Fars —2B 82
Education Rd. Leeds —2J 85
Edward Clo. S'wram —4A 132
Edwards Rd. Hal —3C 130
Edward St. Bgly —1A 60
Edward St. B'frd —5G 99
(nr. Tong St.)
Edward St. B'frd —7B 80 (6F 7)
(nr. Wakefield Rd.)
Edward St. Brigh —5G 133
Edward St. Clif —6J 133
Edward St. Leeds —5J 85 (5F 5)
Edward St. Lit T —3J 135
Edward St. Liv —4J 135
Edward St. Shipl —3F 61
Edward St. Sower B —4K 129
Edward Turner Clo. Low M —1J 115
Edwin Rd. Leeds —3E 84
Eel Holme Vw. St. Kei —1K 39
Eel Mires Gth. Weth —3K 17
Effingham Rd. H'den —3E 58
Egerton Gro. All —4A 78
Egerton St. Sower B —4K 129
*Egerton Ter. Rawd —1B 64*
*(off Town St.)*
Eggleston Dri. B'frd —4H 99
Egglestone Sq. B Spa —3C 36
Eggleston St. Leeds —7D 64
*Egham Grn. B'frd —5D 62*
*(off Ley Fleaks Rd.)*
Egremont Cres. B'frd —1F 115
Egremont St. Sower B —5J 129
*Egremont Ter. Sower B —5J 129*
*(off Egremont St.)*
**Egypt. —5G 77**
Egypt Rd. T'tn —5G 77
Eighth Av. Leeds —7D 84
Eighth Av. Liv —3D 134
Eighth Av. Rothw —7J 105
**Eightlands. —7G 137**
Eightlands Av. Leeds —3H 83
Eightlands La. Leeds —3H 83
Eightlands Rd. Dew —7G 137
Ekota Pl. Leeds —1B 86
Elam Wood Rd. Riddl —6A 22
(in two parts)
*Eland Ho. Ell —2K 143*
*(off Southgate)*
Elbow La. B'frd —3D 80
Elbow La. Hal —6G 111
*Elder Bank. Cull —6B 58*
*(off Keighley Rd.)*
Elder Clo. Bat —5D 118
Elder Cft. Leeds —4G 83
Elder Gth. Gar —7B 90
Elder Mt. Leeds —4G 83
Elder Pl. Leeds —4G 83
Elder Ri. Rothw —1C 124
Elder Rd. Leeds —4G 83
Elder St. B'frd —5G 63
Elder St. Kei —1J 39
Elder St. Leeds —4G 83
Eldon Mt. Guis —2G 45
Eldon Pl. B'frd —5K 79 (2C 6)
Eldon Pl. Cut H —2F 99
Eldon St. Hal —7G 113
Eldon St. Heck —4B 136
Eldon Ter. B'frd —5K 79 (2C 6)
Eldon Ter. Leeds —3H 85 (1C 4)
Eldroth Mt. Hal —3E 130
Eldroth Rd. Hal —3E 130
**Eldwick. —7C 42**
**Eldwick Beck. —5C 42**
Eleanor Dri. C'ley —5H 63
Eleanor St. Brigh —7G 133
Eleventh Av. Liv —3E 134
Elford Gro. Leeds —2B 86
Elford Pl. E. Leeds —2B 86
Elford Pl. W. Leeds —2B 86
Elford Rd. Leeds —2B 86
Elia St. Kei —3B 40
*Elim Wlk. Dew —7G 137*
*(off Willan's Rd.)*
Eliot Gro. Guis —3H 45
Eli St. B'frd —3B 98
Elizabeth Av. Wyke —3K 115
Elizabeth Clo. Wyke —3K 115
Elizabeth Ct. Coll —2F 35
Elizabeth Cres. Wyke —3K 115
Elizabeth Dri. C'frd —6J 127
Elizabeth Dri. Wyke —3K 115
Elizabeth Gro. Morl —2C 120
*Elizabeth Ho. Hal —4C 112*
*(off Furness Pl.)*
Elizabeth Pl. Leeds —7J 69
Elizabeth St. Bgly —1A 60
Elizabeth St. B'frd —1A 98 (7D 6)
Elizabeth St. Ell —3K 143
Elizabeth St. G'lnd —2H 143
Elizabeth St. Leeds —2E 84
Elizabeth St. Liv —4G 135
Elizabeth St. Oakw —2F 57
Elizabeth St. Wyke —3J 115
**Elland. —3K 143**
Elland Bri. Ell —2K 143
Elland Hall Farm Cvn. Pk. Ell —2J 143
Elland La. Ell —2A 144
(in two parts)
**Elland Lower Edge. —2D 144**
Elland Riorges Link. Lfds B —2A 144
Elland Road. —3E 102
Elland Rd. Brigh —6G 133
Elland Rd. Ell —7A 132
Elland Rd. Leeds —4D 102
(nr. Beeston Ring Rd.)
Elland Rd. Leeds —2F 103
(nr. Tilbury Rd.)
Elland Rd. Morl —7B 102
Elland Rd. Sower B —5G 141
Elland Rd. Ind. Pk. Leeds —3D 102
Elland St. C'frd —6F 126
Elland Ter. Leeds —1H 103
**Elland Upper Edge. —3C 144**
Elland Way. Leeds —4D 102
Elland Wood Bottom. G'lnd —7H 131
Ellar Carr Rd. B'frd —2E 62
Ellar Carr Rd. Cull —5A 58
Ellar Gdns. Men —4C 26
Ella St. Kei —3B 40
Ellen Holme Rd. Hal —2F 129
Ellen Royd La. L'ft —7E 110
(in two parts)
Ellen Royd St. Hal —7G 113
Ellen St. Bgly —1A 60
Ellenthorpe Rd. Bail —2E 60
Ellerby La. Leeds —7A 86
Ellerby Rd. Leeds —6A 86
Eller Ct. Leeds —6E 68
Ellercroft Av. B'frd —7G 79
Ellercroft Rd. B'frd —7G 79

Ellercroft Ter.—Farnham Clo.


Ellercroft Ter. B'frd —7G 79
Ellerker La. T'ner —6F 53
Ellerker Rd. T'ner —5E 52
Ellers Gro. Leeds —1B 86
Ellers Rd. Leeds —1B 86
Ellers Rd. Sut Cr —7A 20
Ellerton St. B'frd —6E 80
Ellicott Ct. Men —6C 26
Ellinthorpe St. B'frd —1D 98
Elliot Ct. Q'bry —5H 95
Elliott St. Shipl —4G 61
Elliott St. Sils —1F 21
Ellis Ct. Nor G —5F 115
Ellis Fold. Leeds —6B 84
Ellis La. Gar —3H 89
Ellison Fold. Bail —7J 43
Ellison St. Hal —6E 112
Ellis St. B'frd —3K 97
Ellis Ter. Leeds —6D 66
Ellistones Gdns. G'lnd —2E 142
Ellistones La. G'lnd —3E 142
Ellistones Pl. G'lnd —3E 142
Ellton Gro. B'frd —5G 97
Ellwood Clo. Mean —5F 67
Elm Av. Kip —3K 107
Elm Av. Sower B —3K 129
Elm Ct. B'shaw —3K 117
Elm Cres. E Mor —3H 41
Elm Cft. Leeds —4A 70
Elmet Dri. Bar E —5J 71
Elmete Av. Leeds —5E 68
Elmete Av. Scholes —6D 70
Elmete Clo. Leeds —6F 69
Elmete Ct. Leeds —6E 68
Elmete Cft. Scholes —6D 70
Elmete Dri. Leeds —5F 69
Elmete Grange. Men —6C 26
Elmete Gro. Leeds —5E 68
Elmete Hill. Leeds —6F 69
Elmete La. Leeds —5F 69
Elmete Mt. Leeds —6F 69
Elmete Rd. C'frd —6K 127
Elmete Wlk. Leeds —6E 68
Elmete Way. Leeds —6F 69
Elmet Rd. Bar E —6J 71
Elmet Towers. Leeds —1A 88
Elmfield. Bail —7K 43
Elmfield. Oult —2B 124
Elmfield Bus. Pk. Gar —5A 90
Elmfield Ct. Morl —4B 120
Elmfield Dri. B'frd —6J 97
Elmfield Gro. Leeds —7D 84
Elmfield Pl. Leeds —7D 84
Elmfield Rd. Cro H —3A 20
Elmfield Rd. Leeds —7D 84
Elmfield Rd. Morl —5B 120
Elmfield Ter. Hal —3F 131
Elmfield Way. Leeds —4H 83
Elm Gdns. Hal —3G 131
Elm Gro. Bur W —2B 26
Elm Gro. E Mor —3H 41
Elm Gro. Gom —7J 117
Elm Gro. Hal —1D 114
Elm Gro. Heck —3A 136
Elm Gro. Kei —7J 39
Elm Gro. Shipl —5A 62
Elm Gro. Sils —1F 21
Elm Ho. Leeds —7G 87
Elmhurst Clo. Leeds —7C 50
Elmhurst Gdns. Leeds —7C 50
Elm Pl. Sower B —3K 129
Elm Rd. Dew —7D 136
Elm Rd. Shipl —5K 61
Elmroyd. Rothw —3H 123
Elmsall St. B'frd —5K 79 (1C 6)
Elmsley St. Steet —5E 20
Elms, The. Guis —2G 45
Elms, The. Leeds —6K 67
Elm St. Holy G —5E 142
Elm St. Leeds —1H 85
Elm St. Oxe —3E 74
Elm Ter. Brigh —3H 133
Elm Ter. Otley —2A 28
Elmton Clo. Leeds —7K 103
Elm Tree Av. B'frd —6J 97
Elm Tree Clo. B'frd —6K 97
Elm Tree Clo. Kei —5B 40
Elm Tree Clo. Leeds —7C 88
Elm Tree Clo. Liv —6A 136
Elm Tree Clo. Pud —7C 82
Elm Tree Gdns. B'frd —5J 97
Elmtree La. Leeds —2K 103
Elm Vw. Steet —4D 20
Elm Wlk., The. Leeds —1K 105
Elm Way. Birs —5E 118
Elmwood Av. Bar E —5H 71
Elmwood Chase. Bar E —5H 71
Elmwood Ct. Bar E —5H 71
Elmwood Dri. Brigh —5F 133
Elmwood Dri. Kei —7H 39
Elmwood Gro. Bat —5H 137
Elmwood La. Bar E —5H 71
Elmwood La. Leeds —4J 85 (3F 5)
Elmwood Rd. Kei —1H 57
Elmwood Rd. Leeds —4J 85 (3E 4)
Elm Wood St. Brigh —4H 133
Elmwood St. Hal —3E 130
Elmwood Ter. Dew —7G 137
Elmwood Ter. Kei —1H 57
Elphanborough Clo. H Bri —7A 110
Elsdon Gro. B'frd —1A 98 (7D 6)
Elsham Ter. Leeds —3C 84
Elsie St. Cro R —4H 57
Elsie St. Kei —1K 39
Elsinore Av. Ell —3J 143
Elsinore Ct. Ell —3J 143
Elsworth Av. B'frd —4F 81
Elsworth Ho. Kirks —2K 83
Elsworth St. B'frd —1C 98
Elsworth St. Leeds —6D 84
Eltham Av. Leeds —2H 85
Eltham Clo. Leeds —2H 85
Eltham Ct. Leeds —2H 85
Eltham Dri. Leeds —2H 85
Eltham Gdns. Leeds —2H 85
Eltham Gro. B'frd —6G 97
Eltham Ri. Leeds —2H 85
Elvaston Rd. Morl —4A 120
Elvey Clo. B'frd —1F 81
Elwell Clo. Hal —7D 96
Elwell St. Thpe —6A 122
Elwyn Gro. B'frd —3A 98
Elwyn Rd. B'frd —3B 98
Ely St. G'lnd —3H 143
Ely St. Leeds —5C 84
Embleton Rd. Meth —6G 125
Emerald St. Bat —2F 137
Emerald St. Kei —7J 39
Emerson Av. B'frd —2D 78
Emily Ct. B'frd —3H 97
(off Oakwell Clo.)
Emily St. Kei —3A 40
Emmanuel Trad. Est. Leeds —7F 85
(off Springwell Rd.)
Emmeline Clo. B'frd —4D 62
Emmet Clo. B'shaw —2K 117
Emmfield Dri. B'frd —1G 79
Emm La. B'frd —2G 79
Emmott Dri. Rawd —1B 64
Emmott Farm Fold. Haw —6E 56
Emmott Vw. Leeds —1B 64
Empire Arc. Leeds —6F 5
Empire Av. Leeds —5J 85
Empsall Row. Brigh —5H 133
(off Camm St.)
Emscote Av. Hal —3E 130
Emscote Gdns. Hal —3E 130
Emscote Gro. Hal —3E 130
Emscote Pl. Hal —3E 130
Emscote St. S. Hal —3E 130
Emsley Clo. B'frd —6D 98
Emville Av. Leeds —6E 50
Enderley Rd. T'tn —7H 77
Endor Cres. Bur W —3B 26
Endor Gro. Bur W —3B 26
Endsleigh Pl. Cytn —2B 96
Enfield. Yead —5K 45
Enfield Av. Leeds —3A 86 (2J 5)
Enfield Clo. Bat —2D 136
Enfield Dri. Bat —2D 136
Enfield Dri. B'frd —5G 97
Enfield Pde. B'frd —5G 97
Enfield Rd. Bail —2J 61
Enfield Side Rd. Stanb —7A 56
Enfield St. Kei —4K 39
Enfield St. Leeds —3K 85 (1H 5)
Enfield Ter. Leeds —3A 86 (1J 5)
Enfield Wlk. B'frd —5G 97
Englefield Cres. B'frd —4G 99
Ennerdale Av. Dew —6J 137
Ennerdale Clo. Weth —3G 17
Ennerdale Cres. Dew —6J 137
Ennerdale Dri. B'frd —2D 80
Ennerdale Rd. B'frd —2C 80
Ennerdale Rd. Dew —6J 137
Ennerdale Rd. Leeds —4H 101
Ennerdale Way. Leeds —3H 101
Enterprise 5 La. Ends. B'frd —6D 62
Enterprise Pk. Ind. Est. Leeds —5F 103
Enterprise Way. B'frd —6D 62
Enterprise Way. C'frd —7C 126
Enterprise Way. Leeds —5B 104
Envoy St. Leeds —2J 103
Epsom Rd. Kip —4K 107
Epworth Pl. Leeds —2A 104
Epworth Pl. Oakw —1D 56
Equity Chambers. B'frd —3E 6
Eric St. Kei —3A 40
Eric St. Leeds —7G 65
Erivan Pk. Weth —3A 18
Ernest St. Dew —7H 137
Erringden Rd. H Bri —6A 110
Escroft Clo. Wyke —6K 115
Eshald La. W'ford —2B 124
Eshald Mans. Rothw —1B 124
Eshald Pl. W'ford —1B 124
Eshalt Pl. Dew —7G 137
(off Bradford Rd.)
**Esholt. —6E 44**
Esholt Av. Guis —4F 45
Esholt La. Bail —7B 44
Eshton Av. Oaken —2B 116
Esk Av. C'frd —7H 127
Eskdale Av. Hal —2B 114
Eskdale Clo. Dew —5J 137
Eskdale Clo. Guis —3G 45
Eskdale Cft. Guis —3G 45
Eskdale Gro. Gar —7A 90
Eskdale Ho. Sower B —5K 129
(off Quarry Hill)
Eskdale Ri. All —5B 78
Esk Gdns. Weth —1J 17
Eskine Pde. B'frd —1F 115
Esmond St. B'frd —3F 97
Esmond St. Leeds —6C 84
Esmond Ter. Leeds —6C 84
Essex St. B'frd —7C 80 (6H 7)
Essex St. Hal —2D 130
Estcourt Av. Leeds —7C 66
Estcourt Gro. B'frd —1G 97
Estcourt Rd. B'frd —1G 97
Estcourt Ter. Leeds —7C 66
Esthwaite Gdns. Leeds —7G 87
Ethel St. Kei —2K 39
Etna St. B'frd —3F 97
Eton St. Hal —1D 130
Eureka. (Museum for Children, The) —2H 131
Eurocam Technology Pk. B'frd —4A 98
Euroway Trad. Est. Euro I —1C 116
Euston Gro. Leeds —2F 103
Euston Mt. Leeds —2F 103
Euston Ter. Leeds —2F 103
Evanston Av. Leeds —4C 84
Evans Towers. B'frd —7D 6
Evelyn Av. B'frd —5G 81
Evelyn Pl. Leeds —7C 84
Evens Ter. B'frd —6A 98
Everall Ga. Gar —6B 90
Everall Pas. Kip —5B 108
Everest Av. Shipl —5A 62
Everleigh St. Leeds —5C 86
Eversley Dri. B'frd —2G 99
Eversley Mt. Hal —2C 130
(off Bk. Eversley Mt.)
Eversley Pl. Hal —2C 130
Eversley Vw. S'cft —4A 52
Everson All. Leeds —5J 87
Evesham Gro. B'frd —5D 62
Ewart Pl. B'frd —3G 97
Ewart St. B'frd —3G 97
Ewart St. Q'bry —5J 95
**Ewood. —6B 110**
Ewood Dri. H Bri —6B 110
Ewood Hall Av. H Bri —6B 110
Excell Gdns. Leeds —3H 101
Excell Ter. B'frd —4H 99
Excelsior Clo. Ripp —6E 140
Exchange St. Cleck —6F 117
Exchange St. G'lnd —3H 143
Exe St. B'frd —3J 97
Exeter Dri. Leeds —7K 103
Exeter St. Hal —5H 131
Exeter St. Sower B —4A 130
Exhibition Rd. Shipl —4F 61
**Exley. —7H 131**
Exley Av. Kei —7J 39
Exley Bank. Hal —6H 131
Exley Bank Top. Hal —7H 131
Exley Cres. Kei —6J 39
Exley Dri. Kei —6J 39
Exley Gdns. Hal —7H 131
Exley Gro. Kei —6J 39
**Exley Head. —6H 39**
Exley Head Vw. Kei —3G 39
Exley La. Hal & Ell —7H 131
Exley Mt. B'frd —7F 79
Exley Mt. Kei —6J 39
Exley Rd. Kei —6J 39
Exley St. Kei —5J 39
Exley Way. Kei —7J 39
Exmoor St. Hal —2D 130
Exmouth Pl. B'frd —4B 80
Exton Pl. Leeds —6G 87
Eyres Av. Leeds —5C 84
Eyres Gro. Leeds —5C 84
(off Eyres Ter.)
Eyres Mill Side. Leeds —5B 84
Eyres St. Leeds —5C 84
(off Eyres Ter.)
Eyres Ter. Leeds —5C 84
Eyre St. Bat —4H 137
Eyrie App. Morl —4C 120

Factory La. B'frd —4D 98
Factory St. B'frd —4D 98
**Fagley. —3F 81**
Fagley Cres. B'frd —3E 80
Fagley Cft. B'frd —3F 81
Fagley Dri. B'frd —3E 80
Fagley La. B'frd —1F 81
Fagley Pl. B'frd —4E 80
Fagley Rd. B'frd —4E 80
Fagley Ter. B'frd —4E 80
Fair Bank. Shipl —6J 61
Fairbank Rd. B'frd —4G 79
Fairbank Ter. B'frd —4G 79
Fairburn Dri. Gar —6A 90
Fairburn Gdns. B'frd —1E 80
Fairburn Ho. H'fth —5F 65
(off Regent Cres.)
Fairburn Ings Centre. —3J 127
Fairburn St. C'frd —7C 126
Fairclough Gro. Hal —4D 112
Fairfax Av. B'frd —5E 98
Fairfax Av. Dlgtn —1E 118
Fairfax Av. Men —5C 26
Fairfax Clo. Leeds —2K 87
Fairfax Cres. B'frd —5E 98
Fairfax Cres. Hal —3A 132
Fairfax Gdns. Men —5B 26
Fairfax Gro. Yead —4H 45
Fairfax Ho. B'frd —3G 7
Fairfax Rd. Bgly —6K 41
Fairfax Rd. Cull —5B 58
Fairfax Rd. Leeds —3G 103
Fairfax Rd. Men —5B 26
Fairfax St. B'frd —1B 98 (7G 7)
Fairfax St. Haw —5F 57
Fairfax St. Otley —3K 27
Fairfax St. Sils —1F 21
Fairfax Vw. E Bier —7H 99
Fairfax Vw. H'fth —7F 47
Fairfield. Denh —5B 76
Fairfield. H'fth —3G 65
Fairfield Av. Heck —3C 136
Fairfield Av. Leeds —3E 82
Fairfield Av. Pud —5C 82
Fairfield Av. Ting —1D 138
Fairfield Clo. C'frd —6K 127
Fairfield Clo. Leeds —3F 83
Fairfield Clo. Rothw —3D 122
Fairfield Ct. Bail —7A 44
Fairfield Ct. Gar —6H 89
Fairfield Ct. Leeds —6A 50
Fairfield Ct. Liv —4H 135
Fairfield Cres. Dew —7E 136
Fairfield Cres. Leeds —3E 82
Fairfield Dri. Bail —7A 44
Fairfield Dri. Heck —3C 136
Fairfield Dri. Rothw —3D 122
Fairfield Gdns. Rothw —3D 122
Fairfield Gro. Leeds —3F 83
Fairfield Gro. Rothw —3D 122
Fairfield Hill. Leeds —3F 83
Fairfield La. Rothw —3D 122
Fairfield M. Dew —7E 136
Fairfield Mt. Leeds —3F 83
Fairfield Pde. Heck —3C 136
Fairfield Rd. B'frd —4H 79
Fairfield Rd. Heck —3C 136
Fairfield Rd. Leeds —3E 82
Fairfield Rd. Wyke —4K 115
Fairfield Sq. Leeds —3F 83
Fairfield St. B'frd —5F 99
Fairfield St. Leeds —3E 82
Fairfield Ter. Cleck —1G 135
Fairfield Ter. Leeds —3F 83
Fairford Av. Leeds —3J 103
Fairford Ter. Leeds —3J 103
Fairhaven Grn. B'frd —5E 62
Fair Isle Ct. Kei —4A 40
(off Alice St.)
Fairleigh Cres. Ting —7F 121
Fairleigh Rd. Ting —7F 121
Fairless Av. Hal —1G 133
Fairmoor Way. Heck —3C 136
Fairmount. B'frd —3J 79
Fairmount Pk. Shipl —5E 60
Fairmount Ter. Kei —5D 40
Fair Rd. B'frd —5H 97
Fair Vw. Leeds —5D 102
Fair Vw. Liv —3H 135
Fairview Av. Bat —2D 136
Fairview Clo. Hal —6F 113
Fairview Ct. Bail —3H 61
Fairview Cres. Bat —2E 136
Fairview Rd. Bat —2E 136
Fairview Ter. Hal —6E 112
Fairway. B'frd —5F 97
(BD7)
Fairway. B'frd —3J 63
(BD10)
Fairway. Guis —2D 44
Fairway. Shipl —5F 61
Fairway Av. B'frd —5F 97
Fairway Clo. B'frd —5F 97
Fairway Clo. Guis —3E 44
Fairway Cres. Haw —6F 57
Fairway Dri. B'frd —4F 97
Fairway Gro. B'frd —4F 97
Fairway Ind. Pk. Bat —5D 118
Fairways, The. B'frd —7E 60
Fairways, The. Low U —7J 21
Fairway, The. Hal —7D 94
Fairway, The. Hud —5G 145
Fairway, The. Leeds —5H 49
Fairway, The. S'ley —4K 81
Fairway Wlk. B'frd —4F 97
**Fairweather Green. —5D 78**
Fairweather M. B'frd —6E 78
Fairwood Gro. B'frd —2G 81
Fairy Dell. Bgly —5A 60
Falcon Cliffe. Steet —5F 21
Falcon Clo. Otley —3J 27
Falcon M. B'frd —5C 78
Falcon M. Morl —4C 120
Falcon Rd. Bgly —6K 41
Falcon Sq. Hal —5H 131
Falcon St. B'frd —1H 97
Falcon St. Hal —5H 131
Falkland Ct. Bgly —1A 60
Falkland Ct. Leeds —3J 67
Falkland Cres. Leeds —3J 67
Falkland Gdns. Leeds —3K 67
Falkland Gro. Leeds —3J 67
Falkland Mt. Leeds —3J 67
Falkland Ri. Leeds —3J 67
Falkland Rd. B'frd —1G 81
Falkland Rd. Leeds —3J 67
Fall Brow Clo. Cytn —3A 96
Fall La. E Ard —7K 121
Fall La. Hal —2H 113
Fall La. Harts —6F 135
Fall La. Norl —5B 130
Fallowfield Clo. B'frd —6E 98
Fallowfield Dri. B'frd —5E 98
Fallowfield Gdns. B'frd —5E 98
Fallow La. Oakw —5C 38
Fall Rd. Mir —7G 135
Fall Spring Gdns. Holy G —6D 142
Fall Spring Grn. Slnd —6D 142
Fallswood Gro. Leeds —1H 83
**Fall, The. —1K 139**
Fallwood St. Haw —6F 57
Falmouth Av. B'frd —4B 80 (1G 7)
Falsgrave Av. B'frd —3F 81
Faltis Sq. B'frd —6E 62
Fancett Mt. Bgly —7A 42
Fancett Vw. Wilsd —7G 59
Fanny St. Kei —5K 39
Fanny St. Shipl —3F 61
Farah Ct. Leeds —2G 83
Farcliffe Pl. B'frd —4H 79
Farcliffe Rd. B'frd —4H 79
Farcliffe Ter. B'frd —4H 79
Far Comn. Rd. Mir —7G 135
Far Cft. Ter. Leeds —7D 84
Far Crook. Thack —3B 62
Fardene St. Sils —7F 9
Fardew Ct. Bgly —7K 41
Farfield Av. Bat —2D 136
Farfield Av. B'frd —7E 96
Farfield Av. Fars —2A 82
Farfield Cres. B'frd —7F 97
Farfield Dri. Fars —3A 82
Farfield Gro. B'frd —7F 97
Farfield Gro. Fars —2A 82
Farfield Ri. Fars —2A 82
Farfield Rd. Bail —2K 61
Farfield Rd. B'frd —7G 97
Farfield Rd. Shipl —5F 61
Farfield St. B'frd —3G 79
Farfield St. Cleck —6F 117
Farfield Ter. B'frd —3G 79
**Far Headingley. —5E 66**
Far La. Hal —5C 110
Farlea Dri. B'frd —2E 80
Farleton Dri. B'frd —3F 81
Farm Ct. Leeds —3K 87
Far Mead Cft. Bur W —7A 14
Farm Hill Ct. B'frd —7D 62
Farm Hill Cres. Leeds —7G 67
Farm Hill M. Morl —1J 119
Farm Hill N. Leeds —6G 67
Farm Hill Ri. Leeds —7G 67
Farm Hill Rd. B'frd —6D 62
Farm Hill Rd. Morl —1K 119
Farm Hill S. Leeds —7G 67
Farm Hill Way. Leeds —7G 67
Farm Mt. Leeds —3A 88
Far Moss. Leeds —6G 49
Farm Pond Dri. Hov E —3E 132
Farm Rd. Leeds —3K 87
Farmstead Rd. B'frd —6E 62
Farndale App. Leeds —7A 70
Farndale Clo. Leeds —7A 70
Farndale Clo. Weth —3F 17
Farndale Ct. Gar —1K 107
Farndale Ct. Leeds —7A 70
Farndale Gdns. Leeds —6A 70
Farndale Gth. Leeds —6A 70
Farndale Pl. Leeds —6A 70
Farndale Rd. Bail —2G 61
Farndale Rd. Wilsd —1G 77
Farndale Sq. Leeds —7A 70
Farndale Ter. Leeds —7A 70
Farndale Vw. Leeds —6A 70
(off Farndale Gdns.)
Farnham Clo. Bail —7K 43
Farnham Clo. Leeds —3K 69


A-Z Leeds & Bradford 165

# Farnham Cft.—Foster Av.



Farnham Cft. Leeds —3K 69
Farnham Rd. B'frd —1H 97
**Farnhill. —1A 20**
Farnley Clo. Men —6D 26
Farnley Cres. Leeds —7J 83
Farnley Cres. Oakw —1D 56
Farnley La. Otley —1J 27
Farnley Pk. F'ley —1D 28
Farnley Rd. Men —6C 26
Farnley Vw. Dlgtn —2E 118
Far Peat La. Oxe —6D 74
Farrar Cft. Leeds —7A 48
Farrar Gro. Leeds —7A 48
Farrar Height La. Sower B —5D 140
Farrar La. Leeds —7K 47
(in two parts)
Farrar Mill La. Hal —4H 131
Farra St. Oxe —3E 74
Far Reef Clo. H'fth —2G 65
Farrer La. Oult —2A 124
Farriers Cft. B'frd —1B 80
Farringdon Clo. B'frd —2F 99
Farringdon Dri. B'frd —3G 99
Farringdon Gro. B'frd —7G 97
Farringdon Sq. B'frd —2G 99
Farrow Bank. Leeds —6J 83
Farrow Grn. Leeds —6K 83
Farrow Hill. Leeds —6K 83
Farrow Rd. Leeds —6J 83
Farrow Va. Leeds —6J 83
Farr Royd. Bur W —7A 14
Farside Grn. B'frd —3J 97
**Farsley. —2B 82**
**Farsley Beck Bottom. —2C 82**
**Fartown. —7G 145**
Fartown. Pud —7B 82
Fartown Clo. Pud —1C 100
Fartown Grn. Rd. Hud —7H 145
Far Vw. Hal —1C 112
Farway. B'frd —2G 99
Far Well. Rawd —1B 64
Far Well Fold. Rawd —1B 64
Far Well Rd. Rawd —1B 64
*Fascination Pl. Q'bry —4G 95*
*(off Mill La.)*
Faulkland Ho. B'frd —1A 6
Faversham Wlk. B'frd —2G 99
Fawcett Av. Leeds —1B 102
Fawcett Bank. Leeds —1A 102
Fawcett Clo. Leeds —1A 102
Fawcett Dri. Leeds —1A 102
Fawcett Gdns. Leeds —1A 102
Fawcett La. Leeds —1A 102
Fawcett Pl. B'frd —6E 98
Fawcett Pl. Leeds —1A 102
Fawcett Rd. Leeds —1A 102
*Fawcett Va. Leeds —1A 102*
*(off Fawcett Bank)*
*Fawcett Vw. Leeds —1A 102*
*(off Fawcett Dri.)*
Fawcett Way. Leeds —1A 102
Fawkes Dri. Otley —4F 27
Faxfleet St. B'frd —5K 97
Faye Gdns. B'frd —5F 99
Fearnley Clo. Leeds —6D 84
Fearnley Pl. Leeds —6D 84
Fearnsides St. B'frd —5H 79
Fearnsides Ter. B'frd —5H 79
**Fearn's Island. —7A 86**
**Fearnville. —1F 87**
Fearnville Av. Leeds —1F 87
Fearnville Clo. Leeds —7F 69
Fearnville Dri. B'frd —1F 99
Fearnville Dri. Leeds —1F 87
Fearnville Gro. Leeds —7F 69
Fearnville Mt. Leeds —7F 69
Fearnville Pl. Leeds —7G 69
Fearnville Rd. Leeds —1F 87
Fearnville Ter. Leeds —7G 69
Fearnville Vw. Leeds —1F 87
Feast Fld. H'fth —3F 65
Featherbank Av. H'fth —5F 65
Featherbank Gro. H'fth —4F 65
Featherbank La. H'fth —4F 65
Featherbank Mt. H'fth —4F 65
Featherbank Ter. H'fth —5F 65
Featherbank Wlk. H'fth —5F 65
Featherbed Clo. G'Ind —3H 143
Featherbed La. G'Ind —3H 143
Feather Rd. B'frd —6D 80 (3K 7)
Feather St. Kei —5B 40
Federation St. B'frd —4B 98
Felbrigg Av. Kei —5H 39
Felcourt Dri. B'frd —4G 99
Fell Cres. Kei —6H 39
Fell Greave Cres. Hud —5J 145
Fell Greave Rd. Hud —4H 145
Fell Gro. Hud —5J 145
Fell Gro. Kei —5H 39
Fell La. Kei —6G 39
Fellside Clo. W Bowl —4B 98
Fellwood Av. Haw —4G 57
Fellwood Clo. Haw —4G 57
Felnex Clo. Leeds —1E 104
Felnex Cres. Leeds —1E 104
Felnex Rd. Leeds —1D 104
Felnex Sq. Leeds —1D 104
Felnex Way. Leeds —1E 104
Fenby Av. B'frd —2D 98
(in two parts)
Fenby Clo. B'frd —3E 98
Fenby Gdns. B'frd —3E 98
Fenby Gro. B'frd —3E 98
Fencote Cres. B'frd —2F 81
*Fencote Ho. B'frd —6E 62*
*(off Rowantree Dri.)*
Fender Rd. B'frd —5F 97
Fenned Rd. Bail —7A 44
Fenton Av. W'ford —7K 105
Fenton Clo. W'ford —7K 105
Fenton Fold. Oaken —3B 116
Fenton Rd. Hal —3D 130
Fenton Rd. Stan —7H 123
Fentonsgate. Loft —6E 122
Fenton St. Bur W —1B 26
Fenton St. Leeds —4H 85 (3D 4)
Fenton St. Ting —6F 121
Fenwick Dri. B'frd —7F 97
*Fenwick Ho. B'frd —5B 98*
*(off Parkway)*
Ferguson St. Hal —2G 131
Fern Bank. Otley —2K 27
Fernbank Av. Bgly —1B 60
Fernbank Av. Leeds —2D 82
Fernbank Av. Oakw —7H 39
Fernbank Clo. Leeds —2D 82
Fernbank Dri. Bail —3G 61
Fernbank Dri. Bgly —1A 60
Fernbank Dri. Leeds —2D 82
Fernbank Gdns. Leeds —2D 82
Fernbank Pl. Leeds —2D 82
Fernbank Rd. B'frd —4D 80
Fernbank Rd. Leeds —2D 82
Fernbank St. Bgly —1A 60
Fernbank Ter. Bgly —1A 60
*Fern Bank Ter. Yead —4J 45*
*(off Park Av.)*
Fernbank Wlk. Leeds —2D 82
Fern Chase. Leeds —4J 51
**Ferncliffe. —1B 60**
Ferncliffe Ct. Shipl —4F 61
Ferncliffe Dri. Bail —1H 61
Ferncliffe Dri. Kei —1H 39
Ferncliffe Rd. Bgly —1K 59
Ferncliffe Rd. Leeds —3G 83
Ferncliffe Rd. Shipl —4F 61
Ferncliffe Ter. Leeds —3F 83
Fern Clo. Bat —3K 137
Fern Ct. Kei —1J 39
Fern Cft. Leeds —4J 51
Fern Cft. Liv —4E 134
Ferndale. Cytn —3A 96
Ferndale Av. Cytn —3A 96
Ferndale Ct. I'ly —6A 12
Ferndale Gro. B'frd —1J 79
Ferndene. Bgly —1B 60
Ferndene Av. Birs —4D 118
Ferndown Grn. B'frd —3K 97
Fernfield Ter. Hal —5G 113
Fern Gdns. I'ly —6A 12
Fernhill. Bgly —6A 42
Fern Hill Av. Shipl —5F 61
Fern Hill Gro. Shipl —5F 61
Fern Hill Mt. Shipl —5F 61
Fern Hill Rd. Shipl —5F 61
Ferniehurst. Bail —3J 61
*Fern Lea. Q'bry —5K 95*
*(off Scarlet Heights)*
Fernlea. Rothw —1H 123
Fernlea Clo. Heck —5C 136
Fern Lea Flats. Lind —7A 144
Fern Lea Rd. Hud —7A 144
Fern Lea St. Sower B —3K 129
Fern Lea Vw. S'ley —3C 82
Fernley Gdns. Wyke —3J 115
*Fern Pl. Shipl —4F 61*
*(off George St.)*
Fern St. B'frd —3F 99
Fern St. Hal —5F 113
(in two parts)
Fern St. Kei —3A 40
Fern Ter. Far —3C 82
Fern Way. Leeds —4J 51
Fernwood. Leeds —3C 68
Fernwood Ct. Leeds —3C 68
Ferrand Av. B'frd —6E 98
Ferrand La. Bgly —1K 59
Ferrand La. Gom —6J 117
Ferrand Rd. Shipl —4F 61
Ferrands Clo. H'den —3F 59
Ferrands Pk. Way. H'den —3F 59
Ferrand St. Bgly —1A 60
Ferriby Clo. B'frd —2F 81
Ferriby Towers. Leeds —3K 5
Ferrybridge Rd. C'frd —7E 126
Festival Av. Shipl —7K 61
Feversham St. B'frd —7C 80 (5H 7)
Fewston Av. Leeds —7B 86
Fewston Ct. Leeds —7B 86
Fiddle La. Ripp —5H 141
Fidler Clo. Gar —6J 89
Fidler La. Gar —6J 89
Field Clo. Heck —2B 136
Fieldedge La. Riddl —1E 40
Field End. Leeds —6J 87
Fld. End Clo. Leeds —6J 87
Fld. End Ct. Leeds —6J 87
Fld. End Cres. Leeds —6J 87
Fld. End Gdns. Leeds —6J 87
Fld. End Gth. Leeds —6J 87
Fld. End Gro. Leeds —6J 87
(nr. Fld. End Gdns.)
Fld. End Gro. Leeds —5K 87
(nr. Selby Rd.)
Fld. End Mt. Leeds —6J 87
Fld. End Rd. Leeds —6J 87
Fieldens Pl. Bat —2E 136
Fieldgate Rd. B'frd —5F 63
Fieldhead Ct. B Spa —3C 36
Fieldhead Cres. Birs —4C 118
Fieldhead Dri. Bar E —5K 71
Fieldhead Dri. Guis —3E 44
Fieldhead Gdns. Dew —5B 138
Fieldhead Gro. Guis —3E 44
Fld. Head La. Birs —5C 118
Fld. Head La. Dlgtn —3C 118
Fld. Head La. Hal —7B 94
Fld. Head La. Oxe —7C 56
Fieldhead Paddock. B Spa —2C 36
Fieldhead Rd. Guis —3E 44
Fieldhead St. Field B —7H 79
Fieldhead Way. Heck —3A 136
Fieldhouse Clo. Leeds —2J 67
Fld. House Clo. Weth —4G 17
*Fieldhouse Cotts. Hal —3E 130*
*(off Carlton Ho. Ter.)*
Fieldhouse Dri. Leeds —2J 67
Fieldhouse Gro. Fars —3A 82
Fieldhouse Lawn. Leeds —2J 67
Fieldhouse St. B'frd —6F 81
Fieldhouse Wlk. Leeds —2J 67
(in two parts)
Field Hurst. Schol —1B 134
Fieldhurst Ct. Bier —6E 98
Fielding Ga. Leeds —5D 84
Fielding Ga. M. Leeds —5D 84
**Field Lane. —1F 145**
Field La. Aber —5E 72
Field La. Bat —4G 137
Field La. Brigh —1F 145
Field Side. Pel —7D 112
Fields Rd. Low M —2A 116
Fields, The. Loft —6F 123
Field St. B'frd —6B 80 (4F 7)
Field Ter. Leeds —5J 87
(nr. Cross St.)
Field Ter. Leeds —4K 87
(nr. Hermon Rd.)
Fld. Top Rd. Brigh —1F 145
Field Vw. Hal —2C 112
Fieldway. Cytn —1B 96
Fieldway. I'ly —4E 12
Fieldway Av. Leeds —1E 82
Fieldway Chase. Oult —2B 124
Fieldway Clo. Leeds —1E 82
Fieldway Ri. Leeds —1E 82
Fife St. Haw —5F 57
Fifth Av. B'frd —4E 80
Fifth Av. Rothw —7J 105
Fifth Av. E. Liv —3D 134
Fifth Av. W. Liv —4D 134
Fifth St. Low M —1A 116
Filey St. B'frd —7B 80
Filley Royd. Cleck —2F 135
Fillingfir Dri. Leeds —4K 65
Fillingfir Rd. Leeds —4K 65
Fillingfir Wlk. Leeds —4K 65
Finchley St. B'frd —3K 97
Finchley Way. Morl —4A 120
Finch St. B'frd —2K 97
Findon Ter. B'frd —1G 81
Fine Gth. Clo. B'ham —7D 36
Fink Hill. H'fth —4E 64
Finkil St. Brigh —3E 132
Finkle La. Gild —1G 119
Finkle St. Sower B —4F 129
Finsbury Dri. B'frd —7B 62
Finsbury Rd. Leeds —4H 85 (3C 4)
Fir Bank. Dew —7E 136
Firbank Grn. B'frd —2F 81
Firbank Gro. Leeds —7G 87
Firbeck. H'den —4F 59
Firbeck Rd. B'ham —7D 36
Firethorn Clo. B'frd —5G 79
First Av. Bard —5C 34
First Av. B'frd —4E 80
First Av. Hal —4F 131
First Av. Kei —5K 39
First Av. Leeds —6D 84
First Av. Liv —3E 134
First Av. Rawd —6A 46
First Av. Rothw —7H 105
First Av. S'ley —4C 82
First Av. Weth —4K 17
Firs, The. S'cft —4A 52
Fir St. Haw —6E 56
Fir St. Kei —7K 39
Fir St. Wilsd —1G 77
First St. Low M —1A 116
Firth Av. Brigh —5G 133
Firth Av. Leeds —4G 103
Firth Carr. Shipl —7H 61
Firthcliffe Dri. Liv —3K 135
Firthcliffe Gro. Liv —3K 135
Firthcliffe La. Liv —3K 135
Firthcliffe Mt. Liv —2K 135
Firthcliffe Pde. Liv —3K 135
Firthcliffe Pl. Liv —3A 136
Firthcliffe Rd. Liv —3K 135
Firthcliffe Ter. Liv —3K 135
Firthcliffe Vw. Liv —3K 135
Firthcliffe Wlk. Liv —3K 135
Firthfields. Gar —6A 90
Firth Gro. Leeds —4G 103
Firth Ho. La. Bklnd —7A 142
Firth Ho. La. Brigh —2H 145
Firth La. Wilsd —7G 59
Firth Mt. Leeds —4G 103
Firth Rd. B'frd —2G 79
Firth Rd. Leeds —4G 103
*Firths Ter. Hal —5D 112*
*(off Ramsden St.)*
Firth St. Brigh —7G 133
Firth St. Leeds —4K 85 (3H 5)
Firth St. T'tn —7H 77
Firth Ter. Leeds —4A 86 (3J 5)
Firth Vw. Leeds —4G 103
Fir Tree App. Leeds —7H 49
Firtree Av. Gar —7B 90
Fir Tree Clo. Leeds —7J 49
Fir Tree Gdns. B'frd —6F 63
Fir Tree Gdns. Leeds —7H 49
Fir Tree Grn. Leeds —7J 49
Fir Tree Gro. Leeds —1J 67
Fir Tree La. Leeds —1K 67
Fir Tree Ri. Leeds —1J 67
Fir Tree Va. Leeds —1J 67
Fishbeck La. Sils —5J 9
(in two parts)
Fish St. Leeds —5J 85 (6F 5)
Fitts La. E Kes —2J 33
Fitts La. Hare —2C 32
Fitzgerald St. B'frd —1K 97 (7D 6)
Fitzroy Dri. Leeds —6C 68
Fitzroy Rd. B'frd —6D 80
Fitzwilliam St. B'frd —1B 98 (7F 7)
**Five Lane Ends. —6D 62**
Five Oaks. Bail —2G 61
Five Rise Locks. —7K 41
**Fixby. —4G 145**
Fixby Av. Hal —3C 130
Fixby Fold. Ell —3C 144
Fixby Pk. Dri. Hud —7F 145
Fixby Rd. Hud —4F 145
**Flappit Springs. —6J 57**
Flasby St. Kei —3A 40
Flat Nook. Bgly —1B 60
Flats La. Bar E —6H 71
**Flatts, The. —7F 137**
Flawith Dri. B'frd —3F 81
Flaxen Ct. B'frd —5K 97
Flaxman Rd. B'frd —1E 80
Flax Mdw. Lind —7A 144
Flax Mill Rd. Leeds —3A 104
Flax Pl. Leeds —6A 86 (7J 5)
Flaxton Clo. Leeds —3H 103
Flaxton Gdns. Leeds —3H 103
Flaxton Grn. B'frd —3F 81
Flaxton Pl. B'frd —7H 79
Flaxton St. Leeds —3H 103
Flaxton Vw. Leeds —3H 103
Fledborough Rd. Weth —4G 17
Fleece St. B'frd —7F 97
Fleece St. Kei —4A 40
Fleet La. Q'bry —4H 95
Fleet La. W'ford & Oult —2B 124
(in two parts)
Fleet Thro' Rd. H'fth —6F 65
Fleming St. Bat —3G 137
Fletcher Av. Sils —7G 9
Fletcher Cres. Brigh —3E 144
Fletcher La. B'frd —1K 79
Fletcher Rd. B'frd —5H 97
Fletton Ter. B'frd —3D 80
Flexbury Av. Morl —4A 120
Flight Ho. Rd. Sower B —5B 140
Flintmill La. B Spa —6C 18
Flinton Gro. B'frd —2F 81
Flockton Av. B'frd —2C 98
Flockton Clo. B'frd —2C 98
Flockton Cres. B'frd —2C 98
Flockton Dri. B'frd —2C 98
Flockton Gro. B'frd —2C 98
Flockton Rd. B'frd —2C 98
Flockton Ter. B'frd —2C 98
Floral Av. Leeds —6J 67
Floreat Clo. Bat —7E 118
Florence Av. Leeds —3C 86
Florence Av. Wilsd —6F 59
Florence Gro. Leeds —3C 86
Florence Mt. Leeds —3C 86
Florence Pl. Leeds —3C 86
Florence St. B'frd —7E 80
Florence St. C'frd —7D 126
Florence St. Hal —1E 130
Florence St. Leeds —3C 86
Florence St. Wort —7C 84
*Florence Ter. Morl —4B 120*
*(off South Pde.)*
Florida Rd. All —1A 78
Florist St. Kei —2C 40
*Flower Acre. Ell —3K 143*
*(off Elizabeth St.)*
Flower Bank. B'frd —1B 80
Flower Bank. Sower B —5H 129
Flower Clo. Yead —4J 45
Flower Ct. H'fth —5F 65
Flower Cft. Kei —6H 39
Flowerfields. Hip —6E 114
Flower Gth. B'frd —6F 63
*Flower Gth. H'fth —5F 65*
*(off Regent Rd.)*
Flower Haven. B'frd —1D 78
Flower Hill. B'frd —1F 79
Flower Mt. Bail —7K 43
*Flower Mt. Yead —4A 46*
*(off Alexandra Ter.)*
*Flowers Mt. Bail —7K 43*
*(off Ashfield Dri.)*
Floyd St. B'frd —3H 97
**Flush. —4A 136**
Flush. Liv —4A 136
Foldings Av. Schol —7B 116
Foldings Clo. Schol —7A 116
Foldings Ct. Schol —7A 116
Foldings Gro. Schol —7A 116
Foldings Pde. Schol —7A 116
Foldings Rd. Schol —7A 116
Fold, The. Haw —5D 56
Fold, The. Leeds —1C 88
Folkestone St. B'frd —6D 80
(in two parts)
Folkton Holme. B'frd —3F 81
Follingworth Rd. Bat —3K 137
Folly Hall Av. B'frd —6H 97
Folly Hall Clo. B'frd —6H 97
Folly Hall Gdns., The, B'frd —6H 97
Folly Hall La. Cra V —6A 128
Folly Hall Mt. Ting —7E 120
Folly Hall Rd. B'frd —6H 97
Folly Hall Rd. Ting —7E 120
Folly Hall Wlk. B'frd —6H 97
Folly La. B'ham —1D 54
Folly La. Leeds —2H 103
Folly La. Ripp —7F 141
Folly Rd. Hud —6G 145
Folly Vw. B'ham —1D 54
Folly Vw. Rd. Haw —6F 57
Fontmell Clo. B'frd —4G 99
Football. Yead —4A 46
Forber Gro. B'frd —1G 99
Forber Pl. Leeds —6G 87
*Forbes Ho. B'frd —3G 99*
*(off Stirling Cres.)*
Ford. Q'bry —6G 95
Ford Hill. Q'bry —6G 95
Ford St. Kei —2C 40
Fore La. Sower B —5J 129
Fore La. Av. Sower B —5H 129
Foreside Bottom La. Denh —2B 94
Foreside La. Denh —1K 93
Forest Av. Hal —3C 112
Forest Bank. Gild —7G 101
Forest Cres. Hal —3C 112
*Forester Ct. Denh —5B 76*
*(off Main Rd.)*
Forester Sq. Denh —5B 76
Forest Ga. Otley —3J 27
Forest Grn. Hal —4C 112
Forest Gro. Hal —4D 112
Forest Hill Rd. Holy G & Outl —7B 142
Forest Ridge. E Ard —6J 121
Forge La. Leeds —5D 84
Forge La. Liv —5K 135
(in two parts)
Forge La. Wike —2F 51
Forge Row. Leeds —3H 101
Forge Vw. Steet —5E 20
Forman's Dri. Rob H —4C 122
Formby Av. Hud —6F 145
Forrester's Ter. Holy G —6D 142
Forster Ct. B'frd —6A 80 (3F 7)
Forster Dri. Heck —5C 136
Forster Pl. Leeds —2A 102
Forster Sq. B'frd —6B 80 (4F 7)
Forster St. Leeds —1A 104
Forsythia Av. E Ard —7J 121
Fort Ann Rd. Bat —4K 137
Forth Ct. Leeds —7G 85
Fortshot La. Leeds —2C 50
Foss Av. Weth —2H 17
Fosse Way. Gar —7B 90
Foss Wlk. C'frd —7H 127
Foster Av. Sils —7F 9

Foster Av.—Ghyll, The


Foster Av. T'tn —7K 77
Foster Clo. Bur W —1B 26
Foster Clo. Morl —2A 120
Foster Cres. Morl —2A 120
Foster Gdns. Kei —4H 39
Foster Pk. Denh —4C 76
Foster Pk. Gro. Denh —4C 76
Foster Pk. Rd. Denh —4C 76
Foster Pk. Vw. Denh —4C 76
(in two parts)
Foster Rd. Kei —7K 39
Foster's Ct. Hal —1G 131
(off Union St.)
Foster Sq. Denh —5B 76
Foster St. Morl —2A 120
Foster St. Q'bry —5J 95
Foster Ter. Leeds —2H 83
Foston Clo. B'frd —3G 81
Foston La. B'frd —3F 81
Foulcauseway La. Otley —3B 28
Foulds Ter. Bgly —7A 42
Foundry App. Leeds —3D 86
Foundry Av. Leeds —2D 86
Foundry Dri. Leeds —2D 86
Foundry Hill. Bgly —1K 59
Foundry La. B'frd —2D 98
Foundry La. Leeds & Seac —2F 87
Foundry La. S'ley —3C 82
Foundry Mill Cres. Leeds —2H 87
Foundry Mill Dri. Leeds —2G 87
(in two parts)
Foundry Mill Gdns. Leeds —7G 69
Foundry Mill Mt. Leeds —2H 87
Foundry Mill St. Leeds —2H 87
Foundry Mill Ter. Leeds —2H 87
Foundry Mill Vw. Leeds —2H 87
Foundry Mill Wlk. Leeds —2H 87
Foundry Pl. Leeds —2D 86
Foundry Rd. S'ley —4C 82
Foundry St. Brigh —7J 133
Foundry St. Cleck —7G 117
Foundry St. Dew —7H 137
Foundry St. Hal —1G 131
Foundry St. Leeds —6A 86 (7J 5)
(nr. Saxton La.)
Foundry St. Leeds —7H 85
(nr. Water La.)
Foundry St. Sower B —5K 129
Foundry St. N. Hal —4D 112
Foundry Ter. Cleck —1G 135
Foundry Wlk. Leeds —2C 86
Fountain Clo. Liv —7H 135
Fountain Ct. Gild —3J 119
Fountain Dri. Liv —7H 135
Fountains Av. Bat —4D 136
Fountains Av. B Spa —3C 36
Fountain St. B'frd —6A 80 (3D 6)
Fountain St. Chur —6C 102
Fountain St. Hal —1G 131
Fountain St. Heck —3B 136
Fountain St. Leeds —5G 85 (6B 4)
Fountain St. Liv —7H 135
Fountain St. Low M —1J 115
Fountain St. Morl —5K 119
Fountain St. Q'bry —5J 95
Fountain St. Sower B —5F 141
Fountain St. T'tn —7H 77
Fountain Ter. Wyke —4K 115
Fountain Way. Shipl —5J 61
Fourlands. —4E 62
Fourlands Ct. B'frd —4E 62
Fourlands Cres. B'frd —4E 62
Fourlands Dri. B'frd —4E 62
Fourlands Gdns. B'frd —4E 62
Fourlands Gro. B'frd —4E 62
Fourlands Rd. B'frd —4E 62
Four Lane Ends. —5F 79
Fourteenth Av. Leeds —7D 84
Fourth Av. B'frd —4E 80
Fourth Av. Kei —5J 39
Fourth Av. Liv —3D 134
Fourth Av. Rothw —7J 105
Fourth Av. Weth —4K 17
Fourth St. Low M —1A 116
Fowler's Pl. S'ley —3C 82
Fowler St. B'frd —1D 98
Fox Ct. G'lnd —2H 143
Foxcroft Clo. Leeds —7B 66
Fox Cft. Clo. Q'bry —7G 95
Foxcroft Dri. Brigh —1F 145
Foxcroft Grn. Leeds —7B 66
Foxcroft Mt. Leeds —7B 66
Foxcroft Rd. Leeds —7B 66
Foxcroft Wlk. Leeds —7B 66
Foxcroft Way. Leeds —7B 66
Foxen La. Sower B —3E 140
Foxglove Av. Leeds —6E 68
Foxglove Rd. Birs —5C 118
Foxhill. Bail —1G 61
Foxhill. Weth —3J 17
Foxhill Av. Leeds —3C 66
Foxhill Av. Q'bry —5H 95
Foxhill Clo. Q'bry —5H 95
Foxhill Ct. Leeds —3C 66
Foxhill Cres. Leeds —3D 66
Foxhill Dri. Leeds —3C 66
Foxhill Dri. Q'bry —5H 95
Foxhill Grn. Leeds —3D 66
Foxhill Gro. Leeds —3D 66
Foxhill Gro. Q'bry —5H 95
Foxhills, The. Leeds —7H 47
Foxholes Cres. C'ley —6K 63
Foxholes La. C'ley —6K 63
Fox Hollies Rd. Hud —5H 145
Foxstone Ri. Bail —1A 62
Foxstones La. Ripp —7F 141
Fox St. Bat —4H 137
Fox St. Bgly —1K 59
Fox St. Cleck —1D 134
Fox Vw. Stainc —5E 136
Foxwood Av. Leeds —7G 69
Foxwood Clo. Leeds —7G 69
Foxwood Farm Way. Leeds —7G 69
Foxwood Gro. Leeds —7G 69
Foxwood Ho. B'frd —1F 99
(off Westbury St.)
Foxwood Ri. Leeds —7G 69
Foxwood Wlk. Leeds —7G 69
Foxwood Wlk. Weth —2K 17
Frances St. Brigh —5G 133
Frances St. Ell —3K 143
Frances St. Fars —3B 82
Frances St. Kei —3J 39
France St. Bat —4J 137
Francis Clo. Hal —1E 130
Francis Ct. Leeds —2K 85
(off Francis St.)
Francis Gro. Leeds —3H 103
Francis Ho. B'frd —3D 80
(off Hatfield Rd.)
Francis Sq. Cull —6B 58
(off Station Rd.)
Francis St. B'frd —1C 98 (7H 7)
Francis St. C'frd —7E 126
Francis St. Hal —1E 130
Francis St. Heck —5C 136
Francis St. Leeds —2K 85
Frank Clo. Steet —4D 20
Frankel Gdns. Brigh —5G 133
Frankland Gro. Leeds —2A 86
Frankland Pl. Leeds —2A 86 (1K 5)
Frank La. Hal —5D 110
Franklin Ho. B'frd —2G 7
Franklin St. Hal —1D 130
Frank Parkinson Ct. Guis —2G 45
(off Kelcliffe Av.)
Frank Parkinson Homes. Guis —2G 45
(off Oxford St.)
Frank Peel Clo. Heck —4B 136
Frank Pl. B'frd —2H 97
Frank St. B'frd —2H 97
Frank St. Hal —2E 130
Fraser Av. H'fth —4D 64
Fraser Rd. C'ley —6H 63
Fraser St. B'frd —5J 79 (1A 6)
Fraser St. Leeds —4B 86
Freakfield La. Brigh —6D 134
Frederick Av. Leeds —7C 86
Frederick Clo. B'frd —3B 62
Frederick St. Fars —2A 82
Frederick St. Kei —4B 40
Frederick St. Liv —5K 135
Frederick Walker Gdns. Bat —4H 137
Fred's Pl. B'frd —3E 98
Fred St. Kei —5K 39
Freely La. B'ham —1D 54
Freeman Rd. Hal —3A 132
Freemans Way. Weth —3K 17
Freemantle Pl. Leeds —6G 87
Freemont St. Leeds —3E 82
Free School La. Hal —3E 130
Freestone M. Leeds —6G 83
Fremantle Gro. B'frd —1G 99
Frensham Av. Morl —4K 119
Frensham Dri. B'frd —3D 96
Frensham Gro. B'frd —3D 96
Frensham Way. B'frd —3D 96
Freshfield Gdns. All —4B 78
Friar Ct. B'frd —6E 62
Friars Ind. Est. B'frd —5D 62
Friendly. —3J 129
Friendly Av. Sower B —3J 129
Friendly Fold. Hal —5E 112
Friendly Fold Ho. Hal —5E 112
(off Lentilfield St.)
Friendly Fold Rd. Hal —5E 112
Friendly St. Hal —5E 112
Friendly St. T'tn —7H 77
Frimley Dri. B'frd —4J 97
Frith St. Cro R —4G 57
Frizinghall. —7J 61
Frizinghall Rd. B'frd —2J 79
Frizley Gdns. B'frd —1J 79
Frodingham Vs. B'frd —3F 81
Frogmere Ter. Oaken —2B 116
Frogmore Av. Oaken —2B 116
Frontline Clo. Leeds —6C 68
Front Row. Leeds —7H 85
(in two parts)
Front St. B'ham —1C 54
Front St. Leeds —7H 85
Frost Hill. Liv —4K 135
Fruit St. Kei —3C 40
Fryston Rd. C'frd —7J 127
Fuchsia Cft. Rothw —1C 124
Fulford Av. Hud —7G 145
Fulford Wlk. B'frd —3F 81
Fulham Pl. Leeds —3H 103
Fulham Sq. Leeds —3H 103
(off Fulham St.)
Fulham St. Leeds —3H 103
Fullerton St. B'frd —7C 80 (5H 7)
Fulmar Ct. Leeds —2K 121
Fulmar M. B'frd —6C 78
Fulneck. —1C 100
Fulneck. Pud —2B 100
Fulneck Clo. Hud —6F 145
Fulton St. B'frd —6K 79 (4D 6)
Furever Feline Museum. —4J 61
Furnace Gro. B'frd —2B 116
Furnace Inn St. B'frd —1F 99
Furnace La. B'shaw —1J 117
Furnace Rd. Oaken —2B 116
(in three parts)
Furness Av. Hal —2B 112
Furness Cres. Hal —2B 112
Furness Dri. Hal —2B 112
Furness Gdns. Hal —3C 112
Furness Gro. Hal —3B 112
Furness Pl. Hal —3C 112
Fusden La. Gom —6J 117
Futures Way. B'frd —1B 98 (7F 7)
Fyfe Cres. Bail —2K 61
Fyfe Gro. Bail —2A 62
Fyfe La. Bail —1A 62

Gable End Ter. Pud —6D 82
Gables, The. Bail —1A 62
(nr. Kirklands Rd.)
Gables, The. Bail —2A 62
(off Dewhirst Rd.)
Gables, The. H'fth —2G 65
Gainest. Hal —3D 130
Gainford Dri. Gar —7K 89
Gain La. B'frd & Fag —4F 81
Gainsborough Clo. B'frd —3C 80
Gainsborough Pl. Leeds —3J 101
(off Well Holme Mead)
Gainsbro' Av. Leeds —6B 48
Gainsbro' Dri. Leeds —6B 48
Gaisby. —6K 61
Gaisby La. B'frd & Shipl —1J 79
Gaisby Mt. Shipl —7K 61
Gaisby Pl. Shipl —6K 61
Gaisby Ri. Shipl —6K 61
Gaitskell Ct. Leeds —1G 103
Gaitskell Grange. Leeds —1G 103
Gaitskell Wlk. Leeds —1G 103
Galefield Grn. B'frd —1F 115
Gale St. Cro R —4H 57
Gale St. Kei —3A 40
Gallery & Studio Theatre. —4H 85 (3D 4)
Gallogate La. Wee —1E 30
Galloway Ct. Pud —5J 81
Galloway La. Pud —4J 81
Galloway Rd. B'frd —5F 63
Galsworthy Av. B'frd —2C 78
Gamble Hill. Leeds —5H 83
Gamble Hill Chase. Leeds —5H 83
Gamble Hill Clo. Leeds —5H 83
Gamble Hill Cft. Leeds —5H 83
(off Gamble Hill Vw.)
Gamble Hill Cross. Leeds —5H 83
(off Gamble Hill Lawn)
Gamble Hill Dri. Leeds —5H 83
Gamble Hill Fold. Leeds —5H 83
(off Gamble Hill Dri.)
Gamble Hill Grange. Leeds —5H 83
(off Gamble Hill Lawn)
Gamble Hill Grn. Leeds —5H 83
Gamble Hill Lawn. Leeds —5H 83
Gamble Hill Path. Leeds —5H 83
(off Gamble Hill Grn.)
Gamble Hill Pl. Leeds —5H 83
Gamble Hill Ri. Leeds —5H 83
Gamble Hill Rd. Leeds —5H 83
Gamble Hill Va. Leeds —5H 83
Gamble Hill Vw. Leeds —5H 83
Gamble Hill Wlk. Leeds —5H 83
(off Gamble Hill Ri.)
Gamble La. Leeds —7G 83
Gambles Hill. Fars —2B 82
Gamel Vw. Steet —4D 20
Game Scar La. Oakw —5D 38
Ganners Clo. Leeds —1G 83
Ganners Gth. Leeds —1H 83
Ganners Grn. Leeds —1G 83
Ganners Gro. Leeds —1H 83
Ganners Hill. Leeds —1H 83
Ganners La. Leeds —1G 83
Ganners Mt. Leeds —1G 83
Ganners Ri. Leeds —1H 83
Ganners Rd. Leeds —1G 83
Ganners Wlk. Leeds —1G 83
Ganners Way. Leeds —1G 83
Gannerthorpe Clo. Wyke —4J 115
Ganny Rd. Brigh —6H 133
Ganton Clo. Leeds —1H 85
Ganton Way. Hud —6F 145
Gaol La. Hal —1G 131
(in two parts)
Garden Av. Liv —2J 135
Garden Clo. Liv —3J 135
Garden Clo. Wyke —3J 115
Gardeners Ct. Leeds —2K 103
Gardener's Sq. Hal —7C 114
Garden Fld. Wyke —4J 115
Garden Fold. Hip —7C 114
Garden Ho. Clo. Meth —4H 125
Garden Ho. La. Ting —7G 121
Garden La. B'frd —2F 79
Garden Pde. Liv —2J 135
Garden Pl. Dew —7D 136
Garden Pl. Sut Cr —5A 20
(off Sutton La.)
Garden Rd. Brigh —4F 133
Gardens, The. Bgly —1D 60
Gardens, The. Fars —2A 82
Gardens, The. Hal —3G 131
Gardens, The. Midd —3J 121
Gardens, The. Morl —5K 119
Garden St. B'frd —1F 79
Garden St. Cro R —4H 57
Garden St. Heck —5B 136
Garden St. N. Hal —7H 113
Garden Ter. B'frd —2G 79
Garden Vw. Bgly —1C 60
Garden Vw. Liv —2J 135
Garden Vw. Ct. Leeds —3D 68
Garden Village. M'fld —7G 91
Garden Wlk. Liv —3J 135
Gardiner Row. B'frd —4D 98
Garfield Av. B'frd —3H 79
Garfield Ho. B'frd —2K 97
(off Hutson St.)
Garfield St. All —4A 78
Garfield St. Hal —6E 112
Garfit Hill. Gom & Birs —7B 118
Garforth. —6J 89
Garforth Av. Steet —4E 20
Garforth Bridge. —1G 107
Garforth Rd. Kei —3C 40
Garforth St. All —4B 78
Gargrave App. Leeds —5B 86
Gargrave Clo. Brigh —1D 144
Gargrave Ct. Leeds —4B 86
Gargrave Ho. B'frd —2H 7
Gargrave Pl. Leeds —4B 86
Garibaldi St. B'frd —6G 81
(in two parts)
Garland Dri. Leeds —6B 88
Garlick St. Brigh —3E 144
Garmont M. Leeds —6K 67
Garmont Rd. Leeds —6K 67
Garnet Av. Leeds —3J 103
Garnet Cres. Leeds —3J 103
Garnet Gro. Leeds —3J 103
Garnet Pde. Leeds —3J 103
Garnet Pl. Leeds —3J 103
Garnet Rd. Leeds —4J 103
Garnet Ter. Leeds —3J 103
Garnett St. B'frd —6C 80 (4H 7)
Garnett St. Dew —5D 136
Garnett St. Otley —2J 27
Garnet Vw. Leeds —3J 103
Garrowby Ho. B'frd —4D 62
(off Thorp Gth.)
Garsdale Av. B'frd —5E 62
Garsdale Cres. Bail —7A 44
Garsdale Fold. Coll —1E 34
Garside Ct. Leeds —2H 85
Garth Av. Coll —2F 35
Garth Av. Leeds —3H 67
Gth. Barn Clo. B'frd —2G 79
Garth Dri. Leeds —3H 67
Garth End. Coll —2F 35
Garth Fold. B'frd —4D 62
Garth Gro. Men —6C 26
Gth. Land Way. B'frd —3E 98
Garth Rd. Leeds —3H 67
Garth St. Kei —4K 39
Garth, The. Coll —2F 35
Garth, The. Gar —6A 90
Garth, The. Leeds —6A 86 (7J 5)
Garthwaite Mt. All —3B 78
Garth Wlk. Leeds —3H 67
Garton Av. Leeds —6C 86
Garton Dri. B'frd —7F 63
Garton Gro. Leeds —6C 86
Garton Rd. Leeds —6C 86
Garton Ter. Leeds —6C 86
Garton Vw. Leeds —6C 86
Garvey Vw. B'frd —2A 98
Garwick Ter. G'lnd —2H 143
Gascoigne Av. Bar E —6H 71
Gascoigne Ct. Bar E —6J 71
Gascoigne Rd. Bar E —6H 71
Gascoigne Rd. Wake —6A 122
Gascoigne Vw. Bar E —6H 71
Gas Ho. Yd. Oaken —2A 116
Gas Works La. Ell —2K 143
Gas Works Rd. Kei —3D 40
(in two parts)
Gas Works Rd. Sower B —4B 130
Gasworks St. Liv —4K 135
Gas Works Yd. Rothw —2H 123
(off Commercial St.)
Gatefield Mt. B'frd —1G 115
Ga. Head La. G'lnd —4D 142
Ga. House Ct. Rothw —7C 106
Gateland Dri. Leeds —7G 51
Gateland La. Leeds —1G 69
Gateon Ho. La. E Kes —6J 33
Gatesgarth Cres. Hud —7A 144
Ga. Way Dri. Yead —4J 45
Gathorne Clo. Leeds —2A 86
Gathorne St. B'frd —2H 97
Gathorne St. Brigh —5H 133
Gathorne St. Leeds —2A 86
(in two parts)
Gathorne Ter. Leeds —2A 86
Gaukroger La. Hal —3H 131
Gavin Clo. B'frd —6G 81
Gawcliffe Rd. Shipl —5J 61
Gawthorpe. —7C 138
Gawthorpe Av. Bgly —6A 42
Gawthorpe Dri. Bgly —6A 42
Gawthorpe La. Bgly —7A 42
Gawthorpe La. Oss & K'gte —7D 138
Gawthorpe St. Wilsd —6F 59
Gay La. Otley —3J 27
Gayle Clo. Wyke —5J 115
Gaynor St. B'frd —6K 79 (3B 6)
Gaythorne Rd. B'frd —3A 98
Gaythorne Rd. Fag —2E 80
Gaythorne Ter. Cytn —2C 96
Gaythorn Ter. Hal —6C 114
Geecroft La. Sick —4A 16
Geelong Clo. B'frd —2B 80
Gelderd Clo. Leeds —2D 102
Gelderd La. Leeds —2D 102
Gelderd Pl. Leeds —1E 102
Gelderd Rd. Birs —6D 118
Gelderd Rd. Gild —2G 119
Gelderd Rd. Leeds —2D 102
Gelderd Trad. Est. Leeds —1E 102
Gelder Rd. Leeds —6B 84
Genista Dri. Leeds —6K 103
George Cres. Leeds —5J 85
George La. Sower B —7D 140
George M. Weth —4J 17
George Pl. Morl —4A 120
George's Pl. B'frd —1A 98 (7D 6)
George Sq. Hal —1G 131
George's Sq. Cull —6B 58
George's Sq. Kei —5K 39
George's St. Hal —4D 112
George St. Add —1D 10
George St. Bail —3J 61
George St. Bat —4G 137
George St. B'frd —7B 80 (5G 7)
George St. Brigh —6J 133
George St. Cleck —7F 117
George St. Denh —4C 76
George St. Dew M —7D 136
George St. Ell —3K 143
George St. G'lnd —2H 143
George St. Hal —1G 131
George St. H Bri —7A 110
George St. Heck —4B 136
George St. Hip —1D 132
George St. Leeds —5J 85 (6F 5)
George St. Lind —7B 144
George St. Liv —4J 135
George St. Ras —7G 133
George St. Rawd —7K 45
George St. Shipl —4F 61
George St. Sower B —5K 129
George St. T'tn —7H 77
Geraldton Av. B'frd —2A 80
Gerard Av. Morl —3K 119
Gerard Ho. B'frd —5E 62
(off Fairhaven Grn.)
Gerard St. Hal —1F 131
Germaine Ter. T'ner —1C 70
Gernhill Av. Hud —4F 145
Ghyllbank. Sils —7G 9
Ghyll Beck Dri. Otley —4F 27
Ghyll Beck Dri. Rawd —1C 64
Ghyll Clo. Steet —5E 20
Ghyll Grange La. Sils —1A 22
Ghyll Lodge. Bgly —4A 60
Ghyll M. I'ly —6A 12
Ghyll Mt. Yead —5H 45
Ghyll Rd. Leeds —6A 66
Ghyll Rd. Yead —6J 45
Ghyll Royd. Guis —3G 45
(in two parts)
Ghyllroyd Av. B'shaw —2K 117
Ghyllroyd Dri. B'shaw —2K 117
Ghyll, The. Bgly —4A 60

Ghyll, The—Grange St.


Ghyll, The. Hud —5G 145
Ghyll Wood. I'ly —6J 11
Ghyll Wood Dri. Bgly —4A 60
Gibbet St. Hal —1B 130
Gibb La. Hal —4K 111
Gibraltar Av. Hal —2C 130
Gibraltar Island Rd. Leeds —2B 104
Gibraltar Rd. Hal —1C 130
Gibraltar Rd. Pud —6K 81
Gibson Dri. Leeds —6A 88
Gibson La. Kip —4B 108
Gibson St. B'frd —7D 80
Gilbert Chase. Leeds —2A 84
Gilbert Clo. Leeds —2B 84
Gilbert Gdns. Bklnd —3B 142
Gilbert Mt. Leeds —2B 84
Gilbert St. Fars —3B 82
**Gildersome. —7G 101**
Gildersome La. Gild & Leeds —6F 101
Gildersome Spur. Gild —2H 119
**Gildersome Street. —1F 119**
Giles Hill La. Hal —7A 96
(in two parts)
Giles St. B'frd —1K 97 (7C 6)
Giles St. Wibs —5G 97
Gill Bank Rd. I'ly —3A 12
Gill Beck Clo. Bail —7A 44
Gill Clo. Add —1B 10
Gillett Dri. Rothw —2H 123
Gillett La. Rothw —2H 123
Gilling Av. Gar —5B 90
Gillingham Grn. B'frd —3G 99
Gill La. Cowl —7C 38
Gill La. Nesf —2G 11
Gill La. T'tn —1G 95
Gill La. Yead —7G 45
Gillrene Av. Wilsd —1H 77
**Gillroyd. —3C 120**
Gillroyd Pde. Morl —4B 120
Gillroyd Pl. Morl —4B 120
Gillroyd Ri. B'frd —6H 79
Gillroyd Ter. Morl —3C 120
Gill's Ct. Hal —1G 131
Gills, The. Morl —3C 120
Gills, The. Otley —7J 15
Gillstone Dri. Haw —5F 57
Gilmour St. Hal —6E 112
Gilpin Pl. Leeds —7D 84
Gilpin St. B'frd —5D 80 (3K 7)
Gilpin St. Leeds —7D 84
Gilpin Ter. Leeds —7D 84
Gilpin Vw. Leeds —7D 84
**Gilstead. —1C 60**
Gilstead Ct. Bgly —1C 60
Gilstead Dri. Bgly —1C 60
Gilstead La. Bgly —1B 60
Gilstead Way. I'ly —4A 12
Gilynda Clo. B'frd —6E 78
Ginnel, The. Bard —1A 52
(in two parts)
Ginnel, The. Weth —4J 17
Gipsy Hill. W'ford —1K 123
Gipsy La. Leeds —6G 103
Gipsy La. W'ford —1K 123
Gipsy Mead. W'ford —1K 123
Gipsy St. B'frd —5G 81
**Gipton. —2E 86**
Gipton App. Leeds —4E 86
Gipton Av. Leeds —2A 86
Gipton Ga. E. Leeds —2E 86
Gipton Ga. W. Leeds —2D 86
Gipton Sq. Leeds —4F 87
Gipton St. Leeds —2A 86
**Gipton Wood. —7D 68**
Gipton Wood Av. Leeds —7D 68
Gipton Wood Cres. Leeds —7D 68
Gipton Wood Gro. Leeds —7D 68
Gipton Wood Pl. Leeds —7D 68
Gipton Wood Rd. Leeds —7D 68
**Girlington. —4G 79**
Girlington Rd. B'frd —4F 79
Gisburn St. Kei —3K 39
Glade, The. S'cft —4K 51
Glade, The. S'ley —3J 81
*Gladstone Ct. Dew —7E 136*
*(off School La.)*
*Gladstone Ct. S'ley —3D 82*
*(off Gladstone Ter.)*
Gladstone Cres. Rawd —6K 45
Gladstone Pl. Denh —5B 76
Gladstone Rd. Hal —1E 130
Gladstone Rd. Rawd —7K 45
*Gladstone Sq. Morl —3B 120*
*(off Middleton Rd.)*
Gladstone St. All —4B 78
Gladstone St. Bgly —2K 59
Gladstone St. B'frd —7E 80
Gladstone St. Cleck —1F 135
Gladstone St. Fars —2B 82
Gladstone St. Holy G —5E 142
Gladstone St. Kei —5K 39
Gladstone St. Q'bry —5K 95
Gladstone Ter. C'frd —7E 126
Gladstone Ter. Morl —3A 120
Gladstone Ter. S'ley —3D 82
Gladstone Vw. Hal —5J 131
Gladstone Vs. Leeds —1G 69
Gladwin St. Bat —4F 137
Glaisdale Clo. Sils —2G 21
Glaisdale Ct. All —2A 78
Glaisdale Gro. Hal —1D 132
*Glaisdale Ho. B'frd —5E 62*
*(off Garsdale Av.)*
Glamis Clo. Gar —5B 90
Glanville Ter. Rothw —2G 123
Glasshouse St. Leeds —1K 103
Glasshouse Vw. Leeds —3H 121
Glazier Rd. Q'bry —4G 95
Gleanings Av. Hal —1A 130
Gleanings Dri. Hal —1K 129
Glebe Av. Leeds —1B 84
Glebe Fld. Chase. Weth —3H 17
Glebe Fld. Clo. Weth —3H 17
Glebe Fld. Cft. Weth —3H 17
Glebe Fld. Dri. Weth —3H 17
Glebe Fld. Gth. Weth —3H 17
Glebe Fld. Holt. Weth —3H 17
Glebe Fold. Riddl —1D 40
Glebelands Clo. Gar —7K 89
Glebelands Dri. Leeds —6D 66
Glebe Mt. Pud —7C 82
Glebe Pl. Leeds —1B 84
Glebe St. C'frd —7D 126
(in two parts)
Glebe St. Pud —7C 82
Glebe Ter. Leeds —5D 66
*Gledcliffe. Hal —7H 113*
*(off Charlestown Rd.)*
Gleddings Clo. Hal —5E 130
Gledhill Rd. B'frd —7D 80 (5K 7)
*Gledhills Yd. Hal —3D 130*
*(off King Cross Rd.)*
Gledhill Ter. Dew —7D 136
**Gledhow. —5B 68**
Gledhow Av. Leeds —4B 68
Gledhow Ct. Leeds —5A 68
Gledhow Dri. Oxe —1E 74
Gledhow Grange Vw. Leeds —5B 68
Gledhow Grange Wlk. Leeds —5B 68
Gledhow La. Leeds —5K 67
Gledhow La. End. Leeds —5K 67
Gledhow Mt. Leeds —3A 86 (1K 5)
Gledhow Pk. Leeds —5A 68
Gledhow Pk. Av. Leeds —6A 68
Gledhow Pk. Cres. Leeds —6A 68
Gledhow Pk. Dri. Leeds —6K 67
Gledhow Pk. Gro. Leeds —6A 68
Gledhow Pk. Rd. Leeds —6A 68
Gledhow Pk. Vw. Leeds —6A 68
Gledhow Pl. Leeds —3A 86 (1K 5)
Gledhow Ri. Leeds —6D 68
Gledhow Rd. Leeds —3A 86 (1K 5)
Gledhow Ter. Leeds —3A 86 (1K 5)
Gledhow Towers. Leeds —5A 68
Gledhow Valley Rd. Leeds —4K 67
Gledhow Wood Av. Leeds —5B 68
Gledhow Wood Clo. Leeds —5B 68
Gledhow Wood Ct. Leeds —7C 68
Gledhow Wood Gro. Leeds —5B 68
Gledhow Wood Rd. Leeds —6B 68
Glenaire. Shipl —3A 62
Glenaire Dri. Bail —3G 61
Glen Av. Bat —2G 137
Glenbrook Dri. B'frd —6E 78
Glencoe Clo. Kip —6K 107
Glencoe Cft. Kip —6K 107
Glencoe Gdns. Kip —6K 107
Glencoe Ter. Kip —6K 107
Glencoe Ter. Liv —5K 135
Glencoe Vw. Leeds —7B 86
Glendale. Bgly —5K 59
Glendale Av. Gar —7K 89
Glendale Clo. B'frd —7G 97
Glendale Dri. B'frd —7G 97
Glendale Ho. Morl —4B 120
Glendare Av. B'frd —7F 79
Glendare Rd. B'frd —7F 79
Glendare Ter. B'frd —7F 79
Glendene. Bgly —5K 59
Glen Dene. Men —7D 26
Glendower Pk. Leeds —2D 66
Gleneagles Rd. Leeds —7H 49
Gleneagles Way. Hud —6F 145
Glenfield. Shipl —3A 62
Glenfield Av. B'frd —6K 97
Glenfield Av. Weth —5K 17
Glenfield Cvn. Pk. Leeds —2J 51
Glenfield Mt. B'frd —6K 97
Glen Gth. Kei —6B 40
Glen Gro. Morl —4B 120
Glenholme. Shipl —3A 62
Glenholme Heath. Hal —1C 130
Glenholme Rd. B'frd —4H 79
Glenholme Rd. Fars —3A 82
Glenholme Ter. Oss —7C 138
Glenholm Rd. Bail —2J 61
Glenhurst. B'frd —5F 99
Glenhurst Av. Kei —6A 40
Glenhurst Dri. Kei —6B 40
Glenhurst Gro. Kei —6B 40
Glenhurst Rd. Shipl —4E 60
Glenlea Clo. S'ley —2E 82
Glenlea Gdns. S'ley —2E 82
Glen Lee La. Kei —7B 40
Glenlee Rd. B'frd —6F 79
Glenlow Rd. Dew —5K 137
Glenlyon Av. Kei —2J 39
Glenlyon Dri. Kei —2J 39
Glenmere Mt. Yead —4B 46
Glenmore Clo. B'frd —4E 80
Glenmore Ct. B'hpe —7J 29
Glenmount. Bgly —5K 59
Glen Mt. Men —7D 26
Glen Mt. Morl —4B 120
Glen Mt. Clo. Hal —5C 112
Glen Ri. Bail —2F 61
Glen Rd. Bail —7D 42
Glen Rd. Bgly —6C 42
Glen Rd. Leeds —5C 66
Glen Rd. Morl —4B 120
Glenrose Dri. B'frd —7E 78
Glenroyd. Shipl —3A 62
Glenroyd Av. B'frd —6K 97
Glenroyd Clo. Pud —6A 82
Glensdale Gro. Leeds —6B 86
Glensdale Mt. Leeds —6B 86
Glensdale Rd. Leeds —6B 86
Glensdale St. Leeds —6B 86
Glensdale Ter. Leeds —6B 86
Glenside Av. Shipl —3A 62
Glenside Rd. Shipl —3A 62
Glenstone Gro. B'frd —6F 79
Glen Ter. Hal —3F 131
Glen Ter. Hip —1C 132
Glenthorpe Av. Leeds —5C 86
Glenthorpe Cres. Leeds —5C 86
Glenthorpe Ter. Leeds —5C 86
Glenton Sq. B'frd —3H 79
Glen Vw. Hal —3F 131
Glen Vw. H'den —3F 59
Glenview Av. B'frd —2E 78
Glenview Clo. Shipl —5C 60
Glenview Dri. Shipl —6C 60
(in two parts)
Glenview Gro. Shipl —5D 60
Glen Vw. Rd. Bgly —6C 42
Glenview Rd. Shipl —6C 60
Glenview Ter. Shipl —4F 61
Glen Way. Eld —6D 42
(nr. Glen Rd.)
Glen Way. Eld —5C 42
(nr. Otley Rd.)
Glenwood Av. Bail —2E 60
Global Av. Leeds —5E 102
Globe Ct. Liv —4K 135
Globe Fold. B'frd —5J 79 (1A 6)
Globe Rd. Leeds —6G 85
*Glossop Gro. Leeds —1H 85*
*(off Glossop Vw.)*
Glossop Mt. Leeds —1H 85
Glossop St. Leeds —1H 85
Glossop Vw. Leeds —1H 85
Gloucester Av. B'frd —4F 81
Gloucester Av. Sils —1E 20
Gloucester Rd. Bgly —2B 60
Gloucester Ter. Leeds —6E 84
Glover Ct. B'frd —2A 98
Glovershaw La. Bgly —5E 42
Glover Way. Leeds —4J 103
Glydegate. B'frd —7A 80 (5D 6)
Glyndon Ct. Brigh —1H 145
Glynn Ter. B'frd —5H 79
Gobind Marg. B'frd —6C 80
Godfrey Rd. Hal —6G 131
Godfrey St. B'frd —6D 78
Godley Branch Rd. Hal —7J 113
Godley Gdns. Hal —6K 113
Godley La. Hal —7J 113
Godley Rd. Hal —7H 113
Godwin St. B'frd —6A 80 (4D 6)
Goff Well La. Kei —1A 58
Gog Hill. Ell —2K 143
Goit Side. B'frd —6K 79
(in two parts)
Goit Stock La. H'den —4F 59
Goit Stock Ter. H'den —4F 59
Goldcrest Av. B'frd —6B 78
Golden Acre Park. —3B 48
Golden Bank. H'fth —3G 65
Golden Butts Rd. I'ly —5C 12
Golden Ter. Leeds —2A 102
Golden Vw. Dri. Kei —5D 40
Goldfields Av. G'lnd —1F 143
Goldfields Clo. G'lnd —1F 143
Goldfields Vw. G'lnd —1F 143
Goldfields Way. G'lnd —1F 143
Golf Av. Hal —1A 130
Golf Cres. Hal —1A 130
Golf La. Morl —6J 119
**Gomersal. —7A 118**
**Gomersal Hill Top. —7K 117**
Gomersal La. Cleck —1H 135
Gomersal Rd. Heck —2A 136
Gondal Ct. B'frd —3J 97
Gooder La. Brigh —7G 133
Gooder St. Brigh —6G 133
**Goodley. —2D 56**
Goodman St. Leeds —1A 104
Goodrick La. Leeds —5H 49
*Goodwin Ho. Q'bry —5J 95*
*(off Minstrel Dri.)*
Goodwin Rd. Leeds —7C 84
Goodwood. I'ly —3K 11
Goodwood Av. Kip —4K 107
**Goody Cross. —4H 107**
Goody Cross La. Swil —4F 107
Goody Cross Va. Swil —4F 107
Goose Cote La. Oakw —1G 57
**Goose Eye. —5D 38**
Goose Eye. Oakw —5D 38
Goose Eye Brow. Oakw —5D 38
Goosefield Ri. Gar —1H 107
**Goose Hill. —4D 98**
Goose Hill. Heck —4B 136
Goose La. Guis —1H 43
Goose Nest La. Norl —6K 129
Goose Pond La. Norl —7C 130
Gordale Clo. Bat —3F 137
Gordale Clo. B'frd —3H 99
Gordon Dri. Leeds —6E 66
Gordon Larkin Ct. Otley —3G 27
Gordon Pl. Leeds —6F 67
Gordon St. B'twn —5F 113
Gordon St. B'frd —1B 98 (7F 7)
Gordon St. Cytn —2B 96
Gordon St. Cro R —4G 57
Gordon St. E Ard —7A 122
Gordon St. Ell —3K 143
Gordon St. I'ly —5C 12
Gordon St. Kei —4K 39
Gordon St. Sower B —5J 129
Gordon Ter. B'frd —3D 62
Gordon Ter. Leeds —6F 67
Gordon Vw. Leeds —6F 67
Gorse Av. Bail —3E 60
Gorse Lea. Leeds —6K 103
Gosling La. Bklnd —7H 141
Gothic St. Q'bry —5J 95
Gotts Pk. Av. Leeds —4K 83
Gotts Pk. Cres. Leeds —4K 83
Gotts Pk. Vw. Leeds —3K 83
Gotts Rd. Leeds —6F 85 (7A 4)
Gotts Ter. Kei —1J 39
Gott St. Cro R —4H 57
Gough La. Sower B —2D 140
Goulbourne St. Kei —5K 39
Gower St. B'frd —2A 98
Gower St. Leeds —5K 85 (5G 5)
Goy Cres. Slnd —6D 142
Goy Fld. Lwr W —2A 102
Goy Gth. B Spa —2C 36
Goy La. Steet —5E 20
Goy Rd. Ell —3K 143
Goy Ter. Leeds —6E 66
Gracechurch St. B'frd —5K 79 (2B 6)
Grace Leather La. Bat —3J 137
Grace St. Kei —4B 40
Grace St. Leeds —5G 85 (6B 4)
Gracey La. B'frd —5F 97
Grafton Clo. Bail —7K 43
Grafton Pl. Hal —4E 112
Grafton Rd. Kei —6J 39
Grafton St. Bat —5H 137
Grafton St. B'frd —1A 98 (7D 6)
Grafton St. Kei —6K 39
Grafton St. Leeds —4J 85 (4F 5)
Grafton Vs. Leeds —1B 88
Graham Av. Leeds —2D 84
Graham Dri. C'frd —7H 127
Graham Gro. Leeds —2D 84
*Graham Ho. Leeds —2K 83*
*(off Broad La.)*
Graham Mt. Leeds —2D 84
Graham St. B'frd —3G 79
Graham St. Leeds —2D 84
Graham Ter. Leeds —2D 84
Graham Vw. Leeds —2D 84
Graham Wlk. Gild —7H 101
Grain St. B'frd —4H 97
*Grammar School Pl. Brigh —1F 145*
*(off Church St.)*
Grammar School St. B'frd —5A 80 (2D 6)
Granary Wharf. Leeds —6H 85
Granby Av. Leeds —7D 66
*Granby Clo. Leeds —1D 84*
*(off St Michael's Rd.)*
Granby Dri. Riddl —2D 40
Granby Gro. Leeds —1D 84
Granby La. Kei —2D 40
Granby Mt. Leeds —7D 66
Granby Pl. Leeds —7D 66
Granby Rd. Leeds —1D 84
Granby St. B'frd —1B 98
(in two parts)
Granby St. Leeds —7D 66
Granby St. Q'bry —5J 95
Granby Ter. Leeds —7D 66
Granby Vw. Leeds —7D 66
Grandage Ter. B'frd —5H 79
Grand Arc. Leeds —5F 5
Grandsmere Pl. Hal —4F 131
Grand Theatre. —5J 85 (5F 5)
*Grand Vw. Hal —6E 112*
*(off Ovenden Av.)*
Grand Vw. Q'bry —3G 95
*Grand Vw. Sower B —5K 129*
*(off Clyde St.)*
*Grand Vw. Sower B —2F 141*
*(off Lumb La.)*
Grange Av. All —5C 78
Grange Av. Bat —5F 137
Grange Av. B'frd —5H 81
(BD3)
Grange Av. B'frd —6J 99
(BD4)
Grange Av. Gar —6K 89
Grange Av. Hal —2D 112
Grange Av. I'ly —5D 12
Grange Av. Leeds —1A 86
Grange Av. Men —5B 26
Grange Av. Shipl —4E 60
Grange Av. Thor A —6G 19
Grange Av. Yead —5A 46
Grange Bank. She —1B 114
Grange Clo. Bard —6B 34
Grange Clo. H'fth —4D 64
Grange Clo. H'let —2K 103
Grange Clo. I'ly —5D 12
Grange Ct. Bgly —5A 60
Grange Ct. Hal —5A 132
Grange Ct. Leeds —7F 67
(nr. N. Grange Mt.)
Grange Ct. Leeds —6J 49
(nr. Primley Pk. Rd.)
Grange Ct. Scholes —6D 70
Grange Cres. Leeds —1A 86
Grange Cres. Riddl —2C 40
Grange Cres. Yead —5A 46
Grange Cft. Leeds —6J 49
Grange Dri. All —5C 78
Grange Dri. H'fth —4D 64
Grange Est. I'ly —5D 12
Grangefield Av. Bat —5F 137
Grangefield Av. Bur W —1B 26
Grangefield Ct. Gar —6K 89
Grangefield Ind. Est. S'ley —4C 82
Grangefield Rd. S'ley —3C 82
(in three parts)
Grange Fields Mt. Leeds —7B 104
Grange Fields Rd. Leeds —1B 122
Grange Fields Way. Leeds —1B 122
Grange Fold. All —5B 78
Grange Gro. B'frd —5H 81
Grange Gro. Riddl —2C 40
Grange Heights. Hal —5A 132
Grange Holt. Leeds —6J 49
Grange La. Brigh —6A 134
Grange La. Kild —1C 20
Grange La. Kip —4B 108
Grange La. Oakw —1A 56
Grange Mt. Yead —5A 46
Grange Pk. Bail —1A 62
Grange Pk. Hal —5F 131
Grange Pk. Av. Leeds —7F 69
Grange Pk. Clo. All B —2A 126
Grange Pk. Clo. Leeds —7G 69
Grange Pk. Clo. Morl —7B 102
Grange Pk. Cres. Leeds —7F 69
Grange Pk. Dri. Bgly —4A 60
Grange Pk. Dri. Morl —7B 102
Grange Pk. Gro. Leeds —7F 69
Grange Pk. M. Leeds —7F 69
Grange Pk. M. Morl —7B 102
Grange Pk. Pl. Leeds —7F 69
Grange Pk. Ri. Leeds —7F 69
Grange Pk. Rd. Bgly —4A 60
Grange Pk. Rd. Leeds —7F 69
Grange Pk. Ter. Leeds —7G 69
Grange Pk. Wlk. Leeds —7F 69
Grange Pk. Way. Morl —7B 102
Granger Ct. Hal —7C 112
Granger Gdns. Kei —5J 39
Grange Rd. All —5C 78
Grange Rd. Bat & Dew —4J 137
(in two parts)
Grange Rd. Bgly —7B 42
Grange Rd. Bur W —1B 26
Grange Rd. C'frd —6K 127
Grange Rd. Cleck —7E 116
Grange Rd. Ebrn —5C 20
Grange Rd. H'let —2K 103
Grange Rd. Kild —1A 20
Grange Rd. Riddl —2C 40
Grange Rd. Stainc —5E 136
Grange Rd. Yead —5A 46
Grange Rd., The. Leeds —3B 66
Grange St. Chur —6C 102
Grange St. Hal —6E 112
Grange St. Kei —3A 40

# Grange Ter.—Griffin Gro.



Grange Ter. All —5C 78
Grange Ter. Ebrn —5C 20
Grange Ter. Leeds —1K 85
Grange Ter. Morl —7B 102
Grange Ter. Pud —5C 82
Grange Ter. Shipl —6H 61
*Grange Ter. Yead —5A 46*
*(off Grange Rd.)*
Grange, The. Gar —6B 90
Grange, The. Hal —5F 131
Grange Vw. B'frd —5H 81
Grange Vw. Colt —7B 88
Grange Vw. Ebrn —5C 20
Grange Vw. Leeds —1A 86
Grange Vw. Otley —1H 27
Grange Vw. Pud —5C 82
Grange Vw. Weth —5J 17
Grange Vw. Gdns. Leeds —3H 69
Grange Way. All —5C 78
Grangewood Ct. Leeds —3B 66
Grangewood Gdns. Leeds —3B 66
*Grange Yd. Sower B —4A 130*
*(off Wharf St.)*
Granhamthorpe. Leeds —3G 83
Granny Av. Chur —6C 102
Granny Hall Gro. Brigh —4F 133
Granny Hall La. Brigh —4F 133
Granny Hall Pk. Brigh —4F 133
Granny Hill. Hal —3C 130
Granny La. Leeds —1A 102
Granny Pl. Chur —6C 102
Grant Av. Leeds —3A 86 (1J 5)
Grantham Pl. B'frd —1J 97 (7A 6)
Grantham Pl. Hal —5F 113
Grantham Rd. B'frd —1J 97 (7A 6)
Grantham Rd. Hal —5F 113
Grantham Ter. B'frd —1J 97 (7A 6)
Grantham Towers. Leeds —3K 5
Grantley Pl. Hud —4K 145
Granton Rd. Leeds —7K 67
Granton St. B'frd —6E 80
Grant St. B'frd —6C 80 (3J 7)
Grant St. Kei —4J 39
Grant St. Oxe —3E 74
Granville Mt. Otley —3H 27
Granville Pl. All —4B 78
Granville Pl. Otley —3H 27
Granville Rd. Leeds —4A 86 (3K 5)
Granville Rd. Shipl & B'frd —7H 61
Granville St. Cytn —1C 96
Granville St. Dew —7G 137
Granville St. Ell —3K 143
*Granville St. Kei —4K 39*
*(off Drewery Rd.)*
Granville St. Liv —5K 135
Granville St. Pud —5A 82
Granville St. S'ley —3D 82
Granville Ter. Bgly —1A 60
*Granville Ter. Guis —1H 45*
*(off Moor La.)*
Granville Ter. Otley —3H 27
Granville Ter. Shipl —7H 61
Granville Ter. Yead —4A 46
Grape St. All —4C 78
Grape St. Hal —1F 131
Grape St. Kei —3C 40
Grape St. Leeds —1K 103
Grasleigh Av. All —3A 78
Grasleigh Way. All —3K 77
Grasmere Av. Weth —4G 17
Grasmere Clo. Leeds —7D 84
Grasmere Ct. Leeds —6D 84
Grasmere Dri. Ell —2B 144
Grasmere Dri. Weth —4G 17
Grasmere Pl. Hal —3E 112
Grasmere Rd. B'frd —2C 80
Grasmere Rd. Dew —6J 137
Grasmere Rd. Leeds —7D 84
Grasmere Rd. Wyke —6A 116
Grass Rd. Riddl —7G 23
Gratrix La. Sower B —3A 130
Grattan Rd. B'frd —6K 79 (4B 6)
**Graveleythorpe. —4J 87**
Graveleythorpe Ri. Leeds —4K 87
Graveleythorpe Rd. Leeds —4K 87
Gray Av. Shipl —7K 61
Gray Ct. Leeds —5B 88
Grayrigg Clo. Leeds —6G 87
Grayshon Dri. Wibs —5J 97
Grayshon St. Dlgtn —2D 118
Grayson Crest. Leeds —2B 84
Grayson Heights. Leeds —2B 84
Gray St. Liv —4G 135
Grayswood Cres. B'frd —3F 99
Grayswood Dri. B'frd —2F 99
Gt. Albion St. Hal —1G 131
Gt. Cross St. B'frd —7B 80 (5F 7)
Gt. Edge Rd. Hal —1H 129
Gt. George St. Leeds —5H 85 (5C 4)
**Great Horton. —2G 97**
Gt. Horton Rd. B'frd —4D 96 (7A 6)
Gt. House La. Sower B —6C 140
Gt. Northern Rd. Kei —5A 40
Gt. Northern St. Morl —4A 120
Gt. North Rd. B Spa —1K 35
Gt. North Rd. M'fld —4F 91
Gt. Pasture. Bur W —7B 14
**Great Preston. —6J 107**
Gt. Russell Ct. Field B —6J 79
Gt. Russell St. B'frd —6J 79
Gt. Wilson St. Leeds —7J 85
Gt. Wood St. Bat —4G 137
Greave Clo. Hud —5H 145
Greave Ho. Dri. L'ft —1F 129
Greave Ho. Fields. L'ft —7G 111
Greave Ho. Pk. L'ft —1F 129
Greave Rd. Sower B —3A 140
Greaves Fold. Holy G —5G 143
Greaves Rd. Dew —7G 137
Greaves St. B'frd —3K 97
Greaves St. C'frd —7D 126
Greaves Yd. Pud —1C 100
Greek St. C'frd —7E 126
Greek St. Leeds —5H 85 (6D 4)
Greenacre Av. Wyke —5K 115
Green Acre Clo. Bail —1K 61
Greenacre Clo. Wyke —5K 115
Greenacre Ct. Gar —6A 90
Greenacre Dri. Wyke —5K 115
Greenacre Pk. Rawd —6K 45
Greenacre Pk. Av. Rawd —6K 45
Greenacre Pk. M. Rawd —6A 46
Greenacre Pk. Ri. Rawd —6K 45
Greenacres. Oss —7D 138
Greenacres. She —1D 114
Greenacres. Sower B —5G 141
Greenacres Av. Hal —1D 114
Greenacres Clo. Oss —7D 138
Greenacres Dri. Birs —5D 118
Greenacres Dri. Hal —1D 114
Greenacres Dri. Kei —2J 39
Greenacres Gro. Hal —1D 114
Greenacre Way. Wyke —5K 115
Greenaire Pl. B'frd —6K 79 (4C 6)
Green Av. Heck —4C 136
Green Av. Kip —3K 107
Green Av. Sils —7F 9
Greenbank. Bail —3H 61
Green Bank. Cleck —2H 135
Green Bank. Loft —6F 123
Greenbank Rd. All —5C 78
Greenbanks Av. H'fth —2G 65
Greenbanks Clo. H'fth —2G 65
Greenbanks Dri. H'fth —2F 65
**Greenbottom. —3G 45**
Green Chase. Leeds —5E 66
Greencliffe Av. Bail —1H 61
Green Clo. Bat —3J 137
Green Clo. B'frd —5E 78
Green Clo. Dew —6E 136
Green Clo. Ebrn —4B 20
Green Clo. Leeds —5F 67
Green Ct. B'frd —1F 97
Green Ct. Leeds —2K 67
Green Ct. Schol —7B 116
Green Ct. Scholes —5D 70
Green Cres. Leeds —5E 66
Greencroft Av. Hal —4B 114
Greendown Clo. I'ly —5D 12
**Green End. —2J 41**
Green End. Brigh —7G 133
Green End. Cytn —2B 96
Green End Rd. B'frd —6H 97
Green End Rd. E Mor —2J 41
Greenfell Clo. Kei —5H 39
Green Fld. Bail —2H 61
Greenfield. Haw —5E 56
Greenfield Av. Gild —7F 101
Greenfield Av. Guis —4D 44
Greenfield Av. Hal —1G 133
Greenfield Av. Kip —4A 108
Greenfield Av. Shipl —6J 61
Greenfield Clo. Kip —4A 108
Greenfield Clo. N'wram —4A 114
Greenfield Clo. Sow —7D 142
Greenfield Ct. Kei —4J 39
Greenfield Cres. Cull —6C 58
Greenfield Dri. Gild —7F 101
*Greenfield Dri. Schol —7B 116*
*(off New Rd. E.)*
Greenfield Gdns. Ebrn —5B 20
Greenfield Gth. Kip —4A 108
Greenfield La. Bier —1D 116
Greenfield La. Gt Hor —2F 97
Greenfield La. Guis —4C 44
Greenfield La. Idle —3D 62
Greenfield Pl. B'frd —4J 79
Greenfield Pl. Hal —1G 133
Greenfield Ri. Kip —4A 108
Greenfield Rd. Leeds —6A 86 (7K 5)
Greenfields. Heck —3A 136
Greenfields Way. Bur W —3B 26
Greenfield Ter. Haw —5E 56
Greenfield Ter. Meth —4J 125
Greenfield Va. Kip —4A 108
Greenfield Vw. Kip —4A 108
Greenfinch Way. All —6B 78
Greenfold La. Weth —4K 17
Greengate. Oult —1A 124
Greengate. Sils —7F 9
Greengate Rd. Kei —5A 40
**Greengates. —6F 63**
Greengates Av. Wyke —6J 115
Green Hall Pk. She —2D 114
Green Head Av. Kei —1J 39
Green Head Dri. Kei —1J 39
Greenhead La. Brigh —3E 144
Grn. Head La. Kei —1J 39
Grn. Head Rd. Kei —1J 39
Greenhead Rd. Leeds —4B 66
**Green Hill. —4E 72**
Green Hill. Warley —2K 129
Grn. Hill Chase. Leeds —7B 84
Grn. Hill Clo. Leeds —4K 83
Grn. Hill Cres. Leeds —7B 84
Grn. Hill Cft. Leeds —7B 84
Greenhill Dri. Bgly —4J 41
Grn. Hill Dri. Leeds —4J 83
Grn. Hill Gdns. Leeds —7B 84
Grn. Hill Holt. Leeds —7B 84
Greenhill La. Bgly —5K 41
Greenhill La. B'frd —6E 80
Grn. Hill La. Leeds —1A 102
Grn. Hill Mt. Leeds —4J 83
Grn. Hill Pk. Hal —6D 96
Grn. Hill Pl. Leeds —4J 83
Grn. Hill Rd. Leeds —4J 83
Greenhills. Rawd —1A 64
Greenhill St. B'frd —6E 80
Grn. Hill Way. Leeds —4J 83
Greenholme Clo. Bur W —7B 14
Greenholme Ct. B'frd —4H 99
Greenholme Trad. Est. Bur W —7B 14
Greenhouse Rd. Hud —7G 145
Greenhow Clo. Leeds —3D 84
Greenhow Gdns. Leeds —3D 84
Greenhow Pk. Bur W —1K 25
Greenhow Rd. Leeds —3D 84
Greenhow Wlk. Leeds —3D 84
Greenland Av. Q'bry —6J 95
Greenland Vs. Q'bry —6J 95
Green La. Add —1C 10
Green La. Bail —3G 61
(in two parts)
Green La. B Top —2J 131
Green La. Bees —5F 103
Green La. B Spa —3E 36
Green La. B'frd —1G 97
(BD7)
Green La. B'frd —4J 79 (1A 6)
(BD8)
Green La. Bshw —6C 94
Green La. Brigh —3E 132
Green La. Bur W —6A 14
(nr. Leather Bank)
Green La. Bur W —4H 25
(nr. Moor Rd.)
Green La. C'frd —6F 127
Green La. Clif —6A 134
Green La. Coll —2E 34
Green La. Cook —7H 47
Green La. Dew —7E 136
Green La. Ebrn —4C 20
Green La. Fag —2F 81
Green La. F'ley —1G 101
Green La. Gar —6A 90
(nr. Ninelands La.)
Green La. Gar —7B 90
(nr. Severn Dri.)
Green La. G'lnd —3G 143
Green La. Hal —3C 130
(HX2)
Green La. Hal —7D 96
(HX3)
Green La. H'fth —5F 65
Green La. Huns —5F 117
Green La. Idle —4E 62
(nr. Apperley St.)
Green La. Idle —5C 62
(nr. Highfield Rd.)
Green La. Kip —3K 107
(in two parts)
Green La. Leds —1D 126
Green La. Leeds —4K 87
Green La. Liv —5F 135
Green La. Loft —6E 122
Green La. L'ft —6F 111
Green La. Meth —6K 125
Green La. N Wort —7E 84
Green La. N'wram —2J 113
Green La. Oaken —3B 116
Green La. Oakw —2F 57
(nr. Keighley Rd.)
Green La. Oakw —7B 38
(nr. Whitehill Rd.)
Green La. Otley —1H 27
Green La. Oxe —3A 74
(nr. Bodkin La.)
Green La. Oxe —5F 75
(nr. Isle La.)
Green La. Pud —7B 82
Green La. Q'bry —1J 113
Green La. Ragg —4F 95
Green La. She —1D 114
(in two parts)
Green La. Shipl —7G 43
Green La. Sils —3C 8
Green La. Sower B —7E 128
(nr. Bowood La.)
Green La. Sower B —6D 140
(nr. Ripponden Old La.)
Green La. Sow —7D 142
Green La. T'tn —1J 95
Green La. Whinm —4J 69
Green La. Wyke —5H 115
Green La. Yead —6K 45
Greenlay Dri. K'gte —6H 139
Green Lea. Oult —1K 123
Greenlea Av. Yead —5H 45
Green Lea Clo. B Spa —3E 36
Greenlea Clo. Yead —6H 45
Greenlea Fold. Yead —6H 45
Greenlea Mt. Yead —5H 45
Greenlea Rd. Yead —5H 45
Greenley Hill. Wilsd —1F 77
Green Mdw. Wilsd —1H 77
Greenmoor Av. Leeds —6H 83
Greenmoor Av. Loft —6E 122
Greenmoor Clo. Loft —6E 122
Greenmoor Cres. Loft —6F 123
Green Mt. Bail —2G 61
Green Mt. Cut H —3F 99
*Greenmount Ct. Leeds —3H 103*
*(off Fulham St.)*
Greenmount La. Leeds —3H 103
Greenmount Pl. Leeds —3H 103
Greenmount Retail Pk. Hal —1F 131
Green Mt. Rd. T'tn —7J 77
Greenmount St. Leeds —3H 103
Greenmount Ter. Leeds —3H 103
Greenock Pl. Leeds —5A 84
Greenock Rd. Leeds —5A 84
Greenock St. Leeds —5A 84
Greenock Ter. Leeds —5A 84
Green Pk. Leeds —2A 68
Green Pk. Av. Hal —6G 131
Green Pk. Dri. Hal —6G 131
Green Pk. Ga. Hal —6G 131
Green Pk. Rd. Hal —6G 131
Green Pk. St. Hal —5G 131
Green Pl. B'frd —3D 80
Green Rd. Bail —2G 61
Green Rd. Leeds —4E 66
Green Rd. Liv —3J 135
Green Row. B'frd —6D 62
Green Row. Meth —6H 125
Green Row Fold. Meth —6H 125
Green Royd. G'lnd —3G 143
(in two parts)
Green Royd. Nor G —5G 115
Greenroyd Av. Cleck —5F 117
Greenroyd Av. Hal —5F 131
Greenroyd Clo. Hal —6F 131
Greenroyd Cres. Hal —6D 112
Greenroyd La. Hal —6C 112
Greenshank M. Morl —3D 120
Greenshaw Ter. Guis —2F 45
**Green Side. —6F 79**
Greenside. Bail —2H 61
Greenside. Cleck —1G 135
Greenside. Heck —4A 136
Greenside. Oaken —3C 116
Greenside. Pud —7B 82
Grn. Side Av. Leeds —1B 102
Greenside Clo. Leeds —1C 102
Greenside Ct. Gild —7H 101
Greenside Dri. Leeds —1C 102
Greenside Gro. Pud —7B 82
Greenside La. B'frd —6F 79
Greenside La. Cull —6B 58
Greenside Rd. Leeds —1C 102
Greenside Ter. Dew —6C 136
Grn. Side Ter. Leeds —1B 102
Greenside Wlk. Leeds —1B 102
Green's Sq. Hal —7C 112
Green's Sq. Kip —5A 108
Green's Ter. Oaken —3B 116
Green St. B'frd —6B 80 (4G 7)
Green St. C'frd —6D 126
Green St. Haw —6E 56
Green St. Holy G —5G 143
Green St. Oxe —3E 74
Greensway. Gar —6J 89
Green Sykes Rd. Lay —2B 38
Green Ter. B'frd —3D 80
Green Ter. Dew —7E 136
Green Ter. Guis —3G 45
Green Ter. Leeds —3J 103
Green Ter. Sq. Hal —4E 130
**Green, The. —1B 82**
**(nr. Farsley)**
**Green, The. —7K 69**
**(nr. Seacroft)**
Green, The. Bgly —5A 42
(nr. College Rd.)
Green, The. Bgly —1D 60
(nr. Sheriff La.)
Green, The. Birs —5D 118
Green, The. B'frd —4D 62
Green, The. C'frd —7K 127
(in two parts)
Green, The. E Bier —7H 99
Green, The. Eld —5C 42
Green, The. Fars —1B 82
Green, The. Gar —7A 90
Green, The. Gild —7H 101
Green, The. Guis —3G 45
Green, The. H'fth —4F 65
Green, The. Hud —4K 145
Green, The. Kip —5A 108
Green, The. Leeds —1J 87
(in two parts)
Green, The. M'wte —4J 41
Green, The. Otley —1H 27
Green, The. Seac —2A 68
Greenthorpe Hill. Leeds —6J 83
Greenthorpe Mt. Leeds —5J 83
Greenthorpe Rd. Leeds —5J 83
Greenthorpe St. Leeds —6J 83
Greenthorpe Wlk. Leeds —5J 83
Greenton Av. Schol —6A 116
Greenton Cres. Q'bry —6H 95
Green Top. Leeds —1B 102
Greentop. Pud —7B 82
Grn. Top Gdns. Leeds —1B 102
Green Top St. B'frd —6E 78
Greentrees. B'frd —1H 115
Greenups Ter. Sower B —4K 129
Green Vw. Leeds —5E 66
Green Vw. S'cft —3A 52
Greenview Ct. Leeds —4C 68
Greenville Av. Leeds —1B 102
Greenville Dri. Low M —7A 98
Greenville Gdns. Leeds —1B 102
Greenway. B'frd —5C 80 (1H 7)
Greenway. Guis —4E 44
Green Way. Hal —6C 94
Greenway. Leeds —4A 88
Green Way. S'cft —3A 52
Greenway Clo. Leeds —4A 88
Greenway Dri. All —6B 78
Greenway Rd. B'frd —4A 98
Greenwell Ct. Leeds —5E 86
Greenwell Row. Cytn —2B 96
Greenwood Av. B'frd —7C 62
Greenwood Ct. B'frd —7A 80 (5F 7)
Greenwood Ct. Leeds —4E 66
Greenwood Dri. B'frd —1C 80
Greenwood Mt. B'frd —1C 80
Greenwood Mt. Leeds —5E 66
Greenwood Pk. Leeds —5E 66
Greenwood Rd. Bail —3H 61
Greenwood Rd. Ting —7F 121
*Greenwood Row. Morl —3B 120*
*(off Commercial St.)*
Greenwood Row. Pud —6D 82
Greenwood's Ter. Hal —6D 112
**Greetland. —2E 142**
Greetland Rd. Bklnd —1A 20
Gregory Ct. Cytn —2C 96
Gregory Cres. B'frd —4E 96
Gregory St. Bat —3J 137
Grenfell Dri. B'frd —5F 81
Grenfell Rd. B'frd —5F 81
Grenfell Ter. B'frd —5F 81
Gresham Av. B'frd —1B 80
*Gresley Ho. H'fth —1G 65*
*(off Sussex Av.)*
Gresley Rd. Kei —4A 40
Greycourt Clo. B'frd —6C 62
Greycourt Clo. Hal —2E 130
*Greycourt Ho. Hal —2E 130*
*(off King Cross Rd.)*
Greyfriar Wlk. B'frd —3E 96
Grey Hall Clo. Slnd —6D 142
Greyhound Dri. B'frd —7H 79
Grey Scar Rd. Oakw —2C 56
Greyshiels Av. Leeds —1C 84
Greyshiels Clo. Leeds —1C 84
Greystone Av. Ell —4J 143
Greystone Clo. B Spa —3E 36
Greystone Clo. Bur W —7A 14
Greystone Ct. Brigh —2G 145
Greystone Cres. B'frd —6E 62
Greystone Mt. Leeds —6G 87
Greystone Pk. Aber —3E 72
Greystones Clo. Aber —3E 72
Greystones Ct. Leeds —7J 49
Greystones Dri. Kei —2H 57
Greystones La. Lay —4A 38
Greystones Mt. Kei —2H 57
Greystones Ri. Kei —1H 57
Griffe Dri. Wyke —6J 115
Griffe Gdns. Oakw —1D 56
Griffe Head Cres. Wyke —5J 115
Griffe Head Rd. Wyke —5J 115
Griffe Rd. Wyke —5J 115
Griffe Ter. Wyke —6J 115
Griffe Vw. Oakw —1D 56
Griff Ho. La. Wake —7H 121
Griffin Av. Leeds —3H 121
Griffin Gro. Otley —2J 27

Hardwick Cft.—Heathcliffe Clo.


Hardwick Cft. Leeds —6K 67
Hardwick St. Kei —5J 39
Hardy Av. B'frd —6J 97
Hardy Av. Chur —6C 102
Hardy Ct. Morl —3B 120
Hardy Gro. Leeds —3G 103
Hardy Pl. Hov E —3E 132
Hardy St. B'frd —7B 80 (6F 7)
Hardy St. Brigh —5H 133
Hardy St. Leeds —3G 103
Hardy St. Morl —3B 120
Hardy St. Wibs —5J 97
Hardy Ter. Leeds —3H 103
Hardy Vw. Leeds —3G 103
Harecroft Rd. Otley —1J 27
Hare Farm Av. Leeds —6H 83
Hare Farm Clo. Leeds —6H 83
Harefield Clo. Ebrn —5C 20
Harefield Dri. Bat —6E 118
Harefield E. Leeds —6G 87
Harefield W. Leeds —6G 87
Harehill Clo. B'frd —3D 62
Hare Hill Edge. Oldf —3A 56
Harehill Rd. B'frd —3D 62
**Harehills. —3D 86**
Harehills Av. Leeds —1A 86
**Harehills Corner. —1C 86**
Harehills La. Leeds —7A 68
Harehills La. Oldf —3A 56
Harehills Pk. Av. Leeds —3D 86
Harehills Pk. Cotts. Leeds —3E 86
Harehills Pk. Rd. Leeds —3D 86
Harehills Pk. Ter. Leeds —3D 86
Harehills Pk. Vw. Leeds —3D 86
Harehills Pl. Leeds —2B 86
Harehills Rd. Leeds —1B 86
Hare La. Pud —1C 100
Hare Pk. Av. Liv —4E 134
Hare Pk. Clo. Liv —4E 134
Hare Pk. Dri. Liv —4E 134
*Hare Pk. Grange. Liv —4E 134 (off Hare Pk. La.)*
Hare Pk. La. Liv —5E 134
Hare Pk. Mt. Leeds —6G 83
Hares Av. Leeds —1B 86
Hares Mt. Leeds —1A 86
Hares Rd. Leeds —1A 86
Hares Ter. Leeds —1B 86
Hare St. Hal —1D 130
Hares Vw. Leeds —1B 86
**Harewood. —3C 32**
Harewood Av. Ebrn —5C 20
Harewood Av. Hal —7B 112
Harewood Av. Hare —4D 32
Harewood Av. Heck —5C 136
Harewood Ct. Leeds —1J 87 (LS14)
Harewood Ct. Leeds —3K 67 (LS17)
Harewood Cres. Oakw —1G 57
Harewood Ga. Hare —3C 32
Harewood Gro. Heck —5C 136
Harewood House. —4A 32
Harewood M. Hare —3C 32
Harewood Pl. Hal —2C 130
Harewood Ri. Oakw —1H 57
Harewood Rd. Coll —2C 34
Harewood Rd. E Kes —3J 33
Harewood Rd. Oakw —2G 57
Harewood St. B'frd —6D 80 (3J 7)
Harewood St. Leeds —5J 85 (6F 5)
Harewood Way. Leeds —5F 83
Hargrave Cres. Men —6B 26
Hargreaves Clo. Morl —7K 101
Harker Rd. Low M —7J 97
*Harker St. Sut Cr —5A 20 (off Sutton La.)*
Harker Ter. S'ley —4B 82
Harland Clo. B'frd —3A 80
Harlech Av. Leeds —4H 103
Harlech Cres. Leeds —4H 103
Harlech Gro. Leeds —4H 103
Harlech Mt. Leeds —4H 103
Harlech Rd. Leeds —4H 103
Harlech St. Leeds —4H 103
Harlech Ter. Leeds —4H 103
Harlech Way. Gar —6B 90
Harley Clo. Leeds —5E 82
Harley Ct. Leeds —5E 82
Harley Dri. Leeds —5E 82
Harley Gdns. Leeds —5E 82
Harley Grn. Leeds —5E 82
*Harley Pl. Brigh —7G 133 (off Harley St.)*
Harley Ri. Leeds —5E 82
Harley Rd. Leeds —5E 82
Harley St. Brigh —7G 133
Harley Ter. Leeds —5E 82
Harley Vw. Leeds —5E 82
Harley Wlk. Leeds —5E 82
Harlington Ct. Morl —5A 120
Harlington Rd. Morl —5A 120
Harlow Ct. Leeds —5E 68
Harlow Rd. B'frd —1G 97
Harmon Clo. B'frd —6E 98
Harold Av. Leeds —3E 84
Harold Gro. Leeds —3E 84
Harold Mt. Leeds —3E 84
Harold Pl. Leeds —3E 84
Harold Pl. Shipl —4F 61
Harold Rd. Leeds —3E 84
Harold Sq. Leeds —3E 84
Harold St. Bgly —7J 41
Harold St. Leeds —3E 84
Harold Ter. Leeds —3E 84
Harold Vw. Leeds —3E 84
Harold Wlk. Leeds —3E 84
Harper Av. Idle —3D 62
Harper Cres. Idle —3E 62
Harper Gro. B'frd —3D 62
Harper Gro. Sut Cr —6A 20
Harper La. Yead —5K 45
*Harper Rock. Yead —5K 45 (off Harper La.)*
Harper Royd La. Sower B —6K 129
Harper St. Leeds —6K 85 (7G 5)
*Harper Ter. Yead —5K 45 (off Harper La.)*
Harp La. Q'bry —4H 95
Harrier Clo. B'frd —6B 78
Harrier Way. Morl —3D 120
Harriet St. B'frd —5H 79
Harriet St. Brigh —4G 133
Harriet St. Leeds —2K 85
Harris Ct. B'frd —3G 97
Harrison Cres. Leeds —4F 87
Harrison Rd. Hal —2G 131
Harrison's Av. S'ley —3D 82
Harrison St. Bgly —2A 60
Harrison St. Leeds —5J 85 (5F 5)
Harrison Va. Bgly —1A 60
Harris St. Bgly —2A 60
Harris St. B'frd —6C 80 (4H 7)
Harrogate Av. B'frd —3C 80
Harrogate Pde. Leeds —2K 67
Harrogate Pl. B'frd —3C 80
Harrogate Rd. B'frd —3D 80
Harrogate Rd. B'hpe —3C 46
Harrogate Rd. Hare —1A 32
Harrogate Rd. Leat —1H 29
Harrogate Rd. Leeds —3J 67
Harrogate Rd. Rawd & Leeds (in two parts) —7K 45
Harrogate Rd. Weth —1C 16
Harrogate St. B'frd —3C 80
Harrogate Ter. B'frd —3C 80
Harrogate Vw. Leeds —6E 50
Harrop Av. Morl —5B 120
**Harrop Edge. —3G 77**
Harrop Gro. Morl —5B 120
Harrop La. Wilsd —2E 76
Harrop Ter. Morl —5B 120
Harrowby Cres. Leeds —5B 66
Harrowby Rd. Leeds —5B 66
Harrow St. Hal —1D 130
Harry Clo. Add —1B 10
Harry La. Cytn —2A 96
Harry La. Oxe —2E 74
Harry St. B'frd —3E 98
Harsley Fold. Brigh —6A 134
Harthill. Gild —7H 101
Harthill Av. Gild —7H 101
Harthill Clo. Gild —7H 101
Harthill La. Gild —7H 101
*Harthill Pde. Gild —7H 101 (off Town St.)*
Harthill Ri. Gild —7H 101
Hartington St. Bat —5G 137
Hartington St. Kei —3A 40
Hartington Ter. B'frd —1G 97
Hartland Rd. B'frd —2G 99
Hartley Av. Leeds —1G 85
Hartley Bank La. Hal —5C 114
Hartley Cres. Leeds —1G 85
Hartley Gdns. Leeds —1H 85
Hartley Gro. Dew —6G 137
Hartley Gro. Leeds —1G 85
Hartley Hill. Leeds —4J 85 (4F 5)
Hartley Pl. Morl —4B 120
Hartley's Bldgs. Morl —4B 120
Hartley's Sq. E Mor —2H 41
Hartley St. B'frd —1C 98
Hartley St. Chur —7B 102
Hartley St. Dew —7G 137
Hartley St. Hal —7E 112
Hartley St. Morl —3B 120
Hartley's Yd. Leeds —6B 84
Hartlington Ct. Bail —1A 62
Hartman Pl. B'frd —3F 79
**Hartshead. —6E 134**
Hartshead Hall La. Harts —7E 134
Hartshead La. Harts —6D 134
**Hartshead Moor Side. —2D 134**
**Hartshead Moor Top. —1A 134**
Hart St. B'frd —2G 97
Hartwell Rd. Leeds —3E 84
Harvest Cft. Bur W —1K 25
Harwill App. Chur —7C 102
Harwill Av. Chur —7C 102
Harwill Cft. Chur —7C 102
Harwill Gro. Chur —7C 102
Harwill Ri. Chur —7C 102
Harwill Rd. Morl —7C 102
Haselbury Ho. B'frd —7D 6
Haslam Clo. B'frd —5C 80 (2J 7)
Haslam Gro. Shipl —6A 62
Haslemere Clo. B'frd —3F 99
Haslewood Clo. Leeds —5A 86 (6K 5)
Haslewood Ct. Leeds —5B 86
Haslewood Dene. Leeds —5B 86 (6K 5)
Haslewood Dri. Leeds —5A 86 (5K 5)
Haslewood Grn. Leeds —5B 86
Haslewood Lawn. Leeds —5B 86 (6K 5)
Haslewood M. Leeds —5B 86
Haslewood Pl. Leeds —5B 86
Haslewood Sq. Leeds —5B 86
Hasley Rd. Bur W —2B 26
Haslingden Dri. B'frd —3F 79
Haste St. C'frd —7B 126
Hastings Av. B'frd —4K 97
Hastings Ct. Coll —2F 35
Hastings Ct. Shad —7G 51
Hastings Cres. C'frd —7H 127
Hastings Pl. B'frd —4K 97
Hastings St. B'frd —4K 97
Hastings Ter. B'frd —4K 97
Hastings Wlk. C'frd —7H 127
Hastings Way. Coll —2D 34
Hatchard Bldgs. Leeds —7K 49
Hatchet La. Oaken —3C 116
Hatfield Rd. B'frd —3D 80
Hathaway Av. B'frd —2D 78
Hathaway Dri. Leeds —3K 69
Hathaway La. Leeds —4K 69
Hathaway M. Leeds —3K 69
Hathaway Wlk. Leeds —4K 69
Hathershelf La. Hal —2C 128
Hatters Fold. Hal —1H 131
Hatton Clo. B'frd —6K 97
Haugh End La. Sower B —6J 129
Haugh Shaw Cft. Hal —3E 130
Haugh Shaw Rd. Hal —3E 130
Hauxley Ct. I'ly —5D 12
Hauxwell Dri. Yead —5K 45
Havelock Sq. T'tn —7J 77
Havelock St. B'frd —2F 97
Havelock St. T'tn —7J 77
Haven Chase. Leeds —1J 65
Haven Clo. Leeds —7K 47
Haven Ct. Leeds —1K 65
Haven Cft. Leeds —1K 65
Haven Gdns. Leeds —1J 65
Haven Gth. Leeds —1J 65
Haven Grn. Leeds —1J 65
Haven Mt. Leeds —1J 65
Haven Ri. Leeds —1J 65
Haven, The. B'frd —6E 62
Haven, The. Leeds —5B 88
Haven Vw. Leeds —1J 65
*Havercroft. Bat —3G 137 (off Hanover St.)*
Havercroft. Leeds —1J 101
Havercroft Way. Bat —3D 136
Haverthwaites Dri. Aber —3E 72
Haw Av. Yead —3A 46
Hawber Cote Dri. Sils —7H 9
Hawber Cote La. Sils —7H 9
Hawber La. Sils —1H 21
Hawes Av. B'frd —4J 97
Hawes Clo. C'frd —7H 127 (in two parts)
Hawes Cres. B'frd —4J 97
Hawes Dri. B'frd —4J 97
Hawes Gro. B'frd —4J 97
Hawes Mt. B'frd —4J 97
Hawes Rd. B'frd —4H 97
Hawes Ter. B'frd —4J 97
Haweswater Clo. Weth —4F 17
Hawkcliffe Vw. Sils —1E 20
Hawke Av. Heck —4C 136
Hawke Way. Low M —1A 116
Hawkhill Av. Guis —3F 45
Hawkhill Av. Leeds —3K 87
Hawkhill Dri. Leeds —2K 87
Hawkhill Gdns. Leeds —2K 87
Hawkhills. Leeds —5A 68
Hawkhurst Rd. Leeds —7C 84
Hawkins Dri. Leeds —3J 85 (1E 4)
Hawksbridge La. Oxe —2C 74
Hawkshead Clo. B'frd —1A 98
Hawkshead Cres. Leeds —2H 87
Hawkshead Dri. B'frd —1A 98 (7D 6)
Hawkshead Wlk. B'frd —1A 98 (7D 6)
*Hawkshead Way. B'frd —1A 98 (off Hawkshead Clo.)*
Hawksley Ct. Morl —7K 101
Hawk's Nest Gdns. E. Leeds —7K 49
Hawk's Nest Gdns. S. Leeds —7K 49
Hawk's Nest Gdns. W. Leeds —7K 49
Hawk's Nest Ri. Leeds —7K 49
Hawkstone Av. Guis —4E 44
Hawkstone Dri. Kei —2J 39
Hawkstone Vw. Guis —4E 44
*Hawk St. Kei —3B 40 (off Pheasant St.)*
Hawks Wood Av. B'frd —2F 79
Hawkswood Av. Leeds —5J 65
Hawkswood Cres. Leeds —5J 65
Hawkswood Gro. Leeds —5J 65
Hawkswood Mt. Leeds —5J 65
Hawkswood Pl. Leeds —6J 65
Hawkswood St. Leeds —6K 65
Hawkswood Ter. Leeds —6K 65
Hawkswood Vw. Leeds —5J 65
**Hawksworth. —3B 44 (nr. Guisley)**
**Hawksworth. —5J 65 (nr. Horsforth)**
Hawksworth Av. Guis —4F 45
Hawksworth Clo. Men —7C 26
Hawksworth Dri. Guis —4F 45
Hawksworth Dri. Men —6B 26
Hawksworth Gro. Leeds —6H 65
Hawksworth La. Guis —3B 44
Hawksworth Rd. Bail —5J 43
Hawksworth Rd. H'fth —5H 65 (in two parts)
Hawksworth St. I'ly —5B 12
Haw La. Yead —4K 45
Hawley Clo. Morl —5K 119
Hawley Ter. B'frd —1G 81
Hawley Way. Morl —5K 119
**Haworth. —6F 57**
*Haworth Ct. Yead —4K 45 (off Chapel La.)*
Haworth Gro. B'frd —2E 78
Haworth La. Yead —4K 45
Haworth Rd. All —2A 78
Haworth Rd. Birs —5D 118
Haworth Rd. B'frd —2E 78
Haworth Rd. Cro R —4G 57
Haworth Rd. Cull —6H 57
Haworth Rd. Wilsd —1D 76
Hawthorn Av. Bat —5E 136
Hawthorn Av. B'frd —5G 81
Hawthorn Av. Yead —4K 45
Hawthorn Clo. Brigh —5J 133
Hawthorn Clo. K'gte —5H 139
Hawthorn Cres. Bail —1K 61
Hawthorn Cres. Leeds —5K 67
Hawthorn Cres. Yead —4K 45
Hawthorn Cft. Loft —6E 122
Hawthorn Dri. B'frd —5E 62
Hawthorn Dri. Leeds —7B 64
Hawthorn Dri. Yead —3A 46
Hawthorne Av. Shipl —7K 61
Hawthorne Av. Weth —2H 17
Hawthorne Clo. Gild —7H 101
Hawthorne Dri. Gild —7J 101
Hawthorne Gdns. Leeds —6B 48
*Hawthorne Mills. Leeds —2A 102 (off Cow Clo. Gro.)*
Hawthorne St. Sils —1F 21
Hawthorne Ter. Gar —1G 107
Hawthorne Vw. Gild —7J 101
Hawthorne Way. E Mor —3J 41
Hawthorn Gro. Bur W —2B 26
Hawthorn Gro. Leeds —7B 64
Hawthorn Gro. Rothw —3H 123
Hawthorn La. Leeds —5K 67
Hawthorn Mt. Leeds —5K 67
Hawthorn Ri. Leeds —4A 70
Hawthorn Rd. Leeds —5K 67
Hawthorn Rd. Yead —4K 45
Hawthorn St. B'frd —5G 81
Hawthorn St. Hal —3E 130
Hawthorn St. Hip —7D 114
Hawthorn Va. Leeds —5K 67
Hawthorn Vw. Bail —1A 62
Hawthorn Vw. Leeds —5K 67
Haw Vw. Yead —3A 46
Hayburn Gdns. Bat —3F 137
Hayburn Rd. Bat —3E 136
Haycliffe Av. B'frd —4G 97
Haycliffe Dri. B'frd —4F 97
Haycliffe Gro. B'frd —4G 97
**Haycliffe Hill. —4H 97**
Haycliffe Hill Rd. B'frd —4H 97
Haycliffe La. B'frd —4G 97
Haycliffe Rd. B'frd —3H 97
Haycliffe Ter. B'frd —3H 97
Hayclose Mead. B'frd —1G 115
Hayden St. B'frd —7D 80 (6K 7)
Haydn Pl. Q'bry —5J 95
Haydn's Ter. Far —3C 82
Hayfield Av. B Spa —2C 36
Hayfield Clo. Bail —7A 44
Hayfields, The. Haw —4E 56
Hayfield Ter. Leeds —7C 84
Hayhills La. Sils —5F 9
Hayhills Rd. Sils —7G 9
Hayleigh Av. Leeds —2G 83
Hayleigh Mt. Leeds —2G 83
Hayleigh St. Leeds —3G 83
Hayleigh Ter. Leeds —3G 83
*Hayley Ct. Hal —7G 113 (off Hayley Hill)*
Haynes St. Kei —5B 40
Hays La. Hal —7K 93
Hayson Clo. Dew —7K 137
Haythorns Av. Sils —1F 21
Haythorns Mt. Sils —1F 21
Hayton Dri. Weth —5K 17
Hayton Wood Vw. Aber —4E 72
Haywain, The. I'ly —6D 12
Hazebrouck Dri. Bail —7H 43
Hazel Av. Leeds —4A 70
Hazel Beck. Bgly —4K 59
Hazel Clo. B'shaw —1J 117
Hazel Ct. Rothw —3H 123
Hazelcroft. B'frd —1F 81
Hazel Cft. Shipl —6J 61
*Hazel Dene. Holy G —5F 143 (off Cross St.)*
Hazeldene. Q'bry —6H 95
Hazeldene Cotts. Sick —4A 16
Hazel Gro. Bat —4E 136
Hazel Gro. Hal —1G 133
Hazel Gro. Hud —4H 145
Hazelheads. Bail —7J 43
Hazelhurst Av. Bgly —4K 59
Hazelhurst Brow. B'frd —3D 78
Hazelhurst Ct. B'frd —7E 80 (BD3)
Hazelhurst Ct. B'frd —3D 78 (BD9)
Hazelhurst Ct. Pud —6D 82
Hazelhurst Gro. Q'bry —7H 95
Hazelhurst Rd. B'frd —3D 78
Hazelhurst Rd. Q'bry —7H 95
Hazelhurst Ter. B'frd —3D 78
Hazelmere Av. Bgly —4A 60
Hazel Mt. Shipl —5J 61
Hazel Ri. Meth —6G 125
Hazel Wlk. B'frd —3D 78
Hazelwood Av. Gar —1A 108
Hazelwood Av. Riddl —2D 40
Hazelwood Castle. —7H 55
Hazelwood Rd. B'frd —2C 78
**Headingley. —7D 66**
Headingley. —1D 84
Headingley Av. Leeds —7C 66
Headingley Ct. Leeds —1F 85
Headingley Cres. Leeds —1D 84
**Headingley Hill. —1E 84**
Headingley La. Leeds —1E 84
Headingley Mt. Leeds —7C 66
Headingley Office Pk. Leeds —1F 85
*Headingley Ri. Leeds —2F 85 (off Welton Rd.)*
Headingley Ter. Leeds —1F 85
Headingley Vw. Leeds —1D 84
Headland Gro. B'frd —5F 97
Headlands. Liv —5J 135
Headlands Clo. Liv —5K 135
Headlands Rd. Liv —4J 135
Headlands Rd. Bus. Pk. Liv —4J 135
Headlands St. Liv —5J 135
Headley Cotts. Tad —3G 55
Headley La. B'ham —1D 54
Headley La. T'tn —2G 95
Headrow Cen., The. Leeds —5J 85 (6E 4)
Headrow, The. Leeds —5H 85 (5D 4)
Healdfield Rd. C'frd —7E 126
Healds Av. Liv —4K 135
Healds Rd. Dew —6E 136
Heald St. C'frd —7F 127
Healdwood Clo. C'frd —7G 127
Healdwood Rd. C'frd —7G 127
**Healey. —3D 136**
Healey Av. Bgly —2A 60
Healey Clo. Bat —3D 136
Healey Cft. Wake —1H 139
Healey Cft. La. E Ard —1H 139
Healey La. Bat —4D 136 (in two parts)
Healey La. Bgly —2A 60
Healey St. Bat —3D 136
Healey Wood Cres. Brigh —1G 145
Healey Wood Gdns. Brigh —1G 145
Healey Wood Gro. Brigh —1H 145
Healey Wood Rd. Brigh —1G 145
Heap La. B'frd —6C 80 (3H 7)
Heap St. B'frd —6C 80 (3H 7)
Heap St. Hal —5G 113
Hearn Gth. Hal —1G 131
Heath Av. Hal —4F 131
Heathcliff. Haw —5D 56
Heathcliffe Clo. Birs —4D 118

# Heathcote Av.—Highlands Pk.



Heathcote Av. T'ner —6D 52
Heath Cres. Hal —3G 131
Heath Cres. Leeds —3E 102
Heathcroft Bank. Leeds —4E 102
Heathcroft Cres. Leeds —4E 102
Heathcroft Dri. Leeds —4E 102
Heathcroft Lawn. Leeds —4E 102
Heathcroft Ri. Leeds —4E 102
Heathcroft Va. Leeds —4E 102
Heathdale Av. Hud —7F 145
Heath Dri. B Spa —3B 36
Heatherbank Av. Oakw —7H 39
Heather Bank Clo. Cull —7B 58
Heather Ct. Bgly —6A 42
Heather Ct. Birs —5C 118
Heathercroft. Leeds —6A 68
Heatherdale Ct. Wake —7E 120
Heatherdale Dri. Ting —7E 120
Heatherdale Rd. Ting —7D 120
Heather Dri. Mt Tab —4J 111
Heather Gdns. Leeds —5J 83
Heather Gdns. S'cft —4A 52
Heather Gro. B'frd —1B 78
Heather Gro. Kei —3H 39
Heather Gro. Leeds —5J 83
Heatherlands Av. Denh —3B 76
Heather Pl. Q'bry —4F 95
Heather Ri. Bur W —2A 26
Heather Rd. Bail —7K 43
Heatherside. Bail —7H 43
Heatherstones. Hal —4F 131
Heather Va. S'cft —4K 51
Heather Vw. Bgly —6D 42
**Heathfield. —2A 144**
Heathfield. Leeds —7A 48
Heathfield Av. Ell —2B 144
Heathfield Clo. Bgly —7A 42
Heathfield Clo. Ting —1F 139
Heathfield Cft. Leeds —2D 84
Heathfield Gro. B'frd —2E 96
*Heathfield Gro. Hal —4G 131*
*(off Heath Rd.)*
Heathfield Ind. Est. Ell —2A 144
Heathfield La. B Spa —2B 36
Heathfield Pl. Hal —4G 131
Heathfield St. Ell —3A 144
Heathfield Ter. Hal —4G 131
Heathfield Ter. Leeds —6D 66
Heathfield Vw. B'frd —3E 78
Heathfield Wlk. Leeds —6A 48
Heath Gdns. Hal —4G 131
Heath Gro. Bat —3K 137
Heath Gro. E Mor —3H 41
Heath Gro. Leeds —3E 102
Heath Gro. Pud —7A 82
Heath Hall. Hal —3G 131
Heath Hall Av. B'frd —5D 98
Heath Hill Rd. Hal —7J 111
Heath La. Hal —4G 131
Heath Lea. Hal —3G 131
Heathmoor Clo. Hal —2B 112
Heathmoor Clo. Idle —4C 62
Heathmoor Mt. Hal —1B 112
Heathmoor Pk. Rd. Hal —7B 94
Heathmoor Way. Hal —1B 112
Heath Mt. Hal —4F 131
Heath Mt. Leeds —3E 102
Heath Mt. Rd. Brigh —1G 145
Heathness Rd. Add —1B 10
Heath Pk. I'ly —6K 11
Heath Pk. Av. Hal —3G 131
Heath Pl. Leeds —3E 102
Heath Ri. Leeds —4E 102
Heath Rd. B'frd —4D 80 (1K 7)
Heath Rd. Hal —4G 131
Heath Rd. Leeds —3E 102
Heath Rd. Pud —7A 82
Heath Royd. Hal —4G 131
Heath St. Bgly —1A 60
Heath St. B'frd —6E 80
Heath St. Hal —4F 131
Heath St. Liv —6K 135
Heath Ter. B'frd —6D 80
Heath Vs. Hal —4G 131
Heathy Av. Hal —2E 112
Heathy La. Hal —1D 112
**Heaton. —2G 79**
Heaton Av. Cleck —1E 134
Heaton Av. Leeds —1C 102
Heaton Av. Sandb —4G 41
Heaton Clo. Bail —7H 43
Heaton Clo. Bgly —7B 42
Heaton Cres. Bail —6H 43
Heaton Cres. Bgly —7B 42
Heaton Dri. Bail —6H 43
Heaton Dri. Bgly —7B 42
**Heaton Grove. —1H 79**
Heaton Gro. B'frd —1H 79
Heaton Gro. Cleck —1E 134
Heaton Gro. Shipl —5J 61
Heaton Hill. B'frd —7E 96
Heaton Pk. Dri. B'frd —2F 79
Heaton Pk. Rd. B'frd —2F 79
Heaton Rd. Bat —1G 137
Heaton Rd. B'frd —2G 79
**Heaton Royds. —7F 61**
Heaton Royds La. B'frd —7F 61
Heaton's Ct. Leeds —6J 85 (7E 4)
**Heaton Shay. —7F 61**
Heaton St. B'frd —1C 98 (7H 7)
Heaton St. Cleck —7F 117
Heatons Yd. Brigh —7H 133
Hebble Brook Clo. Mix —3A 112
Hebble Cotts. Hal —6C 112
Hebble Ct. Hal —3B 112
Hebble Dean. Hal —6D 112
Hebble Gdns. Hal —6C 112
Hebble La. Hal —6D 112
*Hebble Row. Oakw —3E 56*
*(off Providence La.)*
Hebble Va. Dri. Hal —5C 112
Hebble Vw. Hal —5C 112
Hebb Vw. B'frd —4E 96
Hebden App. Leeds —6K 69
Hebden Bri. Rd. H Bri & Oxe —1A 92
Hebden Chase. Leeds —6K 69
Hebden Clo. Leeds —6K 69
Hebden Grn. Leeds —6K 69
Hebden Path. Leeds —6K 69
Hebden Pl. Leeds —6K 69
Hebden Rd. Haw —6F 57
Hebden Wlk. Leeds —6K 69
Heber Clo. Sils —2H 21
Heber's Ghyll Dri. I'ly —6H 11
Heber's Gro. I'ly —6J 11
Heber St. Kei —5K 39
**Heckmondwike. —5B 136**
Heckmondwike Rd. Dew —6C 136
Hector Clo. B'frd —5J 97
Heddon Clo. B'frd —1A 98 (7D 6)
Heddon Gro. B'frd —1A 98 (7E 6)
Heddon Pl. Leeds —6E 66
Heddon St. Leeds —6E 66
Heddon Wlk. B'frd —7D 6
Hedge Clo. B'frd —4D 78
Hedge Nook. Wyke —3J 115
Hedge Side. B'frd —5E 78
Hedge Top La. Hal —4A 114
Hedge Way. B'frd —4E 78
Hedley Chase. Leeds —6E 84
Hedley Grn. Leeds —6E 84
Heidelberg Rd. B'frd —3G 79
Height Grn. Sower B —4K 129
Height La. Oxe —3F 75
Height Rd. H Bri —4A 110
Heights Bank. Leeds —6K 83
Heights Clo. Leeds —6J 83
Heights Dri. Leeds —5J 83
Heights E., The. Leeds —6K 83
Heights Gth. Leeds —6J 83
Heights Grn. Leeds —6K 83
Heights La. Bgly —2K 41
Heights La. B'frd —2D 78
Heights La. Heck —5C 136
Heights La. Leeds —6K 83
Heights La. Sils —5C 8
Heights Pde. Leeds —6J 83
Heights Wlk. Leeds —6K 83
Heights Way. Leeds —6J 83
Heights W., The. Leeds —6J 83
Height Wlk. Ripp —6G 141
Helena Pl. Kip —6K 107
Helena St. Kip —6K 107
Helena Way. B'frd —6E 98
Helen Rose Ct. Shipl —3A 62
Helen St. Shipl —4F 61
Helen Ter. Brigh —5F 133
Hellewell St. B'frd —7F 97
Hellwood La. S'cft —4A 52
Helm La. Sower B —7E 128
Helmshore Dri. B'frd —5D 78
Helmsley Ct. Midd —3J 121
Helmsley Dri. Leeds —5B 66
Helmsley Rd. B Spa —3C 36
Helmsley Rd. Leeds —5B 66
Helmsley St. B'frd —2C 98
Helston Cft. Leeds —2G 121
Helston Gth. Leeds —2G 121
Helston Grn. Leeds —2G 121
Helston Pl. Leeds —2G 121
Helston Rd. Leeds —1G 121
Helston Sq. Leeds —1F 121
Helston St. Leeds —1F 121
Helston Wlk. Leeds —2G 121
(in three parts)
Helston Way. Leeds —1G 121
*Hembrigg Ter. Morl —5A 120*
*(off Dartmouth Av.)*
Hemingway Clo. Leeds —2A 104
Hemingway Gth. Leeds —3A 104
Hemingway Grn. Leeds —3A 104
Hemingway Rd. B'frd —4F 63
Hemishor Dri. W'ford —6J 107
*Hemsby Gro. Kei —7K 39*
*(off Hemsby St.)*
Hemsby St. Kei —7K 39
Henacrewood Ct. Q'bry —7J 95
Henage St. Q'bry —5H 95
Henbury St. Leeds —4K 85 (3H 5)
Henconner Av. Leeds —6J 67
Henconner Cres. Leeds —6J 67
Henconner Dri. Leeds —6J 67
Henconner Gdns. Leeds —6J 67
Henconner Gth. Leeds —6J 67
Henconner Gro. Leeds —6J 67
Henconner La. Bmly —4J 83
Henconner La. Chap A —6J 67
Henconner Rd. Leeds —6J 67
Henderson Pl. B'frd —5J 97
Hendford Dri. B'frd —6C 80 (3J 7)
Hendy Cotts. G'lnd —2H 143
Hendy Pas. Leeds —2J 67
Henfield Av. B'frd —5C 62
Hen Holme La. Sils —2G 21
Henley Av. B'frd —4A 98
Henley Av. Leeds —3G 83
Henley Av. Rawd —1B 64
Henley Clo. Rawd —1B 64
Henley Ct. B'frd —4B 98
Henley Cres. Leeds —3G 83
Henley Cres. Rawd —1B 64
Henley Dri. Rawd —1A 64
Henley Gro. B'frd —4A 98
Henley Gro. Leeds —3G 83
Henley Hill. Rawd —1A 64
Henley Mt. Rawd —1B 64
Henley Pl. Leeds —3G 83
Henley Rd. B'frd —4B 98
Henley Rd. Leeds —3G 83
Henley St. Leeds —3G 83
Henley Ter. Leeds —3G 83
Henley Vw. Leeds —3G 83
Henley Vw. Rawd —1A 64
Henrietta St. Bat —3G 137
Henry Av. Leeds —1C 102
Henry Moore Ct. C'frd —7H 127
Henry Pl. Morl —3A 120
Henry Price Bldgs. Leeds —3G 85 (1A 4)
Henry St. Bat —6G 137
Henry St. Brigh —4G 133
Henry St. Cytn —2C 96
Henry St. Hal —2F 131
Henry St. Kei —4A 40
Henry St. T'tn —7H 77
Henry Ter. Yead —4H 45
**Henshaw. —5J 45**
Henshaw Av. Yead —5K 45
Henshaw Cres. Yead —5K 45
Henshaw La. Yead —6J 45
Henshaw Oval. Yead —5K 45
Hepton Ct. Leeds —5D 86
Hepworth Av. Chur —6B 102
Hepworth Cres. Chur —6B 102
Hepworth St. C'frd —6F 127
Herbalist St. Leeds —7E 84
Herbert Pl. B'frd —5G 81
Herbert St. Bgly —1A 60
Herbert St. B'frd —2K 97
Herbert St. Cytn —3C 96
Herbert St. Ctly —6B 60
Herbert St. Hal —2D 130
Herbert St. Shipl —3F 61
Hereford St. Leeds —5C 84
Hereford Way. B'frd —2C 98
Heritage Pk. Bgly —5A 42
Heritage Rd. Bat —4G 137
Heritage Way. Oakw —2E 56
**Hermit Hole. —2J 57**
Hermit St. Oakw —2J 57
Hermon Av. Hal —2E 130
Hermon Gro. Hal —2E 130
Hermon Rd. Leeds —4K 87
Hermon St. Leeds —4K 87
Heron Clo. Leeds —7B 50
Heron Clo. Q'bry —4G 95
Heron Clo. Steet —4D 20
Heron Ct. Morl —3D 120
Heron Gro. Leeds —7B 50
Herschel Rd. B'frd —6D 78
Hertford Chase. Leeds —7A 88
Hertford Clo. Leeds —7B 88
Hertford Cft. Leeds —7B 88
Hertford Fold. Leeds —7A 88
Hertford Lawn. Leeds —7A 88
Heshbon St. B'frd —3E 98
Hesketh Av. Leeds —7A 66
Hesketh Av. Ting —7D 120
Hesketh La. Ting —7D 120
Hesketh Mt. Leeds —7A 66
Hesketh Pl. Hal —1G 133
Hesketh Pl. Leeds —7A 66
Hesketh Rd. Leeds —7A 66
Hesketh Ter. Leeds —1A 84
Hessle Av. Leeds —2E 84
*Hessle Ho. B'frd —5E 62*
*(off Idlethorp Way)*
Hessle Mt. Leeds —2E 84
Hessle Pl. Leeds —2E 84
Hessle Rd. Leeds —2E 84
Hessle St. Leeds —2E 84
Hessle Ter. Leeds —2E 84
Hessle Vw. Leeds —2E 84
Hessle Wlk. Leeds —2E 84
Hetchell Vw. Bard —1B 52
Hetton Ct. H'let —3K 103
Hetton Rd. Leeds —7D 68
Heuthwaite Av. Weth —5K 17
Heuthwaite La. Weth —5A 18
Hew Clews. B'frd —3E 96
**Hey Beck. —3C 138**
Hey Beck La. Dew —3C 138
Heybeck Wlk. B'frd —4H 99
Heyford Ct. B'frd —2K 79
Heygate Clo. Bail —7K 43
Heygate La. Bail —7K 43
Heygate La. B'ham —7E 36
Hey La. Stanb —4B 56
Heys Av. T'tn —7K 77
Heys Cres. T'tn —7A 78
Heysham Dri. B'frd —4G 99
*Heys Ho. Hal —7E 112*
*(off Crossley Gdns.)*
Heys La. Hal —1D 110
Heys La. Ripp —7F 141
Hey St. B'frd —6K 79 (4B 6)
Hey St. Brigh —4H 133
Heywood Clo. Hal —5A 114
Hick La. Bat —3H 137
Hicks La. Meth —4H 125
Hick St. B'frd —6B 80 (4G 7)
Higgin La. Hal —3J 131
Higham and Dob La. Sower B —4E 128
High Ash. Shipl —5A 62
High Ash Av. Leeds —6A 50
High Ash Cres. Leeds —6A 50
High Ash Dri. Leeds —6A 50
High Ash Mt. Leeds —6A 50
High Ash Pk. All —4K 77
High Bank App. Leeds —6B 88
High Bank Clo. Add —1D 10
High Bank Clo. Leeds —6B 88
High Bank Gdns. Leeds —6C 88
High Bank Ga. Leeds —6B 88
High Bank La. Shipl —6D 60
High Bank Pl. Leeds —6B 88
High Banks Clo. Riddl —1D 40
High Bank Vw. Leeds —6B 88
High Bank Way. Leeds —6C 88
High Binns La. Oxe —3F 75
Highbridge Ter. B'frd —5B 98
High Brooms. Hud —7E 144
Highbury Clo. Leeds —6E 66
Highbury Clo. Q'bry —6G 95
Highbury La. Leeds —6E 66
Highbury Mt. Leeds —6E 66
Highbury Pl. Bmly —5E 82
Highbury Pl. Leeds —6E 66
Highbury Rd. Leeds —6E 66
Highbury St. Leeds —6E 66
Highbury Ter. Dew —7H 137
Highbury Ter. Leeds —6E 66
High Busy La. Shipl & B'frd —4A 62
(in three parts)
Highcliffe Av. Hud —7F 145
High Cliffe Clo. T'tn —7J 77
Highcliffe Dri. Hal —1B 130
Highcliffe Ind. Est. Morl —2K 119
Highcliffe Rd. Bat —5G 137
Highcliffe Rd. Morl —3K 119
High Cliffe Ter. Weth —4J 17
High Clo. Guis —3D 44
High Clo. Oss —7D 138
High Clo. Rawd —1K 63
High Cote. Riddl —1B 40
High Ct. Leeds —6K 85 (7G 5)
High Ct. La. Leeds —6K 85 (7G 5)
*Highcroft. Bat —5G 137*
*(off Highcliffe Rd.)*
Highcroft. Coll —2E 34
High Cft. Q'bry —5J 95
Highcroft Clo. Pud —5A 82
Highcroft Gdns. Kei —5D 40
Highcroft Way. F'hll —1A 20
High Cross La. Q'bry —7K 95
Highdale. Dew —6J 137
Highdale Cft. B'frd —4D 62
High End. Esh —6E 44
Higher Brockwell. Sower B —5H 129
Higher Coach Rd. Bail —2C 60
(in two parts)
Higher Downs. B'frd —5D 78
Higher Grange Rd. Pud —5C 82
Higher Intake Rd. B'frd —4E 80
Higher Pk. Royd Dri. Sower B —2G 141
Higher School St. Shipl —4F 61
Higherwood Clo. Kei —5C 40
Highfell Ri. Kei —6G 39
High Fernley Ct. Wyke —3J 115
High Fernley Rd. Wyke —4G 115
(in two parts)
**Highfield. —4J 39**
Highfield. B'frd —5F 99
Highfield. S'wram —2B 114
Highfield. Ting —6D 120
Highfield Av. B'frd —5C 62
Highfield Av. Brigh —7H 115
Highfield Av. G'lnd —2F 143
Highfield Av. Hal —7D 96
Highfield Av. Leeds —7C 84
Highfield Clo. E Mor —2H 41
Highfield Clo. Gild —7J 101
Highfield Clo. Leeds —1D 102
*Highfield Ct. Leeds —1C 102*
*(off Highfield Av.)*
Highfield Ct. Oakw —2E 56
*Highfield Cres. All B —2K 125*
*(off Highfield Dri.)*
Highfield Cres. Bail —7J 43
Highfield Cres. B'frd —1D 78
Highfield Cres. Leeds —7D 84
Highfield Cres. Pud —5B 82
Highfield Cres. W'ford —7A 106
Highfield Dri. All B —2K 125
Highfield Dri. Birs —5C 118
Highfield Dri. B'frd —1D 78
Highfield Dri. Gar —1K 107
Highfield Dri. Gild —7H 101
Highfield Dri. Liv —4G 135
Highfield Dri. L'ft —7G 111
Highfield Dri. Rawd —1A 64
Highfield Gdns. B'frd —2D 78
Highfield Gdns. Gild —7H 101
Highfield Gdns. Leeds —7C 84
Highfield Gth. Leeds —1D 102
Highfield Grn. All B —1K 125
Highfield Grn. Pud —5B 82
Highfield Gro. All B —1K 125
Highfield Gro. B'frd —6C 62
Highfield Gro. Ell —1J 143
Highfield Gro. Leeds —7D 84
*Highfield Ho. B'frd —4J 79*
*(off Church St.)*
Highfield La. Bar E —7H 71
Highfield La. Dew —5D 136
Highfield La. Kei —3J 39
Highfield La. M'fld —2J 109
High Fld. La. Oakw —1E 56
Highfield La. Sils —7G 9
High Fld. La. Sower B —3F 141
Highfield La. W'ford —7A 106
Highfield M. Bail —7J 43
Highfield M. E Mor —2H 41
Highfield Mt. Oult —1A 124
Highfield Pl. All B —1A 126
*Highfield Pl. B'frd —4J 79*
*(off Church St.)*
Highfield Pl. Hal —2D 130
Highfield Pl. Morl —4B 120
Highfield Rd. Aber —4E 72
Highfield Rd. Brigh —1E 144
Highfield Rd. Cleck —1E 134
Highfield Rd. Ell —3K 143
Highfield Rd. Five E & Idle —7C 62
Highfield Rd. Friz —7J 61
Highfield Rd. Kei —4J 39
Highfield Rd. Leeds —3H 83
Highfield Rd. L'ft —7G 111
Highfield Rd. Pud —5A 82
High Fields. Sower B —4C 130
Highfield St. Kei —4K 39
Highfield St. Leeds —3H 83
Highfield St. Pud —5A 82
Highfield Ter. Bgly —1A 60
Highfield Ter. Cleck —1E 134
Highfield Ter. Cull —6B 58
*Highfield Ter. Hal —2D 130*
*(off Highfield Pl.)*
Highfield Ter. Pud —6A 82
Highfield Ter. Q'bry —6H 95
Highfield Ter. Rawd —1A 64
Highfield Ter. Shipl —4E 60
Highfield Ter. Sower B —4G 141
Highfield Vw. Gild —7J 101
High Fold. Bail —7J 43
High Fold. Bgly —3J 41
High Fold. Kei —6H 39
Highfold. Yead —6J 45
High Fold La. Kei —1J 39
Highgate. B'frd —1F 79
Highgate. Denh —7C 76
Highgate Clo. Q'bry —4C 96
Highgate Gro. Q'bry —4C 96
Highgate Rd. Dew —7H 137
(in two parts)
Highgate Rd. Q'bry —5A 96
Highgate St. Bat —5K 137
High Ga. St. Leeds —2A 104
High Grn. Dri. Sils —7F 9
High Gro. La. Hal —3J 131
High Ho. Av. B'frd —1C 80
High Ho. La. Hal —3E 110
High Ho. M. Add —1D 10
High Ho. Rd. B'frd —1C 80
Highlands Clo. B'frd —3E 96
Highlands Clo. Leeds —6B 104
Highlands Dri. Leeds —6B 104
Highlands Gro. B'frd —3E 96
Highlands Gro. Leeds —6B 104
Highlands La. Hal —1D 112
Highlands Pk. Hal —1D 112



172 A-Z Leeds & Bradford

Highlands, The—Holmes St.

Highlands, The. Liv —3F 135
Highlands Wlk. Leeds —6B 104
Highland Ville. Hal —1D 132
High La. Hal —7K 111
Highlea Clo. Yead —6H 45
Highlee La. Sower B —2H 141
High Lees Rd. Hal —2K 111
High Level Way. Hal —7D 112
Highley Hall Cft. Clif —5K 133
Highley Pk. Clif —6A 134
High Mdw. Kei —2J 39
High Meadows. G'lnd —2G 143
High Meadows. Wilsd —7G 59
High Mill La. Add —1E 10
Highmoor. Bail —1G 61
High Moor Av. Leeds —2A 68
High Moor Clo. Leeds —1A 68
High Moor Ct. Leeds —2A 68
Highmoor Cres. Brigh —5K 133
High Moor Cres. Leeds —1A 68
High Moor Dri. Leeds —1A 68
High Moor Gro. Leeds —1A 68
Highmoor La. Brigh & Cleck (in two parts) —5K 133
Highmoor Wlk. Bail —2G 61
High Oxford St. C'frd —7C 126
High Pk. Cres. B'frd —2E 78
High Pk. Dri. B'frd —2E 78
High Pk. Gro. B'frd —2E 78
High Poplars. B'frd —1B 80
High Ridge Av. Rothw —7F 105
High Ridge Ct. Rothw —1G 123
High Ridge Pk. Rothw —7F 105
High Ridge Way. B'hpe —1K 47
**Highroad Well. —7B 112**
Highroad Well. Hal —1B 130
Highroad Well Ct. Hal —1B 130
Highroad Well La. Hal —1A 130
High Royds Dri. Men —7D 26
High Shaw Rd. W. Hal —3D 130
High Spring Gdns. La. Kei —2J 39
High Spring Rd. Kei —5D 40
High Stones Rd. Cra V —5A 128
High St. Birstall, Birs —6C 118
High St. Boston Spa, B Spa —2B 36
High St. Bramham, B'ham —1D 54
High St. Brighouse, Brigh —5G 133
High St. Castleford, C'frd —7C 126
High St. Cleckheaton, Cleck —7F 117
High St. Clifford, Cliff —5D 36
High St. Ct. Ludd —6G 111
High St. Farsley, Far —2B 82
High St. Greetland, G'lnd —3H 143
High St. Halifax, Hal —2F 131
High St. Hanging Heaton, Hang H —5J 137
High St. Heckmondwike, Heck —5B 136
High St. Idle, Idle —4D 62
High St. Keighley, Kei —4K 39
High St. Kippax, Kip —5B 108
High St. Luddenden, Ludd —6G 111
High St. Morley, Morl —5A 120
High St. Ossett, Oss —7C 138
High St. Pl. Idle —4D 62
High St. Queensbury, Q'bry —5J 95
High St. Shipley, Shipl —5J 61
High St. Stainland, Slnd —6C 142
High St. Steeton, Steet —5E 20
High St. Thornton, T'tn —7H 77
High St. Wetherby, Weth —5J 17
High St. Wibsey, Wibs —5H 97
High St. Yeadon, Yead —4K 45
High Sunderland La. Hal —6H 113
Highthorne Av. B'frd —4E 80
Highthorne Ct. Shad —7B 50
Highthorne Dri. Shad —7B 50
Highthorne Gro. A'ley —5A 84
Highthorne Gro. Shad —7C 50
Highthorne Mt. Leeds —7B 50
Highthorne St. A'ley —5A 84
Highthorne Vw. A'ley —5A 84
**Hightown. —3F 135**
**Hightown Heights. —3D 134**
Hightown Rd. Cleck & Liv —1F 135
Hightown Vw. Liv —3F 135
High Trees La. G'lnd —3C 142
**High Utley. —2J 39**
Highway. Guis —2D 44
Highways. Leeds —4G 87
High Weardley La. Arth & Hare —4G 31
High Wheatley. I'ly —6E 12
High Wicken Clo. T'tn —7H 77
High Wood. I'ly —6F 13
Highwood Av. Leeds —1J 67
High Wood Ct. Leeds —7E 66
Highwood Cres. Leeds —1J 67
Highwood Gro. Leeds —2J 67
High Woodlands. E Ard —1J 139
Hilberoyd Rd. Bat —4H 137
Hilda St. H'tn —1G 79
Hillam Rd. B'frd —2K 79
Hillam St. B'frd —3H 97
Hillary Pl. Leeds —3H 85 (2C 4)
Hillary Rd. Shipl —5A 62
Hillary St. Dew —5D 136
Hillbrook Ri. I'ly —6K 11
Hill Brow Clo. All —4A 78
Hill Clo. Bail —2H 61
Hill Clough Gro. Lay —4E 38
Hillcote Dri. B'frd —2A 98
Hill Ct. Av. Leeds —1G 83
Hillcourt Cft. Leeds —1G 83
Hillcourt Dri. Leeds —1G 83
Hill Ct. Fold. Leeds —1G 83
Hillcourt Gro. Leeds —1G 83
Hill Cres. Birs —5E 118
Hill Cres. Bur W —3B 26
Hill Cres. Hal —3K 131
Hill Cres. Rawd —6A 46
Hillcrest. Coll —2C 34
Hillcrest. Gild —6F 101
*Hill Crest. Sower B —3K 129 (off Dalton St.)*
Hill Crest. Swil —5E 106
Hillcrest Av. Bat —3E 136
Hill Crest Av. Denh —4C 76
Hillcrest Av. Leeds —2A 86
Hillcrest Av. Oss —7C 138
Hillcrest Av. Q'bry —6K 95
Hillcrest Av. Sils —7G 9
*Hill Crest Av. Sower B —3K 129 (off Dearden St.)*
Hillcrest Clo. Swil —5D 106
Hill Crest Dri. Denh —4B 76
Hillcrest Dri. Q'bry —6K 95
Hill Crest Mt. Denh —4B 76
Hillcrest Mt. Leeds —7J 47
Hillcrest Mt. Schol —1B 134
Hillcrest Pl. Leeds —1A 86
Hillcrest Ri. Leeds —7H 47
Hillcrest Rd. C'frd —2E 128
Hill Crest Rd. Denh —4B 76
Hillcrest Rd. Q'bry —6K 95
Hill Crest Rd. T'tn —6H 77
Hill Crest Vw. Denh —4B 76
Hillcrest Vw. Leeds —1A 86
Hill Cft. T'tn —6J 77
Hill End Clo. Hip —1C 132
Hill End Clo. Leeds —5K 83
Hill End Clo. Nor G —5G 115
Hill End Cres. Leeds —5K 83
Hill End Gro. B'frd —3E 96
Hill End La. H'den —5C 58
Hill End La. Q'bry —6H 95
Hill End Rd. Leeds —5K 83
Hillesley Rd. Dew —5A 138
**Hillfoot. —5K 81**
Hillfoot. Shipl —5E 60
Hillfoot Av. Pud —5K 81
Hillfoot Cotts. Pud —5J 81
Hillfoot Cres. Pud —5K 81
Hillfoot Dri. Pud —5K 81
Hillfoot Ri. Pud —5K 81
**Hill Green. —4C 100**
Hill Grn. Ct. B'frd —4C 100
Hill Gro. Hud —7K 143
Hillhead Dri. Bat —6D 118
Hill Ho. Edge La. Oxe —4D 74
Hill Ho. La. Oxe —4E 74
Hill Ho. La. Sower B —6H 129
Hillidge Rd. Leeds —2K 103 (in three parts)
Hillidge Sq. Leeds —2K 103
Hillingdon Way. Leeds —5G 49
Hillings La. Men & Guis —6K 25
Hill Lands. Wyke —2J 115
Hill Pk. Av. Hal —6D 112
Hill Ri. Av. Leeds —1G 83
Hill Ri. Gro. Leeds —1G 83
Hill Rd. Hal —1J 131
Hillside. Gar —7A 90
Hillside Av. Guis —7F 27
Hillside Av. Hal —7H 145
Hillside Av. L'ft —1F 129
Hillside Av. Oakw —2D 56
Hillside Av. Sower B —3G 141
*Hillside Bldgs. Leeds —3G 103 (off Beeston Rd.)*
Hillside Clo. Add —1C 10
Hillside Ct. Leeds —5A 68
Hillside Ct. Men —6B 26
Hillside Gro. Oakw —2D 56
Hillside Gro. Pud —6D 82
Hill Side Mt. Far —3C 82
Hillside Mt. Pud —6E 82
Hillside Ri. Guis —7F 27
Hill Side Ri. Liv —5J 135
Hillside Rd. Bgly —7K 41
Hill Side Rd. B'frd —6C 80 (3H 7)
Hillside Rd. Leeds —5K 67
Hillside Rd. Shipl —6J 61
Hillside Ter. Bail —1J 61
Hill Side Ter. B'frd —6C 80 (2H 7)
Hillside Vw. Pud —6E 82
Hillside Vw. Sower B —4J 129
**Hillside Villas. —6J 7**
Hillside Works Ind. Est. Cleck —5F 117
Hill St. B'frd —1D 98 (7K 7) (BD4)
Hill St. B'frd —5G 97 (BD6)
Hill St. Cleck —1E 134
Hill St. Hal —2F 131
Hill St. Haw —6E 56
Hill St. Leeds —4A 86 (3J 5) (LS9)
Hill St. Leeds —3H 103 (LS11)
Hillthorpe Ct. Leeds —4K 121
Hillthorpe Ri. Pud —1C 100
Hillthorpe Rd. Pud —1C 100
Hillthorpe Sq. Pud —1C 100
Hillthorpe St. Pud —1C 100
Hillthorpe Ter. Pud —1C 100
**Hill Top. —4E 66 (nr. Meanwood)**
**Hill Top. —6G 77 (nr. Thornton)**
Hill Top. Bur W —1A 26
Hill Top. C'frd —7K 125
Hill Top. Hal —3C 130
Hill Top. I'ly —7A 12
Hill Top. Q'bry —4H 95
Hill Top. Steet —5E 20
Hilltop Av. Leeds —1B 86
Hill Top Clo. Leeds —5K 83
Hill Top Clo. Ting —2E 138
Hill Top Cotts. B'frd —3E 78
Hill Top Ct. Ting —2E 138
Hill Top Est. Heck —5C 136
Hill Top Gdns. Ting —2E 138
Hill Top Grn. Ting —2D 138
Hill Top Gro. All —4A 78
Hill Top Gro. Ting —2E 138
Hill Top La. All —4A 78
Hill Top La. Bgly —3K 41 (in two parts)
Hill Top La. Ting —2D 138
Hill Top Mt. Leeds —1B 86
Hill Top Pl. Leeds —1B 86 (LS8)
Hill Top Pl. Leeds —3F 85 (LS6)
Hill Top Rd. Hain —3J 57
Hill Top Rd. Leeds —5K 83 (LS12)
Hill Top Rd. Leeds —3F 85 (LS6)
Hill Top Rd. Oakw —2D 56
Hill Top Rd. T'tn —6F 77
Hill Top St. Leeds —3F 85
Hill Top Vw. Ting —2D 138
Hill Top Wlk. Kei —4H 39
Hill Top Way. Kei —4H 39
Hill Vw. Hal —7D 94
Hill Vw. Av. Leeds —5K 67
Hillview Gdns. Hal —6A 114
Hill Vw. Mt. Leeds —5K 67
Hill Vw. Pl. Leeds —5K 67
Hill Vw. Ri. B'frd —2G 99
Hill Vw. Ter. Leeds —5K 67
Hillway. Guis —4E 44
Hilton Av. Shipl —7H 61
Hilton Ct. B'hpe —6E 28
Hilton Cres. Bail —2J 61
Hilton Dri. Shipl —7H 61
Hilton Grange. B'hpe —6E 28
Hilton Gro. B'frd —7G 79
Hilton Gro. Leeds —7B 68
Hilton Gro. Shipl —7H 61
Hilton M. B'hpe —7E 28
Hilton Pl. Leeds —1B 86
Hilton Rd. B'frd —7G 79
Hilton Rd. Leeds —1B 86
Hilton Rd. Shipl —7H 61
Hilton St. Leeds —1B 86
Hilton Ter. Leeds —1B 86
Hinchcliffe St. B'frd —5D 80 (1K 7)
Hinchliffe Av. Bail —2K 61
Hindle Pl. Chur —7B 102
Hindley Rd. Liv —5J 135
Hindley Wlk. B'frd —4D 96
Hind St. B'frd —5J 79 (2A 6)
Hind St. Wyke —5J 115
Hions Clo. Brigh —1G 145
**Hipperholme. —6D 114**
Hipswell St. B'frd —5E 80
Hird Av. B'frd —6J 97
Hird Rd. Low M —1K 115
Hird St. Kei —6K 39
Hird St. Leeds —3G 103
Hird St. Shipl —4H 61
Hirst Av. Heck —3B 136
Hirst La. Shipl —3E 60
Hirst Lodge Ct. B'frd —7B 62
Hirst Mill Cres. Shipl —3E 60
Hirst Rd. Dew —7G 137
Hirst St. All B —7J 107
Hirst's Yd. Leeds —7F 5
Hirst Wood Cres. Shipl —4E 60
Hirst Wood Rd. Shipl —4D 60
Hive St. Kei —5J 39
Hobart Rd. C'frd —7K 127
Hobart Rd. Dew —7K 137
Hobb End. T'tn —5G 77
Hobberley La. Shad —7H 51
Hobb Nook La. Askw —2C 14
Hob Cote La. Oakw —3B 56
Hob La. Hal —7C 110
Hob La. Ripp —4E 140
Hob La. Sower B —7K 129
Hobson Fold. Wyke —5K 115
Hockney Rd. B'frd —5H 79
Hodgson Av. B'frd —5F 81
Hodgson Av. Leeds —1C 68
Hodgson Cres. Leeds —1C 68
Hodgson Fold. Add —1B 10
Hodgson Fold. B'frd —1B 80
Hodgson La. B'shaw —7K 99
Hodgson La. Dlgtn —1B 118
Hodgson Pl. Morl —7B 102
Hodgson St. Morl —6C 120
Hodgson Yd. B'frd —7E 62
**Holbeck. —1G 103**
Holbeck La. Leeds —7F 85
Holbeck Moor Rd. Leeds —1G 103
Holbeck Towers. Leeds —1G 103
Holborn App. Leeds —2G 85
Holborn Ct. Leeds —2H 85
Holborn Ct. Low M —1J 115
Holborn Gdns. Leeds —2G 85
Holborn Grn. Leeds —2G 85
Holborn Gro. Leeds —2G 85
Holborn St. Leeds —2H 85
Holborn Ter. Leeds —2H 85
Holborn Towers. Leeds —2H 85
Holborn Vw. Leeds —2G 85
Holborn Wlk. Leeds —2G 85
Holden Ing Way. Bat —3E 118
Holden La. Bail —7K 43 (in two parts)
Holden La. Oxe —4B 74
Holden La. Sils —2J 21
Holden Rd. B'frd —5H 97
Holdforth Clo. Leeds —6E 84
Holdforth Gdns. Leeds —6E 84
Holdforth Grn. Leeds —6E 84
Holdforth Pl. Leeds —6E 84
**Holdsworth. —7E 94**
Holdsworth Av. Heck —1C 136
Holdsworth Ct. Cleck —1F 135
Holdsworth Pl. Leeds —6B 84
Holdsworth Rd. H'fld —7E 94
Holdsworth Sq. B'frd —1F 81
Holdsworth St. B'frd —5B 80 (2F 7)
Holdsworth St. Cleck —7F 117
Holdsworth St. Shipl —6J 61
Holdsworth Ter. Hal —3H 131
Hole La. Sils —5C 8
Holgate La. B Spa —2D 36
Holker St. Kei —3A 40
Holker St. Mann —5H 79
Holland Rd. Kip —4C 108
Holland St. Bat —3H 137
Holland St. B'frd —7F 81
Hollas La. Norl —6C 130 (in two parts)
Hollerton La. Ting —7F 121
Hollinbank La. Heck —3C 136
Hollin Clo. La. B'frd —2A 80 (in three parts)
Hollin Ct. Leeds —5D 66
Hollin Ct. Shipl —6J 61
Hollin Cres. Leeds —5D 66
Hollin Dri. Leeds —5E 66
Hollin Gdns. Leeds —5C 66
Hollin Ga. Otley —1F 27
Hollingbourne Rd. Leeds —3D 88
Hollin Greaves La. Hal —6H 113
Hollings Rd. B'frd —4H 79
Hollings Sq. B'frd —5H 79
Hollings St. Bgly —6B 60
Hollings St. B'frd —5H 79
Hollings Ter. B'frd —5H 79
Hollings, The. Meth —4F 125
Hollingwood Av. B'frd —2F 97
Hollingwood Ct. B'frd —3E 96
Hollingwood Dri. B'frd —2E 96
Hollingwood Ga. I'ly —6K 11
Hollingwood La. Gt Hor —3D 96
Hollingwood Mt. B'frd —2E 96
Hollingwood Ri. I'ly —6K 11
Hollin Hall Dri. I'ly —6J 11
Hollin Hall Rd. Shipl —6E 60
Hollin Head. Bail —7B 44
Hollin Hill Av. Leeds —7E 68
Hollin Hill Cotts. Leeds —7E 68
Hollin Hill Dri. Leeds —7E 68
Hollinhurst. All B —1J 125
Hollin La. Hal —2C 110
Hollin La. Leeds —5D 66
Hollin La. Ripp —6B 140
Hollin La. Shipl —6K 61
Hollin La. Sower B —7K 129
Hollin M. Leeds —5D 66
Hollin Mt. Leeds —5C 66
**Hollin Park. —7F 69**
Hollin Pk. Av. Leeds —7F 69
Hollin Pk. Ct. C'ley —6J 63
Hollin Pk. Cres. Leeds —7F 69
Hollin Pk. Dri. C'ley —6J 63
Hollin Pk. Mt. Leeds —6F 69
Hollin Pk. Pde. Leeds —7E 68
Hollin Pk. Pl. Leeds —7E 68
Hollin Pk. Rd. Leeds —7E 68
Hollin Pk. Ter. Leeds —7E 68
Hollin Pk. Vw. Leeds —7E 68
Hollin Pl. Leeds —6D 66
Hollin Ri. Shipl —6J 61
Hollin Rd. Leeds —5D 66
Hollin Rd. Shipl —6J 61
Hollinroyd Rd. Dew —7J 137
Hollins Av. Dew —5D 136
Hollins Bank. Sower B —4K 129
Hollins Bank La. Steet —5F 21
Hollins Beck Clo. Kip —6A 108
Hollins Clo. Kei —1H 39
Hollins Gro. All B —1K 125
Hollins Hey Rd. Ell —5H 143
Hollins Hill. Bail & Guis —6C 44
Hollins La. Hal —2A 112
Hollins La. Kei —7H 21
Hollins La. L'ft —3D 128
Hollins La. Sower B —3J 129
Hollins Mill La. Sower B —4J 129
Hollins Pk. Kip —5A 108
Hollins Rd. Dew —6D 136
Hollin St. Sower B —7G 129
Hollin Ter. Shipl —6J 61
**Hollinthorpe. —2E 106**
Hollin Vw. Leeds —5D 66
Hollin Wood Clo. Shipl —5E 60
Hollinwood Vw. Bgly —4H 41
Hollis Pl. Leeds —4F 85
Hollowfield Cft. Oaken —2D 116
Holly Av. Leeds —1H 65
Holly Bank. Gar —7B 90
Holly Bank. Guis —2F 45
Holly Bank. Leeds —6D 66
Hollybank Av. Bat —1G 137
Holly Bank Dri. Hal —7D 114
Hollybank Gdns. B'frd —3E 96
Hollybank Gro. B'frd —3E 96
*Holly Bank Ho. Brigh —1F 145 (off Field La.)*
Holly Bank Pk. Brigh —1F 145
Hollybank Rd. B'frd —3E 96
Holly Bank Rd. Brigh —1E 144
Holly Bank Rd. Hud —7B 144
Holly Bush Ct. B Spa —3E 36
Hollybush Grn. Coll —2G 35
Holly Ct. Guis —3F 45
Holly Ct. Ting —2E 138
Holly Cres. Sower B —6E 140
Hollycroft Ct. Leeds —1A 66
Hollycroft St. Kei —5K 39
Holly Dri. Leeds —1H 65
Holly Gro. Bat —4F 137
Holly Gro. Hal —2E 130
Holly Gro. Lind —7C 144
Holly Hall La. Wyke —3J 115
Hollynsmill. G'lnd —2H 143
Hollyns Ter. G'lnd —2H 143
Holly Pk. C'ley —6J 63
Holly Pk. Dri. B'frd —2E 96
Holly Pk. Gro. B'frd —2E 96
Holly Rd. B Spa —2B 36
Hollyshaw Cres. Leeds —5A 88
Hollyshaw Gro. Leeds —5A 88
Hollyshaw La. Leeds —4A 88
Hollyshaw St. Leeds —5A 88
Hollyshaw Ter. Leeds —5A 88
Hollyshaw Wlk. Leeds —4A 88
Holly St. B'frd —4D 96
Holly Tree La. Leeds —7C 88
Hollywell Gro. Leeds —5B 84
Hollywell La. Leeds —6B 84
Holman Av. Gar —1K 107
Holmecarr Ct. Bgly —7A 42
Holme Dri. Hal —2K 129
Holme Farm La. Bard & Woth —6C 34
Holme Gro. Bur W —3B 26
Holme Ho. La. Hal —3G 111
Holme Ho. La. Oakw —5D 38 (in two parts)
Holme Ho. La. Ripp —7E 140 (in three parts)
Holme Ings. Add —2G 11
Holme La. B'frd —3H 99
Holme Mill La. Kei —5H 39
Holme Pk. Bur W —3B 26
Holme Rd. Hal —2K 129
Holmes Rd. Sower B —4A 130
Holmes St. B'frd —5K 79 (2B 6)
Holmes St. Leeds —7J 85

# Holme's Ter.—Ingrow



Holme's Ter. *Hal* —7C **112**
Holme St. *B'frd* —2K **97**
Holme St. *Hal* —1G **133**
Holme St. *Liv* —4K **135**
Holme St. *Oxe* —3E **74**
**Holme Top. —2K 97**
Holme Top La. *B'frd* —2K **97**
Holme Top St. *B'frd* —2K **97**
Holme Vw. *Arth* —4C **30**
**Holme Village. —3H 99**
Holme Well Rd. *Leeds* —2A **122**
**Holme Wood. —3F 99**
Holme Wood Rd. *B'frd* —3F **99**
Holme Wood Rd. *Kei* —5H **39**
**Holmfield. —2D 112**
Holmfield Cotts. *Meth* —4J **125**
Holmfield Dri. *Leeds* —3C **68**
Holmfield Gdns. *Hal* —2E **112**
Holmfield Ho. *Hal* —2E **112**
Holmfield Ind. Est. *H'fld* —7E **94**
Holmfield Ind. Est. Rd. *Hal* —1E **112**
Holmfield St. *B'frd* —6K **79** (4C **6**)
Holmsley Crest. *W'ford* —1J **123**
Holmsley Fld. Ct. *W'ford* —1A **124**
Holmsley Fld. La. *W'ford* —1K **123**
Holmsley Gth. *W'ford* —7K **105**
Holmsley Ho. *Rothw* —1K **123**
Holmsley La. *W'ford* —1J **123**
Holmsley Wlk. *W'ford* —1K **123**
Holmwood. *Leeds* —2C **68**
Holmwood Av. *Leeds* —4E **66**
Holmwood Clo. *Leeds* —4F **67**
Holmwood Cres. *Leeds* —4F **67**
Holmwood Dri. *Leeds* —4E **66**
Holmwood Gro. *Leeds* —4F **67**
Holmwood Mt. *Leeds* —4F **67**
Holmwood Vw. *Leeds* —4E **66**
Holroyd Hill. *B'frd* —5J **97**
Holroyd Mill La. *Bgly* —3J **41**
*Holroyd Sq. Holy G —5D **142***
*(off Stainland Rd.)*
Holroyd St. *Leeds* —3K **85** (2H **5**)
Holsworthy Rd. *B'frd* —4G **99**
Holt Av. *Hud* —6J **145**
Holt Av. *Leeds* —6C **48**
Holtby Gro. *Hal* —1G **133**
Holt Clo. *Leeds* —7C **48**
Holt Cres. *Leeds* —6K **47**
Holtdale App. *Leeds* —6J **47**
Holtdale Av. *Leeds* —6K **47**
Holtdale Clo. *Leeds* —6K **47**
Holtdale Cft. *Leeds* —6K **47**
Holtdale Dri. *Leeds* —6K **47**
Holtdale Fold. *Leeds* —6K **47**
Holtdale Gdns. *Leeds* —6K **47**
Holtdale Gth. *Leeds* —6K **47**
Holtdale Grn. *Leeds* —6K **47**
Holtdale Gro. *Leeds* —6J **47**
Holtdale Lawn. *Leeds* —6K **47**
Holtdale Pl. *Leeds* —6K **47**
Holtdale Rd. *Leeds* —6K **47**
Holtdale Vw. *Leeds* —6K **47**
Holtdale Way. *Leeds* —6K **47**
Holt Dri. *Leeds* —6A **48**
Holt Farm Clo. *Leeds* —6K **47**
Holt Farm Ri. *Leeds* —6K **47**
Holt Gdns. *Idle* —4C **62**
Holt Gdns. *Leeds* —6C **48**
Holt Gth. *Leeds* —6A **48**
Holt Ga. *Leeds* —6A **48**
Holt Grn. *Leeds* —6A **48**
Holt La. *Leeds* —6J **47**
Holt La. Ct. *Leeds* —7B **48**
**Holt Park. —6A 48**
Holt Pk. App. *Leeds* —6A **48**
Holt Pk. Av. *Leeds* —6A **48**
Holt Pk. Clo. *Leeds* —6A **48**
Holt Pk. Cres. *Leeds* —6K **47**
Holt Pk. Dri. *Leeds* —6A **48**
Holt Pk. Gdns. *Leeds* —6A **48**
Holt Pk. Ga. *Leeds* —6A **48**
Holt Pk. Grange. *Leeds* —6A **48**
Holt Pk. Grn. *Leeds* —6A **48**
Holt Pk. Gro. *Leeds* —6K **47**
Holt Pk. La. *Leeds* —6A **48**
Holt Pk. Ri. *Leeds* —6A **48**
Holt Pk. Rd. *Leeds* —6A **48**
Holt Pk. Va. *Leeds* —6A **48**
Holt Pk. Vw. *Leeds* —6K **47**
Holt Pk. Way. *Leeds* —6A **48**
Holt Ri. *Leeds* —6A **48**
Holt Rd. *Leeds* —6A **48**
Holts La. *Cytn* —1B **96**
Holts Ter. *Hal* —4H **131**
Holt, The. *Shipl* —4J **61**
Holt Va. *Leeds* —6A **48**
Holt Wlk. *Leeds* —6A **48**
Holt Way. *Leeds* —6A **48**
Holybrook Av. *B'frd* —6F **63**
**Holy Croft. —5K 39**
Holyoake Av. *Bat* —3E **136**
Holyoake Av. *Bgly* —3K **59**
Holy Rood La. *S Mil* —6K **109**
Holywell Ash La. *B'frd* —4K **79**
**Holywell Green. —5F 143**
Holywell La. *Leeds* —6F **51**
Holywell Vw. *Leeds* —6F **51**
Home Farm. (Rare Breeds) —1K **105**
Home Farm Clo. *B'frd* —5D **96**
Homefield Av. *Morl* —5A **120**
Home Lea. *Rothw* —7F **105**
Home Lea Dri. *Rothw* —1F **123**
Homepaddock Ho. *Weth* —3K **17**
Homestead, The. *Heck* —4C **136**
Home Vw. Ter. *B'frd* —4H **79**
Hoods, The. *Brigh* —2F **145**
Hopbine Av. *B'frd* —4A **98**
Hopbine Rd. *B'frd* —4A **98**
Hope Av. *B'frd* —4J **97**
Hope Av. *Shipl* —4K **61**
Hopefield Chase. *Rothw* —3D **122**
Hopefield Clo. *Rothw* —3D **122**
Hopefield Ct. *E Ard* —1J **139**
Hopefield Ct. *Rothw* —3D **122**
Hopefield Cres. *Rothw* —3D **122**
Hopefield Dri. *Rothw* —3D **122**
Hopefield Gdns. *Rothw* —3D **122**
Hopefield Grn. *Rothw* —3D **122**
Hopefield Gro. *Rothw* —3D **122**
Hopefield M. *Rothw* —3D **122**
Hopefield Pl. *Rothw* —3D **122**
Hopefield Vw. *Rothw* —3D **122**
Hopefield Wlk. *Rothw* —3D **122**
Hopefield Way. *B'frd* —5D **98**
Hopefield Way. *Rothw* —3D **122**
Hope Hall St. *Hal* —2G **131**
Hope Hill Vw. *Bgly* —5A **60**
Hope La. *Bail* —7H **43**
Hope Pl. *Kei* —6A **40**
Hope Rd. *Leeds* —5K **85** (5H **5**)
Hopes Farm Mt. *Leeds* —7B **104**
Hopes Farm Rd. *Leeds* —7B **104**
Hopes Farm Vw. *Leeds* —7B **104**
Hope St. *C'frd* —5J **127**
Hope St. *Dew* —7G **137**
Hope St. *Hal* —1F **131**
Hope St. *Morl* —3A **120**
Hope St. *She* —3B **114**
Hope St. *Sower B* —5K **129**
Hope St. E. *C'frd* —7D **126**
Hope Vw. *Shipl* —5K **61**
Hopewell Pl. *Leeds* —3E **84**
Hopewell St. *Bat* —2F **137**
Hopewell Ter. *H'fth* —5F **65**
Hopewell Ter. *Kip* —5B **108**
Hopewell Vw. *Leeds* —2K **121**
Hopkinson Dri. *B'frd* —6E **98**
Hopkinson Rd. *Hud* —5H **145**
Hopkinson St. *Hal* —4D **112**
Hopkin St. *B'frd* —5G **99**
Hopton Av. *B'frd* —5D **98**
*Hopton Ct. Leeds —6B **84***
*(off Hopton M.)*
Hopton M. *Leeds* —6B **84**
Hopwood Bank. *H'fth* —2G **65**
Hopwood Clo. *H'fth* —2G **65**
Hopwood Gro. *C'frd* —7H **127**
Hopwood La. *Hal* —2C **130**
Hopwood Rd. *H'fth* —2G **65**
Horace Waller V.C. Pde. *Shaw B* —6K **137**
Horley Grn. La. *Hal* —6J **113**
Horley Grn. Rd. *Hal* —6J **113**
Hornbeam Clo. *All* —1K **77**
Hornbeam Way. *Leeds* —4A **70**
Hornby St. *Hal* —2D **130**
Hornby Ter. *Hal* —2D **130**
Horncastle St. *Cleck* —1G **135**
Horner Av. *Bat* —2D **136**
Horner Cres. *Bat* —2D **136**
Horne St. *Hal* —1F **131**
Horn La. *Sils* —4D **8**
Hornsea Dri. *Wilsd* —1G **77**
Horsefair. *Weth* —4K **17**
Horsefair Cen. *Weth* —4K **17**
Horsfall Ct. *Hal* —3E **130**
Horsfall St. *Morl* —1K **119**
**Horsforth. —4F 65**
Horsforth New Rd. *Leeds* —6C **64**
Horsham Ct. *Kei* —6G **39**
Horsham Rd. *B'frd* —4G **99**
Horsley St. *B'frd* —5J **97**
Horsman St. *B'frd* —5G **99**
**Horton Bank. —4D 96**
**Horton Bank Bottom. —3G 97**
**Horton Bank Top. —4C 96**
Horton Clo. *Rod* —1D **82**
Horton Gth. *Rod* —1D **82**
Horton Grange Rd. *B'frd* —7H **79**
Horton Hall Clo. *B'frd* —1K **97**
Horton Pk. Av. *B'frd* —1H **97**
Horton Ri. *Rod* —1D **82**
Horton St. *Hal* —2G **131**
Horton St. *Heck* —5B **136**
Horton Ter. *Hal* —7B **114**
Hospital La. *Leeds* —2K **65**
Hospital Rd. *Riddl* —2D **40**
Hothfield St. *Sils* —1F **21**
Hough. *Hal* —6K **113**
Hough Clo. *Leeds* —5F **83**
**Hough End. —5G 83**
Hough End Av. *Leeds* —4H **83**
Hough End Clo. *Leeds* —4H **83**
Hough End Ct. *Leeds* —4H **83**
Hough End Cres. *Leeds* —4G **83**
Hough End Gdns. *Leeds* —4H **83**
Hough End Gth. *Leeds* —4G **83**
Hough End La. *Leeds* —4G **83**
Hough Gro. *Leeds* —3G **83**
Hough La. *Leeds* —3G **83**
Houghley Av. *Leeds* —3K **83**
Houghley Clo. *Leeds* —3J **83**
Houghley Cres. *Leeds* —3K **83**
Houghley La. *Leeds* —3J **83**
Houghley Pl. *Leeds* —3K **83**
Houghley Rd. *Leeds* —3K **83**
Houghley Sq. *Leeds* —3K **83**
**Hough Side. —6E 82**
Hough Side Clo. *Pud* —6F **83**
Hough Side La. *Pud* —6E **82**
Hough Side Rd. *Pud* —6D **82**
Hough Ter. *Leeds* —3G **83**
Houghton Pl. *B'frd* —5K **79** (2C **6**)
Houghton St. *Brigh* —5H **133**
Houghton Towers. *Sower B* —4K **129**
Hough Top. *Leeds* —6E **82**
Hough Tree Rd. *Leeds* —5G **83**
Hough Tree Ter. *Leeds* —5G **83**
Hougomont. *Q'bry* —3G **95**
Hoults La. *G'lnd* —1F **143**
**Hove Edge. —3F 133**
Hovingham Av. *Leeds* —1C **86**
Hovingham Gro. *Leeds* —1C **86**
Hovingham Mt. *Leeds* —1C **86**
Hovingham Ter. *Leeds* —1C **86**
Howard Av. *Leeds* —6H **87**
Howard Ct. *Leeds* —6H **87**
Howard Pk. *Cleck* —1G **135**
Howard Pl. *Bat* —5G **137**
Howard St. *Bat* —5G **137**
Howard St. *B'frd* —7K **79** (6C **6**)
Howard St. *Hal* —7E **112**
Howarth Av. *B'frd* —7C **62**
Howarth Cres. *B'frd* —7C **62**
Howbeck Av. *Riddl* —2E **40**
Howbeck Dri. *Riddl* —3F **41**
Howcans La. *B'twn* —3E **112**
(in two parts)
Howden Av. *Kei* —1J **39**
Howden Brook. *Hal* —7D **96**
Howden Clo. *B'frd* —5H **99**
**Howden Clough. —4F 119**
Howden Clough Ind. Est. *Bat* —4G **119**
Howden Clough Rd. *Morl* —4G **119**
Howden Gdns. *Leeds* —3E **84**
Howden Pl. *Leeds* —3E **84**
Howden Rd. *Sils* —1G **21**
Howden Way. *Morl* —4H **119**
Howes La. *N'wram* —4K **113**
Howgate. *B'frd* —4E **62**
Howgill Grn. *B'frd* —1G **115**
Howley Mill La. *Bat* —1H **137**
Howley Pk. Clo. *Morl* —5K **119**
Howley Pk. Rd. *Morl* —5K **119**
Howley Pk. Rd. E. *Morl* —5K **119**
Howley Pk. Ter. *Morl* —5K **119**
Howley Pk. Trad. Est. *Morl* —5K **119**
Howley St. *Bat* —2H **137**
Howley Wlk. *Bat* —3J **137**
Howroyd La. *Bklnd* —5K **141**
Howson Clo. *Guis* —2H **45**
Hoxton Mt. *Leeds* —3F **103**
Hoxton St. *B'frd* —5G **79**
Hoylake Av. *Hud* —6F **145**
Hoyle Ct. Av. *Bail* —1A **62**
Hoyle Ct. Dri. *Bail* —1A **62**
Hoyle Ct. Rd. *Bail* —1A **62**
Hoyle Fold. *Kei* —6H **39**
Hoyle Ing Rd. *I'tn* —7K **77**
**Hubberton Green. —6E 128**
Hubberton Grn. Rd. *Sower B* —6E **128**
Hubert St. *B'frd* —7D **80**
Hubert St. *Hal* —1B **130**
Huddersfield Rd. *Brigh* —2H **145**
Huddersfield Rd. *Ell* —5A **144**
Huddersfield Rd. *Hal* —3G **131**
(in two parts)
Huddersfield Rd. *Heck & Bat* —1C **136**
Huddersfield Rd. *Hud* —6A **144**
Huddersfield Rd. *Liv* —7J **135**
Huddersfield Rd. *Wyke & B'frd* —7H **115**
(in three parts)
Hud Hill. *Hal* —3B **114**
Hudson Av. *B'frd* —2H **97**
Hudson Clo. *B'frd* —3H **97**
Hudson Clo. *Weth* —4J **17**
Hudson Cres. *B'frd* —3H **97**
Hudson Gdns. *B'frd* —3H **97**
Hudson Gro. *Leeds* —4C **86**
Hudson M. *B Spa* —3E **36**
Hudson Pl. *Leeds* —4C **86**
Hudson Rd. *Leeds* —3C **86**
Hudson's Ter. *Yead* —4A **46**
Hudson St. *B'frd* —6F **81**
Hudson St. *Fars* —4B **82**
Hudson St. *Leeds* —4C **86**
Hudson, The. *Wyke* —4J **115**
Hudswell Rd. *Leeds* —2K **103**
*Huggan Row. Pud —6D **82***
*(off Hammerton Gro.)*
Hughenden Vw. *Morl* —1A **120**
Hughendon Dri. *T'tn* —7A **78**
Hughendon Wlk. *T'tn* —7A **78**
Hugh St. *C'frd* —7D **126**
(in two parts)
Hugill St. *T'tn* —7H **77**
Hulbert St. *Bgly* —2A **60**
Hullenedge Gdns. *Ell* —3H **143**
Hullenedge La. *G'lnd* —3G **143**
Hullenedge Rd. *Ell* —3H **143**
Hullen Rd. *Ell* —3H **143**
Hullett Clo. *H Bri* —6B **110**
Hullett Dri. *H Bri* —6B **110**
Hull St. *Morl* —3B **120**
Hulme Sq. *C'frd* —6K **127**
*Hulme St. Sower B —5K **129***
*(off Syke La.)*
Humber Clo. *C'frd* —7H **127**
Humboldt St. *B'frd* —6C **80** (4H **7**)
Hume Crest. *Bat* —3G **137**
**Hungate. —7C 124**
Hungate La. *Meth* —7C **124**
**Hunger Hill. —6K 95**
Hunger Hill. *Hal* —2G **131**
Hunger Hill. *Midd* —2C **12**
Hunger Hill. *Morl* —4A **120**
Hunger Hills Av. *H'fth* —3E **64**
Hunger Hills Dri. *H'fth* —3E **64**
**Hunslet. —2K 103**
**Hunslet Carr. —5K 103**
Hunslet Distributor. *Leeds* —2K **103**
Hunslet Grn. Way. *Leeds* —2K **103**
Hunslet Hall Rd. *Leeds* —2H **103**
Hunslet La. *Leeds* —7J **85**
Hunslet Rd. *Leeds* —6J **85**
(in two parts)
Hunslet Trad. Est. *Leeds* —2B **104**
**Hunsworth. —4F 117**
Hunsworth La. *Cleck & E Bier* —6F **117**
Hunter Hill Rd. *Hal* —2J **111**
Hunters Ct. *B'frd* —1C **78**
Hunters Grn. *Cull* —5B **58**
Hunters Mdw. *Sils* —7G **9**
Hunters Pk. Av. *Cytn* —1D **96**
Hunters Wlk. *Weth* —1J **17**
Huntingdon Rd. *Brigh* —7J **133**
Huntock Pl. *Brigh* —3F **133**
Huntsmans Clo. *Bgly* —6C **42**
Huntsmans Clo. *Kei* —3J **39**
Hunt St. *C'frd* —6D **126**
(in three parts)
Hunt St. *W'wd M* —7B **126**
Hunt Yd. *B'frd* —2G **97**
Hurstville Av. *B'frd* —1H **117**
Husler Gro. *Leeds* —2K **85**
Husler Pl. *Leeds* —2K **85**
Hustings, The. *Liv* —4H **135**
Hustlergate. *B'frd* —6A **80** (4E **6**)
Hustler's Row. *Leeds* —4D **66**
Hustler St. *B'frd* —4C **80** (1J **7**)
Hutchinson La. *Brigh* —6H **133**
Hutchinson Pl. *Leeds* —2A **84**
Hutson St. *B'frd* —2K **97**
Hutton Dri. *Heck* —4C **136**
Hutton Rd. *B'frd* —4J **97**
Hutton Ter. *B'frd* —7F **63**
Hutton Ter. *Pud* —6C **82**
Hydale Clo. *Kei* —6C **40**
Hydale Ct. *Low M* —1J **115**
*Hydo Gro. Kei —3B **40***
*(off Kirby St.)*
**Hyde Park. —2F 85**
Hyde Pk. *Hal* —2E **130**
Hyde Pk. Clo. *Leeds* —3F **85**
Hyde Pk. Corner. *Leeds* —2F **85**
*Hyde Pk. Gdns. Hal —3E **130***
*(off Haugh Shaw Rd.)*
Hyde Pk. Pl. *Leeds* —2F **85**
Hyde Pk. Rd. *Hal* —3E **130**
Hyde Pk. Rd. *Leeds* —3F **85**
Hyde Pk. St. *Hal* —3E **130**
Hyde Pk. Ter. *Leeds* —2F **85**
Hyde Pl. *Leeds* —4G **85** (4A **4**)
Hyde St. *B'frd* —3D **62**
Hyde St. *Leeds* —4G **85** (4A **4**)
Hyde Ter. *Leeds* —4G **85** (3A **4**)
Hydro Clo. *I'ly* —6F **13**
Hyne Av. *B'frd* —5D **98**
Hyrst Gth. *Bat* —5F **137**
Hyrstlands Rd. *Bat* —5F **137**
Hyrst Wlk. *Bat* —5G **137**
Ibbetson Clo. *Morl* —7A **102**
Ibbetson Ct. *Morl* —7A **102**
Ibbetson Cft. *Morl* —7A **102**
Ibbetson Dri. *Morl* —7A **102**
Ibbetson M. *Morl* —7A **102**
Ibbetson Oval. *Morl* —7A **102**
Ibbetson Ri. *Morl* —7A **102**
Ibbetson Rd. *Morl* —7A **102**
Ida's, The. *Leeds* —4C **104**
Ida St. *B'frd* —3J **97**
Ida St. *Leeds* —4C **104**
Iddesleigh St. *B'frd* —7F **81**
**Idle. —4D 62**
Idlecroft Rd. *B'frd* —4D **62**
**Idle Moor. —5B 62**
Idle Rd. *Five E* —7C **62**
Idlethorp Way. *B'frd* —5E **62**
Ilbert Av. *B'frd* —5E **98**
Ilford St. *Morl* —3B **120**
**Ilkley. —5B 12**
Ilkley Hall M. *I'ly* —6B **12**
Ilkley Hall Pk. *I'ly* —6B **12**
Ilkley Rd. *Add* —2F **11**
Ilkley Rd. *Bur W* —6J **13**
Ilkley Rd. *Otley* —3G **27**
Ilkley Rd. *Riddl* —1D **40**
**Illingworth. —7D 94**
Illingworth Av. *Hal* —6C **94**
*Illingworth Bldgs. Oaken —3B **116***
*(off Illingworth Rd.)*
Illingworth Clo. *Hal* —7C **94**
Illingworth Clo. *Yead* —6A **46**
Illingworth Cres. *Hal* —7C **94**
Illingworth Dri. *Hal* —7C **94**
Illingworth Gdns. *Hal* —1C **112**
Illingworth Gro. *Hal* —7C **94**
Illingworth La. *Hal* —1C **112**
Illingworth Rd. *Oaken* —3B **116**
Illingworth Way. *Hal* —7C **94**
Incline, The. *Hal* —7J **113**
Independent St. *B'frd* —3J **97**
Indus Clo. *Heck* —4C **136**
Industrial Av. *Birs* —6B **118**
Industrial Rd. *Sower B* —4K **129**
Industrial St. *Bgly* —1K **59**
Industrial St. *Brigh* —5H **133**
Industrial St. *Kei* —5J **39**
Industrial St. *Leeds* —4B **86**
Industrial St. *Liv* —4G **135**
Industrial St. *Schol* —7B **116**
Industrial Ter. *Hal* —3F **131**
Infirmary Rd. *Dew* —7F **137**
Infirmary St. *B'frd* —5K **79**
(in two parts)
Infirmary St. *Leeds* —5H **85** (6D **4**)
Ing Fld. *Oaken* —3C **116**
Ingham Clo. *Hal* —6D **94**
Ingham La. *Hal* —5C **94**
Inghams Av. *Pud* —6K **81**
Inghams Ct. *Hal* —6E **112**
Inghams Ter. *Pud* —5K **81**
Inghams Vw. *Pud* —5K **81**
Inghead Gdns. *She* —3B **114**
Ing Head Ter. *Hal* —3B **114**
(in three parts)
Ingle Av. *Morl* —1K **119**
Ingleborough Dri. *Morl* —4C **120**
Ingleby Pl. *B'frd* —7G **79**
Ingleby Rd. *B'frd* —5G **79**
Ingleby St. *B'frd* —6G **79**
Ingleby Way. *Leeds* —7A **104**
Ingle Ct. *Morl* —2K **119**
Ingle Cres. *Morl* —1A **120**
Ingledew Ct. *Leeds* —7K **49**
Ingledew Cres. *Leeds* —2D **68**
Ingledew Dri. *Leeds* —3D **68**
Ingle Gro. *Morl* —2K **119**
Ingle Row. *Leeds* —6K **67**
Ingleton Clo. *Leeds* —3H **103**
Ingleton Dri. *Leeds* —6G **87**
Ingleton Gro. *Leeds* —3H **103**
*Ingleton Ho. B'frd —4G **99***
*(off Arlesford Rd.)*
Ingleton Pl. *Leeds* —3H **103**
Ingleton St. *Leeds* —3H **103**
Inglewood App. *Leeds* —2K **87**
Inglewood Av. *Hud* —7C **144**
Inglewood Dri. *Leeds* —2K **87**
Inglewood Dri. *Otley* —3H **27**
Inglewood Pl. *Leeds* —2K **87**
*Inglewood Ter. Leeds —1G **85***
*(off Delph La.)*
Ingram Clo. *Leeds* —1F **103**
Ingram Ct. *Leeds* —1F **103**
Ingram Cres. *Leeds* —2F **103**
Ingram Gdns. *Leeds* —1F **103**
Ingram Pde. *Rothw* —2G **123**
Ingram Rd. *Leeds* —2F **103**
Ingram Row. *Leeds* —7H **85**
Ingram Sq. *Hal* —3E **130**
Ingram St. *Hal* —3E **130**
Ingram St. *Kei* —1K **57**
Ingram St. *Leeds* —7H **85**
Ingram Vw. *Leeds* —1F **103**
**Ingrow. —7J 39**

Ingrow La.—Kennerleigh Dri.


Ingrow La. Kei —7H 39
Ingrow Railway Centre Museum. —7K 39
Ings Av. Guis —1F 45
Ings Ct. Guis —1E 44
Ings Cres. Guis —2E 44
Ings Cres. Leeds —6D 86
Ings Cres. Liv —4K 135
Ings Dri. Meth —4J 125
Ings Grange. Liv —3K 135
(off Ings Rd.)
Ings La. C'frd —5F 127
Ings La. Guis —2E 44
Ings La. Leds —3D 126
Ings La. Otley —2K 27
Ings La. Thor A —2G 37
Ings Rd. Bat —2E 136
Ings Rd. Dew —7J 137
Ings Rd. Heck —4B 136
Ings Rd. Leeds —6D 86
Ings Rd. Liv —3K 135
Ings Rd. Steet —4D 20
Ings, The. Hal —2G 133
Ing St. B'frd —6F 81
Ings Vw. C'frd —7H 127
Ings Vw. Meth —4J 125
Ings Villa. Liv —6A 136
Ings Way. B'frd —5E 78
Ings Way. Sils —1G 21
Ingwell Ter. Cleck —1G 135
Inholmes La. Wltn —6H 19
Inkerman St. B'frd —2F 99
Inkerman St. Haig —1F 81
Inner Ring Rd. Leeds —4G 85
Institute Rd. B'frd —7E 62
Intake. —1D 82
Intake Gro. B'frd —3E 80
Intake La. Bat —7D 118
Intake La. Leeds —4J 121
Intake La. Oxe —5C 74
Intake La. Rawd —1B 64
Intake La. Rod —2D 82
Intake La. Steet —6B 20
Intake La. T'ner —1B 70
Intake Mt. Leeds —3J 121
Intake Rd. B'frd —3E 80
Intake Rd. Pud —5D 82
Intake Sq. Leeds —3J 121
Intake Ter. B'frd —4E 80
Intake, The. Kip —5B 108
Intake Vw. Int —2E 82
Intake Vw. Leeds —3J 121
Intercity Way. Leeds —4D 82
Invargarry Clo. Gar —5B 90
Inverness Rd. Gar —6B 90
Invertrees Av. Rawd —7A 46
Iona Pl. Hal —5G 113
(off Iona St.)
Iona St. Hal —5G 113
Ireland Cres. Leeds —1K 65
Ireland St. Bgly —1J 59
Ireland Ter. Bgly —1J 59
Ireland Wood. —2K 65
Ireton St. B'frd —7H 79
Irish La. Oakw —2C 56
Iron Row. Bur W —1B 26
Iron St. Wgte —1E 134
Ironwood App. Leeds —2J 87
Ironwood Cres. Leeds —2J 87
Ironwood Vw. Leeds —1J 87
Irvine St. Hal —3D 130
Irving Ter. Cytn —3C 96
Irvin Ter. C'frd —7C 126
Irwell St. B'frd —1C 98
Irwin App. Leeds —6H 87
Irwin St. Fars —3B 82
(in two parts)
Isaac St. B'frd —5H 79
Islay Clo. Rothw —2H 123
Isle La. Oxe —6E 74
Isles St. B'frd —5F 79
Islington. —2E 102
Ivanhoe Rd. B'frd —1H 97
Ivegate. B'frd —6A 80 (4E 6)
Ivegate. Yead —4K 45
Ive Ho. La. Hal —7G 111
Iveson App. Leeds —2K 65
Iveson Clo. Leeds —2K 65
Iveson Cres. Leeds —2K 65
Iveson Dri. Leeds —2K 65
Iveson Gdns. Leeds —2K 65
Iveson Gth. Leeds —2A 66
Iveson Grn. Leeds —2K 65
Iveson Gro. Leeds —2K 65
Iveson Lawn. Leeds —2A 66
Iveson Ri. Leeds —2A 66
Iveson Rd. Leeds —2K 65
Ives St. Shipl —4H 61
(in two parts)
Ivory St. Leeds —1J 103
Ivy Av. Leeds —5C 86
Ivy Bank. Wyke —3J 115
Ivy Bank. Yead —4J 45
Ivy Bank Ct. Bail —2K 61
(off Dewhirst Clo.)
Ivy Bank La. Haw —6E 56
Ivy Chase. Leeds —5F 83
Ivy Ct. Leeds —6K 67
Ivy Cres. Hal —1E 132
Ivy Cres. Leeds —5C 86
Ivy Gdns. Bmly —1H 83
Ivy Gth. Leeds —6K 67
Ivy Gro. Leeds —6D 86
Ivy Gro. Shipl —5E 60
Ivy Ho. Rd. B'frd —5A 98
Ivy La. All —4A 78
Ivy La. B Spa —3C 36
Ivy La. Hal —1B 112
Ivy Mt. Hal —6H 131
Ivy Mt. Leeds —5C 86
Ivy Pl. Leeds —1H 83
Ivy Rd. Kei —5C 40
Ivy Rd. Leeds —6C 86
Ivy Rd. Shipl —5E 60
Ivy St. Brigh —5F 133
Ivy St. Hal —3E 130
Ivy St. Kei —3K 39
Ivy St. Leeds —5C 86
Ivy St. S. Hal —3E 130
Ivy St. S. Kei —1K 57
Ivy Ter. Brigh —5F 133
(off Ivy St.)
Ivy Ter. Kei —5D 40
Ivy Ter. Light —1E 132
Ivy Vw. Leeds —5C 86

Jacinth Ct. Far —7J 145
Jackdaw Clo. All —6B 78
Jackdaw La. B Spa —2C 36
Jackie Smart Ct. Leeds —2A 86
Jackie Smart Rd. B'frd —3A 98
Jack La. Bat —6H 137
Jack La. Leeds —1H 103
(in two parts)
Jackman Dri. H'fth —4H 65
Jackson Av. Leeds —5B 68
Jackson Hill. Q'bry —7K 95
Jackson La. Bklnd —4J 141
Jackson Meadows. Bklnd —4J 141
Jackson Rd. Leeds —2J 85
Jackson's La. Sils —4A 8
Jackson St. B'frd —7C 80 (6J 7)
Jacky La. Haw —6E 56
Jacob St. B'frd —2K 97
Jacob St. Leeds —4J 85 (4F 5)
Jacobs Well. B'frd —7A 80 (5E 6)
Jacques Gro. Sils —1H 21
Jade Pl. Far —7J 145
Jagger Green. —6G 143
Jagger Grn. Dean. Holy G —6F 143
Jagger Grn. La. Holy G —7F 143
Jail Rd. Bat —3D 136
Jail Yd. Rothw —2H 123
Jakeman Clo. Ting —7E 120
Jakeman Ct. Ting —7E 120
Jakeman Dri. Ting —7E 120
James Av. Ebrn —5C 20
James Av. Leeds —4B 68
James Baillie Flats. Leeds —7F 67
James Clo. Gar —6A 90
James Ct. Coll —2F 35
(off Station La.)
James Ga. B'frd —6A 80 (4D 6)
James St. All —4C 78
James St. Bat —4F 137
James St. B'shaw —1J 117
James St. B'frd —6A 80 (3D 6)
James St. Brigh —4G 133
James St. C'frd —6D 126
James St. Dew —7F 137
James St. Ell —3K 143
James St. Holy G —5F 143
James St. Liv —4J 135
(nr. Halifax Rd.)
James St. Liv —5K 135
(nr. Union Rd.)
James St. Oakw —2D 56
James St. Rawd —7K 45
James St. T'tn —7H 77
Jamie Ct. B'frd —6F 63
Jane Grn. Hal —4B 94
Jane Hills. Shipl —4G 61
(off Riverside Est.)
Jane St. Denh —4B 76
Jane St. Shipl —4F 61
Janesway. Kip —4K 107
Janet St. Haw —4G 57
Jaques Clo. Leeds —1B 84
Jardine Rd. Bgly —1A 60
Jardine St. Bgly —1A 60
Jarratt St. B'frd —4H 79
Jarratt St. E. B'frd —4H 79
Jarrom Clo. B'frd —2F 99
Jarvis Sq. Rob H —4C 122
Jarvis Wlk. Rob H —4C 122
Jasmin Ter. B'frd —5J 79
Jasper St. B'frd —4D 62
Jasper St. Hal —1D 130
Javelin Clo. B'frd —6D 62
Jaw Hill. —5G 139
Jay Ho. La. Brigh —3J 133
Jay St. Haw —5F 57
(in two parts)
Jean Av. Leeds —6J 87
Jenkinson Clo. Leeds —1G 103
Jenkinson Lawn. Leeds —1G 103
Jenkinsons Pl. Leeds —6K 103
Jenkinson St. Bat —6G 137
Jennetts Cres. Otley —3H 27
Jennings Clo. Sils —2H 21
Jennings Pl. B'frd —2G 97
Jennings St. B'frd —2G 97
Jenny La. Bail —7K 43
Jenson Av. Dew —5D 136
Jepson La. Ell —3K 143
Jeremy La. Heck —4A 136
Jer Gro. B'frd —4E 96
Jer La. B'frd —4E 96
Jermyn St. B'frd —6B 80 (3G 7)
Jerry Clay La. Wren —5K 139
Jerry La. Sower B —5J 129
Jerry Spring Rd. Hal —2F 129
Jersey Clo. Dew —6K 137
Jerusalem La. Hal —3E 110
Jervaulx Clo. B Spa —3C 36
Jervaulx Cres. B'frd —5J 79 (1A 6)
Jerwood Hill Clo. Hal —6H 113
Jerwood Hill Rd. Hal —6H 113
Jesmond Av. B'frd —3F 79
Jesmond Gro. B'frd —3F 79
Jesmond Gro. Dew —7F 137
Jessamine Av. Leeds —5F 103
Jessamine Pl. Cro H —4A 20
Jesse St. B'frd —1A 98
(BD5)
Jesse St. B'frd —6D 78
(BD8)
Jessop Row. Leeds —6A 84
Jessop St. C'frd —7D 126
Jester Pl. Q'bry —4G 95
Jewitt La. Coll —4F 35
Jew La. Oxe —3E 74
Jilley Royd La. Hud —5G 145
(in two parts)
Jill La. Mir —7C 136
Jim Allen La. Hal —6E 110
Jinny Moor La. Rothw —6C 106
Jin-Whin Ct. C'frd —7A 126
Jin-Whin Hill. C'frd —7A 126
Jin-Whin Ter. C'frd —7A 126
Joan Royd. Heck —2B 136
Joba Av. B'frd —6D 80
Joffre Mt. Yead —5A 46
(off Springwell Clo.)
John Booth Clo. Liv —6H 135
John Escritt Rd. Bgly —2A 60
John Naylor La. Hal —3G 129
John Nelson Clo. Bat —6D 118
Johnny La. Otley —4J 27
John O'Gaunts. —7J 105
John O'Gaunts Trad. Est. Rothw —7G 105
John O'Gaunts Wlk. Rothw —1H 123
John Ormsby V.C. Way. Dew —5A 138
Johns La. Ell —5K 143
Johnson St. Bgly —7K 41
Johnson St. B'frd —6F 81
Johnson Ter. Morl —3B 120
Johnston St. Leeds —2H 85
John St. Bail —3J 61
John St. Birs —6C 118
John St. B'frd —6A 80 (3D 6)
(BD1)
John St. B'frd —5G 99
(BD4)
John St. Brigh —5G 133
John St. Cytn —3C 96
John St. Cull —6B 58
John St. Denh —4B 76
John St. Dew —6G 137
John St. Eastb —7J 137
John St. Ell —3K 143
John St. G'lnd —2G 143
John St. Hal —1G 131
John St. Heck —5B 136
John St. Leeds —2E 84
John St. Oakw —2F 57
John St. Rawd —7K 45
John St. Shipl —4G 61
John St. T'tn —7H 77
John St. Mkt. B'frd —6A 80 (3D 6)
John St. W. Sower B —4K 129
John William St. Cleck —7F 117
John William St. Ell —3K 143
John William St. Flush —4A 136
John William St. Liv —5K 135
Jonathan Gth. Add —1C 10
Joseph Av. Hal —5A 114
Joseph Ri. Leeds —5K 67
Joseph St. B'frd —6C 80 (4H 7)
(BD3, in two parts)
Joseph St. B'frd —5G 99
(BD4)
Joseph St. Leeds —2A 104
Joseph's Well. Leeds —5B 4
Joseph Vs. Cytn —2B 96
Joseph Wright Ct. B'frd —3C 62
(off Greenfield La.)
Jowett Pk. Cres. B'frd —2C 62
Jowett's La. Sils —1F 9
Jowett St. B'frd —6J 79 (3A 6)
Jowett Ter. Morl —5A 120
Jubilee Ct. Morl —3B 120
(off Marshall St.)
Jubilee Cres. Dlgtn —7E 100
Jubilee Cft. Dlgtn —7D 100
Jubilee Dri. Kei —6J 39
Jubilee Mt. Brigh —6F 133
Jubilee Pl. Morl —3B 120
Jubilee Rd. Hal —6H 131
Jubilee St. B'frd —4K 79 (1C 6)
Jubilee St. Cut H —2F 99
Jubilee St. Hal —2H 131
Jubilee St. H Bri —6A 110
Jubilee St. Morl —3B 120
Jubilee St. N. Hal —4E 112
Jubilee Ter. Hal —2H 131
(off Jubilee St.)
Jubilee Ter. Morl —3B 120
Jubilee Ter. Sower B —3G 141
Jubilee Trees. Bur W —3J 25
Jubilee Way. Shipl —4K 61
Judy La. Fix —6H 145
Julian Dri. Q'bry —4C 96
Jumb Beck Clo. Bur W —2B 26
Jumble Dyke. Brigh —1F 145
Jumbles Ct. Loft —6E 122
Jumbles La. Loft —6E 122
Jumples. Hal —3B 112
Jumples Clo. Hal —3B 112
Jumples Ct. Hal —3A 112
Jumples Crag. Hal —3B 112
Junction Houses. C'frd —6C 126
Junction Rd. Shipl —4J 61
Junction Row. B'frd —1D 80
(off Bolton Rd.)
Junction St. Leeds —7J 85
Junction Ter. B'frd —1D 80
(off Bolton Rd.)
June St. Kei —3A 40
Juniper Av. Rothw —7C 106
Juniper Clo. B'frd —5H 79
Juniper Pl. Leeds —4D 86

Karnac Rd. Leeds —1B 86
Katherine St. Shipl —4F 61
Kaycell St. B'frd —4D 98
Kay Clo. Morl —1K 119
Kaye Hill. Cull —6B 58
Kaye St. Heck —5B 136
Kay St. Shipl —7J 61
Kearsley Ter. Leeds —4A 104
Keats Dri. Heck —6C 136
Kebble Ct. Gom —1K 135
Keble Gth. Kip —4C 108
Kebroyd. —2G 141
Kebroyd Av. Sower B —2G 141
Kebroyd La. Tri —2G 141
Kebroyd Mt. Sower B —2G 141
Kedleston Rd. Leeds —2B 68
Keeble Ho. B'frd —3F 81
(off St Clare's Av.)
Keelam Ga. H Bri —2A 110
Keelam La. H Bri —2A 110
Keeldar Clo. B'frd —3H 97
Keelham. —1C 94
Keelham La. Kei —1J 39
Keelham Pl. Denh —1D 94
Keel Moorings. Rod —7D 64
Keeper La. B'frd —3B 100
Keeton St. Leeds —5B 86 (6K 5)
Keighley. —6B 40
Keighley & Worth Valley Railway. —4B 40
Keighley Clo. Hal —1C 112
Keighley Dri. Hal —2C 112
Keighley Ind. Pk. Kei —2B 40
Keighley Pl. S'ley —3C 82
Keighley Retail Pk. Kei —2A 40
Keighley Rd. Bgly —7D 40
Keighley Rd. B'frd —1H 79
Keighley Rd. Cro H —3A 20
Keighley Rd. Cull —5A 58
Keighley Rd. Denh —2A 76
Keighley Rd. Oakw —2F 57
Keighley Rd. Ogden —5B 94
(in two parts)
Keighley Rd. Oxe —2E 74
Keighley Rd. Riddl —3J 23
(in two parts)
Keighley Rd. Sils —3F 21
Keighley Rd. Steet —5F 21
Keir Hardie Clo. Liv —4K 135
Kelbrook Ho. B'frd —4G 99
(off Muirhead Dri.)
Kelburn Gro. Oakw —1D 56
Kelcliffe. —1F 45
Kelcliffe Av. Guis —2G 45
Kelcliffe Gro. Guis —2G 45
Kelcliffe La. Guis —1F 45
Keldholme Clo. Leeds —7C 64
Keldholme Rd. Leeds —7C 64
Kell Beck. Otley —7H 15
Kellett Av. Leeds —2C 102
Kellett Bldgs. Low M —2K 115
Kellett Cres. Leeds —2C 102
Kellett Dri. Leeds —2C 102
Kellett Gro. Leeds —2C 102
Kellett La. Leeds —1B 102
Kellett Mt. Leeds —2C 102
Kellett Pl. Leeds —2C 102
Kellett Rd. Leeds —1B 102
Kellett Ter. Leeds —2C 102
Kellett Wlk. Leeds —2C 102
Kell La. Stum X —4K 113
Kelloe St. Cleck —6F 117
Kell St. Bgly —1A 60
Kellymoor Wlk. Idle —5B 62
Kelmore Gro. B'frd —1E 114
Kelmore Ho. B'frd —4E 62
(off Albion Rd.)
Kelmscott Av. Leeds —2B 88
Kelmscott Cres. Leeds —2B 88
Kelmscott Gdns. Leeds —2B 88
Kelmscott Gth. Leeds —1C 88
Kelmscott Grn. Leeds —2B 88
Kelmscott Gro. Leeds —2B 88
Kelmscott La. Leeds —2B 88
Kelsall Av. Leeds —3E 84
Kelsall Gro. Leeds —4E 84
Kelsall Ho. B'frd —2G 7
Kelsall Pl. Leeds —3E 84
Kelsall Rd. Leeds —3E 84
Kelsall Ter. Leeds —3E 84
Kelsey St. Hal —7D 112
Kelso Ct. Leeds —4F 85
Kelso Gdns. Leeds —4F 85
Kelso Pl. Leeds —3F 85
Kelso Rd. Leeds —3F 85 (3A 4)
Kelso St. Leeds —4F 85 (3A 4)
Kelton Ho. B'frd —4C 98
(off Spring Wood Gdns.)
Kelvin Av. Hal —1B 130
Kelvin Cres. Hal —2B 130
Kelvin Ho. B'frd —3H 99
Kelvin Pl. B'frd —1C 98
Kelvin Rd. Ell —3J 143
Kelvin Way. B'frd —3E 80
Kempton Rd. Kip —4A 108
Kemsing Wlk. Leeds —3D 88
Kendal Bank. Leeds —4F 85 (4A 4)
Kendal Carr. Leeds —4A 4
Kendal Clo. C'frd —7K 127
Kendal Clo. Leeds —4F 85 (4A 4)
Kendal Dri. C'frd —7K 127
Kendal Dri. Leeds —6G 87
Kendal Gdns. C'frd —7K 127
Kendal Gth. C'frd —7K 127
Kendal Gro. Leeds —4A 4
Kendal La. Leeds —4F 85 (4A 4)
Kendall Av. Shipl —4E 60
Kendal Mellor Ct. Kei —4K 39
Kendal Ri. Leeds —5A 4
Kendal Rd. Leeds —4G 85 (4A 4)
Kendal St. Kei —5B 40
Kendal Wlk. Leeds —5A 4
Kendell St. Leeds —6J 85 (7F 5)
Kenilworth Av. Gild —1H 119
Kenilworth Dri. Hal —2G 133
Kenilworth Gdns. Gild —7H 101
Kenilworth Rd. Leeds —1C 102
Kenilworth St. B'frd —2D 98
Kenley Av. B'frd —4G 97
Kenley Mt. B'frd —4G 97
Kenley Pde. B'frd —4F 97
Kenmore Av. Cleck —7E 116
Kenmore Clo. Cleck —7E 116
Kenmore Cres. B'frd —4G 97
Kenmore Cres. Cleck —7E 116
Kenmore Dri. B'frd —4G 97
Kenmore Dri. Cleck —7E 116
Kenmore Gro. B'frd —4G 97
Kenmore Gro. Cleck —7E 116
Kenmore Rd. B'frd —4G 97
Kenmore Rd. Cleck —7E 116
Kenmore Vw. Cleck —7E 116
Kenmore Wlk. B'frd —4G 97
Kenmore Way. Cleck —7E 116
Kennedy Av. Hud —5G 145
Kennedy Clo. Dew —5K 137
Kennedy Ho. Kei —7K 39
(off Hainworth La.)
Kennel La. Oxe —3A 74
(in two parts)
Kennel La. Sower B —1C 140
(in two parts)
Kennels La. T'ner —4D 52
Kennerleigh Av. Leeds —4A 88
Kennerleigh Cres. Leeds —4B 88
Kennerleigh Dri. Leeds —4A 88

Kennerleigh Gth.—Lady Ann Rd.


Kennerleigh Gth. Leeds —4B 88
Kennerleigh Glen. Leeds —4A 88
Kennerleigh Gro. Leeds —4B 88
Kennerleigh Ri. Leeds —4B 88
Kennerleigh Wlk. B'frd —4H 99
Kennerleigh Wlk. Leeds —4A 88
Kenneth St. Leeds —1F 103
Kennet La. Gar —7A 90
Kennion St. B'frd —2K 97
Kensington Av. T'ner —5E 52
Kensington Clo. Bat —4F 137
Kensington Clo. Hal —4E 130
Kensington Ct. Leeds —2F 85
Kensington Gdns. Ell —3J 143
Kensington Rd. Hal —4E 130
Kensington St. B'frd —4G 79
Kensington St. Kei —5K 39
*Kensington Ter. Gar —6J 89*
*(off Main St.)*
Kensington Ter. Leeds —2F 85
Kenstone Cres. B'frd —5C 62
**Kent. —6C 82**
Kent Av. Pud —6E 82
Kent Av. Sils —1F 21
Kent Clo. Pud —6E 82
Kent Cres. Pud —6E 82
Kent Dri. Pud —6E 82
Kentmere App. Leeds —7G 69
Kentmere Av. Gar —7B 90
Kentmere Av. Leeds —5H 69
Kentmere Av. Wyke —6A 116
Kentmere Clo. Leeds —7J 69
Kentmere Cres. Leeds —6H 69
Kentmere Gdns. Leeds —6H 69
Kentmere Gth. Leeds —7H 69
Kentmere Ga. Leeds —5H 69
Kentmere Grn. Leeds —6H 69
Kentmere Ri. Leeds —7J 69
Kenton Way. B'frd —2F 99
Kent Rd. Bgly —2B 60
Kent Rd. Pud —6D 82
Kent St. B'frd —7A 80 (6E 6)
Kent St. Hal —2F 131
Kenwood M. H'fth —4H 65
Kenworthy Clo. Leeds —6A 48
Kenworthy Gdns. Leeds —6A 48
Kenworthy Gth. Leeds —6A 48
Kenworthy Ga. Leeds —6A 48
Kenworthy La. Ripp —3G 141
Kenworthy Ri. Leeds —6A 48
Kenworthy Va. Leeds —6A 48
Kenya Mt. Kei —3H 39
Kenyon La. Hal —1B 130
Kepler Gro. Leeds —3A 86 (1K 5)
*Kepler Ho. B'frd —4E 98*
*(off Railway St.)*
Kepler Mt. Leeds —3A 86 (1K 5)
Kepler Ter. Leeds —3A 86 (1K 5)
Kepstorn Clo. Leeds —7A 66
Kepstorn Ri. Leeds —7A 66
Kepstorn Rd. Leeds —5B 66
Kerry Gth. H'fth —3F 65
Kerry Hill. H'fth —4F 65
(in two parts)
Kerry St. H'fth —3F 65
Kerry Vw. H'fth —3G 65
Kershaw Av. C'frd —7H 127
(in two parts)
Kershaw Ct. L'ft —7F 111
Kershaw Cres. L'ft —1F 129
Kershaw Dri. L'ft —7F 111
Kershaw St. B'frd —6F 81
Kester Rd. Bat —3D 136
Kesteven Clo. B'frd —4H 99
Kesteven Ct. B'frd —4H 99
Kesteven Rd. B'frd —4G 99
Kestrel Clo. Leeds —7B 50
Kestrel Dri. B'frd —1C 80
Kestrel Gth. Morl —3D 120
Kestrel Gro. Leeds —7B 50
Kestrel Mt. B'frd —1C 80
Kestrel Vw. Cleck —6F 117
Keswick Clo. Sld —4J 131
Keswick Dri. C'frd —5K 127
Keswick Grange. E Kes —5A 34
Keswick La. Wike —6A 34
Keswick St. B'frd —1F 99
Keswick Vw. Bard —5C 34
Kettleton Chase. Oss —7C 138
Kettlewell Dri. B'frd —3H 97
*Keverne Ho. B'frd —2K 97*
*(off Hutson St.)*
**Kew Hill. —5K 143**
Kew Hill. Hud —6K 143
Kidacre St. Leeds —7J 85
Kiddal La. Pot —1J 71
Kilburn Ho. B'frd —6E 62
Kilburn La. Dew —7G 137
Kilburn Rd. Leeds —6C 84
*Kildale Ho. B'frd —5E 62*
*(off Garsdale Av.)*
Kildare Cres. All —4A 78
Kildare Ter. Leeds —7E 84
**Kildwick. —1A 20**
**Killingbeck. —4G 87**
Killingbeck Bri. Leeds —4G 87
Killingbeck Dri. Leeds —4G 87
Killingbeck Retail Pk. Leeds —3G 87
Killinghall Av. B'frd —4D 80
Killinghall Dri. B'frd —4D 80
Killinghall Gro. B'frd —4D 80
Killinghall Rd. B'frd —3D 80
*Kilncroft. Holy G —6D 142*
*(off Stainland Rd.)*
*Kilner Ho. B'frd —3F 81*
*(off St Clares Av.)*
Kilner Rd. B'frd —5G 97
(in two parts)
Kiln Fold. Brigh —5K 133
Kiln Hill La. Sils —3D 8
Kiln La. Dew —7H 137
Kilnsea Mt. B'frd —3G 99
Kilnsey Fold. Sils —7F 9
Kilnsey Hill. Bat —6H 137
Kilnsey Rd. B'frd —7D 80
Kilpin Hill La. Dew —5D 136
Kilroyd Av. Cleck —5F 117
Kilroyd Dri. Cleck —5G 117
Kimberley Pl. Hal —3E 112
Kimberley Pl. Leeds —3D 86
Kimberley Rd. Leeds —3D 86
Kimberley St. B'frd —7E 80
Kimberley St. Brigh —5H 133
Kimberley St. Hal —3E 112
Kimberley Vw. Leeds —4D 86
Kineholme Dri. Otley —4F 27
King Alfred's Dri. Leeds —3G 67
King Alfred's Grn. Leeds —3G 67
King Alfred's Wlk. Leeds —3G 67
King Alfred's Way. Leeds —3G 67
King Charles St. Leeds —5J 85 (6E 4)
King Clo. Leeds —7G 49
**King Cross. —3C 130**
King Cross Rd. Hal —3D 130
King Cross St. Hal —3E 130
King Dri. Leeds —7F 49
King Edward Av. All B —1K 125
King Edward Av. H'fth —4F 65
King Edward Cres. Leeds —3G 65
King Edward Rd. T'tn —7H 77
King Edward St. Hal —1G 131
King Edward St. Leeds —5J 85 (6F 5)
King Edward Ter. T'tn —7H 77
King Edwins Ct. Leeds —7C 68
Kingfield. Guis —1H 45
Kingfisher Clo. Leeds —7B 50
Kingfisher Gro. B'frd —6C 78
Kingfisher M. Morl —4C 120
Kingfisher Reach. Coll —1F 35
Kingfisher Way. Leeds —7B 50
King George Av. H'fth —3G 65
King George Av. Leeds —5K 67
King George Av. Morl —1B 120
King George Cft. Morl —2B 120
King George Gdns. Leeds —5K 67
King George Gro. Morl —1B 120
King George Rd. H'fth —3G 65
*King Ho. I'ly —5A 12*
*(off Kings Rd.)*
King La. Leeds —2H 67
Kings App. Leeds —3J 83
Kings Av. I'ly —5A 12
Kings Av. Leeds —4E 84
Kingsbury Pl. Hal —2D 130
Kings Chase. Rothw —1H 123
Kings Clo. I'ly —5J 11
Kings Clo. Otley —3A 28
King's Ct. Bgly —1K 59
Kings Ct. Birs —6C 118
Kings Ct. Hal —2F 131
Kings Ct. Leeds —3J 67
Kings Cft. Gar —7H 89
King's Cft. Gdns. Leeds —3K 67
Kingsdale Av. B'frd —2C 80
Kingsdale Av. Dlgtn —1C 118
Kingsdale Ct. Leeds —6G 69
(in two parts)
Kingsdale Cres. B'frd —2C 80
Kingsdale Dri. B'frd —2C 80
Kingsdale Gdns. Dlgtn —1C 118
Kingsdale Gro. B'frd —2B 80
King's Dri. Birs —5C 118
King's Dri. B'frd —6B 62
King's Dri. B'hpe —2A 48
Kingsfield. Rothw —2D 122
King's Ga. B'frd —4A 80
Kings Gro. Bail —3E 60
Kings Gro. Bgly —7A 42
Kings Lea. Hal —6F 131
Kings Lea. Liv —6A 136
Kingsley Av. B'shaw —3K 117
Kingsley Av. B'frd —2A 80
Kingsley Av. Leeds —6B 48
Kingsley Av. Sower B —5H 129
Kingsley Clo. B'shaw —3K 117
Kingsley Cres. Bail —2J 61
Kingsley Cres. B'shaw —3K 117
Kingsley Dri. B'shaw —3K 117
Kingsley Dri. Leeds —6B 48
Kingsley Pl. Hal —2E 130
Kingsley Rd. Leeds —6B 48
Kingsmead. Leeds —4J 69
Kings Mead. Rothw —1J 123
Kingsmead Dri. Leeds —3H 69
Kings Mdw. Clo. Weth —2H 17
Kings Mdw. Dri. Weth —2H 17
Kings Mdw. Gro. Weth —2H 17
Kings Mdw. M. Weth —2H 17
Kings Mdw. Vw. Weth —2H 17
Kingsmill Clo. Morl —2K 119
Kings M. Bklnd —6H 141
King's Mt. Leeds —4J 67
Kings Pl. Leeds —1D 84
King's Rd. Bgly —6J 41
King's Rd. B'frd —3A 80
Kings Rd. B'hpe & Eccup —2A 48
Kings Rd. I'ly —5J 11
King's Rd. Leeds —3E 84
Kingston Clo. Hal —2D 130
Kingston Clo. Wilsd —7G 59
Kingston Ct. Hal —2D 130
Kingston Dri. Hal —2D 130
Kingston Gdns. Leeds —3K 87
Kingston Gro. Thack —3D 62
*Kingston Ho. B'frd —6E 62*
*(off Rowantree Dri.)*
Kingston Rd. B'frd —3D 62
Kingston St. Hal —2D 130
Kingston Ter. Hal —2D 130
Kingston Ter. Leeds —3H 85 (1C 4)
King St. B'frd —7E 62
King St. Brigh —6H 133
King St. Cleck —1G 135
King St. Dlgtn —1C 118
*King St. Ell —3A 144*
*(off Brook St.)*
King St. Hal —1H 131
King St. Haw —6E 56
King St. H Bri —7A 110
King St. Heck —4B 136
King St. Kei —5K 39
King St. Leeds —6H 85 (7C 4)
King St. Morl —4A 120
King St. Rawd —7J 45
King St. Sils —1G 21
King St. Sower B —5G 129
King St. S'ley —4B 82
King St. Yead —4A 46
Kings Vw. Hal —4A 132
Kingsway. Bgly —1A 60
Kingsway. Birs —5C 118
Kingsway. B'frd —5B 62
Kingsway. Dlgtn —1C 118
Kingsway. Gar —7H 89
Kingsway. Leeds —5A 88
Kingsway. Riddl —2E 40
*Kingsway Arc. Dew —7H 137*
*(off Northgate)*
Kingsway Ct. Leeds —3K 67
Kingsway Dri. I'ly —5A 12
Kingsway Gth. Gar —7H 89
Kingswear Clo. Leeds —4B 88
Kingswear Cres. Leeds —4B 88
Kingswear Gth. Leeds —4B 88
Kingswear Glen. Leeds —4B 88
Kingswear Gro. Leeds —4B 88
Kingswear Pde. Leeds —4B 88
Kingswear Ri. Leeds —4B 88
Kingswear Vw. Leeds —4B 88
Kingswood Av. Leeds —1C 68
Kingswood Cres. Leeds —1B 68
Kingswood Dri. Leeds —1B 68
Kingswood Gdns. Leeds —1B 68
Kingswood Gro. Leeds —1C 68
Kingswood Pl. B'frd —2G 97
Kingswood Rd. Leeds —7C 84
Kingswood St. B'frd —2G 97
Kingswood Ter. B'frd —2G 97
Kinnaird Clo. Bat —3K 137
Kinnaird Clo. Ell —1K 143
*Kinross Ho. B'frd —4G 99*
*(off Muirhead Dri.)*
*Kinsey M. Bail —1H 61*
*(off West La.)*
Kipling Ct. B'frd —5F 63
**Kippax. —5B 108**
**Kippax Common. —3K 107**
Kippax Mt. Leeds —6B 86
Kippax Pl. Leeds —6B 86
Kipping La. T'tn —7H 77
Kipping Pl. T'tn —7H 77
Kirby Cote La. Cra V —5A 128
(in two parts)
Kirby St. Kei —3B 40
Kirk Beeston Clo. Leeds —4F 103
Kirkbourne Gro. Bail —2A 62
Kirkburn Pl. B'frd —7H 79
Kirkby Av. Gar —1A 108
Kirkby Leas. Hal —2G 131
Kirkdale. C'frd —7J 127
Kirkdale Av. Leeds —3B 102
Kirkdale Cres. Leeds —3B 102
Kirkdale Dri. Leeds —2B 102
Kirkdale Gdns. Leeds —2B 102
Kirkdale Gro. Leeds —2A 102
*Kirkdale Ho. B'frd —6E 62*
*(off Rowantree Dri.)*
Kirkdale Mt. Leeds —3B 102
Kirkdale Ter. Leeds —3B 102
Kirkdale Vw. Leeds —3B 102
**Kirk Deighton. —1H 17**
Kirk Dri. Bail —7K 43
Kirkfield Av. T'ner —5E 52
Kirkfield Cres. T'ner —5E 52
Kirkfield Dri. Leeds —6B 88
Kirkfield Gdns. Leeds —6B 88
Kirkfield La. T'ner —5E 52
(in two parts)
Kirkfields. Bail —7A 44
Kirkfields Ind. Cen. Yead —4J 45
Kirkfield Vw. Leeds —6B 88
Kirkgate. Bat —5J 137
Kirk Ga. B'shaw —7H 99
Kirkgate. Birs —6B 118
Kirkgate. B'frd —6A 80 (4D 6)
(in three parts)
Kirkgate. Kild —2A 20
Kirkgate. Leeds —5J 85 (6F 5)
(in two parts)
Kirkgate. Otley —2J 27
(in two parts)
Kirkgate. Shipl —5G 61
Kirkgate. Sils —1G 21
Kirkgate Cen. B'frd —6A 80
Kirkgate Mkt. Leeds —5J 85 (6F 5)
Kirkham Av. K'gte —5H 139
**Kirkhamgate. —6H 139**
*Kirkham Ho. B'frd —4B 98*
*(off Parkway)*
Kirkham Rd. B'frd —1H 97
Kirkham St. Leeds —7D 64
Kirk Hills. T'ner —6E 52
Kirklands. Liv —4J 135
Kirklands. T'ner —6D 52
Kirklands Av. Bail —1A 62
Kirklands Clo. Bail —2A 62
Kirklands Clo. Men —6C 26
Kirklands Clo. Yead —4J 45
Kirklands Gdns. Bail —2A 62
Kirklands La. Bail —1A 62
Kirklands Rd. Bail —1K 61
Kirkland Vs. Pud —7C 82
Kirk La. Hal —7C 114
Kirk La. Yead —4H 45
Kirklees Clo. Fars —1B 82
Kirklees Cft. Fars —1B 82
Kirklees Dri. Fars —1B 82
Kirklees Gth. Fars —1B 82
Kirklees Ri. Fars —1B 82
Kirklees Rd. All —6B 78
Kirklees Way. Brigh —4E 144
Kirklees Way. Hud —7C 144
(nr. Burn Rd.)
Kirklees Way. Hud —5E 144
(nr. Cote La.)
Kirklees Way. Hud —3J 145
(nr. Shepherds Thorn La.)
Kirkley Av. Wyke —6J 115
**Kirkstall. —1B 84**
Kirkstall Abbey. —7K 65
Kirkstall Av. Leeds —2K 83
Kirkstall Cen., The. Leeds —4D 84
Kirkstall Gro. B'frd —6D 78
Kirkstall Hill. Leeds —1B 84
Kirkstall La. Leeds —1A 84
Kirkstall Mt. Leeds —2K 83
Kirkstall Rd. Leeds —2B 84
Kirkstone Dri. Gom —7K 117
Kirkstone Dri. Hal —7K 111
Kirkwall Av. Leeds —6D 86
Kirkwall Dri. B'frd —3G 99
Kirkwood Av. Leeds —7H 47
Kirkwood Clo. Leeds —6H 47
Kirkwood Cres. Leeds —6J 47
Kirkwood Dri. Leeds —6H 47
Kirkwood Gdns. Leeds —6J 47
Kirkwood Gro. Leeds —7H 47
Kirkwood Gro. Ting —7F 121
Kirkwood La. Leeds —6H 47
Kirkwood Ri. Leeds —6J 47
Kirkwood Vw. Leeds —6J 47
Kirkwood Way. Leeds —6J 47
Kismet Gdns. B'frd —5E 80
Kitchener Av. Leeds —4D 86
Kitchener Gro. Leeds —3D 86
Kitchener Mt. Leeds —4D 86
Kitchener St. Leeds —4D 86
Kitchener St. Oaken —2C 116
Kitchener St. W'ford —1A 124
Kite M. B'frd —6C 78
Kit La. Sils —4D 8
Kitson Clo. Leeds —7C 84
Kitson Gdns. Leeds —7C 84
Kitson La. Sower B —7B 130
Kitson Rd. Leeds —1K 103
Kitson St. Leeds —6B 86
Kitson St. Shipl —6J 61
Kitson St. Ting —6D 120
Kitten Clough. Hal —6C 112
Kitwood Clo. B'frd —4H 99
Kliffen Pl. Hal —4H 131
Knaresborough Dri. Hud —7G 145
Knavesmire. Rothw —2D 122
Knightsbridge Wlk. B'frd —7D 98
Knights Clo. Leeds —5A 88
Knights Cft. Weth —2K 17
Knightscroft Av. Rothw —1G 123
Knightscroft Dri. Rothw —1G 123
Knight's Fold. B'frd —2G 97
Knightshill. Leeds —5B 88
Knight St. Hal —2D 130
Knightsway. Gar —1H 107
Knightsway. Leeds —4A 88
Knightsway. Rob H —5D 122
Knoll Gdns. Bail —3H 61
Knoll Pk. E Ard —1K 139
Knoll Pk. Dri. Bail —3H 61
Knoll Ter. Bail —3H 61
Knoll, The. B'ham —7C 36
Knoll, The. C'ley —3J 81
Knoll Vw. Bail —2H 61
Knoll Wood Pk. H'fth —4H 65
Knostrop La. Leeds —2D 104
**Knotford. —1C 28**
Knott La. Ebrn —5A 20
Knott La. Rawd —4C 64
Knowle Av. Leeds —2D 84
Knowle Gro. Leeds —2D 84
Knowle La. Wyke —5K 115
Knowle Mt. Leeds —2D 84
**Knowle Park. —6K 39**
Knowle Pl. Leeds —2D 84
Knowler Clo. Liv —3J 135
**Knowler Hill. —3J 135**
Knowler Hill. Liv —4J 135
Knowle Rd. Leeds —2D 84
Knowler Way. Liv —3J 135
Knowles Av. B'frd —4F 99
*Knowles Cft. Dew —6D 136*
*(off Staincliffe Rd.)*
**Knowles Hill. —6E 136**
Knowles Hill. Dew —6D 136
Knowles Hill Rd. Dew —7D 136
Knowles La. Bat —4F 137
Knowles La. B'frd —4E 98
Knowles La. Gom —4K 117
Knowle Spring Rd. Kei —7K 39
(nr. Foster Rd.)
Knowle Spring Rd. Kei —6K 39
(nr. Selborne Rd.)
Knowles Rd. Bat —4F 137
Knowles Rd. Brigh —1G 145
Knowles St. B'frd —4E 98
Knowles St. Denh —5B 76
Knowles Vw. B'frd —4F 99
Knowle Ter. Leeds —3C 84
Knowle Top. Holy G —7E 142
Knowle Top Dri. Hal —7E 114
Knowle Top Rd. Hal —7E 114
Knowsley St. B'frd —6C 80 (5J 7)
**Knowsthorpe. —1B 104**
Knowsthorpe Cres. Leeds —7B 86
Knowsthorpe Ga. Leeds —2D 104
Knowsthorpe La. Leeds —1B 104
(in three parts)
Knowsthorpe Rd. Leeds —1E 104
Knowsthorpe Way. Leeds —2D 104
Knox St. Leeds —7B 64
Knutsford Gro. B'frd —4G 99
**Krumlin. —7K 141**
Kyffin Av. Leeds —6G 87
Kyffin Pl. B'frd —1G 99

Laburnum Clo. E Ard —1J 139
Laburnum Dri. Bail —7K 43
Laburnum Gro. Cro R —4G 57
Laburnum Gro. Gom —6J 117
Laburnum Gro. Hal —2G 133
Laburnum Pl. App B —4G 63
Laburnum Pl. Mann —4J 79
Laburnum Rd. Dew —6C 136
Laburnum Rd. Shipl —7K 61
Laburnum St. B'frd —4J 79
Laburnum St. Far —4B 82
Laburnum St. Pud —5A 82
*Laburnum Ter. Hal —5G 115*
*(off Village St.)*
Lacey Gro. Weth —5K 17
Lacey M. B'frd —4E 98
Lacey St. Dew —7F 137
Lacy Way. Lfds B —1A 144
Ladbroke Gro. B'frd —5G 99
Ladderbanks La. Bail —7K 43
(in two parts)
Ladstone Pk. Cvn. Site. Sower B —2J 141
*Ladstone Towers. Sower B*
*(off Greenups Ter.) —4K 129*
Lady Ann Bus. Pk. Bat —2H 137
Lady Ann Rd. Bat —3H 137

Ladybeck Clo.—Lea Vw.


Ladybeck Clo. Leeds —5K 85 (5G 5)
Lady Fld. T'tn —7H 77 (off West La.)
Lady La. Bgly —5A 42
Lady La. Leeds —5J 85 (6F 5)
Lady Pk. Av. Bgly —5A 42
Lady Pk. Ct. Leeds —7B 50
Lady Pit La. Leeds —2H 103 (in two parts)
Ladyroyd Dri. E Bier —1G 117
Ladysmith Rd. Q'bry —6G 95
Lady's Wlk. Den —2H 13
Ladywell Clo. B'frd —3A 98
Ladywell La. Liv —5D 134
**Lady Wood. —5E 68**
Ladywood Grange. Leeds —6F 69
Ladywood Mead. Leeds —6F 69
Ladywood Rd. Leeds —6D 68
Ladywood Ter. Hal —7E 112
Lairum Ri. Cliff —5D 36
**Laisterdyke. —7F 81**
Laisterdyke. Lais —7F 81
Laisteridge La. B'frd —7J 79 (6A 6)
Laith Clo. Leeds —1K 65
Laithe Clo. Sils —7G 9
Laithecroft Rd. Bat —3J 137
Laithe Gro. B'frd —5G 97
Laithe Rd. B'frd —5H 97
Laith Gdns. Leeds —1A 66
Laith Gth. Leeds —1K 65
Laith Grn. Leeds —1K 65
Laith Rd. Leeds —1K 65
Laith Wlk. Leeds —1K 65
Lakeland Cres. Leeds —5G 49
Lakeland Dri. Leeds —5H 49
Lake Row. B'frd —1D 98
Lakeside. E Mor —1J 41
Lakeside Chase. Rawd —7A 46
Lakeside Clo. I'ly —4A 12
Lakeside Ct. Halt —7G 87
Lakeside Ct. Leeds —4K 103
Lakeside Gdns. Rawd —7A 46
Lakeside Ind. Est. Leeds —7K 83
Lakeside Rd. Leeds —7J 83
Lakeside Ter. Rawd —7A 46
Lakeside Vw. Rawd —7A 46
Lakeside Wlk. Rawd —7A 46 (off Lakeside Ter.)
Lake St. B'frd —1D 98 (7K 7)
Lake St. Kei —2C 40
Lake Ter. Leeds —4K 103
Lake Vw. Hal —7F 113
Lakeview Ct. Leeds —4E 68
Lamb Cote Rd. Hud —3K 145
Lambert Av. Leeds —6B 68
Lambert Clo. G'lnd —2H 143
Lambert Dri. Leeds —6B 68
Lambert Pl. B'frd —3D 80 (off Thirlmere Gdns.)
Lambert's Arc. Leeds —7F 5
Lambert St. G'lnd —2H 143
Lambert Ter. H'fth —4E 64 (nr. Park Side)
Lambert Ter. H'fth —4J 65 (off Low La.)
Lambourne Av. B'frd —7F 63
Lambrigg Cres. Leeds —1J 87
Lambton Gro. Leeds —1B 86
Lambton Pl. Leeds —1B 86
Lambton St. Leeds —1B 86
Lambton Ter. Leeds —1B 86
Lambton Vw. Leeds —1B 86
Lampards Clo. All —3A 78
**Lamplands. —2H 137**
Lamplands. Bat —1H 137
Lanark Dri. H'fth —7F 47
Lancaster Ct. Kei —6K 39 (off Rutland St.)
Lancaster Pl. Rothw —3H 123 (off Springfield St.)
Lancaster St. C'frd —6K 127
Lancastre Av. Leeds —2K 83 (in two parts)
Lancastre Gro. Leeds —2K 83
Landford Ho. B'frd —2K 97 (off Park La.)
Landor St. Kei —3B 40
Lands Beck Way. Liv —4H 135
Landscove Av. B'frd —4G 99
Landsdowne Ho. B'frd —1A 6
Landseer Av. Leeds —2J 83
Landseer Av. Ting —7E 120
Landseer Clo. Leeds —2H 83
Landseer Cres. Leeds —2J 83
Landseer Dri. Leeds —2H 83
Landseer Gdns. Leeds —2H 83
Landseer Grn. Leeds —2H 83
Landseer Gro. Leeds —2J 83
Landseer Mt. Leeds —2J 83
Landseer Ri. Leeds —2H 83
Landseer Rd. Leeds —2H 83
Landseer Ter. Leeds —2J 83
Landseer Vw. Leeds —2J 83
Landseer Wlk. Leeds —2H 83 (off Landseer Clo.)
Landseer Way. Leeds —2H 83
Lands Head La. Hal —3K 113
Landsholme Ct. B'frd —4H 99
Lands La. B'frd —7E 62
Lands La. Guis —2G 45
Lands La. Leeds —5J 85 (6E 4)
Landsmoor Gro. Bgly —6B 42
Land St. Fars —2B 82
Lane Ct. Brigh —5H 133 (off Old La.)
**Lane End. —3B 96 (nr. Horton Bank)**
**Lane End. —2D 56 (nr. Oakworth)**
Lane End. Bail —1J 61
Lane End. H'den —3F 59 (off Spring Row)
Lane End. Pud —5D 82 (in two parts)
Lane End. T'tn —7H 77
Lane End Ct. Leeds —6F 49
Lane End Cft. Leeds —6F 49
Lane End Fold. Pud —5D 82
Lane End Mt. Pud —5D 82
Lane End Pl. Leeds —1H 103
**Lane Ends. —1D 64**
Lane Ends Clo. B'frd —5F 79
Lane Ends Grn. Hal —7B 114
Lane Fox Ct. Yead —5K 45 (off Harper La.)
**Lane Head. —5G 133**
Lane Head La. Caus F —6A 94
Lane Head Rd. Sower B —4D 140
Lane Ho. Gro. L'ft —7G 111
Laneside. Holy G —5F 143
Laneside. Morl —7B 102
Lane Side. Q'bry —3G 95
Lane Side. Wyke —3H 115
Laneside Clo. Morl —7B 102
Laneside Fold. Morl —7B 102
Laneside Gdns. Morl —1B 120
Laneside M. Morl —7B 102
Laneside Ter. Morl —7B 102
Lanes, The. Pud —5D 82 (in two parts)
Lane, The. Alw —6F 49
Lane, The. Leeds —6A 86 (7J 5)
Lane Top. Denh —3B 76
Langbar App. Leeds —6B 70
Langbar Av. B'frd —2D 78
Langbar Clo. Leeds —6B 70
Langbar Gdns. Leeds —7B 70
Langbar Gth. Leeds —6B 70
Langbar Grange. Leeds —7B 70
Langbar Grn. Leeds —6B 70
Langbar Gro. Leeds —7B 70
Langbar Pl. Leeds —6B 70
Langbar Rd. I'ly —3A 12
Langbar Rd. Leeds —7B 70
Langbar Sq. Leeds —7B 70
Langbar Towers. Leeds —7B 70 (off Swarcliffe Av.)
Langbar Vw. Leeds —6B 70
Langdale Av. B'frd —5E 78
Langdale Av. Leeds —7C 66
Langdale Av. Wyke —6A 116
Langdale Clo. Weth —3G 17
Langdale Ct. Bgly —7A 42
Langdale Cres. Hal —6C 112
Langdale Dri. Q'bry —5H 95
Langdale Gdns. Leeds —1C 84
Langdale Rd. B'frd —1G 81
Langdale Rd. Dew —6K 137
Langdale Rd. W'ford —1K 123
Langdale St. Ell —3K 143
Langdale Ter. Leeds —1C 84
Langela Ter. Hal —7C 114
Langford Clo. Bur W —1A 26
Langford Ct. Bur W —1K 25
Langford La. Bur W —1A 26
Langford M. Bur W —1A 26
Langford Ride. Bur W —1B 26
Langford Rd. Bur W —1A 26
Lang Kirk Clo. F'hll —1A 20
Langlands Rd. Bgly —5A 60
Lang La. B'frd —1K 79
**Langley. —7D 122**
Langley Av. Bgly —7A 42
Langley Av. B'frd —5D 98
Langley Av. Leeds —1E 82
Langley Clo. Leeds —1E 82
Langley Cres. Bail —1A 62
Langley Cres. Leeds —1F 83
Langley Gth. Leeds —1E 82
Langley Gro. Bgly —7A 42
Langley La. Bail —7A 44
Langley Mt. Leeds —1F 83
Langley Pl. Leeds —1E 82
Langley Rd. Bgly —7A 42
Langley Rd. Leeds —1E 82
Langley Ter. Leeds —1E 82
Langport Clo. Q'bry —5K 95
Langsett Cft. Hud —4K 145
Langthorne Cres. Morl —5C 120
Langton Av. B'frd —5D 98
Langton Clo. Gom —5K 117
Langton St. Sower B —3K 129
Langtons Wharf. Leeds —7G 5
Langwith Av. Coll —2E 34
Langwith Dri. Coll —2C 34
Langwith M. Coll —2E 34
Langwith Valley Rd. Coll —2C 34 (in two parts)
Lanrick Ho. B'frd —2G 99 (off Broadstone Way)
Lansdale Ct. B'frd —4H 99
Lansdowne Clo. Bail —1B 62
Lansdowne Clo. Bat —2F 137
Lansdowne Ho. B'frd —1A 6
Lansdowne Pl. B'frd —7K 79
Lansdowne St. Leeds —7C 84
Lansdown Pl. B'frd —6C 6
Lanshaw Clo. Leeds —1A 122
Lanshaw Cres. Leeds —2A 122
Lanshaw Pl. Leeds —1A 122
Lanshaw Rd. Leeds —1A 122
Lanshaw Ter. Leeds —2A 122
Lanshaw Vw. Leeds —1A 122
Lanshaw Wlk. Leeds —1A 122
Lapage St. B'frd —6E 80
Lapage Ter. B'frd —7E 80
Lapwing Clo. B'frd —6B 78
Larch Clo. Birs —5E 118
Larch Clo. Liv —5A 136
Larch Clo. Oakw —2F 57
Larch Dale. Hud —5G 145
Larch Dri. B'frd —7J 97
Larchfield Home. Leeds —2A 104
Larchfield Rd. Leeds —1A 104
Larch Gro. Bail —3E 60
Larch Gro. Bgly —6A 42
Larch Hill. B'frd —7K 97
Larch Hill Cres. B'frd —6K 97
Larch La. Gar —7B 90
Larchmont. Cytn —2C 96
Larch St. Kei —7K 39
Larchwood. Rawd —3A 64
Larch Wood. S'cft —4A 52
**Larkfield. —7A 46**
Larkfield. B'frd —2F 79
Larkfield Av. Rawd —7A 46
Larkfield Cres. Rawd —7A 46
Larkfield Dri. Rawd —7A 46
Larkfield Mt. Rawd —7A 46
Larkfield Rd. Pud —5C 82
Larkfield Rd. Rawd —7A 46
Larkfield Ter. Kei —5C 40
Lark Hill. Bat —6E 118
Lark Hill Av. Cleck —2D 134
Lark Hill Clo. Cleck —2D 134
Larkhill Clo. Leeds —4A 68
Lark Hill Dri. Cleck —2D 134
Larkhill Grn. Leeds —3A 68
Larkhill Rd. Leeds —3A 68
Larkhill Vw. Leeds —4A 68
Larkhill Wlk. Leeds —3A 68
Larkhill Way. Leeds —3A 68
Lark St. Bgly —1K 59
Lark St. Haw —5F 57
Lark St. Kei —4K 39
Lark St. Oakw —2F 57
Larne Ho. B'frd —2K 97 (off Roundhill St.)
Larwood Av. B'frd —1G 81
Lascelles Mt. Leeds —2B 86 (off Lascelles Rd. E.)
Lascelles Pl. Leeds —2B 86
Lascelles Rd. Heck —5C 136
Lascelles Rd. E. Leeds —2B 86
Lascelles Rd. W. Leeds —2B 86
Lascelles St. Leeds —2B 86
Lascelles Ter. Leeds —2B 86
Lascelles Vw. Leeds —2B 86
Lastingham Grn. B'frd —5E 96
Lastingham Rd. Leeds —7D 64
Latchmere Av. Leeds —4K 65
Latchmere Clo. Leeds —4A 66
Latchmere Crest. Leeds —4K 65
Latchmere Dri. Leeds —4K 65
Latchmere Gdns. Leeds —3A 66
Latchmere Grn. Leeds —4K 65
Latchmere Rd. Leeds —4K 65
Latchmere Vw. Leeds —4K 65 (in two parts)
Latchmere Wlk. Leeds —3A 66
Latchmore Rd. Leeds —2E 102
Latchmore Rd. Ind. Est. Leeds —2D 102
Latham Ct. Gom —5K 117
Latham La. Gom —4J 117
Latham Lea. Gom —5J 117
Latimer Ho. B'frd —2A 98 (off Manchester Rd.)
Launceston Dri. B'frd —4G 99
Laund Rd. Hud —7J 143
Launton Way. B'frd —2K 97
Laura St. Brigh —7G 133
Laura St. Hal —6G 113
Laura St. Leeds —7F 85
Laurel Bank. Leeds —1B 88
Laurel Bank. Wyke —7J 115
Laurel Bank Clo. H'fld —1E 112
Laurel Bank Ct. Leeds —1C 84
Laurel Clo. E Kes —5A 34
Laurel Clo. Ell —3J 143
Laurel Clo. Hal —7C 96
Laurel Cres. Hal —4D 112
Laurel Dri. Bat —1E 136
Laurel Fold. Leeds —6C 84
Laurel Gro. Bat —1D 136
Laurel Gro. Bgly —6J 41
Laurel Gro. Leeds —6C 84
Laurel Gro. Sils —1F 21
Laurel Hill Av. Leeds —7B 88
Laurel Hill Cft. Leeds —6B 88
Laurel Hill Gdns. Leeds —6B 88
Laurel Hill Gro. Leeds —6B 88
Laurel Hill Vw. Leeds —6B 88
Laurel Hill Way. Leeds —7B 88
Laurel Mt. Hal —3E 130
Laurel Mt. Heck —4B 136
Laurel Mt. Leeds —7K 67
Laurel Mt. S'ley —5C 82
Laurel Pk. Wilsd —1G 77
Laurel Pl. Leeds —6C 84
Laurels, The. Leeds —6B 68
Laurel St. B'frd —7E 80
Laurel St. Hal —3E 130
Laurel St. Leeds —6C 84
Laurel Ter. A'ley —6C 84
Laurel Ter. Holy G —5D 142
Laurel Ter. Leeds —1B 88 (off Laurel Bank)
Laurel Ter. S'ley —5C 82
Laurence Ct. W'ford —7B 106
Lavender Cft. Heck —4C 136
Lavender Cft. Liv —3J 135 (off Carr St.)
Lavender Hill. B'frd —7E 62
Lavender Wlk. Leeds —6B 86 (7K 5)
Laverack Fld. Wyke —4J 115
Laverhills. Liv —3F 135
Laverock Cres. Brigh —3F 133
Laverock La. Brigh —3F 133
Laverock Pl. Brigh —3F 133 (off Huntock Pl.)
Laverton Rd. B'frd —2D 98
Lavinia Ter. Cytn —2D 96
Lawcliffe Cres. Haw —4F 57
Law Clo. Weth —2K 17
Lawefield Av. Rothw —1E 122
Lawkholme Cres. Kei —4A 40
Lawkholme La. Kei —4A 40
Law La. Brigh —2J 133
Law La. Hal —3K 131
Lawler Clo. Oven —4D 112 (off Rugby Ter.)
Lawn Av. Bur W —1B 26
Lawn Rd. Bur W —1B 26
Lawns Av. Leeds —3H 101
Lawns Clo. Leeds —3H 101
Lawns Cres. Leeds —3H 101
Lawns Cft. Leeds —3H 101
Lawns Dene. Leeds —3H 101
Lawns Dri. Leeds —3H 101
Lawns Grn. Leeds —3H 101
Lawns Hall Clo. Leeds —1B 66
Lawns La. Carr G —3K 139
Lawns La. F'ley —2H 101
Lawns La. Leeds —3A 104
Lawns Mt. Leeds —3H 101
Lawns Sq. Leeds —3H 101
Lawns Ter. E Ard —1K 139
Lawns Ter. Leeds —3H 101
**Lawnswood. —2A 66**
Lawnswood Gdns. Leeds —2B 66
Lawnswood Rd. Kei —6J 39
Lawrence Av. Leeds —1E 86
Lawrence Ct. Pud —7B 82
Lawrence Cres. Heck —2B 136
Lawrence Cres. Leeds —1E 86
Lawrence Dri. B'frd —4E 96
Lawrence Gdns. Leeds —7E 68
Lawrence Rd. Hal —5F 131
Lawrence Rd. Leeds —1E 86
Lawrence St. Hal —6E 112
Lawrence Wlk. Leeds —1E 86
Lawson Rd. Brigh —6H 133
Lawson St. B'frd —5B 80 (1F 7)
Lawson St. Leeds —6B 84
Law St. Bat —7D 118
Law St. B'frd —4E 98
Law St. Cleck —6F 117
Laxton Ho. B'frd —2K 97 (off Launton Wlk.)
**Laycock. —4E 38**
Laycock La. Lay —5D 38
Laycock Pl. Leeds —2K 85
Lay Gth. Rothw —2G 123
Lay Gth. Clo. Rothw —2G 123
Lay Gth. Fold. Rothw —3G 123
Lay Gth. Gdns. Rothw —3G 123
Lay Gth. Grn. Rothw —3G 123
Lay Gth. Mead. Rothw —3G 123
Lay Gth. Pl. Rothw —3G 123
Lay Gth. Sq. Rothw —3G 123
Laythorp Ter. E Mor —2H 41
Layton Av. Rawd —1B 64
Layton Clo. Rawd —2C 64
Layton Cres. Rawd —1B 64
Layton Dri. Rawd —1C 64
Layton Ho. B'frd —2K 97 (off Newall St.)
Layton La. Rawd —2C 64
Layton Mt. Rawd —1B 64
Layton Pk. Av. Rawd —2C 64
Layton Pk. Clo. Rawd —1B 64
Layton Pk. Cft. Rawd —2C 64
Layton Pk. Dri. Rawd —1B 64
Layton Ri. H'fth —1D 64
Layton Rd. Rawd & H'fth —1C 64
Lazenby Dri. Weth —3H 17
Lazenby Fold. Weth —3H 17
Lea Av. Hal —5G 131
Leabank Av. Gar —1A 108
Leach Cres. Riddl —1C 40
Leach Ri. Riddl —1C 40
Leach Rd. Riddl —1B 40
Leach Way. Riddl —1C 40
Lea Clo. Brigh —4G 133
Lea Ct. B'frd —4E 96
Lea Cft. Cliff —5D 36
Lea Cft. Otley —3J 27
Leadenhall St. Hal —3D 130
Leadwell La. Rob H & Rothw —4D 122
Lea Farm Cres. Leeds —6K 65
Lea Farm Dri. Leeds —5K 65
Lea Farm Gro. Leeds —6K 65
Lea Farm Mt. Leeds —5J 65
Lea Farm Pl. Leeds —6K 65
Lea Farm Rd. Leeds —5J 65
Lea Farm Row. Leeds —6K 65
Lea Farm Wlk. Leeds —5K 65
Leafield Av. B'frd —1E 80
Leafield Clo. Hud —5K 145
Leafield Clo. Leeds —2H 67
Leafield Cres. B'frd —1D 80
Leafield Dri. B'frd —1E 80
Leafield Dri. Leeds —2H 67
Leafield Dri. Pud —1D 100
Leafield Grange. Leeds —2H 67
Leafield Gro. B'frd —2E 80
Leafield Ho. B'frd —2K 97 (off Newall St.)
Leafield Pl. Yead —4H 45
Leafield Ter. B'frd —2E 80
Leafield Towers. Leeds —2H 67
Leafield Way. B'frd —2E 80
Leafland St. Hal —1E 130
Leaf St. Haw —4G 57
Leah Pl. Leeds —7F 85
Leah Row. Leeds —7F 85
Leake St. C'frd —7E 126
Lea Mill Pk. Clo. Yead —4J 45
Lea Mill Pk. Dri. Yead —4J 45
Leamington Dri. B'frd —4E 62
Leamington Rd. I'ly —4C 12
Leamington St. B'frd —3H 79
Leamington Ter. I'ly —4C 12
Leamside Wlk. B'frd —4G 99
Lea Pk. Clo. Leeds —7B 104
Lea Pk. Cft. Leeds —7C 104
Lea Pk. Dri. Leeds —7B 104
Lea Pk. Gdns. Leeds —7B 104
Lea Pk. Gth. Leeds —7B 104
Lea Pk. Gro. Leeds —7B 104
Lea Pk. Va. Leeds —7C 104
Lea Rd. Bat —1D 136
Leaside Dri. T'tn —6H 77
Leasowe Av. Leeds —4A 104
Leasowe Clo. Leeds —4A 104
Leasowe Ct. Leeds —4A 104 (off Woodhouse Hill Rd.)
Leasowe Gdns. Leeds —4B 104
Leasowe Gth. Leeds —4A 104
Leasowe Rd. Leeds —4A 104
Lea St. Lind —7C 144
Lea Ter. Leeds —3J 67
Lea, The. Gar —1K 107
Leather Bank. Bur W —6A 14
Leathley Av. Men —7D 26
Leathley Cres. Men —7D 26
Leathley Ho. B'frd —2K 97 (off Hutson St.)
Leathley La. Leat —1E 28
Leathley La. Men —6D 26
Leathley Rd. Leeds —1J 103
Leathley Rd. Men —6D 26
Leavens, The. App B —4F 63
**Leaventhorpe. —7C 78**
Leaventhorpe Av. B'frd —6C 78
Leaventhorpe Clo. B'frd —6D 78
Leaventhorpe Gro. T'tn —7C 78
Leaventhorpe La. T'tn —7B 78
Leaventhorpe Way. B'frd —6D 78
Lea Vw. Bat —7D 118


A-Z Leeds & Bradford 177

Lea Vw.—Lit. Horton Grn.

Lea Vw. H'fth —3F 65
Leavington Clo. B'frd —1H 115
Leconfield Ct. Weth —3G 17
Leconfield Ho. B'frd —5E 62
Ledbury Av. Leeds —3B 122
Ledbury Clo. Leeds —3B 122
Ledbury Cft. Leeds —3B 122
Ledbury Dri. Leeds —3B 122
Ledbury Grn. Leeds —3B 122
Ledbury Gro. Leeds —3A 122
Ledbury Pl. B'frd —2D 98
Leddis Ct. Leeds —7H 85
Ledgard Way. A'ley —5C 84
Ledger La. Loft —6E 122
**Ledsham. —6K 109**
**Ledston. —1E 126**
Ledston Av. Gar —1A 108
**Ledston Luck. —4D 108**
Ledston Luck Cotts. Kip —4E 108
Ledston Luck Enterprise Pk. Leeds —4D 108
Ledston Luck Vs. Kip —4D 108
Ledston Mill La. Leds —7E 108
Lee Bank. Hal —6F 113
Lee Beck Gro. Stan —7G 123
Lee Bri. Dean C —7F 113
Lee Bri. Ind. Est. Hal —7F 113
Leech La. H'den —4D 58
Lee Clo. Wilsd —6G 59
Lee Clough Dri. H Bri —6B 110
Lee Ct. Kei —5D 40
Lee Ct. Liv —3J 135
**Leeds. —6J 85 (4F 5)**
Leeds 27 Ind. Est. Morl —3J 119
Leeds and Bradford Rd. S'ley & Leeds —3D 82
Leeds, Bradford Airport Ind. Est. Yead —2C 46
Leeds Bradford International Airport. —4C 46
Leeds Bus. Cen., The. Gild —2J 119
Leeds City Art Gallery. —5H 85 (5D 4)
Leeds City Museum. —5H 85 (5D 4)
Leeds City Office Pk. H'bck —7J 85
Leeds District Cen. Leeds —2K 121
Leeds La. Rothw —1E 106
Leeds Old Rd. B'frd —5F 81
Leeds Old Rd. Heck & Bat —3A 136
Leeds Rhinos Rugby League Football Club. —1D 84
Leeds Rd. All B —1J 125
Leeds Rd. Bar E —7F 71
Leeds Rd. Bat —6D 118
Leeds Rd. B'frd —6B 80
(in two parts)
Leeds Rd. B'hpe —2A 48
Leeds Rd. Coll —3D 34
Leeds Rd. Dew —7H 137
Leeds Rd. Eccl —1D 80
Leeds Rd. Guis —3G 45
Leeds Rd. Hal —6K 113
(nr. Godley La.)
Leeds Rd. Hal —7D 114
(nr. Halifax Rd., in two parts)
Leeds Rd. Hud & D'tn —7K 145
Leeds Rd. Idle —2D 62
Leeds Rd. I'ly —5B 12
Leeds Rd. Kip —2K 107
Leeds Rd. Leeds —1C 88
Leeds Rd. Liv & Heck —4K 135
Leeds Rd. Loft & Wake —5D 122
Leeds Rd. Meth —4F 125
Leeds Rd. Mir —7H 135
Leeds Rd. Oss —7B 138
(in two parts)
Leeds Rd. Otley —3K 27
(in two parts)
Leeds Rd. Rawd —7K 45
Leeds Rd. Shipl —4J 61
Leeds Rd. Tad —7A 54
Leeds Rd. W'wood —7A 126
Leeds Rd. W'ford & Oult —7H 105
Leeds Shop. Plaza. Leeds —6J 85 (7E 4)
Leeds St. Kei —4K 39
Leeds Tykes Rugby Union Club. —1D 84
Leeds United Football Club. —3E 102
Leefield Rd. Bat —2C 136
Lee Grn. Holy G —7G 143
Lee La. Bgly —5G 59
Lee La. Hal —4G 113
Lee La. Oxe —2B 74
Lee La. Wilsd —6F 59
Lee La. E. H'fth —2F 65
Lee La. W. H'fth —2D 64
**Leeming. —4F 75**
Leeming St. B'frd —5B 80 (2F 7)
Lee Moor La. Stan —7G 123
**Lee Mount. —6E 112**
Lee Mt. Gdns. Hal —6E 112
Lee Mt. Rd. Hal —6E 112
Lee Orchards. B Spa —2E 36
**Lees. —4G 57**
Lees Bank Av. Cro R —4G 57
Lees Bank Dri. Cro R —4G 57
Lees Bank Hill. Cro R —4G 57
Lees Bank Rd. Cro R —4G 57
Lees Bldgs. Hal —7C 114
Lees Clo. Cull —6A 58
Leeside Rd. Heck & Bat —2C 136
Lees La. Far —1B 82
Lees La. Hal —6E 114
Lees La. Haw —5F 57
Lees Moor Rd. Cull —6A 58
Lee St. B'frd —7A 80 (4D 6)
Lee St. Brigh —4G 133
Lee St. Liv —3J 135
Lee St. Q'bry —6H 95
Lee Ter. Oaken —2B 116
Legrams Av. B'frd —1F 97
Legrams La. B'frd —1G 97
Legrams Mill La. B'frd —7G 79
Legrams St. B'frd —6H 79
Legrams Ter. Field B —6J 79
Leicester Clo. Leeds —3H 85 (1D 4)
Leicester Gro. Leeds —3H 85 (1D 4)
Leicester Pl. Leeds —3H 85 (1D 4)
Leicester St. B'frd —2C 98
Leicester Ter. Hal —4F 131
Leigh Av. Ting —7G 121
Leigh Rd. Ting —7G 121
Leigh St. Sower B —3A 130
Leighton Pl. Leeds —5C 4
Leighton St. Leeds —5H 85 (5B 4)
Leigh Vw. Ting —7F 121
Leith Ho. B'frd —3G 99
(off Stirling Cres.)
Leith St. Kei —3K 39
Lemans Dri. Dew —5D 136
Lemington Av. Hal —2E 130
Lemon St. B'frd —3J 97
Lemon St. Hal —1D 130
Lenham Clo. Morl —5A 120
Lenhurst Av. Leeds —2K 83
Lennie St. Kei —5K 39
Lennon Dri. B'frd —5H 79
Lennox Rd. Leeds —4D 84
Lens Dri. Bail —7J 43
Lentilfield St. Hal —5E 112
Lentilfield Ter. Hal —5E 112
Lenton Dri. Leeds —4J 103
Lenton Vs. B'frd —3D 62
Leodis Ho. Leeds —5E 104
Leodis Way. Leeds —6D 104
Leonard's Pl. Bgly —2A 60
Leonard St. Bgly —2A 60
Leonard St. Hud —7H 145
Leonard St. Wyke —4K 115
Leopold Gdns. Leeds —2A 86
Leopold Gro. Leeds —2K 85
Leopold St. Leeds —2K 85
Lepton Pl. Gild —7H 101
Leslie Av. Yead —3A 46
Leslie Ter. Leeds —2G 85
Lesmere Gro. B'frd —4F 97
Lessarna Ct. B'frd —1E 98
Leven Gdns. Weth —2H 17
Levens Bank. Leeds —7F 87
Levens Clo. Leeds —7G 87
Levens Gth. Leeds —7G 87
Levens Pl. Leeds —7G 87
Leventhorpe Ct. W'ford —2A 124
Leventhorpe Way. W'ford —2A 124
Lever St. B'frd —5G 97
Levita Gro. B'frd —2F 99
Levita Pl. B'frd —1G 99
Levita Pl. Leeds —5G 87
Lewin Gro. C'frd —7K 127
Lewis Clo. Q'bry —5H 95
Lewisham Ct. Morl —3B 120
Lewisham Gro. Morl —3B 120
Lewisham St. Morl —4J 119
Lewis St. Hal —1F 131
Leyburn Av. Hal —7E 114
Leyburn Av. Heck —2C 136
Leyburne St. B'frd —4J 79
Leyburn Gro. Bgly —7A 42
Leyburn Gro. Shipl —5G 61
Leyden Ri. All —5B 78
Leyfield. Bail —1G 61
Ley Fleaks Rd. B'frd —5D 62
(in two parts)
Leyland Rd. Birs —6B 118
Leyland Rd. C'frd —7J 127
Leylands Av. B'frd —2F 79
Leylands Gro. B'frd —2F 79
Leylands Ho. Kei —5B 40
Leylands La. B'frd —2F 79
Leylands La. Kei —5B 40
Leylands Rd. Leeds —4K 85 (4H 5)
Leylands Ter. B'frd —2F 79
**Leylands, The. —4J 85 (4F 5)**
Ley La. Leeds —5D 84
Leys Clo. Thack —3C 62
Leysholme Cres. Leeds —7A 84
Leysholme Dri. Leeds —1B 102
Leysholme Ter. Leeds —7B 84
Leysholme Vw. Leeds —7B 84
Leyside Dri. All —3B 78
Leys La. B Spa —2B 36
Leys, The. Bail —7J 43
Leyton Cres. B'frd —5D 62
Leyton Dri. B'frd —5D 62
Leyton Gro. B'frd —5D 62
Leyton Ter. B'frd —5D 62
Ley Top La. All —5C 78
Leywell Ter. Leeds —5A 84
Lichen Clo. B'frd —3G 97
Lichfield Mt. B'frd —1A 80
Lichfield Rd. Dew —7K 137
Lickless Av. H'fth —3H 65
Lickless Dri. H'fth —3H 65
Lickless Gdns. H'fth —3H 65
Lickless Ter. H'fth —3H 65
Lidgate Clo. Dew —6G 137
Lidgate Gdns. Dew —6G 137
Lidgate La. Dew —6G 137
**Lidget. —2F 57**
Lidget Av. B'frd —1F 97
**Lidget Green. —7G 79**
Lidget Hill. Pud —6C 82
Lidget Pl. B'frd —1F 97
Lidget St. Hud —7B 144
**Lidgett. —7J 89**
Lidgett Av. Leeds —5B 68
Lidgett Ct. Gar —7J 89
Lidgett Ct. Leeds —4B 68
Lidgett Cres. Leeds —4B 68
Lidget Ter. B'frd —1F 97
Lidget Ter. Cytn —2D 96
Lidgett Gro. Leeds —5B 68
Lidgett Hill. Leeds —5B 68
Lidgett La. Gar —1J 107
Lidgett La. Leeds —3K 67
Lidgett Mt. Leeds —3B 68
**Lidgett Park. —3B 68**
Lidgett Pk. Av. Leeds —3B 68
Lidgett Pk. Ct. Leeds —3B 68
Lidgett Pk. Gdns. Leeds —4B 68
Lidgett Pk. Gro. Leeds —4B 68
Lidgett Pk. M. Leeds —3C 68
Lidgett Pk. Rd. Leeds —3B 68
(in two parts)
Lidgett Pk. Vw. Leeds —3B 68
Lidgett Pl. Leeds —4B 68
Lidgett Towers. Leeds —3A 68
Lidgett Wlk. Leeds —5B 68
(in three parts)
Lifton Pl. Leeds —3G 85 (2A 4)
Light Bank La. Sils —5A 10
**Lightcliffe. —7F 115**
Lightcliffe Rd. Brigh —3G 133
Lightcliffe Royd. Bklnd —3A 142
Lightcliffe Royd La. Bklnd —1A 20
Lighthazles Chapel Rd. Sower B —3C 140
Lighthazles Rd. Sower B —3D 140
Lightowler Clo. Hal —1E 130
Lightowler Rd. Hal —1E 130
Lightowler St. B'frd —5J 97
Lightridge Clo. Hud —5G 145
Lightridge Rd. Hud —5F 145
Lilac Clo. Add —1E 10
Lilac Clo. Brigh —5J 133
Lilac Gro. B'frd —7F 81
Lilac Gro. Gom —6J 117
Lilac Gro. Shipl —7K 61
Lilacs, The. Guis —2G 45
Lilac St. Hal —6E 112
Lilian St. B'frd —3E 98
Lillands Av. Brigh —6F 133
Lillands La. Brigh —7F 133
Lillands Ter. Brigh —6F 133
Lilly La. Hal —2H 131
Lilly St. Sower B —5K 129
Lilycroft. B'frd —4H 79
Lilycroft Pl. B'frd —3H 79
Lilycroft Rd. B'frd —4G 79
Lilycroft Wlk. B'frd —3G 79
(in two parts)
Lily St. B'frd —3H 79
Lilythorne Av. B'frd —4E 62
Lime Clo. Kei —2J 39
Lime Ct. Bgly —5J 41
(off Aire St.)
Lime Gro. Yead —7J 45
Limers Ga. H Bri —5A 92
Limes Av. Hal —4G 131
Lime St. Bgly —1K 59
Lime St. B'frd —2G 97
Lime St. Haw —6E 56
Lime St. Kei —4K 39
Lime Tree Av. Bat —4E 136
Lime Tree Av. B Spa —2D 36
Lime Tree Av. Ell —3A 144
Lime Tree Av. Leeds —2A 68
Lime Tree Clo. Rothw —1B 124
Lime Tree Cres. Kip —5C 108
Lime Tree Gdns. B Spa —3E 36
Limetree Gro. B'shaw —7J 99
Lime Tree Sq. Shipl —3D 60
Limewood App. Leeds —5J 69
Limewood Ct. Leeds —5J 69
Limewood Rd. Leeds —6J 69
Lincoln Av. Heck —3B 136
Lincoln Av. Liv —6H 135
Lincoln Clo. B'frd —4J 79
Lincoln Ct. Fars —3B 82
(off South Dri.)
Lincoln Dri. Liv —6J 135
Lincoln Grn. Rd. Leeds —4A 86 (4J 5)
Lincoln Gro. Liv —6H 135
Lincoln Mt. Leeds —4A 86 (3K 5)
Lincoln Rd. B'frd —5J 79
Lincoln Rd. Dew —7K 137
Lincoln Rd. Leeds —4A 86 (3J 5)
Lincoln St. All —5C 78
Lincoln St. C'frd —7E 126
Lincoln Towers. Leeds —3K 5
Lincoln Wlk. Kip —4C 108
Lincoln Way. B'twn —6F 113
Lincombe Bank. Leeds —4A 68
Lincombe Dri. Leeds —4A 68
Lincombe Mt. Leeds —4A 68
Lincombe Ri. Leeds —4A 68
Lincroft Cres. Leeds —2H 83
Lincs Wold. Liv —4D 134
Lindale Clo. Leeds —7K 103
Lindale Gth. K'gte —6J 139
Lindale Gro. Wake —7K 139
Lindale La. K'gte —6J 139
Lindale Mt. Wake —7J 139
Linden Av. B'frd —5G 81
Linden Av. Leeds —3H 103
Linden Clo. Bard —6B 34
Linden Clo. Brigh —5J 133
Linden Ct. Leeds —5D 66
Linden Gdns. Leeds —3J 103
Linden Gro. Leeds —3J 103
Linden Mt. Av. Leeds —3H 103
Linden Pl. Leeds —3J 103
Linden Ri. Kei —6C 40
Linden Rd. Ell —3J 143
Linden Rd. Hal —4G 131
Linden Rd. Hud —7F 145
Linden Rd. Leeds —3H 103
Linden St. Leeds —3H 103
Linden Ter. Leeds —3J 103
Linden Way. Weth —2H 17
Lindholme Gdns. All —5B 78
Lindisfarne Rd. Shipl —5F 61
Lindley Av. Hud —6A 144
Lindley Dri. B'frd —4F 97
Lindley Moor Rd. Hud —7H 143
Lindley Rd. B'frd —3K 97
Lindley Rd. Ell —5K 143
Lindon St. Haw —6E 56
Lindrick Clo. Hal —7D 94
Lindrick Gro. Hal —7D 94
Lindrick Way. Hal —7D 94
Lindsay Acre. Ting —7G 121
Lindsay Rd. Gar —7K 89
Lindsey Ct. Leeds —4A 86 (4K 5)
Lindsey Gdns. Leeds —4A 86 (4K 5)
Lindsey Mt. Leeds —3K 5
Lindsey Rd. Leeds —4A 86 (4K 5)
**Lindwell. —1H 143**
Lindwell Av. G'lnd —2G 143
Lindwell Gro. G'lnd —2G 143
Lindwell Pl. G'lnd —2G 143
(off Wellgate)
Linefield Rd. Bat —3H 137
Lineham Ct. Liv —5J 135
Lingard St. B'frd —5B 80 (2F 7)
Ling Bob. Hal —7B 112
Ling Bob Clo. Hal —7B 112
Ling Bob Cft. Hal —6B 112
Ling Cft. B Spa —2B 36
Lingcroft Grn. B'frd —4C 98
(off Tristram Av.)
Lingdale Rd. B'frd —1G 115
Lingfield App. Leeds —1H 67
Lingfield Bank. Leeds —1H 67
Lingfield Clo. Leeds —1J 67
Lingfield Cres. Leeds —1H 67
Lingfield Cres. Q'bry —4C 96
Lingfield Dri. Cro R —3J 57
Lingfield Dri. Leeds —1J 67
Lingfield Gdns. Leeds —1H 67
Lingfield Ga. Leeds —1H 67
Lingfield Grn. Leeds —1H 67
Lingfield Gro. Leeds —1J 67
Lingfield Gro. Wilsd —7H 59
Lingfield Hill. Leeds —7H 49
Lingfield Ho. B'frd —6E 62
(off Savile Av.)
Lingfield Mt. Leeds —1J 67
Lingfield Rd. Leeds —1H 67
Lingfield Rd. Wilsd —1G 77
Lingfield Ter. Q'bry —4C 96
Lingfield Vw. Leeds —1H 67
Lingfield Wlk. Leeds —1H 67
Ling La. Leeds —4H 51
Ling Pk. App. Wilsd —1G 77
Ling Pk. Av. Wilsd —1G 77
Ling Royd Av. Hal —7B 112
Lingwell App. Leeds —3J 121
Lingwell Av. Leeds —2J 121
Lingwell Ct. Leeds —3J 121
Lingwell Cres. Leeds —2J 121
Lingwell Gdns. Leeds —3J 121
**Lingwell Gate. —7C 122**
Lingwell Ga. La. Loft & Out —5B 122
Lingwell Grn. Leeds —3J 121
Lingwell Gro. Leeds —3J 121
Lingwell M. Leeds —3J 121
Lingwell Nook La. Loft —7C 122
Lingwell Rd. Leeds —2J 121
Lingwell Vw. Leeds —3J 121
Lingwell Wlk. Leeds —3J 121
Lingwood Av. B'frd —4F 79
Lingwood Rd. B'frd —5F 79
Lingwood Ter. B'frd —5F 79
Links Av. Cleck —6F 117
Link, The. Swil —5D 106
Linkway. Bgly —5A 60
Linnburn M. I'ly —6B 12
Linnet Clo. B'frd —5C 78
Linnet Clo. Mir —7J 135
Linnet Ct. Mir —7J 135
Linnet Ct. Morl —4D 120
Linnet St. Kei —3A 40
Linnhe Av. B'frd —1F 115
**Linton. —7F 17**
Linton Av. Bat —3E 136
Linton Av. Leeds —7B 50
Linton Av. Sils —7G 9
Linton Av. Weth —3H 17
Linton Clo. Leeds —7A 50
Linton Clo. Liv —3H 135
Linton Comn. Lntn —1D 34
Linton Cres. Leeds —7B 50
Linton Cft. Leeds —4K 65
Linton Dri. Leeds —7A 50
Linton Gro. Brigh —1E 144
Linton Gro. Heck —5C 136
Linton Gro. Leeds —7A 50
Linton Hills Rd. Lntn —4G 17
Linton La. Lntn —6G 17
Linton La. Sick —2E 16
Linton Meadows. Weth —4G 17
Linton Ri. Leeds —7A 50
Linton Rd. Coll —1E 34
Linton Rd. Leeds —7A 50
Linton Rd. Weth —4G 17
Linton St. B'frd —2B 98
Linton Vw. Leeds —6A 50
Lion Chambers. Cleck —7F 117
(off Whitcliffe Rd.)
Lippersley La. Sils —3J 9
(in two parts)
Lisbon Sq. Leeds —6A 4
Lisbon St. Leeds —5G 85 (6B 4)
Lisheen Gro. C'frd —7E 126
Lisker Av. Otley —3K 27
Lisker Ct. Otley —3K 27
Lisker Dri. Otley —3K 27
Lismore Clo. Rothw —2H 123
Lismore Rd. Kei —3K 39
Lister Av. B'frd —3D 98
Lister Ct. Hal —1G 131
(off Chapeltown)
Listerdale. Liv —3J 135
Lister Hill. H'fth —2G 65
**Lister Hills. —6J 79 (4A 6)**
Listerhills Rd. B'frd —7J 79 (5A 6)
Lister La. B'frd —3B 80
Lister La. Hal —1E 130
Lister's Clo. Hal —1E 130
Listers Rd. Hal —7J 113
Lister's Rd. Hud —6H 145
Lister St. B'frd —4E 98
Lister St. Brigh —5G 133
Lister St. C'frd —7C 126
Lister St. I'ly —5A 12
Lister St. Kei —5J 39
Lister St. Tong —5G 99
Lister Vw. B'frd —4J 79
Lister Ville. Wilsd —7G 59
Lister Wlk. Morl —1K 119
Listing Av. Liv —3K 135
Listing Ct. Liv —3K 135
Listing Dri. Liv —3K 135
Listing La. Liv & Gom —3K 135
Lit. Baines St. Hal —1E 130
Littlebeck Dri. Bgly —1C 60
Lit. Bradley. G'lnd —3G 143
Lit. Church La. Meth —5G 125
Little Cote. B'frd —3C 62
Lit. Cross St. B'frd —4A 98
Littlefield Wlk. B'frd —6H 97
Lit. Fountain St. Morl —4A 120
Lit. Green. La. Heck —3A 136
**Little Horton. —2H 97**
**Little Horton Green. —1K 97 (7C 6)**
Lit. Horton Grn. B'frd —1K 97

178 A-Z Leeds & Bradford

Lit. Horton La.—Lumley Av.


Lit. Horton La. B'frd —4H 97 (7C 6)
(in four parts)
Lit. King St. Leeds —6H 85 (7D 4)
Littlelands. Bgly —5A 60
Littlelands Ct. Bgly —5A 60
Little La. B'frd —3F 79
Little La. Carl —4G 123
Little La. E Mor —2J 41
Little La. Hal —1A 132
Little La. I'ly —5B 12
Little La. Morl —6C 102
Lit. Lane Ct. Chur —6C 102
**Little London. —3J 85 (2F 5)**
**Little Moor. —5A 96**
Little Moor. Q'bry —5A 96
**Littlemoor Bottom. —7C 82**
Littlemoor Ct. Pud —7C 82
Littlemoor Cres. Pud —1C 100
Littlemoor Cres. S. Pud —1C 100
Littlemoor Gdns. Hal —1C 112
Littlemoor Gdns. Pud —1C 100
Littlemoor La. T'ner —6D 52
Lit. Moor Pl. Leeds —6B 84
Littlemoor Rd. Hal —7C 94
Littlemoor Rd. Pud —7C 82
Littlemoor Vw. Pud —7D 82
Lit. Neville St. Leeds —6H 85
Little Pk. B'frd —3G 63
**Little Preston. —5F 107**
Lit. Queen St. Leeds —6G 85 (7B 4)
Little St. Haw —5E 56
**Little Thorpe. —6F 135**
Littlethorpe Hill. Harts —6F 135
Littlethorpe Rd. Harts —7F 135
**Littletown. —3K 135**
Little Way. Leeds —3J 67
Littlewood Clo. B'frd —7J 97
**Little Woodhouse. —4G 85 (3A 4)**
Lit. Woodhouse. Brigh —7G 133
Lit. Woodhouse St. Leeds —4G 85 (4B 4)
Littondale Clo. Bail —7A 44
Litton Rd. Kei —5J 39
Litton Way. Leeds —4K 69
**Liversedge. —5J 135**
Liversedge Hall La. Liv —5J 135
*Liversedge Row. B'frd —3G 97*
*(off Perseverance La.)*
Livingstone Clo. B'frd —6B 62
Livingstone Rd. B'frd —7B 62
(nr. Cheltenham Rd.)
Livingstone Rd. B'frd —1K 79
(nr. Gaisby La.)
Livingstone St. Hal —6E 112
Livingstone St. N. Hal —2E 112
Livingston Ho. B'frd —6E 62
Livinia Gro. Leeds —3J 85 (1E 4)
Lloyds Dri. Low M —1A 116
Lobley St. Heck —4C 136
Locarno Av. B'frd —3E 78
Locherbie Grn. All —4B 78
Lochry Rd. B'frd —1F 115
Lock La. C'frd —6D 126
Locksley Rd. Brigh —7K 133
Locks, The. Bgly —7K 41
Lock St. Hal —2H 131
*Lock Vw. Bgly —7J 41*
*(off Cemetery Rd.)*
Lockwood Clo. Leeds —5J 103
Lockwood Ct. Leeds —5J 103
Lockwood Pk. Leeds —5J 103
Lockwood St. B'frd —5J 97
Lockwood St. Low M —2A 116
Lockwood St. Shipl —4F 61
Lockwood Way. Leeds —5J 103
Lode Pit La. Bgly —7D 42
Lodge Av. C'frd —7J 127
Lodge Av. Ell —2C 144
Lodge Dri. Ell —2C 144
Lodge Ga. Clo. Denh —4C 76
Lodge Hill. Bail —1F 61
Lodge Hill Clo. Leeds —3J 101
Lodge Hill Rd. Oss —7D 138
Lodge Hill Wlk. Leeds —3J 101
Lodge La. Leeds —3H 103
Lodge La. Liv —6A 136
Lodge Pl. Ell —2C 144
Lodge Rd. Pud —5B 82
*Lodge Row. Leeds —3A 88*
*(off Tranquility Av.)*
Lodge St. Cull —6B 58
Lodge St. Leeds —3H 85 (2C 4)
(in two parts)
Lodge Ter. Leeds —4H 103
Lodore Av. B'frd —2C 80
Lodore Pl. B'frd —2D 80
Lodore Rd. B'frd —2C 80
**Lofthouse. —7F 123**
Lofthouse Pl. Leeds —3H 85 (2D 4)
Loft St. B'frd —5F 79
Loiner Ct. Leeds —1E 104
Lombard St. Hal —3D 130
Lombard St. Leeds —6H 87
Lombard St. Rawd —7J 45
Lomond Av. H'fth —7F 47
Londesboro Gro. Leeds —6C 86
Londesboro Ter. Leeds —6C 86
London La. Rawd —7J 45
London Rd. Norl —5B 130
London Spring Rd. Sower B —5C 140
London Sq. Rawd —7J 45
London St. Rawd —7J 45
Longbottom Av. Sils —1H 21
Longbottom Av. Sower B —5G 129
Longbottom Ter. Hal —4H 131
Long Causeway. Hal —3B 94
Long Causeway. Leeds —1B 104
(LS9)
Long Causeway. Leeds —2D 66
(LS16)
Long Causeway. Oxe —4H 75
Long Causeway, The. Hal —2C 128
Long Clo. Wyke —3H 115
Long Clo. La. Leeds —6B 86
Longcroft. Kei —5A 40
Longcroft Link. B'frd —6K 79 (3C 6)
Longcroft Pl. B'frd —6K 79 (4C 6)
Longcroft Rd. I'ly —6E 12
Longdike Ct. Kip —5B 108
Longdike La. Kip —6C 108
Long Edge Low Rd. Sower B —6D 128
Long Edge Middle Rd. Sower B —5C 128
Long Edge Rd. Sower B —5C 128
(in two parts)
Long Fallas Cres. Brigh —2H 145
Longfield. Holy G —5F 143
Longfield Av. Hal —6A 114
Longfield Av. Pud —6D 82
Longfield Ct. Heck —4B 136
Longfield Ct. Pud —6D 82
Longfield Dri. B'frd —3E 98
Longfield Dri. Halt —5J 87
Longfield Dri. Rod —7D 64
Longfield Gth. Leeds —7D 64
Longfield Gro. Pud —6D 82
Longfield Mt. Pud —6D 82
Longfield Rd. Heck —4B 136
Longfield Rd. Pud —6C 82
*Longfield Ter. Hal —6A 114*
*(off Longfield Av.)*
Longfield Ter. Pud —6C 82
*Longfield Vw. Fars —2B 82*
*(off Croft St.)*
Longford Ter. B'frd —1F 97
Long Heys. G'Ind —3G 143
Long Hill Rd. Hud —5H 145
Longhouse Dri. Denh —5B 76
Longhouse La. Denh —5B 76
Long Ho. Rd. Hal —1A 112
Longlands Dri. Haw —4F 57
Longlands La. Denh —4B 76
Longlands La. Sick —4A 16
Longlands Rd. Dew —6E 136
Longlands St. B'frd —6K 79 (3C 6)
(in two parts)
Longlands Vw. Bat —5E 136
Long La. All —4H 77
Long La. Bar E & Gar —6J 71
Long La. B'frd —7D 60
Long La. Cra V —1A 128
Long La. H'den —3E 58
Long La. Q'bry —7H 95
Long La. S'wram —1J 131
Long La. Sower B —7J 129
Long La. Wheat —5C 112
**Long Lee. —5C 40**
Long Lee La. Kei —6B 40
Longley La. Sower B —7H 129
Longley's Yd. Leeds —4A 104
Long Lover La. Hal —7C 112
Long Mdw. Bklnd —4J 141
Long Mdw. Ct. Gar —1A 108
Long Mdw. Ga. Gar —1K 107
Long Meadows. B'frd —1A 80
Long Meadows. B'hpe —1J 47
Long Meadows. Bur W —7B 14
Long Meadows. Gar —1K 107
Long Preston Chase. App B —5F 63
Long Reach. Hal —4J 111
Long Riddings. Add —1D 10
Long Ridge. Brigh —2G 145
Long Row. H'fth —3G 65
(in two parts)
Long Row. Low M —2K 115
Longrow. T'tn —6G 77
*Long Row Ct. B'frd —3A 98*
*(off Gaythorne Rd.)*
Longroyd. Thack —4B 62
Longroyd Av. Leeds —3J 103
Longroyd Cres. Leeds —3J 103
Longroyd Cres. N. Leeds —3J 103
Long Royd Dri. Bail —7A 44
Longroyde Clo. Brigh —1F 145
Longroyde Gro. Brigh —1F 145
Longroyde Rd. Brigh —7F 133
Longroyd Gro. Leeds —3J 103
Longroyd Pl. Leeds —3J 103
Long Royd Rd. Sower B —6E 128
Longroyd St. Leeds —3J 103
Longroyd St. N. Leeds —3J 103
Longroyd Ter. Leeds —3J 103
Longroyd Vw. Leeds —3J 103
Longside Hall. B'frd —7J 79 (5A 6)
Longside Ind. Est. Leeds —3A 86 (2K 5)
Longside La. B'frd —7J 79 (5A 6)
Long St. B'frd —1D 98 (7K 7)
Longthorpe La. Wake —6B 122
Long Wall. G'Ind —2H 143
Longwood Av. Bgly —6H 41
Longwood Clo. Leeds —6D 50
Longwood Clo. Ting —7D 120
Longwood Ct. Ting —7E 120
Longwood Cres. Leeds —6D 50
Longwood Fold. Ting —7E 120
Longwood Gth. Ting —7E 120
Longwood Ho. Rd. Hud —6G 145
Longwood Rd. Ting —7D 120
Longwood Va. Ting —7E 120
Longwood Vw. Bgly —6J 41
Longwood Way. Leeds —6D 50
Lonsbrough Av. Heck —3B 136
Lonsdale Av. Bat —1D 136
Lonsdale Meadows. B Spa —3D 36
Lonsdale Ri. Ting —7E 120
Lonsdale St. B'frd —5D 80 (2K 7)
*Lonsdale Ter. Liv —4J 135*
*(off Halifax Rd.)*
Lord La. Haw —4D 56
Lord's Bldgs. Morl —5A 120
Lordsfield Pl. B'frd —5F 99
Lord's La. Brigh —7H 133
Lord St. Hal —1G 131
Lord St. Haw —5F 57
Lord St. Kei —4A 40
Lord St. Leeds —7F 85
Lord St. Sower B —3A 130
Lord St. Stainc —4D 136
Lord Ter. Leeds —7F 85
Loris St. B'frd —5F 99
Lorne St. B'frd —3D 98
*Lorne St. Cro R —4H 57*
*(off Bingley Rd.)*
Lorne St. Kei —3C 40
Lotherton Hall. —7H 73
Lotherton La. Aber —6E 72
(in two parts)
Lotherton Way. Gar —5K 89
Lot St. Haw —5F 57
Loughrigg St. B'frd —3A 98
Louisa St. B'frd —4D 62
Louisa St. C'frd —7C 126
Louis Av. B'frd —2J 97
Louis Ct. Leeds —2K 85
Louis Gro. Leeds —2A 86
*Louis Le Prince Ct. Leeds —2B 86*
*(off Bayswater Rd.)*
Louis St. Leeds —2K 85
Love La. Hal —3F 131
Love La. Rothw —2G 123
Lovell Pk. Clo. Leeds —4K 85 (3G 5)
Lovell Pk. Ct. Leeds —3F 5
Lovell Pk. Ga. Leeds —4J 85 (3G 5)
Lovell Pk. Grange. Leeds —3G 5
Lovell Pk. Heights. Leeds —3G 5
Lovell Pk. Hill. Leeds —4J 85 (3F 5)
Lovell Pk. Rd. Leeds —4J 85 (4F 5)
Lovell Pk. Towers. Leeds —3F 5
Lovell Pk. Vw. Leeds —4K 85 (3G 5)
Low Ash Av. Shipl —5K 61
Low Ash Cres. Shipl —5K 61
Low Ash Dri. Shipl —5K 61
Low Ash Gro. Shipl —5K 61
Low Ash Rd. Shipl —6A 62
**Low Baildon. —1K 61**
**Low Bank. —1D 56**
Low Bank Dri. Oakw —1D 56
Low Bank La. Oakw —1D 56
**Low Banks. —1D 40**
Low Bank St. Fars —2B 82
Low Cliff Wlk. Heck —6C 136
Low Clo. Bgly —2B 60
Low Clo. I'ly —3B 12
Low Clo. St. Leeds —2G 85
**Low Common. —6J 125**
Lowcroft. Coll —2E 34
Low Cft. Ct. B'hpe —7J 29
Lowdale. Dew —6J 137
Lowell Av. B'frd —1F 97
Lowell Gro. Leeds —5E 82
Lowell Pl. Leeds —5E 82
Lwr. Ainley. Hal —1D 112
Lwr. Ashgrove. B'frd —7K 79 (6C 6)
Lwr. Balfour St. B'frd —2C 98
Lwr. Bankhouse. Pud —2B 100
Lwr. Bank Houses. Holy G —5B 142
Lwr. Bank St. Far —2B 82
Lwr. Basinghall St. Leeds —5H 85 (6D 4)
Lwr. Bentley Royd. Sower B —4J 129
Lwr. Bower La. Dew —5D 136
Lwr. Brockwell La. Sower B —6H 129
Lwr. Brunswick St. Leeds —4K 85 (4G 5)
Lwr. Cambridge St. C'frd —7E 126
Lwr. Clay Pits. Hal —7D 112
Lwr. Clifton St. Sower B —4A 130
Lwr. Clyde St. Sower B —5K 129
Lwr. Constable Rd. I'ly —6D 12
Lwr. Copy. All —4B 78
Lwr. Cross St. Bat —7G 137
Lwr. Crow Nest Dri. Hal —1H 133
**Lower Edge Bottom. —2B 144**
Lwr. Edge Rd. Ell & Brigh —2B 144
*Lwr. Ellistones. G'Ind —2E 142*
*(off Saddleworth Rd.)*
**Lower Fagley. —2G 81**
Lwr. Finkil St. Brigh —3E 132
Lwr. Fleet. Q'bry —5G 95
Lwr. Fold. Bklnd —3B 142
Lwr. Fold. Brigh —3F 145
Lwr. George St. B'frd —5H 97
Lwr. Globe St. B'frd —5J 79 (2A 6)
**Lower Grange. —6B 78**
Lwr. Grange Clo. B'frd —6C 78
Lwr. Grattan Rd. B'frd —6K 79 (4B 6)
Lower Grn. Bail —2G 61
Lwr. Green Av. Schol —7B 116
Lwr. Hall Clo. Liv —4H 135
Lwr. Hall Dri. Liv —4H 135
Lwr. Hall La. Liv —4H 135
Lwr. Hall Mt. Liv —4H 135
Lwr. Heights Rd. T'tn —5G 77
Lwr. Holme. Bail —3J 61
Lwr. House Clo. Thack —3B 62
Lower Ings. Hal —5A 94
Lwr. Kipping La. T'tn —7H 77
Lwr. Kirkgate. Hal —1H 131
Lower La. B'frd —2D 98
Lower La. E Bier —2F 117
Lower La. Gom —1K 135
Lwr. Langwith. Coll —2E 34
Lwr. Lark Hill. Cleck —1D 134
**Lower Mickletown. —4K 125**
Lwr. Mickletown. Meth —4J 125
Lwr. Mill Bank Rd. Sower B —2F 141
Lwr. Newlands. Brigh —7H 133
Lwr. North St. Bat —4F 137
Lwr. Oxford St. C'frd —7D 126
Lwr. Park Grn. Sils —1E 20
Lwr. Pk. Royd Dri. Sower B —2G 141
Lwr. Peel St. Dew —7G 137
**Lower Popeley. —3A 136**
Lwr. Range. Hal —6G 113
Lwr. Rushton Rd. B'frd —6G 81
Lower Sandhills. T'ner —1C 70
Lwr. School St. B'frd —1J 115
Lwr. School St. Shipl —4F 61
**Lower Soothill. —3J 137**
Lwr. Swift Pl. Sower B —7D 140
Lwr. Tofts Rd. Pud —6C 82
**Lower Town. —3F 75**
Lowertown. Oxe —3E 74
Lwr. Town St. Leeds —2H 83
Lwr. Wellgate. G'Ind —2G 143
Lwr. Wellington Rd. I'ly —5C 12
Lwr. Westfield Rd. B'frd —4G 79
**Lower Woodlands. —2C 116**
Lwr. Wormald. Sower B —7B 140
Lwr. Wortley Rd. Leeds —2A 102
**Lower Wyke. —7J 115**
Lwr. Wyke Grn. Wyke —7H 115
Lwr. Wyke La. Wyke —7H 115
Loweswater Av. B'frd —1F 115
**Low Farm. —7K 47**
Low Farm. W'ford —6J 107
Lowfield Clo. Low M —2A 116
Lowfield Cres. Sils —2H 21
Lowfield Rd. Dew —7D 136
Low Fields Av. Leeds —2E 102
Low Fields Rd. Leeds —2E 102
(in two parts)
Low Fields Way. Leeds —2E 102
Lowfields Way. Lfds B —1A 144
**Low Fold. —4D 64**
Low Fold. B'frd —2B 80
Low Fold. H'fth —5E 64
Low Fold. Leeds —7A 86
Low Fold. Rawd —7K 45
Low Fold. Schol —7B 116
Low Fold. Steet —5E 20
Low Gipton Cres. Leeds —2F 87
Low Grange Cres. Leeds —5A 104
Low Grange Vw. Leeds —6A 104
**Low Green. —1A 64**
Low Grn. B'frd —3G 97
Low Grn. Rawd —1A 64
Low Grn. Ter. B'frd —3H 97
Low Hall Clo. Men —6C 26
Low Hall Pl. Leeds —7G 85
Low Hall Rd. H'fth & Rawd —4C 64
Low Hall Rd. Men —6D 26
Low Hill. Bail —5J 43
Low Ho. Dri. Sils —2G 21
Low Ho. Farm Ct. Sils —2G 21
*Low Ho. Flats. Cleck —1F 135*
*(off Westgate)*
Low Ho. Fold. Liv —4H 135
**Low Laithes. —7H 139**
Low La. Birs —6C 118
Low La. Cytn —1K 95
Low La. Hal —7C 92
Low La. H'fth —2G 65
Low La. Q'bry —3G 95
Low La. Sils —3E 8
Low Mill La. Add —1F 11
Low Mill La. Kei —4B 40
Low Mills Rd. Leeds —2B 102
**Low Mill Village. —2G 11**
**Low Moor. —1K 115**
**Low Moor Side. —4G 101**
Low Moor Side. Leeds —3H 101
Low Moorside Clo. Leeds —3J 101
*Low Moorside Ct. Leeds —3J 101*
*(off Low Moorside Clo.)*
Low Moor Side La. Leeds —4G 101
Low Moor St. Low M —1K 115
Low Moor Ter. Hal —2B 130
Low Moor Ter. Leeds —4H 103
Lowood La. Birs —4C 118
Low Pk. Rd. I'ly —4G 13
Low Rd. Dew M —7D 136
Low Rd. Leeds —2A 104
Lowry Rd. Ting —7D 120
Lowry Vw. Kei —5A 40
Low Shops La. Rothw —1E 122
Low Spring Rd. Kei —5C 40
Low St. Dew —7G 137
Low St. Kei —4A 40
(in two parts)
Low St. Ting —6E 120
Lowther Av. Gar —7J 89
Lowther Cres. Swil —4E 106
Lowther Dri. Gar —7J 89
Lowther Dri. Swil —5D 106
Lowther Gro. Gar —7J 89
Lowther Rd. Gar —7J 89
Lowther St. B'frd —3D 80
Lowther St. Leeds —2B 86
Lowther Ter. Swil C —7E 88
Lowtown. Pud —5D 82
**Low Town End. —4B 120**
**Low Utley. —7J 21**
Low Way. B'ham —1D 54
Low Way. Cliff —4D 36
Low Well St. B'frd —3K 97
Low Whitehouse Row. Leeds —1K 103
Low Wood. Wilsd —1H 77
Low Wood Ct. Utley —7K 21
Low Wood Ri. I'ly —6F 13
Loxley Gro. Weth —1H 17
Loxley St. Bat —1E 136
Lucas Ct. Leeds —2J 85
Lucas Pl. Leeds —1G 85
Lucas St. Leeds —1G 85
Lucy Av. Leeds —5G 87
Lucy Hall Dri. Bail —2E 60
Lucy St. Hal —7H 113
**Luddenden. —6G 111**
**Luddenden Foot. —2F 129**
Luddenden La. L'ft —1F 129
*Luddendon Pl. Q'bry —4G 95*
*(off Mill La.)*
Ludgate Hill. Leeds —5J 85 (6F 5)
Ludlam St. B'frd —1A 98 (7E 6)
Ludlow Av. Gar —6B 90
Ludolf Dri. Leeds —7G 51
Luke Rd. B'frd —2J 97
Lulworth Av. Leeds —4B 88
Lulworth Clo. Leeds —4B 88
Lulworth Cres. Leeds —4B 88
Lulworth Dri. Leeds —5B 88
Lulworth Gth. Leeds —5B 88
Lulworth Gro. B'frd —4F 99
(in two parts)
Lulworth Vw. Leeds —4B 88
Lulworth Wlk. Leeds —4B 88
Lumb Bottom. Dlgtn —7D 100
Lumbfoot Rd. Stanb —5A 56
Lumb Gill La. Add —3F 11
Lumb La. B'frd —4J 79 (1B 6)
Lumb La. Hal —5F 113
Lumb La. Liv —6H 135
Lumb La. Sower B —2E 140
Lumb La. Wains —1H 111
Lumbrook Clo. Hal —4C 114
Lumby Clo. Pud —1D 100
Lumby La. E Kes —3J 33
Lumby La. Pud —1D 100
Lumby St. B'frd —4D 62
Lumley Av. Leeds —2D 84

Lumley Gro.—Marlborough Rd.


Lumley Gro. Leeds —2D 84
Lumley Mt. Leeds —2D 84
Lumley Pl. Leeds —2D 84
Lumley Rd. Dew —6J 137
Lumley Rd. Leeds —2D 84
Lumley St. Leeds —2D 84
Lumley Ter. Leeds —2D 84
Lumley Vw. Leeds —2D 84
Lumley Wlk. Leeds —2D 84
Lunan Pl. Leeds —1B 86
Lunan Ter. Leeds —1B 86
Lund Dri. Heck —5C 136
Lund La. Oakw —5D 38
Lund St. Bgly —1K 59
Lund St. B'frd —6E 78
Lund St. Kei —3A 40
Lundy Ct. B'frd —3A 98
Lune St. Cro R —4H 57
Lupton Av. Leeds —5C 86
Lupton Flats. Leeds —7D 66
Lupton's Bldgs. Leeds —6B 84
Lupton St. B'frd —4A 80 (1D 6)
Lupton St. Leeds —3A 104
Lustre St. Kei —4J 39
Luther St. Leeds —7C 64
Luther Way. B'frd —2B 80
Luton St. Hal —1D 130
Luton St. Kei —4K 39
Luttrell Clo. Leeds —2A 66
Luttrell Cres. Leeds —2A 66
Luttrell Gdns. Leeds —2A 66
Luttrell Pl. Leeds —2A 66
Luttrell Rd. Leeds —2A 66
Lutyens, The. I'ly —5K 11
(nr. Grove Rd.)
Lutyens, The. I'ly —5A 12
(off Westville)
Luxor Av. Leeds —1B 86
Luxor Rd. Leeds —1B 86
Luxor St. Leeds —1B 86
Luxor Vw. Leeds —1B 86
Lydbrook Pk. Cop —6E 130
Lyddon Ter. Leeds —3G 85 (2A 4)
Lydford Ho. B'frd —7D 6
Lydgate. —1E 132
Lydgate. Leeds —4B 86
Lydgate. N'wram —4A 114
Lydgate Pk. Light —1E 132
Lydgate Pl. C'ley —5J 63
Lydgate Rd. Bat —3K 137
Lydgate St. C'ley —5J 63
Lydia Ct. Leeds —5G 5
(off Bridge St.)
Lydia St. Leeds —6G 5
Lyme Chase. Leeds —3H 87
Lymington Dri. B'frd —2G 99
Lynch Av. Gt Hor —3F 97
Lyncroft. B'frd —1B 80
Lyndale. Kip —6A 108
Lyndale Cres. Heck —4C 136
Lyndale Dri. Shipl —5B 62
Lyndale M. Dew —5D 136
Lyndale Rd. Bgly —6C 42
Lyndean Gdns. Idle —5C 62
Lynden Av. Shipl —4A 62
Lynden Ct. B'frd —7G 97
Lyndhurst Av. Brigh —2G 145
Lyndhurst Clo. Scholes —5D 70
Lyndhurst Cres. Scholes —5D 70
Lyndhurst Gro. All —4C 78
Lyndhurst Gro. Rd. Brigh —2G 145
Lyndhurst Rd. Brigh —1G 145
Lyndhurst Rd. Scholes —6D 70
Lyndhurst Vw. Scholes —6D 70
Lyndon Av. B'ham —7C 36
Lyndon Av. Gar —6J 89
Lyndon Clo. B'ham —7C 36
Lyndon Cres. B'ham —7C 36
Lyndon Rd. B'ham —7C 36
Lyndon Sq. B'ham —7C 36
Lyndon Ter. Bgly —1A 60
Lyndon Way. B'ham —7C 36
Lyndsay Acre. Ting —7G 121
Lyndum Gro. Kip —4A 108
Lynfield Dri. B'frd —2C 78
Lynfield Dri. Liv —3D 134
Lynfield Mt. Shipl —4A 62
Lynndale Av. Cro H —3A 20
Lynndale Av. Hud —7F 145
Lynnfield Gdns. Scholes —6D 70
Lynsey Gdns. B'frd —7D 98
Lynthorne Rd. B'frd —1J 79
Lynton Av. B Spa —2D 36
Lynton Av. B'frd —3F 79
Lynton Av. Thpe —5A 122
Lynton Dri. B'frd —3E 78
Lynton Dri. Kei —2D 40
Lynton Dri. Shipl —5G 61
Lynton Gro. B'frd —3F 79
Lynton Gro. Bshw —5D 94
Lynton Ter. Cleck —7F 117
Lynton Vs. B'frd —3F 79
Lynwood Av. Leeds —1C 102
Lynwood Av. Shipl —4A 62
Lynwood Av. W'ford —1B 124
Lynwood Clo. B'shaw —3K 117
Lynwood Ct. B'frd —5C 62
Lynwood Ct. Kei —6G 39
Lynwood Cres. Hal —3D 130
Lynwood Cres. Leeds —1C 102
Lynwood Cres. W'ford —1B 124
Lynwood Gdns. Pud —7A 82
Lynwood Gth. Leeds —1C 102
Lynwood Gro. Leeds —2C 102
Lynwood M. B'frd —4H 99
Lynwood Mt. Leeds —1C 102
Lynwood Ri. Leeds —1C 102
Lynwood Vw. Leeds —1C 102
Lyon Rd. Ebrn —4B 20
Lyons St. Q'bry —5K 95
Lyon St. T'tn —6H 77
Lytham Dri. Q'bry —4B 96
Lytham Gro. Leeds —2A 102
Lytham Pl. Leeds —2A 102
Lytham St. Hal —1D 130
Lythe Ho. B'frd —2H 7
Lytton Rd. B'frd —5F 79
Lytton St. Leeds —3K 103

Mabel Royd. B'frd —1F 97
Mabel St. H Bri —6A 110
Mabgate. —4K 85 (4G 5)
Mabgate. Leeds —5K 85 (5H 5)
Mabgate Grn. Leeds —5K 85 (5H 5)
Macaulay St. Leeds —4A 86 (5J 5)
McBride Way. Weth —4K 17
McBurney Clo. Hal —5F 113
McClaren Fields. Leeds —3H 83
Mackingstone Dri. Oakw —1D 56
Mackingstone La. Oakw —7D 38
Mackintosh St. Hal —2D 130
McMahon Dri. Q'bry —4B 96
Macturk Gro. B'frd —4G 79
Maddocks St. Shipl —4G 61
Madeley Sq. C'frd —6J 127
Madewel Ho. Ell —4A 144
Madison Av. B'frd —5G 99
Madni Clo. Hal —1F 131
Mafeking Av. Leeds —5G 103
Mafeking Gro. Leeds —5G 103
Mafeking Mt. Leeds —5G 103
Mafeking Ter. Shipl —7K 61
Magdalene Clo. Leeds —1A 66
Magnolia Dri. All —1K 77
Magpie La. Morl —4B 120
Maidstone St. B'frd —6E 80
Mail Clo. Leeds —2C 88
Main Rd. Denh —5B 76
Main Rd. Ebrn —4B 20
Main Rd. E Mor —3H 41
Main Rd. Kild —2A 20
Mainspring Rd. Wilsd —7G 59
Main St. Aber —5E 72
Main St. Add —1C 10
Main St. All B —3B 126
Main St. Bar E —5H 71
Main St. Bgly —1K 59
Main St. Bur W —7A 14
Main St. Carl —4F 123
Main St. Coll —2F 35
Main St. Ctly —6B 60
Main St. E Kes —5A 34
Main St. Esh —6E 44
Main St. Gar —6J 89
Main St. Guis —3A 44
Main St. Haw —5E 56
Main St. Leds —2E 126
Main St. Lntn —7F 17
Main St. Low M —1A 116
Main St. Men —5B 26
Main St. Meth —4H 125
Main St. Pool W —3G 29
Main St. Scholes —6D 70
Main St. Shad —6F 51
Main St. Sick —4A 16
Main St. Stanb —5A 56
Main St. Sut Cr —5A 20
Main St. T'ner —7D 52
Main St. Wake —1K 139
Main St. Wltn —5G 19
Main St. Wilsd —7G 59
Main St. Wyke —3J 115
Maitland Clo. All —6B 78
Maitland Pl. Leeds —2G 103
Maizebrook. Dew —7D 136
Maize St. Kei —7J 39
Malham Av. B'frd —2C 78
Malham Av. Brigh —1E 144
Malham Clo. Leeds —1J 87
Malham Ct. Sils —2G 21
(off Ings Way)
Malham Dri. Bat —3E 136
Malham Dri. Liv —7H 135
Malham Rd. Brigh —2E 144
Malin Rd. Dew —5K 137
Mallard Clo. B'frd —7E 62
Mallard Clo. Leeds —7B 104
Mallard Ct. B'frd —6C 78
Mallards, The. Sils —1G 21
Mallard Vw. Oxe —3E 74
Mallard Way. Morl —3D 120
Mallinson St. Dew —7E 136
Mallory Clo. B'frd —7F 79
Malmesbury Clo. B'frd —5G 99
Malmesbury Clo. Leeds —7C 84
Malmesbury Gro. Leeds —7C 84
Malmesbury Pl. Leeds —7C 84
Malmesbury Ter. Leeds —7C 84
Malsis Cres. Kei —5J 39
Malsis Rd. Kei —5J 39
Maltby Ct. Leeds —6B 88
Maltby Ho. B'frd —2K 97
(off Park La.)
Malthouse Clo. S'cft —3A 52
Malting Clo. Rob H —4D 122
Malting Ri. Rob H —4D 122
Maltings Ct. Leeds —2J 103
(off Moorside Maltings)
Maltings Rd. Hal —5B 112
Maltings Rd. Leeds —3J 103
Maltings, The. Cleck —7E 116
Maltings, The. Leeds —3E 84
(off Alexandra Rd.)
Maltings, The. Rob H —4D 122
Maltins, The. C'frd —7E 126
Maltkiln La. C'frd —7E 126
Malt Kiln La. Kip —5B 108
Malt Kiln La. T'tn —1F 95
Malton Ho. B'frd —6E 62
(off Rowantree Dri.)
Malton St. Hal —5G 113
Malton St. Sower B —3K 129
Malt St. Kei —7J 39
Malvern Brow. B'frd —3D 78
Malvern Cres. Riddl —7C 22
Malvern Gro. B'frd —4D 78
Malvern Gro. Leeds —2G 103
Malvern Ri. Leeds —2G 103
Malvern Rd. B'frd —4D 78
Malvern Rd. Dew —7K 137
Malvern Rd. Leeds —2G 103
Malvern St. B'frd —4H 7
Malvern St. Leeds —2G 103
Malvern Vw. Leeds —2G 103
Manchester Rd. B'frd —4K 97 (6E 6)
Manchester Sq. Otley —2J 27
Mancot Ho. B'frd —2A 98
(off Manchester Rd.)
Mandale Gro. B'frd —6D 96
Mandale Rd. B'frd —6D 96
Mandarin Way. Leeds —7B 104
Mandela Ct. Leeds —1K 85
Mandeville Cres. B'frd —6F 97
Mangrill La. Woth —4H 53
Manitoba Pl. Leeds —6A 68
Manley Ct. Gar —1K 107
Manley Dri. Weth —3F 17
Manley Gro. I'ly —5D 12
Manley Ri. I'ly —6D 12
Manley Rd. I'ly —6D 12
Manley St. Brigh —5G 133
Manley St. Pl. Brigh —5G 133
(off Manley St.)
Mannerley Gro. Cleck —2K 135
Mannheim Rd. B'frd —3G 79
Manningham. —3J 79
Manningham La. B'frd —3J 79 (1C 6)
Mann's Bldgs. Bat —5F 119
Mann's Ct. B'frd —4E 6
Mannville Gro. Kei —5J 39
Mannville Pl. Kei —5J 39
Mannville Rd. Kei —6J 39
Mannville St. Kei —5J 39
Mannville Ter. B'frd —7K 79 (5C 6)
Mannville Wlk. Kei —5J 39
(off Mannville St.)
Mannville Way. Kei —5J 39
Manor Av. Leeds —1E 84
Manor Clo. B'frd —5D 78
Manor Clo. B'hpe —7H 29
Manor Clo. Hal —4F 131
Manor Clo. Rothw —1G 123
Manor Clo. Yead —4K 45
Manor Cott. M. S'cft —5A 52
Manor Ct. Aber —5E 72
Manor Ct. Bgly —5A 60
Manor Ct. Leeds —7H 51
Manor Ct. Otley —2J 27
(off Bridge St.)
Manor Ct. Schol —1B 134
Manor Cres. Pool W —3G 29
Manor Cres. Rothw —1F 123
Manor Cft. Leeds —6A 88
Manor Dri. Bgly —4A 60
Manor Dri. Hal —4F 131
Manor Dri. Leeds —1E 84
Mnr. Farm Clo. Bgly —6B 60
Mnr. Farm Clo. Leeds —1K 121
Mnr. Farm Cres. Chur —6C 102
Mnr. Farm Dri. Bat —2K 137
Mnr. Farm Dri. Chur —6C 102
Mnr. Farm Dri. Leeds —1J 121
Mnr. Farm Gdns. Leeds —1J 121
Mnr. Farm Grn. Leeds —1J 121
Mnr. Farm Gro. Leeds —1J 121
Mnr. Farm Ri. Leeds —1K 121
Mnr. Farm Rd. Leeds —1J 121
Mnr. Farm Wlk. Leeds —1K 121
Mnr. Farm Way. Leeds —2J 121
Manorfield. Leeds —3F 103
Manor Gdns. Cull —7B 58
Manor Gdns. Dew —6A 138
Manor Gdns. Pool W —3G 29
Manor Gdns. T'ner —5E 52
Manor Gth. Leeds —6A 88
Manor Gth. S Mil —6K 109
Manor Gth. Rd. Kip —4B 108
Manor Gro. Leeds —6K 67
Manor Gro. Riddl —3E 40
Mnr. Heath Rd. Hal —4F 131
Manor Ho. Otley —2J 27
(off Main St.)
Manor House Art Gallery & Museum. —5B 12
Mnr. House Cft. Leeds —1D 66
Mnr. House La. Leeds —4B 50
Mnr. House Rd. Wilsd —6G 59
Mnr. House St. Pud —6C 82
Manor La. Shipl —5H 61
(in two parts)
Manorley La. B'frd —1E 114
Mnr. Mill La. Leeds —5E 102
Manor Park. —6K 13
Manor Pk. B'frd —5D 78
Manor Pk. Dew —5B 138
(in two parts)
Manor Pk. Oakw —2E 56
Manor Pk. S'cft —4A 52
Manor Pk. Av. All B —2A 126
Mnr. Pk. Gdns. Gom —4K 117
Manor Pl. Kei —1J 39
Manor Ri. I'ly —5D 12
Manor Rd. Bat —3K 137
Manor Rd. Bgly —5A 60
Manor Rd. Chur —6C 102
Manor Rd. H'fth —4E 64
Manor Rd. Kei —1J 39
Manor Rd. Leeds —7H 85
Manor Rd. Rothw —1F 123
Manor Row. B'frd —6A 80 (2D 6)
Manor Row. Low M —7J 97
Manor Royd. Hal —4G 131
Manor Sq. Otley —2J 27
Manor Sq. Yead —4K 45
Manor St. Dew —7H 137
Manor St. Eccl —2D 80
Manor St. Leeds —3K 85 (2H 5)
Manor St. Otley —2J 27
Manor St. Schol —2B 134
Manor Ter. B'frd —2D 80
Manor Ter. Kip —5B 108
Manor Ter. Leeds —1E 84
Manor Ter. Yead —4K 45
Manor, The. Leeds —6E 68
(off Ladywood Rd.)
Manor Vw. Leeds —1E 84
Manor Vw. Pud —6C 82
Manor Way. Bat —4E 136
Manscombe Rd. All —4C 78
Manse Cres. Bur W —1A 26
Mansel M. B'frd —5G 99
Manse Rd. Bur W —1A 26
Manse St. B'frd —6E 80
Mansfield Av. Bgly —6C 42
Mansfield Pl. Leeds —6D 66
Mansfield Rd. B'frd —3J 79
Mansfield Rd. Bur W —1K 25
Mansion La. Hal —4G 131
Mansion La. Leeds —3D 68
Manston. —2A 88
Manston App. Leeds —2A 88
Manston Av. Leeds —2A 88
Manston Cres. Leeds —2A 88
Manston Dri. Leeds —2A 88
Manston Gdns. Leeds —2B 88
Manston Gro. Leeds —3A 88
Manston La. Leeds —3B 88
Manston Ri. Leeds —2A 88
Manston Ter. Leeds —2B 88
Manston Towers. Leeds —7B 70
Manston Way. Leeds —2A 88
Manywells Brow. Cull —1A 76
(in two parts)
Manywells Brow Ind. Est. Cull —7B 58
Manywells Cres. Cull —7B 58
Manywells La. Cull —7K 57
Maple Av. B'frd —5G 81
Maple Av. Oakw —2F 57
Maple Ct. Bgly —2K 59
(off Ash Ter.)
Maple Ct. Leeds —4F 103
Maple Cft. Moort —1A 68
Maple Cft. N Farn —1H 101
Maple Dri. N Farn —1H 101
Maple Dri. Weth —2J 17
Maple Fold. N Farn —1H 101
Maple Gdns. Bard —5C 34
Maple Gro. Bail —3E 60
Maple Gro. Gom —6J 117
Maple Gro. Hud —4G 145
Maple Gro. Kei —2J 39
Maple Gro. N Farn —1J 101
Maple Ri. Rothw —3G 123
Maple St. Hal —3D 130
Maple Ter. Yead —4H 45
Maple Way. Leeds —4A 70
Marbridge Ct. B'frd —4H 97
Marchant St. C'frd —7C 126
Marchbank Rd. B'frd —5E 80
March Cote La. Bgly —6A 60
Marchwood Gro. Cytn —1D 96
Marcus Way. Hud —7H 143
Mardale Cres. Leeds —2J 87
Mardale Rd. Dew —6J 137
Margaret Av. Bard —6B 34
Margaret Clo. Morl —2C 120
Margaret St. Hal —1F 131
Margaret St. Kei —3J 39
Margate. W'ford —1A 124
Margate Rd. B'frd —2C 98
Margate St. Sower B —5J 129
Margerison Cres. I'ly —6E 12
Margerison Rd. I'ly —6E 12
Margetson Rd. Dlgtn —2E 118
Margram Bus. Cen. Hal —7F 113
(off Horne St.)
Marian Gro. Leeds —3H 103
Marian Rd. Leeds —2H 85
Marian Ter. Leeds —2H 85
Maria St. Bur W —7A 14
Marina Cres. Morl —4K 119
Marina Gdns. Sower B —4B 130
(off Park Rd.)
Marion Av. Wake —7K 139
Marion Dri. Shipl —5J 61
Marion Gro. Wake —7K 139
Marion St. Bgly —1A 60
Marion St. B'frd —6J 79
Marion St. Brigh —4G 133
Mark Clo. B'frd —4E 62
Market Ct. T'tn —7J 77
Market Hall. Morl —3A 120
(off Hope St.)
Market Pl. Bat —3G 137
(off Market Sq.)
Market Pl. Cleck —1G 135
(off Albion St.)
Market Pl. Dew —7H 137
Market Pl. Heck —5B 136
Market Pl. Kei —4A 40
Market Pl. Otley —2J 27
Market Pl. Pud —6C 82
Market Pl. Shipl —4H 61
Market Pl. Weth —4J 17
Market Sq. Bat —3G 137
Market Sq. Morl —3A 120
(off Queen St.)
Market Sq. Shipl —5H 61
Market St. Bgly —1K 59
Market St. Birs —6C 118
Market St. B'frd —7A 80 (5D 6)
(in two parts)
Market St. Brigh —6H 133
Market St. Cleck —1G 135
Market St. Hal —1G 131
Market St. Heck —5B 136
(in two parts)
Market St. Kei —5A 40
Market St. Otley —3J 27
Market St. Shipl —5H 61
Market St. Steet —5F 21
Market St. T'tn —7J 77
Market St. Wibs —5J 97
Market St. Arc. Leeds —6J 85 (7F 5)
Markfield Av. Low M —2J 115
Markfield Clo. Low M —2J 115
Markfield Cres. Low M —2J 115
Markfield Dri. Low M —2J 115
Markham Av. Leeds —1B 86
Markham Av. Rawd —6A 46
Markham Cres. Rawd —6A 46
Markham Cft. Rawd —6A 46
Markham St. Bat —4F 137
Markington M. Leeds —4J 121
Markington Pl. Leeds —4J 121
Mark La. Leeds —5J 85 (5E 4)
Mark St. B'frd —3A 98
Mark St. Liv —4K 135
Marland Rd. Kei —3C 40
Marlborough Av. Hal —4F 131
Marlborough Ct. Men —6D 26
Marlborough Gdns. Dew —6F 137
Marlborough Gdns. Leeds —2C 4
Marlborough Grange. Leeds —5A 4
Marlborough Gro. I'ly —6D 12
Marlborough Gro. Leeds —2C 4
Marlborough Ho. Ell —2K 143
(off Southgate)
Marlborough Rd. B'frd —4J 79
Marlborough Rd. Hud —4H 145


180 A-Z Leeds & Bradford

# Marlborough Rd.—Middle Way



Marlborough Rd. Idle —4E 62
Marlborough Rd. Shipl —5G 61
Marlborough Sq. I'ly —6D 12
Marlborough St. Kei —3B 40
Marlborough St. Leeds —5G 85 (6A 4)
*Marlborough Ter. Dew —6F 137 (off Beckett Rd.)*
Marlborough Towers. Leeds —5G 85 (5A 4)
Marlborough Vs. Men —6D 26
Marldon Rd. Hal —6A 114
Marley Clo. B'frd —5E 78
Marley Ct. Bgly —4H 41
Marley Gro. Leeds —3F 103
Marley La. Cytn —3J 95
Marley Pl. Leeds —3F 103
Marley Rd. Kei —3D 40
Marley St. B'frd —6C 80
Marley St. Kei —5K 39
Marley St. Leeds —3F 103
Marley Ter. Leeds —3F 103
Marley Vw. Bgly —4H 41
Marley Vw. Leeds —3F 103
Marling Rd. Hud —6B 144
Marlo Rd. Dew —6A 138
Marlott Rd. Shipl —4K 61
Marlowe Clo. Pud —1D 100
Marlowe Ct. Gar —6K 89
*Marlowe Ct. Guis —2F 45 (off Renton Dri.)*
Marmion Av. B'frd —6C 78
Marne Av. Cytn —3C 96
Marne Cres. B'frd —5D 62
Marquis Av. Oaken —2D 116
Marriner Rd. Kei —5A 40
Marriner's Dri. B'frd —1H 79
Marriner Wlk. Kei —6A 40
Marsden Av. Leeds —4G 103
*Marsden Ct. Far —2B 82 (off Water La.)*
Marsden Gro. Leeds —4G 103
Marsden Mt. Leeds —4G 103
Marsden Pl. Leeds —4G 103
Marsden St. Leeds —7K 83
Marsden Ter. Guis —2F 45
Marsden Vw. Leeds —4G 103
Marsett Way. Leeds —4K 69
**Marsh. —2G 135 (nr. Cleckheaton)**
**Marsh. —1D 74 (nr. Oxenhope)**
Marsh. Pud —6A 82
Marshall Av. Leeds —3B 88
*Marshall Clo. Morl —3A 120 (off Commercial St.)*
Marshall Cres. Morl —5B 120
Marshall Mill. Leeds —7G 85
Marshall St. C'gts —3A 88
Marshall St. Kei —2K 39
Marshall St. Leeds —7H 85
Marshall St. Morl —3A 120
Marshall St. Yead —4K 45
Marshall Ter. Leeds —3A 88
Marsh Delph La. Hal —2K 131
Marsh Delphs. Hal —2K 131
Marshfield Pl. B'frd —3K 97
**Marshfields. —4K 97**
Marshfield St. B'frd —3K 97
Marsh Gro. B'frd —3J 97
Marsh La. B'shaw —3J 117
Marsh La. Hal —2J 131
Marsh La. Leeds —6K 85 (in two parts)
Marsh La. Oxe —2C 74
Marsh Ri. Pud —6A 82
Marsh St. B'frd —4K 97
Marsh St. Cleck —2G 135
Marsh St. Leeds —2G 85
Marsh St. Rothw —3G 123
Marsh Ter. Pud —6A 82
Marsh, The. B'frd —7H 99
**Marsh Top. —1E 74**
Marsh Va. Leeds —2G 85
Marshway. Hal —7E 112
Marsland Ct. Cleck —5F 117
Marsland Pl. B'frd —6F 81
Marston Av. Morl —4A 120
Marston Clo. Q'bry —5K 95
Marston Mt. Leeds —3J 5
Marston Way. Weth —3G 17
Marten Rd. B'frd —3J 97
Martin Clo. Morl —3C 120
Martin Ct. Leeds —5B 88
Martindale Dri. Leeds —4J 83
Martingale Dri. Leeds —4J 121
Martin Grn. La. G'lnd —2E 142
Martin St. Birs —6C 118
Martin St. Brigh —5H 133
Martin Ter. Leeds —3C 84
Martlett Dri. B'frd —4B 98
Marwood Rd. Leeds —6J 83
Maryfield Av. Leeds —3J 87
Maryfield Clo. Leeds —3J 87
Maryfield Ct. Leeds —3K 87
Maryfield Cres. Leeds —3K 87
Maryfield Gdns. Leeds —3J 87
Maryfield Grn. Leeds —3J 87
Maryfield M. Leeds —3J 87
Maryfield Va. Leeds —3J 87
Mary St. B'frd —1E 98
Mary St. Brigh —4G 133
Mary St. Denh —4C 76
Mary St. E Ard —7A 122
Mary St. F'hll —1A 20
Mary St. Fars —1C 82
*Mary St. Oxe —3E 74 (off Denholme Rd.)*
Mary St. Shipl —4F 61
Mary St. T'tn —7H 77
Mary St. Wyke —3J 115
*Mary Sunley Ho. Leeds —2B 86 (off Banstead St. W.)*
Maryville Av. Brigh —3E 132
Masefield Av. B'frd —2C 78
Masefield St. Guis —3H 45
Masham Ct. Leeds —6D 66
Masham Gro. Leeds —6D 84
Masham Pl. B'frd —3F 79
Masham St. Leeds —6D 84
Masonic St. Hal —2C 130
*Mason Sq. Hal —4D 112 (off Keighley Rd.)*
Master La. Hal —4D 130
Matlock St. Hal —6E 112
Matron Heights. Sower B —4J 129
Matterdale Clo. Dew —6J 137
Matterdale Rd. Dew —6J 137
Matthew Clo. Kei —2C 40
Mattyfields Clo. Hal —7C 94
Matty La. Rothw —3D 122
Maud Av. Leeds —4H 103
Maude Av. Bail —2J 61
Maude Cres. Sower B —5G 129
Maude La. Sower B —5F 141
Maude St. G'lnd —2H 143
Maude St. Hal —4E 112
Maude St. Leeds —6K 85 (7G 5)
Maud Pl. Leeds —4H 103
Maudsley St. B'frd —6C 80 (4J 7)
Maud St. B'frd —7D 80 (5K 7)
Maurice Av. Brigh —4F 133
Mavis Av. Leeds —5J 47
Mavis Gro. Leeds —6J 47
Mavis La. Leeds —5J 47
Mavis Rd. Dew —5D 136
Mavis St. B'frd —6D 80 (3K 7)
Mawcroft Clo. Yead —6J 45
Mawcroft Grange Dri. Yead —6J 45
Mawson St. Shipl —4F 61
Maw St. B'frd —1B 98
Maxwell Av. Bat —6G 137
Maxwell Rd. B'frd —6F 97
Maxwell Rd. I'ly —6D 12
Maxwell St. Morl —4K 119
May Av. T'tn —7J 77
Maybrook Ind. Pk. Leeds —5E 84
Mayfair. B'frd —2K 97
Mayfair Av. Sow —7D 142
Mayfair Way. B'frd —1F 99
Mayfield. Hip —6C 114
Mayfield Av. Brigh —7H 115
Mayfield Av. Hal —2E 130
Mayfield Av. I'ly —5D 12
Mayfield Av. Wyke —4J 115
Mayfield Clo. I'ly —5D 12
Mayfield Dri. Hal —2E 130
Mayfield Dri. Sandb —3G 41
Mayfield Gdns. Hal —2E 130
Mayfield Gdns. I'ly —4D 12
*Mayfield Gdns. Sower B —4B 130 (off Park Rd.)*
Mayfield Gro. Bail —1K 61
Mayfield Gro. Brigh —7H 115
Mayfield Gro. Hal —2E 130
Mayfield Gro. Wilsd —6F 59
Mayfield Mt. Hal —2E 130 (nr. Parkinson La.)
*Mayfield Mt. Hal —3E 130 (off King Cross Rd.)*
Mayfield Pl. Dew —7E 136
Mayfield Pl. Wyke —4J 115
Mayfield Ri. Wyke —4K 115
Mayfield Rd. I'ly —5C 12
Mayfield Rd. Kei —3K 39
Mayfield Rd. Leeds —5K 87
Mayfield St. Hal —3E 130
Mayfield Ter. Cytn —3C 96
Mayfield Ter. Cleck —1G 135
Mayfield Ter. Hal —1D 130
Mayfield Ter. Wyke —4K 115
Mayfield Ter. St. Hal —3E 130
Mayfield Vw. Wyke —4K 115
Mayflower Ho. Leeds —4C 104
Maylea Dri. Otley —4F 27
Mayman Clo. Bat —3G 137
Mayman La. Bat —3F 137
Mayo Av. B'frd —4K 97
Mayo Clo. Leeds —6F 69
Mayo Cres. B'frd —5A 98
Mayo Dri. B'frd —5A 98
Mayo Gro. B'frd —5A 98
Mayo Rd. B'frd —5A 98
Maypole M. Bar E —4H 71
Maypole Rd. Hud —6J 145
Mayster Gro. Brigh —2E 144
Mayster Rd. Brigh —2F 145
May St. Cleck —7F 117
May St. Hal —6F 113
May St. Haw —6F 57
May St. Kei —3A 40
May Ter. Leeds —7B 86
Maythorne Av. Bat —5E 136
Maythorne Cres. Cytn —2D 96
Maythorne Dri. Cytn —2E 96
May Tree Clo. Cytn —1D 96
Mayville Av. Leeds —2E 84
Mayville Av. Sandb —3F 41
Mayville Pl. Leeds —2E 84
Mayville Rd. Leeds —2E 84
Mayville St. Leeds —2E 84
Mayville Ter. Leeds —2E 84
Mazebrook Av. Cleck —5G 117
Mazebrook Cres. Cleck —5G 117
Mead Clo. Leeds —7C 88
Mead Gro. Leeds —7C 88
Meadowbank Av. All —4B 78
Meadow Clo. Bard —4C 34
Meadow Clo. Bat —6E 118
Meadow Clo. B Spa —2C 36
Meadow Clo. H'den —3F 59
Meadow Clo. Liv —7H 135
Meadow Clo. She —1D 114
Meadow Ct. All —1A 78
Meadow Ct. Brigh —6A 134
*Meadow Ct. T'tn —7H 77 (off Chapel St.)*
Meadow Cres. Hal —5C 112
Meadowcroft. B'frd —5B 98
Meadow Cft. E Kes —5A 34
Meadow Cft. Kei —5G 39
Meadow Cft. Leeds —1H 103
Meadowcroft. Men —7C 26
Mdw. Croft Clo. B'frd —4B 62
Meadowcroft Cres. C'frd —7G 127
Meadowcroft La. Ripp —4G 141
Meadowcroft M. Leeds —6A 86
Meadowcroft Ri. B'frd —6E 98
Meadow Dri. Hal —5C 112
Meadow Dri. Liv —7H 135
Meadow End. B'hpe —1J 47
Meadow Gth. B'hpe —2K 47
Meadowgate Cft. Loft —5D 122
Meadowgate Dri. Loft —5D 122
Meadowgate Va. Loft —6D 122
Meadowhurst Gdns. Pud —6B 82
Meadowlands. Schol —6A 116
Meadow La. Cnly —3K 21
Meadow La. Dew —7G 137
Meadow La. Hal —5C 112
Meadow La. Leeds —7J 85
Meadow La. Liv —7H 135
Mdw. Park Cres. S'ley —3K 81
Mdw. Park Dri. S'ley —3K 81
Meadow Rd. B'frd —4G 63
Meadow Rd. Gar —6A 90
Meadowside Rd. Bail —7A 44
Meadows, The. All B —1K 125
Meadows, The. Leeds —1C 66
Meadows, The. Wibs —5J 97
Meadow Valley. Leeds —6H 49
Meadow Vw. Bar E —4J 71
Meadow Vw. Leeds —2E 84
Meadow Vw. Oakw —2F 57
Meadow Vw. Wyke —6J 115
*Meadow Wlk. Hal —5C 112 (off Meadow La.)*
Meadow Way. Leeds —6G 49
Meadow Way. Ting —1D 138
Mead Rd. Leeds —7C 88
Mead Vw. B'frd —3G 99
Meadway. B'frd —1E 114
Mead Way. Leeds —7C 88
Meagill Ri. Otley —7F 15
**Meanwood. —6F 67**
Meanwood Clo. Leeds —1H 85
**Meanwood Grove. —3D 66**
Meanwood Gro. Leeds —3E 66
Meanwood Rd. Leeds —6F 67 (1F 5)
Meanwood Towers. Leeds —4G 67
Meanwood Valley Clo. Leeds —6F 67
Meanwood Valley Dri. Leeds —6F 67
Meanwood Valley Grn. Leeds —6F 67
Meanwood Valley Gro. Leeds —6F 67
Meanwood Valley Mt. Leeds —6F 67
Meanwood Valley Urban Farm. —7G 67
Meanwood Valley Wlk. Leeds —6F 67
Mearclough Rd. Sower B —4B 130
Medeway. S'ley —3A 82
Medhurst Av. Kip —4B 108
Medley La. Hal —3K 113
Medley St. C'frd —7E 126
Medway. S'ley —6K 95
Medway Av. Gar —1A 108
Meggison Gro. B'frd —2J 97
Megna Way. B'frd —2A 98
Melba Rd. B'frd —3H 97
Melbourne Gro. B'frd —5G 81
Melbourne Gro. Leeds —3G 83
Melbourne M. Wake —4K 139
Melbourne Pl. B'frd —1K 97 (7C 6)
Melbourne Pl. S'ley —3C 82
Melbourne St. Bmly —3G 83
Melbourne St. Fars —3B 82
Melbourne St. Hal —6E 112
Melbourne St. Leeds —4K 85 (4G 5)
Melbourne St. Liv —5K 135
Melbourne St. Morl —3B 120
Melbourne St. Shipl —4G 61
Melbourne Ter. B'frd —1A 98 (7D 6)
Melbourne Ter. S'ley —3D 82
Melbury Ho. B'frd —2J 7
Melcombe Ho. B'frd —3H 7
Melcombe Wlk. B'frd —2G 99
Melford St. B'frd —4E 98
Mellor Mill La. Holy G —5F 143
Mellor St. Brigh —6H 133
Mellor St. Hal —3E 130
Mellor Ter. Hal —3E 130
Melrose Ct. Ell —3J 143
Melrose Dri. Bur W —7A 14
Melrose Gro. H'fth —4J 65
*Melrose Ho. B'frd —2G 99 (off Ned La.)*
Melrose Pl. H'fth —4H 65
Melrose Pl. Pud —7B 82
Melrose St. B'frd —2G 97
Melrose St. Hal —6E 112
*Melrose Ter. Ell —3K 143 (off Savile Rd.)*
Melrose Ter. H'fth —4H 65
Melrose Wlk. H'fth —4H 65
*Melsonby Ho. B'frd —5E 62 (off Cavendish Rd.)*
Melton Av. Leeds —3B 122
Melton Clo. Leeds —3B 122
Melton Gth. Leeds —3B 122
Melton St. Bat —2F 137
Melton Ter. B'frd —1G 81
Melton Way. Liv —7H 135
Melville Clo. Leeds —2H 85
Melville Gdns. Leeds —1H 85
Melville Gro. I'ly —5E 12
Melville Ho. B'frd —4A 6
Melville Pl. Leeds —1H 85
Melville Rd. Leeds —2H 85
Melville St. B'frd —6J 79 (4A 6)
Memorial Dri. Leeds —5F 67
Mendip Clo. Gar —1K 107
Mendip Rd. Dew —7K 137
Mendip Way. Low M —1H 115
Menin Dri. Bail —6J 43
**Menston. —6B 26**
Menston Dri. Men —7C 26
Menstone St. B'frd —5J 79 (2A 6)
Menston Hall. Men —6D 26
Menston Old La. Men —4B 26
Merchants Ct. B'frd —1C 98
Mercia Way. Leeds —2C 88
Mercury Row. Otley —3J 27
Merewood Rd. C'frd —7K 125
Meriden Av. Gar —1K 107
Merlin Clo. Morl —4C 120
Merlin Ct. Bat —7E 118
Merlin Gro. B'frd —6C 78
Merlinwood Dri. Bail —7K 43
Merrion Cen. Leeds —4J 85 (4E 4)
Merrion Cres. Hal —3J 131
Merrion Pl. Leeds —5J 85 (5F 5) (in two parts)
Merrion St. Hal —3J 131
Merrion St. Leeds —5J 85 (5E 4) (in two parts)
Merrion Way. Leeds —4J 85 (4E 4)
Merrivale Rd. All —5A 78
Merriville. H'fth —5H 65
Merry Bent La. Sower B —4C 140
Merrydale Rd. Euro I —1C 116
Merton Av. Fars —3B 82
Merton Clo. Kip —4C 108
Merton Dri. Fars —3A 82
Merton Fold. B'frd —2A 98
Merton Gdns. Fars —3A 82
Merton Rd. B'frd —1K 97 (7B 6)
Merville Av. Bail —6J 43
Metcalfe St. B'frd —2D 98
**Methley. —5G 125**
Methley Dri. Leeds —6J 67
Methley Gro. Leeds —6J 67
**Methley Junction. —7H 125**
Methley La. Leeds —6K 67
Methley La. Meth —3A 124
**Methley Lanes. —7C 124**
Methley Mt. Leeds —6K 67
Methley Pl. Leeds —6J 67
Methley Rd. C'frd —7A 126
Methley Ter. Leeds —6K 67
Methley Vw. Leeds —6K 67
Methuen Oval. Wyke —6J 115
Mexborough Av. Leeds —1K 85
Mexborough Dri. Leeds —1K 85
Mexborough Gro. Leeds —1K 85
*Mexborough Ho. Ell —2K 143 (off Gog Hill)*
Mexborough Pl. Leeds —2K 85
Mexborough Rd. B'frd —7K 61
Mexborough Rd. Leeds —2K 85
Mexborough St. Leeds —1K 85
Meynell App. Leeds —1G 103
Meynell Av. Rothw —2G 123
Meynell Ct. Leeds —6B 88
Meynell Heights. Leeds —1G 103
Meynell Ho. B'frd —6E 62
Meynell Mt. Rothw —2H 123
Meynell Rd. Leeds —6B 88
Meynell Sq. Leeds —1G 103
Meynell Wlk. Leeds —1G 103
Meyrick Av. Weth —3A 18
Miall St. Hal —7E 112
Michael Gth. B'frd —5H 97
Mickledore Ridge. B'frd —3E 96
**Micklefield. —6G 91**
*Micklefield Ct. Rawd —7K 45 (off Micklefield La.)*
Micklefield La. Rawd —7J 45
Micklefield Rd. Rawd —7K 45
Micklemoss Dri. Q'bry —4G 95
**Micklethwaite. —4K 41**
Micklethwaite Dri. Q'bry —6J 95
Micklethwaite La. Bgly —5J 41
Micklethwaite Vw. Weth —5J 17
**Mickletown. —4H 125**
Mickletown Rd. Meth —4G 125
Mickley St. Leeds —6D 84
Middlebrook Clo. B'frd —6E 78
Middlebrook Cres. B'frd —7D 78
Middlebrook Dri. B'frd —6D 78
Middlebrook Hill. B'frd —6D 78
Middlebrook Ri. B'frd —6D 78
Middlebrook Vw. B'frd —6E 78
Middlebrook Wlk. B'frd —6E 78
Middlebrook Way. B'frd —7D 78
Middlecroft Clo. Leeds —6B 104
Middlecroft Rd. Leeds —6B 104
Middle Cross St. Leeds —6D 84 (in two parts)
Middle Dean St. G'lnd —3G 143
*Middle Ellistones. G'lnd —2E 142 (off Saddleworth Rd.)*
Middle Fold. Leeds —5K 85 (5H 5)
Middlegate. Birs —6C 118
Middle Hall Clo. Liv —4H 135
Middle La. Cytn —1C 96
Middle La. Lntn —7G 17
Middlemoor. Leeds —4K 69
Middle Oxford St. C'frd —7C 126
Middle Rd. Leeds —4F 105
Middle St. B'frd —6A 80 (3E 6)
Middle St. Sower B —7G 129
Middlethorne Clo. Leeds —6D 50
Middlethorne Ri. Leeds —6D 50
**Middleton. —2C 12 (nr. Ilkley)**
**Middleton. —3H 121 (nr. Morley)**
Middleton Av. I'ly —3B 12
Middleton Av. Leeds —4B 86
Middleton Av. Rothw —2C 122
Middleton Clo. Morl —3B 120
Middleton Ct. Liv —4G 135
Middleton Cres. Leeds —4H 103
Middleton Gro. Leeds —5H 103
Middleton Gro. Morl —3C 120
Middleton La. Midd & Thor —4J 121
Middleton La. Rothw —2C 122 (in two parts)
Middleton Pk. Av. Leeds —3H 121
Middleton Pk. Cir. Leeds —2H 121
Middleton Pk. Ct. Leeds —3H 121
Middleton Pk. Cres. Leeds —3J 121
Middleton Pk. Grn. Leeds —3H 121
Middleton Pk. Gro. Leeds —2H 121
Middleton Pk. Mt. Leeds —3H 121
Middleton Pk. Rd. Leeds —2H 121
Middleton Pk. Ter. Leeds —3H 121
Middleton Railway. —5J 103
Middleton Rd. I'ly —5A 12
Middleton Rd. Leeds —7A 104
Middleton Rd. Morl —3B 120
Middleton St. B'frd —4H 79
Middleton Ter. Morl —3C 120
Middleton Way. Leeds —1B 122
Middle Wlk. Leeds —3E 68
Middle Way. Kei —4C 40

Middleway—Moorlands Ct.


Middleway. Sils —1H 21
Midge Hall Clo. Bur W —1A 26
Midgeham Gro. H'den —3E 58
Midgeley Rd. Bail —3G 61
**Midgley. —6E 110**
Midgley Gdns. Leeds —2G 85
Midgley Pl. Leeds —2H 85
Midgley Rd. Bur W —1A 26
Midgley Rd. H Bri —6A 110
Midgley Row. B'frd —5D 98
Midgley Ter. Leeds —2H 85
Midland Clo. Leeds —3B 104
Midland Gth. Leeds —3A 104
Midland Hill. Bgly —1K 59
*Midland Ho. Rothw —1B 124*
*(off Midland St.)*
Midland Pas. Leeds —2F 85
Midland Pl. Leeds —7G 85
Midland Rd. Bail —2K 61
Midland Rd. B'frd —3K 79 (1D 6)
Midland Rd. Friz —7J 61
Midland Rd. Leeds —2F 85
(LS6)
Midland Rd. Leeds —3A 104
(LS10)
Midland St. W'ford —1A 124
Midland Ter. B'frd —2K 79
Midland Ter. Kei —3A 40
Midway Av. Bgly —5A 60
Milan Rd. Leeds —2B 86
Milan St. Leeds —2C 86
Milbrook Gdns. Heck —6E 136
Mildred St. B'frd —4C 80 (1H 7)
Mile Cross Gdns. Hal —2C 130
Mile Cross Pl. Hal —2C 130
Mile Cross Rd. Hal —2C 130
Mile Cross Ter. Hal —2C 130
Miles Gth. Bard —4D 34
**Miles Hill. —6H 67**
Miles Hill Av. Leeds —6H 67
Miles Hill Cres. B'frd —5E 98
Miles Hill Cres. Leeds —6H 67
Miles Hill Dri. B'frd —5E 98
Miles Hill Gro. Leeds —6H 67
Miles Hill Mt. Leeds —5G 67
Miles Hill Pl. Leeds —5H 67
Miles Hill Rd. Leeds —5H 67
Miles Hill Sq. Leeds —6H 67
Miles Hill St. Leeds —6H 67
Miles Hill Ter. Leeds —6H 67
Miles Hill Vw. Leeds —6H 67
Milestone Ct. S'ley —3D 82
Mile Thorn St. Hal —1D 130
Milford Gro. Gom —4J 117
Milford Pl. B'frd —2G 79
Milford Pl. Leeds —4D 84
**Mill Bank. —2F 141**
Mill Bank Clo. Sower B —2E 140
Millbank Ct. Pud —7D 82
Millbank Fold. Pud —7D 82
Mill Bank Rd. Mill B —2F 141
Mill Banks. Sils —1G 21
Millbank Vw. Pud —7D 82
Millbeck App. Morl —3C 120
Millbeck Clo. B'frd —7C 78
Millbeck Clo. T'tn —7C 78
Millbeck Grn. Coll —2E 34
**Mill Bridge. —3K 135**
Millbrook Gdns. Dew —6E 136
Mill Carr Hill Rd. Oaken —2D 116
Mill Clo. La. Q'bry —6G 95
*Mill Ct. Oxe —3E 74*
*(off Yate La.)*
Mill Cft. Gild —7H 101
Millcroft. Pool W —3H 29
Mill Dam. Cliff —5E 36
Millergate. B'frd —6A 80 (4D 6)
Millers Ct. Liv —6K 135
Millers Dale. Morl —1K 119
Millersdale Clo. Euro I —7C 98
Millfields. Sils —1F 21
Mill Fold. Gild —7H 101
Millford Way. Ripp —5F 141
Mill Forest Way. Bat —4K 137
(nr. Oaklands Dri.)
Mill Forest Way. Bat —6G 137
(nr. Town St.)
Mill Gth. Gild —7H 101
Millgarth Ct. Coll —2F 35
Millgarth St. Leeds —5K 85 (6G 5)
Millgate. Bgly —1K 59
Millgate. Ell —2K 143
**Mill Green. —7A 70**
Mill Grn. Leeds —7F 85
Mill Grn. Clo. Leeds —7A 70
Mill Grn. Gdns. Leeds —7A 70
Mill Grn. Gth. Leeds —7A 70
Mill Grn. Pl. Leeds —7A 70
Mill Grn. Rd. Leeds —7A 70
Mill Grn. Vw. Leeds —7A 70
Mill Gro. Brigh —4F 133
Mill Hey. Haw —5F 57
Mill Hill. Haw —5E 56
Mill Hill. Leeds —6J 85 (7E 4)
Mill Hill. Pud —1C 100
Mill Hill. Rothw —2G 123
Mill Hill Grn. Rothw —2G 123
Mill Hill La. Brigh —4F 133
Mill Hill La. Clif —7B 134
Mill Hill Sq. Rothw —2G 123
Mill Hill Top. H'den —4F 59
Mill Ho. Ri. B'frd —5D 98
Milligan Av. B'frd —7B 62
Mill La. Bard —6C 34
Mill La. Bat —4H 137
Mill La. Bgly —5C 42
Mill La. B'shaw —1J 117
Mill La. Birs —5F 119
Mill La. B'twn —5F 113
Mill La. B'frd —1A 98 (7E 6)
Mill La. Brigh —6H 133
Mill La. Butt —1E 114
Mill La. C'frd —6D 126
Mill La. Cleck —4F 117
Mill La. Coll —2F 35
Mill La. E Ard —7K 121
Mill La. Gild —7H 101
Mill La. Guis —4J 43
Mill La. Holy G —5G 143
Mill La. Kear —1G 33
Mill La. Leeds —2E 82
Mill La. Ludd —5G 111
Mill La. Mick M —4G 125
Mill La. Mix —7A 94
Mill La. Oakw —2D 56
Mill La. Otley —2J 27
Mill La. Oxe —2E 74
Mill La. Pool W —3G 29
Mill La. Q'bry —4G 95
Mill La. Steet —5E 20
Mill La. Thor A —2E 36
Mill La. Tong —3D 100
Millmoor Clo. D Hill —3D 78
Mill Pit La. Rothw —7F 105
Mill Pond Clo. Leeds —6E 66
Mill Pond Gro. Leeds —6E 66
Mill Pond La. Leeds —5E 66
Mill Pond Sq. Leeds —5E 66
Mill Rd. Dew —6G 137
Mill Row. Ebrn —4B 20
Mill Royd St. Brigh —6H 133
**Mill Shaw. —5E 102**
Millshaw. Leeds —5D 102
Millshaw Mt. Leeds —6E 102
Millshaw Pk. Av. Leeds —6D 102
Millshaw Pk. Clo. Leeds —6D 102
Millshaw Pk. Dri. Leeds —5D 102
Millshaw Pk. La. Leeds —6D 102
Millshaw Pk. Way. Leeds —5D 102
Millshaw Rd. Leeds —7E 102
Millside Wlk. Morl —3C 120
Millstone Ri. Liv —6K 135
Mill St. Birs —7C 118
Mill St. B'frd —5B 80 (2F 7)
Mill St. C'frd —7B 126
Mill St. Cull —6B 58
Mill St. Hal —7E 130
Mill St. Leeds —6A 86 (7H 5)
Mill St. Morl —4A 120
Mill St. Sut Cr —5A 20
Mill St. Wibs —5G 97
Mill Vw. Bur W —7A 14
Millwright St. Leeds —4K 85 (4H 5)
Milne Ct. Colt —7B 88
Milner Bank. Otley —4F 27
Milner Clo. G'lnd —2G 143
Milner Fold. Pud —1B 100
Milner Gdns. Leeds —7B 86
Milner Ing. Wyke —3J 115
Milner La. G'lnd —2G 143
Milner La. Rob H —4C 122
(in two parts)
Milner La. T'ner —4D 52
Milner Rd. Bail —3H 61
Milner Royd La. Norl —5C 130
Milner's Rd. Yead —4H 45
Milner St. Hal —1F 131
Milner Ct. Oss —7C 138
Milnes St. Leeds —7E 84
Milne St. B'frd —6J 79 (4A 6)
Milnthorpe Clo. B'ham —7C 36
Milnthorpe Gdns. B'ham —7C 36
Milnthorpe Gth. B'ham —7C 36
Milnthorpe La. B'ham —7C 36
Milnthorpe Way. B'ham —7C 36
Milroyd Cres. Bat —5E 118
Milton Av. Liv —5A 136
Milton Av. Sower B —3K 129
Milton Clo. Liv —6A 136
Milton Dri. Liv —6A 136
Milton Dri. Scholes —5D 70
Milton Gdns. Liv —5A 136
Milton Gro. Dew —6G 137
Milton Pl. Hal —1F 131
Milton Rd. Liv —5A 136
Milton Sq. Heck —4B 136
Milton St. B'frd —6J 79 (4A 6)
Milton St. C'frd —7C 126
Milton St. Denh —5C 76
Milton St. Heck —3B 136
Milton St. Sower B —3K 129
Milton Ter. Cleck —7E 116
Milton Ter. Hal —1F 131
Milton Ter. Leeds —1A 84
Milton Ter. Yead —4H 45
*Milton Wlk. Dew —7G 137*
*(off Wellington Wlk.)*
Minerva Ind. Est. Rothw —7C 106
Minnie St. Haw —6E 56
Minnie St. Kei —5K 39
Minorca Mt. Denh —4B 76
Minstead Av. Ell —2D 144
Mint St. B'frd —3D 80
Miramar. Hud —4K 145
Mirey La. Sower B —4D 128
Mirfield Av. B'frd —7C 62
Mirycarr La. T'ner —2C 70
Miry La. Cra V —3B 128
Miry La. Liv —4D 134
Miry La. Pot —2J 71
Miry La. Yead —4K 45
Mission St. Brigh —7J 133
Mistral Clo. Wyke —5J 115
Mistral Gro. Liv —3D 134
Mistress La. Leeds —5C 84
Mitcham Dri. B'frd —3G 79
Mitchell Av. Dew —6F 137
Mitchell Clo. B'frd —3E 62
Mitchell La. B'frd —3E 62
Mitchell La. Sils —1G 21
Mitchell Sq. B'frd —2A 98
Mitchell St. Brigh —5G 133
Mitchell St. Kei —3B 40
Mitchell St. Sower B —4A 130
Mitchell Ter. Bgly —3K 59
Mitford Pl. Leeds —6D 84
Mitford Rd. Leeds —6D 84
Mitford Ter. Leeds —6D 84
Mitford Vw. Leeds —6D 84
Mitre Ct. B'frd —3F 99
Mitre St. Dew —7E 136
Mitton St. Bgly —6B 60
Mitton St. B'frd —3J 97
**Mixenden. —2A 112**
Mixenden Clo. Hal —2A 112
*Mixenden Ct. Hal —3B 112*
*(off Mixenden Rd.)*
Mixenden La. Hal —1B 112
Mixenden Rd. Hal —1A 112
Moat End. T'ner —6D 52
Moat Hill. Birs —5E 118
Moat Hill Farm Dri. Bat —5E 118
Modder Av. Leeds —6B 84
Modder Pl. A'ley —6B 84
Model Av. Leeds —6D 84
Model Rd. Leeds —6D 84
Model Ter. Leeds —6D 84
Moderna Way. Myth —6C 110
Moffat Clo. B'frd —7F 97
Moffat Clo. Hal —4C 112
*Monckton Ho. B'frd —4B 98*
*(off Parkway)*
Mond Av. B'frd —4F 81
Monk Barn Clo. Bgly —7A 42
Monk Bri. Av. Leeds —6F 67
Monk Bri. Dri. Leeds —6F 67
Monk Bri. Gro. Leeds —6E 66
Monk Bri. Mt. Leeds —6F 67
Monk Bri. Pl. Leeds —6E 66
Monk Bri. Rd. Leeds —6E 66
Monk Bri. St. Leeds —6F 67
Monk Bri. Ter. Leeds —6E 66
Monk Ings. Birs —6B 118
Monk Ings Av. Birs —6A 118
Monkmans Wharfe. Sils —1G 21
Monk St. B'frd —6J 79 (4A 6)
Monkswood. Leeds —6K 65
Monkswood Av. Leeds —4H 69
Monkswood Bank. Leeds —4H 69
Monkswood Clo. Leeds —4H 69
Monkswood Dri. Leeds —4H 69
Monkswood Ga. Leeds —4J 69
Monkswood Grn. Leeds —4H 69
Monkswood Hill. Leeds —4H 69
*Monkswood Ho. Leeds —1K 83*
*(off Broad La.)*
Monkswood Ri. Leeds —4H 69
Monkswood Wlk. Leeds —4J 69
Monson Av. C'ley —6K 63
Montagu Av. Leeds —7D 68
Montagu Ct. Leeds —6D 68
Montagu Cres. Leeds —7E 68
Montagu Dri. Leeds —6D 68
Montague Ct. Leeds —6A 84
Montague Cres. Gar —5A 90
Montague Pl. Gar —6A 90
Montague St. B'frd —3J 97
Montague St. Sower B —5J 129
Montagu Gdns. Leeds —7D 68
Montagu Gro. Leeds —7E 68
Montagu Pl. Leeds —7D 68
Montagu Ri. Leeds —7E 68
Montagu Rd. Weth —4A 18
Montagu Vw. Leeds —7D 68
Montcalm Cres. Leeds —4A 104
Monterey Dri. All —2K 77
Montfort Clo. H'fth —1F 65
Montgomery Ho. B'frd —1A 6
*Mont Gro. B'frd —3J 97*
*(off Montague St.)*
Montpelier Ter. Leeds —1G 85
Montreal Av. Leeds —6K 67
Montreal Ter. Leeds —5E 82
Montrose Pl. Q'bry —4G 95
Montrose St. B'frd —1K 79
Montserrat Rd. B'frd —5H 99
Moody St. B'frd —1B 98 (7F 7)
Moon Clo. Birs —6D 118
**Moor Allerton. —1J 67**
Moor Allerton Av. Leeds —2A 68
Moor Allerton Cen. Leeds —2H 67
Moor Allerton Cres. Leeds —2A 68
Moor Allerton Dri. Leeds —2A 68
Moor Allerton Gdns. Leeds —2K 67
Moor Allerton Way. Leeds —2A 68
Moor Av. Cliff —4D 36
Moor Av. Leeds —6H 87
Moor Bank. B'frd —7J 99
Moorbank Ct. Leeds —7E 66
**Moorbottom. —1D 134**
Moorbottom. Cleck —2D 134
Moor Bottom La. Bgly —1A 60
Moor Bottom La. Cra V —3B 128
Moor Bottom La. G'lnd —7E 130
(in two parts)
Moor Bottom La. Kei —2K 57
Moor Bottom La. Sower B —1J 141
Moor Bottom Rd. Hal —1D 112
Moor Bottom Rd. Ripp —4H 141
Moor Clo. Leeds —4K 103
Moor Clo. Av. Q'bry —6G 95
Moor Clo. Farm M. Q'bry —6G 95
Moor Clo. Pde. Q'bry —5G 95
Moor Clo. Rd. Q'bry —6G 95
Moor Cres. Leeds —2J 103
Moor Cres. Chase. Leeds —2J 103
Moorcroft. Bgly —6B 42
Moorcroft. Dew —7E 136
Moor Cft. Leeds —7D 48
Moorcroft Av. B'frd —4F 81
Moorcroft Av. Oakw —1G 57
Moorcroft Dri. Dew —7D 136
Moorcroft Dri. E Bier —5H 99
Moorcroft Rd. B'frd —5H 99
Moorcroft Rd. Dew —7D 136
Moorcroft Ter. B'frd —5H 99
Moor Dri. Leeds —6E 66
Moor Dri. Oakw —1E 56
Moor Dri. Otley —2B 28
Moor Dri. Pud —1D 100
Moore Av. B'frd & Wibs —3F 97
**Moor Edge. —2E 58**
Moor Edge High Side. H'den —2E 58
Moor Edge Low Side. H'den —2E 58
**Moorend. —7F 117**
**(nr. Cleckheaton)**
**Moor End. —2K 111**
**(nr. Mixenden)**
**Moor End. —6C 62**
**(nr. Springfield)**
Moor End. B Spa —2A 36
Moor End Av. Hal —6A 112
Moor End Gdns. Hal —6B 112
Moor End La. Dew —6C 136
Moor End La. Norl —6B 130
(in two parts)
Moor End Rd. Hal —2K 111
Moor End Vw. Hal —7C 112
Moore St. Kei —5A 40
Moore Vw. B'frd —3F 97
Moor Farm Gdns. Leeds —5J 67
Moorfield. Gild —7G 101
Moorfield Av. B'frd —4F 81
Moorfield Av. Leeds —5A 84
Moorfield Av. Men —6B 26
Moorfield Av. Schol —1A 134
Moorfield Bus. Pk. Yead —5B 46
Moorfield Clo. Yead —5B 46
Moorfield Ct. Yead —5B 46
Moorfield Cres. Leeds —5A 84
Moorfield Cres. Pud —7B 82
Moorfield Cres. Yead —5A 46
Moorfield Cft. Yead —5B 46
Moorfield Dri. Bail —6J 43
Moorfield Dri. Oakw —1F 57
Moorfield Dri. Yead —5B 46
Moorfield Gdns. Pud —7A 82
Moorfield Gro. Leeds —5A 84
Moorfield Gro. Pud —7A 82
Moorfield Ind. Est. Yead —4B 46
Moorfield Pl. B'frd —4D 62
(in two parts)
Moorfield Rd. Bgly —5A 60
Moorfield Rd. Hud —7H 145
Moorfield Rd. I'ly —5F 13
Moorfield Rd. Leeds —5A 84
Moorfield Rd. Yead —5B 46
Moorfields. Bmly —2G 83
Moorfields. Leeds —2K 67
Moorfield St. A'ley —5A 84
Moorfield St. Hal —4E 130
Moorfield St. Leeds —2G 85 (1B 4)
Moorfield Ter. Yead —4A 46
Moorfield Vw. Rbtwn —7G 135
Moorfield Way. Schol —1A 134
Moor Flatts Av. Leeds —2J 121
Moor Flatts Rd. Leeds —2J 121
**Moor Garforth. —6K 89**
Moorgarth Av. B'frd —4F 81
**Moor Gate. —4A 108**
Moorgate. Bail —7J 43
Moorgate Av. B'frd —4E 80
Moorgate Av. Kip —3A 108
Moorgate Clo. Kip —4A 108
Moorgate Dri. Kip —4B 108
Moorgate Ri. Kip —4A 108
Moorgate Rd. Kip —3A 108
Moorgate St. Hal —3D 130
*Moor Grange. Yead —5B 46*
*(off Victoria Av.)*
Moor Grange Ct. Leeds —4K 65
Moor Grange Dri. Leeds —4A 66
Moor Grange Ri. Leeds —4A 66
Moor Grange Vw. Leeds —4A 66
Moor Gro. Hal —7C 96
Moor Gro. Pud —1D 100
Moor Haven. Leeds —1G 67
Moor Haven Ct. Leeds —1G 67
**Moor Head. —6F 101**
**(nr. Gildersome)**
**Moorhead. —5E 60**
**(nr. Shipley)**
Moorhead Cres. Shipl —5E 60
Moorhead La. Shipl —5E 60
Moorhead Ter. Shipl —5E 60
Moorhead Vs. Morl —5F 101
Moor Hey La. Ell —4C 144
Moor Hey La. Holy G —7C 142
*Moorhill. Holy G —7D 142*
*(off Thorn Hill Clo.)*
Moorhouse Av. B'frd —7C 62
Moorhouse Av. Leeds —5F 103
Moor Ho. Clo. Oxe —2E 74
Moor Ho. Ct. Leeds —7D 50
Moorhouse Ct. Oxe —2E 74
Moorhouse Dri. B'shaw —7H 99
Moorhouse La. B'shaw —7J 99
Moorhouse La. Oxe —1D 74
Moorings, The. App B —4F 63
Moorings, The. Leeds —3D 104
(LS10)
Moorings, The. Leeds —6A 50
(LS17)
Moor Knoll Clo. E Ard —7K 121
Moor Knoll Dri. E Ard —7J 121
Moor Knoll La. E Ard —6J 121
Moorland Av. Bail —7K 43
Moorland Av. Bgly —6C 42
Moorland Av. Gild —6F 101
Moorland Av. Guis —2G 45
Moorland Av. Leeds —3F 85
Moorland Clo. Gild —6G 101
Moorland Clo. Hal —4C 112
Moorland Clo. Leeds —3K 67
Moorland Cres. Bail —7K 43
Moorland Cres. Gild —6F 101
Moorland Cres. Guis —1G 45
Moorland Cres. Leeds —3J 67
Moorland Cres. Men —1E 44
(nr. Bradford Rd.)
Moorland Cres. Men —5C 26
(nr. Burley Rd.)
Moorland Cres. Pud —5J 81
Moorland Dri. B'shaw —7K 99
Moorland Dri. Guis —1G 45
Moorland Dri. Leeds —3J 67
Moorland Dri. Pud —4J 81
Moorland Gdns. Leeds —3K 67
Moorland Gth. Leeds —3J 67
Moorland Gro. Leeds —2J 67
Moorland Gro. Pud —4J 81
Moorland Ings. Leeds —3J 67
Moorland Leys. Leeds —3J 67
Moorland Mills. Cleck —6F 117
Moorland Pl. Low M —2A 116
Moorland Pl. Stan —7G 123
Moorland Ri. Leeds —3J 67
Moorland Rd. B'hpe —1F 47
Moorland Rd. Dlgtn —1C 118
Moorland Rd. Leeds —3F 85 (1A 4)
Moorland Rd. Pud —4J 81
Moorlands. I'ly —7A 12
Moorlands Av. B'shaw —7J 99
Moorlands Av. B'frd —4F 81
Moorlands Av. Dew —7F 137
Moorlands Av. Hal —4C 112
Moorlands Av. Oakw —7H 39
Moorlands Av. Oss —7C 138
Moorlands Av. Yead —5B 46
Moorlands Av. N. Dew —7F 137
Moorlands Av. W. Dew —7F 137
Moorlands Clo. Dew —5D 136
Moorlands Ct. G'lnd —1F 143


182 A-Z Leeds & Bradford

**Moorlands Ct.—Naylor St.**

Moorlands Ct. *Weth* —4K **17**
Moorlands Cres. *Hal* —4C **112**
Moorlands Cres. *Hud* —7H **143**
Moorlands Dri. *Hal* —5C **112**
Moorlands Dri. *Yead* —5B **46**
Moorlands Ind. Cen. *Cleck* —6F **117**
Moorlands Pl. *Hal* —3F **131**
Moorlands Rd. *B'shaw* —7J **99**
Moorlands Rd. *Dew* —7F **137**
Moorlands Rd. *G'lnd* —1F **143**
Moorlands Rd. *Hud* —7H **143**
Moorlands, The. *B Spa* —2C **36**
Moorlands, The. *Leeds* —7A **50**
Moorlands, The. *Weth* —4K **17**
Moorlands Vw. *Hal* —3F **131**
Moorlands Vw. *Weth* —4K **17**
Moorland Ter. *Gar* —7J **89**
Moorland Ter. *Kei* —5D **40**
Moorland Vw. *Leeds* —2J **67**
Moorland Vw. *Low M* —2A **116**
Moorland Vw. *Rod* —1F **83**
Moorland Vw. *Sower B* —5H **129**
Moorland Vw. *Wilsd* —1H **77**
Moorland Villa. *Sower B* —7H **129**
Moorland Wlk. *Leeds* —2J **67**
Moor La. *Add* —1A **10**
Moor La. *Askw* —3C **14**
(in two parts)
Moor La. *B'shaw & Gom* —3A **118**
Moor La. *B Spa* —4D **18**
Moor La. *B'ham* —4K **35**
Moor La. *Bur W* —3J **25**
Moor La. *Ebrn* —5B **20**
(in two parts)
Moor La. *E Kes* —4H **33**
Moor La. *Guis* —7G **27**
Moor La. *Hal* —3C **112**
Moor La. *Men* —5K **25**
Moorlea Dri. *Bail* —1K **61**
Moorleigh Clo. *Kip* —4B **108**
Moorleigh Dri. *Kip* —4B **108**
Moor Lodge Cvn. Pk. *Leeds* —2J **51**
Moor Pk. Av. *Leeds* —6D **66**
Moor Pk. Clo. *Add* —1B **10**
Moor Pk. Clo. *B'frd* —5E **80**
Moor Pk. Ct. *Dew* —7J **137**
Moor Pk. Cres. *Add* —1B **10**
Moor Pk. Dri. *Add* —1B **10**
Moor Pk. Dri. *B'frd* —5F **81**
Moor Pk. Dri. *Leeds* —6D **66**
Moor Pk. Gdns. *Dew* —7J **137**
Moor Pk. Gro. *Add* —1C **10**
Moor Pk. La. *Dew* —7J **137**
Moor Pk. Mt. *Leeds* —6D **66**
Moor Pk. Rd. *B'frd* —5E **80**
Moor Pk. Vs. *Leeds* —6E **66**
Moor Pk. Way. *Add* —1C **10**
Moor Rd. *B Spa* —3C **36**
Moor Rd. *B'hpe* —7H **29**
Moor Rd. *H'let* —2J **103**
(in two parts)
Moor Rd. *I'ly* —1E **24**
Moor Rd. *Leeds* —6D **66**
Moor Royd. *Hal* —4E **130**
*Moors Cen., The. I'ly —5B **12***
*(off S. Hawksworth St.)*
**Moor Side. —3E 80**
**(nr. Bradford)**
**Moorside. —1G 83**
**(nr. Bramley)**
**Moorside. —2D 118**
**(nr. Drighlington)**
**Moor Side. —2J 115**
**(nr. Wyke)**
Moor Side. *B Spa* —2B **36**
Moorside. *Cleck* —2C **134**
(in two parts)
Moorside. *D Hill* —3E **78**
Moorside App. *Dlgtn* —2D **118**
Moorside Av. *B'shaw* —7J **99**
Moorside Av. *B'frd* —3E **80**
Moorside Av. *Dew* —6D **136**
Moorside Av. *Dlgtn* —2D **118**
Moorside Av. *Ebrn* —5C **20**
Moorside Clo. *B'frd* —2E **80**
Moorside Clo. *Dlgtn* —2D **118**
Moorside Cres. *Dew* —6D **136**
Moorside Cres. *Dlgtn* —2C **118**
Moorside Cft. *B'frd* —3E **80**
Moorside Dri. *Dlgtn* —2D **118**
Moorside Dri. *Leeds* —1G **83**
Moorside End. *Dew* —6D **136**
Moorside Gdns. *B'frd* —2E **80**
Moorside Gdns. *Dlgtn* —2D **118**
Moorside Gdns. *Hal* —3D **112**
Moorside Grn. *Dlgtn* —2D **118**
*Moorside Ho. Wilsd —1G **77***
*(off Crooke La.)*
Moorside La. *Add* —5C **10**
Moorside La. *Askw* —2B **14**
Moorside La. *B'frd* —6F **81**
Moor Side La. *Oxe* —7B **56**
Moorside Maltings. *Leeds* —2J **103**
Moorside M. *B'frd* —2E **80**
Moorside Mt. *Dlgtn* —2C **118**
Moorside Paddock. *Cleck* —2D **134**
Moorside Pde. *Dlgtn* —2D **118**
Moorside Pl. *B'frd* —6F **81**
Moorside Pl. *Dew* —6D **136**
Moorside Ri. *Cleck* —1D **134**
Moorside Rd. *B'frd* —1E **80**
Moorside Rd. *Dew* —6D **136**
Moorside Rd. *Dlgtn* —2C **118**
Moorside Rd. *Wilsd* —1G **77**
Moorside St. *Leeds* —1G **83**
Moorside St. *Low M* —1H **115**
Moorside Ter. *B'frd* —3F **81**
Moorside Ter. *Dlgtn* —2D **118**
Moorside Ter. *Leeds* —1G **83**
Moorside Va. *Dlgtn* —1D **118**
Moorside Vw. *Dlgtn* —2D **118**
Moorside Wlk. *Dlgtn* —1D **118**
Moor Stone Pl. *She* —2C **114**
Moor St. *Oakw* —1F **57**
Moor St. *Q'bry* —5J **95**
*Moor Ter. B'frd —4E **80***
*(off Glenmore Clo.)*
Moorthorpe Av. *B'frd* —4F **81**
**Moor Top. —7G 135**
**(nr. Liversedge)**
**Moor Top. —1H 115**
**(nr. Wyke)**
Moor Top. *Dlgtn* —1B **118**
(in two parts)
Moor Top. *Leeds* —5G **101**
Moor Top. *Men & Guis* —5F **27**
Moor Top Gdns. *Hal* —6C **94**
Moor Top Rd. *Hal* —7K **111**
Moor Top Rd. *Low M* —1H **115**
**Moortown. —1K 67**
Moortown Corner. *Leeds* —2K **67**
Moor Vw. *A'ley* —6B **84**
Moor Vw. *B'frd* —7J **99**
*Moor Vw. Head —2F **85***
*(off Hyde Pk. Rd.)*
Moor Vw. *Heck* —6C **136**
Moor Vw. *Leeds* —1G **103**
Moor Vw. *Meth* —4K **125**
Moor Vw. *Mir* —7J **135**
Moor Vw. Av. *Shipl* —4G **61**
Moor Vw. Ct. *Sandb* —4G **41**
Moor Vw. Cres. *Bgly* —6J **59**
Moorview Cft. *Men* —5B **26**
Moorview Dri. *Bgly* —6J **59**
Moorview Dri. *Shipl* —5B **62**
Moorview Gro. *Kei* —6B **40**
Moorville Av. *B'frd* —4F **81**
Moorville Clo. *Leeds* —2H **103**
Moorville Ct. *Leeds* —2H **103**
Moorville Dri. *B'shaw* —7J **99**
Moorville Gro. *Leeds* —2G **103**
Moorville Rd. *Leeds* —2H **103**
Moorway. *Guis* —2D **44**
Moor Way. *Oakw* —1E **56**
Moorwell Pl. *B'frd* —1E **80**
Moravian Pl. *B'frd* —2K **97**
Morden Ho. *B'frd* —3H **7**
Moresby Rd. *B'frd* —1E **114**
Moresdale La. *Leeds* —2H **87**
Moreton Ho. *B'frd* —2H **7**
**Morley. —4B 120**
Morley Av. *B'frd* —4F **81**
Morley Bottoms. *Morl* —2A **120**
**Morley Carr. —2K 115**
Morley Carr Rd. *Low M* —2K **115**
Morley Hall La. *L'ft* —2E **128**
**Morley Hole. —2K 119**
*Morley Mkt. Morl —3A **120***
*(off Queen St.)*
Morley St. *B'frd* —7K **79** (6C **6**)
Morley Vw. *Hal* —5J **131**
Morningside. *B'frd* —4H **79**
Morningside. *Denh* —3B **76**
Morning St. *Kei* —7K **39**
Mornington Rd. *Bgly* —1A **60**
Mornington Rd. *I'ly* —5C **12**
Mornington St. *Kei* —3K **39**
Mornington Vs. *B'frd* —4K **79**
Morpeth Pl. *Leeds* —6A **86**
Morpeth St. *B'frd* —6J **79** (4A **6**)
Morpeth St. *Q'bry* —5J **95**
Morris Av. *Leeds* —7A **66**
Morris Gro. *Leeds* —1A **84**
Morris La. *Leeds* —7A **66**
Morris Mt. *Kirks* —1A **84**
Morrison St. *C'frd* —7E **126**
Morris Pl. *Morl* —2K **119**
Morris Vw. *Leeds* —1A **84**
Morritt Av. *Leeds* —4K **87**
Morritt Dri. *Leeds* —5H **87**
Morritt Gro. *Leeds* —5H **87**
Mortimer Av. *Bat* —3D **136**
Mortimer Av. *B'frd* —4F **81**
Mortimer Clo. *Gar* —7J **89**
Mortimer Row. *B'frd* —6F **81**
Mortimer St. *Bat* —3D **136**
Mortimer St. *B'frd* —5F **79**
Mortimer St. *Cleck* —1F **135**
Mortimer Ter. *Bat* —3D **136**
Morton Cres. *C'frd* —7F **127**
Morton Gro. *E Mor* —3H **41**
Morton La. *E Mor* —3H **41**
Morton Rd. *B'frd* —1F **99**
Mortons Clo. *Sid* —5J **131**
Morton Ter. *Guis* —2F **45**
Morwick Gro. *Scholes* —6D **70**
Moseley Pl. *Leeds* —2H **85**
Moseley Wood App. *Leeds* —7H **47**
Moseley Wood Av. *Leeds* —5H **47**
Moseley Wood Bank. *Leeds* —6H **47**
Moseley Wood Clo. *Leeds* —7H **47**
Moseley Wood Cres. *Leeds* —7H **47**
Moseley Wood Cft. *Leeds* —7G **47**
Moseley Wood Dri. *Leeds* —6H **47**
Moseley Wood Gdns. *Leeds* —6H **47**
Moseley Wood Grn. *Leeds* —6H **47**
Moseley Wood Gro. *Leeds* —6H **47**
Moseley Wood La. *Leeds* —6J **47**
Moseley Wood Ri. *Leeds* —6H **47**
Moseley Wood Vw. *Leeds* —6J **47**
Moseley Wood Wlk. *Leeds* —7H **47**
Moseley Wood Way. *Leeds* —5H **47**
Moser Av. *B'frd* —7C **62**
Moser Cres. *B'frd* —7C **62**
*Mosley Ho. B'frd —1F **99***
*(off Parsonage Rd.)*
Moss Bri. Rd. *Leeds* —7D **64**
Moss Bldgs. *Cleck* —7F **117**
Moss Carr Av. *Kei* —6D **40**
Moss Carr Gro. *Kei* —6D **40**
Moss Carr Rd. *Kei* —6D **40**
Mosscar St. *B'frd* —6C **80** (4J **7**)
Moss Cotts. *Leeds* —7D **48**
Mossdale Av. *B'frd* —2C **78**
Moss Dri. *Hal* —1C **112**
Moss Fld. *B'frd* —4G **7**
Moss Gdns. *Leeds* —6G **49**
Moss Grn. *Men* —6C **26**
Moss La. *Hal* —1C **112**
Mosslea. *Chur* —7B **102**
Moss Mans. *Bat* —6D **118**
Moss Mt. *I'ly* —5B **12**
Moss Pl. *Swil* —5E **106**
Moss Ri. *Leeds* —6G **49**
Moss Ri. *Mean* —6F **67**
Moss Rd. *Leeds* —7B **68**
Moss Row. *Wilsd* —6G **59**
Moss Side. *B'frd* —3E **78**
Moss St. *C'frd* —7B **126**
Moss St. *Cro R* —4G **57**
Moss St. *Gild* —7H **101**
Moss St. *T'tn* —6G **77**
Moss Syke. *S'cft* —3A **52**
Mosstree Clo. *Q'bry* —4G **95**
Moss Valley. *Leeds* —6G **49**
Mossy Bank Clo. *Q'bry* —4J **95**
Mostyn Gro. *B'frd* —6G **97**
Mostyn M. *Hal* —4E **112**
Mostyn Vs. *Bat* —2H **137**
Motley La. *Guis* —1G **45**
*Motley Row. Guis —1G **45***
*(off Motley La.)*
Mouldson Pl. *Bklnd* —3A **142**
Moule Ri. *Gar* —4B **90**
Moulson Ct. *B'frd* —3A **98**
Moulson Ter. *Denh* —5B **76**
**Mountain. —4G 95**
Mountain Vw. *Shipl* —6K **61**
*Mount Av. Bat —5H **137***
*(off Mount St.)*
Mount Av. *B'frd* —7D **62**
Mount Av. *Hal* —1A **130**
Mount Av. *Heck* —2C **136**
Mountbatten Ct. *B'frd* —4A **98**
Mt. Cliffe Vw. *Morl* —7B **102**
Mount Cres. *Cleck* —7F **117**
Mount Cres. *Hal* —1A **130**
Mount Dri. *Leeds* —5H **49**
Mountfields. *Hal* —7E **114**
Mount Gdns. *Cleck* —7F **117**
Mount Gdns. *Leeds* —5H **49**
Mount Gro. *B'frd* —7D **62**
Mount La. *Brigh* —2E **144**
Mountleigh Clo. *Euro I* —1C **116**
Mt. Pellon. *Hal* —7D **112**
Mt. Pellon Rd. *Hal* —7C **112**
Mt. Pisgah. *Otley* —3J **27**
Mount Pl. *Shipl* —4G **61**
**Mount Pleasant. —5G 137**
**(nr. Batley)**
**Mount Pleasant. —6B 108**
**(nr. Kippax)**
Mt. Pleasant. *Add* —1D **10**
Mt. Pleasant. *Bmly* —1F **83**
Mt. Pleasant. *Brigh* —3E **144**
Mt. Pleasant. *Butt* —7E **96**
Mt. Pleasant. *Denh* —5B **76**
Mt. Pleasant. *Guis* —1G **45**
Mt. Pleasant. *I'ly* —6C **12**
Mt. Pleasant. *Kip* —6B **108**
Mt. Pleasant. *Leeds* —2J **121**
Mt. Pleasant. *Ripp* —5G **141**
Mt. Pleasant. *Sandb* —4G **41**
Mt. Pleasant Av. *Hal* —7F **113**
Mt. Pleasant Av. *Leeds* —7B **68**
Mt. Pleasant Ct. *Pud* —5C **82**
Mt. Pleasant Dri. *Myth* —6A **110**
Mt. Pleasant Gdns. *Kip* —6B **108**
*Mt. Pleasant Gdns. Leeds —7B **68***
*(off Mt. Pleasant Av.)*
Mt. Pleasant Rd. *Pud* —5C **82**
Mt. Pleasant St. *Pud* —5D **82**
Mt. Pleasant St. *Q'bry* —5J **95**
Mt. Preston St. *Leeds* —4G **85** (3A **4**)
Mount Ri. *Leeds* —5H **49**
Mount Rd. *B'frd* —7E **62**
Mount Rd. *Wibs* —5G **97**
Mt. Royal. *Holy G* —7D **142**
Mt. Royal. *H'fth* —4F **65**
Mt. Royd. *B'frd* —3K **79**
Mount St. *Bat* —5H **137**
Mount St. *B'frd* —7C **80** (5J **7**)
Mount St. *Cleck* —7F **117**
Mount St. *Eccl* —7D **62**
Mount St. *Hal* —1G **131**
Mount St. *Kei* —4K **39**
Mount St. *Sower B* —4K **129**
Mt. Street W. *Hal* —7C **112**
**Mount Tabor. —4J 111**
Mt. Tabor Rd. *Hal* —2H **111**
Mt. Tabor St. *Pud* —6A **82**
Mount Ter. *Bat* —5G **137**
Mount Ter. *B'frd* —7D **62**
Mount Ter. *Hal* —6C **112**
Mount Ter. *L'ft* —6E **110**
Mount, The. *Alw* —5H **49**
Mount, The. *Bar E* —6H **71**
Mount, The. *Birs* —5C **118**
Mount, The. *C'frd* —7J **127**
Mount, The. *Kip* —5A **108**
Mount, The. *Leeds* —4K **87**
Mount, The. *Rothw* —7H **105**
Mount, The. *Wren* —7K **139**
Mt. Vernon Rd. *Rawd* —7A **46**
Mount Vw. *Bgly* —1B **60**
Mount Vw. *Hal* —4J **111**
Mount Vw. *Morl* —7B **102**
Mount Vw. *Oakw* —2D **56**
Mount Vw. *Q'bry* —5H **95**
Mowat Ct. *Liv* —3D **134**
Mowbray Chase. *W'ford* —7K **105**
Mowbray Clo. *Cull* —7A **58**
Mowbray Ct. *Leeds* —2J **87**
Mowbray Cres. *Leeds* —2J **87**
Mozeley Dri. *Hal* —1D **112**
Mucky La. *Ell* —5H **143**
Muddy La. *Lntn* —7F **17**
Muffit La. *Gom & Heck* —7A **118**
Muff St. *B'frd* —1D **98** (7K **7**)
Muff Ter. *B'frd* —5G **97**
*Muir Ct. Leeds —1D **84***
*(off St Michael's Gro.)*
Muirhead Dri. *B'frd* —4G **99**
Muirlands, The. *Hud* —4K **145**
Mulberry Av. *Leeds* —7D **48**
Mulberry Gdns. *Meth* —5F **125**
Mulberry Gth. *Leeds* —1E **66**
Mulberry Gth. *Thor A* —1E **36**
Mulberry Ri. *Leeds* —7D **48**
Mulberry St. *Kei* —3B **40**
Mulberry St. *Pud* —6C **82**
Mulberry Vw. *Leeds* —1D **66**
Mulcture Hall Rd. *Hal* —1H **131**
Mulgrave St. *B'frd* —7D **80** (6K **7**)
Mullins Ct. *Leeds* —6B **86**
Mumford St. *B'frd* —3A **98**
Munby St. *B'frd* —6E **78**
Muncaster Rd. *Gar* —5B **90**
Munster St. *B'frd* —3D **98**
Munton Clo. *B'frd* —1E **114**
Murdoch St. *Kei* —3D **40**
Murdstone Clo. *B'frd* —3A **98**
Murgatroyd St. *B'frd* —4A **98**
(in two parts)
Murgatroyd St. *Shipl* —4H **61**
Murray St. *B'frd* —3J **97**
Murton Clo. *Leeds* —1J **87**
Museum Ct. *B'frd* —3E **80**
Museum St. *Leeds* —4B **86**
Musgrave Bank. *Leeds* —3J **83**
Musgrave Bldgs. *Pud* —5D **82**
Musgrave Dri. *B'frd* —3E **80**
Musgrave Gro. *B'frd* —3E **80**
Musgrave Mt. *B'frd* —3E **80**
Musgrave Mt. *Leeds* —3J **83**
Musgrave Ri. *Leeds* —3J **83**
Musgrave Rd. *B'frd* —3E **80**
Musgrave St. *Bat* —6C **118**
Musgrave Vw. *Leeds* —3J **83**
Mushroom St. *Leeds* —4K **85** (3H **5**)
Musselburgh St. *B'frd* —6J **79**
Mutton La. *All* —3H **77**
Myers Av. *B'frd* —1C **80**
Myers Cft. *Otley* —3J **27**
Myers La. *B'frd* —1C **80**
Myrtle Av. *Bgly* —2K **59**
Myrtle Av. *Hal* —3C **112**
Myrtle Ct. *Bgly* —2K **59**
Myrtle Dri. *Cro R* —3H **57**
Myrtle Dri. *Hal* —3C **112**
Myrtle Gdns. *Hal* —3C **112**
Myrtle Gro. *Bgly* —2K **59**
Myrtle Gro. *Hal* —3C **112**
Myrtle Gro. *Q'bry* —7G **95**
Myrtle Pl. *Bgly* —1K **59**
Myrtle Pl. *Hal* —3C **112**
Myrtle Pl. *Shipl* —4F **61**
Myrtle Rd. *Ell* —4K **143**
Myrtle St. *Bgly* —1A **60**
Myrtle St. *B'frd* —7E **80**
Myrtle Vw. *Oakw* —1F **57**
*Myrtle Wlk. Bgly —1K **59***
*(off Ferncliffe Rd.)*
**Mytholmes. —4E 56**
Mytholmes La. *Haw* —5E **56**
(in two parts)
**Mytholmroyd. —6A 110**

**N**ab End Rd. *G'lnd* —2H **143**
Nab La. *Birs* —5E **118**
(in two parts)
Nab La. *Shipl* —5D **60**
Naburn App. *Leeds* —3K **69**
Naburn Chase. *Leeds* —5A **70**
Naburn Clo. *Leeds* —5A **70**
Naburn Ct. *Leeds* —4K **69**
Naburn Dri. *Leeds* —5K **69**
Naburn Fold. *Leeds* —5A **70**
Naburn Gdns. *Leeds* —5K **69**
Naburn Grn. *Leeds* —5K **69**
Naburn Pl. *Leeds* —4K **69**
Naburn Rd. *Leeds* —5K **69**
Naburn Vw. *Leeds* —5A **70**
Naburn Wlk. *Leeds* —5K **69**
Nab Vw. *Sils* —6H **9**
Nab Water La. *Oxe* —7D **74**
**Nab Wood. —5D 60**
Nab Wood Bank. *Shipl* —5D **60**
Nab Wood Clo. *Shipl* —5E **60**
Nab Wood Cres. *Shipl* —5D **60**
Nab Wood Dri. *Shipl* —6D **60**
Nab Wood Gdns. *Shipl* —5E **60**
Nab Wood Gro. *Shipl* —5D **60**
Nab Wood Mt. *Shipl* —5D **60**
Nab Wood Pl. *Shipl* —5D **60**
Nab Wood Ri. *Shipl* —5D **60**
Nab Wood Rd. *Shipl* —6D **60**
Nab Wood Ter. *Shipl* —5D **60**
Nancroft Cres. *Leeds* —6C **84**
Nancroft Mt. *Leeds* —6C **84**
Nancroft Ter. *Leeds* —6C **84**
Nanny Goat La. *Gar* —5J **89**
Nansen Av. *Leeds* —3F **83**
Nansen Gro. *Leeds* —3F **83**
Nansen Mt. *Leeds* —3F **83**
Nansen Pl. *Leeds* —3F **83**
Nansen St. *Leeds* —3E **82**
Nansen Ter. *Leeds* —3F **83**
Nansen Vw. *Leeds* —3F **83**
Napier Rd. *B'frd* —6F **81**
Napier Rd. *Ell* —3J **143**
Napier St. *B'frd* —6F **81**
Napier St. *Kei* —5B **40**
Napier St. *Q'bry* —5K **95**
Napier Ter. *B'frd* —6F **81**
Naples St. *B'frd* —4H **79**
Nares St. *Cro R* —4G **57**
Nares St. *Kei* —4K **39**
Narrow La. *H'den* —3F **59**
Narrows, The. *H'den* —3F **59**
Naseby Gdns. *Leeds* —5A **86** (5J **5**)
Naseby Gth. *Leeds* —5A **86** (4J **5**)
Naseby Grange. *Leeds* —5J **5**
Naseby Ho. *B'frd* —5H **99**
Naseby Pl. *Leeds* —5A **86** (5J **5**)
Naseby Ri. *Q'bry* —5K **95**
Naseby Ter. *Leeds* —5A **86** (5K **5**)
Naseby Vw. *Leeds* —5A **86** (5J **5**)
Naseby Wlk. *Leeds* —5A **86** (5K **5**)
Nashville Rd. *Kei* —5J **39**
Nashville St. *Kei* —5J **39**
*Nashville Ter. Kei —5J **39***
*(off Nashville Rd.)*
Nassau Pl. *Leeds* —2A **86**
Nathan La. *Sower B* —2E **140**
Nathans Folly. *Sower B* —2F **141**
National Museum of Photography, Film & T.V. —7A **80** (6D **6**)
National Rd. *Hun P* —1A **104**
*National Waterhouse Homes. Hal —2G **131***
*(off Harrison Rd.)*
Navigation Rd. *C'frd* —6D **126**
Navigation Rd. *Hal* —2H **131**
Navigation Wlk. *Leeds* —6J **85** (7F **5**)
Naylor Gth. *Leeds* —7F **67**
Naylor La. *Hal* —7E **110**
Naylor Pl. *Leeds* —2H **103**
Naylor St. *Dew* —6F **137**
Naylor St. *Hal* —1D **130**

*A-Z Leeds & Bradford 183*

Neal Pl.—Norristhorpe La.

Neal Pl. Leeds —7K 85
Neal St. B'frd —7A 80 (6D 6)
Nearcliffe Rd. B'frd —3G 79
Near Crook. Thack —3B 62
Near Peat La. Oxe —6C 74
Near Royd. Oven —4E 112
Neath Gdns. Leeds —2F 87
Necropolis Rd. B'frd —1F 97
Ned Hill Rd. Hal —4C 94
Ned La. B'frd —2G 99
Needless Inn La. W'ford —7A 106
Nelson Ct. I'ly —5B 12
(off Nelson Rd.)
Nelson Ct. Morl —5K 119
Nelson Cft. Gar —1H 107
Nelson Pl. Morl —2A 120
(off S. Nelson St.)
Nelson Pl. Q'bry —5J 95
Nelson Pl. Sower B —4B 130
Nelson Rd. I'ly —5B 12
Nelson St. All —4C 78
Nelson St. Bat —3E 136
Nelson St. Birs —6D 118
Nelson St. B'frd —7A 80 (6E 6)
Nelson St. Cro R —4G 57
(nr. East Ter., in two parts)
Nelson St. Cro R —4G 57
(nr. Albion St.)
Nelson St. Liv —5K 135
Nelson St. Otley —3J 27
Nelson St. Q'bry —5J 95
Nelson St. Sower B —4A 130
Nene St. B'frd —2J 97
Nepshaw La. Gild —3H 119
Nepshaw La. Morl —2K 119
Nepshaw La. N. Gild —2J 119
Nepshaw La. S. Gild —2J 119
Neptune St. Leeds —6K 85
**Nesfield. —2G 11**
Nesfield Clo. Leeds —1B 122
Nesfield Cres. Leeds —1B 122
Nesfield Gdns. Leeds —1A 122
Nesfield Gth. Leeds —1A 122
Nesfield Grn. Leeds —1A 122
Nesfield La. Nesf —1G 11
Nesfield Rd. I'ly —4K 11
Nesfield Rd. Leeds —1A 122
Nesfield St. B'frd —5K 79 (1C 6)
Nesfield Vw. I'ly —5J 11
Nesfield Vw. Leeds —1A 122
Nesfield Wlk. Leeds —1A 122
Nessfield Dri. Kei —6H 39
Nessfield Gro. Kei —6H 39
Nessfield Rd. Kei —6H 39
Neston Way. Oss —7D 138
Netherby St. B'frd —6D 80
Nethercliffe Cres. Guis —1F 45
Nethercliffe Rd. Guis —1F 45
Netherdale Ct. Weth —3A 18
Netherfield Clo. Yead —4K 45
Netherfield Ct. Guis —2F 45
(off Netherfield Rd.)
Netherfield Dri. Guis —1F 45
Netherfield Pl. Cleck —1G 135
Netherfield Ri. Guis —2F 45
Netherfield Rd. Guis —1F 45
Netherfield Ter. Guis —2F 45
(off Netherfield Rd.)
Netherfield Ter. Yead —4K 45
Netherhall Rd. Bail —1K 61
Netherlands Av. B'frd —7J 97
Netherlands Sq. Low M —1K 115
Nether Moor Vw. Bgly —1A 60
**Netheroyd Hill. —6G 145**
Netheroyd Hill Rd. Hud —6G 145
Nether St. Fars —2B 82
**Nethertown. —7E 100**
Netherwood Clo. Hud —6G 145
**Nether Yeadon. —7K 45**
Nettle Gro. Hal —6A 114
Nettleton Clo. B'frd —4C 100
Nettleton Ct. Leeds —5B 88
Neville App. Leeds —7E 86
Neville Av. B'frd —5D 98
Neville Av. Leeds —7E 86
Neville Clo. Leeds —7E 86
Neville Ct. Shipl —4F 61
Neville Cres. Leeds —5F 87
Neville Gth. Leeds —7E 86
Neville Gro. Leeds —7E 86
Neville Gro. Swil —4E 106
Neville Mt. Leeds —7E 86
Neville Pde. Leeds —7E 86
Neville Pl. Leeds —6F 87
Neville Rd. B'frd —2D 98
Neville Rd. Leeds —5F 87
Neville Rd. Otley —3K 27
Neville Row. Leeds —7E 86
Neville Sq. Leeds —6F 87
Neville St. Kei —3B 40
Neville St. Leeds —7H 85 (7D 4)
Neville St. Mar —2G 135
Neville Ter. Leeds —7E 86
Neville Vw. Leeds —7E 86
Neville Wlk. Leeds —6E 86
Nevill Gro. B'frd —2D 78
New Adel Av. Leeds —1A 66
New Adel Gdns. Leeds —1A 66
New Adel La. Leeds —2A 66
**Newall. —1H 27**
Newall Av. Otley —1H 27
Newall Carr Rd. Otley & N Clift —3G 15
Newall Clo. Men —5D 26
Newall Clo. Otley —1H 27
Newall Hall Pk. Otley —1J 27
Newall Mt. Otley —2H 27
Newall St. B'frd —2K 97
Newark Ho. B'frd —2K 97
(off Roundhill St.)
Newark Rd. Bgly —6K 41
Newark St. B'frd —1C 98 (7K 7)
New Augustus St. B'frd —7B 80 (6G 7)
New Bank. Hal —7H 113
New Bank St. Morl —2B 120
New Bond St. Hal —1F 131
New Briggate. Leeds —5J 85 (6F 5)
**New Brighton. —6C 60**
**(nr. Cottingley)**
**New Brighton. —3A 120**
**(nr. Morley)**
New Brighton. Bgly —6C 60
New Brook St. I'ly —5B 12
New Brunswick St. Hal —1F 131
Newburn Rd. B'frd —1H 97
Newbury Rd. Brigh —2F 145
Newby Gth. Leeds —6D 50
Newby Ho. B'frd —3D 80
(off Otley Rd.)
Newby Rd. F'hll —1A 20
Newby St. B'frd —2A 98
Newby St. Cro H —3A 20
Newcastle Clo. Dlgtn —2B 118
Newcastle Ho. B'frd —3G 7
New Clayton Ter. Cull —7B 58
New Clo. Av. Sils —1G 21
New Clo. Rd. Shipl —5C 60
New Clough Rd. Norl —6B 130
Newcombe St. Ell —4A 144
New Craven Ga. Leeds —1J 103
New Cres. H'fth —4F 65
New Cft. H'fth —4F 65
New Cross St. B'frd —4A 98
(in two parts)
New Cross St. Oaken —2D 116
New Delight. Hal —7A 94
New England Rd. Kei —6A 40
New Farmers Hill. W'ford —7B 106
**New Farnley. —3H 101**
Newfield Dri. Gar —2B 108
Newfield Dri. Men —6C 26
Newfield La. S Mil —6K 109
New Fold. B'frd —7E 96
Newforth Gro. B'frd —4J 97
**New Fryston. —4J 127**
Newgate St. Bat —5K 137
**Newhall. —5C 98**
Newhall Bank. Leeds —2K 121
Newhall Chase. Leeds —1K 121
Newhall Clo. Leeds —1K 121
Newhall Cres. Leeds —1K 121
Newhall Cft. Leeds —7A 104
Newhall Dri. B'frd —6B 98
Newhall Gdns. Leeds —2K 121
Newhall Gth. Leeds —2K 121
Newhall Ga. Leeds —7K 103
Newhall Grn. Leeds —1A 122
Newhall Mt. B'frd —6B 98
Newhall Mt. Leeds —2K 121
Newhall Rd. B'frd —5D 98
Newhall Rd. Leeds —1K 121
Newhall Wlk. Leeds —1A 122
New Hey Rd. B'frd —2C 98
New Hey Rd. Fix & Brigh —5B 144
Newhold. Gar —5A 90
New Holme Rd. Haw —6F 57
New Ho. La. Q'bry —6B 96
New Ho. Rd. Hud —5K 145
Newill Clo. B'frd —4C 98
Newington St. B'frd —5J 79 (2A 6)
New Inn Ct. Otley —3J 27
New Inn St. Leeds —6A 84
New John St. B'frd —6K 79 (4D 6)
New Kirkgate. Shipl —4H 61
New Laithe. Holy G —7D 142
New Laithe Rd. B'frd —5G 97
Newlaithes Gdns. H'fth —5F 65
Newlaithes Gth. H'fth —6E 64
Newlaithes Rd. H'fth —6E 64
Newlands. Fars —3B 82
Newlands Av. B'frd —4F 81
Newlands Av. Hal —3A 114
Newlands Av. Sower B —5G 129
Newlands Av. Yead —3J 45
Newlands Clo. Brigh —7H 133
Newlands Cres. Hal —4A 114
Newlands Cres. Morl —3D 120
Newlands Dri. Bgly —5J 41
Newlands Dri. Cro H —3A 20
Newlands Dri. Hal —4A 114
Newlands Dri. Morl —2D 120
Newlands Gro. Hal —4A 114
Newlands Pl. B'frd —5D 80 (1K 7)
Newlands Ri. Yead —4J 45
Newlands Rd. Hal —1J 129
Newlands, The. Sower B —6G 129
Newlands Vw. Hal —4A 114
New La. B'frd —7F 81
New La. Cleck —2C 134
New La. Cra V —5A 128
New La. Dlgtn —6E 100
New La. E Ard —7H 121
(in two parts)
New La. Hal —4H 131
New La. Leeds —2H 121
(LS10)
New La. Leeds —7H 85
(LS11)
New La. L'ft —3D 128
New La. Sils —7B 8
New La. Ski G —5E 130
New La. Tong —4K 99
**Newlay. —6F 65**
Newlay Bridle Path. H'fth —5F 65
Newlay Clo. B'frd —5G 63
Newlay Gro. H'fth —6F 65
Newlay La. Bmly —1G 83
Newlay La. H'fth —5F 65
Newlay La. Pl. Leeds —1G 83
Newlay Mt. H'fth —6F 65
Newlay Wood Av. H'fth —5G 65
Newlay Wood Clo. H'fth —5G 65
Newlay Wood Cres. H'fth —5G 65
Newlay Wood Dri. H'fth —5G 65
Newlay Wood Fold. H'fth —5F 65
Newlay Wood Gdns. H'fth —5G 65
Newlay Wood Ri. H'fth —5G 65
Newlay Wood Rd. H'fth —5F 65
New Leeds. Leeds —7F 65
Newley Av. Bat —7D 118
New Line. B'frd —5F 63
New Longley La. Sower B —7J 129
Newlyn Rd. Riddl —2E 40
Newman St. B'frd —4D 98
New Mkt. Otley —3J 27
Newmarket App. Leeds —1D 104
Newmarket Grn. Leeds —7D 86
Newmarket La. Leeds —1D 104
Newmarket La. Stan & Meth —7K 123
New Mkt. St. Leeds —6J 85 (7F 5)
**New Micklefield. —1G 109**
New Mill La. Cliff —5E 36
New N. Rd. Heck —3A 136
New Occupation La. Pud —7A 82
New Otley Rd. B'frd —5C 80 (2H 7)
New Pk. Av. Fars —2C 82
New Pk. Clo. Fars —2C 82
New Pk. Cft. Fars —2C 82
New Pk. Gro. Fars —3B 82
New Pk. Pl. Fars —2B 82
New Pk. Rd. Q'bry —4H 95
New Pk. St. Morl —4K 119
New Pk. Va. Fars —2C 82
New Pk. Vw. Fars —3C 82
New Pk. Wlk. Fars —3B 82
New Pk. Way. Fars —2C 82
New Pepper Rd. Leeds —3B 104
New Popplewell La. Schol —7B 116
Newport Av. Leeds —3E 82
Newport Cres. Leeds —2D 84
Newport Gdns. Leeds —2D 84
Newport Mt. Leeds —2D 84
Newport Pl. B'frd —4J 79
Newport Rd. B'frd —4J 79 (1A 6)
Newport Rd. Leeds —2D 84
Newport Vw. Leeds —1D 84
New Princess St. Leeds —1H 103
New Pudsey Sq. Far —4A 82
New Rd. B'ham —7D 36
New Rd. Carl —4F 123
New Rd. Denh —5B 76
New Rd. G'lnd —2E 142
New Rd. Hal —2G 131
New Rd. H Bri —7A 110
New Rd. Holy G —6G 143
New Rd. L'ft —6F 111
New Rd. Sils —1F 21
New Rd. S Mil —5K 109
New Rd. Yead —4H 45
New Rd. E. Schol —7B 116
**New Road Side. —3K 115**
New Rd. Side. H'fth —4E 64
New Rd. Side. Rawd —6K 45
New Rd. Sq. Brigh —3E 144
(off New Hey Rd.)
New Row. Bgly —4B 60
New Row. C'ley —2H 81
New Row. D Hill —3E 78
New Row. Holy G —5G 143
New Row. K'gte —6H 139
New Row. Leeds —7C 88
New Row. Wyke —5K 115
Newroyd Rd. B'frd —4A 98
Newsam Ct. Leeds —6J 87
Newsam Dri. Leeds —6G 87
**Newsam Green. —4B 106**
Newsam Grn. Rd. Leeds —4B 106
**New Scarborough. —4H 83**
**(nr. Bramley)**
**New Scarborough. —4G 45**
**(nr. Guisley)**
**Newsholme. —7C 38**
Newsholme New Rd. Oakw —7C 38
Newsomes Row. Bat —4F 137
(off Brown's Pl.)
Newsomes Row. Gom —6K 117
(off Oxford Rd.)
Newsome St. Dew —7F 137
New Station St. Leeds —6H 85 (7D 4)
Newstead Av. Hal —1C 130
Newstead Gdns. Hal —1C 130
Newstead Gro. Hal —1C 130
Newstead Heath. Hal —1C 130
Newstead Pl. Hal —1C 130
Newstead Rd. Otley —3J 27
Newstead Ter. Hal —1C 130
Newstead Wlk. B'frd —2K 97
New St. Bail B —1H 133
New St. Bat —3G 137
New St. Bier —6D 98
New St. Bgly —4J 41
New St. C'frd —6E 126
New St. Clif —5K 133
New St. Denh —5B 76
New St. Far —4B 82
New St. Hal —7C 112
New St. Hang H —5J 137
New St. Haw —6E 56
New St. H'fth —4F 65
New St. Idle —4D 62
New St. Kip —5B 108
New St. Oaken —2D 116
New St. Oakw —2F 57
New St. Pud —7B 82
New St. Rawf —2H 135
New St. S'wram —4A 132
New St. Slnd —6D 142
New St. Clo. Pud —7C 82
New St. Gdns. Pud —7C 82
New St. Gro. Pud —7C 82
New Sturton La. Gar —5B 90
New Temple Ga. Leeds —7J 87
**New Toftshaw. —6F 99**
New Toftshaw. B'frd —6F 99
**Newton. —3H 127**
Newton Clo. Rothw —3D 122
Newton Ct. Leeds —6E 68
Newton Ct. Rothw —3D 122
Newton Dri. C'frd —7H 127
Newton Gth. Leeds —7A 68
Newton Gro. Leeds —1A 86
Newton Hill Rd. Leeds —7K 67
**Newton Kyme. —4K 37**
Newton La. Fair —3J 127
Newton La. Leds —3D 126
Newton Lodge Clo. Leeds —7J 67
Newton Lodge Dri. Leeds —7J 67
Newton Pde. Leeds —7K 67
Newton Pk. Brigh —2F 133
Newton Pk. Ct. Leeds —7A 68
Newton Pk. Dri. Leeds —7A 68
Newton Pk. Vw. Leeds —1A 86
Newton Pl. B'frd —2K 97
Newton Rd. Leeds —1K 85
Newton Sq. Leeds —3H 101
Newton St. B'frd —2A 98
(in two parts)
Newton St. Sower B —4K 129
Newton Vw. Leeds —7K 67
Newton Vs. Leeds —6J 67
Newton Wlk. Leeds —1A 86
Newton Way. Bail —7J 43
**New Town. —1D 10**
**(nr. Addingham)**
**New Town. —5J 39**
**(nr. Keighley)**
**New Town. —3A 86 (2K 5)**
**(nr. Leeds)**
New Town Clo. Kei —4K 39
New Town Ct. Kei —4K 39
New Wlk. Leeds —3D 68
New Way. Bat —3G 137
New Way. Guis —2D 44
New Windsor Dri. Rothw —1H 123
New Works Rd. Low M —2J 115
New York Cotts. Rawd —2B 64
New York La. Rawd —2B 64
New York Rd. Leeds —5K 85 (5G 5)
(in two parts)
New York St. Leeds —6K 85 (7F 5)
Nibshaw La. Gom —7J 117
Nibshaw Rd. Gom —7J 117
Nice Av. Leeds —1B 86
Nice St. Leeds —1C 86
Nice Vw. Leeds —1B 86
Nicholas Clo. B'frd —6F 79
Nichols Clo. Weth —4G 17
Nicholson Clo. Bgly —5A 42
Nichols Way. Weth —4F 17
Nickleby Rd. Leeds —5C 86
Nicolsons Pl. Sils —1G 21
Nidd App. Weth —1H 17
Nidd Ct. Sils —1G 21
Nidd Dri. C'frd —7H 127
Nidderdale Clo. Gar —1B 108
Nidderdale Wlk. Bail —7A 44
Nidd St. B'frd —7D 80
Nightingale St. Kei —3A 40
(off Linnet St.)
Nile Cres. Kei —5H 39
Nile Rd. I'ly —5B 12
Nile St. Cro R —4G 57
Nile St. Kei —5H 39
Nile St. Leeds —4K 85 (4G 5)
Nina Rd. B'frd —3F 97
Ninelands La. Gar —1A 108
Ninelands Spur. Gar —7A 90
Ninelands Vw. Gar —6A 90
Ninevah La. All B —2K 125
Nineveh Gdns. Leeds —1G 103
Nineveh Pde. Leeds —1G 103
Nineveh Rd. Leeds —1G 103
Ninth Av. Liv —3D 134
Nippet La. Leeds —5A 86 (5K 5)
Nixon Av. Leeds —6D 86
Noble St. B'frd —1H 97
Nog La. B'frd —1G 79
**Nook. —6E 118**
Nook Gdns. Scholes —4D 70
Nooking, The. K'gte —5H 139
Nook La. Sower B —1B 140
Nook Rd. Scholes —4D 70
Nooks, The. Gild —7H 101
Nook, The. Cleck —7G 117
Nook, The. Leeds —6K 49
Nook, The. Sower B —5K 129
Nook, The. Ting —2E 138
Nook Vw. Ting —2E 138
**Noon Nick. —7B 60**
Nora Pl. Leeds —2E 82
Nora Rd. Leeds —2E 82
Nora Ter. Leeds —2E 82
Norbreck Dri. Cro R —4G 57
Norbury Rd. B'frd —7G 63
Norcroft Brow. B'frd —7K 79 (5B 6)
Norcroft St. B'frd —6J 79 (4A 6)
Norfield. Fix —5G 145
Norfolk Av. Bat —5F 137
Norfolk Clo. Leeds —5K 67
Norfolk Clo. Oult —2B 124
Norfolk Dri. Oult —2B 124
Norfolk Gdns. B'frd —7A 80 (5E 6)
Norfolk Gdns. Leeds —5K 67
Norfolk Grn. Leeds —5K 67
Norfolk Mt. Leeds —5K 67
Norfolk Pl. Hal —2E 130
Norfolk Pl. Leeds —5K 67
Norfolk St. Bat —4F 137
Norfolk St. Bgly —1A 60
Norfolk Ter. Leeds —5K 67
Norfolk Vw. Leeds —5K 67
Norfolk Wlk. Leeds —5K 67
Norgarth Clo. Bat —3K 137
Norham Gro. Wyke —5K 115
Norland Rd. G'lnd —2B 142
Norland Rd. Sower B —5K 129
Norland St. B'frd —3F 97
**Norland Town. —6C 130**
Norland Town Rd. Norl —6B 130
Norland Vw. Hal —4E 130
(off Albert Promenade)
Norland Vw. Sower B —4B 130
Norman Av. B'frd —7D 62
Norman Av. Ell —3A 144
Norman Cres. B'frd —7D 62
Norman Gro. B'frd —7D 62
Norman Gro. Ell —3A 144
Norman Gro. Leeds —1A 84
Norman La. B'frd —7D 62
Norman Mt. B'frd —7D 62
Norman Mt. Leeds —1A 84
Norman Pl. Leeds —2C 68
Norman Rd. Hud —7G 145
Norman Row. Leeds —1A 84
Norman St. Bgly —1A 60
Norman St. Ell —3A 144
Norman St. Hal —3D 130
Norman St. Haw —5F 57
Norman St. Leeds —1A 84
Norman Ter. B'frd —7D 62
Norman Ter. Ell —3A 144
Norman Ter. Leeds —2C 68
Normanton Gro. Leeds —2G 103
Normanton Pl. Leeds —2G 103
Norman Towers. Leeds —6A 66
Norman Vw. Leeds —1A 84
Norquest Ind. Pk. Birs —4E 118
**Norr. —6H 59**
Norr Grn. Ter. Wilsd —6H 59
**Norristhorpe. —6J 135**
Norristhorpe Av. Liv —6J 135
Norristhorpe La. Liv —6J 135

Nortech Clo.—Oakwell Gro.


Nortech Clo. Leeds —3K 85 (2H 5)
Northallerton Rd. B'frd —4B 80
Northampton St. B'frd —4B 80 (1G 7)
North App. H'wd —6G 55
North Av. B'frd —2K 79
North Av. C'frd —7K 125
North Av. Otley —2J 27
N. Bank Rd. Bat —3E 136
N. Bank Rd. Bgly —7A 60
North Bolton. Hal —7B 94
North Bri. Hal —7G 113
N. Bridge St. Hal —7G 113
N. Broadgate La. H'fth —3G 65
Northbrook Pl. Leeds —5K 67
N. Brook St. B'frd —5B 80 (2F 7)
Northbrook St. Leeds —5K 67
North Cliffe. Sower B —6K 129
N. Cliffe Av. T'tn —7K 77
N. Cliffe Clo. T'tn —6J 77
N. Cliffe Dri. T'tn —7J 77
N. Cliffe Gro. T'tn —6J 77
Northcliffe La. Hal —2K 131
N. Cliffe La. T'tn —6K 77
Northcliffe Rd. Shipl —6G 61
North Clo. Leeds —6F 69
Northcote. Oss —7C 138
Northcote Cres. Leeds —2H 103
Northcote Dri. Leeds —2H 103
Northcote Fold. Lntn —7F 17
Northcote Grn. Leeds —2H 103
Northcote Rd. B'frd —3D 80
Northcote St. Fars —3B 82
North Ct. Leeds —5J 85 (5F 5)
N. Croft Gro. Rd. I'ly —5A 12
Northcroft Ri. B'frd —4E 78
N. Cross Rd. Hud —7F 145
North Cut. Brigh —6F 133
Northdale Av. B'frd —4J 97
Northdale Cres. B'frd —4J 97
Northdale Mt. B'frd —4J 97
Northdale Rd. B'frd —1H 79
N. Dean Av. Kei —4G 39
N. Dean Bus. Pk. G'lnd —7G 131
N. Dean Rd. G'lnd —7E 130
N. Dean Rd. Kei —4G 39
N. Dene Rd. Sils —7G 9
North Dri. B'hpe —1K 47
North Dri. Sher E —1B 108
*North Edge. Hal —6C 114 (off Brighouse and Denholme Ga. Rd.)*
Northedge La. Hal —6C 114
Northedge Mdw. B'frd —6D 62
Northedge Pk. Hal —6D 114
Northern Clo. B'frd —4F 97
Northern St. Leeds —6G 85 (7B 4)
N. Farm Rd. Leeds —2D 86
Northfield Av. Rothw —3E 122
Northfield Av. Weth —3J 17
*Northfield Clo. Ell —3K 143 (off Victoria Av.)*
Northfield Cres. Bgly —5A 60
Northfield Gdns. B'frd —5J 97
Northfield Gro. B'frd —5J 97
Northfield Ho. B'frd —5E 62
Northfield M. Weth —3K 17
Northfield Pl. B'frd —4J 79
Northfield Pl. Dew —7F 137
Northfield Pl. Rothw —3D 122
Northfield Pl. Weth —3J 17
Northfield Rd. B'frd —5H 97
Northfield Rd. Dew —7F 137
Northfields. Wltn —6G 19
Northfield St. Dew —7G 137
Northfield Ter. Q'bry —5A 96
North Fold. B'frd —4D 62
Northgate. Bail —7J 43
Northgate. B'frd —6A 80 (3D 6)
Northgate. Cleck —1F 135
Northgate. Dew —7H 137
Northgate. Ell —2K 143
Northgate. Hal —1G 131
Northgate. Heck —4A 136
Northgate. Oult —1A 124
*Northgate Ho. Weth —4J 17 (off Northgate La.)*
Northgate La. Lntn —4E 16
Northgate Ri. Lntn —7F 17
Northgates. Weth —4J 17
N. Grange M. Leeds —1F 85
N. Grange Mt. Leeds —7E 66
N. Grange Rd. Leeds —1E 84
N. Grove App. Weth —2J 17
N. Grove Av. Weth —2J 17
N. Grove Clo. Leeds —6F 69
N. Grove Ct. Weth —3J 17
N. Grove Cres. Weth —2J 17
N. Grove Dri. Leeds —6F 69
N. Grove Dri. Weth —2J 17
N. Grove Mt. Weth —3J 17
N. Grove Ri. Leeds —6F 69
N. Grove Rd. Weth —2J 17
N. Grove Way. Weth —3J 17
N. Hall Av. B'frd —2C 62
North Hill. S'cft —3B 52
N. Hill Clo. Leeds —6E 68
N. Hill Ct. Leeds —7F 67
N. Hill Rd. Leeds —1F 85
N. Holme St. B'frd —5A 80 (2E 6)
N. John St. Q'bry —5J 95
N. King St. Bat —4H 137
North La. Head —7D 66
North La. Round —5E 68
North La. W'ford & Oult —1A 124
N. Lane Gdns. Leeds —6E 68
Northlea Av. B'frd —3C 62
N. Lingwell Rd. Leeds —2J 121
N. Lodge Fold. Dew —5D 136
N. Mead. B'hpe —1K 47
Northolme Av. Leeds —5B 66
Northolme Cres. Leeds —5B 66
**Northowram. —5A 114**
Northowram Grn. Hal —4A 114
North Pde. All —3A 78
North Pde. B'frd —6A 80 (3D 6)
North Pde. Bur W —7A 14
North Pde. Hal —1G 131
North Pde. I'ly —5C 12
North Pde. Leeds —4A 66
*North Pde. Morl —4B 120 (off Wide La.)*
North Pde. Otley —2J 27
N. Park Av. Leeds —4B 68
N. Park Gro. Leeds —4C 68
N. Park Pde. Leeds —3B 68
N. Park Rd. B'frd —2H 79
N. Park Rd. Leeds —4C 68 (in two parts)
N. Park St. Dew —7E 136
N. Park Ter. B'frd —3J 79
N. Parkway. Leeds —7G 69
N. Queen St. Kei —4A 40
North Ri. Hud —7J 145
North Rd. Bklnd —4K 141
North Rd. B'frd —5H 97
North Rd. H'fth —1F 65
North Rd. Leeds —3E 104 (LS9)
North Rd. Leeds —3A 88 (LS15)
N. Road E. Leeds —3F 105
Northrop Clo. B'frd —4F 79
Northrop Yd. Pud —6C 82
N. Royd. Hip —6C 114
Northside Av. B'frd —7G 79
Northside Bus. Pk. Leeds —1G 5
Northside Rd. B'frd —7F 79
Northside Shop. Cen. Leeds —5F 67
Northside Ter. B'frd —7F 79
North St. Add —1E 10
North St. Bat —2F 137
North St. B'frd —6B 80 (3G 7)
North St. C'frd —7C 126
North St. Dew —7G 137
North St. Fry —4J 127
North St. G'lnd —2H 143
North St. Haw —5D 56
North St. Heck —5B 136
North St. Holy G —5G 143
North St. Idle —2D 62
North St. Kei —4A 40
North St. Leeds —4K 85 (4G 5)
North St. Oaken —3C 116
North St. Otley —2J 27
North St. Pud —5C 82
North St. Rawd —7K 45
North St. Sils —7G 9
North St. Sut Cr —5A 20
North St. Weth —4J 17
North Ter. Birs —6D 118
*North Ter. Leeds —3A 88 (off Tranquility Av.)*
North Ter. Yead —4K 45
North Vw. All —4H 77
North Vw. Bur W —1B 26
North Vw. Ebrn —4B 20
North Vw. Leeds —6F 69
North Vw. Men —6C 26
*North Vw. Rothw —3H 123 (off Royds La.)*
*North Vw. Sut Cr —5A 20 (off North St.)*
North Vw. Wilsd —7G 59
N. View Rd. B'frd —3B 80 (nr. Bolton Rd.)
N. View Rd. B'frd —7J 99 (nr. Bradford Rd.)
N. View St. Kei —2K 39
N. View St. S'ley —3C 82
*N. View Ter. Dew —6F 137 (off Halifax Rd.)*
*N. View Ter. Dew —6D 136 (off Staincliffe Rd.)*
N. View Ter. Haw —4E 56
N. View Ter. S'ley —3C 82
North Wlk. H'den —3E 58
North Way. Leeds —6F 69
Northwell Ga. Otley —1G 27
N. West Bus. Pk. Leeds —2H 85 (1D 4)
N. West Rd. Leeds —2H 85 (1D 4)
North Wing. B'frd —5B 80 (2G 7)
Northwood Clo. Pud —1D 100
Northwood Clo. W'ford —7A 106
Northwood Cres. B'frd —5E 62
Northwood Falls. W'ford —7A 106
Northwood Gdns. Colt —6C 88
Northwood Mt. Pud —1D 100
Northwood Pk. W'ford —7A 106
Northwood Vw. Pud —1D 100
Norton Clo. Ell —4K 143
Norton Clo. Hal —1K 129
Norton Dri. Hal —1K 129
Norton Rd. Leeds —2C 68
Norton St. Ell —4K 143
Norton St. Sils —1F 21
**Norton Tower. —1K 129**
Norton Way. Morl —1A 120
Norwich Av. Leeds —4K 103
Norwood Av. B'shaw —3K 117
Norwood Av. Bur W —1B 26
Norwood Av. Shipl —6H 61
Norwood Clo. Bur W —1B 26
Norwood Cres. B'shaw —3K 117
Norwood Cres. S'ley —3D 82
Norwood Cft. S'ley —3D 82
Norwood Dri. Bat —7D 118
Norwood Dri. B'shaw —3K 117
**Norwood Green. —5F 115**
Norwood Grn. Hill. Hal —5F 115
Norwood Gro. B'shaw —3K 117
Norwood Gro. Leeds —2E 84
Norwood Pk. Hud —7D 144
Norwood Pl. Leeds —2E 84
Norwood Pl. Shipl —6H 61
Norwood Rd. Bkby —7E 144
Norwood Rd. Leeds —2E 84
Norwood Rd. Shipl —6H 61
Norwood St. B'frd —4K 97
Norwood St. Shipl —6H 61
Norwood Ter. Bur W —1B 26
Norwood Ter. Hal —5G 115
Norwood Ter. Leeds —2E 84
Norwood Ter. Shipl —6H 61
Norwood Vw. Leeds —2E 84
Nostell Clo. B'frd —5K 79 (2B 6)
Noster Gro. Leeds —3F 103
Noster Hill. Leeds —3F 103
Noster Pl. Leeds —3F 103
Noster Rd. Leeds —3F 103
Noster St. Leeds —3F 103
Noster Ter. Leeds —3F 103
Noster Vw. Leeds —3F 103
Nottingham St. B'frd —6G 81
Nova La. Birs —5B 118
Nowell App. Leeds —4D 86
Nowell Av. Leeds —4D 86
Nowell Clo. Leeds —4D 86
Nowell Cres. Leeds —4D 86
Nowell End Row. Leeds —4D 86
Nowell Gdns. Leeds —4D 86
Nowell Gro. Leeds —4D 86
Nowell La. Leeds —4D 86
Nowell Mt. Leeds —4D 86
Nowell Pde. Leeds —4D 86
Nowell Pl. Leeds —4D 86
Nowell Sq. Leeds —4D 86
Nowell St. Leeds —4D 86
Nowell Ter. Leeds —4D 86
Nowell Vw. Leeds —4D 86
Nowell Wlk. Leeds —4D 86
Nunburnholme Wlk. B'frd —6E 62
Nunington Av. Leeds —5C 84
Nunington St. Leeds —5C 84
Nunington Ter. Leeds —5C 84
Nunington Vw. Leeds —4C 84
Nunlea Royd. Hal —2G 133
Nunnery La. Brigh —2D 144
**Nunroyd. —3B 136**
Nunroyd. Heck —3B 136
Nunroyd Av. Guis —3H 45
Nunroyd Av. Leeds —3K 67
Nunroyd Gro. Leeds —3K 67
*Nunroyd Ho. B'frd —7F 81 (off Sticker La.)*
Nunroyd Lawn. Leeds —3K 67
Nunroyd Rd. Leeds —3K 67
Nunroyd St. Leeds —3K 67
Nunroyd Ter. Leeds —3K 67
Nunthorpe Rd. Leeds —7D 64
Nurser La. B'frd —2J 97
Nurser Pl. B'frd —2J 97
Nursery Av. Hal —4D 112
Nursery Clo. Bail —2F 61
Nursery Clo. Hal —5D 112
Nursery Clo. Kei —1J 39
Nursery Clo. Leeds —7J 49
Nursery Gth. Weth —3K 17
Nursery Gro. Hal —4D 112
Nursery Gro. Leeds —7G 49
Nursery La. Hal —4C 112
Nursery La. Leeds —7G 49
Nursery La. Sower B —6D 140
Nursery Mt. Leeds —5A 104
Nursery Mt. Rd. Leeds —4A 104
Nursery Rd. B'frd —4F 97
Nursery Rd. Cytn —2B 96
Nursery Rd. Guis —7F 27
Nursery Way. B Spa —2B 36
Nursery Way. Cliff —5D 36
Nursery Wood Rd. Bat —5H 137
Nussey Av. Birs —5C 118
Nuttall Rd. B'frd —6C 80 (3H 7)
Nutter La. Birs —5A 118
Nutter St. Cleck —1E 134
Nutting Gro. Ter. Leeds —1J 101

**O**ak Av. Bgly —3K 59
Oak Av. B'frd —3J 79
Oak Av. Bur W —2B 26
Oak Av. Gar —6K 89
Oak Av. Morl —4B 120
Oak Av. Sower B —3K 129
Oak Bank. Bail —2J 61
Oak Bank. Bgly —2A 60
Oak Bank. Shipl —7K 61
Oakbank Av. Kei —6H 39
Oakbank B'way. Oakw —7H 39
Oakbank Ct. Oakw —7H 39
Oakbank Cres. Oakw —7H 39
Oakbank Dri. Kei —6H 39
Oakbank Gro. Kei —6H 39
Oakbank La. Oakw —7H 39
Oakbank Mt. Oakw —7H 39
Oakburn Rd. I'ly —6A 12
Oak Clo. Bur W —2B 26
Oak Cres. Gar —6K 89
Oak Cres. Leeds —6H 87
Oakdale. Bgly —6A 42
Oakdale Av. B'frd —5H 97
Oakdale Av. Shipl —6K 61
Oakdale Clo. B'frd —2G 81
Oakdale Clo. Hal —5E 112
Oakdale Cres. B'frd —5H 97
Oakdale Dri. B'frd —2G 81
Oakdale Dri. Shipl —6A 62
Oakdale Gth. Leeds —3K 69
Oakdale Gro. Shipl —6A 62
Oakdale Mdw. Leeds —3K 69
Oakdale Pk. Pool W —3H 29
Oakdale Rd. Shipl —6A 62
Oakdale Ter. B'frd —5H 97
Oakdean. Hud —5G 145
Oakdene Clo. Pud —1D 100
Oakdene Ct. Leeds —7C 50
Oakdene Dri. Leeds —7C 50
Oakdene Gdns. Leeds —7C 50
Oakdene Va. Leeds —7C 50
Oakdene Way. Leeds —7C 50
Oak Dri. Gar —6K 89
Oak Dri. Leeds —2B 66
**Oakenshaw. —2B 116**
Oakenshaw Ct. Wyke —5J 115
Oakenshaw La. Schol —5C 116
Oakes Gdns. Holy G —5F 143
Oakfield. Leeds —1E 84
Oakfield Av. Bgly —2C 60
Oakfield Av. Rothw —1G 123
Oakfield Clo. Ell —3J 143
Oakfield Clo. Gar —7K 89
Oakfield Dri. Bail —2K 61
Oakfield Gro. B'frd —3J 79
Oakfield Rd. Kei —7J 39
*Oakfield Ter. H'fth —4J 65 (off Low La.)*
Oakfield Ter. Shipl —5K 61
Oak Gro. Gar —6A 90
Oak Gro. Kei —1J 57
Oak Gro. Morl —4B 120
Oakhall Pk. T'tn —6H 77
Oakhampton Ct. Leeds —5E 68
Oakham Wlk. B'frd —2C 98
Oak Head Ter. Cro H —2A 20
Oak Hill. Sower B —1G 141
Oakhill Rd. Bat —1E 136
Oak Hill Rd. Brigh —5H 133
Oak Ho. Leeds —7G 87
Oak Ho. Msde —1K 83
Oakhurst Av. Leeds —5G 103
Oakhurst Ct. B'frd —3K 79
Oakhurst Gro. Leeds —5F 103
Oakhurst Mt. Leeds —5F 103
Oakhurst Rd. Leeds —5F 103
Oakhurst St. Leeds —5G 103
Oaklands. B'frd —4C 62
Oaklands. Brigh —7F 133
Oaklands. I'ly —6A 12
Oaklands. Rob H —4C 122
Oaklands. Shipl —5D 60
Oaklands Av. Adel —1D 66
Oaklands Av. Hal —4A 114
Oaklands Av. Leeds —7C 64
Oaklands Dri. Adel —2D 66
Oaklands Dri. Bat —3K 137
Oaklands Fold. Adel —1D 66
Oaklands Gro. Adel —1D 66
Oaklands Gro. Leeds —7C 64
Oaklands Rd. Rod —7C 64
Oaklands Rd. Trad. Est. Leeds —7C 64
Oakland St. Sils —1F 21
Oak La. B'frd —3H 79
Oak La. Hal —1E 130
Oak La. Sower B —1G 141
Oaklea Gdns. Leeds —2D 66
Oaklea Hall Clo. Leeds —2D 66
Oaklea Rd. Scholes —6D 70
Oakleigh Av. Cytn —3B 96 (in two parts)
Oakleigh Av. Hal —5G 131
Oakleigh Clo. Cytn —2B 96
Oakleigh Gro. Cytn —3B 96 (in two parts)
Oakleigh Rd. Cytn —3B 96
Oakleigh Ter. Cytn —2B 96
Oakleigh Vw. Bail —1H 61
Oakley Gro. Leeds —3J 103
*Oakley Ho. B'frd —2K 97 (off Park La.)*
Oakley St. Thpe —6A 122
Oakley Ter. Leeds —4J 103
Oakley Vw. Leeds —4J 103
Oak Mt. B'frd —3K 79
Oak Mt. Hal —7E 114
Oak Pl. Bail —7B 44
Oak Pl. Gar —6J 89
Oak Pl. Hal —1E 130
Oak Pl. Sower B —3K 129
Oak Ridge. Weth —4G 17
Oakridge Av. Men —6D 26
Oakridge Ct. Bgly —7A 42
Oak Ri. Cleck —5F 117
Oak Rd. A'ley —6E 84
Oak Rd. Gar —6J 89
Oak Rd. Leeds —6H 87
Oak Rd. Morl —4K 119
Oak Rd. Pott —7K 67
Oak Royd. Gar —6K 89
Oakroyd. Rothw —3H 123
Oakroyd Av. B'frd —5J 97
Oakroyd Clo. B'shaw —2J 117
Oakroyd Clo. Brigh —3H 133
Oak Royd Cotts. Hal —6F 131
Oakroyd Dri. B'shaw —3J 117
Oakroyd Dri. Brigh —3H 133
Oakroyd Fold. Chur —6C 102
Oakroyd Mt. S'ley —5C 82
Oakroyd Rd. B'frd —5H 97
Oakroyd Ter. Bail —2K 61
Oakroyd Ter. B'frd —3K 79
Oakroyd Ter. Chur —6C 102
Oakroyd Ter. S'ley —5C 82
Oakroyd Vs. B'frd —3K 79
Oaks Dri. All —5C 78
Oaksfield. Meth —5H 125
Oaks Fold. B'frd —3A 98
Oaks Grn. Mt. Brigh —2F 145
Oaks La. All —5C 78
Oaks La. B Spa —2C 36
Oaks La. B'frd —6D 78
Oaks Rd. Bat —4J 137
Oaks, The. Guis —1G 45
Oaks, The. Morl —7B 102
Oak St. Chur —7B 102
Oak St. Cytn —2B 96
Oak St. Ell —3K 143
Oak St. Haw —5F 57
Oak St. Heck —4B 136
Oak St. Oxe —2E 74
Oak St. Pud —5A 82
Oak St. Sower B —3K 129
Oak St. Wilsd —1G 77
*Oak Ter. Hal —1E 130 (off Acorn St.)*
Oak Ter. Holy G —5E 142
*Oak Ter. Leeds —2B 88 (off Church La.)*
Oak Tree Bus. Pk. Leeds —5J 69
Oak Tree Clo. Leeds —2E 86
*Oak Tree Ct. Leeds —2E 86 (off Oak Tree Pl.)*
Oak Tree Ct. Sils —7F 9
Oak Tree Cres. Leeds —2E 86
Oak Tree Dri. Leeds —2E 86
Oak Tree Gro. Leeds —2E 86
Oak Tree Mt. Leeds —2E 86
Oak Tree Pl. Leeds —2E 86
Oak Tree Wlk. Leeds —2E 86
Oak Vw. Sils —7G 9
Oak Vw. Ter. Bat —7D 118
Oak Vs. B'frd —3K 79
Oakway. B'shaw —3K 117
**Oakwell. —4B 118**
Oakwell Av. Bat —2C 136
Oakwell Av. Leeds —6C 68
Oakwell Clo. B'frd —3H 97
Oakwell Clo. Dlgtn —2E 118
Oakwell Ct. Bat —4E 118
Oakwell Cres. Leeds —6C 68
Oakwell Dri. Leeds —6C 68
Oakwell Gdns. Leeds —6C 68
Oakwell Gro. Leeds —2G 83


A-Z Leeds & Bradford 185

# Oakwell Hall—Palmer M.



Oakwell Hall. —4B 118
Oakwell Ind. Est. Bat —4F 119
Oakwell Ind. Pk. Bat —4E 118
Oakwell Mt. Leeds —6C 68
Oakwell Oval. Leeds —6C 68
Oakwell Rd. Dlgtn —2E 118
Oakwell Ter. Fars —2B 82
Oakwell Way. Birs —4E 118
**Oakwood. —6D 68**
Oakwood Av. B'shaw —3J 117
Oakwood Av. B'frd —1K 79
Oakwood Av. Leeds —6D 68
Oakwood Boundary Rd. Leeds —6D 68
Oakwood Ct. B'frd —5J 79
Oakwood Ct. Leeds —6E 68
Oakwood Dri. Bgly —6K 41
Oakwood Dri. Leeds —6D 68
Oakwood Dri. Rothw —7F 105
Oakwood Gdns. Leeds —6D 68
Oakwood Gth. Leeds —6E 68
Oakwood Grange. Leeds —6E 68
Oakwood Grange La. Leeds —6E 68
Oakwood Grn. Leeds —6E 68
Oakwood Gro. B'frd —4G 79
Oakwood Gro. Leeds —6D 68
Oakwood La. Leeds —6D 68
Oakwood Mt. Leeds —6D 68
Oakwood Nook. Leeds —6D 68
Oakwood Pk. Leeds —7E 68
Oakwood Pl. Leeds —6D 68
Oakwood Ri. Leeds —6E 68
Oakwood Rd. Bat —3J 137
Oak Wood Rd. Weth —2H 17
Oakwood Ter. Pud —7C 82
Oakwood Vw. Leeds —6E 68
Oakwood Wlk. Leeds —6E 68
**Oakworth. —2E 56**
Oakworth Hall. Oakw —2E 56
Oakworth Rd. Oakw & Kei —7H 39
*Oakworth Ter. Oakw —2E 56*
*(off Dockroyd La.)*
Oasby Cft. B'frd —5G 99
Oast Ho. Cft. Rob H —4D 122
Oastler Pl. Low M —1K 115
Oastler Rd. C'ley —6K 63
Oastler Rd. Shipl —4F 61
Oastler St. Dew —7F 137
Oates St. Dew —7H 137
Oatland Clo. Leeds —3J 85 (1F 5)
Oatland Ct. Leeds —3J 85 (2F 5)
Oatland Dri. Leeds —3J 85 (2F 5)
Oatland Gdns. Leeds —3J 85 (2F 5)
Oatland Grn. Leeds —3J 85 (1F 5)
Oatland La. Leeds —3J 85 (1E 4)
Oatland Pl. Leeds —2J 85 (1E 4)
Oatland Rd. Leeds —3J 85 (1E 4)
Oatlands Dri. Otley —1J 27
Oatland Towers. Leeds —3J 85 (2F 5)
Oat St. Kei —7J 39
Oban Clo. Ting —6D 120
Oban Pl. Leeds —5A 84
Oban St. Leeds —5B 84
Oban Ter. Leeds —5B 84
Oban Ter. Ting —6D 120
Occupation La. B'hpe —7F 29
Occupation La. Hal —1C 112
Occupation La. Oakw —7F 39
Occupation La. Pud —7A 82
Occupation La. Stainc —5D 136
Occupation La. Tad —7D 54
Occupation Rd. Sheep —6J 145
Octagon Ter. Hal —4C 130
Odda La. Guis —2A 44
Oddfellows Ct. B'frd —6A 80 (5D 6)
Oddfellows St. Brigh —5H 133
Oddfellows St. Schol —7B 116
Oddfellow St. Morl —3A 120
Oddy Pl. B'frd —5H 97
Oddy Pl. Leeds —6D 66
Oddy's Fold. Leeds —4E 66
Oddy St. B'frd —5G 99
**Odsal. —6A 98**
Odsal Rd. B'frd —6K 97
(in two parts)
Odsal Stadium. —6A 98
**Odsal Top. —6A 98**
**Ogden. —4B 94**
Ogden Cres. Denh —3B 76
Ogden Ho. B'frd —3H 99
Ogden La. Brigh —1F 145
Ogden La. Denh —3B 76
Ogden La. Hal —4B 94
Ogden St. Sower B —5J 129
Ogden Vw. Clo. Hal —7B 94
Ogden Water Countryside Centre. —4B 94
Ogilby Ct. W'ford —7K 105
Ogilby M. W'ford —7K 105
O'Grady Sq. Leeds —6B 86
Old Allen Rd. T'tn —2E 76
*Old Arc., The. Hal —1G 131*
*(off Old Mkt.)*
Old Bank. Hal —1H 131
(in two parts)
Old Bank. Ripp —5G 141
Old Bank Rd. Dew —7K 137
Old Barn Clo. Leeds —6G 49
*Old Bell Ct. Hal —2G 131*
*(off Trinity Pl.)*
**Old Bramhope. —7E 28**
Old Brandon La. Leeds —7G 51
Old Bri. Ri. I'ly —5A 12
Old Brookfoot La. Brigh —5F 133
Old Canal Rd. B'frd —5A 80 (1E 6)
Old Causeway. Sower B —4A 130
Old Clo. Leeds —6D 102
Old Cock Yd. Hal —1G 131
Old Corn Mill La. B'frd —2F 97
Old Corn Mill, The. Brigh —6D 82
Old Dalton La. Kei —4B 40
Old Dan La. Holy G —4G 143
**Old Dolphin. —4A 96**
Old Earth. Ell —2B 144
Old Farm App. Leeds —4K 65
Old Farm Clo. Leeds —4A 66
Old Farm Cross. Leeds —4A 66
Old Farm Dri. Leeds —4K 65
Old Farm Gth. Leeds —4A 66
Old Farm Pde. Leeds —4A 66
Old Farm Wlk. Leeds —4K 65
Oldfield Av. Leeds —7C 84
Old Fieldhouse La. Hud —7K 145
Oldfield La. Coll —1H 35
Oldfield La. Haw —4C 56
Oldfield La. Heck —5B 136
Oldfield La. Leeds —7C 84
Oldfield La. Oldf —4A 56
Oldfield St. Hal —3E 112
Oldfield St. Leeds —7C 84
Old Fold. Fars —2B 82
Old Forge M. B'hpe —7H 29
Old Godley La. Hal —7J 113
Old Gt. N. La. M'fld —5F 91
Old Guy Rd. Q'bry —4F 95
Old Hall Clo. Haw —6E 56
Old Hall M. Bat —1G 137
Old Hall Rd. Bat —1G 137
Old Hall Rd. Ting —7F 121
Oldham Rd. Ripp —7E 140
*Oldham St. Brigh —7G 133*
*(off Bridge End)*
Old Haworth La. Yead —4K 45
Old Hollins Hill. Esh & Guis —5E 44
Old La. Add —3G 11
Old La. B'shaw —1J 117
Old La. Brigh —5H 133
Old La. Cro H —4A 20
Old La. Cull —6B 58
Old La. Dlgtn —7D 100
Old La. Guis —3K 43
Old La. Hal —4E 112
Old La. Hud —4J 145
Old La. I'ly —6D 12
Old La. Leeds —4F 103
Old La. L'ft —6F 111
Old La. Otley & B'hpe —6C 28
*Old La. Ct. Brigh —5H 133*
*(off Old La.)*
Old Langley La. Bail —7K 43
Old Lee Bank. Hal —6F 113
**Old Lindley. —6G 143**
Old Lindley Rd. Holy G —6G 143
Old Lodge Hill. I'ly —4K 11
Old Main St. Bgly —7K 41
Old Mkt. Hal —1G 131
Old Marsh. Pud —6A 82
*Old Marsh. Sower B —3K 129*
*(off Burnley Rd.)*
**Old Micklefield. —6F 91**
Old Mill Clo. Bur W —7B 14
Old Mill La. Cliff —5E 36
Old Mill La. Hun P —2A 104
Old Mill Rd. Shipl —4G 61
Old Mill, The. Weth —4J 17
Old Oak Clo. Leeds —5A 66
Old Oak Dri. Leeds —5A 66
Old Oak Gth. Leeds —5K 65
Old Oak Lawn. Leeds —5A 66
Old Orchard, The. Pool W —3G 29
Old Oxenhope La. Oxe —7D 56
Old Pk. Rd. B'frd —4E 62
Old Pk. Rd. Leeds —4C 68
(in two parts)
Old Pool Bank. Pool W —6F 29
Old Popplewell La. Schol —7A 116
Old Power Way. Lfds B —1A 144
Old Riding La. Ludd —4H 111
Old Rd. B'frd —4E 96
Old Rd. Chur —6C 102
Old Rd. Denh —5B 76
Old Rd. Far —4A 82
Old Rd. T'tn —7K 77
*Old Robin. Cleck —1F 135*
*(off Westgate)*
Oldroyd Cres. Leeds —4E 102
Oldroyd Way. Dew —7F 137
Old Run Rd. Leeds —4K 103
Old Run Vw. Leeds —6K 103
Old Sawmills, The. Ripp —7E 140
Old Sch. M. Chur —6C 102
Old Side Ct. E Mor —2J 41
Old Souls Way. Bgly —5J 41
Old Sta. Way. Add —1D 10
*Old Tannery. Bgly —1A 60*
*(off Clyde St.)*
*Old Tannery. Bgly —1K 59*
*(off Industrial St.)*
Old Well Head. Hal —2G 131
Old Whack Ho. La. Yead —5H 45
Old Wood La. Bgly —2G 43
Olicana Pk. I'ly —4A 12
Olive Gro. B'frd —5E 78
Oliver Ct. Dlgtn —2B 118
Oliver Hill. H'fth —5G 65
Oliver Meadows. Ell —2B 144
Oliver Rd. Heck —3C 136
Oliver's Mt. Kirks —1B 84
Oliver St. B'frd —1C 98 (7H 7)
Olive Ter. Bgly —1A 60
Olivia's Ct. B'frd —3E 78
Ollerdale Av. All —2A 78
(in two parts)
Ollerdale Clo. All —3A 78
Olympic Pk. Low M —2A 116
Olympic Way. Low M —2A 116
Omar St. Heck —4A 136
One St. B'frd —4C 6
Onslow Cres. B'frd —4D 98
Ontario Pl. Leeds —6K 67
Opal St. Kei —7J 39
Orange St. B'frd —7E 80
Orange St. Hal —1G 131
Orange Tree Gro. E Ard —1J 139
Orchard Clo. E Ard —2K 139
Orchard Clo. Hal —2B 130
Orchard Ct. B'ham —1D 54
*Orchard Ct. Guis —2G 45*
*(off Orchard La.)*
*Orchard Ct. Leeds —6D 66*
*(off St Chads Rd.)*
Orchard Cft. Bat —5E 136
Orchard Cft. Leeds —3K 87
Orchard Dri. Lntn —6F 17
*Orchard Ga. Otley —3J 27*
*(off Market St.)*
Orchard Gro. B'frd —5F 63
Orchard Gro. Men —6C 26
*Orchard Ho. B Spa —2D 36*
*(off Albion St.)*
Orchard La. Add —1E 10
Orchard La. Guis —2G 45
Orchard Mt. Leeds —3A 88
Orchard Rd. Leeds —3K 87
Orchard Sq. Leeds —3K 87
Orchards, The. Bgly —6A 42
Orchards, The. Gom —7A 118
Orchards, The. Halt —3K 87
Orchards, The. Meth —5G 125
Orchard St. Otley —3K 27
Orchard, The. B Spa —2D 36
Orchard, The. Holy G —6D 142
Orchard, The. Kei —4D 40
Orchard Vw. Weth —1J 17
Orchard Wlk. H Bri —6B 110
Orchard Way. Brigh —4G 133
Orchard Way. Guis —2G 45
Orchard Way. Rothw —1G 123
Orchid Ct. Loft —5D 122
Oriental St. Leeds —6C 84
Orion Cres. Leeds —7A 104
Orion Dri. Leeds —7A 104
Orion Gdns. Leeds —7B 104
Orion Vw. Leeds —7B 104
Orion Wlk. Leeds —6B 104
Orleans St. B'frd —7F 97
Ormonde Dri. All —5A 78
Ormonde Pl. Leeds —2J 85 (1F 5)
Ormond Rd. B'frd —5H 97
Ormondroyd Av. B'frd —6J 97
Ormond St. B'frd —2G 97
Orville Gdns. Leeds —1E 84
Osborne Gro. Hal —1D 132
Osborne St. B'frd —1K 97 (7C 6)
Osborne St. Hal —7D 112
Osborne Ter. Bat —2F 137
Osbourne Ct. Leeds —4H 83
Osbourne Dri. Q'bry —5H 95
*Osdal Rd. B'frd —6K 97*
*(off Glenfield Mt.)*
Osmond Ho. B'frd —7D 6
**Osmondthorpe. —6F 87**
Osmondthorpe Cotts. Leeds —6E 86
Osmondthorpe La. Leeds —5E 86
Osmondthorpe Ter. Leeds —5D 86
Osprey Clo. Coll —1F 35
Osprey Clo. Leeds —7B 50
Osprey Ct. B'frd —6C 78
Osprey Gro. Leeds —7B 50
Osprey Mdw. Morl —3D 120
Osterley Gro. B'frd —7G 63
Oswald St. B'frd —5G 79
Oswald St. Shipl —5K 61
Oswaldthorpe Av. B'frd —4F 81
**Otley. —2J 27**
Otley La. Yead —4K 45
Otley Mills. Otley —3G 27
Otley Mt. E Mor —3J 41
Otley Old Rd. Leeds —6J 47
Otley Old Rd. Otley, Yead, H'fth & Leeds —6C 28
Otley Rd. Bgly —6B 42
Otley Rd. B'frd —6B 80 (1H 7)
Otley Rd. Bur W —1C 26
Otley Rd. E Mor —2J 41
Otley Rd. Guis —2E 44
Otley Rd. Leeds & Head —3B 48
Otley Rd. Men —5D 26
Otley Rd. Pool W —3G 31
Otley Rd. Shipl & C'twn —6H 61
Otley St. Hal —1D 130
Otley St. Kei —5K 39
Ottawa Pl. Leeds —6K 67
Otterburn Clo. B'frd —1K 97
Otterburn Gdns. Leeds —1B 66
Otterburn St. Kei —3A 40
Otter Lee La. Sower B —1D 140
Otterwood Bank. Weth —2K 17
**Oulton. —2A 124**
Oulton Dri. Oult —4A 124
Oulton La. Oult —7A 106
Oulton La. Rothw —2H 123
Oulton Ter. B'frd —1J 97 (6A 6)
Ouse Dri. Weth —1H 17
**Ousel Hole. —1J 41**
Ouse St. Haw —5F 57
Out Gang. Leeds —2H 83
Out Gang La. Leeds —2J 83
Outlands Ri. B'frd —4F 63
Outside La. Oxe —3A 74
Outwood Av. H'fth —5H 65
Outwood Chase. H'fth —4H 65
Outwood La. H'fth —5G 65
Outwood Wlk. H'fth —5G 65
**Ouzlewell Green. —6F 123**
Ouzlewell Grn. Loft —5F 123
**Oval, The. —3H 87**
Oval, The. Bail —3H 61
Oval, The. Bgly —2B 60
Oval, The. B'frd —5E 78
Oval, The. Gar —6A 90
Oval, The. Guis —3E 44
Oval, The. H'let —2K 103
Oval, The. Leeds —3H 87
Oval, The. Liv —3E 134
Oval, The. Otley —1H 27
Oval, The. Rothw —2H 123
**Ovenden. —5D 112**
Ovenden Av. Hal —6E 112
Ovenden Clo. Hal —6E 112
Ovenden Cres. Hal —5E 112
Ovenden Grn. Hal —5D 112
Ovenden Rd. Ter. Hal —5E 112
Ovenden Ter. Hal —5E 112
Ovenden Way. Hal —5C 112
**Ovenden Wood. —5A 112**
Ovendon Wood Rd. Hal —5A 112
Overdale. Sower B —2G 141
Overdale Av. Leeds —6C 50
Overdale Clo. Weth —3H 17
Overdale Dri. B'frd & Shipl —3B 62
Overdale Mt. Sower B —3A 130
Overdale Ter. Haw —5E 56
Overdale Ter. Leeds —5J 87
Overend St. B'frd —5G 97
Overland Cres. B'frd —4F 63
Overland Trad. Est. Gild —2G 119
Over La. Rawd —1A 64
Overmoor Fold. Idle —5B 62
Overton Dri. B'frd —4D 96
*Overton Ho. B'frd —2K 97*
*(off Newstead Wlk.)*
Ovington Dri. B'frd —5G 99
Owen Ct. Bgly —5A 42
Owlcotes Dri. Pud —5A 82
Owlcotes Gdns. Pud —5A 82
Owlcotes Gth. Pud —5K 81
Owlcotes La. Far —4A 82
(in two parts)
Owlcotes La. Pud —5A 82
Owlcotes Rd. Pud —5K 81
Owlcotes Shop. Cen. S'ley —4B 82
Owlcotes Ter. Pud —5A 82
Owler Ings Rd. Brigh —6G 133
Owler La. Birs —4C 118
Owler Meadows. Heck —3A 136
Owler Pk. Rd. I'ly —2J 11
**Owlet. —7K 61**
Owlet Grange. Shipl —6J 61
Owlet Hurst La. Liv —6K 135
Owlet Rd. Shipl —5J 61
Owlett Mead. Thpe —6A 122
Owlett Mead Clo. Thpe —6A 122
Owl La. Dew & Oss —5A 138
(in two parts)
Owl Ridge. Morl —4C 120
Oxenford Ct. Leeds —1A 66
**Oxenhope. —3E 74**
Oxenhope Station Railway Museum. —2E 74
Oxford Av. Guis —1F 45
Oxford Clo. Gom —7K 117
Oxford Clo. Q'bry —6G 95
Oxford Ct. Gdns. C'frd —7C 126
Oxford Cres. Cytn —2B 96
Oxford Cres. Hal —4H 131
Oxford Dri. Gom —7K 117
Oxford Dri. Kip —5K 107
Oxford La. Hal —4H 131
Oxford Pl. Bail —2A 62
Oxford Pl. B'frd —5B 80 (1G 7)
Oxford Pl. Leeds —5H 85 (5C 4)
Oxford Pl. S'ley —4C 82
Oxford Rd. Birs —6C 118
Oxford Rd. B'frd —3C 80
Oxford Rd. Dew —7E 136
Oxford Rd. Gom —4K 117
Oxford Rd. Guis —2F 45
Oxford Rd. Hal —2G 131
Oxford Rd. Leeds —2J 85
Oxford Rd. Q'bry —6G 95
Oxford Row. Leeds —5H 85 (5C 4)
(in two parts)
Oxford St. Bat —4F 137
Oxford St. Cytn —2B 96
Oxford St. E Ard —7A 122
Oxford St. Guis —2G 45
Oxford St. Kei —5J 39
Oxford St. Morl —5K 119
Oxford St. Sower B —4B 130
*Oxford Ter. Bail —2A 62*
*(off Union St.)*
Oxford Ter. Bat —4H 137
Oxford Vs. Guis —2G 45
Oxford Wlk. Cleck —7K 117
Ox Heys Mdw. T'tn —7A 78
Oxley Gdns. Low M —7J 97
Oxley Rd. Hud —5J 145
Oxley St. B'frd —5J 79 (2A 6)
Oxley St. Leeds —6B 86
Oxton Clo. Leeds —5B 86
Oxton Gdns. Leeds —5B 86
Oxton Mt. Leeds —5B 86
Oxton Pl. Leeds —5B 86
Oxton Way. Leeds —5B 86
Oyster Clo. Morl —4C 120

**P**acaholme Rd. Wake —7K 139
Packington St. T'tn —5G 77
Padan St. Hal —4H 131
Paddock. B'frd —1J 79
Paddock Clo. Dlgtn —2C 118
Paddock Clo. Gar —7A 90
Paddock Clo. Wyke —6J 115
*Paddock Corner. Leeds —6A 88*
*(off Colton Rd.)*
Paddock Dri. Dlgtn —2C 118
Paddock Grn. E Kes —5A 34
Paddock Ho. La. Sick —6A 16
Paddock La. Eld —5D 42
Paddock La. Hal —7A 112
Paddock Rd. Hal —2J 113
Paddock, The. Bail —7B 44
Paddock, The. Cull —6B 58
Paddock, The. E Kes —4A 34
Paddock, The. Leeds —5F 67
Paddock, The. Rothw —2G 123
Paddock, The. Schol —7B 116
Paddock, The. Sils —1G 21
Paddock, The. T'ner —6D 52
*Padgate Ho. B'frd —2K 97*
*(off Park La.)*
Padgum. Bail —7J 43
Padma Clo. B'frd —6H 79
Padmans La. B Spa —2D 36
Padstow Av. Leeds —2G 121
Padstow Gdns. Leeds —2G 121
Padstow Pl. Leeds —3G 121
Padstow Row. Leeds —3G 121
Page Hill. Hal —4C 112
Paget Cres. Hud —7D 144
Paget St. Kei —4J 39
Page Wood Clo. B'frd —3C 62
Paignton Ct. Leeds —4H 83
Paisley Gro. Leeds —5A 84
Paisley Pl. Leeds —5A 84
Paisley Rd. Leeds —5A 84
Paisley St. Leeds —5A 84
Paisley Ter. Leeds —5A 84
Paisley Vw. Leeds —5A 84
Pakington St. B'frd —2K 97
Paley Pl. B'frd —1C 98
Paley Rd. B'frd —2C 98
Paley Ter. B'frd —2C 98
Palin Av. B'frd —4F 81
Palm Clo. B'frd —6H 97
Palmer Bldgs. Leeds —3C 86
Palmer Cres. Guis —2G 45
Palmer Cft. Leeds —7B 104
Palmer Mans. Yead —4K 45
Palmer M. Ting —7E 120

Palmer Rd.—Peel St.


Palmer Rd. B'frd —5D 80 (1K 7)
Palmer Sq. Oss —7C 138
Palmerston St. B'frd —3D 80
Palm St. Hal —5F 113
Pannal St. B'frd —3G 97
Pannel Hill. Leeds —7D 108
Panorama Dri. I'ly —7J 11
Paper Hall, The. —6B 80 (3G 7)
Parade, The. Bat —4E 136
Parade, The. Bgly —5A 60
Parade, The. Head —7D 66 (off North La.)
Parade, The. H Wd —3G 99
Parade, The. Leeds —6A 86 (7J 5)
Parade, The. Otley —1G 27
Parade, The. Yead —5H 45 (off Westfield Dri.)
Paradise Fold. B'frd —2E 96
Paradise Green. —2F 97
Paradise La. H'wd —6H 55
Paradise La. Warley —2K 129
Paradise Pl. H'fth —4J 65
Paradise Rd. B'frd —1F 79
Paradise Row. Hal —3D 130
Paradise St. B'frd —6K 79 (3B 6)
Paradise St. Hal —2F 131
Parc Mont. Leeds —4E 68
Parish Ghyll Dri. I'ly —6K 11
Parish Ghyll La. I'ly —6K 11
Parish Ghyll Rd. I'ly —6A 12
Parish Ghyll Wlk. I'ly —6A 12
Park. —7B 44
Park Av. All B —3C 126
Park Av. A'ley —5B 84
Park Av. Bat —2H 137
Park Av. Bgly —2K 59
Park Av. B'frd —2D 62
Park Av. C'frd —7F 127
Park Av. C'gts —3B 88
Park Av. Dlgtn —1C 118
Park Av. Ell —3J 143
Park Av. Kei —5K 39
Park Av. Kip —5C 108
Park Av. Liv —6J 135
Park Av. Morl —4K 119
Park Av. Oakw —2F 57
Park Av. Pud —6C 82
Park Av. Rawd —7A 46
Park Av. Round —4E 68
Park Av. Shipl —4G 61
Park Av. Swil —5E 106
Park Av. Yead —4J 45
Pk. Bottom. Low M —2J 115
Pk. Cliffe Rd. B'frd —3C 80
Park Clo. Bat —5F 137
Park Clo. Bgly —7A 42
Park Clo. B'frd —7E 62
Park Clo. Dlgtn —1C 118
Park Clo. Hal —5K 111
Park Clo. Kei —6A 40
Park Clo. Leeds —2G 83
Park Clo. Light —1E 132
Park Clo. Q'bry —5H 95
Park Copse. H'fth —3E 64
Park Cotts. Leeds —3D 68
Park Ct. B'frd —3J 79
Park Ct. Pool W —4H 29
Park Cres. Add —1E 10
Park Cres. A'ley —5B 84
Park Cres. B'frd —4C 80
Park Cres. C'frd —7J 127
Park Cres. Gild —1H 119
Park Cres. Guis —4E 44
Park Cres. Hal —6E 112
Park Cres. Leeds —2C 68
Park Cres. Rothw —1J 123
Park Cres. Sower B —4B 130 (off Grove St.)
Park Cft. Bat —4F 137
Park Cft. Dew —7E 136
Parkcroft. Fars —3C 82
Pk. Cross St. Leeds —5H 85 (6C 4)
Park Dale. C'frd —6J 127 (in two parts)
Park Dale. Men —6C 26
Parkdale Dri. Sower B —2G 141
Park Dri. Bat —1E 136
Park Dri. Bgly —6B 42
Park Dri. B'frd —1G 79
Park Dri. Hal —2E 130 (HX1)
Park Dri. Hal —3B 130 (HX2)
Park Dri. H'fth —4D 64
Park Dri. Sut Cr —5A 20
Park Dri. Rd. Kei —6A 40
Pk. Edge Clo. Leeds —5E 68
Parker's La. Kei —7J 21
Parker St. E Ard —1J 139
Parker St. Heck —4B 136
Parker St. Liv —5A 136
Pk. Farm Ind. Est. Leeds —6H 103
Park Fld. Men —6C 26
Parkfield Av. Ell —3K 143 (off Catherine St.)
Parkfield Av. Leeds —3G 103
Parkfield Clo. Kip —4B 108
Parkfield Clo. Pud —6B 82
Parkfield Ct. Leeds —2G 87
Parkfield Dri. B Spa —2C 36
Parkfield Dri. Q'bry —5H 95
Parkfield Dri. Sower B —6J 129
Parkfield Gro. Leeds —3G 103
Parkfield Mt. Leeds —3G 103
Parkfield Mt. Pud —6C 82
Parkfield Pl. Leeds —3G 103
Parkfield Rd. B'frd —3K 79
Parkfield Rd. Leeds —3G 103
Parkfield Rd. Shipl —4E 60
Parkfield Row. Leeds —3G 103
Park Fields. Hal —5K 111
Parkfield St. Leeds —1J 103
Parkfield Ter. Pud —6C 82
Parkfield Ter. S'ley —4C 82 (in two parts)
Parkfield Vw. Leeds —3G 103
Parkfield Way. Leeds —2G 87
Park Gdns. Hal —3B 130
Park Ga. B'frd —6B 80 (3G 7)
Pk. Gate Clo. H'fth —4F 65
Pk. Gate Cres. Guis —3F 45
Park Grn. Hal —6K 113
Park Grn. Sils —1E 20
Park Gro. B'frd —1J 79
Park Gro. Gild —1H 119
Park Gro. Hal —6A 114
Park Gro. H'fth —4D 64
Park Gro. Kei —3A 40
Park Gro. Leeds —3J 121
Park Gro. Midd —6D 66
Park Gro. Q'bry —5H 95
Park Gro. Shipl —4F 61
Park Gro. Swil —6E 106
Park Gro. Yead —4J 45
Pk. Grove Ct. B'frd —1J 79
Parkhead Clo. B'frd —1G 115
Pk. Hill Clo. B'frd —4D 78
Pk. Hill Dri. B'frd —4D 78
Pk. Hill Gro. Bgly —7A 42
Pk. Holme. Leeds —1A 86
Pk. House Clo. Low M —7A 98
Pk. House Cres. Low M —7A 98
Pk. House Gro. Low M —7A 98
Pk. House Rd. Low M —1K 115
Pk. House Wlk. Low M —7A 98
Parkin Hall La. Sower B —7D 128
Parkin La. B'frd —4H 63
Parkinson App. Gar —5K 89
Parkinson La. Hal —2C 130
Parkinson Rd. Denh —5C 76
Parkinson St. B'frd —2K 97
Parkin St. Liv —3E 134
Parkland Av. Morl —4J 119
Parkland Cres. Leeds —3G 67
Parkland Dri. B'frd —5E 62
Parkland Dri. Leeds —3G 67
Parkland Gdns. Leeds —4G 67
Parklands. —1J 87
Parklands. Bgly —6B 42
Parklands. B'hpe —7H 29
Parklands. I'ly —5D 12
Parklands Cres. B'hpe —7J 29
Parklands Dri. Sower B —7G 129
Parklands Ga. B'hpe —7J 29
Parkland Ter. Leeds —4G 67
Parkland Vw. Yead —4K 45 (off Town St.)
Park La. All B —3B 126
Park La. Bail —7B 44
Park La. B'frd —2K 97 (7C 6)
Park La. Cytn —2B 96
Park La. Guis —4E 44
Park La. Hal —6H 131
Park La. Kei —5A 40
Park La. Kip —6C 108
Park La. Led —5J 109 (in two parts)
Park La. Leeds —5F 85 (5A 4)
Park La. Meth —6E 124
Park La. Q'bry —5K 95
Park La. Rothw —2H 123
Park La. Round —2D 68
Park La. Sow —7D 142
Park La. Sut Cr —5A 20
Park La. M. Leeds —7D 50
Park Lea. Leeds —2J 121
Parklee Ct. Kei —5B 40
Park Mead. B'frd —2D 62
Parkmere Clo. B'frd —6D 98
Park M. Pool W —4H 29
Pk. Mill La. Oss —7F 139
Park Mt. A'ley —5A 84
Park Mt. Kirks —1A 84
Park Mt. Pool W —5F 29
Park Mt. Av. Bail —1A 62
Park Pde. Leeds —7C 86
Park Pde. Morl —4K 119
Park Pl. Idle —2D 62
Park Pl. Leeds —5H 85 (6C 4)
Park Pl. E. Hal —1E 132
Park Pl. W. Hal —1E 132
Park Ri. C'frd —7F 127
Park Ri. Leeds —1G 83
Park Rd. A'ley —5A 84
Park Rd. Bat —3H 137
Park Rd. Bgly —1K 59
Park Rd. B Spa —2C 36
Park Rd. B'frd —1A 98 (7D 6)
Park Rd. Dew —7E 136
Park Rd. Eccl —7E 62 (in two parts)
Park Rd. Ell —1K 143
Park Rd. Guis —4E 44
Park Rd. Hal —2F 131
Park Rd. Heck —4B 136
Park Rd. Leeds —2G 83 (LS13)
Park Rd. Leeds —7B 88 (LS15)
Park Rd. Low M —7J 97
Park Rd. Men —6C 26
Park Rd. Rawd —7K 45
Park Rd. Shipl —5J 61
Park Rd. Sower B —3A 130
Park Rd. Thack —2D 62
Park Rd. Yead —4J 45
Park Row. Brigh —6H 133
Park Row. Bur W —7B 14
Park Row. Leeds —5H 85 (6D 4)
Park Row. Otley —2K 27 (off Cross Grn.)
Park Row. S'ley —4C 82
Parkside. —4C 98
Parkside. Bgly —7A 42
Park Side. Cytn —2B 96
Parkside. Cleck —1G 135
Park Side. Gom —1J 135
Parkside. Hal —4F 131
Park Side. H'fth —4E 64
Parkside Av. Leeds —5F 67
Parkside Av. Q'bry —5H 95
Parkside Clo. Leeds —4F 67
Parkside Ct. Cro R —4G 57
Parkside Cres. Leeds —4F 67
Parkside Dri. B'frd —2G 79
Parkside Gdns. Leeds —5F 67
Parkside Grn. Leeds —5F 67
Parkside Gro. B'frd —2G 79
Parkside Gro. Leeds —5G 103
Parkside Ind. Est. Leeds —5J 103
Parkside La. Leeds —4J 103
Parkside Lawns. Leeds —5F 67
Parkside Mt. Leeds —5G 103
Parkside Pde. Leeds —5G 103
Parkside Pl. Leeds —4F 67
Parkside Rd. B'frd —4K 97
Parkside Rd. Fars —3B 82
Parkside Rd. Leeds —3E 66
Parkside Row. Leeds —5G 103
Parkside Ter. Cull —6B 58
Parkside Vw. Leeds —4F 67
Parkside Wlk. Fars —3C 82
Parks La. Midd —1A 12
Park Spring. —6G 83
Pk. Spring Gdns. Leeds —4F 83
Pk. Spring Ri. Leeds —5F 83
Park Sq. B'frd —6F 97
Park Sq. Hal —5A 114 (off Hough)
Park Sq. Pool W —4H 29
Park Sq. Pud —6C 82
Park Sq. E. Leeds —5H 85 (6C 4)
Park Sq. N. Leeds —5H 85 (6C 4)
Park Sq. S. Leeds —5H 85 (6C 4)
Park Sq. W. Leeds —5H 85 (6C 4)
Parkstone Av. Leeds —3A 66
Parkstone Dri. B'frd —7E 62
Parkstone Grn. Leeds —3A 66
Parkstone Gro. Leeds —3A 66
Parkstone Mt. Leeds —3A 66
Parkstone Pl. Leeds —3A 66
Pk. Stone Ri. She —1B 114
Park St. A'ley —5A 84
Park St. Bat —3H 137
Park St. Birs —7C 118
Park St. Brigh —6H 133
Park St. Chur —6C 102
Park St. Cleck —2D 134
Park St. Dew —7H 137
Park St. Gom —7A 118
Park St. Halt —5K 87
Park St. Haw —5E 57
Park St. Heck —4B 136
Park St. Leeds —5H 85 (5C 4)
Park St. Shipl —4G 61
Park St. Sower B —4B 130
Park St. Yead —4J 45
Park Ter. Hal —2E 130 (in two parts)
Park Ter. Hip —1D 132
Park Ter. Kei —4B 40
Park Ter. Leeds —6D 66
Park Ter. Low M —1J 115 (off Park Rd.)
Park Ter. Otley —2K 27 (off Cross Grn.)
Park Ter. Pool W —5E 28
Park Ter. Shipl —4G 61
Park Ter. T Brow —5D 40 (off Bank Top Way)
Park, The. S'wram —4A 132
Park Top. S'ley —4C 82
Pk. Top Cotts. Bgly —6B 42
Pk. Top Row. Haw —5E 56
Park Vw. B'shaw —2J 117
Park Vw. Cleck —7E 116
Park Vw. Hal —2E 130
Park Vw. Kip —5B 108
Park Vw. Leeds —3G 103 (LS11)
Park Vw. Leeds —2G 83 (LS13)
Park Vw. Light —1E 132
Park Vw. Pud —6C 82
Park Vw. Q'bry —4H 95
Park Vw. Swil —5E 106
Park Vw. Yead —4H 45
Pk. View Av. Cro R —4G 57
Pk. View Av. Leeds —2D 84
Pk. View Av. Rawd —7A 46
Parkview Ct. Leeds —2D 68
Parkview Ct. Shipl —5G 61
Pk. View Cres. Leeds —3D 68
Pk. View Gro. Leeds —2D 84
Pk. View Rd. B'frd —3H 79
Pk. View Rd. Hal —6A 114
Pk. View Rd. Leeds —3D 84
Pk. View Ter. B'frd —2H 79
Pk. View Ter. Leeds —5J 87 (off Park St.)
Pk. View Ter. Rawd —7K 45
Pk. Villa Ct. Leeds —3C 68
Park Villas. —3C 68
Park Vs. Leeds —3C 68
Parkville Pl. Leeds —2G 83
Parkville Rd. Leeds —2G 83
Park Way. Bail —3F 61
Parkway. B'frd —4B 98
Parkway. Gild —1G 119
Parkway. Kei —6A 40
Park Way. Men —6C 26
Park Way. Pool W —4H 29
Parkway. Q'bry —5H 95
Parkway. Steet —5D 20 (in two parts)
Parkway Clo. Leeds —1G 87
Parkway Ct. Leeds —2G 87
Parkway Grange. Leeds —2G 87
Parkway M. Leeds —7K 69
Parkways. W'ford —1K 123
Parkways Av. W'ford —2K 123
Parkways Clo. W'ford —1K 123
Parkways Ct. W'ford —1K 123
Parkways Dri. W'ford —1K 123
Parkways Gth. W'ford —2K 123
Parkways Gro. W'ford —1K 123
Parkway Towers. Leeds —1G 87
Parkway Va. Leeds —2G 87 (in two parts)
Park W. Rothw —2G 123
Parkwood. —5A 40
Pk. Wood Av. Leeds —6F 103
Parkwood Av. Round —5C 68
Park Wood Bottom. —5B 40
Pk. Wood Clo. Leeds —7F 103
Parkwood Ct. Round —4C 68
Pk. Wood Cres. Leeds —7F 103
Pk. Wood Dri. Leeds —6F 103
Parkwood Gdns. C'ley —6J 63
Parkwood Gdns. Round —5C 68
Parkwood Ri. Kei —5A 40
Parkwood Rd. C'ley —6K 63
Pk. Wood Rd. Leeds —7F 103
Parkwood Rd. Shipl —5F 61
Parkwood St. Kei —5A 40
Parkwood Way. Round —5C 68
Parliament Pl. Leeds —5D 84
Parliament Rd. Leeds —6D 84
Parlington Ct. Bar E —5J 71
Parlington Dri. Aber —5E 72
Parlington La. Gar —2K 89
Parlington Mdw. Bar E —6J 71
Parlington Vs. Aber —5E 72
Parma St. B'frd —1A 98
Parnaby Av. Leeds —5B 104
Parnaby Rd. Leeds —5B 104
Parnaby St. Leeds —5B 104
Parnaby Ter. Leeds —5B 104
Parratt Row. B'frd —6F 81
Parrish Pl. Kei —4A 40
Parrish Rd. Leeds —3H 103
Parrish Vw. Hal —4A 132
Parrish Wlk. Q'bry —5J 95
Parrott St. B'frd —5F 99
Parry La. B'frd —1E 98
Parsonage La. Brigh —5G 133
Parsonage Rd. Lais —1F 99
Parsonage Rd. Meth —4H 125
Parsonage Rd. W Bowl —3A 98
Parsonage St. Hal —6H 113
Parsons Grn. Weth —4K 17
Parson's La. Sils —2H 9
Parsons Rd. B'frd —1G 79
Parson St. Kei —3A 40
Partington Ho. B'frd —5E 62 (off Fairhaven Grn.)
Partridge Clo. Morl —3D 120
Pasture Av. Leeds —5K 67
Pasture Clo. Cytn —2D 96
Pasture Cres. Leeds —5K 67
Pasture Fold. Bur W —7A 14
Pasture Grn. Clo. Leeds —5E 86
Pasture Gro. Leeds —5K 67
Pasture La. Cytn & B'frd —2C 96
Pasture La. Kear —1G 33
Pasture La. Leeds —5K 67
Pasture Mt. Leeds —5B 84
Pasture Pde. Leeds —5K 67
Pasture Pl. Leeds —5K 67
Pasture Ri. Cytn —2D 96
Pasture Rd. Bail —2K 61
Pasture Rd. Leeds —1A 86
Pastureside Ter. E. Cytn —2D 96
Pastureside Ter. W. Cytn —2C 96
Pasture St. Leeds —5K 67
Pasture Ter. Leeds —5K 67
Pasture Vw. Leeds —5B 84
Pasture Vw. Rd. Rothw —2G 123
Pasture Wlk. Cytn —2C 96
Patchett Sq. Q'bry —5B 96 (off Western Pl.)
Pateley Cres. Hud —7G 145
Patent St. B'frd —3H 79
Paternoster La. B'frd —2G 97
Patterdale App. Weth —4F 17
Patterdale Ho. B'frd —2K 97 (off Hutson St.)
Patterdale Rd. Dew —6J 137
Pattie St. Kei —2K 39
Paulena Ter. Morl —5B 120 (off Britannia Rd.)
Pauline Ter. C'frd —7C 126
Pavement La. Hal —6C 94
Paw La. Q'bry —7K 95
Pawson St. B'frd —7F 81
Pawson St. Loft —5D 122
Pawson St. Morl —4K 119
Pawson St. Wake —7A 122
Peabody St. Hal —6E 112
Peace St. B'frd —1E 98
Peace St. Ind. Est. B'frd —7E 80
Peach Wlk. B'frd —2D 98
Peacock Grn. Morl —4C 120
Peacock Ter. Shipl —5G 61
Peak Vw. Dew —6D 136
Pearl St. Bat —2E 136
Pearl St. Kei —7J 39
Pearsall Gro. B'frd —6B 80
Pearson Av. Leeds —2E 84
Pearson Fold. Oaken —3B 116
Pearson Gro. Leeds —2E 84
Pearson La. B'frd —4D 78
Pearson Rd. B'frd —6K 97
Pearson Rd. W. B'frd —6K 97
Pearson Row. Wyke —4K 115
Pearsons Bldgs. Otley —3K 27
Pearson St. B'frd —7E 80
Pearson St. C'ley —5K 63
Pearson St. Cleck —2G 135
Pearson St. Leeds —1K 103
Pearson St. Msde —2D 134
Pearson Ter. Leeds —2E 84
Pear St. Hal —2D 130
Pear St. Kei —1J 57
Pear St. Oxe —3E 74
Pear Tree Acre. Thor A —1E 36
Pear Tree Ct. Sils —7G 9
Peas Acre. —3J 41
Peas Acre. Bgly —3J 41
Peasborough Vw. Bur W —2B 26
Peasefold. Kip —5B 108
Peasehill Clo. Rawd —7A 46
Peasehill Pk. Rawd —7A 46
Peaseland Av. Cleck —1E 134
Peaseland Clo. Cleck —1F 135
Peaseland Rd. Cleck —1F 135
Peaselands. Shipl —5G 61
Peat Ponds. Hud —7J 143
Peckover Dri. Pud —4H 81
Peckover St. B'frd —6B 80 (4G 7)
Peel Av. Bat —3G 137
Peel Clo. Tyer —1G 99
Peel Ct. B'frd —3B 80
Peel Ho. Bgly —2B 60
Peel Pk. Dri. B'frd —3D 80
Peel Pk. Ter. B'frd —3D 80
Peel Pk. Vw. B'frd —4C 80
Peel Pl. Bur W —1A 26
Peel Row. B'frd —2G 97
Peel Sq. B'frd —5K 79 (2C 6)
Peel Sq. Leeds —1A 84
Peel St. Bgly —1B 60


A-Z Leeds & Bradford 187

Peel St.—Priestley Hill


Peel St. Heck —4A 136
Peel St. Morl —3B 120
Peel St. Q'bry —5K 95
Peel St. Sower B —4K 129
Peel St. T'tn —7H 77
Peel St. Wilsd —1G 77
Peep Grn. La. Liv —6E 134
Peep Grn. Rd. Liv —6E 134
Pegholme Dri. Otley —4F 27
Pelham Ct. B'frd —2D 80
Pelham Pl. Leeds —5J 67
Pelham Rd. B'frd —2D 80
**Pellon. —7C 112**
Pellon La. Hal —7D 112
Pellon New Rd. Hal —7C 112
Pellon Ter. B'frd —3D 62
Pellon Wlk. B'frd —3D 62
Pemberton Dri. B'frd —7K 79 (6B 6)
Pemberton Rd. C'frd —7G 127
Pembroke Clo. Morl —2K 119
Pembroke Dri. Morl —2K 119
Pembroke Dri. Pud —5C 82
Pembroke Grange. Leeds —3F 87
*Pembroke Ho. B'frd —4G 99 (off Launceston Dri.)*
Pembroke Ri. Kip —4C 108
Pembroke Rd. Pud —5C 82
Pembroke St. B'frd —2A 98
Pembroke Towers. Leeds —2F 87
Pembury Mt. Leeds —2D 88
Penarth Rd. Leeds —3K 87
Pendas Dri. Leeds —3B 88
**Pendas Fields. —2D 88**
Pendas Gro. Leeds —2B 88
Pendas Wlk. Leeds —3B 88
Pendas Way. Leeds —3B 88
Pendil Clo. Leeds —5A 88
Pendle Ct. Q'bry —7J 95
Pendle Rd. Bgly —1B 60 (in two parts)
Pendragon. B'frd —2C 80
Pendragon La. B'frd —2D 80
Pendragon Ter. Guis —2F 45
Penfield Gro. Cytn —2C 96
Penfield Rd. Dlgtn —1D 118
Pengarth. Bgly —6B 42
Penistone Hill Country Park. —6C 56
Penistone M. Haw —5E 56
Penlands Cres. Leeds —6B 88
Penlands Lawn. Leeds —6B 88
Penlands Wlk. Leeds —6B 88
*Pennard Ho. B'frd —2K 97 (off Launton Way)*
Penn Clo. B'frd —1D 80
Penn Dri. Liv —2F 135
Penn Gro. Liv —2F 135
Pennine Clo. Q'bry —7H 95
Pennine Rd. Dew —7J 137
Pennine Vw. Birs —4E 118
Pennington Ct. Leeds —2G 85
Pennington Gro. Leeds —1G 85
Pennington La. Oult —5K 123
Pennington Pl. Leeds —2G 85
Pennington St. Leeds —2G 85
Pennington Ter. B'frd —2J 97
Pennington Ter. Leeds —1G 85
Pennithorne Av. Bail —7J 43
Penn St. Hal —7E 112
*Pennwell Cft. Leeds —7B 70 (off Whinmoor Way)*
Pennwell Dean. Leeds —7B 70
Pennwell Fld. Leeds —7C 70
Pennwell Gth. Leeds —7B 70
Pennwell Ga. Leeds —7B 70
Pennwell Grn. Leeds —7B 70
Pennwell Lawn. Leeds —7B 70
Pennygate. Bgly —6D 42
Penny Hill Cen., The. Leeds —2A 104
Penny Hill Dri. Cytn —2D 96
Penny La. Way. Leeds —2K 103
Penny St. B'frd —6C 80 (5J 7)
Penraevon Av. Pen I —2J 85
Penrith Cres. C'frd —5K 127
Penrith Gro. Leeds —7C 84
Penrose Dri. Gt Hor —3F 97
Pentland Av. Cytn —2C 96
Pentland Clo. Kei —5J 39
Pentland Dri. Gar —1K 107
Pentland Way. Morl —4A 120
Penuel Pl. Hal —5H 131
Pepper Gdns. Bmly —1J 83
**Pepper Hill. —1A 114**
Pepper Hills. Leeds —7K 49
Pepper La. Leeds —3B 104
Pepper La. Msde —1H 83
Pepper Rd. Leeds —4B 104
Pepper Royd St. Dew —7H 137
Percival St. B'frd —6C 80 (4J 7)
Percival St. Leeds —4H 85 (4D 4)
Percy St. Bgly —1A 60
Percy St. Hud —7G 145
Percy St. Kei —7K 39
Percy St. Leeds —7D 84
Percy St. Q'bry —4G 95
Peregrine Av. Morl —3D 120
Peridot Fold. Far —7J 145
*Perkin La. B'frd —3B 62 (off Far Crook)*
Per La. Hal —7B 94
Perry Clo. Kei —1J 57
Perseverance La. B'frd —3G 97
Perseverance Rd. Hal —3E 94
Perseverance St. Bail —7K 43
Perseverance St. C'frd —7C 126
Perseverance St. Hal —3E 130
Perseverance St. Pud —6A 82
Perseverance St. Sower B —3K 129
Perseverance St. Wyke —3J 115
Perseverance Ter. Bat —5G 137
Perseverance Ter. Rothw —3G 123
Perth Av. B'frd —2A 80
Perth Dri. Ting —7F 121
*Perth Ho. B'frd —1F 99 (off Parsonage Rd.)*
Perth Mt. H'fth —7F 47
Peterborough Pl. B'frd —2D 80
Peterborough Rd. B'frd —3D 80
Peterborough Ter. B'frd —2D 80
Petergate. B'frd —6B 80 (4F 7)
Peter Hill. Bat —6H 137
Peterhouse Dri. Otley —3A 28
Peter La. Hal —1K 129
Peter La. Morl —2D 120
Petersfield Av. Leeds —7A 104
Petersgarth. Shipl —4E 60
Pether Hill. Slnd —6D 142
Petrel Way. Morl —4C 120
Petrie Cres. Leeds —7B 64
Petrie Gro. B'frd —6G 81
Petrie Rd. B'frd —6G 81
Petrie St. Leeds —7B 64
Peverell Clo. B'frd —3G 99
Peveril Mt. B'frd —2E 80
Pheasant Dri. Birs —4E 118
Pheasant St. Kei —3B 40
Philip Ho. Leeds —4A 4
Philippa Way. Leeds —3C 102
Phillips St. C'frd —7B 126
*Phil May Ct. Leeds —7E 84 (off Green La.)*
Philpotts Pl. Kei —6K 39
Phipp Av. Leeds —1B 86
Phipp Ho. Sils —1G 21
Phoebe La. Hal —4H 131
Phoebe La. Ind. Est. Hal —4H 131
Phoenix Bldgs. B'frd —7J 79 (6A 6)
Phoenix St. Brigh —6H 133
Phoenix Way. B'frd —7G 81
Piccadilly. B'frd —6A 80 (3D 6)
Pickard Bank. Leeds —7F 67
Pickard Ct. Leeds —5A 88
Pickard La. Sils —7G 9
Pickard Way. Dew —7F 137
Pickering Av. Gar —5B 90
Pickering Dri. Oss —7C 138
Pickering La. Oss —7C 138
Pickering Mt. Leeds —5D 84
Pickerings, The. Q'bry —6J 95
Pickering St. Leeds —5D 84
Pickersgill St. Oss —7C 138
Picklesfield. Bat —6F 137
**Pickles Hill. —4F 97**
Pickles La. B'frd —4F 97
Pickles St. Bat —6F 137
Pickles St. Kei —6K 39
Pickpocket La. Rothw —7J 105
Pickwood La. Norl —6C 130
**Pickwood Scar. —6C 130**
Picton St. B'frd —4K 79
Piece Hall Yd. B'frd —6A 80 (4E 6)
Piece Wood Rd. Leeds —1H 65
Pigeon Cote Clo. Leeds —6J 69
Pigeon Cote Rd. Leeds —6J 69
Piggott St. Brigh —5G 133
Pigman La. Hal —2J 129
Pilden La. E Ard —2J 139
Pilot St. Leeds —4A 86 (3J 5)
Pinder Av. Leeds —2K 101
**Pinder Green. —6G 125**
Pinder Gro. Leeds —2K 101
Pinders Grn. Ct. Meth —6G 125
Pinders Grn. Dri. Meth —6G 125
Pinders Grn. Fold. Meth —6G 125
Pinders Grn. Wlk. Meth —7G 125
Pinder St. Leeds —2K 101
Pinder Vw. Leeds —2K 101
Pine Clo. Weth —2J 17
Pine Ct. Leeds —6K 85 (7G 5)
Pine Cft. Kei —2J 39
Pinedale. Bgly —6K 41
Pine Gro. Bat —4F 137
*Pinehurst Ct. Lind —7B 144 (off Lidget St.)*
Pines Gdns. I'ly —6K 11
Pine St. B'frd —6B 80 (3G 7)
Pine St. Hal —2G 131
Pine St. Haw —6E 56
Pine Tree Av. B Spa —2E 36
Pinewood Clo. I'ly —6A 12
Pinewood Gdns. Holy G —5F 143
Pinfold Clo. Bklnd —4J 141
Pinfold Clo. Mick M —4J 125
Pinfold Ct. Leeds —5K 87
Pinfold Gro. Leeds —5J 87
Pinfold Hill. Leeds —5K 87
Pinfold La. A'ley —6B 84
Pinfold La. Cook —5J 47
Pinfold La. Ell —3D 144
Pinfold La. Gar —6K 89
Pinfold La. Leeds —5J 87
Pinfold La. Meth —4J 125
Pinfold La. Sower B —4F 129
Pinfold Mt. Leeds —6K 87
Pinfold Ri. Aber —4E 72
Pinfold Rd. Leeds —6K 87
Pinfold Sq. Leeds —5J 87
Pin Hill La. Hal —6F 111
Pink St. Haw —7E 56
Pinnar Cft. Hal —4A 132
Pinnar La. Hal —3K 131
Pipe & Nook La. Leeds —6K 83
Pipercroft. B'frd —1E 114
Piper La. Otley —3H 27
Pipit Mdw. Morl —4C 120
Pippins Grn. Av. K'gte —6H 139
Pirie Clo. B'frd —2B 80
Pitchstone Ct. Leeds —6H 83
Pitcliffe Way. B'frd —2B 98
Pitfall St. Leeds —6J 85 (7F 5)
Pit Fld. Rd. Carl —5F 123
Pit La. B'frd —6C 80
Pit La. Butt —7F 97
Pit La. Dew —6D 136
Pit La. Gom —5K 117
Pit La. Meth —3H 125
Pit La. M'fld —2E 108 (in two parts)
Pit La. Q'bry —3G 95
Pit Row. Leeds —6J 85 (7E 4)
Pits La. Schol —2A 134
Pitt Hill La. Bklnd —7A 142
Pitt Row. Leeds —7E 4
Pitts St. B'frd —2F 99
Pitt St. Kei —4B 40
Pitt St. Liv —6K 135
Place's Rd. Leeds —6A 86
Plaid Row. Leeds —5A 86 (6K 5)
Plain La. Sower B —6E 128
Plains La. Ell —1K 143
Plane Tree Av. Leeds —7B 50
Plane Tree Clo. Leeds —7B 50
Plane Tree Cft. Leeds —7B 50
Plane Tree Gdns. Leeds —7B 50
Plane Tree Gro. Yead —5B 46
Plane Tree Nest. Hal —2C 130
Plane Tree Nest La. Hal —2C 130
Plane Tree Ri. Leeds —7B 50
Plane Tree Rd. Sower B —3K 129
Plane Trees Clo. Cleck —4F 117
Planetrees Rd. B'frd —7E 80
Planetrees St. All —4A 78
Plane Tree Vw. Leeds —7B 50
Plantation Av. Leeds —6H 87
Plantation Av. Shad —6C 50
Plantation Gdns. Leeds —6C 50
Plantation Pl. B'frd —2F 99
Plantation Way. Bail —1K 61
*Platt Sq. Cleck —1F 135 (off Westgate)*
Playfair Rd. Leeds —4K 103
Playground. Leeds —3H 101
Pleasance, The. Swil —5E 106
*Pleasant Ct. Leeds —2G 85 (off Rampart Rd.)*
Pleasant Mt. Leeds —1G 103
Pleasant Pl. All —4A 78
Pleasant Pl. Leeds —1G 103
Pleasant Row. Q'bry —6G 95
Pleasant St. B'frd —2G 97
Pleasant St. Leeds —1G 103
Pleasant St. Sower B —4A 130
Pleasant Ter. Leeds —1G 103
Pleasant Vw. Loft —7B 122
Pleasant Vw. L'ft —6E 110
Pleasant Views. Denh —4C 76
*Pleasant Vw. Ter. Rothw —3D 122 (off Copley La.)*
Plevna St. Leeds —4C 104
Plevna Ter. Bgly —7K 41
Plimsoll St. B'frd —2C 98
Ploughcroft La. Hal —5F 113
Ploughman's Cft. B'frd —1A 80
Plover Dri. Bat —3D 136
Plover St. B'frd —3J 97
Plover St. Kei —3A 40
Plover Way. Morl —4C 120
Plumpton Av. B'frd —6B 62
Plumpton Clo. B'frd —7C 62
Plumpton Dri. B'frd —6B 62
Plumpton End. B'frd —6C 62
Plumpton Gdns. B'frd —6A 62
Plumpton Lea. B'frd —6B 62
Plumpton Mead. B'frd —6B 62
Plumpton St. B'frd —5G 79
Plumpton Wlk. B'frd —6B 62
Plum St. Hal —2D 130
Plum St. Kei —1J 57
*Plymouth Gro. Hal —7E 112 (off Diamond St.)*
Poets Pl. H'fth —2G 65
*Pogson's Cotts. Leeds —7K 69 (off York Rd.)*
Pohlman St. Hal —3D 130
Pole Rd. Sut Cr —3A 38
Pollard Av. Bgly —6B 42
Pollard Av. Gom —6K 117
Pollard Clo. Gom —6K 117
Pollard La. B'frd —4D 80
Pollard La. Leeds —6F 65
Pollard St. Bgly —6B 60
Pollard St. B'frd —1B 98 (7F 7)
Pollard St. Hud —7H 145
Pollard St. N. Hal —7H 113
Pollard Way. Gom —6K 117
Pollit Av. Sower B —5G 129
Pomfret Pl. Gar —5B 90
Ponderosa Clo. Leeds —2B 86
Pondfields Clo. Kip —5B 108
Pondfields Crest. Kip —4B 108
Pondfields Dri. Kip —4B 108
Pondfields Ri. Kip —4B 108
Pond St. Kei —4A 40
Pond Ter. Brigh —3E 132
Pontefract Av. Leeds —6B 86
Pontefract La. Leeds —5B 86 (6K 5)
Pontefract La. Clo. Leeds —6B 86
Pontefract Rd. C'frd —7E 126
Pontefract Rd. Leeds —4C 104
Pontefract Rd. Rothw —6F 105
Pontefract St. Leeds —6B 86
**Pool. —3G 29**
Pool Bank Clo. Pool W —3H 29
Pool Bank Ct. Pool W —4H 29
Pool Bank New Rd. B'hpe & Pool W —6F 29
Pool Ct. B'frd —6C 80 (3J 7)
Poole Cres. Leeds —3K 87
Poole Mt. Leeds —4K 87
Poole Rd. Leeds —3K 87
Poole Sq. Leeds —4K 87
Pool Rd. Otley —2A 28
Pool St. Kei —2C 40
Popeley Rd. Heck —2A 136
Pope St. Kei —3B 40
Poplar Av. B'frd —4F 97
Poplar Av. C'frd —7J 127
Poplar Av. Gar —6J 89
Poplar Av. Leeds —3B 88
Poplar Av. Shipl —7J 61
Poplar Av. Sower B —3A 130
Poplar Av. Weth —2H 17
Poplar Clo. Bur W —2B 26
Poplar Clo. Leeds —5K 83
Poplar Ct. B'frd —7H 79
Poplar Ct. Leeds —5J 83
Poplar Cres. Hal —7D 94
Poplar Cres. Shipl —6J 61
Poplar Cres. Ting —6C 120
Poplar Cft. Leeds —5J 83
Poplar Dri. H'fth —4D 64
Poplar Dri. Sandb —4G 41
Poplar Dri. Shipl —7J 61
Poplar Gdns. Leeds —5J 83
Poplar Gth. Leeds —5J 83
Poplar Ga. Leeds —5J 83
Poplar Grn. Leeds —5J 83
Poplar Gro. Bail —3E 60
Poplar Gro. B'frd —4E 96
Poplar Gro. Cleck —2D 134
Poplar Gro. H'den —3E 58
Poplar Gro. Shipl —7J 61
Poplar Mt. Leeds —5J 83
Poplar Pl. Pud —6K 81
Poplar Ri. Leeds —4J 83
Poplar Rd. B'frd —4G 97
Poplar Rd. Shipl —7J 61
Poplars Pk. Rd. B'frd —1A 80
Poplar Sq. Fars —3B 82
Poplars, The. B'hpe —1K 47
Poplars, The. Guis —1G 45
Poplars, The. Leeds —1E 84
Poplars, The. Loft —7E 122
Poplars, The. Nor G —5G 115
Poplar St. Bkby —7G 145
Poplar St. Hal —7G 113
*Poplar Ter. Kei —4J 39 (off W. Leeds St.)*
Poplar Ter. Sandb —4H 41
Poplar Vw. B'frd —4E 96
Poplar Vw. Hal —2G 133
Poplar Vw. Leeds —5J 83
Poplar Way. Leeds —5J 83
Popples Dri. Hal —7D 94
Poppleton Ct. Ting —6E 120
Poppleton Dri. Ting —6E 120
Poppleton Ri. Ting —7E 120
Poppleton Rd. Ting —6E 120
Poppleton Way. Ting —6E 120
*Porritt St. Cleck —6F 117 (off Heaton St.)*
Portage Av. Leeds —6H 87
Portage Cres. Leeds —6G 87
Portal Cres. Mir —7J 135 (in two parts)
Portal Dri. Mir —7J 135
Portland Cres. Leeds —5H 85 (5D 4)
Portland Ga. Leeds —4H 85 (4D 4) (in two parts)
*Portland Ho. B'frd —7F 81 (off Fearnville Dri.)*
*Portland Ho. Ell —2K 143 (off Huddersfield Rd.)*
Portland Pl. Bgly —2A 60
Portland Rd. Hal —7H 113
Portland Rd. Leeds —7C 84
Portland St. B'frd —7A 80 (6E 6)
Portland St. Hal —2G 131
Portland St. Haw —5F 57
Portland St. Leeds —5H 85 (5C 4)
Portland St. Pud —5E 82
Portland Way. Leeds —4H 85 (4D 4)
Portman St. C'ley —6K 63
Portsmouth Av. B'frd —4C 80
Portwood St. B'frd —3D 78
Post Hill Ct. Leeds —6H 83
Post Office Rd. B'frd —7E 62
Post Office St. Rawf —2H 135
Pothouse Rd. B'frd —6H 97
Pot La. Steet —5E 20
Potter Brow Rd. Bail —4J 43
**Potternewton. —1A 86**
Potternewton Av. Leeds —6H 67
Potternewton Ct. Leeds —6J 67
Potternewton Cres. Leeds —7H 67
Potternewton Gro. Leeds —6H 67
Potternewton Heights. Leeds —6J 67
Potternewton La. Leeds —6G 67
Potternewton Mt. Leeds —6H 67
Potternewton Vw. Leeds —6H 67
**Potterton. —1J 71**
Potterton Clo. Bar E —4J 71
*Potterton Ct. Bar E —4J 71 (off Potterton Clo.)*
Potterton Hall. —1K 71
Potterton La. Pot —2J 71
**Pottery Field. —1K 103**
Pottery La. W'ford —7B 106
Pottery Rd. Leeds —2K 103
Pottery St. C'frd —7B 126
Poulton Pl. Leeds —3J 103
Poverty La. Sower B —7C 128
Powell Av. B'frd —2J 97
Powell Rd. Bgly —1B 60
Powell Rd. Shipl —7K 61
Powell St. C'frd —7D 126
Powell St. Hal —1G 131 (in two parts)
Powell St. Heck —5C 136
Poxon Ct. Leeds —6A 48
Poxon Grn. Gar —6J 89
Poxon La. B'frd —6K 79
Poxon Yd. Leeds —4K 69
Pratt La. Shipl —6J 61
Premiere Pk. I'ly —6J 11
Prescott St. Hal —2G 131
Prescott Ter. All —4B 78
Preston La. Hal —6A 112 (in two parts)
Preston La. W'ford & All B —7J 107
Preston Pde. Leeds —4G 103
Preston Pl. Hal —1E 130
Preston St. Bat —4G 137
Preston St. B'frd —6J 79 (4A 6)
*Preston Ter. Bgly —6K 41 (off Sleningford Rd.)*
Preston Vw. Swil —5F 107
Prestwich Dri. Hud —6F 145
Prestwick Clo. Otley —4F 27
Pretoria Rd. B'frd —6F 81
Pretoria St. C'frd —7E 126
Pretoria Ter. Hal —7B 112
Priest Bank Rd. Kild —2A 20
**Priest Hill. —1H 17**
Priest Hill Gdns. Weth —2H 17
**Priesthorpe. —1A 82**
Priesthorpe Av. S'ley —3K 81
Priesthorpe Ct. Fars —1B 82
Priesthorpe La. Fars —2K 81
Priesthorpe Rd. Fars —1J 81 (in two parts)
Priest La. Ripp —5G 141
Priestley Av. B'frd —6J 97
Priestley Av. Heck —2B 136
Priestley Clo. Pud —5D 82
Priestley Dri. Pud —4D 82
Priestley Gdns. Heck —3A 136
Priestley Gdns. Pud —5D 82
**Priestley Green. —6D 114**
Priestley Hill. Q'bry —1G 113

Priestley Pl. Sower B —5J 129
Priestley Sq. Birs —5C 118
Priestley St. B'frd —5B 80 (2F 7)
Priestley St. T'tn —7H 77
Priestley Ter. B'frd —5J 97
Priestley Theatre, The. —4G 7
Priestley Vw. Pud —5D 82
Priestley Wlk. Pud —5D 82
Priestman Clo. B'frd —4J 79
Priestman St. B'frd —4J 79 (1A 6)
**Priestthorpe. —7A 42**
Priestthorpe Clo. Bgly —7A 42
Priestthorpe La. Bgly —7A 42
Priestthorpe Rd. Bgly —1A 60
Primitive St. Carl —4F 123
Primley Gdns. Leeds —7J 49
Primley Pk. Av. Leeds —7J 49
Primley Pk. Clo. Leeds —7K 49
Primley Pk. Ct. Leeds —6J 49
Primley Pk. Cres. Leeds —7J 49
Primley Pk. Dri. Leeds —7J 49
Primley Pk. Gth. Leeds —6K 49
Primley Pk. Grn. Leeds —6K 49
Primley Pk. Gro. Leeds —7J 49
Primley Pk. La. Leeds —7J 49
Primley Pk. Mt. Leeds —7K 49
Primley Pk. Ri. Leeds —7K 49
Primley Pk. Rd. Leeds —7J 49
Primley Pk. Vw. Leeds —6J 49
Primley Pk. Wlk. Leeds —6K 49
Primley Pk. Way. Leeds —6J 49
Primrose Av. Leeds —5J 87
Primrose Av. Swil —5F 107
Primrose Bank. Bgly —2B 60
Primrose Clo. Leeds —5J 87
*Primrose Ct. Guis —2G 45*
*(off Orchard Way)*
Primrose Ct. Leeds —6K 49
Primrose Cres. Leeds —4J 87
Primrose Dri. Bgly —2B 60
Primrose Dri. Leeds —5J 87
Primrose Gdns. Leeds —4J 87
Primrose Gth. Leeds —5H 87
Primrose Gro. Kei —4C 40
Primrose Gro. Leeds —4J 87
Primrose Hill. Bat —2H 137
Primrose Hill. Bgly —3C 60
Primrose Hill. S'ley —4C 82
Primrose Hill Clo. Swil —5F 107
Primrose Hill Dri. Swil —5F 107
Primrose Hill Gdns. Swil —5F 107
Primrose Hill Gth. Swil —6F 107
Primrose Hill Grn. Swil —6F 107
Primrose Hill Gro. Swil —5F 107
Primrose La. Bgly —3B 60
Primrose La. B Spa —3C 36
Primrose La. B'frd —1K 79
Primrose La. Halt —5H 87
(in three parts)
Primrose La. Leeds —3J 103
Primrose La. Liv —3H 135
Primrose Rd. Leeds —5J 87
Primrose Row. Bail —7B 44
Primrose St. B'frd —5J 79
Primrose St. Kei —4C 40
Primrose Wlk. Chur —6C 102
Primrose Way. Hal —7D 96
Primrose Yd. Oult —2A 124
Prince Albert Sq. Q'bry —4B 96
Prince Edward Gro. Leeds —2A 102
Prince Edward Rd. Leeds —2A 102
Prince Henry Rd. Otley —7J 15
**Prince Royd. —7C 144**
Princeroyd Way. B'frd —6G 79
Princes Av. Leeds —5D 68
Prince's Ct. Leeds —3J 67
Prince's Cres. B'frd —2A 80
Prince's Ga. Hal —4F 131
Prince's Gro. Leeds —7D 66
Princess Ct. Colt —7B 88
Princess Ct. Leeds —1K 67
Princess Fields. Colt —7B 88
*Princess Gdns. Dew —7F 137*
*(off Halliley St.)*
Princess Rd. I'ly —6A 12
Princess St. Bat —2G 137
Princess St. C'frd —6E 126
Princess St. G'lnd —2H 143
Princess St. Hal —1G 131
Princess St. Rawd —7J 45
Princess St. Sower B —4A 130
Prince's St. B'frd —6H 97
(nr. Pothouse Rd.)
*Prince's St. B'frd —5J 97*
*(off Horsley St.)*
Prince's St. Butt —7E 96
Princes St. Heck —4C 136
Prince St. All B —7K 107
Prince St. Bat —2G 137
Prince St. B'frd —5E 98
Prince St. Haw —6F 57
Prince St. Sils —1F 21
Prince's Way. B'frd —7A 80 (5D 6)
**Princeville. —6G 79**
Princeville Rd. B'frd —6G 79
Princeville St. B'frd —6H 79
Prince Wood La. Hud —7C 144
Prior St. Kei —3C 40
Priory Clo. Bgly —7A 42
Priory Clo. Weth —2K 17
Priory Ct. Bgly —7A 42
Priory Ct. B'frd —5K 79 (1B 6)
Priory Gro. Bgly —7A 42
*Priory Ho. B'frd —5E 62*
*(off Cavendish Rd.)*
Priory Rd. Brigh —7J 133
Privilege St. Leeds —7B 84
Procter Ter. B'frd —5F 99
Proctor St. B'frd —5F 99
Prod La. Bail —2E 60
Progress Av. H'den —3E 58
Prospect Av. Hal —4C 130
Prospect Av. Leeds —2G 83
Prospect Av. Pud —5B 82
Prospect Av. Shipl —5J 61
Prospect Bank. B'ham —7D 36
Prospect Clo. Hal —4C 130
Prospect Clo. Shipl —5J 61
Prospect Ct. Hal —7K 111
Prospect Ct. T'ner —6D 52
Prospect Cres. Kei —6G 39
Prospect Cres. Leeds —3K 103
Prospect Dri. Kei —6G 39
Prospect Gdns. Leeds —5K 87
Prospect Gro. Pud —5B 82
Prospect Gro. Shipl —5J 61
Prospect La. B'shaw —2K 117
Prospect Mt. Kei —6G 39
Prospect Mt. Shipl —5J 61
Prospect Pl. B'frd —4F 79
Prospect Pl. Brigh —6G 133
Prospect Pl. Eccl —3E 80
Prospect Pl. Hal —4D 112
Prospect Pl. H'fth —4F 65
Prospect Pl. Leeds —2G 83
Prospect Pl. Loft —5D 122
*Prospect Pl. Nor G —5G 115*
*(off Village St.)*
Prospect Pl. Q'bry —5J 95
Prospect Pl. Rothw —3H 123
Prospect Rd. Bgly —6C 42
Prospect Rd. B'frd —5B 80 (1G 7)
(in two parts)
Prospect Rd. Bur W —2A 26
Prospect Rd. Cleck —7F 117
Prospect Rd. Harts —7F 135
Prospect Rd. Heck —2A 136
Prospect Row. Broc —7A 94
Prospect Row. Bur W —4J 25
Prospect Row. Hal —4D 112
Prospect Sq. Fars —3B 82
Prospect St. Bat —2G 137
Prospect St. B'frd —1B 98 (7G 7)
Prospect St. Butt —7F 97
Prospect St. Cleck —1F 135
Prospect St. Eccl —7E 62
Prospect St. Far —2B 82
Prospect St. Hal —7H 113
Prospect St. Haw —6E 56
Prospect St. Kei —5H 39
Prospect St. Pud —5A 82
Prospect St. Rawd —1A 64
Prospect St. Shipl —5J 61
Prospect St. T'tn —7J 77
Prospect Ter. All —4C 78
Prospect Ter. Bmly —2G 83
Prospect Ter. Cleck —7F 117
Prospect Ter. Fars —3B 82
Prospect Ter. H'fth —3G 65
Prospect Ter. Leeds —6B 86
Prospect Ter. Liv —4H 135
Prospect Ter. L'ft —5E 94
Prospect Ter. M'fld —7G 91
Prospect Ter. Rod —7C 64
Prospect Ter. Rothw —3H 123
Prospect Vw. Leeds —2G 83
Prospect Vw. Liv —6F 135
Prospect Vs. Weth —3J 17
Prospect Wlk. Shipl —5J 61
Prosper St. Leeds —2A 104
Providence Av. Bail —7J 43
Providence Av. Leeds —1G 85
*Providence Bldgs. Hal —4A 132*
*(off New St.)*
Providence Ct. Morl —2A 120
(nr. Victoria Rd.)
Providence Ct. Morl —4B 120
(nr. Wide La.)
*Providence Ct. Morl —2A 120*
*(off Troy Rd.)*
Providence Ct. Oakw —2E 56
Providence Cres. Oakw —2E 56
Providence Hill. Slnd —6C 142
Providence La. Oakw —2E 56
Providence Pl. All B —4B 126
Providence Pl. Brigh —7J 133
Providence Pl. Gar —6J 89
Providence Pl. Leeds —4J 85 (3E 4)
Providence Pl. Morl —3J 119
Providence Pl. S'ley —4C 82
Providence Pl. Swil C —7E 88
Providence Pl. Wyke —3J 115
Providence Rd. Leeds —1G 85
Providence Row. Bail —7J 43
Providence Row. E Mor —1J 41
Providence Row. Hal —7A 94
Providence Row. Oven —4D 112
Providence St. Bat —3G 137
Providence St. B'frd —6K 79 (4C 6)
Providence St. Cleck —7G 117
Providence St. Ell —2K 143
Providence St. Fars —3B 82
(in two parts)
Providence St. Schol —6A 116
Providence Ter. Leeds —2G 85
Providence Ter. T'tn —7H 77
Providence Vs. Schol —6A 116
Prune Pk. La. All —2J 77
**Pudsey. —7B 82**
Pudsey Bus. Cen. Pud —6D 82
Pudsey Rd. Leeds —6F 83
Pule Grn. La. Hal —4F 113
**Pule Hill. —4F 113**
Pullan Av. B'frd —1D 80
Pullan Dri. B'frd —1E 80
Pullan Gro. B'frd —1E 80
Pullan La. Esh —6E 44
Pullan St. B'frd —1K 97
Pulmans Pl. Hal —6G 131
Pulmans Yd. Hal —6G 131
Pump La. Hal —7K 113
Pump La. Wake —3E 138
Pump St. B'frd —1F 99
*Purbeck Ct. H Wd —4G 99*
*(off Dorchester Cres.)*
Purbeck Gro. Gar —7K 89
Purcell Dri. Sils —7F 9
Purley Wlk. B'frd —6H 97
Purlwell Av. Bat —5F 137
Purlwell Cres. Bat —5F 137
Purlwell Hall Rd. Bat —5G 137
Purlwell La. Bat —4G 137
**Pye Nest. —3C 130**
Pye Nest Av. Hal —3B 130
Pye Nest Dri. Hal —4C 130
Pye Nest Gdns. Hal —3C 130
Pye Nest Gro. Hal —3C 130
Pye Nest Ri. Hal —4C 130
Pye Nest Rd. Sower B —4B 130
Pyenot Av. Cleck —1G 135
Pyenot Dri. Cleck —2G 135
Pyenot Gdns. Cleck —2G 135
Pyenot Hall La. Cleck —1G 135
Pymont Ct. Loft —6E 122
Pymont Dri. W'ford —7J 105
Pymont Gro. W'ford —7K 105
Pym St. Leeds —1K 103
Pynate Rd. Bat —2E 136
Pyrah Fold. Wyke —3J 115
Pyrah Rd. Low M —7K 97
Pyrah St. Dew —7G 137
Pyrah St. Wyke —3K 115

QBM Bus. Pk. Bat —5D 118
Q.M. Ind. Pk. Hud —7K 145
Quail St. Kei —3B 40
Quaker La. B'frd —3H 97
Quaker La. Cleck & Liv —1F 135
Quakers La. Rawd —6K 45
Quakers La. Ripp —7F 141
Quarrie Dene Ct. Leeds —6J 67
Quarry Bank Ct. Leeds —6K 65
Quarry Cotts. H'fth —3F 65
*Quarry Ct. Brigh —3E 132*
*(off Spout Ho. La.)*
Quarry Dene. Leeds —4D 66
Quarry Farm Rd. Pool W —5E 28
Quarryfield Ter. E Ard —1K 139
Quarry Gdns. Leeds —5G 49
**Quarry Hill. —5K 85 (6H 5)**
*Quarry Hill. Far —2B 82*
*(off Wesley St.)*
Quarry Hill. Sower B —5K 129
Quarry Hill. W'ford —2A 124
Quarry Hill La. Weth —2H 17
(in two parts)
Quarry Ho. Leeds —5A 86 (6J 5)
Quarry La. Bat —7D 118
Quarry La. Dew —2A 138
Quarry La. Morl —5B 120
Quarry Mt. Leeds —1G 85
*Quarry Mt. Yead —4A 46*
*(off King St.)*
Quarry Mt. Pl. Leeds —1G 85
Quarry Mt. St. Leeds —1G 85
Quarry Mt. Ter. Leeds —1G 85
Quarry Pl. B'frd —3D 80
Quarry Pl. Leeds —2G 85
Quarry Rd. Brigh —2G 145
Quarry Rd. Cleck —1F 135
Quarry Rd. Gom —1K 135
Quarry Rd. Hal —5C 112
Quarry Rd. Liv —4J 135
Quarry Rd. Pool W —5E 28
Quarry Rd. W'ford —1B 124
Quarry St. H'tn —1G 79
Quarry St. Kei —4B 40
Quarry St. Leeds —2G 85
Quarry Ter. H'fth —3F 65
Quarry, The. Leeds —5G 49
Quarry Vw. Dew —7D 136
Quayside. Shipl —4H 61
Quayside, The. App B —4G 63
Quebec St. B'frd —7A 80 (5D 6)
Quebec St. Ell —2A 144
Quebec St. Kei —5K 39
Quebec St. Leeds —6H 85 (6D 4)
Queen's Arc. Leeds —5J 85 (6E 4)
Queen's Av. B'frd —2B 80
**Queensbury. —5J 95**
Queensbury Rd. Hal —3F 113
Queensbury Sq. Q'bry —5J 95
Queens Clo. Bgly —2B 60
Queen's Clo. Leeds —4J 67
Queens Ct. Bgly —1K 59
*Queens Ct. Gom —5K 117*
*(off Queen St.)*
Queen's Ct. Leeds —7F 5
Queens Ct. Moort —3J 67
Queens Ct. Shipl —5F 61
Queens Dri. Carl —4F 123
Queens Dri. Hal —4A 132
Queen's Dri. I'ly —6K 11
Queens Dri. Pud —5B 82
Queen's Dri. Wren —7K 139
Queen's Dri. La. I'ly —6K 11
Queen's Gdns. I'ly —6A 12
Queensgate. B'frd —6A 80 (4E 6)
Queen's Ga. Hal —4F 131
Queen's Gro. Kei —6K 39
Queens Gro. Morl —4K 119
Queenshill App. Leeds —2J 67
Queenshill Av. Leeds —2J 67
Queenshill Clo. Leeds —2J 67
Queenshill Ct. Leeds —2J 67
Queenshill Cres. Leeds —1J 67
Queenshill Dri. Leeds —2H 67
Queenshill Gdns. Leeds —2H 67
Queenshill Gth. Leeds —2J 67
*Queenshill Lawn. Leeds —2J 67*
*(off Queenshill App.)*
Queenshill Rd. Leeds —2J 67
Queenshill Vw. Leeds —2J 67
Queenshill Wlk. Leeds —2J 67
Queenshill Way. Leeds —2J 67
Queens Mead. N'wram —4A 114
Queens Pde. Guis —2F 45
Queen's Pk. Clo. C'frd —7H 127
Queen's Pk. Dri. C'frd —7G 127
Queen's Pl. Otley —3J 27
Queen's Pl. Shipl —4F 61
Queen's Promenade. Morl —2A 120
Queen Sq. Leeds —4J 85 (4D 4)
Queen's Ri. B'frd —2B 80
Queen's Rd. Bgly —5J 41
Queen's Rd. B Spa —2C 36
Queen's Rd. B'frd —3B 80
(BD2)
Queen's Rd. B'frd —3K 79
(BD8)
Queen's Rd. Hal —1D 130
Queen's Rd. I'ly —6A 12
Queen's Rd. Kei —7J 39
Queen's Rd. Leeds —3E 84
Queens Rd. Morl —4K 119
Queen's Rd. Nor G —5F 115
Queen's Rd. Shipl —4F 61
Queens Ter. Otley —3J 27
Queensthorpe Av. Leeds —5H 83
Queensthorpe Clo. Leeds —5J 83
Queensthorpe Ri. Leeds —5H 83
Queen St. Bail —3J 61
Queen St. Bgly —1K 59
Queen St. Butt —7E 96
Queen St. Carl —4F 123
Queen St. C'frd —6E 126
Queen St. Cull —6B 58
Queen St. E Ard —7K 121
Queen St. Gom —5K 117
Queen St. Gre —5F 63
Queen St. G'lnd —3G 143
Queen St. Haw —6E 56
Queen St. Heck —5A 136
Queen St. H'let —4C 104
Queen St. Leeds —6G 85 (6B 4)
Queen St. Mar —2G 135
Queen St. Morl —2A 120
(in two parts)
Queen St. Myth —7A 110
Queen St. Rawd —7K 45
Queen St. Sils —1G 21
Queen St. Sower B —5G 129
Queen St. Steet —5E 20
Queen St. Wilsd —1G 77
Queen St. W'ford —1J 125
Queensview. Leeds —7K 69
Queen's Wlk. Leeds —6A 66
Queensway. Bgly —1B 60
Queensway. Gar —6H 89
Queensway. Guis & Yead —2G 45
Queensway. Hal —7D 112
*Queensway. Kei —4A 40*
*(off Airedale Shop. Cen.)*
Queensway. Leeds —5A 88
Queensway. Morl —3A 120
Queensway. Rothw —1G 123
Queenswood Clo. Leeds —6A 66
Queenswood Ct. Leeds —1C 84
Queenswood Dri. Leeds —5A 66
Queenswood Gdns. Leeds —1C 84
Queenswood Grn. Leeds —5A 66
Queenswood Heights. Leeds —7C 66
Queenswood Mt. Leeds —7B 66
Queenswood Ri. Leeds —7B 66
Queenswood Rd. Leeds —7B 66
Queen Victoria Cres. Hal —4B 114
Quincy Clo. B'frd —1E 80
Quinsworth St. B'frd —2D 98

Raby Av. Leeds —2K 85
**Raby Park. —3J 17**
Raby Pk. Weth —4H 17
Raby St. Leeds —2K 85
Raby Ter. Leeds —2K 85
Race Moor La. Oakw —1D 56
Rachel Grn. B'frd —2B 80
Radcliffe Av. B'frd —7C 62
Radcliffe Gdns. Pud —7C 82
Radcliffe Gro. Pud —7C 82
Radcliffe La. L'ft —5E 110
Radcliffe La. Pud —6C 82
Radcliffe Ter. Pud —7C 82
Radfield Dri. B'frd —5A 98
Radfield Rd. B'frd —5A 98
Radnor St. B'frd —6E 80
Radnor St. Leeds —7E 84
Radwell Dri. B'frd —1A 98 (7D 6)
Raeburn Dri. B'frd —7G 97
Rae Rd. Shipl —6H 61
Rafborn Av. Hud —7J 143
Rafborn Gro. Hud —7J 143
Raglan Av. Kei —5H 39
Raglan Clo. C'frd —7A 126
*Raglan Ct. Hal —1E 130*
*(off Raglan St.)*
Ragland Ind. Est. C'frd —7A 126
Raglan Dri. B'frd —6F 81
*Raglan Gdns. Hal —1E 130*
*(off Lister's Clo.)*
Raglan Rd. Leeds —2G 85 (1B 4)
(in two parts)
Raglan St. B'frd —6F 81
Raglan St. Hal —1E 130
Raglan St. Kei —5H 39
Raglan St. Q'bry —5K 95
Raglan Ter. B'frd —6G 81
Raikes La. Birs —5C 118
Raikes La. B'frd —4J 99
Raikes La. E Bier —6G 99
Raikes Wood Dri. E Bier —7G 99
Rail Balk La. Weth —2H 17
(in two parts)
Railes Clo. L'ft —6F 111
Railsfield Mt. Leeds —4G 83
Railsfield Ri. Leeds —4G 83
Railsfield Way. Leeds —3H 83
Railway Cotts. M'fld —7G 91
Railway Rd. C'gts —3A 88
(in two parts)
Railway Rd. Idle —4D 62
Railway Rd. I'ly —5B 12
Railway St. B'frd —5E 98
Railway St. Brigh —7H 133
Railway St. Cleck —1F 135
Railway St. Heck —5B 136
Railway St. Kei —2A 40
Railway St. Leeds —6A 86 (7J 5)
*Railway Ter. Brigh —6J 133*
*(off Clifton Comn.)*
Railway Ter. E Ard —6J 121
Railway Ter. Hal —6E 130
Railway Ter. Low M —2A 116
Railway Vw. C'frd —7B 126
Raincliffe Gro. Leeds —5C 86
Raincliffe Mt. Leeds —6C 86
Raincliffe Rd. Leeds —5C 86
Raincliffe St. Leeds —5C 86
Raincliffe Ter. Leeds —6C 86
*Rainton Ho. B'frd —2K 97*
*(off Park La.)*
Raistrick Way. Shipl —4K 61
Rakehill Rd. Bar E —5G 71
Rakehill Rd. Scholes —5D 70
(in three parts)
Raleigh St. Hal —3D 130
Rampart Rd. Leeds —2G 85
Ramsden Av. B'frd —1E 96
Ramsden Ct. B'frd —2G 97
Ramsden Pl. Cytn —1B 96
Ramsden St. Hal —5C 112
Ramsden St. Kip —6K 107
Ramsey St. B'frd —3K 97

**Ramsgate—Ripley Ter.**


Ramsgate. *Loft* —6D **122**
Ramsgate Cres. *Loft* —6D **122**
Ramsgate St. *Hal* —1D **130**
Ramshead App. *Leeds* —6J **69**
Ramshead Clo. *Leeds* —5J **69**
Ramshead Cres. *Leeds* —5H **69**
Ramshead Dri. *Leeds* —5H **69**
Ramshead Gdns. *Leeds* —5H **69**
Ramshead Gro. *Leeds* —6J **69**
Ramshead Heights. *Leeds* —6J **69**
(in two parts)
Ramshead Hill. *Leeds* —6J **69**
Ramshead Pl. *Leeds* —6J **69**
Ramshead Vw. *Leeds* —6J **69**
Randall Pl. *B'frd* —2G **79**
Randall Well St. *B'frd*
—7K **79** (5C **6**)
Randolph St. *B'frd* —5G **81**
Randolph St. *Hal* —6G **113**
Randolph St. *Leeds* —3E **82**
Random Clo. *Kei* —6H **39**
Rand Pl. *B'frd* —1J **97** (7A **6**)
Rand St. *B'frd* —1J **97** (7A **6**)
Ranelagh Av. *B'frd* —7G **63**
Range Bank. *Hal* —6G **113**
*Range Bank Top. Hal —6G **113***
*(off Range La.)*
*Range Ct. Hal —6G **113***
*(off All Saint's St.)*
Range Gdns. *Hal* —6G **113**
Range La. *Hal* —7G **113**
Ranger's Wlk. *M'fld* —3J **91**
Range St. *Hal* —6G **113**
Ransdale Dri. *B'frd* —3K **97**
Ransdale Gro. *B'frd* —3K **97**
Ransdale Rd. *B'frd* —3K **97**
Ranson St. *Dew* —6D **136**
Raper Vw. *Aber* —4E **72**
**Rastrick. —1F 145**
Rastrick Comn. *Brigh* —1G **145**
Rathlin Rd. *Dew* —6K **137**
Rathmell Rd. *Leeds* —6G **87**
Rathmell St. *B'frd* —5K **97**
Ratten Row Rd. *Sower B* —7E **128**
*Ravenham Wlk. B'frd —4G **99***
*(off Launceston Dri.)*
Raven Rd. *Leeds* —1E **84**
Ravenscar Av. *Leeds* —6C **68**
Ravenscar Mt. *Leeds* —6C **68**
Ravenscar Ter. *Leeds* —6C **68**
Ravenscar Vw. *Leeds* —6C **68**
Ravenscar Wlk. *Leeds* —6C **68**
**Ravenscliffe. —1G 81**
Ravenscliffe Av. *B'frd* —7F **63**
Ravenscliffe Rd. *C'ley* —6H **63**
Ravenscroft Rd. *Hal* —5F **131**
Ravens Mt. *Pud* —6D **82**
Ravenstone Dri. *G'lnd* —3G **143**
Ravenstone Gdns. *Sut Cr* —5A **20**
Raven St. *Bgly* —1K **59**
Raven St. *Hal* —1D **130**
Raven St. *Kei* —4K **39**
Ravensville. *Cro H* —4A **20**
Ravensworth Clo. *Leeds* —2D **88**
Ravensworth Way. *Leeds* —2D **88**
Raven Ter. *B'frd* —6C **78**
Rawden Hill. *Arth* —4E **30**
**Rawdon. —7A 46**
Rawdon Dri. *Rawd* —1K **63**
Rawdon Hall Dri. *Rawd* —1K **63**
Rawdon Rd. *Haw* —5E **56**
Rawdon Rd. *H'fth* —2C **64**
Rawdon St. *Kei* —5J **39**
Raw End Rd. *Hal* —6H **111**
**Rawfolds. —2H 135**
Rawfolds Av. *Birs* —5D **118**
Rawfolds Way. *Rawf* —2H **135**
Rawgate Av. *C'frd* —7A **126**
Raw Hill. *Brigh* —1F **145**
Raw La. *Hal* —2B **112**
Raw La. *Wadsw* —4A **110**
Rawling St. *Kei* —6K **39**
Rawling Way. *Leeds* —7G **67**
**Raw Nook. —1B 116**
Rawnook. *Low M* —2A **116**
*Rawnsley Ho. B'frd —2K **97***
*(off Manchester Rd.)*
Rawroyds. *G'lnd* —4G **143**
Rawson Av. *B'frd* —5F **81**
Rawson Av. *Hal* —5F **131**
Rawson Pl. *B'frd* —6A **80** (3D **6**)
Rawson Pl. *Sower B* —5J **129**
Rawson Rd. *B'frd* —6K **79** (3C **6**)
Rawson Sq. *B'frd* —6A **80** (3D **6**)
Rawson Sq. *Idle* —3D **62**
Rawson St. *Hal* —1G **131**
Rawson St. *Wyke* —3K **115**
Rawson St. N. *Hal* —6F **113**
Rawson Ter. *Leeds* —3J **103**
Rawson Wood. *Sower B* —6G **129**
Ray Ga. *H Bri* —7B **92**
Raygill Clo. *Leeds* —6D **50**
Raylands Clo. *Leeds* —1B **122**
Raylands Ct. *Leeds* —1B **122**
Raylands Fold. *Leeds* —1B **122**
Raylands Gth. *Leeds* —1B **122**
Raylands La. *Leeds* —1B **122**
Raylands Pl. *Leeds* —1B **122**
Raylands Rd. *Leeds* —1B **122**
Raylands Way. *Leeds* —2A **122**
Rayleigh St. *B'frd* —2C **98**
Raymond Dri. *B'frd* —4A **98**
Raymond St. *B'frd* —4A **98**
Raynbron Cres. *B'frd* —4B **98**
Raynel App. *Leeds* —1A **66**
Raynel Clo. *Leeds* —7K **47**
Raynel Dri. *Leeds* —1A **66**
Raynel Gdns. *Leeds* —7A **48**
Raynel Gth. *Leeds* —1A **66**
Raynel Grn. *Leeds* —1A **66**
Raynel Mt. *Leeds* —7A **48**
Raynel Way. *Leeds* —7K **47**
Rayner Av. *B'frd* —4F **79**
Rayner Av. *Heck* —2B **136**
Rayner Dri. *Brigh* —4G **133**
Rayner Mt. *All* —5A **78**
Rayner Rd. *Brigh* —4G **133**
Rayners Av. *Liv* —4E **134**
Raynham Cres. *Kei* —3G **39**
Raynville App. *Leeds* —3J **83**
Raynville Av. *Leeds* —2J **83**
Raynville Clo. *Leeds* —2J **83**
Raynville Ct. *Leeds* —3J **83**
Raynville Cres. *Leeds* —3K **83**
Raynville Dene. *Leeds* —2K **83**
Raynville Dri. *Leeds* —2J **83**
*Raynville Grange. Leeds —3J **83***
*(off Raynville Rd.)*
Raynville Grn. *Leeds* —3J **83**
Raynville Gro. *Leeds* —2J **83**
Raynville Mt. *Leeds* —2J **83**
Raynville Pl. *Leeds* —3J **83**
Raynville Ri. *Leeds* —3J **83**
Raynville Rd. *Leeds* —2H **83**
Raynville St. *Leeds* —2J **83**
Raynville Ter. *Leeds* —2J **83**
Raynville Wlk. *Leeds* —3J **83**
Raywood Clo. *Yead* —3J **45**
Reap Hirst Rd. *Hud* —7D **144**
Rebecca St. *B'frd* —5K **79** (2B **6**)
Recreation Cres. *Leeds* —2F **103**
Recreation Gro. *Leeds* —2F **103**
Recreation La. *Ell* —3J **143**
Recreation Mt. *Leeds* —2F **103**
Recreation Pl. *Leeds* —2F **103**
Recreation Rd. *Leeds* —4F **103**
Recreation Rd. *Sower B* —4A **130**
Recreation Row. *Leeds* —2F **103**
Recreation St. *Leeds* —2F **103**
Recreation Ter. *Leeds* —2F **103**
Recreation Vw. *Leeds* —2F **103**
Rectory Av. *C'frd* —7D **126**
Rectory Clo. *Gar* —6K **89**
Rectory Dri. *Bat* —6E **118**
Rectory Row. *Kei* —4K **39**
Rectory St. *C'frd* —7D **126**
Rectory St. *Leeds* —4A **86** (3K **5**)
Redbeck Cotts. *H'fth* —4C **64**
Red Beck Rd. *Hal* —6K **113**
Red Beck Va. *Shipl* —7G **61**
Red Brink La. *Sower B* —6D **128**
Red Brink Rd. *Sower B* —6D **128**
Redburn Av. *Shipl* —7G **61**
Redburn Dri. *Shipl* —7G **61**
Redburn Rd. *Shipl* —7H **61**
Redcar La. *Steet* —1D **38**
Redcar Rd. *B'frd* —6G **63**
Redcar St. *Hal* —1D **130**
Redcliffe Av. *Kei* —4J **39**
Redcliffe Gro. *Kei* —4J **39**
Redcliffe St. *Kei* —4J **39**
Redcote La. *Leeds* —5B **84**
(in two parts)
Red Doles La. *Hud* —7J **145**
Red Doles Rd. *Hud* —7J **145**
Redesdale Gdns. *Leeds* —1A **66**
Redfearn Av. *Heck* —3B **136**
Red Hall App. *Leeds* —3J **69**
Red Hall Av. *Leeds* —3H **69**
Red Hall Chase. *Leeds* —3J **69**
Redhall Clo. *Leeds* —5E **102**
Red Hall Ct. *Leeds* —3J **69**
Redhall Cres. *Leeds* —5E **102**
Red Hall Cft. *Leeds* —3J **69**
Red Hall Dri. *Leeds* —3J **69**
Red Hall Gdns. *Leeds* —3H **69**
Red Hall Gth. *Leeds* —3J **69**
Redhall Ga. *Leeds* —5E **102**
Red Hall Grn. *Leeds* —3J **69**
Red Hall La. *Leeds* —3H **69**
Red Hall Va. *Leeds* —4J **69**
Red Hall Vw. *Leeds* —3J **69**
Red Hall Wlk. *Leeds* —3J **69**
Red Hall Way. *Leeds* —3J **69**
**Red Hill. —7G 127**
Redhill Av. *Ting* —3E **138**
Redhill Clo. *Ting* —3E **138**
Redhill Cres. *Ting* —3E **138**
Redhill Dri. *C'frd* —7G **127**
Redhill Dri. *Ting* —3E **138**
Redhill Rd. *C'frd* —7G **127**
Redhouse La. *Leeds* —5A **68**
Red House Museum. —6K **117**
Red La. *Fars* —2A **82**
Red Lodge Clo. *Leeds* —1F **87**
Redman Clo. *Haw* —5D **56**
Redman Gth. *Haw* —5D **56**
Redmire Ct. *Leeds* —1J **87**
Redmire Dri. *Leeds* —1J **87**
Redmire St. *B'frd* —6G **81**
Redmire Vw. *Leeds* —1J **87**
Redshaw Rd. *Leeds* —7D **84**
Redvers Clo. *Leeds* —3A **66**
Redwood Av. *Ting* —7G **121**
Redwood Clo. *Kei* —6C **40**
Redwood Clo. *Rothw* —1C **124**
Redwood Clo. *Yead* —4J **45**
Redwood Dri. *Hud* —4K **145**
Redwood Gro. *Yead* —4H **45**
Redwood Way. *Yead* —4H **45**
Reedling Dri. *Morl* —4C **120**
Reed Rd. *Leeds* —7D **84**
Reedsdale Av. *Gild* —7G **101**
Reedsdale Dri. *Gild* —7G **101**
Reedsdale Gdns. *Gild* —7G **101**
Rees Way. *B'frd* —5B **80** (1G **7**)
Reeth Rd. *Brigh* —1E **144**
Reevy Av. *B'frd* —7F **97**
Reevy Cres. *B'frd* —7E **96**
Reevy Dri. *B'frd* —6G **97**
Reevylands Dri. *B'frd* —6G **97**
Reevy Rd. *B'frd* —6F **97**
Reevy Rd. W. *B'frd* —6D **96**
Reevy St. *B'frd* —5G **97**
*Reevy Yd. B'frd —6H **97***
*(off Green End Rd.)*
Reform St. *Gom* —6K **117**
Regal Pde. *Leeds* —3K **87**
Regency Ct. *B'frd* —5H **79**
Regency Ct. *Leeds* —1E **84**
Regency Gdns. *Ting* —7G **121**
Regency Pk. Gro. *Pud* —1C **100**
Regency Pk. Rd. *Pud* —1C **100**
Regency Vw. *B'frd* —3C **80**
Regent Av. *H'fth* —5G **65**
Regent Clo. *Brigh* —3E **144**
Regent Clo. *H'fth* —5G **65**
Regent Ct. *H'fth* —5G **65**
Regent Ct. *Leeds* —7F **5**
Regent Cres. *H'fth* —5F **65**
Regent Ho. *Ell* —2K **143**
Regent M. *Bat* —4K **137**
Regent Pk. Av. *Leeds* —1F **85**
*Regent Pk. Cross Av. Leeds —1F **85***
*(off Regent Pk. Av.)*
Regent Pk. Ter. *Leeds* —1F **85**
Regent Pl. *B'frd* —3C **62**
Regent Pl. *Sower B* —3K **129**
Regent Rd. *H'fth* —5F **65**
Regent Rd. *I'ly* —5A **12**
Regent St. *B'frd* —3C **62**
Regent St. *Chap A* —5K **67**
Regent St. *Gre* —5F **63**
Regent St. *Hal* —2G **131**
Regent St. *Haw* —5F **57**
Regent St. *Heck* —5A **136**
Regent St. *Leeds* —5K **85** (5H **5**)
Regent St. *Q'bry* —5K **95**
Regent Ter. *Chap A* —5K **67**
Regent Ter. *Leeds* —3F **85**
Regina Dri. *Leeds* —6K **67**
Regina Ho. *Leeds* —5H **83**
Reginald Mt. *Leeds* —1K **85**
Reginald Pl. *Leeds* —1K **85**
Reginald Row. *Leeds* —1K **85**
Reginald St. *B'frd* —3K **97**
Reginald St. *Leeds* —1K **85**
Reginald Ter. *Leeds* —1K **85**
Reginald Vw. *Leeds* —1K **85**
Reighton Cft. *B'frd* —6G **63**
Rein Ct. *Aber* —4E **72**
Rein Gdns. *Ting* —7C **120**
Rein M. *Ting* —7C **120**
Rein Rd. *H'fth* —6F **65**
(in two parts)
Rein Rd. *Morl & Ting* —6B **120**
Reins Av. *Bail* —3H **61**
Reins Rd. *Brigh* —1E **144**
Rein St. *Morl* —6C **120**
Rein, The. *Leeds* —6H **69**
Reinwood Av. *Leeds* —7F **69**
Rembrandt Av. *Wake* —7F **121**
Rembrant Av. *Wake* —7F **121**
Renee Clo. *B'frd* —6E **98**
Renshaw St. *B'frd* —3D **62**
Renton Av. *Guis* —2F **45**
Renton Dri. *Guis* —3F **45**
Renton Lea. *Guis* —3F **45**
Reservoir Pl. *Dew* —7E **136**
Reservoir Pl. *Q'bry* —4G **95**
Reservoir Rd. *Bat* —4D **136**
Reservoir Rd. *Hal* —7C **112**
Reservoir Rd. *Sower B* —1A **140**
Reservoir Rd. *Stanb* —5A **56**
Reservoir St. *Dew* —7E **136**
Reservoir Vw. *T'tn* —7G **77**
Restmore Av. *Guis* —7F **27**
Retford Pl. *B'frd* —1J **97** (7A **6**)
Reuben St. *Liv* —3J **135**
Reva Clo. *Bgly* —7B **42**
Reva Syke Rd. *Cytn* —3B **96**
Revie Rd. *Leeds* —3F **103**
Revie Rd. Ind. Est. *Leeds* —3F **103**
Reydon Wlk. *B'frd* —5F **97**
Reyhill Gro. *B'frd* —1A **98** (7E **6**)
Reyner Ho. M. *B'frd* —7E **6**
Reynolds Av. *B'frd* —1E **96**
Reynor Ho. M. *B'frd* —1A **98**
Rhine St. *B'frd* —1C **98**
Rhodes Av. *Heck* —2B **136**
Rhode's Hill La. *B'ham* —7E **36**
Rhodesia Av. *All* —5C **78**
Rhodesia Av. *Hal* —5G **131**
Rhodes La. *B Spa* —4B **36**
Rhodes Pl. *Shipl* —4H **61**
Rhodes St. *C'frd* —7C **126**
Rhodes St. *Hal* —1F **131**
Rhodes St. *Liv* —4A **136**
Rhodes St. *Shipl* —4G **61**
Rhodes Ter. *B'frd* —1D **80**
Rhodes Ter. *Leeds* —7E **84**
Rhodesway. *B'frd* —6D **78**
Rhondda Pl. *Hal* —2C **130**
Rhum Clo. *B'frd* —1F **115**
Rhyddings Gdns. *I'ly* —5D **12**
Rhylstone Mt. *B'frd* —6F **79**
*Ribble Ct. Sils —1G **21***
*(off Howden Rd.)*
Ribblesdale Av. *Gar* —7B **90**
Ribble St. *Kei* —3C **40**
Ribbleton Gro. *B'frd* —5C **80** (2J **7**)
Ribstone St. *H Bri* —6A **110**
Riccall Nook. *B'frd* —6F **63**
*Richard Pl. Brigh —4G **133***
*(off Richard St.)*
Richardshaw Dri. *S'ley* —4C **82**
Richardshaw La. *S'ley* —4C **82**
Richardshaw Rd. *S'ley* —4C **82**
Richardson Av. *B'frd* —6J **97**
Richardson Cres. *Leeds* —6D **86**
Richardson Rd. *Leeds* —6D **86**
Richardson St. *Oaken* —3C **116**
Richard St. *B'frd* —6C **80** (4H **7**)
Richard St. *Brigh* —4G **133**
Richmond Av. *Hud* —7G **145**
Richmond Av. *Leeds* —1E **84**
Richmond Av. *Sower B* —5H **129**
Richmond Clo. *Bmly* —3E **82**
Richmond Clo. *Hal* —7G **113**
Richmond Clo. *Morl* —4A **120**
Richmond Clo. *Rothw* —1H **123**
Richmond Ct. *Leeds* —6B **86** (7K **5**)
Richmond Ct. *Rothw* —1H **123**
Richmond Cft. *Leeds* —6B **86**
Richmondfield Av. *Bar E* —6J **71**
Richmondfield Clo. *Bar E* —6J **71**
Richmondfield Cres. *Bar E* —6J **71**
Richmondfield Cross. *Bar E* —6J **71**
Richmondfield Dri. *Bar E* —6J **71**
Richmondfield Gth. *Bar E* —5J **71**
Richmondfield Gro. *Bar E* —6J **71**
Richmondfield La. *Bar E* —6J **71**
Richmondfield Mt. *Bar E* —6J **71**
Richmondfield Way. *Bar E* —6J **71**
Richmond Gdns. *Pud* —6E **82**
Richmond Gdns. *Sower B* —5H **129**
Richmond Gro. *Gom* —5K **117**
**Richmond Hill. —6B 86**
Richmond Hill App. *Leeds*
—6A **86** (7K **5**)
Richmond Hill Clo. *Leeds*
—6A **86** (7K **5**)
*Richmond Ho. Leeds —2D **68***
*(off Street La.)*
Richmond M. *Shipl* —4F **61**
Richmond Mt. *Leeds* —1E **84**
Richmond Pl. *I'ly* —6C **12**
Richmond Pl. *Shipl* —4F **61**
Richmond Rd. *Bat* —6H **137**
Richmond Rd. *B'frd* —6J **79** (4A **6**)
Richmond Rd. *Fars* —3A **82**
Richmond Rd. *Hal* —7F **113**
Richmond Rd. *Heck* —2C **136**
Richmond Rd. *Leeds* —1E **84**
Richmond Rd. *Shipl* —4F **61**
Richmond St. *C'frd* —7D **126**
Richmond St. *Cleck* —1F **135**
Richmond St. *Hal* —7F **113**
Richmond St. *Kei* —3K **39**
Richmond St. *Leeds* —6A **86** (7J **5**)
Richmond Ter. *Guis* —2F **45**
Richmond Ter. *Otley* —3H **27**
Richmond Ter. *Pud* —6E **82**
Richmond Way. *Gar* —1K **107**
Rickard St. *Leeds* —7F **85**
Ridding Ga. *Otley* —1G **27**
**Riddings. —6K 145**
Riddings Clo. *Hud* —6K **145**
Riddings Ri. *Hud* —6K **145**
Riddings Rd. *Hud* —6K **145**
Riddings Rd. *I'ly* —6B **12**
**Riddlesden. —1E 40**
Riddlesden St. *Riddl* —2D **40**
Rider Rd. *Leeds* —1H **85**
Rider St. *Leeds* —5A **86** (5J **5**)
Ridge Clo. *Guis* —3E **44**
Ridge Gro. *Leeds* —7G **67**
Ridge Hill. *Brigh* —7E **132**
Ridge La. *Sils* —1E **8**
Ridge Lea. *Brigh* —7F **133**
Ridge Mt. *Leeds* —1G **85**
Ridgemount Rd. *Riddl* —1C **40**
Ridge Rd. *Kip* —6D **108**
Ridge Rd. *Leeds* —1H **85**
Ridge Ter. *Leeds* —7E **66**
Ridge, The. *Lntn* —6G **17**
Ridgeview. *Ell* —3C **144**
Ridge Vw. *Leeds* —5G **83**
Ridge Vw. Dri. *Bkby* —7D **144**
Ridge Vw. Gdns. *B'frd* —5E **62**
Ridge Vw. Rd. *Brigh* —7F **133**
Ridgeway. *All* —5A **78**
Ridgeway. *Guis* —3D **44**
Ridge Way. *Leeds* —6B **68**
Ridgeway. *Q'bry* —6K **95**
Ridgeway. *Shipl* —6A **62**
Ridge Way Clo. *Leeds* —6B **68**
Ridgeway Dri. *Bat* —6E **118**
Ridgeway Gdns. *Brigh* —3E **132**
Ridgeway Mt. *Kei* —6H **39**
*Ridgeway Ter. Leeds —1G **85***
*(off Delph La.)*
Ridgewood Clo. *Bail* —1A **62**
Riding Head La. *Ludd* —6G **111**
Riding Hill. *Hal* —1E **114**
Riding La. *Hal* —4A **112**
Ridings Cft. *B'frd* —5D **98**
Ridings, The. *Utley* —7K **21**
Riding St. *Bat* —2C **136**
Ridings Way. *B'frd* —5E **96**
Ridleys Fold. *Add* —1D **10**
Rievaulx Av. *B'frd* —5J **79** (1A **6**)
Rievaulx Clo. *B Spa* —3C **36**
Rigton App. *Leeds* —5A **86** (5K **5**)
Rigton Bank. *Bard* —5K **34**
Rigton Clo. *Leeds* —5B **86** (5K **5**)
Rigton Dri. *Leeds* —5A **86** (5K **5**)
Rigton Grn. *Bard* —6C **34**
Rigton Grn. *Leeds* —5A **86** (5K **5**)
**Rigton Hill. —4C 34**
Rigton Lawn. *Leeds* —5A **86** (5K **5**)
Rigton M. *Leeds* —5A **86** (5K **5**)
Rigton St. *B'frd* —3K **97**
Riley La. *Hal* —6D **94**
Rillbank La. *Leeds* —4F **85**
*Rillbank St. Leeds —4F **85***
*(off Rillbank La.)*
Rillington Mead. *B'frd* —6F **63**
Rills Mead. *Otley* —3J **27**
Rilston St. *B'frd* —7H **79**
Rimswell Holt. *B'frd* —6G **63**
Ringby La. *Hal* —3F **113**
Ring Rd. Adel. *Adel* —2D **66**
Ring Rd. Beeston. *Leeds* —2C **102**
Ring Rd. Beeston Pk. *Leeds*
—6G **103**
Ring Rd. Bramley. *Bmly* —5H **83**
Ring Rd. Cross Gates. *Leeds*
—2A **88**
Ring Rd. Farnley. *Leeds* —6H **83**
Ring Rd. Farsley. *Far* —3K **81**
Ring Rd. Halton. *Leeds* —4A **88**
Ring Rd. Horsforth. *H'fth* —4J **65**
Ring Rd. Lwr. Wortley. *Lwr W*
—7K **83**
Ring Rd. Meanwood. *Mean* —2E **66**
Ring Rd. Middleton. *Midd* —2K **121**
Ring Rd. Moortown. *Moort* —2G **67**
Ring Rd. Seacroft. *Leeds* —4H **69**
Ring Rd. Seacroft. *Seac* —7K **69**
Ring Rd. Shadwell. *Shad* —1E **68**
Ring Rd. Weetwood. *Weet* —3B **66**
Ring Rd. W. Pk. *W Park* —3K **65**
Ringway. *Gar* —7H **89**
Ringwood Av. *Leeds* —4H **69**
Ringwood Cres. *Leeds* —3J **69**
Ringwood Dri. *Leeds* —4J **69**
Ringwood Edge. *Ell* —3H **143**
Ringwood Gdns. *Leeds* —4J **69**
Ringwood Mt. *Leeds* —4J **69**
Ringwood Rd. *B'frd* —3H **97**
*Rink Pde. Bat —5H **137***
*(off Rink St.)*
Rink St. *Bat* —5H **137**
Rink Ter. *Bat* —5H **137**
Ripley La. *Guis* —7G **27**
Ripley Rd. *B'frd* —2B **98**
Ripley Rd. *Liv* —4H **135**
Ripley St. *All* —3A **78**
Ripley St. *B'frd* —2A **98**
(in two parts)
Ripley St. *Hal* —1G **133**
Ripley St. *Riddl* —2D **40**
Ripley Ter. *B'frd* —2B **98**
Ripley Ter. *L'ft* —1F **129**

Ripon Av.—Royd La.


Ripon Av. Hud —7G 145
Ripon Ho. Ell —2K 143
Ripon Ho. Far —2B 82
Ripon Rd. Dew —7K 137
Ripon St. Hal —2C 130
Ripon Ter. Hal —6F 113
**Ripponden. —5F 141**
Ripponden Old Bank. Ripp —5G 141
Ripponden Old La. Sower B —5C 140
**Ripponden Wood. —3G 141**
Risedale Av. Birs —5F 119
Risedale Clo. Birs —5F 119
Rise, The. Hal —5A 114
Rise, The. Kip —5A 108
Rise, The. Leeds —7A 66
**Rishworth. —7E 140**
Rishworthian Ct. Hal —7E 130
Rishworth New Rd. Sower B —7E 140
Rishworth Rd. Bklnd —5J 141
Rishworth St. Kei —5H 39
Rivadale Vw. I'ly —4B 12
Riverdale. Weth —5K 17
Riverdale Ct. Otley —2J 27
Riverdale Gdns. B Spa —3F 37
Riverdale Gdns. Otley —2J 27
Riverdale Rd. Otley —2J 27
Riverside. Kei —4C 40
Riverside Av. Otley —7K 15
Riverside Bus. Pk. I'ly —4C 12
Riverside Clo. Otley —1K 27
Riverside Ct. Bail —3G 61
Riverside Ct. Leeds —7F 5
Riverside Cres. Otley —7K 15
Riverside Dri. Otley —7K 15
Riverside Est. Shipl —4G 61
Riverside Pk. Otley —1K 27
Riverside Wlk. I'ly —4K 11
River St. Brigh —7J 133
River St. Haw —5F 57
River Vw. B Spa —3F 37
River Vw. C'frd —7B 126
River Vw. H'fth —3F 65
River Vw. I'ly —4E 12
River Wlk. Bgly —1K 59
Riverwood Dri. Hal —6F 131
Riviera Gdns. Leeds —6J 67
Rivock Av. Low U —7H 21
Rivock Av. Steet —4F 21
Rivock Gro. Kei —7H 21
Roach Grange Av. Kip —3A 108
Road End. G'lnd —2G 143
Roans Brae. B'frd —6G 63
Robb Av. Leeds —5G 103
Robb St. Leeds —5G 103
Roberson Ter. Gom —7J 117
Robert Ct. Liv —5J 135
Roberts Av. Leeds —3D 86
*Roberts Bldgs. Hal —1B 130*
*(off Gibbet St.)*
Roberts Ct. Leeds —3D 86
Robertsgate. Loft —6D 122
*Robertsgate Sq. Loft —6D 122*
*(off Robertsgate)*
Roberts Gro. Leeds —4D 86
Robertshaw Pl. Bgly —2A 60
Robertson Av. Brigh —1G 145
Roberts Pl. B'frd —6K 79 (3C 6)
Robert's St. Cleck —1E 134
Roberts St. Lay —5E 38
Roberts St. W'ford —1A 124
Roberts St. N. Hal —5G 113
Robert St. B'frd —7C 80 (5H 7)
Robert St. Cro R —4H 57
Robert St. Hal —5E 112
**Roberttown. —7G 135**
*Roberttown Grange. Liv —6G 135*
*(off School St.)*
Roberttown La. Liv —7G 135
Robin Chase. Pud —6D 82
Robin Clo. B'frd —1E 80
Robin Clo. Dew —6F 137
Robin Dri. B'frd —1E 80
Robin Dri. Steet —4D 20
Robin Hill. Bat —7E 118
**Robin Hood. —4D 122**
Robin Hood Gro. Hud —5J 145
Robin Hood Rd. Hud —5J 145
Robin Hood St. C'frd —7E 126
Robin Hood Way. Brigh —6A 134
Robin La. Dew —5D 136
Robin La. Pud —6C 82
Robin's Gro. Rothw —2H 123
Robinson Ct. B'frd —7F 79
Robinson La. Kip —5B 108
Robinson St. All B —3B 126
Robins, The. Bur W —2A 26
Robin St. B'frd —2J 97
Robin Wlk. Shipl —6K 61
Robinwood Ct. Leeds —3C 68
Rochdale Dri. Sower B —6H 129
Rochdale Rd. G'lnd —2B 142
Rochdale Rd. Ripp —6A 140
Rochdale Rd. Sower B —1G 141
(nr. Halifax Rd.)
Rochdale Rd. Sower B & Hal
(nr. Pye Nest Rd.) —3B 130
Rocheford Clo. Leeds —3B 104
Rocheford Ct. Leeds —3B 104
Rocheford Gdns. Leeds —3B 104
Rocheford Gro. Leeds —3B 104
Rocheford Wlk. Leeds —3B 104
Rochester Gdns. Leeds —2D 82
*Rochester Pl. Ell —3K 143*
*(off Savile Rd.)*
Rochester Rd. Birs —4C 118
Rochester St. B'frd —6E 80
Rochester St. Shipl —6J 61
Rochester Ter. Leeds —1D 84
Rochester Wynd. Leeds —7C 50
Rockcliffe Av. Bail —3J 61
Rock Cliffe Mt. L'ft —1F 129
Rock Edge. Liv —3J 135
Rockery Cft. H'fth —2G 65
Rockery Rd. H'fth —2G 65
*Rockfield. Yead —4A 46*
*(off Rockfield Ter.)*
Rockfield Ter. Yead —4A 46
Rockhill Clo. Bat —6D 118
Rockhill La. B'frd —7C 98
Rock Ho. Dri. Dew —6G 137
Rockingham Clo. Leeds —2D 88
Rockingham Rd. Leeds —2D 88
Rockingham Way. Leeds —2D 88
Rockland Cres. B'frd —1E 96
Rocklands Av. Bail —7J 43
Rocklands Pl. Bail —7J 43
Rock La. Leeds —1F 83
Rock La. T'tn —5G 77
Rock Lea. Q'bry —5K 95
Rockley Grange Gdns. Gar —1H 107
Rockley St. Dew —7H 137
Rock Rd. Hud —7B 144
Rocks La. Hal —6B 94
Rocks Rd. Hal —5E 130
Rock St. Brigh —5G 133
Rocks Vw. Hal —4E 130
Rock Ter. Hip —7D 114
Rock Ter. Hud —7B 144
Rock Ter. Leeds —5H 87
Rock Ter. Morl —2B 120
Rock Vw. Holy G —5G 143
Rockville Ter. Hal —3E 130
*Rockville Ter. Yead —5A 46*
*(off S. View Ter.)*
Rockwell La. B'frd —6E 62
Rockwood Cres. C'ley —3J 81
Rockwood Gro. C'ley —2K 81
Rockwood Hill Ct. C'ley —3J 81
Rockwood Rd. C'ley —3J 81
Roderick St. Leeds —6B 84
Rodin Av. B'frd —6D 78
**Rodley. —7C 64**
Rodley La. C'ley —6A 64
Rodley La. Rod —1E 82
Rods Vw. Morl —4B 120
Roebuck La. N Clift —5H 15
Roebuck St. Birs —6D 118
Roebuck Ter. N Clift —5H 15
*Roe Ho. Bail —3H 61*
*(off Fairview Ct.)*
Roger Ct. B'frd —4D 80
Roger Fold. Kip —5B 108
Rogerson Sq. Brigh —5G 133
Rogers Pl. Pud —5D 82
Roils Head Rd. Hal —1K 129
Rokeby Gdns. B'frd —6G 63
Rokeby Gdns. Leeds —7C 66
Roker La. Pud —1D 100
**Roker Lane Bottom. —2F 101**
Roman Av. Leeds —2C 68
Romanby Shaw. B'frd —6F 63
Roman Ct. Leeds —2D 68
Roman Cres. Leeds —2D 68
Roman Dri. Leeds —2D 68
Roman Gdns. Leeds —2C 68
Roman Gro. Leeds —2C 68
Roman Mt. Leeds —2D 68
Roman Pl. Leeds —2D 68
Roman Rd. Bat —7D 118
Roman Ter. Leeds —2C 68
Roman Vw. Leeds —2D 68
Rombalds Av. Leeds —5C 84
Rombalds Ct. Men —6B 26
Rombalds Cres. Leeds —4C 84
Rombalds Cres. Sils —2H 21
Rombalds Dri. Bgly —1B 60
Rombalds Gro. Leeds —5C 84
Rombalds La. I'ly —6E 12
Rombalds Pl. Leeds —4C 84
Rombalds St. Leeds —4C 84
Rombalds Ter. Leeds —5C 84
Rombald's Vw. I'ly —4D 12
Rombalds Vw. Leeds —4C 84
Rombalds Vw. Otley —7F 15
Romford Av. Morl —4A 120
Romford Ct. B'frd —1F 115
Romney Mt. Pud —1E 100
Romsey Clo. Hud —7K 143
Romsey Gdns. B'frd —3F 99
Romsey M. B'frd —3F 99
Rona Cft. Rothw —2J 123
Ronald Dri. B'frd —7G 79
Rookery La. Hal —5H 131
Rookery Pl. Brigh —5H 133
Rookery, The. Add —1D 10
Rookes Av. B'frd —6J 97
Rookes La. Hal —6G 115
Rook La. B'frd —4D 98
Rooks Av. Cleck —7E 116
Rooks Clo. Wyke —6K 115
Rook St. Bgly —1K 59
Rookwith Pde. B'frd —6F 63
Rookwood Av. Kip —6A 108
Rookwood Av. Leeds —5E 86
Rookwood Cres. Leeds —5E 86
Rookwood Cft. Leeds —6E 86
Rookwood Gdns. Leeds —6E 86
Rookwood Hill. Leeds —5E 86
Rookwood Mt. Leeds —5E 86
Rookwood Pde. Leeds —5F 87
Rookwood Pl. Leeds —5E 86
Rookwood Rd. Leeds —5E 86
Rookwood Sq. Leeds —5F 87
Rookwood St. Leeds —6E 86
Rookwood Ter. Leeds —5E 86
Rookwood Va. Leeds —6E 86
Rookwood Vw. Leeds —5E 86
Rookwood Wlk. Leeds —5E 86
Rooley Av. B'frd —6K 97
Rooley Banks. Sower B —5G 129
Rooley Clo. B'frd —5A 98
Rooley Cres. B'frd —5A 98
Rooley Heights. Sower B —5F 129
**Rooley Hill. —5F 129**
Rooley La. B'frd —5K 97
Rooley La. Sower B —6F 129
**Rooms. —6K 101**
Rooms Fold. Morl —1A 120
Rooms La. Morl —6K 101
Roper Av. Leeds —4B 68
Roper Gdns. Hal —3B 112
Roper Grn. Hal —3B 112
Roper Gro. Leeds —4B 68
Roper Ho. Hal —3B 112
Roper La. Hal —6D 94
Roper La. Q'bry —3F 95
Roper St. Kei —4K 39
Rope Wlk. Hal —7H 93
Roscoe St. Leeds —3K 85 (1H 5)
Roscoe Ter. Leeds —6B 84
Roseate Grn. Morl —4C 120
Rose Av. H'fth —5F 65
Rose Bank. Bur W —2A 26
Rosebank Cres. Leeds —3F 85
Rosebank Gdns. Leeds —4F 85
*Rosebank Ho. Leeds —3F 85*
*(off Belle Vue Rd.)*
Rose Bank Pl. B'frd —6E 78
Rosebank Rd. Leeds —4F 85
Rosebank Row. Leeds —4F 85
Rosebank St. Bat —2E 136
Roseberry St. Oakw —2F 57
Rosebery Av. Hal —4H 131
Rosebery Av. Shipl —5J 61
Rosebery Mt. Shipl —5K 61
Rosebery Rd. B'frd —3J 79
Rosebery St. Ell —3K 143
Rosebery St. Pud —5A 82
Rosebery Ter. Hal —7E 112
Rosebery Ter. S'ley —3D 82
Rosebud Wlk. Leeds —3A 86 (1J 5)
Rosecliffe Mt. Leeds —2F 83
Rosecliffe Ter. Leeds —3G 83
Rose Ct. Gar —6A 90
Rose Cft. E Kes —4A 34
Rosedale. Rothw —1H 123
Rosedale Av. All —3K 77
Rosedale Av. Harts —6F 135
Rosedale Bank. Leeds —5K 103
Rosedale Clo. Bail —2G 61
Rosedale Gdns. Leeds —5K 103
(in two parts)
Rosedale Grn. Leeds —5K 103
Rosedale Ho. B'frd —6F 63
*Rosedale Ho. Sower B —5K 129*
*(off Sowerby St.)*
Rosedale Ri. B Spa —3C 36
Rosedale Wlk. Leeds —5K 103
Rose Gth. Bur W —3J 25
Rose Gro. H Bri —7A 110
Rose Gro. Rothw —1F 123
Rose Gro. La. Hal —3H 129
Rose Heath. I'wth —7B 94
Rose Hill Cres. Low M —3J 115
Roselee Clo. Sid —5J 131
Rosemary Clo. Brigh —7G 133
Rosemary Gro. Hal —5J 131
(in two parts)
Rosemary La. Brigh —1G 145
Rosemary La. Sid —5J 131
Rosemary Ter. Hal —5J 131
Rose Meadows. Kei —6G 39
Rosemont Av. Leeds —3G 83
Rosemont Av. Pud —5D 82
Rosemont Dri. Pud —5D 82
Rosemont Gro. Leeds —3F 83
Rosemont La. Bail —2A 62
Rosemont Pl. Leeds —3G 83
Rosemont Rd. Leeds —3G 83
Rosemont St. Leeds —3G 83
Rosemont St. Pud —5D 82
Rosemont Ter. Leeds —3G 83
Rosemont Ter. Pud —5D 82
Rosemont Vw. Leeds —3F 83
Rosemont Vs. Pud —5D 82
Rosemont Wlk. Leeds —3G 83
**Rosemount. —4A 144**
Rose Mt. B'frd —2C 80
(BD2)
Rose Mt. B'frd —6J 99
(BD4)
Rose Mt. Hal —4E 130
*Rosemount. Leeds —6J 67*
*(off Henconner La.)*
Rosemount Av. Ell —3A 144
*Rosemount Clo. Kei —4K 39*
*(off Well St.)*
Rose Mt. Pl. Leeds —7D 84
Rosemount Ter. Ell —3A 144
*Rosemount Wlk. Kei —4K 39*
*(off Well St.)*
Roseneath Pl. Leeds —7D 84
Roseneath St. Leeds —7D 84
Roseneath Ter. Leeds —7D 84
Rose Pl. L'ft —3G 129
Rose St. B'frd —4H 79
Rose St. Hal —2D 130
Rose St. Haw —6E 56
Rose St. H'fth —4F 65
Rose St. Kei —4D 40
Rose Ter. Add —1D 10
Rose Ter. Hal —4E 130
(HX2)
*Rose Ter. Hal —1E 130*
*(off West St.)*
Rose Ter. H'fth —4E 64
Rosetta Dri. B'frd —6F 79
Roseville Rd. Leeds —3A 86 (2J 5)
Roseville St. Leeds —3A 86 (1K 5)
*Roseville Ter. Leeds —2B 88*
*(off Church La.)*
Roseville Way. Leeds —3A 86 (2J 5)
Rosewood Av. Kip —3K 107
Rosewood Av. Riddl —2D 40
Rosewood Ct. Rothw —7H 105
Rosewood Gro. B'frd —1F 99
Rosgill Dri. Leeds —7H 69
Rosgill Grn. Leeds —7J 69
Rosgill Wlk. Leeds —7H 69
Rosley Mt. B'frd —1F 115
Roslyn Pl. B'frd —7H 79
Rossall Rd. Leeds —1B 86
Rossefield App. Leeds —4H 83
Rossefield Av. Leeds —3H 83
Rossefield Chase. Leeds —3H 83
Rossefield Clo. Leeds —3H 83
Rossefield Dri. Leeds —3H 83
Rossefield Gdns. Leeds —3H 83
Rossefield Gth. Leeds —3H 83
*Rossefield Grn. Leeds —3H 83*
*(off Rossefield Dri.)*
Rossefield Gro. Leeds —3H 83
Rossefield Lawn. Leeds —3H 83
*Rossefield Pde. Leeds —3H 83*
*(off Rossefield Gro.)*
Rosse Fld. Pk. B'frd —1H 79
Rossefield Pl. Leeds —3H 83
Rossefield Rd. B'frd —1G 79
Rossefield Ter. Leeds —3H 83
Rossefield Vw. Leeds —3H 83
Rossefield Wlk. Leeds —3H 83
Rossefield Way. Leeds —3H 83
Rossendale Pl. Shipl —5G 61
Rosse St. B'frd —6G 79
Rosse St. Shipl —4H 61
Rossett Ho. B'frd —2G 7
Ross Gro. Leeds —1E 82
Rossington Gro. Leeds —1A 86
Rossington Pl. Leeds —1A 86
Rossington Rd. Leeds —7C 68
Rossington St. Leeds —5H 85 (5D 4)
Rosslyn Gro. Haw —6E 56
Rossmore Dri. All —4C 78
Ross Ter. Leeds —1E 82
Rosy St. Cro R —4H 57
Rothbury Gdns. Leeds —1B 66
Rothesay Ter. B'frd —7J 79
**Rothwell. —2G 123**
Rothwell Dri. Hal —3F 131
**Rothwell Haigh. —7G 105**
Rothwell La. Oult —1J 123
Rothwell Mt. Hal —3F 131
Rothwell Rd. Hal —3F 131
Rough Hall La. Hal —2G 111
Roundell Av. B'frd —6D 98
**Roundhay. —3C 68**
Roundhay Av. Leeds —7B 68
Roundhay Cvn. & Camping Pk. Leeds —4F 69
Roundhay Cres. Leeds —7B 68
Roundhay Gdns. Leeds —7B 68
Roundhay Gro. Leeds —7B 68
Roundhay Mt. Leeds —1B 86
Roundhay Park. —4E 68
Roundhay Pk. La. Leeds —6D 50
Roundhay Pl. Leeds —7B 68
Roundhay Rd. Leeds —3K 85 (1H 5)
Roundhay Vw. Leeds —7B 68
Roundhead Fold. App B —4G 63
Round Hill. Hal —1D 112
Roundhill Av. Bgly —4B 60
Round Hill Clo. Hal —1D 112
Round Hill Clo. Q'bry —4B 96
Roundhill Mt. Bgly —5B 60
Roundhill Pl. B'frd —6K 79 (4C 6)
Round Hill Pl. Q'bry —4B 96
Roundhill St. B'frd —2K 97
Round St. B'frd —3A 98
(in two parts)
Round Thorn Pl. B'frd —5G 79
Roundway, The. Morl —3J 119
Roundwell Rd. Liv —3E 134
Roundwood. Shipl —5E 60
Roundwood Av. Bail —1B 62
Roundwood Av. B'frd —7G 63
Roundwood Glen. B'frd —7G 63
Roundwood Rd. Bail —1A 62
Roundwood Vw. B'frd —6G 63
Rouse Fold. B'frd —1B 98 (7G 7)
Rouse Mill La. Bat —4H 137
Rouse St. Liv —4J 135
Rowan Av. B'frd —6G 81
Rowanberry Clo. B'frd —1D 80
Rowan Clo. Birs —5E 118
Rowan Ct. B'frd —4E 80
Rowan Ct. Rawd —6K 45
Rowan Ct. Rothw —1C 124
Rowan Dri. Brigh —5J 133
Rowan Pl. Gar —7B 90
Rowans, The. Bail —1F 61
Rowans, The. B'hpe —1K 47
Rowans, The. Leeds —2D 82
Rowans, The. Weth —3A 18
Rowan St. Kei —1J 39
Rowantree Av. Bail —7H 43
Rowantree Dri. B'frd —6D 62
Row Bottom Ter. Sower B —4F 129
Rowland Pl. Leeds —3H 103
Rowland Rd. Leeds —3H 103
Rowland Ter. Leeds —3H 103
Row La. Sower B —5F 129
Rowlestone Ri. B'frd —6G 63
Rowley Dri. I'ly —6F 13
Rowsley St. Kei —4B 40
Row, The. Rawd —7J 45
Rowton Thorpe. B'frd —6G 63
Roxburgh Gro. All —5B 78
Roxby Clo. Leeds —4A 86 (4K 5)
Roxby St. B'frd —3K 97
Roxholme Av. Leeds —7A 68
Roxholme Gro. Leeds —7A 68
*Roxholme Ho. B'frd —4E 98*
*(off Prince St.)*
Roxholme Pl. Leeds —7A 68
Roxholme Rd. Leeds —7A 68
Roxholme Ter. Leeds —7A 68
Royal Armouries Museum. —7K 85
Royal Clo. Gt Hor —3F 97
Royal Clo. Leeds —4K 103
Royal Ct. Leeds —4K 103
Royal Dri. Leeds —4K 103
Royal Gdns. Leeds —4K 103
Royal Gro. Leeds —4K 103
Royal Pk. Av. Leeds —3F 85
Royal Pk. Gro. Leeds —2F 85
Royal Pk. Mt. Leeds —2F 85
Royal Pk. Rd. Leeds —3E 84
Royal Pk. Ter. Leeds —3F 85
Royal Pk. Vw. Leeds —2F 85
Royal Pl. Leeds —4K 103
Royal Ter. B Spa —2D 36
Royd Av. Ain T —6A 144
Royd Av. Bgly —1C 60
Royd Av. Heck —2B 136
Royd Cres. Hal —7C 112
Royd Cres. H Bri —6B 110
Royden Gro. B'frd —3G 79
*Royd Farm. Hal —7C 94*
*(off Causeway Foot)*
Roydfield St. Hud —7H 145
Royd Ho. Gro. Kei —6C 40
Royd Ho. Rd. Kei —6C 40
Royd Ho. Wlk. Kei —6C 40
Royd Ho. Way. Kei —6C 40
Royd Ings Av. Kei —2A 40
Roydlands St. Hal —1D 132
Roydlands Ter. Hal —1D 132
Royd La. Hal —3E 112


A-Z Leeds & Bradford 191

Royd La. I'wth —7C 94
Royd La. Kei —2K 39
Royd La. Ripp —5E 140
Royd Mt. Hal —5G 113
Royd Pl. Hal —5G 113
Royds Av. B'shaw —2K 117
Royds Av. Brigh —7H 115
Royds Av. C'frd —7J 127
Royds Av. Oss —7C 138
Roydscliffe Dri. B'frd —1F 79
Roydscliffe Rd. B'frd —2F 79
Royds Clo. Leeds —2C 102
Royds Ct. Rothw —2H 123
(off Marsh St.)
Royds Cres. Brigh —1H 133
Roydsdale Way. Euro I —1C 116
Royds Farm Rd. Leeds —4C 102
**Royds Green. —5J 123**
Royds Hall Av. B'frd —6J 97
Royds Hall La. B'frd —2G 115
Royds Hall La. Butt —1G 115
Royds Hall Rd. Leeds —3C 102
Royds La. Leeds —2C 102
Royds La. Rothw —3H 123
Royds Pk. Cres. Wyke —3K 115
Roydstone Rd. B'frd —5F 81
Roydstone Ter. B'frd —5F 81
Royd St. Kei —1K 39
(in two parts)
Royd St. T'tn —7G 77
Royd St. Wilsd —1G 77
Royd St. Wyke —3J 115
Royd Vw. H Bri —6A 110
Royd Vw. Pud —7A 82
Royd Way. Kei —2A 40
Royd Wood. Cleck —2F 135
Royd Wood. Oxe —1F 75
Roydwood Ter. Cull —6B 58
Royle Fold. Heck —4B 136
Roy Rd. B'frd —5D 96
Royston Clo. E Ard —2K 139
Royston Hill. E Ard —2K 139
Ruby St. Bat —2E 136
Ruby St. Kei —7J 39
Ruby St. Leeds —4A 86 (3J 5)
Rudding Av. All —4A 78
Rudding Cres. All —4A 78
Rudding Dri. Bat —2D 136
Rudd St. B'frd —2G 97
Rudgate. Newt K —4K 37
Rudgate. Thor A —6J 19
Rudgate Pk. Wltn —6G 19
(in two parts)
Ruffield Side. Wyke —2J 115
Rufford Av. Yead —5K 45
Rufford Bank. Yead —5A 46
Rufford Clo. Yead —5A 46
Rufford Cres. Yead —5A 46
Rufford Dri. Yead —5A 46
**Rufford Park. —5A 46**
Rufford Pl. Hal —4F 131
Rufford Ridge. Yead —5A 46
Rufford Ri. Yead —5K 45
Rufford Rd. Ell —3K 143
Rufford Rd. Hal —4F 131
Rufford St. B'frd —6E 80
Rufford Vs. Hal —4F 131
Rufforth Ho. B'frd —6E 62
(off Rowantree Dri.)
Rufus St. B'frd —3H 97
Rufus St. Kei —3A 40
Rugby Av. Hal —4D 112
Rugby Dri. Hal —4D 112
Rugby Gdns. Hal —4D 112
Rugby League Hall of Fame. —3A 124
Rugby Mt. Hal —4D 112
Rugby Pl. B'frd —7H 79
Rugby Ter. Hal —4D 112
Rumble Rd. Dew —7K 137
Rumple Cft. Otley —7G 15
Runnymeade Ct. B'frd —5D 62
(off Cobden St.)
Runswick Av. Leeds —1F 103
Runswick Gro. B'frd —5K 97
Runswick Pl. Leeds —1F 103
Runswick St. B'frd —5K 97
Runswick St. Leeds —1F 103
Runswick Ter. B'frd —5K 97
Runswick Ter. Leeds —1G 103
Rupert Rd. I'ly —4A 12
Rupert St. Cro R —4H 57
Rupert St. Kei —3A 40
Rushcroft Ter. Bail —1J 61
Rushdene Ct. Wyke —6J 115
Rushmoor Rd. B'frd —4F 99
Rusholme Dri. Fars —2A 82
Rusholme St. B'frd —4E 98
Rushton Av. B'frd —5G 81
Rushton Hill Clo. Hal —6A 112
Rushton Rd. B'frd —5F 81
Rushton St. C'ley —6K 63
Rushton St. Hal —7D 112
Rushton Ter. B'frd —6G 81
Rushworth St. Hal —6E 112

Ruskin Av. B'frd —2D 78
Ruskin Clo. C'frd —7H 127
Ruskin Cres. Guis —3H 45
Ruskin Dri. C'frd —7G 127
Ruskin Gro. Hud —6K 145
Ruskin Pl. C'frd —7H 127
Ruskin St. S'ley —4A 82
Rusling M. Schol —7B 116
Russel Ho. B'frd —6E 62
(off Yewdall Way)
Russell Av. Q'bry —6J 95
Russell Clo. Bat —3G 137
Russell Clo. Heck —5C 136
Russell Ct. Bard —7B 34
Russell Gro. B'shaw —2K 117
Russell Gro. Leeds —1B 86
Russell Hall La. Q'bry —5J 95
Russell Rd. Q'bry —6H 95
Russell St. B'frd —1K 97 (7C 6)
Russell St. Dew —7E 136
Russell St. Kei —4K 39
Russell St. Leeds —5H 85 (6D 4)
Russell St. Q'bry —5J 95
Russell St. Shipl —7J 61
Russel St. Hal —1G 131
Russet Fold. Liv —4J 135
Rustic Av. Hal —4A 132
Ruswarp Cres. B'frd —6F 63
Ruth Ho. B'frd —6C 80
(off Otley Rd.)
Ruth St. Cro R —4G 57
Ruthven Vw. Leeds —2C 86
Rutland Clo. Kip —4B 108
Rutland Clo. W'ford —1B 124
Rutland Ct. Pud —5C 82
(off Richardshaw La.)
Rutland Dri. Kip —4B 108
Rutland Ho. Bgly —1A 60
(off Lyndon Ter.)
Rutland Mt. Leeds —5F 85
Rutland Rd. Bat —2H 137
Rutland St. B'frd —2C 98 (7J 7)
Rutland St. Kei —6K 39
Rutland St. Leeds —5G 85 (5A 4)
Rutland Ter. Leeds —5F 85 (5A 4)
Ryan Gro. Kei —3F 39
Ryan Pl. Leeds —1C 86
Ryan St. B'frd —3K 97
Ryburn Ct. Hal —1D 130
(off Hanson La.)
Ryburn Ho. Hal —1D 130
(off Clay St.)
Ryburn La. Sower B —4G 141
Ryburn St. Sower B —5K 129
Ryburn Ter. Hal —1D 130
Ryburn Ter. Ripp —7E 140
Ryburn Vw. Hal —3C 130
Ryburn Vw. Sower B —6E 140
Rycroft Av. Bgly —6A 60
Rycroft Av. Leeds —4E 82
Rycroft Clo. Leeds —4F 83
Rycroft Ct. Leeds —4F 83
Rycroft Dri. Leeds —4F 83
Rycroft Grn. Leeds —4F 83
Rycroft Pl. Leeds —4F 83
Rycroft Sq. Leeds —4F 83
Rycroft St. Shipl —7K 61
Rycroft Towers. Leeds —4E 82
Rydal Av. Bail —3E 60
Rydal Av. B'frd —1J 79
Rydal Av. Gar —7K 89
Rydal Dri. Morl —2D 120
Rydal Gro. Liv —7J 135
Rydall Pl. Leeds —1F 103
Rydall St. Leeds —1F 103
Rydall Ter. Leeds —1F 103
Rydal St. C'frd —7K 127
Rydal St. Kei —5J 39
Ryder Gdns. Leeds —5C 68
Rydings Av. Brigh —5G 133
Rydings Clo. Brigh —5F 133
Rydings Dri. Brigh —5F 133
Rydings, The. Brigh —5G 133
(off Halifax Rd.)
Rydings Wlk. Brigh —5F 133
Rydings Way. Brigh —5F 133
Ryebread. C'frd —6E 126
Ryecroft. H'den —3D 58
Rye Cft. I'wth —1D 112
Ryecroft Cres. Hal —6B 112
Ryecroft Dri. Hud —7B 144
Ryecroft La. Brigh —1J 145
Ryecroft La. Hal —7B 112
Ryecroft Rd. H'den —2B 58
Ryecroft Ter. Hal —6B 112
Ryedale Av. Leeds —2B 102
Ryedale Ct. Leeds —7H 69
Ryedale Holt. Leeds —1C 102
Ryedale Pk. I'ly —6D 12
Ryedale Way. All —3A 78
Ryedale Way. Ting —1E 138
Ryefield Av. Cytn —1B 96
Rye Gth. Weth —1H 17
Ryelands Gro. B'frd —1D 78
Rye La. Hal —6A 112

Rye Pl. Leeds —4H 87
Rye St. Kei —7K 39
Rye Way. C'frd —7H 127
Rylands Av. Bgly —1B 60
Rylstone Gdns. B'frd —3C 80
Rylstone Rd. Bail —2F 61
Rylstone St. Kei —3B 40
Ryshworth Av. Bgly —4H 41
Ryshworth Bri. Bgly —5H 41
Ryton Dale. B'frd —6G 63

Sable Crest. B'frd —1B 80
Sackville App. Leeds —2J 85 (1F 5)
Sackville Rd. Sils —7G 9
Sackville St. B'frd —6A 80 (4D 6)
Sackville St. Leeds —3J 85 (1F 5)
Sackville Ter. Leeds —3J 85
Saddlers Cft. I'ly —5A 12
Saddler St. Wyke —3J 115
Saddleworth Rd. Bklnd & Ell —6J 141
Sadler Clo. Leeds —7C 48
Sadler Copse. Leeds —7C 48
Sadlers Wlk. Weth —3K 17
Sadler Way. Leeds —7C 48
Saffron Dri. All —4B 78
Sagar Pl. Leeds —1D 84
(off St Michael's Rd.)
Sagar St. C'frd —7D 126
Sage St. B'frd —2J 97
Sahara Ct. B'frd —3K 79
St Abbs Clo. B'frd —7J 97
St Abbs Dri. B'frd —7J 97
St Abbs Fold. B'frd —7J 97
St Abbs Ga. B'frd —7J 97
St Abbs Wlk. B'frd —7J 97
St Abbs Way. B'frd —7J 97
St Aidan's Rd. Bail —2K 61
St Aidans Rd. W'ford —6J 107
St Aidans Sq. Bgly —5J 41
(off Micklethwaite La.)
St Alban App. Leeds —4E 86
St Alban Clo. Leeds —4E 86
St Alban Cres. Leeds —4E 86
St Alban Gro. Leeds —4E 86
St Alban Mt. Leeds —4E 86
St Alban Rd. Leeds —4E 86
St Albans Av. Hal —5G 131
St Alban's Av. Hud —6A 144
St Albans Cft. Hal —4H 131
St Alban's Pl. Leeds —4J 85 (4F 5)
St Albans Rd. Hal —5G 131
St Alban Vw. Leeds —4E 86
St Andrews Av. Morl —4J 119
St Andrew's Clo. Hal —2E 112
St Andrew's Clo. Leeds —7C 64
St Andrews Clo. Morl —4J 119
St Andrew's Clo. Yead —3A 46
St Andrew's Ct. Leeds —5F 85
(off Cavendish St.)
St Andrew's Ct. Yead —3A 46
(off St Andrew's Rd.)
St Andrew's Cres. Oaken —3C 116
St Andrew's Cft. Leeds —7H 49
St Andrews Dri. Brigh —4G 133
St Andrew's Dri. Leeds —7J 49
St Andrews Gro. Morl —4K 119
St Andrews Pl. B'frd —7J 79 (5A 6)
St Andrew's Pl. Leeds —5F 85
St Andrew's Rd. C'frd —6K 127
St Andrew's Rd. Yead —3A 46
St Andrew's Sq. Bgly —5J 41
(off Mickelthwaite La.)
St Andrew's St. Leeds —5F 85
St Andrew's Vs. B'frd —6J 79 (4A 6)
St Andrew's Wlk. Leeds —7J 49
St Anne's Av. Hud —6A 144
St Anne's Dri. Leeds —1C 84
St Anne's Grn. Leeds —1C 84
St Anne's Pl. Hal —7E 112
(off Pellon La.)
St Anne's Pl. Holy G —5C 142
St Anne's Rd. Hal —6G 131
St Anne's Rd. Leeds —7C 66
St Annes Ter. Bail —2K 61
St Ann's Av. Leeds —3D 84
St Ann's Clo. Leeds —2C 84
St Ann's Ct. Hal —2B 112
St Ann's Gdns. Leeds —2C 84
St Ann's La. Leeds —1C 84
St Ann's Mt. Leeds —2D 84
St Ann's Ri. Leeds —2B 84
St Ann's Sq. Head —2C 84
St Ann's Sq. Leeds —6J 5
St Anns Sq. Sower B —4A 130
St Ann St. Leeds —5H 85 (5D 4)
St Ann's Way. Leeds —2C 84
St Anthony's Dri. Leeds —4F 103
St Anthonys Gdns. Shipl —6K 61
(off Snowden Rd.)
St Anthony's Rd. Leeds —4E 102
St Anthony's Ter. Leeds —5E 102
St Armands Ct. Gar —6K 89

St Augustines Ct. Leeds —2B 86
(off Harehills Pl.)
St Augustine's Ter. B'frd —4C 80 (1H 7)
St Augustine's Ter. Hal —1E 130
St Baise Ct. B'frd —1A 98 (7E 6)
St Barnabas Rd. Leeds —7H 85
St Barnabas Rd. Liv —3E 134
St Bartholomews Clo. Leeds —6C 84
St Bevan's Rd. Hal —5G 131
St Blaise Sq. B'frd —6A 80 (3E 6)
St Catherines Cres. Leeds —1H 83
St Catherine's Dri. Leeds —1H 83
St Catherine's Grn. Leeds —1H 83
St Catherine's Hill. Leeds —1H 83
St Catherines Wlk. Leeds —6C 68
St Chad's Av. Brigh —3E 132
St Chad's Av. Leeds —6C 66
St Chad's Dri. Leeds —6C 66
St Chad's Gro. Leeds —6C 66
St Chads Pl. Leeds —6D 66
St Chad's Ri. Leeds —6C 66
St Chad's Rd. B'frd —4H 79
St Chads Rd. Leeds —6D 66
St Chad's Vw. Leeds —7C 66
St Christopher's Av. Rothw —2H 123
St Christophers Dri. Add —2D 10
St Clair Ter. Otley —2K 27
(off St Clair Rd.)
St Clair Rd. Otley —2K 27
(in two parts)
St Clair St. Otley —2K 27
St Clare's Av. B'frd —3F 81
St Clements Av. Rothw —3G 123
St Clements Clo. Rothw —3F 123
St Clements Ri. Rothw —2F 123
St Cyprian's Gdns. Leeds —3D 86
St David's Rd. Otley —7G 15
St Edmund's Clo. C'frd —7J 127
St Edward's Ter. Cliff —5D 36
St Elmo. Q'bry —7G 95
St Elmo Gro. Leeds —5C 86
St Eloi Av. Bail —7J 43
St Enoch's Rd. B'frd —5H 97
St Francis Gdns. Fix —4G 145
St Francis Pl. Leeds —7H 85
St George's Av. Hud —6A 144
St George's Av. Rothw —7E 104
St George's Cres. Rothw —7E 104
St George's Pl. B'frd —2D 98
St George's Rd. Hal —6E 112
St George's Rd. Leeds —4H 85 (4C 4)
St George's Sq. Hal —6F 113
St George's St. B'frd —7D 80 (5K 7)
St George's Ter. Hal —6F 113
St Giles Clo. Brigh —3E 132
St Giles Ct. Light —1E 132
St Giles Gth. B'hpe —7J 29
St Giles Rd. Hal —1E 132
St Helena Rd. B'frd —5H 97
St Helens Av. Leeds —1D 66
St Helens Clo. Leeds —1D 66
(in two parts)
St Helens Cft. Leeds —1C 66
St Helen's Dri. M'fld —5F 91
St Helens Gdns. Leeds —1C 66
St Helens Gro. Leeds —1C 66
St Helens La. Leeds —1B 66
St Helens Pl. C'frd —7E 126
St Helens Sq. Holy G —5G 143
(off Station Rd.)
St Helen's St. Leeds —1K 103
St Helen's Way. I'ly —5D 12
St Helens Way. Leeds —1D 66
St Helier Gro. Bail —7K 43
St Hilda's Av. Leeds —7B 86
St Hilda's Cres. Leeds —7B 86
St Hilda's Gro. Leeds —7B 86
St Hilda's Mt. Leeds —7B 86
St Hilda's Pl. Leeds —7B 86
St Hilda's Rd. Leeds —7B 86
St Hilda's Ter. B'frd —5G 81
St Ians Cft. Add —2D 10
St Ives Gdns. Hal —5G 131
St Ives Gro. H'den —2G 59
St Ives Gro. Leeds —5A 84
St Ives Mt. Leeds —5A 84
St Ives Pl. H'den —2G 59
St Ives Rd. Hal —5G 131
St Ives Rd. H'den —2G 59
St James App. Leeds —1J 87
St James Av. H'fth —3G 65
St James Bus. Pk. B'frd —7C 80 (6H 7)
St James Clo. Leeds —5K 83
St James Ct. Brigh —5H 133
St James Ct. Hal —1G 131
(off St James Rd.)
St James Cres. Pud —6K 81
St James Dri. H'fth —3H 65
St James Mkt. B'frd —7C 80 (6H 7)
St James M. Leeds —5K 83

St James Pl. Bail —7B 44
(off Otley Rd.)
St James Rd. Bail —7B 44
St James Rd. Hal —1G 131
St James Rd. I'ly —6A 12
St James's Ct. Leeds —3A 86 (1K 5)
St James Sq. B'frd —1A 98
St James's Sq. B'frd —7E 6
St James's Sq. Hal —5A 114
St James's St. Weth —4J 17
St James St. Bat —3G 137
St James St. Hal —1G 131
St James St. Heck —5B 136
St James Ter. H'fth —3H 65
St James Wlk. H'fth —3H 65
**St John's. —3E 72**
St Johns. I'ly —6A 12
St Johns Av. Add —1D 10
St John's Av. Bat —2E 136
St John's Av. Fars —3B 82
St John's Av. Leeds —3F 85
St John's Av. T'ner —6D 52
St John's Cen. Leeds —5J 85 (5E 4)
St John's Clo. Aber —3E 72
St John's Clo. Cleck —1G 135
(in two parts)
St John's Clo. Leeds —3F 85
St John's Ct. Bail —2A 62
St John's Ct. Leeds —1K 85
St John's Ct. Low U —1J 39
(off St John's Rd.)
St John's Ct. T'ner —6D 52
St John's Ct. Yead —5J 45
St Johns Cres. B'frd —5E 78
St John's Dri. Yead —5J 45
St John's Gth. Aber —4E 72
St John's Gro. Leeds —3F 85
St John's La. Hal —2G 131
St John's Pk. Men —5B 26
St John's Pl. B'shaw —1J 117
St John's Pl. Cleck —1G 135
St John's Rd. B Spa —3D 36
St John's Rd. I'ly —5E 12
St John's Rd. Leeds —4F 85
St John's Rd. Low U —1J 39
St John's Rd. Yead —5J 45
St John's St. Cnly —1G 21
St John's St. Oult —2A 124
St John's Ter. Leeds —3F 85
St John St. Brigh —7G 133
St John St. Dew —7F 137
St John's Vw. Bat —2E 136
St John's Vw. B Spa —3C 36
St Johns Way. Kei —5H 39
St John's Way. Yead —5J 45
St John's Yd. Oult —2A 124
St Jude's Pl. B'frd —5K 79 (1C 6)
St Jude's St. B'frd —5K 79 (1B 6)
St Judes St. Hal —3F 131
St Laurence's Clo. B'frd —7K 61
St Lawrence Clo. Pud —6B 82
St Lawrence St. Leeds —6K 67
St Lawrence Ter. Pud —6C 82
St Leonards Clo. Add —2D 10
St Leonard's Farm Park. —6E 44
St Leonard's Gro. B'frd —4F 79
St Leonard's Rd. B'frd —4F 79
St Lukes Clo. Bat —4J 137
St Luke's Clo. Cleck —1D 134
St Luke's Clo. Cliff —5D 36
St Luke's Cres. Leeds —2G 103
St Luke's Grn. Leeds —2G 103
St Luke's Rd. Leeds —2G 103
St Luke's St. Leeds —2G 103
St Luke's Ter. Cleck —1D 134
(off St Luke's Clo.)
St Luke's Ter. E Mor —3H 41
St Luke's Vw. Leeds —2G 103
St Margaret's Av. B'frd —4F 99
St Margaret's Av. H'fth —3F 65
St Margaret's Av. Leeds —6C 68
St Margaret's Av. Meth —4H 125
St Margaret's Clo. H'fth —2F 65
St Margaret's Dri. H'fth —2F 65
St Margaret's Dri. Leeds —6C 68
St Margaret's Gro. Leeds —6C 68
St Margaret's Pl. B'frd —1H 97
St Margaret's Rd. B'frd —7H 79
St Margaret's Rd. H'fth —2F 65
St Margaret's Rd. Meth —4H 125
St Margaret's Ter. B'frd —1H 97
St Margaret's Ter. I'ly —6B 12
St Margaret's Vw. Leeds —6C 68
St Mark's Av. Leeds —3G 85 (1B 4)
St Mark's Av. Low M —2J 115
St Mark's Flats. Leeds —2G 85
(off Low Clo. St.)
St Mark's Pl. B'frd —2J 115
St Mark's Rd. Leeds —2G 85 (1C 4)
(in two parts)
St Mark's St. Leeds —3G 85 (1B 4)
St Mark's Ter. Low M —2J 115
St Martins Av. Field B —6J 79

St Martin's Av. Leeds —7J 67
St Martin's Av. Otley —7H 15
St Martin's Cres. Leeds —7K 67
St Martin's Dri. Leeds —6K 67
St Martin's Gdns. Leeds —7J 67
St Martin's Gro. Leeds —7K 67
St Martin's Rd. Leeds —7K 67
St Martin's Ter. Leeds —7K 67
St Martin's Vw. Brigh —5G 133
St Martin's Vw. Leeds —7K 67
St Mary Magdalenes Clo. B'frd —5J 79 (1A 6)
St Mary's Av. Bat —5F 137
St Mary's Av. Swil —5E 106
St Mary's Av. Wyke —5J 115
St Mary's Clo. Gar —7K 89
St Marys Clo. I'ly —5C 12
St Mary's Clo. Leeds —7D 84
St Mary's Clo. Pott —7K 67
St Mary's Clo. Wyke —5H 115
St Mary's Ct. All B —3B 126
St Mary's Ct. Hal —2B 112
St Mary's Ct. Leeds —7K 67
St Mary's Cres. Wyke —6H 115
St Mary's Dri. Wyke —5J 115
St Mary's Gdns. Wyke —5J 115
St Mary's Gth. E Kes —5K 33
St Mary's Ga. Ell —2K 143
St Mary's Heights. Hal —2B 112
St Mary's Mt. Wyke —5H 115
St Mary's Pk. App. Leeds —5K 83
St Mary's Pk. Ct. Leeds —5K 83
St Mary's Pk. Cres. Leeds —5K 83
St Mary's Pk. Grn. Leeds —5K 83
St Mary's Pl. C'frd —7C 126
St Mary's Rd. B'frd —1F 99
St Mary's Rd. Leeds —7K 67
St Mary's Rd. Mann & B'frd —3J 79
St Mary's Rd. Riddl —1D 40
St Mary's Sq. Morl —3A 120
St Mary's Sq. Wyke —5J 115
St Mary's St. B Spa —2D 36
St Mary's St. Leeds —5K 85 (5H 5)
St Mary St. Hal —2F 131
St Mary's Wlk. M'fld —6F 91
St Matthews Clo. Wilsd —1F 77
St Matthew's Dri. N'wram —4A 114
St Matthews Gro. Wilsd —1G 77
St Matthews Rd. B'frd —5K 97
St Matthew's St. Leeds —1G 103
St Matthews Wlk. Leeds —4J 67
St Matthias Ct. Leeds —3D 84
St Matthias Gro. Leeds —3D 84
St Matthias St. Leeds —4D 84
(in two parts)
St Matthias Ter. Leeds —3D 84
St Michael Ct. Leeds —2G 83
St Michaels Clo. Bgly —6B 60
St Michael's Ct. Leeds —7D 66
St Michael's Cres. Leeds —1D 84
St Michael's Gro. Leeds —1D 84
St Michael's La. Leeds —2C 84
St Michael's Rd. B'frd —5J 79 (2A 6)
St Michael's Rd. Leeds —1D 84
St Michael's Ter. Leeds —1D 84
St Michael's Vs. Leeds —1D 84
(off St Michael's Cres.)
St Michaels Way. Add —1D 10
St Michael's Way. Bur W —2B 26
St Nicholas Rd. I'ly —4A 12
St Oswald's Gth. Guis —2H 45
St Oswald's Ter. Guis —2G 45
St Oswald St. C'frd —7D 126
St Paul's Av. B'frd —6H 97
St Paul's Clo. Mann —4J 79
(off Church St.)
St Paul's Dri. Wake —7K 139
St Paul's Gro. B'frd —6H 97
St Paul's Gro. I'ly —5D 12
St Paul's Pl. Leeds —5H 85 (6C 4)
St Pauls Ri. Add —2D 10
St Paul's Rd. B'shaw —2K 117
St Paul's Rd. Hal —3D 130
St Paul's Rd. Kei —5B 40
St Paul's Rd. Mann —3J 79
St Paul's Rd. Shipl —5G 61
St Paul's Rd. Wibs —6H 97
St Paul's St. Leeds —5G 85 (6B 4)
St Paul's St. Morl —4B 120
St Paul's Wlk. Wake —7K 139
St Peg Clo. Cleck —1G 135
St Peg La. Cleck —1G 135
St Peter's Av. Rothw —2H 123
St Peter's Av. Sower B —5G 129
St Peter's Clo. Birs —6B 118
St Peters Ct. Add —2D 10
St Peter's Ct. Leeds —2J 103
(LS11)
St Peter's Ct. Leeds —2H 83
(LS13)
St Peter's Cres. Morl —1A 120
St Peter's Gdns. Leeds —2G 83
St Peter's Gth. T'ner —5E 52
St Peter's Mt. Leeds —3H 83
St Peter's Pl. Leeds —5K 85 (6H 5)
St Peter's Sq. Leeds —5K 85 (6H 5)
St Peters Sq. Sower B —5G 129
(off Dean La.)
St Peter's St. Leeds —5K 85 (6G 5)
St Peter's Way. Men —6B 26
St Philip's Av. Leeds —2H 121
St Philip's Clo. Bur W —2B 26
St Philip's Clo. Dew —7H 137
St Philip's Clo. Leeds —2H 121
St Philips Ct. Hud —7B 144
St Philip's Dri. Bur W —2B 26
St Philip's Way. Bur W —1B 26
St Richard's Rd. Otley —7G 15
St Rouse Fold. B'frd —1B 98
St Stephen's Ct. Hal —6E 130
St Stephen's Ct. Leeds —5B 86 (5K 5)
St Stephen's Ct. Steet —4E 20
St Stephen's Rd. B'frd —3K 97
St Stephen's Rd. C'ley —5J 63
St Stephen's Rd. Leeds —5B 86 (5K 5)
St Stephen's Rd. Steet —5E 20
St Stephen's St. Hal —6E 130
St Stephen's Ter. B'frd —3A 98
St Stephen's Ter. Hal —7F 131
Saint St. B'frd —2G 97
St Thomas Row. Leeds —4K 85 (4G 5)
St Thomas's Rd. B'frd —6K 79 (3C 6)
St Vincent Rd. Pud —7C 82
St Wilfred's. Hal —2B 112
St Wilfrid's Av. Leeds —1C 86
St Wilfrid's Cir. Leeds —2D 86
St Wilfrid's Clo. B'frd —1F 97
St Wilfrid's Cres. B'frd —1F 97
St Wilfrid's Cres. Leeds —1D 86
St Wilfrid's Dri. Leeds —1C 86
St Wilfrid's Gth. Leeds —2D 86
St Wilfrid's Gro. Leeds —1C 86
St Wilfrid's Rd. B'frd —1F 97
St Wilfrid's St. C'ley —5K 63
Salcombe Pl. B'frd —4G 99
Salem Pl. Gar —6J 89
Salem Pl. Leeds —7J 85
Salem St. B'frd —5A 80 (2D 6)
Salem St. Q'bry —5H 95
Salisbury Av. Bail —1J 61
Salisbury Av. Leeds —5C 84
Salisbury Clo. Dew —7K 137
Salisbury Ct. H'fth —3H 65
Salisbury Gro. Leeds —5C 84
Salisbury M. H'fth —3H 65
Salisbury Pl. C'ley —5J 63
Salisbury Pl. Hal —6F 113
Salisbury Rd. B'frd —7J 61
Salisbury Rd. Kei —5J 39
Salisbury Rd. Leeds —5C 84
Salisbury Rd. Low M —1J 115
Salisbury Rd. Schol —7B 116
Salisbury St. C'ley —6J 63
Salisbury St. Rawd —7K 45
Salisbury St. Sower B —5J 129
Salisbury Ter. Hal —6F 113
Salisbury Ter. Leeds —5C 84
Salisbury Vw. H'fth —3H 65
Salisbury Vw. Leeds —5C 84
Salmon Cres. H'fth —3G 65
Sal Nook Clo. Low M —7K 97
Sal Royd Rd. Low M —2A 116
**Saltaire. —4G 61**
Saltaire. Cro R —4H 57
Saltaire Rd. Bgly —6D 42
Saltaire Rd. Shipl —4F 61
Saltburn Pl. B'frd —3F 79
Saltburn St. Hal —1D 130
Salt Drake. Sower B —1D 140
**Salterhebble. —5H 131**
Salterhebble Hill. Hal —5H 131
Salterhebble Ter. Hal —5H 131
(off Huddersfield Rd.)
Salter St. Bat —6F 137
Salt Horn Clo. Oaken —2B 116
Saltonstall La. Hal —2F 111
Salt St. B'frd —4J 79 (1A 6)
Salt St. Hal —7E 112
Sampson St. Liv —4K 135
Samuel St. Kei —4K 39
Sandacre Clo. B'frd —2G 81
Sandale Wlk. B'frd —7F 97
Sandall Clo. Kip —4B 108
Sandal Magna. Hal —7E 96
Sandals Rd. Bail —1J 61
Sandal Way. Birs —6D 118
Sandbeck Ind. Est. Weth —2K 17
Sandbeck La. Weth —2K 17
(in two parts)
Sandbeck Way. Weth —2K 17
Sandbed Ct. Leeds —2B 88
Sandbed La. Leeds —2B 88
Sandbed Lawns. Leeds —2B 88
Sand Beds. Q'bry —5J 95
Sandbeds Cres. Hal —6C 112
Sandbeds Rd. Hal —7B 112
Sandbeds Ter. Hal —6C 112
Sanderling Ct. B'frd —6C 78
Sanderling Gth. Leeds —2K 121
Sanderling Way. Leeds —2K 121
Sanderson Av. B'frd —5J 97
Sanderson La. Oult —5J 123
Sandfield Av. Leeds —6E 66
Sandfield Gth. Leeds —6E 66
Sandfield Rd. B'frd —6D 62
Sandfield Vw. Leeds —6E 66
(off Sandfield Av.)
**Sandford. —7J 65**
Sandford Pl. Kirks —1A 84
Sandford Rd. B'frd —6E 80
Sandford Rd. Leeds —2B 84
Sandforth Dri. Hal —5G 113
Sandgate Dri. Kip —3B 108
Sandgate La. M'fld —5C 108
(in two parts)
Sandgate Ri. Kip —4C 108
Sandgate Ter. Kip —5C 108
Sandgate Wlk. B'frd —4H 99
Sandhall Av. Hal —1B 130
Sandhall Cres. Hal —7B 112
(off Sandhall Grn.)
Sandhall Dri. Hal —1B 130
Sandhall Grn. Hal —1B 130
(in two parts)
Sandhall La. Hal —1B 130
Sandhill Ct. Leeds —1K 67
Sandhill Cres. Leeds —7A 50
Sandhill Dri. Leeds —7K 49
Sandhill Gro. Leeds —6A 50
Sand Hill La. Leeds —1K 67
Sandhill Lawns. Leeds —1K 67
Sandhill Mt. B'frd —6D 62
Sandhill Mt. Leeds —6A 50
Sandhill Oval. Leeds —6A 50
**Sandhills. —7C 52**
Sandholme Cres. Hip —1D 132
Sandholme Dri. B'frd —6D 62
Sandholme Dri. Bur W —2B 26
Sandhurst Av. Leeds —2C 86
Sandhurst Gro. Leeds —2C 86
Sandhurst Mt. Leeds —1C 86
Sandhurst Pl. Leeds —2C 86
Sandhurst Rd. Leeds —2C 86
Sandhurst St. C'ley —6J 63
Sandhurst Ter. Leeds —2C 86
Sandiford Clo. Leeds —2B 88
Sandiford Ter. Leeds —2B 88
Sandleas Way. Leeds —3D 88
Sandlewood Clo. Leeds —1G 103
Sandlewood Grn. Leeds —1H 103
Sandmead Clo. B'frd —3G 99
Sandmead Clo. Morl —1A 120
Sandmead Cft. Morl —1A 120
Sandmead Way. Morl —1A 120
Sandmoor Av. Leeds —5K 49
Sandmoor Chase. Leeds —6K 49
Sandmoor Clo. Leeds —6K 49
Sandmoor Clo. T'tn —7J 77
Sandmoor Ct. Leeds —6K 49
Sandmoor Dri. Leeds —5K 49
Sandmoor Gdns. Hal —2B 114
Sandmoor Gth. B'frd —3D 62
Sandmoor Grn. Leeds —5J 49
Sandmoor Ho. B'frd —5E 62
(off Fairhaven Grn.)
Sandmoor La. Leeds —5K 49
Sandmoor M. Leeds —6K 49
Sandon Gro. Leeds —4A 104
Sandon Mt. Leeds —4A 104
Sandon Pl. Leeds —4A 104
Sandown Av. Hal —3C 112
Sandown Rd. Hal —3C 112
Sandpiper App. Morl —4C 120
Sandpiper M. B'frd —6C 78
Sandringham App. Leeds —1A 68
Sandringham Av. Pud —7C 82
Sandringham Clo. Cytn —1D 96
Sandringham Clo. Morl —2C 120
Sandringham Ct. Cytn —1D 96
Sandringham Ct. Hud —4K 145
Sandringham Ct. Morl —2C 120
Sandringham Cres. Leeds —1K 67
Sandringham Dri. Leeds —1K 67
Sandringham Gdns. Leeds —1K 67
Sandringham Grn. Leeds —7A 50
Sandringham Mt. Leeds —1A 68
Sandringham Rd. Cytn —1D 96
Sandringham Rd. Weth —3J 17
Sandringham Way. Leeds —1K 67
Sandsend Clo. B'frd —2D 78
Sandside Clo. B'frd —4B 98
Sandstone Dri. Leeds —6G 83
Sand St. Haw —6E 56
Sand St. Kei —4A 40
Sandway. Leeds —3K 87
Sandway Gdns. Leeds —3K 87
Sandway Gro. Leeds —3K 87
Sandwich Cres. Hud —6F 145
Sandyacres. Rothw —1H 123
Sandyacres Cres. Rothw —1H 123
Sandyacres Dri. Rothw —1H 123
Sandy Bank Av. Rothw —1H 123
Sandy Banks. H'den —4F 59
Sandy Beck. All —2A 78
Sandy Dike La. Sower B —1G 141
Sandyfield Ter. Bat —2F 137
(off Bradford Rd.)
Sandyfoot. Bklnd —1A 20
Sandy Ga. Hare —3K 31
Sandy Ga. Kei —3J 39
Sandygate Ter. B'frd —1F 99
Sandy Gro. Rothw —1H 123
Sandylands. Cro H —3A 20
(off Anderton St.)
**Sandy Lane. —1K 77**
Sandy Lobby. Pool W —4G 29
Sandymoor. All —1A 78
Sandy Wlk. B'hpe —1K 47
Sandy Way. Yead —4K 45
Sandywood Ct. H'fth —5G 65
Sandywood St. Kei —3A 40
Sangster Way. B'frd —5C 98
Santa Monica Cres. B'frd —5C 62
Santa Monica Gro. B'frd —5C 62
Santa Monica Rd. B'frd —5C 62
Santon Ho. B'frd —2A 98
(off Manchester Rd.)
Sapgate La. T'tn —7J 77
Sapling Gro. Cotts. Hal —4D 130
Saplin St. B'frd —4H 79
Sapphire Ct. Bat —2E 136
Sarah St. E Ard —7K 121
Sardinia St. Leeds —1K 103
Savile Av. B'frd —6E 62
Savile Av. Leeds —2K 85
Savile Clo. Brigh —5K 133
Savile Cres. Hal —2F 131
Savile Dri. Hal —3F 131
Savile Dri. Leeds —1K 85
Savile Glen. Hal —2F 131
Savile Grn. Hal —2G 131
Savile La. Brigh —5K 133
Savile Lea. Hal —2F 131
Savile Mt. Hal —3F 131
Savile Mt. Leeds —2K 85
Savile Pde. Hal —3F 131
**Savile Park. —3F 131**
Savile Pk. Hal —3F 131
(in three parts)
Savile Pk. Gdns. Hal —3F 131
Savile Pk. Rd. Cleck —4F 117
Savile Pk. Rd. Hal —3F 131
Savile Pk. St. Hal —3E 130
Savile Pk. Ter. Hal —3E 130
(off Moorfield St.)
Savile Pit La. Dew —7A 138
Savile Pl. Leeds —2K 85
Savile Precinct. C'frd —7C 126
Savile Rd. C'frd —7C 126
Savile Rd. Ell —3K 143
Savile Rd. Hal —2F 131
Savile Rd. Leeds —2K 85
Savile Rd. Meth —4H 125
Savile Royd. Hal —3F 131
Savile St. Dew & Bat —6H 137
Savile Way. Lfds B —1A 144
Saville Clo. Loft —6E 122
Saville Ct. Otley —3H 27
Saville Grn. Leeds —5B 86
Saville's Sq. Morl —3A 120
(off Queen St.)
Saville St. Cleck —6F 117
Saville Wlk. Dew —7G 137
(off Swindon Rd.)
Sawley St. Kei —5K 39
Saw Mill St. Leeds —7H 85
**Sawood. —5H 75**
Sawood La. Oxe —4H 75
(in two parts)
Sawrey Pl. B'frd —7K 79 (6C 6)
Sawyers Gth. Add —1E 10
Saxon Ct. Leeds —1H 67
Saxon Ga. Leeds —2H 67
Saxon Grn. Leeds —2G 67
Saxon Gro. Leeds —1G 67
Saxon Mt. Leeds —1H 67
Saxon Rd. Leeds —2G 67
Saxon St. B'frd —5J 79
Saxon St. Hal —1D 130
Saxon Way. C'frd —7G 127
Saxton Av. B'frd —5E 96
Saxton Ct. Gar —5K 89
Saxton Gdns. Leeds —7J 5
(in three parts)
Saxton Ho. Yead —5K 45
(off Well La.)
Saxton La. Leeds —6A 86 (7J 5)
Saxton St. Liv —3A 136
Sayers Clo. Leeds —1B 84
Sayle Av. B'frd —5D 98
Sayner La. Leeds —7K 85
Sayner Rd. H'let —7K 85
Scafell Ct. Dew —6J 137
Scalebor Pk. Clo. Bur W —2A 26
Scale Hill. Hud —7G 145
Scales La. B'frd —6D 98
Scaley St. B'frd —6F 81
Scammonden Rd. Bklnd —3J 141
Scarborough Gro. Shipl —5G 61
Scarborough Junct. Leeds —4G 83
Scarborough La. Ting —6D 120
Scarborough Rd. Otley —3H 27
Scarborough Rd. Shipl —5G 61
Scarborough St. Ting —6D 120
Scarborough Ter. Ell —3K 143
**Scar Bottom. —4D 130**
Scar Bottom. Hal —4D 130
Scar Bottom La. G'lnd —2D 142
**Scarcroft. —3A 52**
Scarcroft Ct. S'cft —3B 52
**Scarcroft Hill. —4C 52**
Scarcroft Ho. B'frd —5B 98
(off Parkway)
Scarcroft Vw. Leeds —5H 51
Scargill Clo. Leeds —4B 86
Scargill Grange. Leeds —5B 86
Scargill Ho. B'frd —2G 7
Scar Head Rd. Sower B —6K 129
Scar Hill. Oxe —4G 75
**Scarlet Heights. —5K 95**
Scarlet Heights. Q'bry —5K 95
Scarr End La. M'end —6D 136
Scarr End Vw. Dew —6D 136
Scarsdale La. Bard —4C 34
Scarsdale Ridge. Bard —4C 34
Scarth Av. Leeds —3C 86
Scarwood Clo. Bgly —7A 42
Scatcherd La. Morl —4K 119
Schofield Ct. Morl —3A 120
(off Queensway)
Scholars Wlk. B'frd —2D 80
**Scholebrook. —3A 100**
Scholebrooke Ct. B'frd —5G 99
(off Broadfield Clo.)
Scholebrook La. B'frd & Pud —3A 100
**Scholemoor. —1E 96**
Scholemoor Av. B'frd —2E 96
Scholemoor La. B'frd —1E 96
Scholemoor Rd. B'frd —1F 97
**Scholes. —7B 116**
**(nr. Cleckheaton)**
**Scholes. —3B 56**
**(nr. Oakworth)**
**Scholes. —6D 70**
**(nr. Whinmoor)**
Scholes La. G'lnd —7E 130
Scholes La. Oakw —3B 56
Scholes La. Schol —7B 116
Scholes La. Whinm —4C 70
Scholes Rd. C'frd —6K 127
Scholes Rd. Hud —7G 145
Scholes St. B'frd —4K 97
Scholey Av. Brigh —1G 145
**Scholey Hill. —7E 124**
Scholey Rd. Brigh —1G 145
School Av. Dew —7D 136
School Clo. Hal —1D 112
School Clo. Leeds —3H 101
School Clo. Sower B —5G 141
School Cote Brow. H'fld —1F 113
School Cote Ter. Hal —1F 113
School Cres. Dew —7D 136
School Cres. Hal —7D 94
School Cft. Rothw —1G 123
School Fold. Low M —1H 115
**School Green. —7A 78**
School Grn. B'hpe —1J 47
School Grn. Brigh —1G 145
School Grn. T'tn —7A 78
School Grn. Av. T'tn —7K 77
School Gro. Dew —7D 136
School Ho. Hal —4A 114
School La. Aber —5E 72
School La. Add —1C 10
School La. B'frd —4J 97
(BD5)
School La. B'frd —5H 97
(BD6)
School La. Chap A —6J 67
School La. Coll —2F 35
School La. Colt —7C 88
School La. Dew —7D 136
School La. E Kes —5A 34
School La. Halt —5J 87
School La. Harts —6F 135
School La. I'wth —1D 112
School La. Kei —4B 40
School La. Leeds —6E 66
School La. S'wram —5A 132
School La. Wltn —5F 19
School La. Wike —3D 50
School Pl. S'ley —3D 82
School Pl. Wyke —3J 115
School Ridge. T'tn —5G 77
School Rd. Kei —4H 39
School Rd. Weth —3K 17
School Sq. B'frd —6K 81
School St. Birs —6D 118

School St.—Silver Birch Av.

School St. B'frd —6A 80 (3E 6)
(BD1, in two parts)
School St. B'frd —6D 98
(BD4)
School St. Butt —7E 96
School St. C'frd —7C 126
(nr. Savile Rd.)
School St. C'frd —6E 126
(nr. Wheldon Rd.)
School St. Chur —6C 102
School St. Cytn —2B 96
School St. Cleck —2D 134
School St. Ctly —5B 60
School St. Cull —6B 58
School St. Cut H —3E 98
School St. Denh —5C 76
School St. Far —2B 82
School St. G'lnd —1F 143
School St. Hal —2H 131
School St. Kei —1J 39
School St. Low M —1J 115
School St. Morl —3B 120
School St. Norr —6K 135
School St. Oaken —3C 116
School St. Oss —7C 138
School St. Pud —7B 82
(in two parts)
School St. Rbtwn —6G 135
School St. Steet —5E 20
(in two parts)
School St. Ting —3D 138
School St. Wilsd —7G 59
School Vw. Leeds —2E 84
School Wlk. Kei —4H 39
Sconce La. H Eld —3G 43
Score Hill. Hal —3A 114
Scoresby St. B'frd —6B 80 (4G 7)
Scotchman Clo. Morl —5K 119
Scotchman La. Morl —1H 137
Scotchman Rd. B'frd —3F 79
Scotch Pk. Ind. Est. Leeds —5D 84
Scotland. —6F 47
Scotland Clo. H'fth —1F 65
Scotland La. Hal —5D 110
Scotland La. H'fth —3E 46
Scotland Mill La. Leeds —2F 67
Scotland St. Birs —5A 118
Scotland Way. H'fth —7E 46
Scotland Wood Rd. Leeds —2F 67
Scott Av. Heck —2B 136
Scott Bldgs. Leeds —6D 66
(off Oddy Pl.)
Scott Clo. Heck —4C 136
Scott Clo. Swil —5E 106
Scott Green. —7F 101
Scott Grn. Gild —6F 101
Scott Grn. Cres. Gild —6F 101
Scott Grn. Dri. Gild —6F 101
Scott Grn. Gro. Gild —6G 101
Scott Grn. Mt. Gild —6F 101
Scott Grn. Vw. Gild —6G 101
Scott Hall. —7J 67
Scott Hall Av. Leeds —7J 67
Scott Hall Cres. Leeds —6H 67
Scott Hall Dri. Leeds —1J 85
Scott Hall Grn. Leeds —7J 67
Scott Hall Gro. Leeds —7J 67
Scott Hall Pl. Leeds —7J 67
Scott Hall Rd. Leeds —5H 67
Scott Hall Row. Leeds —1K 85
Scott Hall Sq. Leeds —7J 67
Scott Hall St. Leeds —1J 85
Scott Hall Ter. Leeds —7J 67
Scott Hall Wlk. Leeds —1J 85
Scott Hall Way. Leeds —6J 67
Scott La. Cleck —7G 117
Scott La. Gom —6K 117
Scott La. Leeds —7K 83
Scott La. Morl —5H 119
Scott La. Riddl —1C 40
Scott La. Weth —4J 17
Scott La. W. Riddl —1B 40
Scott M. Woth —4J 17
Scotts Almshouse's. Leeds —5A 104
Scotts Hill Clo. T'ner —6D 52
Scott Sq. Leeds —7K 83
Scott St. Kei —4K 39
Scott St. Pud —7D 82
Scott Va. Hud —6K 145
Scott Wood La. Leeds —7H 67
(in three parts)
Scotty Bank. Brigh —6G 133
(off Bridge End)
Scotty Cft. La. Brigh —7G 133
(off Bramston St.)
Scout Bottom La. H Bri —7B 110
Scout Clo. Myth —7B 110
Scout La. H Bri —7A 110
Scratcherd Gro. Morl —3K 119
Sculptor Pl. Brigh —5G 133
(off Waterloo Rd.)
Seacroft. —7K 69
Seacroft Av. Leeds —7K 69
Seacroft Cres. Leeds —7K 69
Seacroft Ga. Leeds —7K 69
(in two parts)
Seacroft Ho. B'frd —6E 62
(off Rowantree Dri.)
Seacroft Ind. Est. Leeds —5K 69
(nr. Coal Rd.)
Seacroft Ind. Est. Leeds —5J 69
(nr. Ramshead App.)
Seaforth Av. Leeds —2C 86
Seaforth Gro. Leeds —2C 86
Seaforth Mt. Leeds —2C 86
Seaforth Pl. Leeds —2C 86
Seaforth Rd. Leeds —2C 86
Seaforth Ter. Leeds —2C 86
Seaton St. B'frd —6D 80 (4K 7)
Second Av. Bard —5C 34
Second Av. B'frd —4E 80
Second Av. Hal —4F 131
Second Av. Kei —5K 39
Second Av. Leeds —6E 84
Second Av. Liv —4D 134
Second Av. Rawd —6A 46
Second Av. Rothw —7H 105
Second Av. Weth —4K 17
Second St. Low M —1A 116
Sedan St. Hal —2G 131
(off Trinity Rd.)
Sedbergh Dri. I'ly —6C 12
Sedbergh Pk. I'ly —6B 12
Sedburgh Chambers. I'ly —6B 12
(off Chantry Dri.)
Sedburgh Clo. Leeds —6F 87
Sedburgh Rd. Hal —3H 131
Sedgefield Ter. B'frd —3B 6
Sedge Gro. Haw —4E 56
Sedgewick Clo. B'frd —2B 6
Sedgewick St. Birs —6C 118
Sedgfield Ter. B'frd —6K 79
Sedgwick Clo. B'frd —5K 79
Seed Hill Ter. Hal —1A 112
Seed Hill Ter. Steet —5E 20
Seed Row. B'frd —6D 98
Seed St. Low M —1K 115
See Mill La. Hal —5F 113
Sefton Av. Brigh —3F 133
Sefton Av. Leeds —3G 103
Sefton Cres. Brigh —3F 133
Sefton Dri. Brigh —3F 133
Sefton Dri. I'ly —6B 12
Sefton Gro. B'frd —2D 80
Sefton Pl. B'frd —2D 80
Sefton Pl. Kei —3A 40
Sefton St. Hal —7E 112
Sefton St. Kei —3A 40
Sefton St. Leeds —3H 103
Sefton Ter. Hal —7E 112
Sefton Ter. Leeds —3G 103
Selborne Gro. B'frd —3H 79
Selborne Gro. Kei —6J 39
Selborne Mt. B'frd —3J 79
Selborne Ter. B'frd —3H 79
Selborne Ter. Shipl —6H 61
Selborne Vs. B'frd —2H 79
(off Selborne Gro.)
Selbourne Vs. Cytn —3C 96
Selby. Hal —1B 112
Selby Av. Leeds —5G 87
Selby Rd. Leeds —5G 87
Selby Rd. M'fld —1H 107
Seldon St. B'frd —3H 97
Selene Clo. Gom —5A 118
Sellars Fold. —2G 97
Sellerdale Av. Wyke —6K 115
Sellerdale Dri. Wyke —5K 115
Sellerdale Ri. Wyke —5K 115
Sellerdale Way. Wyke —6K 115
Sellers Fold. B'frd —2G 97
Selside Ho. B'frd —5E 62
(off Garsdale Av.)
Selso Rd. Dew —7K 137
Seminary St. Leeds —4G 85 (3B 4)
Semon Av. B'frd —7B 62
Senior Way. B'frd —7A 80
(in two parts)
Serpentine Rd. Cleck —7F 117
Servia Dri. Leeds —2J 85 (1E 4)
Servia Gdns. Leeds —2J 85 (1E 4)
Servia Hill. Leeds —2H 85 (1D 4)
Servia Rd. Leeds —2H 85 (1D 4)
Service Rd. Leeds —4E 104
Sevenoaks Mead. All —4B 78
Seventh Av. Liv —3D 134
Seventh Av. Rothw —1J 123
Severn Dri. Gar —1B 108
Severn Rd. B'frd —2C 80
Severn Rd. H'let —3B 104
Severn Way. H'let —2B 104
Sewage Works Rd. Leeds —3E 104
Sewell Rd. B'frd —7D 80
Seymour St. B'frd —7C 80 (5J 7)
Shackleton Ter. H'den —3E 58
(off Hill End La.)
Shadwell. —7H 51
Shadwell La. Leeds —2K 67
Shadwell Pk. Av. Leeds —6E 50
Shadwell Pk. Clo. Leeds —6E 50
Shadwell Pk. Ct. Leeds —7E 50
Shadwell Pk. Dri. Leeds —7E 50
Shadwell Pk. Gdns. Leeds —6E 50
Shadwell Pk. Gro. Leeds —7E 50
Shadwell Wlk. Leeds —1A 68
Shaftesbury Av. B'frd —4D 78
Shaftesbury Av. Brigh —2H 145
Shaftesbury Av. Leeds —3C 68
Shaftesbury Av. Shipl —5J 61
Shaftesbury Ct. B'frd —4D 78
Shaftesbury Rd. Leeds —2C 68
Shafton La. Leeds —1F 103
Shafton Pl. Leeds —1F 103
Shafton St. Leeds —1F 103
Shafton Vw. Leeds —1F 103
Shakespeare App. Leeds —4B 86
Shakespeare Av. Leeds —4B 86
Shakespeare Clo. Guis —3H 45
Shakespeare Clo. Leeds —4B 86
Shakespeare Ct. Leeds —4B 86
Shakespeare Gdns. Leeds —4B 86
Shakespeare Grange. Leeds —4B 86
Shakespeare Lawn. Leeds —4B 86
Shakespeare Rd. Guis —3G 45
Shakespeare St. Hal —2G 131
Shakespeare St. Leeds —3B 86
Shakespeare Towers. Leeds —4B 86
Shakespeare Va. Leeds —4B 86
Shakespeare Wlk. Leeds —4B 86
Shalimar St. Hal —1D 130
Shambles, The. Weth —4J 17
Shann Av. Kei —3H 39
Shann Cres. Kei —3H 39
Shann La. Kei —3H 39
Shannon Clo. Brigh —2E 144
Shannon Clo. I'ly —6K 11
Shannon Rd. Brigh —2E 144
Shannon Rd. Leeds —5A 86 (6K 5)
Shannon St. Leeds —5A 86 (6J 5)
Shann St. B'frd —1K 79
Shapla Clo. Kei —5J 39
Sharp Av. B'frd —6J 97
Sharpe St. B'frd —7A 80 (6D 6)
Sharpe St. Heck —5B 136
Sharp Ho. Rd. Leeds —3A 122
Sharp La. Leeds & Rob H —2A 122
(nr. Throstle Rd.)
Sharp La. Leeds —2K 121
(nr. Town St.)
Sharp M. Leeds —7F 67
Sharp Row. Pud —7C 82
Sharp St. B'frd —5J 97
Sharp St. Dew —7H 137
Shaw. —3D 74
Shaw Barn Cft. Weth —4G 17
Shaw Barn La. Weth —4G 17
Shaw Booth La. Hal —3H 111
Shaw Clo. Gar —1A 108
Shaw Clo. Guis —3H 45
Shaw Clo. Holy G —5G 143
Shaw Cross. —6A 138
Shaw Hill. Hal —3G 131
(in two parts)
Shaw Lane. —3J 45
Shaw La. Ell —1C 144
Shaw La. Guis —2H 45
Shaw La. Hal —3H 131
Shaw La. Holy G —5F 143
Shaw La. Kei —2B 58
Shaw La. Leeds —7D 66
Shaw La. Oxe —3D 74
Shaw La. Q'bry —1K 113
Shaw La. Ripp —7E 140
Shaw La. Sower B —7K 129
Shaw La. Gdns. Guis —2H 45
Shaw Leys. Yead —3J 45
Shaw Lodge. Hal —3H 131
Shaw Mt. L'ft —7G 111
Shaw Royd. Yead —3J 45
Shaw Royd Ct. Yead —3J 45
(off Shaw Royd)
Shaws La. Bar E —6G 71
Shaw's La. Sower B —7C 128
Shaw St. Cleck —1D 134
Shaw St. Holy G —5G 143
Shaw St. Low M —1H 115
Shaw Vs. Guis —2H 45
(off Queensway)
Shay Brow. —2K 77
Shay Clo. B'frd —1F 79
Shay Cres. B'frd —1E 78
Shay Dri. B'frd —1E 78
Shayfield La. Carl —4F 123
Shay Fold. B'frd —1E 78
Shaygate. Wilsd —1J 77
Shay Grange. B'frd —7E 60
Shay Gro. B'frd —1F 79
Shay La. B'frd —7E 60
Shay La. H Wd —3H 99
Shay La. Oven —4E 112
Shay La. Wilsd —7H 59
Shay St. Leeds —2H 85 (1C 4)
Shay Syke. Hal —2H 131
Shay, The. —3G 131
Sheaf St. Leeds —7K 85
Shearbridge. —7J 79 (6A 6)
Shearbridge Grn. B'frd —7J 79 (6A 6)
Shearbridge Pl. B'frd —7J 79 (6A 6)
Shearbridge Rd. B'frd —7J 79 (5A 6)
Shearbridge Ter. B'frd —1J 97 (6A 6)
Shear's Yd. Leeds —6K 85 (7G 5)
Shed St. Kei —4A 40
Sheep Hill La. Q'bry —4B 96
Sheepridge Gro. Hud —6J 145
Sheepridge Rd. Hud —6J 145
Sheepscar. —3K 85
Sheepscar Ct. Leeds —3K 85 (1G 5)
Sheepscar Gro. Leeds —4K 85 (3G 5)
Sheepscar Row. Leeds —3K 85 (2H 5)
Sheepscar St. N. Leeds
(in two parts) —2J 85 (1G 5)
Sheepscar St. S. Leeds —3K 85 (2H 5)
Sheepscar Way. Leeds —2K 85
Sheila Ter. Heck —5A 136
Sheldon Ridge. Bier —7D 98
Sheldrake Av. B'frd —6C 78
Shelf. —1C 114
Shelf Hall La. Hal —2B 114
Shelf Moor. Hal —7C 96
Shelldrake Dri. Leeds —2K 121
Shelley Av. Heck —6C 136
Shelley Clo. W'ford —4A 124
Shelley Cres. Oult —4A 124
Shelley Gro. B'frd —5E 78
Shell La. C'ley —6K 63
(in two parts)
Shepcote Clo. Leeds —1K 65
Shepcote Cres. Leeds —1K 65
Shepherds Fold. Hal —4K 113
Shepherd's Gro. Leeds —1A 86
Shepherd's La. Leeds —1A 86
Shepherd's Pl. Leeds —1B 86
Shepherds Thorn La. Brigh & Hud —2H 145
Shepherd St. B'frd —2G 97
Shepton Ho. B'frd —7D 6
Sherborne Dri. Kei —6G 39
Sherborne Rd. Gt Hor —7K 79 (6A 6)
Sherborne Rd. Idle —3D 62
Sherbrooke Av. Leeds —6H 87
Sherburn App. Leeds —6A 70
Sherburn Clo. B'shaw —1K 117
Sherburn Clo. Leeds —6A 70
(off Sherburn Pl.)
Sherburn Ct. Leeds —6A 70
(off York Rd.)
Sherburn Gro. B'shaw —1K 117
Sherburn Pl. Leeds —6A 70
Sherburn Rd. Brigh —1D 144
Sherburn Rd. Leeds —6A 70
Sherburn Rd. N. Leeds —4K 69
Sherburn Row. Leeds —6A 70
(off York Rd.)
Sherburn Sq. Leeds —6A 70
(off Sherburn Pl.)
Sherburn Wlk. Leeds —6A 70
(off York Rd.)
Sheridan Clo. Pud —7D 82
Sheridan Ct. Pud —7D 82
Sheridan St. B'frd —2C 98
Sheridan Way. Pud —7D 82
Sheriff La. Bgly —6C 42
Sherwell Gro. All —4C 78
Sherwell Ri. All —4C 78
Sherwood Av. Gom —7K 117
Sherwood Clo. Bgly —6C 42
Sherwood Clo. Dew —5D 136
Sherwood Clo. Gom —7K 117
Sherwood Grn. Rob H —4C 122
Sherwood Gro. Shipl —4E 60
Sherwood Ind. Est. Rob H —4D 122
Sherwood Pl. B'frd —3D 80
Sherwood Rd. Brigh —6J 133
Sherwood Works. Brigh —7K 133
Shetcliffe La. B'frd —6D 98
Shetcliffe Rd. B'frd —6D 98
Shetland Clo. B'frd —1B 80
Shibden Dri. Bat —2D 136
Shibden Gth. Shib —1A 132
Shibden Grange Dri. Hal —6K 113
Shibden Hall. —7K 113
Shibden Hall Cft. Hal —1A 132
Shibden Hall Rd. Hal —7J 113
Shibden Head. —1G 113
Shibden Head La. Q'bry —7G 95
Shibden Vw. Q'bry —7H 95
Shield Clo. Leeds —2C 88
Shield Hall La. Sower —4E 128
Shipley. —4H 61
Shipley Airedale Rd. B'frd —5B 80 (2F 7)
Shipley Fields Rd. Shipl —7H 61
(in two parts)
Shipley Glen Cable Tramway. —2F 61
Ship St. Brigh —6H 133
Shipton M. Morl —4B 120
Ship Yd. Leeds —6E 4
Shire Clo. B'frd —7F 97
Shire Oak Rd. Leeds —7E 66
Shire Oak St. Leeds —7D 66
Shirley Av. Birs —5B 118
Shirley Av. Gom —7K 117
Shirley Av. Wyke —6H 115
Shirley Clo. Otley —3K 27
Shirley Cres. Wyke —6H 115
Shirley Dri. Leeds —1G 83
Shirley Gro. Gom —7K 117
Shirley Gro. Hal —1G 133
Shirley Mnr. Gdns. B'frd —6F 81
(off Moorside La.)
Shirley Mt. Gom —7K 117
Shirley Pde. Gom —7J 117
Shirley Pl. Gom —7K 117
Shirley Pl. Wyke —6J 115
Shirley Rd. B'frd —5F 99
(BD4)
Shirley Rd. B'frd —7H 79
(BD7)
Shirley Rd. Gom —1K 135
Shirley Sq. Gom —7K 117
Shirley St. Haw —5D 56
Shirley St. Shipl —4F 61
Shirley Ter. Gom —7K 117
Shirley Wlk. Gom —7K 117
Shoebridge Av. Ebrn —4B 20
Sholebroke Av. Leeds —1K 85
Sholebroke Ct. Leeds —1K 85
Sholebroke Mt. Leeds —1J 85
Sholebroke Pl. Leeds —1K 85
Sholebroke St. Leeds —1J 85
Sholebroke Ter. Leeds —7K 67
Sholebroke Vw. Leeds —1K 85
Shop La. Loft —7D 122
Shore End La. Hal —5C 92
Shoreham Rd. Leeds —6C 84
Short Clo. Wyke —2H 115
Short La. Leeds —5J 67
Short Row. Low M —1K 115
Short Way. S'ley —4J 81
Shortway. T'tn —7A 78
Shroggs Rd. Hal —5D 112
Shroggs St. Hal —7E 112
Shroggs, The. Steet —5E 20
Shroggs Va. Ter. Hal —7E 112
Shuttleworth La. B'frd —5E 78
Shuttocks Clo. Kip —3A 108
Shuttocks Fold. Kip —3B 108
Shutts La. Nor G —5E 114
Sickleholme Ct. Hud —4K 145
Sickle St. Cleck —7G 117
Sicklinghall. —4A 16
Sicklinghall Rd. Weth —4D 16
Siddal. —5J 131
Siddal Gro. Hal —4H 131
Siddal La. Hal —4J 131
Siddall St. Leeds —7H 85
Siddal New Rd. Hal —3H 131
Siddal Pl. Hal —5J 131
Siddal St. Hal —5J 131
Siddal Top La. Hal —4J 131
Siddal Vw. Hal —4J 131
Side Copse. Otley —2K 27
Sidings Clo. B'frd —2K 79
Sidings, The. Guis —2F 45
Sidings, The. Shipl —4J 61
Sidney St. Leeds —5J 85 (6F 5)
Siegen Clo. Morl —3A 120
Siegen Mnr. Morl —3A 120
(off Wesley St.)
Silcoates Av. Wren —7K 139
Silcoates Ct. Wake —7K 139
Silcoates La. Wren —7K 139
Silk Mill App. Leeds —2J 65
Silk Mill Av. Leeds —1H 65
Silk Mill Bank. Leeds —2H 65
Silk Mill Clo. Leeds —1H 65
Silk Mill Dri. E Mor —2J 41
Silk Mill Dri. Leeds —2H 65
Silk Mill Gdns. Leeds —2H 65
Silk Mill Grn. Leeds —2J 65
Silk Mill M. Leeds —2K 65
Silk Mill Rd. Leeds —2H 65
Silk Mill Way. Leeds —2J 65
Silkstone Clo. Gar —4B 90
Silkstone Ct. Leeds —4A 88
Silkstone Way. Leeds —4A 88
Silk St. B'frd —3G 79
Silsbridge St. B'frd —4B 6
Silsden. —1G 21
Silsden Rd. Add —2K 9
Silsden Rd. Riddl —6C 22
Silson La. Bail —7A 44
Silver Birch Av. Wyke —5K 115

Silver Birch Clo.—Southway


Silver Birch Clo. Wyke —5K 115
Silver Birch Dri. Wyke —5K 115
Silver Birch Gro. Wyke —5K 115
Silver Ct. Leeds —4D 82
Silverdale Av. Guis —3G 45
Silverdale Av. Leeds —6D 50
Silverdale Av. Riddl —2C 40
Silverdale Clo. Guis —4G 45
Silverdale Cres. Guis —3G 45
Silverdale Dri. Guis —4G 45
Silverdale Grange. Guis —4G 45
Silverdale Gro. Guis —4F 45
Silverdale Mt. Guis —4G 45
Silverdale Rd. B'frd —4A 98
Silverdale Rd. Guis —4F 45
Silverdale Ter. G'lnd —3E 142
Silverhill Av. B'frd —4F 81
Silverhill Dri. B'frd —5F 81
Silverhill Rd. B'frd —4E 80
Silver La. Yead —4K 45
Silver Mill Hill. Otley —4K 27
Silver Royd Av. Leeds —7K 83
Silver Royd Clo. Leeds —7K 83
Silver Royd Dri. Leeds —7K 83
Silver Royd Gth. Leeds —7K 83
Silver Royd Gro. Leeds —7K 83
Silver Royd Hill. Leeds —7K 83
Silver Royd Pl. Leeds —7K 83
Silver Royd Rd. Leeds —7K 83
Silver Royd St. Leeds —7K 83
Silver Royd Ter. Leeds —7K 83
Silver St. Bees —7G 85
Silver St. B'frd —4H 79
Silver St. Hal —1G 131
Silverwood Av. Hal —6A 112
Silverwood Wlk. Hal —6A 112
(in two parts)
Silwood Dri. B'frd —2E 80
Simes St. B'frd —6K 79 (3C 6)
Simm Carr La. Shib —3H 113
Simmonds La. Hal —3H 131
Simmons Ct. Leeds —7B 86
Simms Dene. All —1A 78
Simon Clo. B'frd —4H 99
Simon Fld. Wyke —5J 115
*Simon Marks Ct. Leeds —1C 102*
*(off Lynwood Gth.)*
**Simpson Green. —3E 62**
Simpson Gro. B'frd —3E 62
Simpson Gro. Leeds —6D 84
Simpson Rd. H Bri —7A 110
Simpson St. E Ard —7A 122
Simpson St. Hal —5F 113
Simpson St. Kei —4J 39
Sinclair Rd. B'frd —7B 62
Sinden M. B'frd —2D 62
Singleton St. B'frd —5A 80 (1E 6)
Sion Hill. Sid —5J 131
*Sir Francis Crossley's Almshouses.*
*(off Margaret St.) Hal —1F 131*
Sir George Martin Dri. Leeds
—7D 48
Sir Isaac Holden Pl. List —6H 79
Sir Karl Cohen Sq. Leeds —6B 84
Sir Wilfred Pl. B'frd —4D 62
Siskin Ct. Morl —4B 120
Sissons Av. Leeds —3H 121
Sissons Cres. Leeds —4H 121
Sissons Dri. Leeds —3H 121
Sissons Grn. Leeds —3H 121
Sissons Gro. Leeds —3H 121
Sissons La. Leeds —3H 121
Sissons Mt. Leeds —4G 121
Sissons Pl. Leeds —2H 121
Sissons Rd. Leeds —3G 121
Sissons Row. Leeds —3H 121
Sissons St. Leeds —3H 121
Sissons Ter. Leeds —3G 121
Sissons Vw. Leeds —4G 121
Six Heights. Ripp —6F 141
Sixth Av. B'frd —4E 80
Sixth Av. Liv —3D 134
Sixth Av. Rothw —7J 105
Sizers Ct. Yead —6J 45
Skelda Ri. I'ly —6B 12
Skelton Av. Leeds —5D 86
Skelton Cres. Leeds —5D 86
Skelton Grange Cotts. Leeds
—3E 104
Skelton Grange Rd. Leeds —4D 104
Skelton Mt. Leeds —5D 86
*Skelton Pl. Leeds —5D 86*
*(off Skelton Av.)*
Skelton Rd. Leeds —5D 86
Skeltons La. T'ner —3K 69
Skelton St. Leeds —5D 86
Skelton Ter. Leeds —5D 86
Skelton Wlk. B'frd —5F 63
Skelwith App. Leeds —3J 87
Skelwith Wlk. Leeds —3J 87
Skinner La. B'frd —3J 79
Skinner La. Leeds —4K 85 (3G 5)
Skinner St. Leeds —6A 4
Skippon Ter. T'ner —6D 52
Skipton Av. Hud —7H 145
Skipton Ri. Gar —6B 90
Skipton Rd. Add —1B 10
Skipton Rd. Ebrn —5D 20
Skipton Rd. Kei —3A 40
Skipton Rd. Kild —2A 20
Skipton Rd. Low U —7H 21
Skipton Rd. Sils —1D 20
Skipton St. Bat —5G 137
**Skircoat Green. —5G 131**
Skircoat Grn. Hal —6G 131
Skircoat Grn. Rd. Hal —5G 131
Skircoat Moor Clo. Hal —4E 130
Skircoat Moor Rd. Hal —3D 130
Skircoat Rd. Hal —2G 131
Skirrow St. Bgly —6B 60
Skye Vw. Rothw —2H 123
Slack Bottom Rd. B'frd —6G 97
Slack La. Bklnd —6J 141
Slack La. Hal —3D 110
Slack La. Oakw —1C 56
Slack La. Sower B —7B 128
(nr. Bower Slack Rd.)
Slack La. Sower B —4B 140
(nr. Merry Bent La.)
**Slack Side. —5F 97**
Sladdin Row. Q'bry —6G 95
Slade Clo. B Spa —3D 36
*Slade Ho. B'frd —3F 81*
*(off St Clares Av.)*
Slade La. Brigh —3F 145
Slade La. Riddl —1C 40
Sladen St. Kei —4J 39
Slade Wlk. Bat —6D 118
**Slaid Hill. —6E 50**
Slaid Hill Ct. Leeds —6D 50
Slaters Rd. S'ley —4C 82
Slates La. I'ly —2A 12
Slaymaker La. Oakw —1D 56
Slead Av. Brigh —4F 133
Slead Ct. Brigh —4F 133
Slead Cres. Brigh —4F 133
Slead Gro. Brigh —4F 133
Slead Royd. Brigh —4F 133
**Slead Syke. —4F 133**
Slead Vw. Brigh —4F 133
Sledmere Cft. Leeds —6A 70
Sledmere Gth. Leeds —6A 70
*Sledmere Grn. Leeds —6A 70*
*(off Sledmere Pl.)*
Sledmere La. Leeds —6A 70
Sledmere Pl. Leeds —6A 70
*Sledmere Sq. Leeds —6A 70*
*(off Sledmere Pl.)*
Sleights La. Hare —4D 32
Sleningford Gro. Shipl —4E 60
Sleningford Ri. Bgly —6K 41
Sleningford Rd. Bgly —6J 41
Sleningford Rd. Shipl —4E 60
*Sleningford Ter. Bgly —6K 41*
*(off Sleningford Rd.)*
Sleningford Vs. Bgly —6J 41
*Slicer's Yd. Bgly —1K 59*
*(off Busfield St.)*
Slingsby Clo. App B —4F 63
Slippy La. Hal —2A 112
(in two parts)
Smalewell Clo. Pud —7B 82
Smalewell Dri. Pud —7A 82
Smalewell Gdns. Pud —7A 82
Smalewell Grn. Pud —7B 82
Smalewell Rd. Pud —7A 82
Smalldrink La. Cro H —4A 20
Small Lees Rd. Sower B —6F 141
Small Page Fold. Q'bry —5J 95
Smallwood Gdns. Dew —5B 138
Smallwood Rd. Dew —5A 138
(in two parts)
Smawthorne La. C'frd —7E 126
Smeaton App. Leeds —2C 88
Smeaton Gro. Swil —5E 106
Smiddles La. B'frd —4K 97
Smiddy Hill. Wltn —5G 19
Smith Art Gallery. —5G 133
Smith Av. B'frd —5J 97
Smith Cres. Brigh —1E 144
Smitherd's St. Kei —5K 39
Smithfield Av. Hal —7C 114
Smith Ho. Av. Brigh —2G 133
Smith Ho. Cres. Brigh —3G 133
Smith Ho. Gro. Brigh —3G 133
Smith Ho. La. Brigh —3G 133
Smithies La. Birs —6C 118
Smithies La. Heck —6B 136
Smithies Moor Clo. Bat —1D 136
Smithies Moor Cres. Bat —7D 118
Smithies Moor La. Bat —7C 118
Smithies Moor Ri. Bat —7D 118
Smith La. B'frd —3E 78
Smith La. Sower B —5D 140
Smith Rd. B'frd —3G 97
Smith Rd. Dew —7D 136
Smithson St. Rothw —3H 123
Smith's Ter. Hal —4E 112
Smith St. Bier —6D 98
Smith St. B'frd —6K 79 (4B 6)
Smith St. C'frd —6F 127
(nr. Green La.)
Smith St. C'frd —5J 127
(nr. Wheldon Rd.)
Smith St. Ctly —6B 60
Smith St. Kei —3J 39
Smith St. Liv —5K 135
Smithville. Riddl —2D 40
Smithy Carr La. Brigh —4G 133
Smithy Clough La. Ripp —6C 140
Smithy Ct. Coll —2F 35
Smithy Ct. Schol —6B 116
Smithy Fold. Q'bry —4C 96
Smithy Greaves. Add —2G 11
Smithy Hill. B'frd —5J 97
Smithy Hill. Denh —7C 76
Smithy La. Bard —1A 52
Smithy La. Bur W —1A 26
Smithy La. Leeds —5J 47
Smithy La. Ting —7F 121
Smithy La. Wilsd —6G 59
Smithy Mills La. Leeds —2D 66
(in two parts)
Smithy St. Hal —1H 131
Smools La. Morl —7B 102
Snaith Wood Dri. Rawd —3A 64
Snaith Wood M. Rawd —3A 64
Snake Hill. Oaken —2C 116
Snake La. Leeds —7C 86
Snape Dri. B'frd —4D 96
Snape St. Kei —7A 40
Snelsins La. Cleck —6E 116
Snelsins Rd. Cleck —6E 116
Snowden App. Leeds —2J 83
Snowden Clo. Leeds —3H 83
Snowden Cres. Leeds —3H 83
Snowden Fold. Leeds —3H 83
*Snowden Grn. Leeds —3H 83*
*(off Aston Rd.)*
Snowden Gro. Leeds —3H 83
Snowden Lawn. Leeds —3H 83
Snowden Rd. Shipl —6K 61
(in two parts)
Snowden Royd. Leeds —2H 83
Snowden St. B'frd —5A 80
Snowdens Wlk. Cytn —2D 96
Snowden Va. Leeds —3H 83
Snowden Wlk. Leeds —3H 83
Snowden Way. Leeds —2H 83
Snowdon St. Bat —4F 137
Snowdon St. B'frd —2D 6
Snowdrop M. All —5B 78
Soaper Ho. La. Hal —5C 114
Soaper La. She & B'frd —7C 96
Sod Ho. Grn. Hal —4E 112
Soho Mills. B'frd —4C 6
Soho Sq. B'frd —6K 79
Soho St. B'frd —4C 6
Soho St. Hal —1D 130
**Soil Hill. —3C 94**
Solomon Hill. Hal —6F 111
Solway Rd. Bat —3K 137
Somerdale Clo. Leeds —4H 83
Somerdale Gdns. Leeds —4H 83
Somerdale Gro. Leeds —4H 83
Somerdale Wlk. Leeds —4H 83
Somerset Av. Bail —7H 43
Somerset Av. Brigh —2H 145
Somerset Rd. Pud —5C 82
Somers Pl. Leeds —6C 4
Somers St. Leeds —5H 85 (6B 4)
Somerton Dri. B'frd —4F 99
Somerville Av. B'frd —7H 97
Somerville Av. Leeds —3H 87
Somerville Dri. Leeds —3H 87
Somerville Grn. Leeds —3H 87
Somerville Gro. Leeds —2H 87
Somerville Mt. Leeds —3H 87
Somerville Pk. B'frd —7H 97
Somerville Ter. Otley —2K 27
Somerville Vw. Leeds —3H 87
Sonning Rd. All —5B 78
Soothill La. Bat —4H 137
Sorrin Clo. Idle —5C 62
Soureby Cross Way. E Bier —7H 99
(in two parts)
S. Accommodation Rd. Leeds
—1K 103
Southampton St. B'frd
—4B 80 (1G 7)
South App. Aber —2F 73
South App. B'ham —2K 53
South Av. C'frd —7K 125
South Av. Far —7H 145
South Bank. E Kes —4A 34
South Bank. Q'bry —5K 95
S. Bank Rd. Bat —2E 136
South Bolton. Hal —7B 94
Southbrook Ter. B'frd
—7K 79 (5C 6)
*Southcliffe. S'wram —3J 131*
*(off Bank Top)*
South Cliffe. T'tn —7J 77
Southcliffe Dri. Bail —3H 61
Southcliffe Way. Bail —3J 61
South Clo. Guis —3D 44
S. Clough Head. Hal —1J 129
Southcote Pl. Idle —4D 62
S. Croft Av. B'shaw —1J 117
S. Croft Dri. B'shaw —7J 99
S. Croft Ga. B'shaw —1J 117
S. Cross Rd. Hud —7F 145
Southdown Clo. B'frd —3E 78
*Southdown Ct. B'frd —3E 78*
*(off Southdown Clo.)*
Southdown Rd. Bail —3H 61
South Dri. Fars —2B 82
South Dri. Guis —3D 44
South Edge. Kei —3J 39
South Edge. Shipl —5E 60
Southedge Clo. Hip —1C 132
Southedge Ter. Hal —1D 132
S. End Av. Leeds —4J 83
S. End Ct. Leeds —3J 83
S. End Gro. Leeds —4J 83
S. End Mt. Leeds —4J 83
S. End Ter. Leeds —4J 83
S. Farm Cres. Leeds —3E 86
S. Farm Rd. Leeds —3E 86
Southfield. B'hpe —1K 47
Southfield Av. B'frd —6J 97
Southfield Av. Leeds —2A 68
Southfield Av. Riddl —1D 40
Southfield Dri. Leeds —2A 68
Southfield Dri. Riddl —1E 40
Southfield La. Add —2C 10
Southfield La. B'frd —2G 97
Southfield Mt. A'ley —6C 84
*Southfield Mt. Leeds —5A 104*
*(off S. View Rd.)*
Southfield Mt. Riddl —1D 40
Southfield Rd. Add —1D 10
Southfield Rd. Bgly —3A 60
Southfield Rd. B'frd —3J 97
Southfield Rd. Bur W —1A 26
Southfield Sq. B'frd —4J 79
Southfield St. Leeds —6C 84
Southfield Ter. Add —1D 10
Southfield Ter. B'shaw —1J 117
Southfield Ter. Hal —6C 114
Southfield Way. Riddl —1E 40
Southgate. B'frd —6A 80 (4D 6)
Southgate. Ell —2K 143
Southgate. Guis —4D 44
Southgate. Hal —1G 131
Southgate. Holy G —6G 143
Southgate. Oult —1A 124
South Gro. Brigh —3E 132
South Gro. Shipl —5D 60
S. Hawksworth St. I'ly —5B 12
S. Hill Clo. Leeds —7B 104
S. Hill Cft. Leeds —7B 104
S. Hill Dri. Bgly —2C 60
S. Hill Gdns. Leeds —7B 104
S. Hill Gro. Leeds —7B 104
S. Hill Ri. Leeds —7B 104
S. Hill Way. Leeds —7B 104
S. Holme La. Brigh —4E 132
Southlands. Bail —3H 61
Southlands. Hal —5D 94
Southlands. H'fth —3F 65
Southlands Av. Bgly —3A 60
Southlands Av. Leeds —4J 67
Southlands Av. Rawd —2B 64
Southlands Av. Riddl —2E 40
Southlands Av. T'tn —7C 78
Southlands Clo. Leeds —3J 67
Southlands Cres. Leeds —4J 67
Southlands Dri. Hud —6G 145
Southlands Dri. Leeds —4J 67
Southlands Dri. Riddl —2E 40
Southlands Gro. Bgly —3K 59
Southlands Gro. Riddl —2E 40
Southlands Gro. T'tn —7B 78
Southlands Gro. W. Riddl —1E 40
Southlands Mt. Riddl —2E 40
Southlands Rd. Riddl —1E 40
South La. B'ley —5K 143
South La. She —7B 96
South La. Gdns. Ell —4K 143
Southlea. Oaken —2C 116
Southlea Av. Oakw —2G 57
South Lee. H'fth —3F 65
S. Leeds Bus. Cen. Leeds —2J 103
South Leeds Stadium. —6J 103
Southleigh Av. Leeds —6G 103
Southleigh Cres. Leeds —6G 103
Southleigh Cft. Leeds —6H 103
Southleigh Dri. Leeds —6G 103
Southleigh Gdns. Leeds —6G 103
Southleigh Gth. Leeds —6H 103
Southleigh Grange. Leeds —6H 103
Southleigh Gro. Leeds —6G 103
Southleigh Rd. Leeds —6G 103
Southleigh Vw. Leeds —6G 103
S. Mead. B'hpe —1K 47
Southmere Av. B'frd —3G 97
Southmere Cres. B'frd —3G 97
Southmere Dri. B'frd —3F 97
(in two parts)
Southmere Gro. B'frd —3G 97
Southmere Oval. B'frd —4F 97
Southmere Rd. B'frd —3G 97
Southmere Ter. B'frd —3G 97
South Mt. E Kes —4K 33
S. Nelson St. Morl —2A 120
Southolme Clo. Leeds —6K 65
**Southowram. —4A 132**
Southowram Bank. Hal —1H 131
South Pde. B'frd —4K 79
South Pde. Cleck —7E 116
South Pde. Ell —4K 143
South Pde. Hal —2H 131
South Pde. Head —7D 66
South Pde. I'ly —5A 12
South Pde. Leeds —5H 85 (6D 4)
South Pde. Morl —3B 120
*South Pde. Otley —3K 27*
*(off Albion St.)*
South Pde. Pud —7B 82
South Pde. Slnd —6D 142
S. Parade Clo. Pud —7C 82
S. Park Ter. Pud —2D 100
S. Parkway. Leeds —2G 87
(in three parts)
S. Parkway App. Leeds —2G 87
*South Pl. Morl —3B 120*
*(off South St.)*
S. Queen St. Morl —4B 120
S. Ridge. Kip —5A 108
South Rd. B'frd —1J 79
South Rd. Cull —7B 58
South Row. H'fth —3G 65
S. Royd Av. Hal —4G 131
*Southroyd Pde. Pud —1C 100*
*(off Fartown)*
Southroyd Pk. Pud —1C 100
(in two parts)
Southroyd Ri. Pud —1C 100
South Selby. Hal —1B 112
South Sq. T'tn —7H 77
South St. B'frd —3J 97
South St. Brigh —5G 133
South St. Brun I —2F 131
South St. Denh —5B 76
South St. E Mor —3H 41
South St. Holy G —5F 143
South St. Kei —7K 39
South St. Liv —4K 135
South St. Morl —3B 120
South St. Oaken —3C 116
South St. Rawd —7K 45
South St. T'tn —6H 77
South Ter. N'wram —4A 114
South Vw. Birs —6D 118
South Vw. B'frd —1E 114
South Vw. Far —4A 82
South Vw. Friz —1J 79
South Vw. Fry —5J 127
South Vw. Gre —5F 63
South Vw. Guis —2G 45
South Vw. Hal —4J 131
South Vw. Haw —5E 56
South Vw. H'fth —5G 65
*South Vw. Kild —1A 20*
*(off Hanover St.)*
*South Vw. Leeds —3A 88*
*(off Selby Rd.)*
*South Vw. L'ft —2E 112*
*(off Blackmires)*
South Vw. Men —7C 26
South Vw. Morl —7B 102
South Vw. Pud —6D 82
South Vw. Q'bry —4G 95
South Vw. Rothw —1G 123
South Vw. Sandb —2F 41
South Vw. Schol —1B 134
South Vw. S'wram —4A 132
South Vw. Ting —3D 138
South Vw. Weth —1J 17
South Vw. Wilsd —7G 59
South Vw. Yead —4H 45
S. View Clo. B'frd —7G 99
S. View Clo. Yead —4H 45
S. View Cres. Yead —4H 45
S. View Dri. B'frd —7H 99
S. View Gro. Gom —1K 135
S. View Rd. B'frd —7H 99
S. View Rd. Yead —4K 45
S. View Ter. Bail —1J 61
*S. View Ter. Dew —6F 137*
*(off Tate Naylor St.)*
*S. View Ter. Hal —7D 112*
*(off Queen's Rd.)*
*S. View Ter. Otley —3K 27*
*(off Bermondsey St.)*
S. View Ter. Sils —1F 21
S. View Ter. Yead —5A 46
Southwaite Clo. Leeds —1H 87
Southwaite Gth. Leeds —1H 87
Southwaite La. Leeds —1H 87
Southwaite Lawn. Leeds —1H 87
Southwaite Pl. Leeds —1H 87
South Wlk. H'den —3E 58
Southway. Bgly —6B 42

South Way—Stanningley Gro.

South Way. B'frd —7G 99
Southway. Bur W —6J 13
Southway. Guis —3C 44
Southway. H'fth —1E 64
Southway. I'ly —6D 12
South Way. Shipl —5D 60
Southwood Clo. Leeds —1A 88
Southwood Cres. Leeds —1A 88
Southwood Ga. Leeds —1A 88
Southwood Rd. Leeds —1A 88
Sovereign Clo. Birs —6D 118
Sovereign Ct. Leeds —5A 50
Sovereign St. Hal —1F 131
Sovereign St. Leeds —6J 85
Sowden Bldgs. B'frd —3D 80
Sowden Grange. T'tn —7H 77
Sowden La. Nor G —4F 115
(in two parts)
Sowden La. Wyke —4G 115
Sowden Rd. B'frd —2D 78
Sowden St. B'frd —3H 97
Sowden's Yd. Leeds —6D 66
(off Moor Rd.)
**Sowerby. —5G 129**
**Sowerby Bridge. —5K 129**
Sowerby Cft. La. Sower B —5K 129
Sowerby La. L'ft —1D 128
Sowerby New Rd. Sower B —5G 129
Sowerby St. Sower B —5K 129
**Sowood. —7E 142**
**Sowood Green. —7D 142**
Sowood St. Leeds —3C 84
**Soyland Town. —3F 141**
Soyland Town Rd. Sower B —3F 141
Spa Grn. La. Sower B —6D 140
Spa Hill. Bat —3G 137
Spa Ind. Est. Leeds —1J 85
Spaines Rd. Hud —7G 145
Spa La. Bgly —6A 42
Spa La. B Spa —3E 36
Spalding Towers. Leeds —4K 5
Spa M. B Spa —3E 36
Spanfield La. Hal —3H 111
Sparable La. Bgly —1C 60
Spark Ho. La. Sower B —5A 130
Spartal La. Leds —6E 108
Spartan Rd. Low M —2K 115
Spa St. Bat —3G 137
Speakers Ct. Dew —7F 137
Spear Fir. Bard —1J 51
Spearhead Way. Kei —3A 40
Speedwell Mt. Leeds —2H 85
Speedwell St. Leeds —2H 85
Speeton Av. B'frd —4E 96
Speeton Gro. B'frd —4D 96
Spen App. Leeds —5K 65
Spen Bank. Cleck —1H 135
Spen Bank. Leeds —5K 65
Spence La. Leeds —7F 85
Spenceley St. Leeds —2G 85 (1B 4)
(in two parts)
Spencer Av. B'frd —1G 97
Spencer Av. Morl —5A 120
Spencer Av. Sils —7G 9
Spencer Clo. Cro H —3A 20
Spencer Mt. Leeds —2A 86
Spencer Pl. Leeds —2A 86 (1K 5)
Spencer Rd. B'frd —2F 97
(in two parts)
Spencer St. Kei —4J 39
(in three parts)
Spencer St. Sut Cr —5A 20
(off North St.)
Spencer Ter. Hud —6K 145
Spen Clo. B'frd —7D 98
Spen Comn. La. Tad —5E 54
Spen Cres. Leeds —5K 65
Spen Dri. Leeds —4A 66
Spenfield Ct. Liv —6J 135
Spen Gdns. Leeds —4B 66
Spen Grn. Leeds —5K 65
Spen La. Gom —7H 117
Spen La. Leeds —3A 66
(in two parts)
Spen Lawn. Leeds —5K 65
**Spen Lower. —7H 117**
Spen M. Leeds —5A 66
Spennithorne Av. Leeds —2A 66
Spennithorne Dri. Leeds —3A 66
Spen Rd. Leeds —4A 66
Spenser Ri. Guis —3H 45
Spenser Rd. Guis —3H 45
Spenslea Gro. Morl —5A 120
Spen Va. St. Heck —5B 136
Spen Valley Ind. Pk. Rawf —2H 135
Spen Vw. Dew M —7D 136
Spen Vw. La. B'frd —7D 98
Spen Wlk. Leeds —5K 65
Spibey Cres. Rothw —7F 105
Spibey La. Rothw —7F 105
Spicer St. B'frd —3J 97
Spiers Gth. B'frd —5K 97
Spindles, The. Leeds —6K 103
Spindle St. Hal —2E 112
Spiners Way. Schol —7B 116
(off Scholes La.)
Spink Pl. B'frd —5K 79 (2B 6)
Spinks Gdns. Leeds —1K 87
Spink St. B'frd —5K 79 (2B 6)
Spinkwell Clo. B'frd —4B 80 (1F 7)
Spink Well La. Wake —6F 121
Spinkwell Rd. Dew —7G 137
Spinners Chase. Pud —6C 82
Spinners, The. Haw —6E 56
Spinneyfield. Hud —6G 145
Spinneyfield Ct. Leeds —6A 86 (7K 5)
Spinney, The. Brigh —3G 133
Spinney, The. E Mor —3H 41
Spinney, The. Leeds —6A 86
Spinney, The. Moort —2A 68
Spinney, The. Rawd —2J 63
Spinney, The. Weth —3H 17
Spinning Mill Ct. Shipl —3E 60
Spion Kop. T'ner —6D 52
Spire Heights. Bgly —1D 60
Spofforth Hill. Weth —3G 17
Spofforth Wlk. Gar —6B 90
Spout Hill. Brigh —3E 144
Spout Ho. La. Brigh —2E 132
Spring Av. Gild —7G 101
Spring Av. Kei —5C 40
**Spring Bank. —7A 40**
Spring Bank. Cull —7A 58
Springbank. Gar —1G 107
Spring Bank. Kirks —1A 84
Spring Bank. Liv —6A 136
Springbank Av. Fars —2C 82
Springbank Av. Gild —7G 101
Springbank Clo. Fars —2B 82
Springbank Cres. Gar —7G 89
Springbank Cres. Gild —6G 101
Spring Bank Cres. Leeds —1E 84
Springbank Dri. Fars —2C 82
Spring Bank Dri. Liv —6K 135
Springbank Gro. Fars —2C 82
Spring Bank Pl. B'frd —4K 79
Springbank Ri. Fars —2C 82
Spring Bank Ri. Kei —7A 40
Springbank Rd. Fars —2B 82
Springbank Rd. Gild —6G 101
Spring Bank Ter. Guis —2G 45
Springcliffe. B'frd —4H 79
Springcliffe St. B'frd —4H 79
Spring Clo. Bgly —2B 60
Spring Clo. Gar —7B 90
(nr. Fairburn Dri.)
Spring Clo. Gar —5A 90
(nr. Newhold)
Spring Clo. Kei —5C 40
Spring Clo. Av. Leeds —7B 86
Spring Clo. Gdns. Leeds —7B 86
Spring Clo. St. Leeds —7A 86
Spring Clo. Wlk. Leeds —7B 86
Spring Ct. All —2A 78
Springdale Cres. B'frd —5E 62
Spring Dri. Kei —5C 40
Spring Edge. Hal —4E 130
Spring Edge N. Hal —3E 130
Spring Edge W. Hal —3D 130
Spring Farm La. H'den —3E 58
Spring Farm M. Wilsd —7G 59
**Springfield. —7G 137**
**(nr. Batley)**
**Springfield. —6D 62**
**(nr. Idle)**
Springfield. B Spa —2D 36
Springfield. Cliff —5D 36
Springfield. Q'bry —5H 95
Springfield. Sower B —5J 129
Springfield Av. Bat —3F 137
Springfield Av. B'frd —1F 97
Springfield Av. I'ly —5C 12
Springfield Av. Morl —1K 119
Springfield Clo. H'fth —3J 65
Springfield Commercial Cen. Far —1C 82
Springfield Ct. Kei —3J 39
Springfield Ct. Yead —3J 45
Springfield Cres. Morl —1A 120
Springfield Dri. Liv —3E 134
Springfield Gdns. H'fth —3H 65
Springfield Gdns. Kei —3J 39
Springfield Gdns. Pud —7D 82
Springfield Grn. Leeds —4A 104
Springfield Gro. Bgly —7K 41
Springfield Gro. Brigh —4G 133
Springfield La. B'frd —4D 100
Springfield La. Liv —4G 135
Springfield La. Morl —1A 120
Springfield Mt. Add —1D 10
Springfield Mt. A'ley —5A 84
Springfield Mt. H'fth —3H 65
Springfield Mt. Leeds —4G 85 (3A 4)
Springfield Pl. B'frd —5K 79 (1C 6)
Springfield Pl. Gar —7G 89
Springfield Pl. Guis —2G 45
Springfield Pl. H'let —4C 104
Springfield Pl. Idle —6D 62
Springfield Pl. Leeds —4A 104
Springfield Pl. Otley —3H 27
Springfield Ri. H'fth —3H 65
Springfield Ri. Rothw —3H 123
Springfield Rd. Bail —7H 43
Springfield Rd. Ell —2B 144
Springfield Rd. Guis —3G 45
Springfield Rd. Kei —3J 39
Springfield Rd. Morl —1K 119
Springfields. C'frd —7E 126
Springfield St. B'frd —5J 79 (1A 6)
Springfield St. Rothw —3H 123
Springfield St. T'tn —7J 77
Springfield Ter. B'frd —5J 79 (1A 6)
Springfield Ter. Cull —7C 58
Springfield Ter. Dew —7G 137
Springfield Ter. Guis —3G 45
Spring Fld. Ter. Hal —7C 114
Springfield Ter. Leeds —7C 50
Springfield Ter. L'ft —6E 110
Springfield Ter. Schol —6B 116
Springfield Ter. S'ley —4B 82
Springfield Vs. Gild —6F 101
Springfield Wlk. H'fth —3H 65
**Spring Gardens. —1D 118**
Spring Gdns. Bat —3F 137
Spring Gdns. B'frd —5A 80 (1C 6)
Spring Gdns. Bur W —1B 26
Spring Gdns. Dlgtn —1D 118
Spring Gdns. Hal —4C 112
Spring Gdns. Hare —3C 32
Spring Gdns. Morl —7K 101
Spring Gdns. Nor G —5F 115
Spring Gdns. La. Kei —1J 39
Spring Gdns. Mt. Kei —2K 39
Spring Gdns. Rd. B'frd —2G 79
Spring Garden St. Q'bry —5J 95
Spring Gro. Hal —1C 130
Spring Gro. Leeds —3E 84
Spring Gro. Av. Leeds —3E 84
Spring Gro. Vw. Leeds —3E 84
Spring Gro. Wlk. Leeds —3E 84
Spring Hall Clo. Hal —2B 114
Spring Hall Ct. Hal —7C 112
Spring Hall Dri. Hal —2C 130
Spring Hall Gdns. Hal —1C 130
Spring Hall Gro. Hal —1C 130
Spring Hall La. Hal —2C 130
Spring Hall Pl. Hal —1C 130
Spring Head. She —2C 114
Spring Head Rd. Haw —4D 56
Springhead Rd. Rothw —1J 123
Spring Head Rd. T'tn —7J 77
Spring Hill. Bail —1F 61
Spring Hill. Leeds —7E 48
Spring Hill. Shipl —5A 62
Spring Hill Cotts. Leeds —6E 66
(off Monk Bri. Ter.)
Spring Hill Ter. Leeds —6E 66
(off Monk Bri. Rd.)
Spring Holes La. T'tn —6G 77
Springhurst Rd. Shipl —5G 61
Spring La. Bat —1F 137
Spring La. Bgly —5D 42
Spring La. G'Ind —2E 142
Spring La. Kear —4C 18
Springlodge Pl. B'frd —4K 79 (1C 6)
Springmead Dri. Gar —7K 89
Spring Mill St. B'frd —1A 98
Spring Pk. Rd. Wilsd —6G 59
Spring Pl. B'frd —1J 97 (7A 6)
Spring Pl. Kei —6C 40
Spring Ri. Kei —5C 40
Spring Rd. Leeds —1E 84
Spring Rock. Holy G —5G 143
Spring Row. Hal —7A 94
Spring Row. H'den —3F 59
Spring Row. Kei —5K 39
Spring Row. Oxe —4G 75
Spring Row. Q'bry —5H 95
Springroyd Ter. B'frd —5F 79
Springs La. I'ly —5C 12
Springs La. Wltn —2F 19
Springs Rd. Yead —5G 45
Spring St. Brigh —6G 133
Spring St. Cro R —4H 57
(off Bingley Rd.)
Spring St. Dew —7G 137
Spring St. Idle —5D 62
Spring St. Kei —3A 40
Spring St. Liv —4K 135
Spring St. Ripp —5F 141
Springswood Av. Shipl —5G 61
Springswood Pl. Shipl —5G 61
Springswood Rd. Shipl —5G 61
Spring Ter. Holy G —7C 142
Spring Ter. Kei —5C 40
Spring Ter. N Bnk —7H 113
Spring Ter. Sower B —6A 130
Spring Valley. S'ley —4C 82
Spring Valley Av. Leeds —4G 83
Spring Valley Clo. Leeds —4G 83
Spring Valley Clo. Liv —3J 135
(off Spring Valley St.)
Spring Valley Ct. Leeds —4G 83
Spring Valley Cres. Leeds —4G 83
Spring Valley Cft. Leeds —4G 83
Spring Valley Dri. Leeds —4G 83
Spring Valley Sq. Liv —3J 135
(off Spring Valley St.)
Spring Valley St. Liv —3J 135
Spring Valley Vw. Leeds —4G 83
Spring Valley Wlk. Leeds —4G 83
Spring Vw. Gild —6H 101
Spring Vw. L'ft —2F 129
Spring Vw. Rd. Hal —2F 129
Springville Ter. B'frd —5D 62
Spring Way. Kei —5C 40
Springwell Av. Swil —5E 106
Springwell Clo. Yead —5A 46
Springwell Ct. Leeds —7F 85
Springwell Ct. Ting —6E 120
Springwell Dri. B'frd —2A 98
Springwell Rd. Leeds —7F 85
Springwell Rd. Swil —5E 106
Springwell St. Leeds —7F 85
Springwell Ter. Yead —5A 46
Springwell Vw. Birs —6D 118
Springwell Vw. Leeds —7G 85
Springwood Av. B'frd —3B 98
Spring Wood Av. Hal —6F 131
Springwood Ct. Leeds —6D 68
(off Bk. Wetherby Rd.)
Spring Wood Dri. Hal —6F 131
Spring Wood Gdns. B'frd —4B 98
Spring Wood Gdns. Hal —7F 131
Springwood Gdns. Leeds —6D 68
Springwood Gro. Leeds —6E 68
Springwood Pl. B'frd —3A 80
(off Bolton Rd.)
Springwood Rd. Leeds —6D 68
Springwood Rd. Rawd —1J 63
Springwood Ter. B'frd —3A 80
(off King's Rd.)
Spruce St. Kei —3B 40
Spur Dri. Leeds —2C 88
Spurr St. Bat —4H 137
Square St. B'frd —1C 98 (7J 7)
Square, The. Bat —2D 136
Square, The. B Spa —3E 36
Square, The. B'frd —6C 78
Square, The. C'frd —7J 127
Square, The. Hal —3J 131
Square, The. Hare —3C 32
Square, The. Kip —5A 108
Square, The. N'wram —4A 114
Squire Grn. B'frd —4F 79
Squire La. B'frd —4F 79
Squirrel Clo. Dew —6E 136
Squirrel End. Dew —6D 136
Squirrel Hall Dri. Dew —5D 136
Squirrel La. T'tn —1F 95
Squirrel Wlk. Dew —5E 136
Stable Fold. Wyke —5K 115
Stable La. Hal —6F 113
Stables La. B Spa —3E 36
Stacks La. Cra V —3A 128
Stadium Rd. B'frd —6K 97
Stadium Way. Leeds —3E 102
Stafford Av. Hal —4G 131
Stafford Pde. Hal —5G 131
Stafford Pl. Hal —4G 131
Stafford Rd. Hal —5G 131
Stafford Sq. Hal —5H 131
Stafford St. B'frd —2D 98
Stafford St. C'frd —7C 126
Stafford St. Leeds —2A 104
Stafford St. Morl —5K 119
Stainbeck Av. Leeds —6F 67
Stainbeck Gdns. B'frd —6D 96
Stainbeck Gdns. Leeds —6H 67
Stainbeck La. Leeds —5G 67
Stainbeck Rd. Leeds —6F 67
Stainbeck Wlk. Leeds —6H 67
Stainburn Av. Leeds —3A 68
Stainburn Cres. Leeds —3K 67
Stainburn Dri. Leeds —3K 67
Stainburn Gdns. Leeds —3A 68
Stainburn Mt. Leeds —4A 68
Stainburn Pde. Leeds —3K 67
Stainburn Rd. Leeds —4K 67
Stainburn Ter. Leeds —4K 67
Stainburn Vw. Leeds —3A 68
**Staincliffe. —4F 137**
Staincliffe Clo. Dew —7E 136
Staincliffe Ct. Sils —1F 21
Staincliffe Cres. Dew —6D 136
Staincliffe Hall Rd. Bat —5D 136
Staincliffe Rd. Dew —5D 136
**Stainland. —6D 142**
Stainland Dean. Holy G —7B 142
Stainland Rd. Bklnd —5J 141
Stainland Rd. G'Ind —7H 131
Stainland Rd. Slnd —6D 142
Stainmore Clo. Leeds —2J 87
Stainmore Pl. Leeds —2J 87
Stainton Clo. B'frd —6E 96
Stainton La. Carl —3F 123
Staircase La. Pool W & B'hpe —4H 29
Stairfoot Clo. Leeds —6D 48
Stair Foot La. Leeds —6D 48
Stairfoot Vw. Leeds —6D 48
Stairfoot Wlk. Leeds —6D 48
Staithe Av. Leeds —2K 121
Staithe Clo. Leeds —2K 121
Staithe Gdns. Leeds —2K 121
Staithgate La. B'frd —5B 98
Stake La. Cra V —1B 128
Stakes Fold. Heck —4C 136
Stallabrass St. B'frd —5J 79 (2A 6)
Stamford St. B'frd —1D 98 (7K 7)
Stammergate La. Lntn —1F 35
Stamp Hill Clo. Add —1B 10
Stanacre Pl. B'frd —5B 80 (1G 7)
Stanage La. Hal —7C 96
Standale Av. Pud —5B 82
Standale Cres. Pud —5B 82
Standale Ho. B'frd —4E 98
(off Prince St.)
Standale Ri. Pud —5B 82
Standard Ind. Est. B'frd —2E 80
Standard Vs. Leeds —2B 102
Stanhall Av. S'ley —4B 82
Stanhope Av. H'fth —2G 65
Stanhope Clo. H'fth —2G 65
Stanhope Dri. H'fth —5F 65
Stanhope Gdns. Wake —6A 122
Stanhope Rd. Thpe —6A 122
**Stank. —4J 31**
**Stanks. —7B 70**
Stanks App. Leeds —1B 88
Stanks Av. Leeds —1B 88
Stanks Clo. Leeds —1C 88
Stanks Cross. Leeds —1C 88
Stanks Dri. Leeds —6A 70
Stanks Gdns. Leeds —7B 70
Stanks Gth. Leeds —1C 88
Stanks Grn. Leeds —1C 88
Stanks Gro. Leeds —1B 88
Stanks La. N. Leeds —6A 70
Stanks La. S. Leeds —1B 88
Stanks Pde. Leeds —1B 88
Stanks Ri. Leeds —1C 88
Stanks Rd. Leeds —1B 88
Stanks Way. Leeds —1B 88
Stanley Av. Leeds —3B 86
Stanley Ct. Hal —1D 130
(off Queens Rd.)
Stanley Dri. Leeds —2D 68
Stanley Gth. Heck —4C 136
Stanley Gro. Guis —3G 45
Stanley La. Holy G —6D 142
Stanley La. Liv —3J 135
Stanley Pl. Bat —3H 137
Stanley Pl. Leeds —3C 86
Stanley Rd. Ain T —6A 144
Stanley Rd. B'frd —1K 79
Stanley Rd. Hal —2D 130
Stanley Rd. Kei —7J 39
Stanley Rd. Leeds —2K 85
(LS7)
Stanley Rd. Leeds —3B 86
(LS9)
Stanley Rd. Lind —7C 144
Stanley Rd. Liv —6J 135
Stanley St. Bgly —1A 60
Stanley St. Brigh —5H 133
Stanley St. C'frd —7E 126
Stanley St. Cleck —7F 117
Stanley St. Cro R —4G 57
Stanley St. Gre —5F 63
Stanley St. Idle —4D 62
Stanley St. Kei —3K 39
Stanley St. Shipl —7J 61
Stanley St. Sower B —4A 130
Stanley St. N. Hal —2E 112
(off Shay La.)
Stanley Ter. A'ley —6C 84
Stanley Ter. Leeds —3C 86
(in two parts)
Stanley Vw. Leeds —6C 84
Stanmore Av. Leeds —2C 84
Stanmore Cres. Leeds —2C 84
Stanmore Gro. Leeds —2C 84
Stanmore Hill. Leeds —2D 84
Stanmore Mt. Leeds —2C 84
Stanmore Pl. B'frd —1G 97
Stanmore Pl. Leeds —2C 84
Stanmore Rd. Leeds —2C 84
Stanmore St. Leeds —2C 84
Stanmore Ter. Leeds —2C 84
Stanmore Vw. Leeds —2C 84
Stannary Pl. Hal —7F 113
Stannery. Slnd —5E 142
Stannery End La. Cra V —1B 128
**Stanningley. —3D 82**
Stanningley Av. Hal —2K 111
Stanningley By-Pass. S'ley —4K 81
Stanningley Dri. Hal —2K 111
Stanningley Fld. Clo. Leeds —4E 82
Stanningley Gro. Heck —5B 136

Stanningley Ind. Est.—Sunderland St.


Stanningley Ind. Est. S'ley —4B 82
Stanningley Rd. Hal —2K 111
Stanningley Rd. Leeds —4J 83
Stanningley Rd. S'ley —3D 82
Stansfield Clo. C'frd —6H 127
Stansfield Clo. Hal —1E 130
Stansfield Ct. Sower B —5K 129
Stansfield Dri. C'frd —7J 127
Stansfield Grange. Sower B —7G 129
Stansfield Mill La. Sower B —7G 129
Stansfield Pl. B'frd —4D 62
Stansfield Rd. C'frd —6G 127
Stanwell Av. Hud —7D 144
Stanwick Ho. B'frd —1K 79
Staples La. Kei —5J 57
Stapleton Ho. B'frd —1K 79
Stapper Grn. Wilsd —6F 59
Starkey La. F'hll —1A 20
Starkie St. Kei —5K 39
Starling M. All —6B 78
(off Bell Dean Rd.)
Star St. B'frd —3J 97
Star Ter. Brigh —2E 144
Starting Post. Idle M —5B 62
Stathers Cotts. Wyke —5K 115
Stathers Gdns. Fars —3B 82
Station App. Bur W —2A 26
Station App. Hal —2H 131
Station Av. Leeds —3F 83
Station Clo. Gar —6K 89
Station Cotts. Newt K —4J 37
Station Ct. B'frd —6B 80 (4F 7)
Station Ct. Gar —6K 89
Station Ct. Leeds —4A 88
Station Cres. Leeds —6B 84
Station Fields. Gar —6K 89
Station Gdns. Weth —4H 17
Station Gro. Cro H —3A 20
(off Bk. Station Rd.)
Station La. B'shaw —1J 117
Station La. Coll —2F 35
Station La. Heck —6A 136
Station La. T'ner —5D 52
Station La. Thpe —6K 121
Station La. Ting —6E 120
Station La. W'ford —7B 106
Station Mt. Leeds —3F 83
Station Pde. Leeds —1B 84
Station Pl. Leeds —3G 83
Station Plaza. I'ly —5B 12
(off Station Rd.)
Station Rd. All B —3B 126
Station Rd. A'ley —6B 84
Station Rd. Bail —1J 61
Station Rd. Bat —4H 137
Station Rd. B'frd —3A 80
Station Rd. Brigh —6J 133
Station Rd. Bur W —2A 26
Station Rd. C'frd —7D 126
Station Rd. Cytn —2C 96
Station Rd. Cro H —3A 20
Station Rd. Cull —6A 58
Station Rd. Denh —5B 76
Station Rd. Dlgtn —2C 118
Station Rd. Esh —5D 44
Station Rd. Gar —6K 89
Station Rd. Guis —2F 45
Station Rd. Hal —2E 112
Station Rd. Haw —5E 56
Station Rd. Heck —5B 136
Station Rd. Holy G —5F 143
Station Rd. H'fth —2G 65
Station Rd. I'ly —5B 12
Station Rd. Kip —6K 107
Station Rd. Leeds —3A 88
Station Rd. Low M —2A 116
Station Rd. L'ft —1F 129
Station Rd. Men —6D 26
Station Rd. Meth —4F 125
Station Rd. Morl —2B 120
Station Rd. Nor G —5G 115
Station Rd. Oakw —2F 57
Station Rd. Otley —3J 27
Station Rd. Oxe —2E 74
Station Rd. Pool W —5K 29
Station Rd. Q'bry —5J 95
Station Rd. Scholes —5D 70
Station Rd. Shipl —4H 61
Station Rd. Sower B —5K 129
Station Rd. Steet —5F 21
Station Rd. Wilsd —2D 76
Station St. Pud —7B 82
Station Ter. All B —3C 126
Station Ter. Leeds —4G 83
Station Vw. Leeds —4A 88
Station Vw. Oxe —2E 74
Station Vw. Steet —5F 21
Station Way. Leeds —6B 84
Staups La. Hal —5K 113
Staveley Ct. Bgly —7A 42
Staveley Dri. Shipl —5D 60
Staveley Gro. Kei —1J 57
Staveley M. Bgly —7A 42
Staveley Rd. Bgly —7A 42
Staveley Rd. B'frd —7H 79
Staveley Rd. Kei —1J 57
Staveley Rd. Shipl —4D 60
Staveley Way. Kei —7J 39
Staverton St. Hal —1C 130
Staybrite Av. Bgly —5A 60
**Staygate.** —4A 98
Staygate Grn. B'frd —5A 98
**Stead.** —1G 25
Stead Hill Way. Thack —3B 62
Stead La. Bgly —5D 42
Stead La. T'ner —6D 52
Steadman St. B'frd —7D 80
Steadman Ter. B'frd —7D 80
Stead Rd. B'frd —6G 99
Stead St. Hal —1F 131
Stead St. Shipl —4H 61
Steads Yd. H'fth —2G 65
Steele La. Bklnd —7K 141
Steel Hill. Kei —6F 39
**Steel Lane Head.** —7K 141
Steel Ter. Rothw —2H 123
(off Blackburn Ct.)
**Steep Lane.** —4D 128
Steep La. Sower B —4C 128
**Steeton.** —5E 20
Steeton Gro. Steet —4E 20
Steeton Hall Gdns. Steet —4E 20
Stell Hill. Kei —6F 39
Stephen Clo. Hal —6A 114
Stephen Cres. B'frd —2A 80
Stephen Rd. B'frd —4F 97
Stephen Row. Hal —5A 114
(off Windmill La.)
Stephenson Clo. Dew —7J 137
Stephenson Dri. Leeds —3H 101
Stephenson Rd. All —3H 77
Stephenson St. B'frd —3H 97
Stephensons Way. I'ly —5B 12
Stephenson Way. Leeds —3H 101
Steps La. Sower B —3A 130
Sterne Hill. Hal —4D 130
Stevens Wlk. Cull —6B 58
Stewart Clo. B'frd —7E 62
Stewart Royd. Heck —4C 136
Stewart St. Cro R —4G 57
Sticker La. B'frd —3E 98
**Stile.** —6G 129
Stile Hill Way. Colt —6D 88
Stillington Ho. B'frd —1K 79
Stirling Cres. B'frd —3G 99
Stirling Cres. H'fth —7E 46
Stirling Rd. Bur W —1K 25
Stirling St. Hal —2F 131
Stirling St. Sils —7G 9
Stirling Way. Gar —6B 90
Stirrup Gro. B'frd —1B 80
Stirton St. B'frd —3K 97
**Stockbridge.** —2C 40
Stockeld La. Sick —3B 16
Stockeld Park House. —2C 16
Stockeld Rd. I'ly —5A 12
Stockeld Way. I'ly —4A 12
Stockheld La. Scholes —3D 70
Stockhill Fold. B'frd —4F 63
(in two parts)
Stockhill Rd. B'frd —5F 63
Stockhill St. Dew —7E 136
Stockinger La. Add —1D 10
(in two parts)
Stocking La. Aber —6F 73
Stock La. Hal —2K 129
Stocks App. Leeds —1K 87
Stocks Av. H Bri —7A 110
Stocks Gdns. H Bri —7A 110
Stocks Hill. Leeds —1G 103
(LS11)
Stocks Hill. Leeds —5C 84
(LS12)
Stocks Hill. Men —6B 26
Stocks Hill Clo. E Mor —2H 41
Stocks La. Bat —3G 137
Stocks La. Ludd & Mt Tab —6G 111
Stocks La. Q'bry —5B 96
Stocks La. Sower B —5G 129
Stocks Ri. Leeds —1K 87
Stocks Rd. Leeds —1A 88
Stocks St. Leeds —2J 85
Stockwell Dri. Bat —2G 137
Stod Fold. Hal —6A 94
Stogden Hill. Q'bry —5B 96
Stoneacre Ct. B'frd —4A 98
Stonebridge. B'frd —4D 62
(off Idlecroft Rd.)
Stonebridge App. Leeds —7J 83
Stonebridge Av. Leeds —7K 83
Stonebridge Gro. Leeds —7J 83
Stonebridge La. Leeds —1J 101
Stone Brig Grn. Rothw —3F 123
Stone Brig La. Rothw —3F 123
**Stone Chair.** —3C 114
Stonechat Ri. Morl —3C 120
Stone Cliffe. Hal —5E 130
(off Wakefield Ga.)
Stonecliffe Bank. Leeds —7J 83
Stonecliffe Clo. Leeds —7J 83
Stonecliffe Cres. Leeds —7J 83
Stonecliffe Dri. Leeds —7J 83
Stonecliffe Gdns. Leeds —7J 83
Stonecliffe Gth. Leeds —7J 83
Stonecliffe Grn. Leeds —7J 83
Stonecliffe Gro. Leeds —7J 83
Stonecliffe Lawn. Leeds —7J 83
Stonecliffe Mt. Leeds —7J 83
Stonecliffe Pl. Leeds —1J 101
(off Stonecliffe Way)
Stonecliffe Ter. Leeds —7J 83
Stonecliffe Vw. Leeds —7J 83
Stonecliffe Wlk. Leeds —1J 101
Stonecliffe Way. Leeds —7J 83
Stone Ct. E Mor —3H 41
Stonecroft. B'frd —1E 80
Stonedale Clo. Pool W —4J 29
Stone Dene. Weth —3K 17
Stonedene Ct. Heck —3B 136
Stonefield. S'cft —3B 52
Stonefield Clo. B'frd —7D 62
Stonefield Pl. Bat —6D 118
Stonefield St. Cleck —2C 134
Stonefield St. Dew —7G 137
Stonefield Ter. Chur —6C 102
Stone Fold. Bail —2G 61
Stonegate. Bgly —6A 42
Stonegate. Leeds —2J 85
(in two parts)
Stonegate App. Leeds —6F 67
Stonegate Chase. Leeds —5F 67
Stonegate Clo. Leeds —1K 67
Stonegate Cres. Mean —5G 67
Stonegate Dri. Leeds —5G 67
Stonegate Edge. Leeds —5G 67
Stonegate Farm Clo. Leeds —5F 67
Stonegate Gdns. Leeds —5F 67
Stonegate Grn. Leeds —6F 67
Stonegate Gro. Leeds —5F 67
(in two parts)
Stonegate La. Mean —5F 67
Stonegate M. Leeds —6F 67
Stonegate Pl. Leeds —6F 67
Stonegate Rd. B'frd —6D 62
Stonegate Rd. Leeds —5F 67
Stonegate Vw. Leeds —5F 67
Stonegate Wlk. Leeds —6G 67
Stone Gro. Steet —5E 20
(in two parts)
Stone Hall M. B'frd —1E 80
Stone Hall Rd. B'frd —1D 80
Stonehaven Ct. Kei —6C 40
Stone Hill. Bgly —7B 42
Stone Ho. Dri. Q'bry —6G 95
Stonehurst. Leeds —1B 88
Stonehyrst Av. Dew —7H 137
Stone La. Oxe —3C 74
Stonelea. Bklnd —4J 141
Stonelea Ct. Head —7D 66
Stonelea Ct. Mean —5G 67
Stonelea Dri. Brigh —2F 145
Stoneleigh. Q'bry —5K 95
Stone Mill App. Leeds —5E 66
Stone Mill Ct. Leeds —5E 66
Stone Mill Way. Leeds —5E 66
Stone Pits La. Gild —1H 119
Stones Bank. Sower B —7E 140
Stones Dri. Sower B —7D 140
Stone St. All —2A 78
Stone St. Bail —2A 62
Stone St. B'frd —6A 80 (3E 6)
Stone St. Cleck —1E 134
Stone St. Haw —6E 56
(off Sun St.)
Stone St. Q'bry —4G 95
Stone Vs. Leeds —6D 66
Stoney Butts La. Bklnd —5K 141
Stoney Cft. Gom —1K 135
Stoneycroft. H'fth —4F 65
Stoneycroft. Rawd —7A 46
(off Batter La.)
Stoneycroft La. Kei —1K 39
Stoney Hill. Brigh —6G 133
Stoneyhurst Sq. B'frd —3G 99
Stoneyhurst Way. B'frd —3F 99
Stoney La. Bat —2H 137
Stoney La. Bur W —4J 25
Stoney La. E Ard —3J 139
Stoney La. Hal —3D 130
Stoney La. H Bri —5C 110
Stoney La. H'fth —4F 65
Stoney La. Leeds —6J 51
Stoney La. Light —1G 133
Stoney La. Meth —7C 124
Stoney La. Oven —4E 112
Stoney La. S'wram —3C 132
Stoney Ridge Av. B'frd —1B 78
Stoney Ridge Rd. Bgly —1B 78
Stoney Ri. H'fth —4F 65
Stoney Rock Ct. Leeds —4B 86
Stoney Rock Gro. Leeds —4B 86
Stoney Rock La. Leeds —4B 86
**Stoney Royd.** —3H 131
Stoney Royd Ter. Hal —4H 131
Stoneys Fold. Wilsd —6F 59
Stoney St. Kei —1K 39
Stoneythorpe. H'fth —4F 65
Stony Cft. La. Bklnd —1A 20
Stony La. All —3K 77
Stony La. B'frd —7E 62
Stony La. G'lnd —1E 142
Stony La. Oakw —5C 38
Stony La. Sower B —4F 141
Stony Royd. Fars —2A 82
Stoodley Ter. Hal —2C 130
Storey Pl. Leeds —4G 87
Storiths Ct. Add —2D 10
Stormer Hill La. Norl —6B 130
Storr Hill. Wyke —3J 115
Storr Hill Ter. Wyke —3J 115
Storth Pl. Hud —7F 145
Storths Rd. Hud —7E 144
Stott Hill. B'frd —6B 80 (3F 7)
Stott Rd. Leeds —2E 84
Stotts Pl. Hal —2J 131
Stott St. Leeds —6D 84
Stott Ter. B'frd —1F 81
**Stourton.** —5C 104
Stourton Rd. I'ly —4K 11
Stowe Gro. Leeds —5E 86
Stowell Mill St. B'frd —2K 97
Stradmore Rd. Denh —5C 76
Strafford Way. App B —4G 63
Straight Acres La. B'frd —7F 63
Straight La. Add —4A 10
Straight La. Hal —2B 112
Straits. Bail —7J 43
(off Northgate)
Stralau St. Bat —2G 137
Strangford Ct. B'frd —4F 63
Stratford Av. Leeds —3G 103
Stratford Ct. Leeds —5J 67
Stratford Rd. B'frd —1H 97
Stratford St. Leeds —4H 103
Stratford Ter. Leeds —3H 103
Strathallan Dri. Bail —1K 61
Strathmore Av. Leeds —3C 86
Strathmore Clo. B'frd —2D 80
Strathmore Dri. Bail —7H 43
Strathmore Dri. Leeds —2C 86
Strathmore Rd. I'ly —5E 12
Strathmore St. Leeds —3D 86
Strathmore Ter. Leeds —3C 86
Strathmore Vw. Leeds —3C 86
Stratton Ho. B'frd —3J 7
Stratton Pk. Ras —1H 145
Stratton Rd. Brigh —7H 133
Stratton Vw. B'frd —2G 99
Stratton Wlk. All —5A 78
Strawberry Av. Gar —7J 89
Strawberry Av. Liv —4J 135
Strawberry Bank. Liv —4J 135
Strawberry Fields. Kei —3A 40
Strawberry La. Leeds —6C 84
(in two parts)
Strawberry Rd. Leeds —6C 84
Strawberry Sq. Heck —5B 136
(off Church La.)
Strawberry St. Kei —3A 40
Strawberry St. Sils —1F 21
Stray, The. B'frd —6C 62
Stream Head Rd. T'tn —3F 77
Streamside. Leeds —6E 66
Streamside Clo. H Bri —7A 110
Street 1. Thor A —2G 37
Street 2. Thor A —2H 37
Street 3. Thor A —1H 37
Street 5. Thor A —7H 19
Street 6. Thor A —6H 19
Street 7. Thor A —6H 19
Street 8. Thor A —7J 19
Street La. E Mor —7F 23
Street La. Leeds —2C 68
(LS8)
Street La. Leeds —2J 67
(LS17)
Street La. Morl —2G 119
Street La. Oakw —3A 56
Street, The. Add —1B 10
(in two parts)
Strensall Grn. B'frd —6E 96
Stretchgate La. Hal —7C 112
Strickland Av. Leeds —7H 51
Strickland Clo. Leeds —7H 51
Strickland Cres. Leeds —7H 51
Strikes La. Sut Cr —7A 20
**Strong Close.** —4C 40
Strong Clo. Gro. Kei —4C 40
Strong Clo. Rd. Kei —4C 40
Strong Clo. Way. Kei —4C 40
(off Strong Clo. Rd.)
Stuart Ct. B'frd —2A 98
(off Swarland Gro.)
Stuart St. C'frd —7E 126
Stubbing La. Sower B —1G 141
Stubbing La. Slnd —5C 142
Stubbings Clo. H Bri —7A 110
Stubbings Rd. Bail —2F 61
Stubbings St. H Bri —7A 110
Stubbing Way. Shipl —6J 61
(in two parts)
Stubbs La. Wake —7A 122
Stubham Ri. I'ly —4A 12
Stubley Farm Rd. Heck —2B 136
Stubley Rd. Heck —2A 136
Stubs Beck La. West I —5F 117
Stub Thorn La. Hal —2K 131
Studdley Cres. Gil —1B 60
Studfold Vw. Leeds —3J 87
Studio Rd. Leeds —4E 84
Studleigh Ter. Brigh —3E 132
(off Brooklyn Ter.)
Studley Av. B'frd —7H 97
Studley Clo. E Mor —2H 41
Studley Rd. B'frd —3B 80
Studley Ter. Pud —5C 82
**Stump Cross.** —6K 113
Stunsteds Rd. Cleck —7F 117
Sturges Gro. B'frd —4D 80
Sturton Av. Gar —5A 90
Sturton Grange La. Gar —6B 90
Sturton Gro. Hal —7C 94
Sturton La. Gar —5A 90
Sturton La. Hal —7C 94
Styebank La. Rothw —1H 123
Stye La. Sower B —4F 129
Sty La. Bgly —5J 41
Styveton Way. Steet —4D 20
Suffolk Av. Bat —5E 136
Suffolk Ct. Yead —4K 45
Suffolk Pl. B'frd —1B 80
Suffolk St. Bat —4F 137
**Sugar Hill.** —7E 118
Sugar Hill. Add —1D 10
Sugar Hill Clo. Oult —4A 124
Sugar La. Dew —7J 137
Sugar Well App. Leeds —7G 67
Sugar Well Mt. Leeds —7G 67
Sugar Well Rd. Leeds —7G 67
Sugden Bank. Sower B —4A 130
(off Sunny Bank St.)
Sugden Clo. Brigh —1G 145
Sugden's Almshouses. Oakw —1F 57
Sugden St. B'frd —6J 79 (3A 6)
Sugden St. Oaken —3B 116
Sulby Gro. B'frd —5G 63
Summerbridge Clo. Bat —2E 136
Summerbridge Cres. B'frd —7F 63
Summerbridge Cres. Gom —5A 118
Summerbridge Dri. B'frd —7F 63
Summerdale. Gom —5K 117
Summerfield Av. Brigh —2H 133
Summerfield Av. Leeds —2E 82
Summerfield Clo. Bail —1G 61
Summerfield Dri. Bail —1H 61
Summerfield Dri. Leeds —2E 82
Summerfield Gdns. Leeds —2E 82
Summerfield Grn. Bail —1H 61
Summerfield Grn. Leeds —2E 82
Summerfield Gro. Bail —1G 61
Summerfield Pk. Bail —1H 61
Summerfield Pl. Leeds —2E 82
Summerfield Pl. Pud —5C 82
(off Richardshaw La.)
Summerfield Rd. B'frd —6E 62
Summerfield Rd. Leeds —2E 82
Summerfield Wlk. Leeds —2E 82
Summergate Pl. Hal —2D 130
Summergate St. Hal —2D 130
Summer Hall Ing. Wyke —3H 115
Summerhill Av. Steet —4F 21
Summerhill Dri. Steet —5F 21
Summerhill Gdns. Leeds —2D 68
Summerhill Gro. Gar —7H 89
Summerhill La. Steet —4F 21
Summerhill Pl. Leeds —2D 68
Summerhill Rd. Gar —6H 89
Summer Hill Rd. Meth —4H 125
Summer Hill St. B'frd —1G 97
Summerlands Gro. B'frd —4C 98
Summerland Ter. Sower B —4B 130
Summerscale St. Hal —7E 112
Summerseat. Rawd —1B 64
Summerseat Pl. B'frd —1J 97
Summersgill Sq. H'fth —4F 65
Summer St. Hal —3D 130
Summerville Rd. B'frd —7J 79 (6A 6)
Summerville Rd. S'ley —4A 82
Summit St. Kei —3K 39
Sunbeam Av. Leeds —3H 103
Sunbeam Gro. Leeds —3H 103
Sunbeam Pl. Leeds —3H 103
Sunbeam Ter. Leeds —3H 103
Sunbridge Rd. B'frd —6K 79 (2A 6)
Sunderland Clo. Brigh —5G 133
(off Thornhill Bri. La.)
Sunderland Rd. B'frd —3H 79
Sunderland Rd. Sils —4A 8
Sunderland St. Cro R —4H 57

## Sunderland St.—Tenth Av.


Sunderland St. Hal —1F 131
Sunderland St. Kei —5K 39
Sundown Av. B'frd —2E 96
Sun Fld. S'ley —4B 82
Sunfield Clo. S'ley —3B 82
Sunfield Dri. S'ley —3B 82
Sunfield Gdns. S'ley —3B 82
Sunfield Pl. S'ley —4B 82
Sunfield Ter. Mar —1G 135
(off Mayfield Ter.)
Sun Fold. Hal —2H 131
Sunhill Dri. Bail —2E 60
Sunhurst Clo. Oakw —2E 56
Sunhurst Dri. Oakw —2E 56
Sun La. Bur W —7K 13
(in three parts)
Sunningdale. B'frd —5D 78
Sunningdale. M'fld —5F 91
Sunningdale Av. Leeds —7G 49
Sunningdale Clo. Leeds —7G 49
Sunningdale Cres. Cull —7C 58
Sunningdale Cft. Hud —6F 145
Sunningdale Dri. Leeds —7G 49
Sunningdale Grn. Leeds —7G 49
Sunningdale Wlk. Leeds —7G 49
Sunningdale Way. Leeds —7G 49
**Sunnybank. —2F 143**
Sunny Bank. H Bri —6A 110
Sunny Bank. Leeds —7B 68
Sunnybank. M'fld —7H 91
Sunny Bank. Nor G —5D 112
Sunny Bank. Q'bry —5K 95
Sunny Bank. Shipl —5H 61
Sunny Bank. Wyke —3A 116
Sunnybank Av. B'frd —5K 97
Sunnybank Av. H'fth —5F 65
Sunnybank Av. Thornb —4H 81
Sunnybank Clo. Schol —2B 134
Sunnybank Ct. Yead —4B 46
Sunnybank Cres. G'lnd —2F 143
Sunnybank Cres. Yead —4B 46
Sunnybank Dri. G'lnd —2F 143
Sunny Bank Dri. Mir —7H 135
Sunny Bank Dri. Sower B —4A 130
Sunny Bank Grange. Brigh
(off Sunny Bank Rd.) —5G 133
Sunny Bank Gro. Leeds —7B 68
Sunnybank Gro. Thornb —4H 81
Sunny Bank La. Bat —1H 137
Sunnybank La. G'lnd —2F 143
Sunny Bank La. Hal —2B 132
Sunny Bank La. S'wram —2B 132
Sunnybank La. Thornb —4H 81
Sunny Bank Mills. Far —2B 82
Sunny Bank Rd. Bat —2H 137
Sunny Bank Rd. B'frd —5K 97
Sunny Bank Rd. Brigh —6G 133
Sunnybank Rd. G'lnd —2E 142
Sunny Bank Rd. Hal —2K 111
Sunnybank Rd. H'fth —5F 65
Sunny Bank Rd. Mir —7H 135
Sunnybank St. H'fth —5F 65
Sunny Bank St. Sower B —4A 130
Sunny Bank Ter. Hal —6G 113
Sunnybank Ter. H'fth —5F 65
Sunny Bank Vw. Leeds —7B 68
Sunny Brae Cres. Bgly —2B 60
Sunny Brow La. B'frd —3D 78
Sunnycliffe. E Mor —3H 41
Sunnydale Av. Brigh —1G 145
Sunnydale Cres. Otley —4F 27
Sunnydale Gro. Kei —5D 40
Sunnydale Pk. E Mor —2J 41
Sunnydale Ridge. Otley —4F 27
Sunnydene. Leeds —4H 87
Sunnyfield. E Ard —1J 139
Sunny Gro. Chur —6C 102
Sunny Hill. Wake —7K 139
Sunnyhill Av. Kei —6H 39
Sunnyhill Cres. Wren —7K 139
Sunnyhill Cft. Wren —6K 139
Sunnyhill Gro. Kei —6H 39
Sunny Mt. H'den —3F 59
Sunny Mt. High —3K 39
Sunny Mt. Sandb —4G 41
Sunnymount Ter. Birs —6D 118
(off Springwell Vw.)
Sunnyridge Av. Pud —5K 81
Sunnyside. Brigh —1K 145
Sunny Side. Hal —1E 132
Sunnyside. Heck —5B 136
Sunnyside. Holy G —7E 142
Sunnyside Av. Liv —6H 135
Sunnyside Av. Ting —7D 120
Sunnyside La. B'frd —4B 80
Sunnyside Rd. Leeds —4F 83
Sunny Side St. Hal —6G 113
Sunnyview. E Ard —1J 139
Sunnyview Av. Leeds —3F 103
Sunny Vw. Cres. Hud —6K 145
Sunnyview Gdns. Leeds —3F 103
Sunnyview Ter. Leeds —3F 103
Sunny Vw. Ter. Q'bry —6G 95
Sunset Av. Leeds —4E 66
Sunset Cres. Hal —3J 131
Sunset Dri. I'ly —4D 12
Sunset Dri. Leeds —5E 66
Sunset Hilltop. Leeds —4E 66
Sunset Mt. Leeds —5E 66
Sunset Ri. Leeds —4E 66
Sunset Rd. Leeds —4E 66
Sunset Ter. I'ly —4E 12
Sunset Vw. Leeds —4E 66
Sunshine Mills. Leeds —6B 84
Sun St. B'frd —5B 80 (2G 7)
Sun St. Ebrn —5B 20
Sun St. Haw —6E 56
Sun St. Kei —5A 40
Sun St. S'ley —4C 82
Sun St. Yead —4A 46
Sun Way. Hal —3K 131
Sun Wood Av. Hal —3B 114
Sun Wood Ter. Hal —3B 114
Suresnes Rd. Kei —4K 39
Surgery St. Haw —6F 57
Surrey Gro. B'frd —2A 98
Surrey Gro. Pud —5C 82
Surrey Rd. Pud —5C 82
Surrey St. Bat —3H 137
Surrey St. Hal —2C 130
Surrey St. Kei —3C 40
Sussex App. Leeds —3B 104
Sussex Av. H'fth —1G 65
Sussex Av. Leeds —3B 104
Sussex Cres. C'frd —7K 127
Sussex Gdns. Leeds —3B 104
Sussex Grn. Leeds —3B 104
Sussex Pl. Leeds —3B 104
Sussex St. Bat —3H 137
Sussex St. Kei —3C 40
Sussex St. Leeds —6A 86
Sutcliffe Ct. Hal —3J 131
(off Bank Top)
Sutcliffe Pl. B'frd —6K 97
Sutcliffe St. Hal —7C 112
Sutcliffe Ter. Hal —6G 113
(off Amblers Ter.)
Sutcliffe Wood La. Hal —1C 132
Sutherland Av. Leeds —3C 68
Sutherland Cres. Leeds —2C 68
Sutherland Mt. Leeds —3C 86
Sutherland Rd. Leeds —3C 86
Sutherland St. Leeds —7E 84
Sutherland Ter. Leeds —3C 86
Sutton App. Leeds —4G 87
Sutton Av. B'frd —7B 62
Sutton Cres. B'frd —2G 99
Sutton Cres. Leeds —4G 87
Sutton Dri. Cull —7B 58
Sutton Gro. B'frd —1G 99
Sutton Gro. Morl —4A 120
Sutton Ho. B'frd —1G 99
**Sutton-in-Craven. —5A 20**
Sutton La. Sut Cr —5A 20
Sutton Rd. B'frd —1G 99
Sutton St. Leeds —7F 85
Swaine Hill Cres. Yead —4J 45
Swaine Hill St. Yead —4J 45
Swaine Hill Ter. Yead —4J 45
**Swain Green. —1E 98**
**Swain House. —7C 62**
Swain Ho. Cres. B'frd —7C 62
Swain Ho. Rd. B'frd —7C 62
Swain Mt. B'frd —7C 62
**Swain Royd Lane Bottom. —2K 77**
Swale Ct. Sils —2G 21
(off Ings Way)
Swale Cres. Gar —7B 90
Swaledale Ho. Sower B —5K 129
(off Sowerby St.)
Swale Dri. C'frd —7H 127
Swale Ri. Weth —1H 17
Swales Moor Rd. Hal —2G 113
Swallow Av. Leeds —7A 84
Swallow Clo. Leeds —7B 50
Swallow Clo. Pool W —4H 29
Swallow Cres. Leeds —7K 83
Swallow Dri. Leeds —7B 50
Swallow Dri. Pool W —4H 29
Swallow Fold. B'frd —6C 78
Swallow Hill. Bat —7E 118
Swallow Mt. Leeds —7A 84
Swallow St. Heck —5B 136
Swallow St. Kei —3B 40
Swallow Va. Morl —3D 120
Swan Bank La. Hal —3H 131
Swan La. Leeds —2D 48
Swan St. B'frd —1A 98 (6D 6)
Swan St. Leeds —5E 4
**Swarcliffe. —1A 88**
Swarcliffe App. Leeds —1A 88
Swarcliffe Av. Leeds —1A 88
Swarcliffe Bank. Leeds —7A 70
Swarcliffe Dri. Leeds —7A 70
Swarcliffe Dri. E. Leeds —1B 88
Swarcliffe Grn. Leeds —1B 88
Swarcliffe Pde. Leeds —1A 88
Swarcliffe Rd. Leeds —7A 70
Swarcliffe Towers. Leeds —7B 70
Swardale Grn. Leeds —1A 88
Swardale Rd. Leeds —1A 88
Swarland Gro. B'frd —2A 98
**Swartha. —7J 9**
Swartha La. Sils —7J 9
Sweet St. Leeds —7H 85
Sweet St. W. Leeds —7G 85
(in two parts)
Swift Pl. Sower B —7D 140
Swift St. Hal —5H 131
**Swillington. —4E 106**
Swillington La. Swil & Leeds —5D 106
Swincar Av. Yead —4J 45
**Swincliffe. —3J 117**
Swincliffe Clo. Gom —3J 117
Swincliffe Cres. Gom —4J 117
Swindon Rd. Dew —7G 137
Swinegate. Leeds —6J 85 (7E 4)
Swine La. Sandb —3F 41
**Swinnow. —4E 82**
Swinnow Av. Leeds —4E 82
Swinnow Clo. Leeds —4E 82
Swinnow Cres. S'ley —3E 82
Swinnow Dri. Leeds —4E 82
Swinnow Gdns. Leeds —4E 82
Swinnow Gth. Leeds —5E 82
Swinnow Grn. Pud —4D 82
Swinnow Gro. Leeds —4E 82
Swinnow La. S'ley & Leeds —3E 82
**Swinnow Moor. —5E 82**
Swinnow Pl. S'ley —3E 82
Swinnow Rd. Pud & Leeds —5D 82
Swinnow Vw. Leeds —4E 82
Swinnow Wlk. Leeds —4E 82
Swinton Pl. B'frd —1H 97
Swinton Ter. Hal —3D 130
Swires Rd. B'frd —4E 80
Swires Rd. Hal —2F 131
Swires Ter. Hal —2F 131
Swiss St. C'frd —6E 126
Swiss Wlk. Bat —5F 137
Swithenbank Av. Oss —7C 138
Swithenbank St. Oss —7C 138
Swithen's Ct. Rothw —3H 123
Swithen's Dri. Rothw —3G 123
Swithen's Gro. Rothw —3G 123
Swithen's La. Rothw —3H 123
Swithen's St. Rothw —3H 123
Sycamore Av. Bgly —2K 59
Sycamore Av. B'frd —6F 79
Sycamore Av. C'gts —5J 87
Sycamore Av. Kip —4K 107
Sycamore Av. Leeds —7B 68
Sycamore Chase. Pud —6D 82
Sycamore Clo. B'frd —5C 80 (1H 7)
Sycamore Clo. B'hpe —2K 47
Sycamore Clo. Leeds —1G 85
Sycamore Clo. Mean —5F 67
Sycamore Ct. B'frd —5C 80 (1H 7)
Sycamore Cft. Leeds —3H 103
Sycamore Dri. Add —1E 10
Sycamore Dri. Cleck —1D 134
Sycamore Dri. Ell —3H 143
Sycamore Dri. Hal —2G 133
Sycamore Fld. Leeds —3H 103
Sycamore Gro. Kei —5B 20
Sycamore Ind. Est. Heck —6B 136
Sycamore Row. Leeds —1E 82
Sycamores, The. B'hpe —2K 47
Sycamores, The. Dew —6F 137
Sycamores, The. Guis —1G 45
Sycamore Vw. Kei —5H 39
Sycamore Wlk. Fars —3B 82
Sycamore Way. Birs —5D 118
Sydenham Pl. B'frd —3C 80
Sydenham Rd. Leeds —7F 85
Sydenham St. Leeds —7F 85
Sydney St. Bgly —1A 60
Sydney St. Fars —3B 82
Sydney St. Liv —5K 135
Sydney St. W'ford —1B 124
Syke Av. Ting —1D 138
Syke Clo. Ting —1C 138
Syke Fold Grange. Cleck —1F 135
Syke Gdns. Ting —1D 138
Syke Grn. S'cft —3A 52
Syke Ho. La. G'lnd —3D 142
Syke La. Caus F —4C 94
Syke La. Hal —6E 114
Syke La. Q'bry —7K 95
Syke La. S'cft —4J 51
Syke La. Sower B —5K 129
Syke Rd. B'frd —2G 79
Syke Rd. Ting —1D 138
Syke Rd. Weth —4A 18
Sykes Av. Heck —3C 136
Sykes Clo. Bat —2J 137
Syke Side. Kei —1K 39
Sykes La. Bat —4K 137
Sykes La. Oaken —3C 116
Sykes La. Oakw —1F 57
Sykes La. Sils —2F 21
Sykes Rd. Bat —2J 137
Sykes St. C'frd —7D 126
Sykes St. Cleck —1F 135
Sykes Yd. Hal —3D 130
(off King Cross Rd.)
Syke Ter. Ting —1C 138
Sylmet Clo. B'frd —5K 79 (2C 6)
Sylvan Av. Q'bry —6H 95
Sylvan Vw. H'fth —3G 65
Syrett Gro. Leeds —5A 84
Syrett Pk. Hal —6E 112
Syringa Av. All —1A 78

Tabbs Ct. Schol —6B 116
Tabbs La. Schol —6A 116
Tackgarth. Brigh —1G 145
Talbot Av. Leeds —2C 84
Talbot Av. Moort & Round —2A 68
Talbot Ct. Leeds —3B 68
Talbot Cres. Leeds —2B 68
Talbot Fold. Leeds —3B 68
Talbot Gdns. Leeds —2B 68
Talbot Gro. Leeds —2B 68
Talbot Ho. Ell —3K 143
Talbot Mt. Leeds —2C 84
Talbot Ri. Leeds —2B 68
Talbot Rd. Leeds —2B 68
Talbot Row. Bat —3H 137
Talbot St. Bat —4G 137
Talbot St. B'frd —6H 79
Talbot St. Kei —4J 39
Talbot Ter. Leeds —2C 84
Talbot Ter. Rothw —3G 123
Talbot Vw. Leeds —2C 84
Tamar St. B'frd —2J 97
Tamworth St. B'frd —7G 81
Tandy Trad. Est. Leeds —4D 84
(off Canal Rd.)
Tanfield Dri. Bur W —7A 14
Tanglewood Ct. B'frd —5G 97
Tan Ho. Ct. B'frd —7D 98
Tanhouse Hill. Hip —1C 132
Tanhouse Hill. H'fth —4J 65
Tan Ho. La. Hal —3A 114
Tan Ho. La. Wilsd —6E 58
Tanhouse Pk. Hal —1C 132
Tan Ho. Yd. Morl —5C 102
Tan La. B'frd —1D 116
Tannerbrook Clo. Cytn —2D 96
Tanner Hill Rd. B'frd —3E 96
Tanner St. Liv —3D 134
Tannett Grn. B'frd —4B 98
Tanton Cres. Cytn —2D 96
Tanton Wlk. Cytn —2D 96
Tarn Clo. C'frd —6K 127
Tarn Ct. Kei —3H 39
Tarnhill M. B'frd —2A 98
Tarn La. Leeds —5E 50
Tarn La. Oakw —3C 38
Tarnside Dri. Leeds —2H 87
Tarn Vw. Rd. Yead —4B 46
Tatefield Gro. Kip —6A 108
Tatefield Pl. Kip —5A 108
Tateley Clo. Oss —7C 138
Tateley La. Oss —7C 138
Tate Naylor St. Dew —6F 137
Tatham's Ct. Hal —3D 130
(off High Shaw Rd. W.)
Tatham Way. Leeds —6E 68
Taunton Ho. B'frd —7D 6
Taunton St. Shipl —4G 61
Taverngate. Guis —3A 44
Tawny Clo. Morl —3D 120
Tay Ct. B'frd —7F 63
Taylor Av. Sils —1F 21
Taylor Gro. Meth —4J 125
Taylor Hall La. Mir —7G 135
(in two parts)
Taylor La. Bar E —6F 71
Taylor La. Hal —3D 94
Taylor Rd. B'frd —6K 97
(in three parts)
Taylors Clo. Leeds —1K 87
Taylor St. Bat —4G 137
Taylor St. Cleck —1F 134
Taylor Va. Brigh —7G 133
Tealbeck App. Otley —3K 27
Tealbeck Ho. Otley —3K 27
Tealby Clo. Leeds —2J 65
Teal Ct. Steet —4D 20
Teal Dri. Morl —3D 120
Teal La. Hal —3K 113
(in two parts)
Teal M. Leeds —2K 121
Teasdale St. B'frd —3D 98
(in two parts)
Teasel Clo. Oaken —3C 116
Techno Cen. H'fth —2G 65
Technology Dri. Bat —4J 137
Tees Clo. C'frd —7H 127
Tees St. B'frd —3J 97
Telephone Pl. Leeds —4K 85 (3H 5)
Telford Clo. C'frd —7B 126
Telford Clo. Leeds —4A 104
Telford Clo. Sils —2H 21
Telford Gdns. Leeds —4A 104
Telford Pl. Leeds —4A 104
Telford St. Leeds —4A 104
Telford Ter. Leeds —4A 104
Telford Wlk. Leeds —4A 104
Telscombe Dri. B'frd —4F 99
Temperance Ct. H'fth —4F 65
Temperance Fld. Schol —7B 116
Temperance Fld. Wyke —4J 115
Temperance St. S'ley —4C 82
Tempest Pl. Leeds —3G 103
Tempest Rd. Leeds —3G 103
Templar Gdns. Weth —2K 17
Templar La. Leeds —5K 85 (5G 5)
(LS2)
Templar La. Leeds —1B 88
(LS15)
Templar Pl. Leeds —5K 85 (6G 5)
Templars Clo. G'lnd —2E 142
Templar St. Leeds —5J 85 (5F 5)
Templars Way. B'frd —5E 78
Templars Way. Gar —7K 89
Templar Ter. Morl —5B 120
Temple Av. Leeds —7J 87
Temple Av. Rothw —7H 105
Temple Clo. Leeds —7J 87
Temple Ct. Leeds —6H 87
Temple Ct. Rothw —7H 105
Temple Cres. Leeds —3G 103
Temple Ga. Leeds —6K 87
Templegate Av. Leeds —7J 87
Templegate Clo. Leeds —6K 87
Templegate Cres. Leeds —7K 87
Temple Ga. Dri. Leeds —6J 87
Templegate Grn. Leeds —6K 87
Templegate Ri. Leeds —7J 87
Templegate Rd. Leeds —7J 87
Templegate Vw. Leeds —7J 87
Templegate Wlk. Leeds —6K 87
Templegate Way. Leeds —7K 87
Temple Grn. Rothw —7J 105
Temple Gro. Leeds —6J 87
Temple La. Leeds —6K 87
Temple Lawn. Rothw —7J 105
Temple Lea. Leeds —6J 87
Temple Newsam Country Park. —1K 105
Templenewsam Rd. Leeds —6H 87
Templenewsam Vw. Leeds —7H 87
Temple Pk. Clo. Leeds —6J 87
Temple Pk. Gdns. Leeds —6J 87
Temple Pk. Grn. Leeds —6J 87
Temple Rhydding. Bail —2J 61
Temple Rhydding Dri. Bail —2J 61
Temple Ri. Leeds —7J 87
Temple Row. Kei —4A 40
(off Temple St.)
Temple Row. Leeds —7C 88
Temple Row Clo. Leeds —7C 88
Templestowe Cres. Leeds —4A 88
Templestowe Dri. Leeds —5A 88
Templestowe Gdns. Leeds —5K 87
Templestowe Hill. Leeds —4K 87
Temple St. B'frd —3H 79
Temple St. Kei —4K 39
Temple Vw. Loft —6E 122
Temple Vw. Gro. Leeds —6C 86
(in two parts)
Temple Vw. Pl. Leeds —6B 86
Temple Vw. Rd. Leeds —5B 86
Temple Vw. Ter. Leeds —6B 86
Temple Wlk. Leeds —5K 87
Tenbury Fold. B'frd —3G 99
Tenby Ter. Hal —7D 112
(off Osborne St.)
Tennis Av. B'frd —5G 99
Tennis Way. Bail —3G 61
Tennyson Av. Sower B —5H 129
Tennyson Clo. Pud —7D 82
Tennyson Pl. B'frd —5C 80 (1K 7)
Tennyson Pl. Cleck —7F 117
Tennyson Pl. Hal —7C 114
Tennyson Rd. B'frd —6H 97
Tennyson St. Far —3B 82
Tennyson St. Guis —3H 45
Tennyson St. Hal —6E 112
Tennyson St. Kei —6K 39
Tennyson St. Morl —3B 120
Tennyson St. Pud —7D 82
Tennyson Ter. Morl —3B 120
Tenter Clo. Birs —2G 137
Tentercroft Pl. Bail —7J 43
Tenterden Way. Leeds —2D 88
Tenterfield Ri. Hal —6A 114
Tenterfields. App B —4F 63
Tenterfields. Hal —3G 129
Tenterfields Bus. Cen. L'ft —3G 129
Tenterfield Ter. Hal —6A 114
(off Bradford Rd.)
Tenter Hill. B'ham —1C 54
(in two parts)
Tenter Hill. Cytn —2B 96
Tenter Hill La. Hud —5K 145
Tenter La. Leeds —6J 85
(off Bridge End)
Tenters Gro. Hud —6K 145
Tenth Av. Liv —3E 134


198 A-Z Leeds & Bradford

Ten Yards La.—Toulston La.

Ten Yards La. T'tn —4D 76
Terminus Pde. Leeds —3A 88
(off Farm Rd.)
Ternhill Gro. B'frd —1A 98 (7D 6)
Tern Pk. Coll —1F 35
Tern St. B'frd —3H 97
Terrace Gdns. Hal —6F 113
Terrace, The. B Spa —3E 36
Terrace, The. B'frd —3B 80
Terrace, The. Cleck —1G 135
Terrace, The. Pud —2C 100
Terrington Crest. Cytn —2D 96
Terry Rd. Low M —2A 116
Tetley Dri. B'shaw —3J 117
Tetley La. Hal —5A 114
Tetley Pl. B'frd —3B 80
Tetley's Brewery Wharf. —6K 85
Tetley St. B'frd —6K 79 (4C 6)
Teville Ct. B'frd —2C 98
Tewit Clo. Hal —7D 94
Tewit Gdns. Hal —7D 94
Tewit Grn. Hal —7D 94
Tewit Hall Gdns. Hal —1D 112
Tewit Hall Rd. B'frd —5E 80
Tewit La. Hal —7D 94
Tewitt Clo. Steet —4D 20
Tewitt La. Bgly —5B 42
Tewitt La. T'tn —3D 76
Texas St. Morl —5B 120
Thackeray Rd. B'frd —1F 81
Thackeray's Medical Museum. —3B 86
Thacker Ga. Rd. Cra V —3C 128
**Thackley. —3C 62**
Thackley Av. B'frd —2C 62
Thackley Ct. Shipl —4J 61
Thackley Old Rd. Shipl —4J 61
Thackley Rd. B'frd —2C 62
Thackley Vw. B'frd —2C 62
Thackray Av. Heck —3C 136
Thackray St. Hal —1B 130
Thackray St. Morl —4A 120
Thames Dri. Gar —7A 90
Thanes Clo. Hud —7E 144
Thanet Gth. Sils —2G 21
Thane Way. Leeds —2C 88
Thatchers Way. Gom —6J 117
Theaker La. Leeds —5B 84
Theakston Mead. Cytn —2C 96
Thealby Clo. Leeds —5A 86 (5J 5)
Thealby Lawn. Leeds —4A 86 (5J 5)
Thealby Pl. Leeds —5A 86 (5J 5)
Thearne Grn. Cytn —2D 96
Theodore St. Leeds —5G 103
Third Av. B'frd —4E 80
Third Av. Hal —4F 131
Third Av. Kei —5K 39
Third Av. Leeds —7D 84
Third Av. Liv —4D 134
Third Av. Rothw —7H 105
Third Av. Weth —4K 17
Third St. Low M —1A 116
Thirkhill Ct. B'frd —2A 98
Thirkleby Royd. Cytn —2C 96
Thirlmere Av. Ell —2B 144
Thirlmere Av. Wyke —6A 116
Thirlmere Clo. Leeds —6E 102
Thirlmere Dri. C'frd —7K 127
Thirlmere Dri. Ting —7G 121
Thirlmere Dri. Weth —3F 17
Thirlmere Gdns. B'frd —3D 80
Thirlmere Gdns. Leeds —6E 102
Thirlmere Gro. Bail —3E 60
Thirlmere Rd. Dew —6K 137
Thirsk Clo. Hud —7H 145
Thirsk Dri. Kip —4A 108
Thirsk Grange. Cytn —2D 96
Thirsk Row. Leeds —6H 85 (7C 4)
Thirteenth Av. Liv —3D 134
Thistle Clo. Hud —7E 144
Thistle Way. Gild —2H 119
Thomas Ct. B'frd —5J 97
Thomas Duggan Ho. Shipl —5H 61
Thomas Fold. B'frd —3D 80
Thomas St. Bat —2F 137
Thomas St. Brigh —7G 133
Thomas St. C'frd —6E 126
Thomas St. Ell —3A 144
Thomas St. Hal —3E 130
(nr. Eldroth Rd.)
Thomas St. Hal —1G 131
(nr. Union St.)
Thomas St. Haw —6F 57
Thomas St. Heck —5B 136
Thomas St. Holy G —5F 143
Thomas St. Leeds —2G 85
Thomas St. Lind —7B 144
Thomas St. Liv —5K 135
(nr. Wormald St.)
Thomas St. Liv —4J 135
(off Valley Rd.)
Thomas St. S. Hal —2D 130
Thompson Av. B'frd —7B 62
Thompson Grn. Bail —2G 61
Thompson La. Bail —3G 61
Thompson St. Hal —1F 131
Thompson St. Shipl —4G 61
Thoresby Dri. Gom —7K 117
Thoresby Gro. B'frd —3E 96
Thoresby Pl. Leeds —5H 85 (5C 4)
Thornaby Dri. Cytn —2C 96
Thornacre Cres. Shipl —6A 62
Thornacre Rd. Shipl —5A 62
Thorn Av. B'frd —1C 78
Thornbank Av. Oakw —7H 39
Thornberry Dri. Liv —3D 134
Thornbridge M. B'frd —1D 80
**Thornbury. —5F 81**
Thornbury Av. B'frd —5F 81
Thornbury Cres. B'frd —5F 81
Thornbury Dri. B'frd —5F 81
Thornbury Gro. B'frd —5F 81
Thornbury Rd. B'frd —6F 81
Thornbury St. B'frd —6F 81
Thorncliffe Est. Bat —5E 136
Thorncliffe Rd. Bat —5E 136
Thorncliffe Rd. B'frd —4K 79
Thorncliffe Rd. Kei —5H 39
Thorncliffe St. Hud —7B 144
Thorn Clo. Leeds —2D 86
Thorn Clo. Shipl —6A 62
Thorn Cres. Leeds —2D 86
Thorncroft Rd. B'frd —5F 97
Thorn Cross. Leeds —1E 86
Thorndale Ri. B'frd —1A 80
Thorndene Way. B'frd —7J 99
Thorn Dri. B'frd —1D 78
Thorn Dri. Leeds —2D 86
Thorn Dri. Q'bry —7G 95
Thorne Clo. Pud —5K 81
Thornefield Cres. Ting —7D 120
Thorne Gro. Rothw —1H 123
**Thorner. —6D 52**
Thorner Gro. Sils —7G 9
Thorner La. B'ham —1G 53
Thorner La. S'cft —3B 52
Thorner La. T'ner —2C 70
Thorner Rd. Woth —4H 53
Thornes Pk. Brigh —7G 133
Thornes Pk. Shipl —7K 61
Thorne St. Holy G —5E 142
Thorney La. L'ft —6E 110
Thornfield. Bgly —7J 41
Thornfield. Haw —6F 57
Thornfield Av. B'frd —6K 97
Thornfield Av. Fars —2A 82
Thornfield Ct. Leeds —3K 87
Thornfield Dri. Leeds —3K 87
Thornfield Hall. T'tn —7J 77
(off Thornton Rd.)
Thornfield M. Leeds —3K 87
Thornfield M. M'wte —4J 41
Thornfield Mt. Birs —6E 118
Thornfield Pl. B'frd —2E 80
Thornfield Ri. G'lnd —2F 143
Thornfield Rd. Leeds —4B 66
Thornfield Sq. B'frd —2E 80
Thornfield St. G'lnd —2F 143
Thornfield Ter. Wilsd —1F 77
Thornfield Way. Leeds —3K 87
Thorn Gth. Cleck —2E 134
Thorn Gth. Kei —2J 39
Thorn Gro. B'frd —1D 78
Thorn Gro. Leeds —2D 86
Thorn Hill. Holy G —7D 142
Thornhill Av. Oakw —1G 57
Thornhill Av. Shipl —7K 61
Thornhill Bri. La. Brigh —5G 133
Thornhill Clo. C'ley —5K 63
Thornhill Ct. Leeds —7C 84
Thornhill Cft. Leeds —7B 84
Thornhill Dri. C'ley —4H 63
Thornhill Dri. Shipl —7K 61
Thornhill Gro. C'ley —5K 63
Thornhill Gro. Shipl —7K 61
Thornhill Gro. Steet —4D 20
Thorn Hill Hey. Holy G —7D 142
(in two parts)
Thornhill Ho. B'frd —5G 81
(off Thornhill Pl.)
Thornhill Pl. B'frd —5G 81
Thornhill Pl. Brigh —7G 133
Thornhill Pl. Leeds —7B 84
Thornhill Rd. Brigh —1F 145
Thornhill Rd. Leeds —7B 84
Thornhill Rd. Steet —3D 20
**Thornhills. —4J 133**
Thornhills Beck La. Brigh —4H 133
Thornhills La. Clif —4J 133
Thornhill St. C'ley —5K 63
Thornhill St. Leeds —7B 84
Thornhill Ter. B'frd —5F 81
**Thornhurst. —5C 34**
Thorn La. B'frd —1D 78
(in two parts)
Thorn La. Leeds —5B 68
Thornlea Clo. Yead —6H 45
Thornleigh Dri. Liv —3K 135
Thornleigh Gdns. Leeds —7B 86
Thornleigh Gro. Leeds —7B 86
Thornleigh Mt. Leeds —7B 86
Thornleigh St. Leeds —7B 86
Thornleigh Vw. Leeds —7B 86
Thornmead Rd. Bail —2K 61
Thorn Mt. Leeds —1E 86
Thorn Royd Dri. B'frd —4H 99
Thornsgill Av. B'frd —3E 98
Thorn St. Birs —6C 118
Thorn St. B'frd —4F 79
Thorn St. Haw —4G 57
Thorn Ter. Leeds —1D 86
**Thornton. —7J 77**
Thornton Av. Leeds —6A 84
Thornton Clo. Birs —4D 118
Thornton Ct. B'frd —5F 79
(off Lane Ends Clo.)
Thornton Gdns. Leeds —6A 84
Thornton Gro. Leeds —6A 84
Thornton La. B'frd —3J 97
Thornton Moor Rd. Oxe —5J 75
Thornton Old Rd. B'frd —6D 78
Thornton Rd. B'frd —5G 79 (3A 6)
Thornton Rd. Brigh —1E 144
Thornton Rd. Denh & T'tn —1C 94
Thornton Rd. Q'bry —4H 95
Thornton's Arc. Leeds —5J 85 (6E 4)
Thornton Sq. B'frd —4K 97
(off Delamere St.)
Thornton Sq. Brigh —6H 133
(off Commercial St.)
Thornton St. B'frd —6J 79 (3A 6)
Thornton St. Bur W —7A 14
Thornton St. Cleck —2C 134
Thornton St. Hal —3D 130
Thornton St. Rawf —1H 135
Thornton Ter. Hal —3D 130
Thornton Vw. Cytn —3C 96
Thornton Vw. Rd. Cytn —3C 96
Thorntonville. Rawf —2H 135
Thorntree St. Hal —3D 130
Thorn Vw. Ell —3A 144
Thorn Vw. Hal —5G 113
Thorn Vw. Leeds —2E 86
Thorn Vw. Myth —7A 110
Thornville. Morl —7B 102
Thornville Av. Leeds —3E 84
Thornville Ct. B'frd —3J 79
Thornville Ct. Leeds —3E 84
(off Thornville Rd.)
Thornville Cres. Leeds —2E 84
Thornville Gro. Leeds —3E 84
Thornville Mt. Leeds —3E 84
Thornville Pl. Leeds —3E 84
Thornville Rd. Leeds —3E 84
Thornville Row. Leeds —3E 84
Thornville St. Leeds —3E 84
Thornville Ter. Leeds —3E 84
Thornville Vw. Leeds —3E 84
Thorn Wlk. Leeds —2E 86
Thorold Ho. B'frd —5E 62
(off Fairhaven Grn.)
**Thorp Arch. —1E 36**
Thorp Arch Grange. B Spa —6F 19
Thorp Arch Trad. Est. Thor A —7H 19
**Thorpe. —5E 62**
Thorpe Arch Pk. Thor A —1E 36
Thorpe Av. T'tn —7A 78
Thorpe Clo. Guis —3D 44
Thorpe Ct. Leeds —4J 121
Thorpe Cres. Leeds —4J 121
Thorpe Dri. Guis —2E 44
**Thorpe Edge. —5E 62**
Thorpe Gdns. Leeds —3J 121
Thorpe Gth. Leeds —4H 121
Thorpe Gro. Leeds —3J 121
Thorpe Gro. T'tn —7B 78
Thorpe La. Guis —3C 44
Thorpe La. Ting —6E 120
(in two parts)
Thorpe Lwr. La. Rob H —5B 122
Thorpe Mill Ct. Sower B —1G 141
Thorpe Mt. Leeds —4H 121
**Thorpe on the Hill. —5A 122**
Thorpe Pl. Sower B —6E 128
Thorpe Rd. E Ard & Leeds —1J 139
Thorpe Rd. Leeds —3J 121
Thorpe Rd. Pud —5B 82
Thorpe Rd. T'tn —7A 78
Thorpe Sq. Leeds —3K 121
Thorpe St. Hal —5F 113
Thorpe St. Halt —5J 87
Thorpe St. Kei —3A 40
Thorpe St. Leeds —3J 121
Thorpe Vw. Leeds —4J 121
Thorp Gth. B'frd —5D 62
Thorverton Dri. B'frd —6G 99
Thorverton Gro. B'frd —6G 99
Threadneedle St. Hal —3D 130
(off Dundas St.)
Threelands Grange. B'shaw —1J 117
Three Nooked M. Idle —5D 62
(off Brecon Clo.)
Threshfield. Bail —1J 61
Threshfield Cres. B'shaw —1J 117
Thrift Way. Bgly —2K 59
Throstle Av. Leeds —4H 121
Throstle Bank. Hal —3D 130
(off Gainest)
Throstle Dri. Leeds —4G 121
Throstle Gro. Leeds —4J 121
Throstle Hill. Leeds —4H 121
Throstle La. Leeds —4H 121
Throstle Mt. Leeds —4H 121
Throstle Mt. L'ft —3H 129
Throstle Nest. Bat —4E 136
Throstle Nest Clo. Otley —7F 15
Throstle Nest Rd. Sils —7F 9
Throstle Nest Vw. H'fth —5G 65
Throstle Pde. Leeds —4H 121
Throstle Pl. Leeds —4H 121
Throstle Rd. Leeds —2A 122
(nr. Ring Rd. Middleton)
Throstle Rd. Leeds —4J 121
(nr. Thorpe La.)
Throstle Row. Leeds —4H 121
Throstle Sq. Leeds —4K 121
Throstle St. Leeds —4H 121
Throstle Ter. Leeds —4J 121
Throstle Vw. Leeds —4K 121
Throstle Wlk. Leeds —4H 121
Throxenby Way. Cytn —2C 96
Thrum Hall Clo. Hal —1D 130
Thrum Hall Dri. Hal —1D 130
Thrum Hall La. Hal —1D 130
Thrush Hill Rd. H Bri —7A 110
Thrush St. Kei —3B 40
Thryberg St. B'frd —6C 80 (5J 7)
Thunderton La. Sower B —6D 128
Thurley Dri. B'frd —4D 98
Thurley Rd. B'frd —4D 98
Thurnscoe Rd. B'frd —5K 79 (1C 6)
Thursby St. B'frd —6D 80 (4K 7)
Thurston Gdns. All —5B 78
**Thwaite Gate. —3C 104**
Thwaite Ga. Leeds —3B 104
Thwaite La. Leeds —3C 104
Thwaite Mills Museum. —3D 104
**Thwaites. —4D 40**
Thwaites Av. I'ly —5C 12
Thwaites Bri. Kei —4C 40
**Thwaites Brow. —5D 40**
Thwaites Brow Rd. Kei —6D 40
Thwaites La. Kei —4C 40
Tibgarth. Lntn —6F 17
Tichborne Rd. B'frd —3A 98
Tichborne St. Liv —4G 135
Tichbourne Rd. W. B'frd —3A 98
Tichbourne St. Bat —4D 136
Tickhill St. B'frd —7D 80 (5K 7)
Tidswell St. Heck —4C 136
Tilbury Av. Leeds —2F 103
Tilbury Gro. Leeds —2F 103
Tilbury Mt. Leeds —2F 103
Tilbury Pde. Leeds —2F 103
Tilbury Rd. Leeds —2F 103
Tilbury Row. Leeds —2F 103
Tilbury Ter. Leeds —2F 103
Tilbury Vw. Leeds —2F 103
Tile La. Leeds —1D 66
(in two parts)
Tile St. B'frd —4H 79
Tile Ter. Brigh —7G 133
Tiley Sq. B'frd —2A 98
Till Carr La. Hal —1G 133
Tillotson Av. Sower B —5J 129
Tillotson St. Sils —7F 9
Timber St. Ell —3K 143
Timber St. Kei —3C 40
Timble Dri. Bgly —7B 42
Tim La. Oakw —2D 56
Timmey La. Sower B —3J 129
Timothy La. Bat —1G 137
**Tingley. —6E 120**
Tingley Av. Ting —6E 120
Tingley Comn. Morl —5B 120
Tingley Cres. Ting —6C 120
Tinkler Stile. Thack —4B 62
Tinsel Rd. Dew —7K 137
**Tinshill. —7J 47**
Tinshill Av. Leeds —1J 65
Tinshill Clo. Leeds —1J 65
Tinshill Cres. Leeds —7J 47
Tinshill Dri. Leeds —6J 47
Tinshill Gth. Leeds —7J 47
Tinshill Gro. Leeds —7J 47
Tinshill La. Leeds —1H 65
**Tinshill Moor. —6J 47**
Tinshill Mt. Leeds —7J 47
Tinshill Rd. Leeds —1H 65
Tinshill Vw. Leeds —7J 47
Tinshill Wlk. Leeds —6J 47
Tintern Av. B'frd —6D 78
Tisma Dri. B'frd —6E 98
Tithe Barn Fold. Bar E —5H 71
Tithe Barn La. Bard —1K 51
Titus St. Shipl —4F 61
Tiverton Ho. B'frd —7D 6
Tiverton Wlk. B'frd —4G 99
Tivoli Pl. B'frd —3J 97
Tivoli Pl. I'ly —6C 12
Toby La. B'frd —2G 97
Todd Ter. B'frd —2H 97
Todley Hall Rd. Oakw —5A 38
Todwell La. B'frd —3J 97
Tofts Av. Wyke —5J 115
Tofts Gro. Brigh —2F 145
Tofts Gro. Gdns. Brigh —2F 145
Tofts Gro. Pl. Brigh —2F 145
(off Tofts Gro.)
**Toftshaw. —6F 99**
Toftshaw Fold. B'frd —6F 99
Toftshaw La. B'frd —6G 99
Toftshaw New Rd. B'frd —6F 99
Tofts Ho. Clo. Pud —6C 82
Tofts Rd. Cleck —1F 135
Tofts Rd. Pud —6B 82
Toft St. Leeds —7D 84
Toll Bar La. Wren —7K 139
Toll Bar Rd. C'frd —7K 125
Toller Dri. B'frd —2E 78
Toller Gro. B'frd —2F 79
Toller La. B'frd —2E 78
Toller Pk. B'frd —2F 79
Tollgate Ct. B'frd —4G 79
Tolson St. Dew —7G 137
Tolworth Fold. All —5B 78
Tomling Cote La. Sils —2J 21
Tomlinson Bldgs. B'frd —3C 62
Tomroyds La. Mir —7B 136
Tonbridge Clo. B'frd —6F 97
Tonbridge St. Leeds —4G 85 (3B 4)
**Tong. —4C 100**
Tong App. Leeds —7H 83
Tong Dri. Leeds —6H 83
Tong Ga. Leeds —6H 83
Tong Grn. Leeds —6H 83
Tong Hall Bus. Pk. B'frd —4B 100
Tong Ho. B'frd —4C 100
Tong La. B'frd —6A 100
**Tong Park. —7B 44**
Tong Pk. Bail —7B 44
Tong Rd. Leeds —2F 101
**Tong Street. —5G 99**
Tong St. B'frd —4E 98
Tongue La. Leeds —4F 67
Tong Wlk. Leeds —6H 83
Tong Way. Leeds —6H 83
**Toothill. —2G 145**
Toothill Av. Brigh —2G 145
Toothill Bank. Brigh —1G 145
Toothill La. Brigh —3G 145
Toot Hill La. Sower B —6D 128
Toothill La. S. Brigh —4F 145
Topaz Clo. Far —7J 145
**Topcliffe. —5C 120**
Topcliffe Av. Morl —3D 120
Topcliffe Ct. Morl —3D 120
Topcliffe Fold. Morl —5C 120
Topcliffe Grn. Morl —3D 120
Topcliffe Gro. Morl —5C 120
Topcliffe La. Morl —5C 120
Topcliffe La. Ting —4D 120
Topcliffe Mead. Morl —3D 120
Topcliffe M. Morl —3D 120
Top Fold. Leeds —7B 84
Top Moor Side. Leeds —1G 103
Top of Carr. Bat —6F 137
(off Upper Rd.)
**Top of Cowcliffe. —6F 145**
Tor Av. Wyke —6J 115
Torcote Cres. Hud —4J 145
Tordoff Av. B'frd —1E 96
Tordoff Grn. B'frd —6H 97
Tordoff Pl. Kirks —1A 84
Tordoff Rd. Low M —1A 116
Tordoff Ter. Leeds —1A 84
Toronto Pl. Leeds —6K 67
Toronto St. Hyde P —3E 84
(off Queen's Rd.)
Toronto St. Leeds —5H 85 (6D 4)
Torre Clo. Leeds —5C 86
Torre Cres. B'frd —5D 96
Torre Cres. Leeds —5D 86
Torre Dri. Leeds —4C 86
Torre Gdns. Leeds —5B 86
Torre Grn. Leeds —5B 86
Torre Gro. B'frd —5D 96
Torre Gro. Leeds —4C 86
Torre Hill. Leeds —5D 86
Torre La. Leeds —5D 86
Torre Mt. Leeds —4C 86
Torre Pl. Leeds —5C 86
Torre Rd. B'frd —5D 96
Torre Rd. Leeds —5B 86
Torre Vw. Leeds —4D 86
Torre Wlk. Leeds —4D 86
Torridon Cres. B'frd —1F 115
Torridon Rd. Dew —6J 137
**Toulston. —5J 37**
Toulston La. B'ham —1E 54

## Tower Bldgs.—Valentine Ct.

*Tower Bldgs. Heck —5B 136*
*(off Church La.)*
Tower Ct. Leeds —5D 84
Tower Dri., The. Pool W —4J 29
Tower Gdns. Hal —4D 130
Tower Gro. Leeds —5A 84
Tower Hill. Sower B —4K 129
Tower Ho. St. Leeds —4J 85 (4F 5)
Tower La. Leeds —5K 83
(in two parts)
Tower Pl. Leeds —5K 83
Tower Rd. Leeds —2F 105
Tower Rd. Shipl —4E 60
Towers Sq. Leeds —4G 67
Tower St. B'frd —3D 80
Towers Way. Leeds —4G 67
Tower Works. Leeds —6H 85
Town Clo. H'fth —3F 65
**Town End. —3J 83**
**(nr. Bramley)**
**Town End. —3A 120**
**(nr. Morley)**
**Town End. —2A 96**
**(nr. Queensbury)**
**Town End. —6E 122**
**(nr. Rothwell)**
Town End. B'frd —2G 97
Town End. Gar —5J 89
Town End. Gild —7H 101
*Town End. Morl —3B 120*
*(off Middleton Rd.)*
Town End Clo. Leeds —4J 83
Townend Pl. Pud —5D 82
Town End Rd. Cytn —1B 96
Townend Rd. Leeds —1B 102
Town End Yd. Leeds —4H 83
Townfield. Wilsd —7G 59
Town Fields Rd. Ell —3J 143
*Towngate. Bail —7K 43*
*(off Northgate)*
Town Ga. B'frd —4D 62
Towngate. Brigh —5K 133
Town Ga. C'ley —5K 63
Town Ga. Guis —2G 45
Towngate. Hip —7C 114
Towngate. Kei —4A 40
Town Ga. L'ft —6D 110
Towngate. N'wram —4A 114
Town Ga. Schol —7B 116
Towngate. Shipl —5K 61
Towngate. S'wram —4A 132
Town Ga. Sower B —5F 129
Town Ga. Wyke —5J 115
Towngate Av. Brigh —5K 133
Town Ga. Clo. Guis —2G 45
Towngate Ho. Ell —3K 143
Towngate Rd. Bat —3E 136
Town Hall Sq. Yead —4K 45
Town Hall St. Ell —3K 143
Town Hall St. Kei —4A 40
Town Hall St. Sower B —5K 129
Town Hall St. E. Hal —1G 131
**Town Head. —7H 9**
Townhead Fold. Add —1C 10
Town Hill. B'ham —1D 54
Town Hill St. Bgly —6B 60
Town La. B'frd —3D 62
Townley Av. Hal —4A 132
Town St. Bat C & Dew —6G 137
Town St. Bees —5E 102
Town St. B'shaw —1J 117
Town St. Bmly —2G 83
Town St. C'ley —6K 63
Town St. Carl —4F 123
Town St. Chap A —5K 67
Town St. Far —2B 82
Town St. Gild —7G 101
Town St. Guis —2G 45
Town St. H'fth —4F 65
Town St. Leeds —5A 84
Town St. Midd —2H 121
Town St. Rawd —1B 64
Town St. Rod —7C 64
Town St. S'ley —4C 82
Town St. Yead —4K 45
Town St. M. Leeds —5K 67
Town St. Wlk. Leeds —5K 67
Town Wells Dri. C'ley —6K 63
Track Mt. Bat —6F 137
Track Rd. Bat —6F 137
Trafalgar Gdns. Morl —4A 120
Trafalgar Rd. Dew —7F 137
Trafalgar Rd. I'ly —5B 12
Trafalgar Sq. Hal —3E 130
Trafalgar St. Bat —4E 136
Trafalgar St. B'frd —5A 80 (2D 6)
Trafalgar St. Hal —3E 130
Trafalgar St. Leeds —5K 85 (5G 5)
Trafford Av. Leeds —3D 86
Trafford Gro. Leeds —2C 86
Trafford Ter. Leeds —3D 86
Tramways. Oaken —2B 116
Tranbeck Rd. Guis —2D 44
Tranfield Av. Guis —2E 44
Tranfield Clo. Guis —2E 44
Tranfield Ct. Guis —2E 44
Tranfield Gdns. Guis —2E 44
Tranmere Dri. Guis —2E 44
**Tranmere Park. —3D 44**
Tranquility. Leeds —3A 88
Tranquility Av. Leeds —3A 88
*Tranquility Ct. Leeds —3A 88*
*(off Tranquility Av.)*
Tranquility Wlk. Leeds —3A 88
Transvaal Ter. Bat —1F 137
Tranter Gro. B'frd —1G 99
Tranter Pl. Leeds —5G 87
Tredgold Av. B'hpe —1J 47
Tredgold Clo. Leeds —1J 47
Tredgold Cres. B'hpe —1J 47
Tredgold Gth. B'hpe —1J 47
Treefield Ind. Est. Gild —1H 119
Tree La. Hal —2H 111
Trees St. B'frd —4J 79
Tree Top Vw. Q'bry —4G 95
Trelawn Av. Leeds —7D 66
Trelawn Cres. Leeds —7D 66
Trelawn Pl. Leeds —7D 66
Trelawn St. Leeds —7D 66
Trelawn Ter. Leeds —7D 66
Tremont Gdns. Leeds —4A 104
Trenam Pk. Dri. B'frd —2C 62
Trenance Dri. Shipl —5F 61
Trenance Gdns. G'lnd —2E 142
Trenholme Av. B'frd —1H 115
*Trenholme Ho. B'frd —5E 62*
*(off Garsdale Av.)*
Trenic Cres. Leeds —2D 84
Trenic Dri. Leeds —2D 84
Trent Av. Gar —1B 108
Trentham Av. Leeds —3H 103
Trentham Gro. Leeds —3H 103
Trentham Pl. Leeds —3H 103
Trentham Row. Leeds —3H 103
Trentham St. Leeds —4H 103
Trentham Ter. Leeds —3H 103
Trenton Dri. B'frd —4J 79
Trenton Rd. Bat —5K 137
Trent Rd. Leeds —5B 86
Trent St. Leeds —1H 103
Trescoe Av. Leeds —4J 83
Tresham Ct. Dew —6K 137
Trevelyan Sq. Leeds —6J 85 (7E 4)
Trevelyan St. Brigh —3G 133
**Triangle. —7G 129**
Triath Ct. Bat —2C 136
Trigg All. Haw —6E 56
Trigg Ter. Liv —4J 135
Trimmingham La. Hal —2B 130
Trimmingham Rd. Hal —2B 130
Trimmingham Vs. Hal —2C 130
*Trinity Fold. Hal —2G 131*
*(off Blackwall)*
Trinity Pl. Bgly —2A 60
Trinity Pl. Hal —2G 131
Trinity Ri. Otley —3K 27
Trinity Rd. B'frd —1K 97 (7B 6)
Trinity Rd. Hal —2G 131
Trinity St. Bat —6G 137
Trinity St. Hal —2G 131
(in two parts)
*Trinity St. Kei —3A 40*
*(off East Av.)*
Trinity St. Leeds —5J 85 (6E 4)
Trinity St. Arc. Leeds —6J 85 (7E 4)
Trinity Ter. Bat —6B 118
Trinity Vw. Hal —2H 131
Trinity Vw. Low M —7A 98
Trinity Wlk. Low M —7A 98
Trip Garth. Lntn —7F 17
Trip La. Lntn —7D 16
Tristram Av. B'frd —4C 98
Troon Dri. Hud —6F 145
Trooper La. Hal —3H 131
Trooper Ter. Hal —3H 131
Tropical World. —3D 68
Trough La. Oxe & Denh —4H 75
Troughton Pl. Pud —1D 100
Troughton St. Pud —1D 100
Trough Well La. Wren —5K 139
Troutbeck Av. Bail —3E 60
**Troy. —2G 65**
**Troydale. —7F 83**
Troydale Gdns. Pud —1F 101
Troydale Gro. Pud —1F 101
Troydale La. Pud —7E 82
**Troy Hill. —2A 120**
Troy Hill. H'fth —2G 65
Troy Hill. Morl —2A 120
Troy Ri. Morl —2B 120
Troy Rd. H'fth —2G 65
Troy Rd. Morl —3A 120
Trueman Av. Heck —4C 136
Trueman Ct. Low M —1A 116
**Truncliffe. —5K 97**
Truncliffe. B'frd —5K 97
*Truncliffe Ho. B'frd —5K 97*
*(off Truncliffe)*
Truro St. Leeds —5C 84
Tubby La. Hud —7H 145
Tucknott Dri. Heck —4B 136
Tudor Barn Ct. Wrose —5K 61
Tudor Clo. Fars —3A 82
*Tudor Ct. B'frd —1A 98*
*(off Swarland Gro.)*
Tudor Gdns. Leeds —4E 102
Tudor St. B'frd —2K 97
Tudor Way. C'frd —7H 127
Tuel La. Sower B —3K 129
Tufton St. Sils —1F 21
Tulip Retail Pk. H'let —3K 103
Tulip St. Haw —7E 56
Tulip St. Leeds —3K 103
Tumbling Hill St. B'frd —7K 79 (5B 6)
Tunnel St. Denh —5B 76
Tunnicliffe Pl. Sils —1F 21
Tunstall Grn. B'frd —3G 99
Tunstall Rd. Leeds —3J 103
Tunwell La. B'frd —1E 80
Tunwell St. B'frd —1E 80
Turbary Av. Fars —3C 82
Turbury La. G'lnd —1C 142
Turf Ct. Cull —7A 58
Turf La. Cull —6A 58
Turgate La. Sower B —7B 128
Turkey Hill. Pud —7D 82
(in two parts)
Turks Head Yd. Leeds —6E 4
Turley Cote La. Holy G —7F 143
Turnberry Av. Leeds —7H 49
Turnberry Clo. Leeds —7H 49
Turnberry Clo. Ting —7D 120
Turnberry Ct. Low U —7J 21
Turnberry Dri. Leeds —7H 49
Turnberry Dri. Ting —7D 120
Turnberry Gdns. Ting —7D 120
Turnberry Gro. Leeds —7H 49
Turnberry Pl. Leeds —7H 49
Turnberry Ri. Leeds —7H 49
Turnberry Vw. Leeds —7H 49
Turnbull Ct. Leeds —7F 69
Turner Av. Bat —3G 137
Turner Av. B'frd —1F 97
Turner Av. N. Hal —2B 112
Turner Av. S. Hal —2C 112
Turner Clo. Ting —7E 120
Turner Cres. Otley —1K 27
Turner Dri. Ting —7E 120
*Turner Farm. Hal —7C 94*
*(off Causeway Foot)*
Turner Ho. Kirks —1K 83
Turner La. Add —3A 10
(in two parts)
Turner La. Hal —6H 113
(in two parts)
Turner Pl. B'frd —1H 97
Turner Pl. Hal —3C 112
Turners Ct. Hal —5F 113
Turner St. Fars —2B 82
Turner's Yd. Fars —2B 82
Turner's Yd. Leeds —3H 83
*Turner Vw. Hal —3C 112*
*(off Bank Edge Rd.)*
Turney St. Hal —5E 112
Turnpike St. Ell —2A 144
Turnshaw Rd. Oakw —2B 56
Turnsteads Av. Cleck —7D 116
Turnsteads Clo. Cleck —7E 116
Turnsteads Cres. Cleck —7E 116
Turnsteads Dri. Cleck —7E 116
Turnsteads Mt. Cleck —7E 116
Turnstone Ct. Leeds —2K 121
Turnways, The. Leeds —1C 84
Turton Grn. Gild —7H 101
Turton Va. Gild —1H 119
Tweed Clo. Birs —6E 118
Tweedy St. Wilsd —7G 59
Twelfth Av. Liv —3D 134
Twickenham Ct. B'frd —3K 79
Twine La. H Bri —6C 110
Twinge La. Hal —2K 131
Twivey St. C'frd —7C 126
Tyas Gro. Leeds —6D 86
**Tyersal. —7F 81**
Tyersal Av. B'frd —6H 81
Tyersal Clo. B'frd —7H 81
Tyersal Ct. B'frd —7G 81
Tyersal Cres. B'frd —7H 81
Tyersal Dri. B'frd —7H 81
Tyersal Gth. B'frd —7H 81
**Tyersal Gate. —2G 99**
Tyersal Grn. B'frd —7H 81
Tyersal Gro. B'frd —7H 81
Tyersal La. B'frd —2G 99
(in two parts)
Tyersal Pk. B'frd —7H 81
Tyersal Rd. B'frd —7G 81
Tyersal Ter. B'frd —7G 81
Tyersal Vw. B'frd —7G 81
Tyersal Wlk. B'frd —7H 81
Tyler Ct. B'frd —4E 62
Tyndale Wlk. Bat —3C 136
Tynedale Ct. Leeds —6G 67
Tyne St. B'frd —5B 80 (2G 7)
Tyne St. Haw —5F 57
Tyne St. Kei —4B 40
Tynwald Clo. Leeds —2G 67
Tynwald Dri. Leeds —1G 67
Tynwald Gdns. Leeds —2G 67
Tynwald Grn. Leeds —1G 67
Tynwald Hill. Leeds —2G 67
Tynwald Mt. Leeds —1G 67
Tynwald Rd. Leeds —2G 67
Tynwald Wlk. Leeds —1G 67
Tyrls, The. B'frd —7A 80 (5D 6)
Tyrrel St. B'frd —6A 80 (4E 6)
Tyson St. B'frd —5K 79 (2C 6)
Tyson St. Hal —2C 130

Ullswater Av. Dew —6J 137
Ullswater Clo. Dew —6J 137
Ullswater Cres. Leeds —6G 87
Ullswater Cres. W'ford —1A 124
Ullswater Dri. B'frd —1F 115
Ullswater Dri. Weth —3G 17
Ullswater Ri. Weth —3G 17
Ullswater Rd. Dew —6J 137
**Undercliffe. —4D 80**
Undercliffe La. B'frd —4C 80 (1H 7)
Undercliffe Old Rd. B'frd —4D 80
Undercliffe Ri. I'ly —7E 12
Undercliffe Rd. B'frd —2D 80
Undercliffe St. B'frd —5D 80 (1K 7)
Underwood Dri. Rawd —2K 63
Underwood Ho. B'frd —2G 7
Union Ct. Otley —3H 27
Union Cross Yd. Hal —1G 131
Union Gro. Liv —5K 135
Union Ho. Q'bry —4C 96
Union Ho. La. Q'bry —4C 96
Union La. Hal —6B 94
Union Pl. Leeds —7H 85
Union Rd. B'frd —1H 97
Union Rd. Liv —5K 135
Union Rd. Low M —7J 97
Union St. Bail —2A 62
Union St. Bgly —4J 41
Union St. Birs —6C 118
Union St. Chur —6C 102
Union St. Dew —7H 137
Union St. G'lnd —2H 143
Union St. Hal —1G 131
Union St. Heck —5A 136
Union St. Leeds —5J 85 (6F 5)
Union St. Otley —3H 27
Union St. Q'bry —5J 95
Union St. Sower B —3A 130
(nr. Albert Rd.)
Union St. Sower B —7G 129
(nr. Butterworth La.)
Union Ter. Leeds —6J 67
Union Yd. B'frd —4D 62
Unity Clo. Leeds —1H 85
Unity Ct. Brigh —1F 145
Unity St. Carl —4F 123
Unity St. Riddl —1D 40
Unity St. N. Bgly —2K 59
Unity St. S. Bgly —2K 59
Unity Ter. Hal —2C 130
University Rd. Leeds —3G 85 (2A 4)
University St. C'frd —7D 126
Unwin Pl. B'frd —3E 78
Upland Cres. Leeds —7C 68
Upland Gdns. Leeds —1C 86
Upland Gro. Leeds —7C 68
Upland Rd. Leeds —1C 86
Uplands. Hud —7E 144
Uplands. Kei —2J 39
Uplands Av. Q'bry —4B 96
Uplands Clo. Q'bry —4B 96
Uplands Cres. Q'bry —4B 96
Uplands Gro. Q'bry —4B 96
Up. Accommodation Rd. Leeds —5A 86 (6K 5)
Up. Ada St. Shipl —4F 61
Up. Addison St. B'frd —1B 98 (7G 7)
Up. Allerton La. All —5J 77
**Upper Armley. —4A 84**
Up. Ashley La. Shipl —4H 61
Up. Bank Hey Bottom. Ripp —6G 141
Up. Barker St. Liv —4J 135
Up. Basinghall St. Leeds —5H 85 (5D 4)
**Upper Batley. —7G 119**
Up. Batley La. Bat —6D 118
Up. Batley Low La. Bat —5F 119
Up. Battye St. Heck —3B 136
Up. Bell Hall. Hal —3E 130
Up. Bolton Brow. Sower B —3B 130
Up. Bonegate. Brigh —5H 133
Up. Brig Royd. Sower B —5F 141
**Upper Brockholes. —6B 94**
Upper Butts. Cleck —1F 135
Up. Calton St. Kei —6K 39
Up. Camroyd St. Dew —7H 137
Up. Carr La. C'ley —6J 63
Up. Carr St. Liv —3J 135
Up. Castle St. B'frd —2A 98
Up. Chelsea St. Kei —6K 39
Up. Commercial St. Bat —3G 137
**Upper Common. —4K 115**
Up. Croft Rd. Bat —4F 137
Up. Cross St. Dew —7H 137
*Up. Ellistones. G'lnd —2E 142*
*(off Martin Grn. La.)*
Up. Ellistones Ct. G'lnd —2E 142
**Upper Exley. —7J 131**
**Upper Fagley. —2G 81**
Up. Ferndown Grn. All —4A 78
Up. Field Ho. La. Tri —6F 129
Upper Forge. Hal —1G 131
Up. Fountaine St. Leeds —5H 85 (5E 4)
Up. Fountain St. Sower B —4K 129
Up. George St. B'frd —5H 97
Up. George St. Heck —4B 136
Up. Grange Av. All —5B 78
**Upper Green. —3F 97**
**(nr. Bradford)**
**Upper Green. —1D 138**
**(nr. East Ardsley)**
Upper Grn. Bail —2H 61
Upper Grn. B'frd —3F 97
Up. Green Av. Schol —7B 116
Up. Green Av. Ting —1D 138
Up. Green Clo. Ting —1E 138
Up. Green Dri. Ting —1E 138
Up. Green La. Brigh —3E 132
Up. Green Way. Ting —1D 138
Up. Hall Vw. N'wram —4A 114
Up. Haugh Shaw. Hal —3E 130
Up. Heights Rd. T'tn —5G 77
Up. Hird St. Kei —6J 39
Up. House Cotts. Q'bry —4A 96
Up. House La. Liv —4E 134
Up. House St. B'frd —1D 98
Up. Hoyle Ing. T'tn —6K 77
Up. Kirkgate. Hal —1H 131
Upper La. Gom —1K 135
Upper La. Hal —3K 113
Up. Langwith. Coll —2C 34
Up. Lombard St. Rawd —7J 45
**Upper Marsh. —7C 56**
Up. Marsh La. Oxe —7B 56
Up. Martin Grn. G'lnd —2E 142
Up. Mary St. Shipl —4F 61
Up. Meadows. Q'bry —6J 95
*Up. Millergate. B'frd —4D 6*
*(off Kirkgate)*
Up. Mill Row. E Mor —1J 41
Uppermoor. Pud —6A 82
Uppermoor Clo. Pud —7B 82
**Upper Moor Side. —4G 101**
Up. Mosscar St. B'frd —6C 80 (4J 7)
Up. Mount St. Bat —5G 137
Up. Nidd St. B'frd —7D 80
Up. North St. Bat —4F 137
Up. North St. Leeds —4H 85 (4D 4)
Up. Parish Ghyll La. I'ly —6K 11
Up. Park Ga. B'frd —6B 80 (3G 7)
Up. Peel St. Dew —7H 137
Up. Piccadilly. B'frd —6A 80 (3D 6)
*Up. Range. Hal —6G 113*
*(off Woodlands Gro.)*
Upper Rd. Bat & Dew —6F 137
Up. Rushton Rd. B'frd —4F 81
Up. Seymour St. B'frd —7D 80 (5K 7)
Up. South St. Dew —7G 137
Up. Station Rd. Bat —4H 137
Up. Sutherland Rd. Hal —7E 114
**Upper Town. —3E 74**
Upper Town. Oxe —3E 74
Up. Town St. Leeds —2G 83
Up. Washer La. Hal —3D 130
Up. Westlock Av. Leeds —4C 86
Up. West St. Bat —3J 137
Up. Willow Hill. Hal —2B 130
Up. Woodlands Rd. B'frd —4G 79
*Up. Woodview Pl. Leeds —4H 103*
*(off Woodview St.)*
Up. Wortley Dri. Leeds —6B 84
Up. Wortley Rd. Leeds —6B 84
**Upper Wyke. —4K 115**
Upton St. Bat —2F 137
Upton Wlk. All —5B 78
Upwood Holiday Pk. Oxe —2G 75
Upwood La. E Mor —1H 41
Ure Cres. B'frd —5K 79 (1A 6)
Ure Gro. Weth —1H 17
Usher St. B'frd —1C 98 (7H 7)
Uttley St. Hal —5F 113

Vale Av. Leeds —2C 68
Vale Gro. Q'bry —5K 95
Vale Gro. Sils —1F 21
Vale Mill La. Haw —3F 57
Valentine Ct. T'tn —6J 77

200 A-Z Leeds & Bradford

Valentine M.—Wards Pl.


Valentine M. Loft —7E 122
Vale St. Brigh —5G 133
Vale St. Kei —2C 40
Vale Ter. Oakw —3F 57
Vale, The. Coll —2E 34
Vale, The. Leeds —7F 67
Valley Av. Hal —7F 115
Valley Clo. Leeds —6G 49
Valley Ct. B'frd —4A 80
Valley Ct. Liv —3K 135
Valley Dri. I'ly —5D 12
Valley Dri. Leeds —4J 87
Valley Dri. W'ford —6J 107
Valley Farm Rd. Leeds —5C 104
Valley Farm Way. Leeds —5C 104
Valley Fold. Q'bry —6J 95
Valley Gdns. Leeds —4J 67
Valley Grn. Pud —7D 82
Valley Gro. Hal —7D 94
Valley Gro. Pud —7D 82
Valley Head. Hud —7C 144
Valley Heights. Hud —7C 144
Valley Mills. Dlgtn —6F 101
Valley Mills Ind. Est. B'frd —4G 63
Valley Mt. Kip —4K 107
Valley Mt. Leeds —5E 82
Valley Parade. —4K 79
Valley Pde. B'frd —4K 79
Valley Pl. B'frd —4A 80
Valley Ridge. Kip —3K 107
(in two parts)
Valley Ri. Leeds —7G 65
*Valley Ri. Sower B —2F 141*
*(off Lumb La.)*
Valley Rd. B'frd —3K 79 (1D 6)
Valley Rd. Cleck —7G 117
Valley Rd. I'ly —4D 12
Valley Rd. Kei —4D 40
Valley Rd. Kip —3K 107
Valley Rd. Leeds —7G 65
Valley Rd. Liv —4J 135
Valley Rd. Morl —2B 120
Valley Rd. Pud —7C 82
Valley Rd. Shipl —5H 61
Valley Rd. Retail Pk. B'frd —5A 80 (1E 6)
Valley Sq. Pud —7D 82
Valley Ter. Leeds —1B 68
Valley, The. Leeds —5G 49
Valley Vw. Bail —3H 61
Valley Vw. Hal —7D 94
Valley Vw. H'den —3E 58
Valley Vw. Clo. Oakw —1G 57
Valley Vw. Gdns. Cro R —4G 57
Valley Vw. Gro. B'frd —3C 80
Valley Way. Hal —7D 94
Vancouver Pl. Leeds —6A 68
Varley St. S'ley —4B 82
(in two parts)
Varleys Yd. Pud —6D 82
Vaughan St. B'frd —6K 79 (3B 6)
Vaughan St. Hal —3D 130
Vegal Cres. Hal —5D 112
Veitch St. Idle —4D 62
Veitch Wlk. Sower B —4B 130
Ventnor Clo. Gom —5K 117
Ventnor St. B'frd —6C 80 (4J 7)
Ventnor Ter. Hal —4F 131
Vento Clo. B'frd —6H 97
Verdun Rd. B'frd —6G 97
Vere Sq. B'frd —2A 98
Verity Spur. Leeds —5G 87
Verity St. B'frd —7H 99
Verity Vw. Leeds —4G 87
Vermont St. Leeds —3E 82
Vernon Ct. Kei —3K 39
Vernon Pl. B'frd —3D 80
Vernon Pl. S'ley —4C 82
Vernon Rd. Leeds —4H 85 (3C 4)
Vernon Rd. Liv & Heck —4K 135
Vernon St. Cro R —4H 57
Vernon St. Leeds —4H 85 (4D 4)
Vesper Clo. Leeds —6K 65
Vesper Ct. Leeds —6J 65
Vesper Ct. Dri. Leeds —6J 65
Vesper Gdns. Leeds —7K 65
Vesper Ga. Cres. Leeds —7K 65
Vesper Ga. Dri. Leeds —6J 65
Vesper Ga. Mt. Leeds —7K 65
Vesper Gro. Leeds —1A 84
Vesper La. Leeds —7K 65
Vesper Mt. Leeds —1A 84
Vesper Pl. Leeds —1A 84
Vesper Ri. Leeds —6J 65
Vesper Rd. Leeds —6H 65
Vesper Ter. Leeds —1A 84
Vesper Wlk. Leeds —7J 65
Vesper Way. Leeds —6J 65
Vestry St. B'frd —3D 98
Viaduct Rd. Leeds —4D 84
Viaduct St. S'ley —4B 82
Vicarage Av. Gild —1G 119
Vicarage Av. Leeds —1B 84
Vicarage Clo. Wyke —5J 115
Vicarage Dri. Pud —6B 82
Vicarage Gdns. B'shaw —2J 117
Vicarage Gdns. Brigh —1F 145
Vicarage Gdns. Otley —3J 27
Vicarage La. B'ham —1D 54
Vicarage Pl. Leeds —1B 84
Vicarage Rd. Leeds —3F 85
Vicarage Rd. Shipl —4A 62
Vicarage Rd. Haw —5F 57
Vicarage St. Leeds —1B 84
Vicarage Ter. Bat —1E 136
Vicarage Ter. Leeds —1B 84
Vicarage Vw. Leeds —1B 84
Vicar La. B'frd —6B 80
(in two parts)
Vicar La. Leeds —5J 85 (7F 5)
Vicar Pk. Dri. Hal —7K 111
Vicar Pk. Rd. Hal —1K 129
Vicars Rd. Leeds —1B 86
Vicars Ter. All B —3B 126
Vicars Ter. Leeds —1B 86
Vicar St. Liv —4J 135
Vickerman St. Hal —2D 130
Vickers Av. Leeds —2K 83
Vickersdale. S'ley —3C 82
*Vickersdale Gro. S'ley —3C 82*
*(off Haydn's Ter.)*
Vickers Pl. S'ley —3C 82
Vickers St. C'frd —7D 126
Vickers St. Morl —4K 119
(in two parts)
Vickers Yd. S'ley —4B 82
Victor Dri. Guis —3G 45
Victoria Av. Bat —4G 137
Victoria Av. Brigh —5J 133
Victoria Av. Cleck —1F 135
Victoria Av. Eccl —1F 81
Victoria Av. Ell —3J 143
Victoria Av. Hal —2D 130
Victoria Av. Haw —4E 56
Victoria Av. H'fth —5E 64
Victoria Av. I'ly —5K 11
Victoria Av. Kei —3A 40
Victoria Av. Leeds —5C 86
Victoria Av. Men —5B 26
Victoria Av. Morl —2A 120
Victoria Av. Rothw —3G 123
Victoria Av. Shipl —4F 61
Victoria Av. Sower B —4A 130
Victoria Av. Yead —5B 46
Victoria Bldgs. Dew —7J 137
Victoria Clo. All B —3B 126
Victoria Clo. H'fth —5E 64
Victoria Clo. I'ly —5A 12
Victoria Clo. Yead —4B 46
Victoria Ct. Birs —6C 118
Victoria Ct. Kei —4K 39
Victoria Ct. Morl —2A 120
*Victoria Ct. Shipl —5F 61*
*(off Victoria Av.)*
Victoria Ct. M. Leeds —2E 84
Victoria Cres. Dew —6F 137
Victoria Cres. Ell —3K 143
Victoria Cres. H'fth —5E 64
Victoria Cres. Pud —6A 82
Victoria Dri. B'frd —1F 81
Victoria Dri. Hal —4B 114
Victoria Dri. H'fth —5E 64
Victoria Dri. I'ly —5K 11
Victoria Dri. Morl —1B 120
Victoria Gdns. H'fth —5F 65
Victoria Gdns. I'ly —5K 11
Victoria Gdns. Pud —6A 82
Victoria Grange Dri. Morl —2A 120
Victoria Grange Way. Morl —2A 120
Victoria Gro. H'fth —6E 64
Victoria Gro. I'ly —5K 11
Victoria Gro. Leeds —5D 86
Victoria Gro. Pud —6A 82
Victoria Ho. Kirks —1A 84
Victoria Ind. Est. B'frd —1E 80
Victoria M. H'fth —5E 64
*Victoria M. Kei —4K 39*
*(off Drewry Rd.)*
Victoria M. Morl —2A 120
Victoria Mills. Bat —2F 137
Victoria Mt. H'fth —4E 64
Victoria Pk. Shipl —5F 61
Victoria Pk. Av. Bmly & Kirks —2J 83
Victoria Pk. Gro. Bmly —2J 83
Victoria Pk. Gro. Kirks —2K 83
Victoria Pk. St. Kei —3B 40
Victoria Pk. Vw. Kei —3B 40
Victoria Pl. B'frd —7E 62
Victoria Pl. Brigh —7H 133
Victoria Pl. C'frd —7E 126
Victoria Pl. Cliff —6D 36
Victoria Pl. Yead —4J 45
Victoria Quarter. Leeds (LS1) —5J 85 (6F 5)
Victoria Quarter. Leeds —5C 86
(LS9)
Victoria Ri. Pud —6A 82
Victoria Rd. Brigh —1H 133
Victoria Rd. Bur W —1A 26
Victoria Rd. Dew —7G 137
Victoria Rd. Eccl & B'frd —7E 62
Victoria Rd. Ell —4H 143
Victoria Rd. Gom —7A 118
Victoria Rd. Guis —3F 45
Victoria Rd. Hal —1E 130
Victoria Rd. Haw —5F 57
Victoria Rd. Hip —1D 132
Victoria Rd. I'ly —5K 11
Victoria Rd. Kei —5K 39
Victoria Rd. Kirks —1A 84
Victoria Rd. Leeds —2E 84
(LS6)
Victoria Rd. Leeds —7H 85
(LS11)
Victoria Rd. Liv —5J 135
Victoria Rd. Morl —2A 120
Victoria Rd. Oakw —2F 57
Victoria Rd. Pud —3B 82
(nr. Northcote St.)
Victoria Rd. Pud —6A 82
(nr. Uppermoor)
Victoria Rd. Rothw —1F 123
Victoria Rd. Shipl —4F 61
Victoria Rd. Sower B —5K 129
Victoria Rd. Wibs —6G 97
Victoria Shop. Cen. B'frd —5G 79
Victoria Sq. Leeds —5H 85 (5C 4)
Victoria St. All —2A 78
Victoria St. All B —3B 126
Victoria St. Bail —3J 61
Victoria St. Bat —2F 137
Victoria St. Bgly —2K 59
Victoria St. Birs —6D 118
Victoria St. B'frd —5K 79 (1C 6)
Victoria St. Brigh —7H 133
Victoria St. C'ley —6J 63
Victoria St. C'frd —7B 126
Victoria St. Chur —7C 102
Victoria St. Cytn —2B 96
Victoria St. Cleck —7F 117
Victoria St. Clif —5J 133
Victoria St. Cull —6C 58
Victoria St. Fag —3E 80
Victoria St. G'lnd —2H 143
Victoria St. Hal —1G 131
Victoria St. Heck —4B 136
Victoria St. Leeds —4F 85
(LS3)
Victoria St. Leeds —5K 67
(LS7)
Victoria St. M'wte —4J 41
Victoria St. Morl —2K 119
*Victoria St. Oakw —2F 57*
*(off Victoria Rd.)*
Victoria St. Q'bry —5K 95
Victoria St. Shipl —4H 61
Victoria St. Sower B —5K 129
Victoria St. Sut Cr —5A 20
Victoria St. Thack —2D 62
Victoria St. Weth —4J 17
Victoria St. Wilsd —1G 77
*Victoria Ter. Guis —2G 45*
*(off Lands La.)*
Victoria Ter. Hal —4E 130
(HX2)
*Victoria Ter. Hal —2E 130*
*(off Park Dri.)*
Victoria Ter. Head —6D 66
Victoria Ter. Hip —1D 132
*Victoria Ter. Kei —4B 40*
*(off Dalton La.)*
Victoria Ter. Leeds —4F 85 (4A 4)
Victoria Ter. L'ft —3G 129
Victoria Ter. Morl —4J 119
Victoria Ter. Shipl —3F 61
Victoria Ter. S'ley —3D 82
Victoria Ter. Yead —4A 46
Victoria Vs. S'ley —4C 82
Victoria Wlk. H'fth —5E 64
Victor Rd. B'frd —3H 79
Victor St. Bat —3H 137
Victor St. B'frd —6G 81
Victor St. Mann —3H 79
Victor Ter. B'frd —3H 79
Victor Ter. Hal —7E 112
Victory Rd. I'ly —5B 12
Vw. Croft Rd. Shipl —4J 61
Viewlands. Hud —5G 145
Viewlands Cres. Men —5F 27
Viewlands Mt. Men —5F 27
Viewlands Ri. Men —6F 27
View Rd. Kei —3J 39
View Row. All —5C 78
View, The. Alw —5F 49
View, The. Round —4B 68
Vigar Mnr. B'frd —6C 78
Vigar Mans. Weth —2J 17
Vigar M. Haw —5F 57
Vignola Ter. Cytn —1C 96
Village Av. Leeds —3D 84
Village Gdns. Leeds —7B 88
(in two parts)
Village M. Wilsd —2A 78
Village Pl. Leeds —3D 84
Village Rd. Eccup —1F 49
Village St. Nor G —4F 115
Village St., The. Leeds —3D 84
Village Ter. Leeds —3D 84
Village, The. Thor A —1E 36
Villa Gro. Bgly —7A 42
Villa Mt. Wyke —4J 115
Villa Rd. Bgly —7A 42
Villas, The. Cleck —1G 135
Villa St. Sower B —4A 130
Villa Ter. Bklnd —7K 141
Villier Ct. All —4B 78
Vincent Av. Ebrn —5C 20
Vincent St. B'frd —6K 79 (4C 6)
Vincent St. Hal —2D 130
Vine Av. Cleck —7E 116
Vine Clo. Clif —6K 133
Vine Ct. Clif —6K 133
Vine Ct. Guis —3G 45
Vine Cres. Cleck —7F 117
Vine Gth. Clif —5K 133
Vine Gro. Clif —6K 133
Vinery Av. Leeds —5C 86
Vinery Gro. Leeds —5C 86
Vinery Mt. Leeds —6C 86
Vinery Pl. Leeds —6C 86
Vinery Rd. Leeds —3D 84
Vinery St. Leeds —5C 86
Vinery Ter. Leeds —6C 86
Vinery Vw. Leeds —6C 86
Vine St. B'frd —1H 97
Vine St. Cleck —7F 117
Vine Ter. Hal —2F 131
Vine Ter. T'tn —7H 77
Vine Ter. E. B'frd —5E 78
Vine Ter. W. B'frd —5E 78
Violet St. Hal —1E 130
Violet St. Haw —7E 56
Violet St. N. Hal —7E 112
Violet Ter. Sower B —4A 130
Virginia St. Cytn —3C 96
Virginia Ter. T'ner —6D 52
Vivian Pl. B'frd —3G 97
Vivien Rd. B'frd —5C 78
Vulcan Gdns. Dew —7G 137
Vulcan St. B'frd —5F 99
Vulcan St. Brigh —7J 133

Waddington St. Kei —5A 40
Wade Ho. Av. Hal —1C 114
Wade Ho. Rd. Hal —1C 114
Wade La. Leeds —5J 85 (5E 4)
Wade St. B'frd —7A 80 (5D 6)
Wade St. Fars —2B 82
Wade St. Hal —1G 131
Wadey Ct. Bat —3G 137
Wadey Fld. Bail —7J 43
Wadlands Clo. Fars —2B 82
Wadlands Dri. Fars —2A 82
Wadlands Gro. Fars —1A 82
Wadlands Ri. Fars —2A 82
Wadsworth Ct. Hal —7E 112
Wadsworth St. Hal —7D 112
(in two parts)
Wagon La. Bgly —3A 60
Waincliffe Cres. Leeds —5F 103
Waincliffe Dri. Leeds —6F 103
Waincliffe Gth. Leeds —5F 103
*Waincliffe Ho. B'frd —7F 81*
*(off Fearnville Dri.)*
Waincliffe Mt. Leeds —5F 103
Waincliffe Pl. Leeds —5F 103
Waincliffe Sq. Leeds —5F 103
Waincliffe Ter. Leeds —6F 103
Waindale Clo. Hal —4J 111
Waindale Cres. Hal —4J 111
*Wainfleet Ho. B'frd —5G 81*
*(off Rushton Rd.)*
Wainhouse Rd. Hal —3D 130
Wainman Sq. Wyke —4J 115
Wainman St. Bail —7K 43
Wainman St. Hal —1D 130
Wainman St. Shipl —4H 61
Wainman St. Wyke —4J 115
**Wainstalls. —1H 111**
Wainstalls La. Hal —2G 111
Wainstalls Rd. Hal —1H 111
Waites Cft. K'gte —6H 121
Waites Ter. Otley —3K 27
Wakefield Av. Leeds —4H 87
Wakefield Ga. Hal —4D 130
Wakefield Old Rd. Dew —7H 137
Wakefield Rd. B'frd —7B 80 (6G 7)
(in two parts)
Wakefield Rd. Brigh —6H 133
Wakefield Rd. Dew —7H 137
Wakefield Rd. Dlgtn —1D 118
(in two parts)
Wakefield Rd. Hip & Bail B —1D 132
Wakefield Rd. Leeds —4B 104
Wakefield Rd. Liv —4K 135
Wakefield Rd. Morl —2G 119
Wakefield Rd. Oult —6K 123
Wakefield Rd. Rothw —2D 122
Wakefield Rd. Sower B —4B 130
Wakefield Rd. W'ford & Gar —6C 106
Walden Dri. B'frd —2C 78
Walden St. C'frd —7D 126
Waldron Ho. B'frd —7D 6
Walesby Ct. Leeds —2J 65
Walford Av. Leeds —5C 86
Walford Gro. Leeds —5C 86
Walford Mt. Leeds —5C 86
Walford Rd. Leeds —5C 86
Walford Ter. Leeds —5C 86
Walker Av. B'frd —1E 96
(in two parts)
Walker Dri. B'frd —5G 79
Walkergate. Otley —3J 27
Walker Ho. Kirks —1K 83
Walker La. Sower B —4B 130
Walker Pl. Morl —7B 102
Walker Pl. Shipl —4K 61
(in two parts)
Walker Rd. H'fth —3F 65
Walker Rd. Men —6B 26
Walker Rd. Oaken —3B 116
Walkers Ct. Leeds —7F 67
Walker's Grn. Leeds —2C 102
Walker's La. Leeds —2C 102
(in two parts)
Walker's La. Sils —2F 9
Walkers Mt. Bat —5G 137
Walkers Mt. Leeds —7F 67
Walker's Pl. Sils —2G 21
Walkers Row. Yead —4J 45
Walker St. B'frd —6D 98
Walker St. Cleck —7F 117
*Walker St. Schol —7B 116*
*(off Tabbs La.)*
Walker Ter. B'frd —2D 98
Walker Ter. Cull —7B 58
Walker Wood. Bail —2F 61
Walkley Av. Heck —5B 136
Walkley Gro. Heck —5B 136
Walkley La. Heck —5B 136
Walkley Ter. Heck —6C 136
Walkley Vs. Heck —6C 136
Walk, The. Fars —3A 82
Walk, The. Kei —5A 40
Wallace St. Hal —2D 130
Wallbank Dri. Shipl —6J 61
Waller Pas. Sils —7G 9
Wallingford Mt. All —6B 78
Wallis St. B'frd —6F 79
(in two parts)
Wallis St. Sower B —4K 129
Wall Rd. Kei —2C 40
Wall St. Kei —5H 39
Walmer Gro. Pud —1D 100
Walmer Vs. B'frd —4K 79
Walmsley Rd. Leeds —2E 84
Walnut Clo. Leeds —4A 70
Walnut St. B'frd —7E 80
Walnut St. Hal —1E 130
Walnut St. Kei —7K 39
Walshaw St. B'frd —2G 97
Walsh La. Bgly —5K 41
Walsh La. Hal —6F 113
Walsh La. Leeds —4G 101
*Walsh's Sq. Hal —3E 130*
*(off Mellor Ter.)*
Walsh St. Hal —1D 130
Walter Clough La. S'wram —3B 132
Walter Cres. Leeds —6B 86 (7K 5)
Walter Pl. Leeds —7K 83
Walter St. B'frd —1K 79
(BD2)
Walter St. B'frd —4D 62
(BD10)
Walter St. Leeds —4D 84
**Walton. —5G 19**
Walton Chase. Wltn —6F 19
Walton Dri. Dlgtn —1D 118
Walton Gth. Dlgtn —2D 118
Walton La. Cleck —3A 134
Walton Rd. Thor A —1F 37
Walton Rd. Weth —4K 17
Walton's Bldgs. Hal —3D 112
Walton St. B'frd —1B 98 (7G 7)
Walton St. Leeds —7H 85
Walton St. Sower B —4K 129
Waltroyd Rd. Cleck —1E 134
Wand La. Hal —7C 114
Wansford Clo. B'frd —4G 99
Wanstead Cres. All —5B 78
**Wapping. —2G 7**
Wapping Nick La. Hud —6J 143
Wapping Rd. B'frd —5B 80 (1F 7)
Warburton Pl. B'frd —5J 97
Ward Ct. Brigh —2F 145
Wardle Cres. Kei —3H 39
Wardman St. Kei —3C 40
Ward's End. Hal —2G 131
Wards Hill. Bat —3G 137
Wards Hill Ct. Bat —3G 137
Wards Pl. Bat —3E 136

# Ward St.—Westborough Dri.



Ward St. *B'frd* —3G **97**
Ward St. *Crack* —7G **137** (in two parts)
Ward St. *Kei* —5K **39**
Wareham Corner. *B'frd* —4G **99**
Warehouse St. *Bat* —4H **137**
Warhurst Rd. *Lfds B* —1A **144**
**Waring Green. —5G 133**
Waring Way. *Dew* —7J **137**
Warlbeck. *I'ly* —5K **11**
Warley Av. *B'frd* —5F **81**
Warley Dene. *Hal* —2K **129**
Warley Dri. *B'frd* —6F **81**
Warley Edge. *Hal* —1A **130**
Warley Edge La. *Hal* —1K **129**
Warley Gro. *B'frd* —5F **81**
Warley Gro. *Hal* —1B **130**
Warley Rd. *Hal* —1B **130**
Warley St. *Hal* —2E **130**
**Warley Town. —2K 129**
Warley Town La. *Hal* —1J **129**
Warley Vw. *Hal* —1B **130**
Warley Vw. *Leeds* —1F **83**
Warley Wood Av. *L'ft* —3H **129**
Warley Wood La. *L'ft* —3G **129**
Warm La. *Yead* —6J **45**
Warmleigh Pk. *Q'bry* —5F **95**
*Warneford Sq. Hal —3D 130 (off King Cross Rd.)*
Warnford Gro. *B'frd* —3F **99**
Warrel's Av. *Leeds* —2G **83**
Warrel's Ct. *Leeds* —3G **83**
Warrel's Gro. *Leeds* —3G **83**
Warrel's Mt. *Leeds* —3G **83**
Warrel's Pl. *Leeds* —2G **83**
Warrel's Rd. *Leeds* —2G **83**
Warrel's Row. *Leeds* —3G **83**
Warrel's St. *Leeds* —3G **83**
Warrel's Ter. *Leeds* —3G **83**
Warren Av. *Bgly* —6B **42**
Warren Clo. *Liv* —6K **135**
Warren Dri. *Bgly* —7B **42**
Warren Ho. La. *Hud* —6A **144**
Warren Ho. La. *Yead* —2B **46**
Warren La. *Arth* —4A **30**
Warren La. *Bgly* —6B **42**
Warren La. *Tad* —3G **55**
Warren Pk. *Brigh* —3E **132**
Warren Pk. Clo. *Brigh* —3E **132**
Warrens La. *Bat* —4B **118**
Warrens La. *Dlgtn* —2C **118**
Warren Ter. *Bgly* —1C **60**
Warrenton Pl. *B'frd* —1G **97**
Warton Av. *B'frd* —5D **98**
Warwick Clo. *B'frd* —2D **98**
*Warwick Clo. Hal —4F 131 (off Free School La.)*
Warwick Ct. *H'fth* —5G **65**
Warwick Dri. *B'frd* —2D **98**
*Warwick Ho. B'frd —4D 62 (off Thorp Gth.)*
Warwick Mt. *Bat* —4H **137**
Warwick Rd. *Bat* —6G **137**
Warwick Rd. *B'frd* —2D **98**
*Waryn Ho. B'frd —5E 62 (off Fairhaven Grn.)*
*Washburn Ct. Sils —1G 21 (off Wharfe Ct.)*
Washburn Ct. *Weth* —1H **17**
Washer La. *Sower B* —4C **130**
Washer La. Ind. Est. *Hal* —4D **130**
Washington Pl. *Leeds* —5E **82**
Washington St. *B'frd* —4F **79**
Washington St. *Hal* —6E **112**
Washington St. *Leeds* —5E **84** (LS3)
Washington St. *Leeds* —5E **82** (LS13)
Washington Ter. *Leeds* —5E **82**
Wasp Nest Rd. *Hud* —7G **145**
Wastwater Dri. *B'frd* —1F **115**
Watercock St. *B'frd* —1C **98**
Waterfront M. *App B* —4G **63**
Watergate. *Hal* —1C **132**
Watergate. *Meth* —7E **124**
Water Grn. La. *Sower B* —3C **140**
Water Hill La. *Sower B* —3J **129**
Water Ho. Ct. *H'fth* —5F **65**
*Waterhouse Ct. Leeds —2K 103 (off Oval, The)*
Waterhouse Dri. *E Ard* —1H **139**
Waterhouse St. *Hal* —1G **131**
Waterhouse St. *Kei* —4J **39**
Watering La. *Morl* —3D **120**
Water La. *B'frd* —6J **79** (4A **6**) (in two parts)
Water La. *Fars* —2B **82**
Water La. *Hal* —2H **131**
Water La. *H'bck* —7G **85**
Water La. *H'fth* —3D **64**
Water La. *Kei* —5A **40**
Water La. *Leeds* —6H **83** (LS12)
*Water La. Leeds —6J 85 (off Meadow La.)*
Waterloo Cres. *B'frd* —4H **63**
Waterloo Cres. *Leeds* —2H **83**
Waterloo Fold. *Wyke* —5K **115**
Waterloo Gro. *Pud* —6K **81**
Waterloo La. *Leeds* —2H **83**
Waterloo Mt. *Pud* —5K **81**
Waterloo Rd. *Bgly* —1K **59**
Waterloo Rd. *Brigh* —5G **133**
Waterloo Rd. *Leeds* —2A **104**
Waterloo Rd. *Pud* —5K **81**
Waterloo St. *Leeds* —6J **85**
Waterloo Ter. *Sower B* —2A **130**
Waterloo Way. *Leeds* —2H **83**
Waterside. *Bgly* —6H **41**
Waterside. *Hal* —2H **131**
Waterside. *Oxe* —3E **74**
Waterside. *Sils* —2H **21**
Waterside Ind. Pk. *Leeds* —3D **104**
Waterside Rd. *B'frd* —5G **79**
Waterside Rd. *Leeds* —4D **104**
Watersole La. *Weth* —5A **18**
Water Stalls Rd. *Cra V* —1A **140** (in two parts)
Water St. *Brigh* —5H **133**
Water St. *Sower B* —5K **129**
Water St. *Wyke* —5J **115**
Waterwood Clo. *Ting* —1F **139**
Waterworks Rd. *Bat* —4D **136**
Watery La. *Sils* —6H **9**
Watford Av. *Hal* —4F **115**
Watkin Av. *T'tn* —7K **77**
Watkinson Av. *Hal* —2E **112**
Watkinson Dri. *Hal* —3D **112**
Watkinson Rd. *Hal* —3D **112**
Watling Rd. *C'frd* —6K **127**
Watmough St. *B'frd* —3G **97**
Watson Av. *Dew* —7B **138**
Watson Clo. *Oxe* —3E **74**
Watson Mill La. *Sower B* —6K **129**
Watson Rd. *Leeds* —4H **87**
Watsons's La. *Newt K* —5J **37**
Watson St. *Morl* —4K **119**
Wattlesyke. *Coll* —1H **35**
Watts St. *Cytn* —2B **96**
Watt St. *B'frd* —1F **99**
Watty Hall Av. *B'frd* —4G **97**
Watty Hall La. *B'frd* —4H **97**
Watty Hall Rd. *B'frd* —4G **97**
*Wauds Gates. Bail —3J 61 (off Baildon Rd.)*
Waveney Rd. *Leeds* —7C **84**
Waverley Av. *B'frd* —1H **97**
Waverley Av. *Sandb* —3F **41**
Waverley Cres. *Hal* —1C **132**
Waverley Gth. *Leeds* —2H **103**
Waverley Pl. *B'frd* —1H **97**
Waverley Rd. *B'frd* —1H **97**
Waverley Rd. *Ell* —4K **143**
Waverley Ter. *B'frd* —1H **97**
Waverley Ter. *Hal* —1C **132**
Waverton Grn. *B'frd* —7F **97**
Wavertree Pk. Gdns. *Low M* —3J **115**
Wayland App. *Leeds* —7D **48**
Wayland Clo. *Leeds* —7D **48**
Wayland Ct. *Leeds* —7D **48**
Wayland Cft. *Leeds* —7D **48**
Wayland Dri. *Leeds* —7D **48**
Wayne Clo. *Bat* —2G **137**
Wayside Av. *S'cft* —2B **52**
Wayside Cres. *B'frd* —7D **62**
Wayside Cres. *S'cft* —1B **52**
**Wayside Gardens. —2B 52**
Wayside Mt. *S'cft* —1B **52**
Weardale Clo. *B'frd* —5E **98**
**Weardley. —4G 31**
Weardley La. *Hare* —4H **31**
Weatherhead Pl. *Sils* —1H **21**
Weatherhill Cres. *Hud* —7A **144**
Weather Hill La. *Cra V* —3A **128**
Weatherhill Rd. *Hud* —6A **144**
Weatherhouse Ter. *Hal* —6B **112**
*Weaver Ct. B'frd —4D 62 (off Moorfield Pl.)*
Weaver Gdns. *Morl* —4D **120**
Weaver Grn. *Pud* —6C **82**
*Weavers Cotts. Oxe —3E 74 (off Waterside)*
Weavers Ct. *Leeds* —6B **84**
Weavers Ct. *Pud* —1D **100**
Weavers Cft. *B'frd* —2C **62**
Weavers Cft. *Pud* —7D **82**
Weavers Ga. *H Bri* —6A **92**
Weavers Grange. *Guis* —1G **45**
Weavers Hill. *Haw* —6E **56**
Weavers Row. *Pud* —7D **82**
Weaver St. *Leeds* —4D **84**
Weavers Wlk. *Sils* —7G **9**
Weaverthorpe Rd. *B'frd* —5G **99**
Webb Dri. *B'frd* —3C **80**
Webber Ga. *Kei* —6H **39**
Webb's Ter. *Hal* —7H **113**
*Weber Ct. B'frd —6E 80 (off Amberley St.)*
Webster Pl. *B'frd* —6D **80** (3K **7**)
Webster Row. *Leeds* —7B **84**
Webster St. *B'frd* —6D **80** (3K **7**)
Webton Ct. *Leeds* —5K **67**
Wedgemoor Clo. *Wyke* —3J **115**
Wedgewood Ct. *Leeds* —3C **68**
Wedgewood Dri. *Leeds* —4C **68**
Wedgewood Gro. *Leeds* —4C **68**
Weetlands Clo. *Kip* —4B **108**
**Weeton. —1E 30**
**Weetwood. —4C 66**
Weetwood Av. *Leeds* —5D **66**
Weetwood Ct. *Leeds* —4C **66**
Weetwood Cres. *Leeds* —4D **66**
Weetwood Grange Gro. *Leeds* —4B **66**
Weetwood Ho. Ct. *Leeds* —4B **66**
Weetwood La. *Leeds* —3C **66**
Weetwood Mnr. *Leeds* —4C **66**
Weetwood Mill La. *Leeds* —4D **66**
Weetwood Pk. Dri. *Leeds* —4B **66**
Weetwood Rd. *B'frd* —5G **79**
Weetwood Rd. *Leeds* —4B **66**
Weetwood Ter. *Leeds* —4D **66**
Weetwood Wlk. *Leeds* —4C **66**
Welbeck Dri. *B'frd* —2E **96**
Welbeck Ri. *B'frd* —2E **96**
Welbeck Rd. *Birs* —5D **118**
Welbeck Rd. *Leeds* —6C **86**
Welbeck St. *C'frd* —7D **126**
Welburn Av. *Hal* —1D **132**
Welburn Av. *Leeds* —5B **66**
Welburn Dri. *Leeds* —5B **66**
Welburn Gro. *Leeds* —5B **66**
Welburn Mt. *B'frd* —6E **96**
Welbury Dri. *B'frd* —3J **79**
Welfare Av. *Bar E* —5J **71**
Welham Wlk. *B'frd* —5C **80** (1H **7**)
Welland Dri. *Gar* —7A **90**
Wellands Grn. *Cleck* —1D **134**
Wellands La. *Schol* —7B **116** (in two parts)
Wellands Ter. *B'frd* —6E **80**
Well Clo. *Rawd* —1A **64**
Well Clo. *W'ford* —6J **107**
Well Clo. Ri. *Leeds* —3J **85** (2E **4**)
Well Clo. St. *Brigh* —5H **133**
Wellcroft. *Otley* —3K **27**
Well Cft. *Shipl* —5H **61**
Wellcroft Gro. *Ting* —1F **139**
*Wellesley Ho. B'frd —7F 81 (off Wellington St.)*
Wellesley St. *B'frd* —6B **80** (3G **7**)
*Wellfield Pl. Leeds —7D 66 (off Chapel St.)*
Wellfield Ter. *Gild* —7G **101**
Well Fold. *Idle* —4D **62**
Wellgarth. *Hal* —3F **131**
Well Gth. *Leeds* —3A **88**
Well Gth. Bank. *Leeds* —1F **83**
Well Gth. Mt. *Leeds* —3A **88**
Well Gth. Vw. *Leeds* —1G **83**
Wellgate. *G'lnd* —1G **143**
Well Grn. Ct. *B'frd* —7G **99**
Well Grn. La. *Brigh* —3F **133**
Well Gro. *Brigh* —3F **133**
Well Gro. *Hud* —6J **145**
Wellhead Clo. *B'hpe* —7J **29**
Well Head Dri. *Hal* —2G **131**
Well Head La. *Hal* —3G **131**
Well Head La. *Sower B* —5E **128**
Well Head Ri. *Hal* —3G **131**
**Well Heads. —6E 76**
Well Heads. *T'tn* —1D **94**
Well Hill. *Otley* —3H **27**
Well Hill. *Yead* —4K **45**
*Well Hill Ct. Yead —5K 45 (off Well Hill)*
Wellholme. *Brigh* —5H **133**
Well Holme Mead. *Leeds* —3J **101**
Well Ho. Av. *Leeds* —7C **68**
Well Ho. Cres. *Leeds* —7C **68**
Well Ho. Dri. *Leeds* —7C **68**
Well Ho. Gdns. *Leeds* —7C **68**
Well Ho. Rd. *Leeds* —7C **68**
*Wellington Arc. Brigh —6G 133 (off Briggate)*
Wellington Bri. Ind. Est. *Leeds* —6F **85**
Wellington Bri. St. *Leeds* —5F **85** (6A **4**)
Wellington Ct. *B'shaw* —1J **117**
Wellington Cres. *Shipl* —5G **61**
Wellington Gdns. *Leeds* —2H **83**
Wellington Gth. *Leeds* —1H **83**
Wellington Gro. *B'frd* —3D **80**
Wellington Gro. *Leeds* —1H **83**
Wellington Gro. *Pud* —6A **82**
**Wellington Hill. —4H 69**
Wellington Hill. *Leeds* —2J **69**
Wellington Mt. *Leeds* —1H **83**
Wellington Pl. *B'frd* —2E **80**
Wellington Pl. *Hal* —2G **131**
Wellington Rd. *B'frd* —2D **80**
Wellington Rd. *I'ly* —5B **12**
Wellington Rd. *Kei* —5A **40**
Wellington Rd. *Leeds* —7E **84** (7A **4**)
Wellington Rd. *Wilsd* —1F **77**
Wellington Rd. E. *Dew* —7G **137**
Wellington St. *All* —4C **78**
Wellington St. *Bat* —3F **137**
Wellington St. *Bgly* —1K **59**
Wellington St. *B'frd* —6B **80** (3F **7**)
Wellington St. *C'frd* —7B **126**
Wellington St. *Eccl* —3D **80**
Wellington St. *Idle* —5D **62**
Wellington St. *Lais* —7F **81**
Wellington St. *Leeds* —5F **85** (6A **4**) (in two parts)
Wellington St. *Liv* —5K **135**
Wellington St. *Morl* —3A **120**
Wellington St. *Q'bry* —5K **95**
Wellington St. *Wilsd* —1G **77**
Wellington St. S. *Hal* —2H **131**
Wellington Ter. *Leeds* —1H **83**
Wellington Wlk. *Dew* —7G **137**
Well La. *Bat* —3H **137**
Well La. *Brigh* —1F **145**
Well La. *Clif* —6A **134**
Well La. *Guis* —2G **45**
Well La. *Hal* —1H **131**
Well La. *Kip* —5A **108**
Well La. *Leeds* —5K **67**
Well La. *Rawd* —1A **64**
Well La. *Schol* —6B **116**
Well La. *Yead* —5K **45**
Well Royd Av. *Hal* —1A **130**
Well Royd Clo. *Hal* —1B **130** (in two parts)
*Wells Ct. I'ly —6B 12 (off Wells Promenade)*
*Wells Ct. Yead —5K 45 (off Well La.)*
Wells Cft. *Leeds* —5E **66**
Wells Gro. *Guis* —2G **45**
*Wells Ho. Sower B —4A 130 (off Church Vw.)*
*Wells M. I'ly —6B 12 (off Wells Wlk.)*
Wells Mt. *Guis* —2G **45**
Wells Promenade. *I'ly* —5B **12**
Wells Rd. *Guis* —2G **45**
Wells Rd. *I'ly* —7A **12**
Wells St. *Guis* —2G **45**
*Wells Ter. Hal —5G 115 (off Village St.)*
Wells, The. *Hal* —3C **130** (nr. Burnley Rd.)
Wells, The. *Hal* —1A **130** (nr. Stock La.)
Wellstone Av. *Leeds* —4F **83**
Wellstone Dri. *Leeds* —4F **83**
Wellstone Gdns. *Leeds* —5F **83**
Wellstone Gth. *Leeds* —5F **83**
Wellstone Grn. *Leeds* —4F **83**
Wellstone Ri. *Leeds* —5F **83**
Wellstone Rd. *Leeds* —5F **83**
Wellstone Way. *Leeds* —5F **83**
Well St. *B'frd* —6B **80** (4F **7**)
Well St. *Denh* —5B **76**
Well St. *Dew* —7J **137**
Well St. *Fars* —2B **82**
Well St. *Holy G* —5F **143**
Well St. *Kei* —4K **39**
Well St. *Lit T* —3J **135**
*Well St. Sut Cr —5A 20 (off Sutton La.)*
Well St. *Wilsd* —7G **59**
Wells Wlk. *I'ly* —6B **12**
*Well Ter. Guis —2G 45 (off Well St.)*
Well Vw. *Guis* —2G **45**
Welton Gro. *Leeds* —2E **84**
Welton Mt. *Leeds* —2E **84**
Welton Pl. *Leeds* —2E **84**
Welton Rd. *Leeds* —2E **84**
Welwyn Av. *Bat* —2D **136**
Welwyn Av. *Shipl* —5B **62**
Welwyn Dri. *Bail* —2J **61**
Welwyn Dri. *Shipl* —5B **62**
Welwyn Rd. *Dew* —5K **137**
Wembley Av. *T'tn* —7K **77**
Wenborough La. *B'frd* —3H **99**
Wendel Av. *Bar E* —5H **71**
Wendover Ct. *Leeds* —1D **66**
Wendron Clo. *Liv* —7H **135**
Wendron Way. *B'frd* —5D **62**
Wenlock St. *B'frd* —7C **80** (5H **7**)
Wenning St. *Kei* —3C **40**
Wensley Av. *Leeds* —5J **67**
Wensley Av. *Shipl* —5G **61**
Wensley Bank. *T'tn* —7G **77**
Wensley Bank Ter. *T'tn* —7G **77**
Wensley Bank W. *T'tn* —7G **77**
Wensley Cres. *Leeds* —5J **67**
Wensleydale Av. *Leeds* —3K **83**
Wensleydale Clo. *Leeds* —3K **83**
*Wensleydale Ct. Leeds —5J 67 (off Stainbeck La.)*
Wensleydale Cres. *Leeds* —3K **83**
Wensleydale Dri. *Leeds* —3K **83**
*Wensleydale Ho. Bat —6G 137 (off Dale Clo.)*
Wensleydale M. *Leeds* —3K **83**
Wensleydale Pde. *Bat* —7D **118**
Wensleydale Ri. *Bail* —7A **44**
Wensleydale Ri. *Leeds* —3K **83**
Wensleydale Rd. *B'frd* —6G **81**
Wensley Dri. *Leeds* —4H **67**
Wensley Gdns. *Leeds* —4H **67**
Wensley Grn. *Leeds* —5H **67**
Wensley Gro. *Brigh* —1E **144**
Wensley Gro. *Leeds* —5J **67**
Wensley Ho. *B'frd* —6F **63**
Wensley Lawn. *Midd* —3J **121**
Wensley Rd. *Leeds* —4H **67**
Wensley Vw. *Leeds* —5J **67**
Wentworth Av. *Leeds* —7H **49**
Wentworth Clo. *Men* —6C **26**
Wentworth Ct. *Brigh* —2F **145**
Wentworth Cres. *Leeds* —7J **49**
Wentworth Dri. *Hal* —7D **94**
Wentworth Farm Res. Pk. *Leeds* —4H **101**
Wentworth Ga. *Weth* —3F **17**
Wentworth Gro. *Hal* —7D **94**
*Wentworth Ter. Rawd —1B 64 (off Town St.)*
Wentworth Way. *Leeds* —7J **49**
Wepener Mt. *Leeds* —4D **86**
Wepener Pl. *Leeds* —4D **86**
Wescoe Hill La. *Wee* —1C **30**
Wesleyan St. *B'frd* —3E **98**
Wesley App. *Leeds* —4F **103**
Wesley Av. *Leeds* —6C **84**
Wesley Av. *Low M* —7A **98**
Wesley Av. S. *Low M* —1A **116**
Wesley Clo. *Birs* —6C **118**
Wesley Clo. *Leeds* —3F **103**
Wesley Ct. *Hal* —1G **131**
Wesley Ct. *Leeds* —4F **103** (LS11)
*Wesley Ct. Leeds —2G 85 (off Woodhouse St.)*
Wesley Cft. *Leeds* —3F **103**
Wesley Dri. *Low M* —7A **98**
Wesley Gth. *Leeds* —3F **103**
Wesley Grn. *Leeds* —4F **103**
Wesley Gro. *B'frd* —3E **62**
Wesley Ho. *Leeds* —4F **103**
Wesley Pl. *Kei* —1J **57**
Wesley Pl. *Leeds* —6A **86** (LS9)
Wesley Pl. *Leeds* —6C **84** (LS12)
*Wesley Pl. Low M —1A 116 (off Main St.)*
**Wesley Place. —1K 115**
Wesley Pl. *Sils* —1G **21**
Wesley Rd. *Leeds* —6C **84**
Wesley Rd. *S'ley* —4A **82**
Wesley Row. *Pud* —5C **82**
Wesley Sq. *Pud* —6C **82**
Wesley St. *C'frd* —7D **126**
Wesley St. *Cleck* —7F **117**
Wesley St. *Far* —2B **82**
Wesley St. *Leeds* —3F **103**
Wesley St. *Morl* —3A **120**
Wesley St. *Otley* —2J **27**
Wesley St. *Rod* —7D **64**
Wesley St. *S'ley* —4B **82**
Wesley Ter. *Gar* —6K **89**
Wesley Ter. *Leeds* —2H **83**
Wesley Ter. *Pud* —6C **82**
Wesley Ter. *Rod* —7D **64**
Wesley Vw. *Leeds* —7D **64**
Wesley Vw. *Pud* —6C **82**
Westacre. *Brigh* —1H **145**
W. Acre Dri. *Bat* —3J **137** (nr. Lady Ann Rd.)
W. Acre Dri. *Bat* —3H **137** (nr. Soothill La.)
**West Ardsley. —7E 120**
West Av. *All* —2K **77**
West Av. *Bail* —1J **61**
West Av. *B Spa* —2C **36**
West Av. *Hal* —4F **131**
West Av. *Light* —1G **133**
West Av. *Round* —4E **68**
West Bank. *Bat* —2F **137**
West Bank. *B'frd* —1F **79**
West Bank. *Hal* —3B **112**
*West Bank. Kei —3H 39 (off W. Bank Ri.)*
W. Bank Clo. *Kei* —3H **39**
W. Bank Gro. *Riddl* —1C **40**
W. Bank Ri. *Kei* —3H **39**
W. Bank Rd. *Riddl* —1B **40**
West Bolton. *Hal* —7B **94**
**Westborough. —7D 136**
Westborough Dri. *Hal* —1B **130**

Westbourne Av.—Weyhill Dri.


Westbourne Av. Gar —7H 89
(in two parts)
Westbourne Av. Leeds —3H 103
Westbourne Clo. Otley —4G 27
Westbourne Cres. Gar —7H 89
Westbourne Cres. Hal —5H 131
Westbourne Dri. Gar —7H 89
Westbourne Dri. Guis —2E 44
Westbourne Dri. Men —5B 26
Westbourne Gdns. Gar —7H 89
Westbourne Gro. Gar —7H 89
Westbourne Gro. Hal —5H 131
Westbourne Gro. Otley —4G 27
Westbourne Mt. Leeds —3H 103
Westbourne Pl. Leeds —3H 103
Westbourne Pl. S'ley —4B 82
Westbourne Rd. B'frd —3H 79
Westbourne St. Leeds —3H 103
Westbourne Ter. Gar —7H 89
Westbourne Ter. Hal —5H 131
**West Bowling. —3B 98**
**West Breary. —7A 30**
Westbrook Clo. H'fth —2F 65
*Westbrook Ct. Hal —7F 113*
*(off Stannary Pl.)*
Westbrook La. H'fth —2F 65
Westbrook Ter. Bat —2F 137
Westburn Av. Kei —5H 39
Westburn Cres. Kei —6H 39
Westburn Gro. Kei —6H 39
Westburn Pl. Cleck —7E 116
Westburn Way. Kei —6H 39
Westbury Clo. B'frd —1F 99
Westbury Ct. Hal —2C 130
Westbury Gro. Leeds —4B 104
Westbury Mt. Leeds —5B 104
Westbury Pl. Hal —2C 130
Westbury Pl. N. Leeds —4B 104
Westbury Pl. S. Leeds —5B 104
Westbury Rd. B'frd —5D 96
Westbury St. B'frd —1F 99
Westbury St. Ell —2A 144
Westbury St. Leeds —5B 104
Westbury Ter. Hal —2C 130
Westbury Ter. Leeds —5B 104
W. Busk La. Otley —4E 26
**West Carlton. —1K 45**
W. Chevin Rd. Men & Otley —5F 27
Westcliffe Av. Bail —7H 43
Westcliffe Dri. Hal —1B 130
Westcliffe Ri. Cleck —1E 134
Westcliffe Rd. Cleck —7E 116
Westcliffe Rd. Shipl —5G 61
West Clo. Hud —7H 145
Westcombe Av. Leeds —2C 68
Westcombe Ct. Wyke —3J 115
Westcott Ho. B'frd —1A 6
West Ct. Bmly —4G 83
West Ct. Leeds —4E 68
West Cft. Add —1D 10
West Cft. Wyke —5J 115
Westcroft Av. Hal —3B 114
Westcroft Dri. Oss —7C 138
*Westcroft Ho. C'frd —7C 126*
*(off West St.)*
Westcroft Rd. B'frd —2G 97
West Dale. B Spa —1C 36
Westdale Dri. Pud —5B 82
Westdale Gdns. Pud —5B 82
Westdale Gro. Pud —5B 82
Westdale Ri. Pud —5B 82
Westdale Rd. Pud —5B 82
West Dene. Leeds —6B 50
West Dene. Sils —7G 9
West Dri. Oxe —2E 74
**West End. —3D 64**
**(nr. Horsforth)**
**West End. —6H 95**
**(nr. Queensbury)**
**West End. —1E 134**
**(nr. Scholes)**
West End. B Spa —1C 36
West End. Gild —7G 101
West End. Leeds —3H 101
West End. Q'bry —6H 95
W. End App. Morl —4J 119
W. End Clo. H'fth —3D 64
W. End Dri. Cleck —2E 134
W. End Dri. H'fth —3D 64
W. End Gro. H'fth —3D 64
W. End La. H'fth —3D 64
W. End Ri. H'fth —3D 64
W. End Rd. C'ley —6K 63
W. End Rd. Hal —2C 130
W. End St. B'frd —6K 79 (4C 6)
W. End Ter. B'frd —7D 62
W. End Ter. Guis —2E 44
W. End Ter. H Bri —6A 110
W. End Ter. Leeds —1F 85
W. End Ter. Shipl —4G 61
Westercroft La. Hal —4A 114
Westercroft Vw. Hal —4B 114
Westerley Cres. Sils —1E 20
Westerly Cft. Leeds —5C 84
*Westerly Ri. Leeds —5C 84*
*(off Stocks Hill)*
Western Av. Birs —6E 118
Western Av. Riddl —7A 22
Western Gro. Leeds —1B 102
Western Mt. Leeds —1B 102
Western Pl. Q'bry —5B 96
Western Rd. Leeds —1B 102
Western St. Leeds —1B 102
Western Way. Butt —7G 97
**Westerton. —1F 139**
Westerton Clo. Ting —7H 121
Westerton Ct. Oaken —2D 116
Westerton Rd. Ting —1D 138
Westerton Wlk. Ting —7H 121
W. Farm Av. Leeds —2H 121
Westfell Clo. Kei —5H 39
Westfell Rd. Kei —5H 39
Westfell Way. Kei —5H 39
**Westfield. —3A 136**
**(nr. Heckmondwike)**
**Westfield. —5H 45**
**(nr. Yeadon)**
Westfield. Leeds —5J 67
Westfield. S'ley —4B 82
Westfield. T'tn —7A 78
Westfield Av. All B —2A 126
Westfield Av. Hal —1D 132
Westfield Av. Kip —5A 108
Westfield Av. Leeds —5K 83
Westfield Av. Yead —5H 45
Westfield Clo. Heck —3A 136
Westfield Clo. Rothw —3E 122
Westfield Clo. Yead —5H 45
*Westfield Ct. Leeds —4F 85*
*(off Westfield Rd.)*
Westfield Ct. Rothw —3E 122
Westfield Cres. B'frd —4D 80
Westfield Cres. K'gte —6H 139
Westfield Cres. Leeds —4F 85
(in two parts)
Westfield Cres. Riddl —1D 40
Westfield Cres. Shipl —6A 62
Westfield Dri. Hal —1D 132
Westfield Dri. Riddl —2D 40
Westfield Dri. Yead —5G 45
Westfield Gdns. Hal —1D 132
Westfield Gdns. Kip —4K 107
Westfield Grn. B'frd —2G 99
Westfield Gro. All B —2A 126
Westfield Gro. B'frd —4C 62
Westfield Gro. Dew —7D 136
Westfield Gro. Shipl —6A 62
Westfield Gro. Yead —5H 45
*Westfield Ho. B'frd —5D 62*
*(off Buckfast Ct.)*
Westfield Ind. Est. Yead —5J 45
Westfield La. Kip —4K 107
Westfield La. Shipl & Idle —6A 62
Westfield La. T'ner —7C 52
Westfield La. Wyke & Schol —5J 115
Westfield M. T'tn —1A 96
Westfield Mt. Yead —6H 45
Westfield Oval. Yead —5G 45
Westfield Pl. Hal —2E 130
Westfield Pl. K'gte —5H 139
Westfield Pl. Morl —3A 120
Westfield Pl. Schol —6A 116
Westfield Rd. B'frd —3G 79
Westfield Rd. Cytn —2B 96
Westfield Rd. Heck —3A 136
Westfield Rd. Leeds —4F 85
Westfield Rd. Morl —3A 120
Westfield Rd. Riddl —2D 40
Westfield Rd. Rothw & Carl —4E 122
Westfield St. Brun I —2F 131
Westfield St. Heck —3A 136
Westfield Ter. All B —2A 126
Westfield Ter. Bail —7J 43
Westfield Ter. B'frd —4D 80
Westfield Ter. Cytn —2B 96
Westfield Ter. Hal —7E 112
Westfield Ter. Leeds —4F 85
(LS3)
Westfield Ter. Leeds —5J 67
(LS7)
Westfield Ter. Myth —6A 110
Westfield Yd. Leeds —1B 102
West Fold. Bail —7J 43
**West Garforth. —1H 107**
Westgarth. Lntn —6F 17
**Westgate. —7E 122**
Westgate. Bail —7J 43
Westgate. B'frd —5K 79 (2B 6)
Westgate. Brigh —6A 134
Westgate. Cleck —1E 134
Westgate. Dew —7H 137
Westgate. Eccl —1E 80
Westgate. Ell —2K 143
Westgate. Guis —3C 44
Westgate. Hal —1G 131
Westgate. Heck —4A 136
*Westgate. Holy G —6D 142*
*(off Stainland Rd.)*
West Ga. Kei —4K 39
Westgate. Leeds —5G 85 (6A 4)
(in two parts)
Westgate. Otley —3H 27
Westgate. Shipl —4H 61
West Ga. Weth —4J 17
Westgate Clo. Loft —7E 122
Westgate Ct. Loft —7E 122
Westgate Gro. Loft —7E 122
**Westgate Hill. —6J 99**
Westgate Hill St. B'frd —6H 99
Westgate La. Loft —7D 122
Westgate Mkt. Hal —1G 131
Westgate Pl. B'frd —6J 99
Westgate Ter. B'frd —6J 99
W. Grange Clo. Leeds —5K 103
W. Grange Dri. Leeds —5K 103
W. Grange Fold. Leeds —5K 103
W. Grange Gdns. Leeds —5K 103
W. Grange Gth. Leeds —5K 103
W. Grange Grn. Leeds —5K 103
W. Grange Rd. Leeds —6K 103
W. Grange Wlk. Leeds —5K 103
West Gro. Bail —7J 43
Westgrove Ct. Cleck —7E 116
W. Grove St. B'frd —6K 79
W. Grove St. S'ley —4B 82
Westgrove Ter. Hal —1F 131
Westhill Av. Cull —7C 58
W. Hill Av. Leeds —5J 67
W. Hill St. Hal —1E 130
W. Hill Ter. Leeds —5J 67
Westholme Rd. Hal —1D 130
Westholme St. B'frd —7K 79
*West Ho. Ell —2K 143*
*(off Gog Hill)*
Westland Clo. Cro H —4A 20
Westland Ct. Leeds —6H 103
Westland Rd. Leeds —5H 103
Westlands Dri. All —4B 78
Westlands Gro. All —4C 78
Westland Sq. Leeds —6H 103
West La. Askw —4K 13
West La. Bail —1F 61
(in two parts)
West La. B Spa —1C 36
West La. Gom —6K 117
West La. Hal —5K 131
West La. Haw —5D 56
West La. Kei —3H 39
West La. T'tn —6H 77
Westlea Av. Riddl —2D 40
W. Lea Clo. Leeds —3H 67
W. Lea Cres. Ting —1D 138
W. Lea Cres. Yead —5H 45
W. Lea Dri. Leeds —3H 67
W. Lea Dri. Ting —1D 138
W. Lea Gdns. Leeds —3H 67
W. Lea Gth. Leeds —3H 67
W. Lea Gro. Yead —5H 45
W. Leeds St. Kei —4J 39
Westleigh. Bgly —7A 42
Westleigh Clo. Bail —2G 61
Westleigh Dri. Bail —2G 61
Westleigh Rd. Bail —1G 61
Westleigh Way. Bail —2F 61
Westlock Av. Leeds —4C 86
W. Lodge Cres. Hud —5B 144
W. Lodge Gdns. Leeds —6J 67
West Mead. C'frd —7G 127
Westmead. S'ley —4J 81
Westminster Av. Cytn —2A 96
Westminster Clo. Rod —1D 82
Westminster Cres. Cytn —2A 96
Westminster Cres. Leeds —6G 87
Westminster Cft. Rod —1D 82
Westminster Dri. Cytn —2A 96
Westminster Dri. Rod —1D 82
Westminster Gdns. Cytn —2A 96
Westminster Pl. B'frd —4B 80 (1G 7)
Westminster Rd. B'frd —4B 80 (1G 7)
Westminster Ter. B'frd —4B 80 (1G 7)
Westmoor Av. Bail —7H 43
Westmoor Clo. Bail —7H 43
Westmoor Pl. Leeds —2F 83
Westmoor Ri. Leeds —2F 83
Westmoor Rd. Leeds —2F 83
Westmoor St. Leeds —2F 83
Westmoreland Mt. Leeds —1H 83
**West Morton. —1G 41**
W. Mount St. Hal —7E 112
W. Mount St. Leeds —3G 103
*Westmuir Ho. B'frd —2K 97*
*(off Launton Way)*
**Weston. —6D 14**
Weston Av. Q'bry —5H 95
Weston Cres. Otley —1G 27
Weston Dri. Otley —7F 15
Weston Hall. —7D 14
Weston La. Otley —1F 27
Weston Moor Rd. Askw —1D 14
Weston Pk. Vw. Otley —7F 15
Weston Ridge Otley —7G 15
Weston Rd. I'ly —5B 12
Weston St. Kei —6H 39
Weston Va. Rd. Q'bry —6H 95
Westover Av. Leeds —2G 83
Westover Clo. Leeds —2H 83
Westover Gdns. Pud —6A 82
Westover Grn. Leeds —2G 83
Westover Gro. Leeds —2G 83
Westover Mt. Leeds —2G 83
Westover Rd. Leeds —2G 83
Westover St. Leeds —2G 83
Westover Ter. Leeds —2G 83
Westover Vw. Leeds —2G 83
West Pde. Guis —2G 45
West Pde. Hal —2F 131
West Pde. I'ly —5C 12
West Pde. Leeds —4A 66
West Pde. Rothw —2H 123
West Pde. Sower B —4B 130
*West Pde. Flats. Hal —2F 131*
*(off West Pde.)*
**West Park. —1C 36**
**(nr. Boston Spa)**
**West Park. —4A 66**
**(nr. Lawnswood)**
West Pk. Guis —1E 44
West Pk. Pud —6B 82
W. Park Av. Leeds —1D 68
W. Pk. Chase. Leeds —1C 68
W. Park Clo. Leeds —1C 68
W. Park Ct. Leeds —1D 68
W. Park Cres. Leeds —2D 68
W. Park Dri. Leeds —4A 66
W. Park Dri. E. Leeds —1C 68
W. Park Dri. W. Leeds —1B 68
W. Park Gdns. Leeds —2D 68
W. Park Gro. Bat —3E 136
W. Park Gro. Leeds —1C 68
W. Park Ind. Est. B'frd —2F 97
W. Park Pl. Leeds —2D 68
W. Park Rd. Bat —4D 136
W. Park Rd. B'frd —5F 79
W. Park Rd. Leeds —2D 68
W. Park St. Brigh —6H 133
W. Park St. Dew —7F 137
W. Park Ter. Bat —4E 136
W. Park Ter. B'frd —5F 79
W. Pasture Clo. H'fth —3D 64
West Riding Folk Museum. —7K 113
West Rd. Leeds —3E 104
W. Road N. Leeds —3E 104
**West Royd. —4A 62**
West Royd. Hal —7C 114
Westroyd. N Clift —6J 15
Westroyd. Pud —7A 82
West Royd. Wilsd —7G 59
W. Royd Av. B'frd —1D 80
Westroyd Av. Cleck —4F 117
W. Royd Av. Hal —2E 130
Westroyd Av. Pud —7A 82
W. Royd Av. Shipl —4K 61
W. Royd Clo. Hal —3E 130
W. Royd Clo. Shipl —4K 61
Westroyd Cres. Pud —1A 100
W. Royd Cres. Shipl —4A 62
W. Royd Dri. Shipl —4A 62
Westroyd Gdns. Pud —7A 82
W. Royd Gro. Shipl —4A 62
**Westroyd Hill. —7A 82**
W. Royd Mt. Shipl —4A 62
W. Royd Rd. Shipl —4A 62
W. Royd Ter. Shipl —4A 62
W. Royd Wlk. Shipl —4A 62
W. Scausby Pk. Hal —7C 94
**West Scholes. —3H 95**
W. Shaw La. Oxe —2C 74
*Westside Ct. B'frd —5G 79*
*(off Bk. Girlington Rd.)*
W. Side Retail Pk. Guis —4H 45
West St. Bail —7J 43
West St. Bail B —1H 133
West St. Bat —3H 137
(in two parts)
West St. B'frd —7B 80
(BD1)
West St. B'frd —2D 80
(BD2)
West St. Brigh —5G 133
West St. C'frd —7C 126
West St. Cleck —1F 135
West St. Dlgtn —2C 118
West St. Gom —6K 117
West St. Guis —2G 45
West St. Hal —1E 130
West St. Heck —4A 136
West St. Holy G —5F 143
West St. Hud —7A 144
West St. I'ly —5B 12
West St. Leeds —5F 85 (6A 4)
West St. Morl —4B 120
West St. She —3B 114
West St. Sower B —5K 129
West St. S'ley —5C 82
W. Terrace St. S'ley —4B 82
**West Vale. —3H 143**
West Va. Leeds —1E 102
Westvale M. Leeds —4J 83
West Vw. Bat —6F 137
West Vw. Bgly —6C 42
West Vw. B'shaw —3K 117
West Vw. B'twn —5F 113
*West Vw. B'frd —2C 98*
*(off New Hey Rd.)*
*West Vw. Fars —3B 82*
*(off New St.)*
*West Vw. Hal —2D 130*
*(off Hopwood La.)*
West Vw. Holy G —5E 142
West Vw. I'ly —6B 12
West Vw. Kip —4B 108
West Vw. K'gte —6H 139
West Vw. Leeds —3G 103
West Vw. M'fld —7H 91
West Vw. Otley —3K 27
West Vw. Pool W —4K 29
West Vw. Schol —6B 116
West Vw. Sils —7G 9
West Vw. Sower B —4A 130
West Vw. W'ford —2A 124
West Vw. Yead —4H 45
W. View Av. Bur W —1A 26
W. View Av. C'frd —7G 127
W. View Av. Hal —1C 130
Westview Av. Kei —3J 39
W. View Av. Shipl —5A 62
W. View Clo. Shipl —5A 62
Westview Ct. Kei —3J 39
W. View Ct. Yead —4H 45
W. View Cres. Hal —1C 130
W. View Dri. Hal —1B 130
Westview Gro. Kei —3J 39
W. View Rd. Bur W —1A 26
W. View Rd. Hal —5F 113
W. View St. Cro R —4H 57
W. View Ter. Bshw —5D 94
W. View Ter. Pel —7C 112
Westview Way. Kei —3K 39
W. Villa Rd. Guis —2G 45
Westville. I'ly —5A 12
Westville Av. I'ly —5A 12
Westville Clo. I'ly —5A 12
Westville Rd. I'ly —5A 12
Westville Way. T'tn —7H 77
Westward Cft. Hud —7C 144
Westward Ho. Hal —3E 112
Westward Ho. Q'bry —5H 95
Westway. Bat —5K 137
Westway. Bgly —6B 42
Westway. B'frd —3C 78
Westway. Fars —2A 82
Westway. Gar —7H 89
Westway. Guis —3D 44
Westway. Kei —3H 39
Westway. Shipl —5D 60
Westways Dri. Leeds —5E 68
West Winds. Men —5A 26
Westwinn Gth. Leeds —4A 70
Westwinn Vw. Leeds —3A 70
Westwood. B'frd —1F 79
Westwood Av. B'frd —7D 62
Westwood Clo. Morl —1B 120
W. Wood Ct. Leeds —2G 121
Westwood Cres. Bgly —4A 60
Westwood Dri. I'ly —7K 11
Westwood Gro. B'frd —7D 62
Westwood Ri. Morl —1B 120
W. Wood Rd. Morl —3F 121
Westwood Side. Morl —7A 102
Westwood Way. B Spa —3D 36
W. Yorkshire Ind. Est. B'frd —6F 99
West Yorkshire Playhouse. —5K 85 (6H 5)
**Wetherby. —4J 17**
Wetherby Bus. Pk. Weth —3K 17
Wetherby Grange. Weth —7A 18
Wetherby Gro. Leeds —3C 84
Wetherby Pl. Leeds —3D 84
Wetherby Racecourse. —3B 18
Wetherby Rd. Bard —6C 34
Wetherby Rd. B'ham —7C 36
Wetherby Rd. Coll —1H 35
Wetherby Rd. Kirk D —1H 17
Wetherby Rd. Leeds —6D 68
Wetherby Rd. S'cft & Leeds —5G 69
Wetherby Rd. Sick —4B 16
Wetherby Rd. Wltn —5E 18
Wetherby Ter. Leeds —3C 84
Wetherhill St. Bat —3F 137
*Wetherill Ter. Dew —5D 136*
*(off Kilpin Hill La.)*
Wet Shod La. Brigh —4E 132
*Weybridge Ho. B'frd —4J 79*
*(off Trenton Dri.)*
Weyhill Dri. All —5B 78


A-Z Leeds & Bradford 203

Weymouth Av.—Wilsden Hill Rd.


Weymouth Av. All —5A 78
Weymouth St. Hal —1G 131
Whack Ho. Yead —5H 45 (off Whack Houses)
Whack Ho. Clo. Yead —5J 45
Whack Ho. La. Yead —5J 45
Whalley La. Denh —3B 76
Wharfbank Ho. Otley —3G 27
Wharfe Bank. Coll —2C 34
Wharfe Clo. Leeds —7D 48
Wharfe Ct. Bur W —1B 26
Wharfe Ct. Sils —1G 21
Wharfe Cres. Pool W —3H 29
Wharfedale Av. Leeds —1H 85
Wharfedale Ct. Leeds —7H 69
Wharfedale Ct. Otley —2J 27
Wharfedale Cres. Gar —1K 107
Wharfedale Dri. I'ly —5C 12
Wharfedale Gdns. Bail —7A 44
Wharfedale Gro. Leeds —1H 85
Wharfedale Ho. Sower B —5K 129 (off Quarry Hill)
Wharfedale M. Otley —2J 27
Wharfedale Mt. Hal —2B 114
Wharfedale Mt. Leeds —1H 85
Wharfedale Pl. Leeds —1H 85
Wharfedale Ri. B'frd —3C 78
Wharfedale Ri. Ting —1D 138
Wharfedale Rd. Euro I —7C 98
Wharfedale St. Leeds —1H 85
Wharfedale Vw. Add —1C 10
Wharfedale Vw. Leeds —1H 85
Wharfedale Vw. Men —6C 26
Wharfe Grange. Weth —4H 17
Wharfe Gro. Weth —4H 17
Wharfe Pk. Add —1E 10
Wharfe Rein. Coll —2C 34
Wharfeside. B Spa —3F 37
Wharfeside La. I'ly —4C 12
Wharfe St. B'frd —5B 80 (1F 7)
Wharfe St. Otley —2K 27
Wharfe Vw. Pool W —3G 29
Wharfe Vw. Weth —4H 17
Wharfe Vw. Rd. I'ly —5B 12
Wharfe Way. C'frd —7H 127 (in two parts)
Wharf St. Brigh —6H 133
Wharf St. Leeds —6K 85 (7G 5)
Wharf St. Shipl —4H 61
Wharf St. Sower B —4A 130
Wharncliffe Cres. B'frd —1F 81
Wharncliffe Dri. B'frd —1F 81
Wharncliffe Gro. B'frd —1F 81
Wharncliffe Gro. Shipl —6H 61
Wharncliffe Rd. Shipl —7H 61
Wharton Sq. Q'bry —5B 96 (off Highgate Rd.)
Whartons, The. Otley —7J 15
Wharton St. Liv —4K 135
Wharton Ter. Heck —5B 136 (off Church La.)
Wheat Clo. Dew —7D 136
Wheatcroft. Bat —3G 137 (off Bayldons Pl.)
Wheatcroft Av. Bat —4G 137
Wheater Rd. B'frd —1G 97
Wheatfield Ct. Pud —7B 82
Wheat Head Cres. Kei —6G 39
Wheat Head Dri. Kei —6H 39
Wheat Head La. Kei —6G 39
Wheatlands. Fars —2A 82
Wheatlands. I'ly —5C 12
Wheatlands Av. B'frd —3E 78
Wheatlands Cres. B'frd —3E 78
Wheatlands Dri. B'frd —3E 78
Wheatlands Dri. Liv —6H 135
Wheatlands Gro. B'frd —3E 78
Wheatlands Sq. B'frd —3E 78
**Wheatley. —5C 112**
Wheatley Av. I'ly —6E 12
Wheatley Clo. Hal —6E 112
Wheatley Ct. Hal —3B 112
Wheatley Gdns. I'ly —6E 12
Wheatley Gro. I'ly —6E 12
Wheatley La. Ben R —6E 12
Wheatley La. Hal —6E 112
Wheatley Ri. I'ly —6E 12
Wheatley Rd. Hal —5C 112
Wheatley Rd. I'ly —6C 12
Wheaton Av. Leeds —5J 87
Wheaton Ct. Leeds —5J 87 (off Wheaton Av.)
Wheat St. Kei —7J 39
Wheelwright Av. Leeds —1A 102
Wheelwright Clo. Leeds —1A 102 (in two parts)
Wheelwright Dri. Dew —6E 136
**Wheldale. —5K 127**
Wheldale Ct. C'frd —6H 127 (off Stansfield Clo.)
Wheldale La. C'frd —5K 127
Wheldon Road. —6F 127
Wheldon Rd. C'frd —7E 126
Whernside Mt. B'frd —4E 96
Whernside Way. Mt Tab —4J 111
Wherwell Rd. Brigh —7H 133
Whetley Clo. B'frd —5J 79 (1A 6)
Whetley Gro. B'frd —4G 79
Whetley Hill. B'frd —4H 79
Whetley La. B'frd —5G 79
Whetley Ter. B'frd —5J 79 (1A 6)
Whewell St. Birs —6C 118
Whimbrel Clo. B'frd —6C 78
Whimbrel M. Morl —4C 120
Whinberry Pl. Birs —4D 118
Whinbrook Ct. Leeds —3J 67
Whinbrook Cres. Leeds —3J 67
Whinbrook Gdns. Leeds —3J 67
Whinbrook Gro. Leeds —3J 67
Whincop Av. C'frd —7A 126
Whincover Bank. Leeds —1K 101
Whincover Clo. Leeds —1K 101
Whincover Cross. Leeds —1K 101
Whincover Dri. Leeds —1J 101
Whincover Gdns. Leeds —1K 101
Whincover Grange. Leeds —1K 101
Whincover Gro. Leeds —1K 101
Whincover Hill. Leeds —1K 101
Whincover Mt. Leeds —1K 101
Whincover Rd. Leeds —1J 101
Whincover Vw. Leeds —1K 101
Whincup Gdns. Leeds —4A 104 (off Woodhouse Hill Rd.)
Whiney Hill. Q'bry —5K 95 (off Sand Beds)
Whinfield. Leeds —7B 48
Whinfield Av. Kei —4G 39
Whinfield Clo. Kei —3H 39
Whinfield Dri. Kei —3G 39
Whingate. Leeds —5A 84
Whingate Av. Leeds —6A 84
Whingate Clo. Leeds —6A 84
Whingate Grn. Leeds —6A 84
Whingate Gro. Leeds —6A 84
Whingate Rd. Leeds —6A 84
Whin Knoll Av. Kei —3H 39
**Whinmoor. —4K 69**
Whinmoor Ct. Leeds —3J 69
Whinmoor Cres. Leeds —3J 69
Whinmoor Gdns. Leeds —3H 69
Whinmoor La. Leeds —1G 69
Whinmoor Way. Leeds —5A 70 (in four parts)
Whinmore Gdns. Gom —1A 136
Whinney Fld. Hal —4G 131
Whinney Hill Pk. Brigh —3G 133
Whinney Royd La. Hal —2A 114
Whinn Wood Grange. Leeds —4K 69
Whins La. Sick —2A 16
Whins La. Thor A —1F 37
Whin St. Kei —4J 39
Whiskers La. Hal —4J 113
Whitaker Av. B'frd —2E 80
Whitaker Clo. B'frd —2E 80
Whitaker St. Bat —4H 137
Whitaker St. Fars —4B 82
Whitburn Way. All —5B 78
Whitby Av. Hud —7G 145
Whitby Cres. Dew —7K 137
Whitby Rd. B'frd —4G 79
Whitby Ter. B'frd —4G 79
Whitcliffe Rd. Cleck —7E 116
Whitcliffe Sq. Cleck —7F 117 (off Whitecliffe Rd.)
White Abbey Rd. B'frd —5J 79 (1A 6)
Whitebeam La. Leeds —6K 103
Whitebeam Wlk. B'frd —7D 62
White Birch Ter. Hal —5C 112
Whitebridge Av. Leeds —5G 87
Whitebridge Cres. Leeds —4G 87
Whitebridge Spur. Leeds —4G 87
Whitebridge Vw. Leeds —4G 87
White Castle Ct. Q'bry —4F 95
Whitechapel Clo. Leeds —6D 68
Whitechapel Gro. Schol —6C 116
Whitechapel Rd. Cleck —6D 116
Whitechapel Way. Leeds —6D 68
Whitecliffe Cres. Swil —4E 106
Whitecliffe Dri. Swil —4E 106
Whitecliffe La. Swil —4E 106
Whitecliffe Ri. Swil —4E 106
**Whitecote. —7G 65**
Whitecote Gdns. Leeds —1F 83
Whitecote Hill. Leeds —1F 83
Whitecote Ho. Leeds —7F 65
Whitecote La. Leeds —1F 83
Whitecote Ri. Leeds —1F 83
**White Cross. —2D 44**
White Cross Rd. Dew —7J 137
Whitefield Pl. B'frd —5G 79
Whitegate. E Kes —4A 34
Whitegate. Hal —4H 131
White Ga. Ogden —7B 94
Whitegate Dri. Hal —4H 131
Whitegate Rd. Hal —3H 131
Whitegate Ter. Hal —4H 131
Whitegate Top. Hal —4J 131
White Gro. Leeds —4C 68
Whitehall Av. Wyke —6J 115
Whitehall Cft. Rothw —7H 123
Whitehall Est. Leeds —2K 101
Whitehall Gro. B'shaw —2K 117
Whitehall Gro. Dlgtn —1B 118
White Hall La. Hal —1J 111
Whitehall Pk. Leeds —2A 102
Whitehall Rd. Cleck & Wyke —5E 116
Whitehall Rd. Dlgtn —1B 118
Whitehall Rd. Hal & Wyke —6F 115
Whitehall Rd. Leeds —2B 102 (7B 4)
Whitehall Rd. E. B'shaw —3J 117
Whitehall Rd. W. Cleck & B'shaw —5F 117
Whitehall St. Hal —1D 132
Whitehall Way. Dew —7H 137
Whitehaven Clo. B'frd —7F 97
Whitehead Gro. Fag —4E 80
Whitehead Pl. B'frd —3E 80
Whitehead's Ter. Hal —1D 130
Whitehead St. B'frd —7D 80 (5K 7)
Whitehill Cotts. Hal —2C 112
Whitehill Cres. Hal —1C 112
Whitehill Dri. Hal —1C 112
Whitehill Grn. Hal —1D 112
Whitehill Rd. H'fld —2C 112
Whitehill Rd. Oakw —6A 38
White Horse Clo. Birs —5F 119
Whitehouse Av. W'ford —6H 107
Whitehouse Cres. W'ford —6J 107
Whitehouse Dri. W'ford —6H 107
Whitehouse La. W'ford —3G 107
Whitehouse La. Yead —3C 46
White Houses. H Bri —6A 110
Whitehouse St. Leeds —1K 103
White Laithe App. Leeds —4K 69
White Laithe Av. Leeds —4K 69
White Laithe Clo. Leeds —4K 69
White Laithe Ct. Leeds —4K 69
White Laithe Cft. Leeds —4K 69
White Laithe Gdns. Leeds —4K 69
White Laithe Gth. Leeds —3K 69
White Laithe Grn. Leeds —4A 70
Whitelaithe Gro. Leeds —4A 70
White Laithe Rd. Leeds —4K 69
White Laithe Wlk. Leeds —4A 70
Whitelands. Pud —5D 82
White Lands. Rawd —7J 45
Whitelands Cres. Bail —1K 61
Whitelands Rd. Bail —1K 61
White La. B'frd —5K 97
White La. Oakw —2B 56
White La. Top. B'frd —5K 97 (off White La.)
White Lea Cft. H Bri —6B 110
**White Lee. —1C 136**
White Lee Clo. Bat —2C 136
White Lee Gdns. H Bri —6B 110
White Lee Rd. Heck & Bat —1C 136
White Lee Side. Heck —2C 136
Whiteley Av. Sower B —5H 129
Whiteley Cft. Otley —3J 27
Whiteley Cft. Clo. Otley —3J 27
Whiteley Cft. Gth. Otley —3H 27
Whiteley Cft. Ri. Otley —3J 27
Whiteley Cft. Rd. Otley —3H 27
Whiteley Ter. Sower B —7D 140
Whitelock St. Leeds —4K 85 (3G 5)
White Moor La. Oxe —6E 74
White Rose Av. Gar —6K 89
White Rose Mead. Gar —6A 90
White Rose Shop. Cen., The. Leeds —7E 102
White Rose Way. Gar —6A 90
Whites Clo. B'frd —2D 78
White's Ter. B'frd —4H 79
Whitestone Cres. Yead —4K 45
White St. W'ford —1B 124
White's Vw. B'frd —5H 79
White Va. B'frd —2C 98
Whiteways. B'frd —2A 80
White Wells Spa Cottage. —7B 12
Whitfield Av. Leeds —2A 104
Whitfield Gdns. Leeds —2A 104
Whitfield Pl. Leeds —2A 104
Whitfield Sq. Leeds —2A 104
Whitfield St. Cleck —7F 117
Whitfield St. H'let —2A 104
Whitfield St. Leeds —2B 86
Whitfield Way. Leeds —2A 104
Whitham Clo. B Spa —2D 36
Whitham Rd. Shipl —4E 60
**Whitkirk. —4K 87**
Whitkirk Clo. Leeds —5C 88
Whitkirk La. Leeds —5B 88
**Whitkirk Lane End. —6B 88**
Whitlam St. Shipl —4F 61
Whitley Gdns. Leeds —2A 86 (off Bayswater Rd.)
Whitley La. S'wram —3A 132
Whitley Pl. All B —3B 126
Whitley Rd. Kei —6J 39
Whitley St. Bgly —1K 59
Whitley St. B'frd —6C 80 (4H 7)
Whitley St. Hal —2F 131
Whitteron Clo. Hud —7B 144
Whittle Cres. Cytn —1B 96
Whitton Cft. Rd. I'ly —5B 12
Whitty La. Sower B —2K 129
Whitwell Av. Ell —2B 144
Whitwell Dri. Ell —2B 144
Whitwell Grn. La. Ell —3B 144
Whitwell Gro. Ell —2B 144
Whitwell St. B'frd —1C 98
Whitwood La. Brigh —1J 133
**Whitwood Mere. —7A 126**
**Wholestone Hill. —7J 141**
Whytecote End. Wyke —3J 115
**Wibsey. —5J 97**
Wibsey Bank. B'frd —5K 97
Wibsey Pk. Av. B'frd —6F 97
Wicken Clo. B'frd —6E 62
Wicken La. T'tn —6H 77
Wickets Clo. B'frd —6K 97
Wickets, The. Colt —6C 88
Wickets, The. Leeds —5F 67
Wicket, The. C'ley —5K 63
Wickham Av. B Spa —3C 36
Wickham Av. B'frd —6J 97
Wickham Clo. B Spa —2C 36
Wickham St. Leeds —3G 103
Wickham St. Schol —6B 116
Wicking La. Sower B —1B 140
Wide La. Morl —4B 120
Wide La. Oakw —1C 56
Wigan St. B'frd —6K 79 (4B 6) (in two parts)
Wigeon App. Morl —3C 120
Wiggan La. Hud —5K 145
Wighill La. Wltn —5G 19
Wightman St. B'frd —4C 80
Wignall St. Kei —1K 39
Wigton Chase. Leeds —6C 50
Wigton Ga. Leeds —5A 50
Wigton Grn. Leeds —5B 50
Wigton Gro. Leeds —5A 50
Wigton La. Leeds —5A 50
Wigton Pk. Clo. Leeds —5B 50
**Wike. —2F 51**
Wike La. Bard —1H 51
Wike La. Hare —7D 32
Wike Ridge Av. Leeds —6D 50
Wike Ridge Clo. Leeds —5D 50
Wike Ridge Ct. Leeds —5D 50
Wike Ridge Fold. Leeds —5C 50
Wike Ridge Gdns. Leeds —6D 50
Wike Ridge Gro. Leeds —6D 50
Wike Ridge La. Leeds —6D 50
Wike Ridge M. Leeds —6D 50
Wike Ridge Mt. Leeds —6D 50
Wike Ridge Vw. Leeds —6D 50
Wilby St. Cleck —1F 135
Wilcock La. Sils —5B 8
Wilday Clo. Bgly —5J 41
Wild Gro. Pud —6J 81
Wilfred Av. Leeds —5K 87
Wilfred St. Cytn —2D 96
Wilfred St. Leeds —5K 87
Wilfred Ter. Leeds —2A 102
Wilkinson Fold. Wyke —4J 115
Wilkinson Ter. B'frd —1F 97
Wilkinson Way. Otley —1G 27
Wilkin St. Kei —4K 39
Willan's Rd. Dew —7G 137
Willerton Clo. Dew —5B 138
Willgutter La. Oakw —2B 56
William Av. Leeds —5G 87
William Henry St. Brigh —5G 133
William Henry St. Shipl —4F 61
William Hey Ct. Leeds —3D 86
William Ri. Leeds —5G 87
Williams Ct. Fars —2B 82
Williams Dri. Steet —5D 20
Williamson St. Hal —7E 112
Williams Rd. Steet —5D 20
William St. B'frd —7A 80 (6D 6)
William St. Brigh —7G 133
William St. Butt —7F 97
William St. C'frd —6D 126 (nr. Lock La., in two parts)
William St. C'frd —6E 126 (nr. Wheldon Rd.)
William St. Chur —6C 102
William St. Denh —4B 76
William St. Dew —7J 137
William St. Fry —5J 127
William St. G'lnd —3H 143
William St. Leeds —2E 84
William St. Liv —4K 135
William St. Stain —5D 136
William St. S'ley —4B 82 (nr. Sun Fld.)
William St. S'ley —3D 82 (nr. Town St.)
William St. Tong —5F 99
William Vw. Leeds —5G 87
Willians Av. Rothw —7G 105
Willington St. W. Hal —2F 131
Willis St. Leeds —6A 86
Willoughby Ter. Leeds —1F 103
Willow App. Leeds —4E 84
Willow Av. B'frd —6C 62
Willow Av. Cliff —4D 36
Willow Av. Leeds —4E 84
Willow Bank. Hal —3E 130
Willow Clo. B'frd —7J 97
Willow Clo. Bur W —1A 26
Willow Clo. Gom —1K 135
Willow Clo. Guis —2G 45
Willow Clo. Hal —2B 130
Willow Clo. Leeds —4E 84
Willow Clough. Ripp —7F 141
Willow Ct. Bat —2G 137
Willow Ct. Pool W —4H 29
Willow Cres. B'frd —6C 62
Willow Cres. Cliff —4D 36
Willow Cres. Leeds —6H 87
Willow Cres. Sower B —3A 130
Willowcroft. Cleck —2E 134
Willow Cft. Men —6C 26
Willow Dene Av. Hal —3B 130
Willow Dri. B'frd —7J 97
Willow Dri. Hal —2B 130
**Willow Field. —2B 130**
Willowfield Av. Hal —3B 130
Willowfield Clo. Hal —2B 130
Willowfield Cres. B'frd —7C 62
Willowfield Cres. Hal —2B 130
Willowfield Dri. Hal —3B 130
Willowfield Lodge. Brigh —2E 144
Willowfield Rd. Hal —2B 130
Willowfield St. B'frd —6H 79
Willowfield Ter. Hal —3C 130
Willowfield Vw. Hal —2B 130
Willow Gdns. B'frd —6C 62
Willow Gdns. Guis —2G 45
Willow Gdns. Hal —3C 130
Willow Gth. Leeds —4E 84
Willow Gth. Av. Cro H —3A 20
Willow Gth. Av. Leeds —4K 69
Willow Gth. Clo. Leeds —4K 69
Willow Glade. Cliff —5D 36
Willow Gro. B'frd —6C 62
Willow Gro. Cliff —5D 36
Willow Gro. Kei —1J 57
Willow Gro. Kip —3K 107
Willow Hall Dri. Sower B —3B 130
Willow Hall Fold. Sower B —3B 130 (off Bairstow La.)
Willow Hall La. Sower B —3B 130
Willow Houses. Sower B —3B 130 (off Rochdale Rd.)
Willow La. Cliff —4D 36
Willow La. Guis —5B 44
Willow Mt. Hal —1D 114 (off Witchfield Hill)
Willow Mt. Sower B —3A 130 (off Overdale Mt.)
Willow Pk. Dri. Hal —1D 114
Willow Ri. Hal —2B 130
Willow Rd. Bat —4J 137
Willow Rd. Fars —3A 82
Willow Rd. Leeds —4E 84 (LS4)
Willow Rd. Leeds —6E 84 (LS12)
Willow Sq. Oult —2A 124
Willows, The. H'den —3F 59
Willows, The. I'wth —7C 94
Willows, The. Leeds —2J 67
Willow St. B'frd —5F 79
Willow St. Cleck —6F 117
Willow St. Hal —2E 130
Willow St. Sower B —4B 130
Willow Ter. Bat —4J 137
Willow Ter. Leeds —4G 85 (3B 4)
Willow Ter. Sower B —3A 130
Willow Tree Clo. Kei —6B 40
Willow Tree Gdns. Bgly —6C 42
Willow Tree Gdns. Bur W —7B 14
Willow Va. Weth —2H 17
Willow Vw. Sower B —3B 130 (off Bairstow Mt.)
Willow Vs. B'frd —6C 62
Willow Wlk. Liv —5J 135
Willow Well Clo. Leeds —5H 87
Wills Gill. Guis —2H 45
Will St. B'frd —2F 99
Wilman Hill. B'frd —5H 97
Wilmer Dri. B'frd —1G 79
Wilmer Dri. Shipl —7G 61
Wilmer Rd. B'frd —2G 79
Wilmington Gro. Leeds —2J 85 (1F 5)
Wilmington St. Leeds —3J 85 (1G 5)
Wilmington Ter. Leeds —3J 85
Wilmot Rd. I'ly —5C 12
Wilmur Mt. L'ft —2G 129
**Wilsden. —7G 59**
Wilsden Hill Rd. Wilsd —7F 59

Wilsden Old Rd.—Woodroyd Gdns.

Wilsden Old Rd. H'den —3F 59
Wilsden Rd. All —1J 77
Wilsden Rd. H'den —3F 59
Wilson Av. Steet —4D 20
Wilson Fold. Low M —2K 115
Wilson Grn. Sower B —4K 129
Wilson Hill. Bklnd —7J 141
Wilson Rd. Bgly —7K 41
Wilson Rd. Hal —3D 130
Wilson Rd. Wyke —3K 115
Wilson Sq. B'frd —4J 79
Wilson's Row. Meth —4K 125
Wilson St. B'frd —4J 79
Wilson St. C'frd —7C 126
Wilson St. Sut Cr —5A 20
Wilsons Yd. S'ley —4B 82
Wilson Wood St. Bat —6G 137
Wilson Yd. Leeds —5E 82
Wilton Gro. Leeds —6E 66
Wilton Ind. Ct. Bat —7D 118
Wilton Rd. I'ly —6A 12
Wilton St. B'frd —7K 79 (6C 6)
Wilton St. Brigh —5F 133
Wilton Ter. Cleck —1F 135
Wimborne Dri. All —4C 78
Wimborne Dri. Kei —3H 39
Winbrooke Ter. B'frd —5G 97
Winburg Rd. B'frd —1G 97
*Winchester Ho. Sower B —4A 130 (off Church Vw.)*
Winchester St. Leeds —6D 84
Windermere Av. Men —4C 26
Windermere Dri. Gar —7K 89
Windermere Dri. Leeds —5F 49
Windermere Rd. Bail —3F 61
Windermere Rd. B'frd —3E 96
Windermere Rd. Dew —5J 137
Windermere Ter. B'frd —3E 96
Winders Dale. Morl —1K 119
Windgate. Sils —2H 21
**Windhill. —5J 61**
Windhill Old Rd. B'frd & Shipl —3B 62
Winding Rd. Hal —1G 131
Winding Way. Leeds —6H 49
Windle Royd La. Hal —1A 130
Windmill App. Leeds —6A 104
Windmill Chase. Rothw —3G 123
Windmill Clo. Leeds —7A 104
*Windmill Cotts. Colt —6B 88 (off Colton La.)*
Windmill Ct. Leeds —6K 69
Windmill Cres. Hal —5A 114
Windmill Dri. Hal —5A 114
Windmill Fld. Rd. Rothw —3G 123
*Windmill Fold. Yead —4A 46 (off Windmill La.)*
Windmill Grn. Rothw —3G 123
Windmill Gro. Cleck —2K 135
**Windmill Hill. —7A 82**
Windmill Hill. B'frd —5G 97
Windmill Hill. Hal —6A 114
Windmill Hill. Pud —7A 82
Windmill La. Bat —2F 137
Windmill La. Birs —6E 118
Windmill La. B'frd —5J 97
Windmill La. Gild —1H 119
Windmill La. Hal —5A 114
Windmill La. Men —6F 27
Windmill La. Rothw —3G 123
Windmill La. Yead —5A 46
*Windmill Pl. Yead —5A 46 (off Windmill La.)*
Windmill Ri. Aber —6E 72
Windmill Rd. B'ham —7D 36
Windmill Rd. Leeds —6A 104
Windsor Av. Leeds —5K 87
Windsor Av. Sils —1F 21
Windsor Clo. Dew —5B 138
Windsor Clo. Kip —4A 108
*Windsor Ct. B'frd —1A 98 (off Swarland Gro.)*
Windsor Ct. Leeds —2A 68
Windsor Ct. Morl —3A 120
Windsor Cres. Hal —6C 112
Windsor Cres. Oakw —2D 56
Windsor Cres. Rothw —1G 123
Windsor Dri. Liv —6K 135
Windsor Gdns. Dew —5B 138
Windsor Grn. Gar —6B 90
Windsor Gro. Oakw —2D 56
Windsor Gro. T'tn —7H 77
Windsor Mt. Leeds —5K 87
Windsor Rd. Bat —6E 118
Windsor Rd. Dew —6A 138
Windsor Rd. Oakw —2D 56
Windsor Rd. Shipl —5H 61
Windsor St. B'frd —1C 98 (7H 7)
Windsor St. Hal —2G 131
Windsor Ter. Gild —7H 101
Windsor Vw. Dew —6B 138
Windsor Wlk. Bat —5F 119
Windsor Wlk. Hal —2G 133
Windy Bank La. Liv —3D 134
Windy Bank La. Q'bry —1F 113
Windy Gro. Wilsd —1H 77
Windy Ridge. T'tn —6G 77
Wine Tavern La. Sower B —5D 128
Wine Tavern Rd. Sower B —5D 128 (in two parts)
Winfield Dri. E Bier —1G 117
Winfield Gro. Leeds —1C 4
Winfield Pl. Leeds —3H 85 (1D 4)
Winfield Ter. Leeds —1D 4
Wingate Av. Kei —5H 39
Wingate Way. Kei —5H 39
Wingfield Ct. Bgly —7A 42
Wingfield Mt. B'frd —5D 80 (1K 7)
Wingfield St. B'frd —5D 80 (2K 7)
Winnipeg Pl. Leeds —6K 67
Winnow La. B Spa —3A 36
Winrose App. Leeds —7A 104
Winrose Av. Leeds —6K 103
Winrose Clo. Wyke —3J 115
Winrose Cres. Leeds —6K 103
Winrose Dri. Leeds —6K 103
Winrose Gth. Leeds —6A 104
Winrose Gro. Leeds —6A 104
Winrose Hill. Leeds —5A 104
Winslow Rd. B'frd —1G 81
*Winstanley Ter. Leeds —2E 84 (off Victoria Rd.)*
Winston Av. Cro H —3A 20
Winston Gdns. Leeds —7C 66
Winston Mt. Leeds —7C 66
Winston Ter. B'frd —1G 97
Winterbourne Av. Morl —1B 120
Winterburn La. Warley —1J 129
Winterburn St. Kei —3A 40
Winter Ct. All —2A 78
Winter St. Hal —3D 130
Winterton Dri. Low M —2J 115
Winthorpe Av. Thpe —5K 121
Winthorpe Cres. Thpe —5K 121
Winthorpe St. Leeds —6F 67
Winthorpe Vw. Wake —5A 122
Winton Grn. B'frd —1H 115
*Winton Ho. B'frd —2K 97 (off Hutson St.)*
*Winton Mill. Sower B —4A 130 (off Wharf St.)*
Wintoun St. Leeds —4K 85 (3G 5)
Wira Ho. Leeds —3K 65
Wistons La. Ell —2A 144 (in two parts)
**Witchfield. —1D 114**
*Witchfield Ct. Hal —1D 114 (off Shelf Moor Rd.)*
Witchfield Grange. Hal —1C 114
Witchfield Hill. Hal —1D 114
Witham Way. Gar —7A 90
Withens Hill Cft. Hal —7B 94
Withens New Rd. Hal —4H 93 (in two parts)
Withens Rd. Birs —5C 118
Withens Rd. Wains —4G 93
Within Fields. Hal —4A 132
Withins Clo. B'frd —4H 97
*Woburn Ho. B'frd —2K 97 (off Park La.)*
Woburn Ter. Cytn —2B 96
Wold Clo. T'tn —7H 77
Wolley Av. Leeds —3H 101
Wolley Ct. Leeds —3H 101
Wolley Dri. Leeds —3H 101
Wolley Gdns. Leeds —3H 101
Wolseley Rd. Leeds —4D 84 (in two parts)
Wolseley St. Cytn —1C 96
Wolston Clo. B'frd —4G 99
Womersley Pl. Pud —7B 82
Womersley Pl. S'ley —4K 81
Womersley St. Hal —1D 130
Woodacre Cres. Bard —7A 34
Woodacre Grn. Bard —6A 34
Woodacre La. Bard —6A 34
Woodale Av. B'frd —2D 78
Wood Av. Heck —3B 136
Woodbine Gro. B'frd —5D 62
Woodbine Rd. Hud —7H 145
Woodbine St. B'frd —6C 80 (3H 7)
Woodbine St. Hal —3E 130
Woodbine Ter. B'frd —5D 62
Woodbine Ter. Bmly —2G 83
*Woodbine Ter. H'fth —5G 65 (off Wood La.)*
Woodbine Ter. Leeds —6E 66
**Woodbottom. —4C 64**
Wood Bottom La. Brigh —3D 132
Woodbourne. Leeds —5E 68
Woodbourne Av. Leeds —3J 67
Woodbridge Av. Gar —4C 90
Woodbridge Clo. Leeds —7B 66
Woodbridge Cres. Leeds —6A 66
Woodbridge Fold. Leeds —7A 66
Woodbridge Gdns. Leeds —7A 66
Woodbridge Gth. Leeds —7B 66
Woodbridge Grn. Leeds —7B 66
Woodbridge Lawn. Leeds —7A 66
Woodbridge Pl. Leeds —7A 66
Woodbridge Rd. Leeds —7A 66
Woodbridge Va. Leeds —7A 66
Woodbrook Av. Hal —2A 112
Woodbrook Clo. Hal —2A 112
Woodbrook Pl. Hal —2A 112
Woodbrook Rd. Hal —2A 112
Wood Clo. Bail —2H 61
Wood Clo. Leeds —5J 67
Wood Clo. Rothw —1F 123
Woodcot Av. Bail —2K 61
Wood Ct. Chur —6D 102
Wood Cres. Rothw —1F 123
Wood Cft. Brigh —1F 145
Wood Cft. Sower B —5G 129
Woodcross. Morl —1A 120
Woodcross End. Morl —7A 102
Woodcross Fold. Morl —1A 120
Woodcross Gdns. Morl —1A 120
Woodcross Gth. Morl —7A 102
Wood Dri. Rothw —1E 122
**Woodend. —1K 125 (nr. Allerton Bywater)**
**Woodend. —5K 61 (nr. Shipley)**
Woodend. All B —1K 125
Wood End Clo. Hal —5F 131
Woodend Ct. B'frd —4B 98
Woodend Cres. All B —2K 125
Wood End Cres. Shipl —4K 61
Wood End La. Bklnd —3B 142
Woodfield Av. Bat —4E 136
Woodfield Av. G'lnd —2F 143
Woodfield Ct. Bat —6F 137
Woodfield Dri. G'lnd —3F 143
Woodfield Rd. Cull —5C 58
*Woodfield Ter. Pud —7D 82 (off Sheridan Way)*
Woodford Av. Hal —4H 131
Woodford Clo. All —5A 78
Woodgarth Gdns. B'frd —3H 99
Wood Gro. Leeds —6H 83
**Woodhall. —3J 81**
Woodhall Av. B'frd —5G 81
Woodhall Av. Leeds —6J 65
Woodhall Clo. S'ley —3J 81
Woodhall Ct. C'ley —7J 63
Woodhall Ct. Leeds —7B 88
Woodhall Cres. Hal —5E 130
Woodhall Cft. S'ley —3J 81
Woodhall Dri. Bat —4E 136
Woodhall Dri. Leeds —6J 65
Woodhall Gro. Meth —4H 125
**Woodhall Hills. —2J 81**
Woodhall Hills. C'ley —2H 81
Woodhall La. S'ley —2J 81
**Woodhall Park. —3K 81**
Woodhall Pk. N'wram —3A 114
Woodhall Pk. Av. S'ley —3J 81
Woodhall Pk. Cres. E. S'ley —4K 81
Woodhall Pk. Cres. W. S'ley —4J 81
Woodhall Pk. Dri. S'ley —4J 81
Woodhall Pk. Gdns. S'ley —4K 81
Woodhall Pk. Gro. S'ley —4J 81
Woodhall Pk. Mt. S'ley —3J 81
Woodhall Pl. B'frd —4G 81
Woodhall Rd. B'frd —5G 81
Woodhall Rd. C'ley —1J 81
Woodhall Ter. B'frd —4G 81
Woodhall Vw. B'frd —4H 81
Woodhams Clo. Yead —5A 46
Woodhead Clo. Hud —6J 145
Woodhead La. Brigh —7A 134
Woodhead La. Gild —7G 101
Woodhead Rd. Bat —4F 119
Woodhead Rd. B'frd —1H 97 (5A 6)
Woodhead St. Hal —7C 112
Woodhead St. Mar —2G 135
**Wood Hill. —6G 137**
Wood Hill. Rothw —1F 123
Wood Hill Ct. Leeds —7H 47
Wood Hill Cres. Leeds —1G 65
Wood Hill Gdns. Leeds —7H 47
Wood Hill Gth. Leeds —7H 47
Wood Hill Gro. Leeds —1G 65
Wood Hill La. N Clift —5G 15
Woodhill Ri. App B —4G 63
Wood Hill Ri. Leeds —7H 47
Wood Hill Rd. Leeds —1H 65
Woodhill Vw. Weth —3J 17
**Woodhouse. —6A 40 (nr. Keighley)**
**Woodhouse. —3G 85 (1A 4) (nr. Leeds)**
**Woodhouse. —1J 145 (nr. Rastrick)**
Woodhouse. Bgly —2A 60
Woodhouse Av. Hud —7H 145
Woodhouse Av. Kei —6A 40
**Woodhouse Carr. —2G 85**
**Woodhouse Cliff. —1G 85**
Woodhouse Cliff. Leeds —1G 85
Woodhouse Clo. E Ard —2H 139
Woodhouse Clo. Kei —6A 40
Woodhouse Dri. Kei —7A 40
Woodhouse Gdns. Brigh —1J 145
Woodhouse Gro. All —1A 78
Woodhouse Gro. Hud —7J 145
Woodhouse Gro. Kei —6A 40
Woodhouse Hall Rd. Hud —7J 145
**Woodhouse Hill. —7J 145 (nr. Brackenhall)**
**Woodhouse Hill. —4A 104 (nr. Hunslet)**
Woodhouse Hill. Hud —7J 145
Woodhouse Hill Av. Leeds —4A 104
Woodhouse Hill Gro. Leeds —4A 104
Woodhouse Hill Pl. Leeds —4A 104
Woodhouse Hill Rd. Leeds (in two parts) —4A 104
Woodhouse La. Brigh —2H 145
Woodhouse La. Hal —5E 130
Woodhouse La. K'gte & E Ard —5G 139
Woodhouse La. Leeds —2G 85 (1B 4)
Woodhouse Rd. Kei —6A 40
Woodhouse Sq. Leeds —5G 85 (5B 4)
Woodhouse St. Leeds —2G 85
Woodhouse Ter. B'frd —6A 98
Woodhouse Wlk. Kei —6A 40
Woodhouse Way. Kei —6A 40
**Woodkirk. —1C 138**
Woodkirk Av. Ting —7C 120
Woodkirk Gdns. Dew —2B 138
Woodkirk Gro. Wake —7D 120
Woodkirk Gro. Wyke —6J 115
Woodland Av. Swil —5E 106
Woodland Clo. B'frd —1C 78
Woodland Clo. Leeds —5A 88
Woodland Ct. Bgly —6J 41
Woodland Ct. Leeds —7C 68
Woodland Cres. B'frd —1B 78
Woodland Cres. Rothw —1F 123
Woodland Cres. Swil —5E 106
Woodland Cft. H'fth —2G 65
Woodland Dri. Brigh —5F 133
Woodland Dri. Hal —3B 130
Woodland Dri. Leeds —5K 67
Woodland Dri. Swil —5D 106
Woodland Gro. B'frd —7C 60
Woodland Gro. Dew —7D 136
Woodland Gro. Leeds —1A 86
Woodland Gro. Swil —5E 106
Woodland Hill. Leeds —5K 87
*Woodland Ho. B'frd —5E 62 (off Garsdale Av.)*
Woodland La. Leeds —5K 67
Woodland Mt. Leeds —1A 86
Woodland Pk. W'ford —3A 124
Woodland Pk. Rd. Leeds —7E 66
Woodland Ri. Leeds —5A 88
Woodland Rd. Leeds —5K 87
**Woodlands. —6G 113**
Woodlands. Bail —7A 44
Woodlands. E Ard —1J 139
Woodlands. I'ly —5D 12
Woodlands. Leeds —2A 68
Woodlands. Sower B —6H 129
Woodlands Av. Gom —6J 117
Woodlands Av. Hal —6G 113
Woodlands Av. Q'bry —5B 96
Woodlands Av. S'ley —4A 82
Woodlands Clo. App B —3H 63
Woodlands Clo. E Ard —1J 139
Woodlands Clo. I'ly —5K 11
Woodlands Clo. Leeds —3A 52
Woodlands Ct. Leeds —3B 66
Woodlands Ct. Pud —1C 100
Woodlands Cres. Gom —6J 117
Woodlands Cft. Kip —6B 108
Woodlands Dri. B'frd & Rawd —3H 63
Woodlands Dri. E Ard —1H 139
Woodlands Dri. Gar —7B 90
Woodlands Dri. Gom —6J 117
Woodlands Dri. Morl —1K 119
Woodlands Fold. B'shaw —2K 117
Woodlands Gdns. S'cft —5A 52
Woodlands Gro. Bail —2F 61
Woodlands Gro. Bgly —5B 60
Woodlands Gro. Hal —6G 113
Woodlands Gro. I'ly —5K 11
Woodlands Gro. Kip —6C 108
Woodlands Gro. Q'bry —5A 96
Woodlands Gro. S'ley —4A 82
Woodlands La. Dew —7D 136
Woodlands Mt. Hal —5G 113
Woodlands Pk. Gro. Pud —1B 100
Woodlands Pk. Rd. Pud —1B 100
Woodland Sq. Brigh —7J 133
Woodland Sq. Leeds —5K 83
Woodlands Ri. Haw —7E 56
Woodlands Ri. I'ly —5J 11
Woodlands Rd. Bat —7E 118
Woodlands Rd. Bgly —7C 42
Woodlands Rd. B'frd —5G 79
Woodlands Rd. Ell —1K 143
Woodlands Rd. Gom —6J 117
Woodlands Rd. Hal —6G 113
Woodlands Rd. Q'bry —5A 96
Woodlands St. B'frd —5J 79 (2A 6)
Woodlands Ter. B'frd —4G 79
Woodlands Ter. Oaken —2D 116
Woodlands Ter. S'ley —4A 82
Woodlands Vw. Kip —6C 108
Woodlands Vw. S'cft —4A 52
Woodland Ter. Leeds —5G 67
Woodland Vw. C'ley —5J 63
Woodland Vw. Leeds —5K 67
Wood Land Vs. Leeds —1B 88
Wood La. Bard —7B 34
Wood La. Bat —5H 137
Wood La. Bgly —4K 41
Wood La. B'frd —1A 80 (in two parts)
Wood La. Bmly —1G 83
Wood La. Chap A —5J 67 (in two parts)
Wood La. Dew —7G 137
Wood La. Hal —1D 110
Wood La. Head —7D 66
Wood La. Hip —6B 114
Wood La. H'fth —5G 65
Wood La. Leeds —5H 83
Wood La. N Farn —4H 101
Wood La. Oven W —6B 112
Wood La. Pud —5K 63
Wood La. Rothw —7D 104
Wood La. Scholes —7C 70
Wood La. S'wram —5B 132
Wood La. Sower B —5G 129
Wood La. Wltn —5E 18
Wood La. W'ford —1J 125
Wood La. Ct. Leeds —7E 66
Woodlea. B Spa —2D 36
Woodlea App. Mean —3F 67
Woodlea App. Yead —5H 45
Woodlea Chase. Mean —4F 67
Woodlea Clo. Yead —6H 45
Woodlea Ct. Leeds —7D 50
Woodlea Ct. Mean —4F 67
Woodlea Cft. Mean —3F 67
Woodlea Dri. Mean —3F 67
Woodlea Dri. Yead —6H 45
Woodlea Gdns. Mean —3F 67
Woodlea Gth. Mean —3F 67
Woodlea Grn. Leeds —3F 67
*Woodlea Gro. Leeds —3F 103 (off Woodlea St.)*
Woodlea Gro. Mean —3F 67
Woodlea Gro. Yead —5H 45
Woodlea Holt. Leeds —3F 67
Woodlea La. Leeds —3F 67
Woodlea Lawn. Mean —3F 67
Woodlea Mt. Leeds —3F 103
Woodlea Mt. Yead —5H 45
Woodlea Pk. Mean —3F 67
Woodlea Pl. Leeds —3G 103
Woodlea Pl. Mean —3F 67
Woodlea Rd. Yead —5H 45
Woodlea Sq. Mean —4F 67
Woodlea St. Leeds —3F 103
Woodlea Vw. Mean —4F 67
Woodlea Vw. Yead —6H 45
Woodleigh Av. B'frd —5A 98
Woodleigh Av. Gar —6J 89
**Woodlesford. —7A 106**
Woodlesford Cres. Hal —5K 111
Woodliffe Ct. Leeds —5J 67
Woodliffe Cres. Leeds —5J 67
Woodliffe Dri. Leeds —5J 67
Woodman Av. Ell —4K 143
*Woodman Ct. B'frd —7F 97 (off Pit La.)*
Woodman Ct. Butt —1E 114
Woodman St. Leeds —5J 87
Woodman Works. Ell —4K 143
Wood Mt. Hal —4D 130
Wood Mt. Rothw —1E 122
Woodnook Clo. Leeds —2H 65
Woodnook Dri. Leeds —2H 65
Woodnook Gth. Leeds —2H 65
Wood Nook La. Sower B —3A 130
Woodnook Rd. Leeds —1H 65
Wood Nook Ter. S'ley —4A 82
Woodpecker Clo. All —6B 78
Wood Pl. B'frd —5J 79 (BD8)
Wood Pl. B'frd —1J 79 (BD9)
Wood Rd. B'frd —2A 98
Wood Rd. Friz —1J 79
**Wood Row. —4F 125**
Wood Row. Meth —4F 125
Woodrow Cres. Meth —4E 124
Woodrow Dri. Low M —1A 116
Woodroyd Av. B'frd —4B 98
Woodroyd Dri. Hal —5D 112
Woodroyd Gdns. I'ly —6F 13
Woodroyd Gdns. L'ft —3H 129

A-Z Leeds & Bradford 205

Woodroyd Rd. *B'frd* —3A **98**
(in three parts)
Woodroyd Ter. *B'frd* —4B **98**
**Woodside.** —7F **113**
(nr. Halifax)
**Woodside.** —7G **97**
(nr. Shelf)
Woodside. *C'frd* —6J **127**
Woodside. *Kei* —2J **39**
Woodside. *Shipl* —4K **61**
Woodside Av. *Bgly* —5K **59**
Woodside Av. *Leeds* —3C **84**
Woodside Av. *Mean* —5F **67**
Woodside Av. *Shipl* —4E **60**
Woodside Clo. *Morl* —1A **120**
Woodside Ct. *H'fth* —4J **65**
Woodside Ct. *Leeds* —3K **65**
Woodside Cres. *Bat* —4E **136**
Woodside Cres. *Bgly* —5K **59**
Woodside Cres. *Hal* —6F **113**
Woodside Dri. *Bgly* —5K **59**
Woodside Dri. *Morl* —7A **102**
Woodside Gdns. *Morl* —7A **102**
Woodside Gro. *All B* —1K **125**
Woodside Gro. *G'lnd* —3G **143**
Woodside Gro. *Hal* —6G **113**
Woodside Hill Clo. *H'fth* —4J **65**
Woodside La. *Hud* —5H **145**
Woodside La. *Morl* —7A **102**
Woodside M. *Mean* —5F **67**
Woodside Mt. *Hal* —7F **113**
Woodside Pk. Av. *H'fth* —4H **65**
Woodside Pk. Dri. *H'fth* —4H **65**
Woodside Pl. *Hal* —6F **113**
Woodside Pl. *Leeds* —3C **84**
Woodside Rd. *B Spa* —3B **36**
Woodside Rd. *Hal* —7F **113**
Woodside Rd. *Sils* —1E **20**
Woodside Rd. *Wyke* —4J **115**
Woodside St. *All B* —1K **125**
Woodside Ter. *G'lnd* —3H **143**
Woodside Ter. *Hal* —6G **113**
Woodside Ter. *Leeds* —3C **84**
Woodside Vw. *Bgly* —5K **59**
Woodside Vw. *G'lnd* —3H **143**
(off Woodside Ter.)
Woodside Vw. *Hal* —6F **113**
Woodside Vw. *Leeds* —2C **84**
Woodsley Grn. *Leeds* —3F **85**
Woodsley Rd. *Leeds* —6C **62**
Woodsley Rd. *Leeds* —4E **84** (2A **4**)
Woodsley Ter. *Leeds*
—4G **85** (3A **4**)
Woods M. *I'ly* —5C **12**
Woodsome Est. *Bat* —4E **136**
Woods Row. *S'ley* —4C **82**
Woodstock Clo. *Leeds* —1D **66**
Woodstock Wlk. *B'frd* —7D **6**
Wood St. *All* —4C **78**
Wood St. *Bail* —3J **61**
Wood St. *Bat* —3G **137**
Wood St. *Bgly* —5J **41**
Wood St. *B'frd* —5J **79** (1A **6**)
Wood St. *Brigh* —6H **133**
Wood St. *C'frd* —7C **126**
Wood St. *Cleck* —1E **134**
Wood St. *Dew* —7H **137**
Wood St. *E Ard* —7K **121**
Wood St. *Ell* —3A **144**
Wood St. *Haw* —6E **56**
Wood St. *Heck* —5B **136**
Wood St. *H'fth* —2G **65**
Wood St. *Low M* —1K **115**
Wood St. *Morl* —2K **119**
Wood St. *Oss* —7D **138**
Wood St. *Steet* —5E **20**
Woodthorne Cft. *Leeds* —7C **50**
Woodtop. *Brigh* —3E **132**
Woodvale Clo. *B'frd* —1G **99**

Woodvale Cres. *Bgly* —6A **42**
Woodvale Gro. *B'frd* —1E **96**
Woodvale Rd. *Brigh* —5H **133**
Woodvale Ter. *H'fth* —5H **65**
Woodvale Way. *B'frd* —1E **96**
Wood Vw. *Bkby* —7D **144**
Wood Vw. *B'frd* —2K **79**
Wood Vw. *C'frd* —7A **126**
Wood Vw. *Cull* —2A **76**
Woodview. *Dlgtn* —7B **100**
Wood Vw. *Oaken* —3C **116**
Woodview Av. *Bail* —7B **44**
Wood Vw. Av. *C'frd* —7A **126**
Wood Vw. Bungalows. *C'frd*
—7A **126**
Wood Vw. Clo. *C'frd* —7A **126**
Woodview Clo. *H'fth* —7A **126**
Wood Vw. Cres. *C'frd* —7A **126**
Wood Vw. Dri. *B'frd* —3E **80**
Wood Vw. Gro. *Brigh* —4F **133**
Woodview Gro. *Leeds* —4H **103**
Woodview Mt. *Leeds* —4H **103**
Woodview Pl. *Leeds* —4H **103**
Woodview Rd. *Oakw* —7H **39**
Woodview St. *Leeds* —4H **103**
Woodview. Ter. *B'frd* —2K **79**
Wood Vw. Ter. *Chur* —6D **102**
Woodview Ter. *Kei* —7K **39**
(off Haincliffe Pl.)
Woodview Ter. *Leeds* —4H **103**
Woodville Av. *H'fth* —4H **65**
Woodville Ct. *Leeds* —3D **68**
Woodville Cres. *H'fth* —4H **65**
Woodville Gro. *Cro R* —4H **57**
Woodville Gro. *H'fth* —4H **65**
Woodville Gro. *Leeds* —5A **104**
Woodville Mt. *Leeds* —5A **104**
Woodville Pl. *B'frd* —1F **79**
Woodville Pl. *H'fth* —4J **65**
Woodville Rd. *Dew* —7H **137**
Woodville Rd. *Kei* —3K **39**
Woodville Sq. *Leeds* —5A **104**
Woodville St. *Hal* —6E **112**
Woodville St. *H'fth* —4J **65**
Woodville St. *Shipl* —4K **61**
Woodville Ter. *B'frd*
—1K **97** (7C **6**)
Woodville Ter. *Cro R* —4H **57**
(off Vernon St.)
Wood Vine St. *S'ley* —4A **82**
Woodway. *Bgly* —5K **59**
Woodway. *H'fth* —5G **65**
Woodway Dri. *H'fth* —5G **65**
Woodworth Gro. *Kei* —1K **57**
Wooler Av. *Leeds* —4G **103**
Wooler Dri. *Leeds* —4G **103**
Wooler Gro. *Leeds* —4G **103**
Wooler Pl. *Leeds* —4F **103**
Wooler Rd. *Leeds* —4F **103**
Wooler St. *Leeds* —4F **103**
Wool Exchange, The. —4E **6**
Wooller Rd. *Low M* —2K **115**
Woollin Av. *Ting* —3E **138**
Woollin Cres. *Ting* —2E **138**
Woolpack. *Hal* —1G **131**
Woolrow La. *Brigh* —2J **133**
Woolshops Sq. *Hal* —1G **131**
Wool St. *Bat* —3H **137**
Wool St. *Heck* —5B **136**
Wootton St. *B'frd* —2A **98**
Worcester Av. *Leeds* —3B **122**
Worcester Dri. *E Ard* —6J **121**
Worcester Dri. *Leeds* —3B **122**
Worcester Pl. *B'frd* —2C **98**
Worden Gro. *B'frd* —2E **96**
Wordsworth Ct. *W'ford* —4A **124**
Wordsworth Dri. *Oult* —4A **124**

Wordsworth Way. *Bgly* —6A **42**
Workhouse La. *G'lnd* —3H **143**
Workhouse La. *Hal* —1J **129**
Workhouse La. *Midg* —5D **110**
World's End. *Yead* —4A **46**
Wormald Lea. *B'frd* —3G **99**
(off Stirling Cres.)
Wormald Row. *Leeds*
—5J **85** (5E **4**)
Wormald St. *Liv* —5A **136**
Worrall St. *Morl* —4K **119**
Worsnop Bldgs. *Wyke* —3J **115**
Worsnop St. *Low M* —1K **115**
Worstead Rd. *Cro R* —3H **57**
Worth Av. *Kei* —2C **40**
Worth Bri. Rd. *Kei* —4C **40**
Worthing Head Clo. *Wyke* —4K **115**
Worthing Head Rd. *Wyke* —4J **115**
Worthing St. *Wyke* —4K **115**
Worthington St. *B'frd*
—5J **79** (2A **6**)
**Worth Village.** —3C **40**
Worthville Clo. *Kei* —6A **40**
Worth Way. *Kei* —5A **40**
Wortley Heights. *Leeds* —7D **84**
Wortley La. *Leeds* —7F **85**
Wortley Moor La. *Leeds* —7B **84**
Wortley Moor La. Trad. Est. *Leeds*
—7B **84**
Wortley Moor Rd. *Leeds* —6A **84**
Wortley Pk. *Leeds* —7D **84**
Wortley Rd. *Leeds* —6A **84**
Wortley St. *Bgly* —1B **60**
Wortley Towers. *Leeds* —7E **84**
(off Tong Rd.)
Wrangthorn Av. *Leeds* —2F **85**
Wrangthorn Pl. *Leeds* —2F **85**
Wrangthorn Ter. *Leeds* —2F **85**
Wren Av. *B'frd* —1E **96**
Wrenbeck Av. *Otley* —7J **15**
Wrenbeck Clo. *Otley* —7J **15**
Wrenbeck Dri. *Otley* —7J **15**
Wrenbury Av. *Leeds* —6H **47**
Wrenbury Cres. *Leeds* —6H **47**
Wrenbury Gro. *Leeds* —6J **47**
Wren Dri. *Morl* —4D **120**
Wren Hill. *Bat* —7E **118**
Wren Nest Rd. *Sower B* —5C **140**
Wren St. *Haw* —5F **57**
Wren St. *Kei* —3A **40**
Wrenthorpe La. *Wren* —7J **139**
Wrexhall Rd. *Dew* —6J **137**
Wrexham Rd. *Bur W* —1K **25**
Wright Av. *Oakw* —1F **57**
Wright St. *Oakw* —2F **57**
Wright St. *Sut Cr* —5A **20**
(off North St.)
Wrigley Av. *B'frd* —5D **98**
Wrigley Hill. *Hal* —2C **112**
Wroe Cres. *Wyke* —4J **115**
Wroe Pl. *Wyke* —4J **115**
Wroe St. *Dew* —7D **136**
Wroe Ter. *Wyke* —4J **115**
**Wrose.** —6K **61**
Wrose Av. *B'frd* —7C **62**
Wrose Av. *Shipl* —6K **61**
Wrose Brow Rd. *Shipl* —4K **61**
Wrosecliffe Gro. *B'frd* —4B **62**
Wrose Dri. *Shipl* —6K **61**
Wrose Gro. *B'frd* —6B **62**
Wrose Gro. *Shipl* —6K **61**
Wrose Hill Pl. *B'frd* —7K **61**
Wrose Mt. *Shipl* —6A **62**
Wrose Rd. *Shipl & B'frd* —6K **61**
Wrose Vw. *Bail* —7J **43**
Wrose Vw. *Shipl* —6K **61**
Wycliffe Clo. *Leeds* —7B **64**
Wycliffe Dri. *Leeds* —2K **67**
Wycliffe Gdns. *Shipl* —4G **61**

Wycliffe Rd. *Leeds* —7B **64**
Wycliffe Rd. *Shipl* —4G **61**
Wycoller Rd. *Wyke* —3J **115**
Wycombe Grn. *B'frd* —3G **99**
**Wyke.** —5J **115**
Wykebeck Av. *Leeds* —6F **87**
Wykebeck Cres. *Leeds* —5F **87**
Wykebeck Gdns. *Leeds* —5F **87**
Wykebeck Gro. *Leeds* —5F **87**
Wykebeck Mt. *Leeds* —6F **87**
Wykebeck Pl. *Leeds* —5G **87**
Wykebeck Rd. *Leeds* —5F **87**
Wykebeck Sq. *Leeds* —5F **87**
Wykebeck St. *Leeds* —5F **87**
Wykebeck Ter. *Leeds* —5F **87**
Wykebeck Valley Rd. *Leeds*
—3F **87**
Wykebeck Vw. *Leeds* —5F **87**
**Wyke Bottoms.** *Oaken* —3B **116**
**Wyke Common.** —5K **115**
Wyke Cres. *Wyke* —5K **115**
Wyke La. *Wyke* —5J **115**
Wykelea Clo. *Wyke* —4K **115**
Wyke Old La. *Brigh* —1H **133**
Wyncliffe Ct. *Leeds* —2J **67**
Wyncliffe Gdns. *Leeds* —2K **67**
Wyncroft Ct. *Bar E* —6J **71**
Wyncroft Gro. *B'hpe* —1K **47**
Wyncroft Ri. *Shipl* —7K **61**
Wyndham Av. *B'frd* —2B **80**
Wynford Av. *Leeds* —3B **66**
Wynford Gro. *Leeds* —3B **66**
Wynford Mt. *Leeds* —3A **66**
Wynford Ri. *Leeds* —3A **66**
Wynford Ter. *Leeds* —3A **66**
Wynford Way. *Low M* —6A **98**
Wynmore Av. *B'hpe* —1J **47**
Wynmore Cres. *B'hpe* —1K **47**
Wynmore Dri. *B'hpe* —1K **47**
Wynne St. *B'frd* —5H **79** (3B **6**)
Wynyard Dri. *Morl* —3K **119**
Wyther Av. *Kirks* —2K **83**
Wyther Dri. *Wyth I* —2A **84**
Wyther Grn. *Wyth I* —2A **84**
Wyther La. *Leeds* —2K **83**
Wyther La. Ind. Est. *Kirks* —2A **84**
Wyther Pk. Av. *Leeds* —4K **83**
Wyther Pk. Clo. *Leeds* —4K **83**
Wyther Pk. Cres. *Leeds* —4K **83**
Wyther Pk. Gro. *Leeds* —3K **83**
Wyther Pk. Hill. *Leeds* —3K **83**
Wyther Pk. Mt. *Leeds* —4K **83**
(in three parts)
Wyther Pk. Pl. *Leeds* —3K **83**
Wyther Pk. Rd. *Leeds* —4J **83**
(in three parts)
Wyther Pk. Sq. *Leeds* —4J **83**
Wyther Pk. St. *Leeds* —4K **83**
Wyther Pk. Ter. *Leeds* —4K **83**
Wyther Pk. Vw. *Leeds* —3K **83**
Wyvern Clo. *Bat* —2G **137**
Wyvern Clo. *B'frd* —1F **97**
Wyvern Pl. *Hal* —7C **112**
Wyvern Ter. *Hal* —7C **112**
Wyvil Cres. *I'ly* —5E **12**

**Y**arborough Cft. *N'wram* —3A **114**
Yardley Way. *Low M* —1A **116**
Yard No.4. *Bat* —7D **118**
Yarn St. *Leeds* —1A **104**
Yarra Ct. *Gild* —7H **101**
Yarwood Gro. *B'frd* —3E **96**
Yate La. *Oxe* —3E **74**
Yates Flat. *Shipl* —6K **61**
**Yeadon.** —4K **45**
Yeadon Dri. *Hal* —4A **132**
Yeadon Moor Rd. *Yead* —5C **46**
(in two parts)

Yeadon Row. *H'fth* —5G **65**
(off South Vw.)
Yeadon Stoops. *Yead* —5B **46**
(off Bayton La.)
Ye Farre Clo. *Brigh* —4G **133**
Yewbank Clo. *I'ly* —5A **12**
Yewbank Ter. *I'ly* —5A **12**
Yewdall Rd. *Leeds* —7B **64**
Yewdall Way. *B'frd* —6E **62**
Yew La. *Gar* —7B **90**
Yew Pk. *Brigh* —3E **132**
**Yews Green.** —3J **95**
Yew St. *Hud* —7G **145**
Yew Tree Av. *B'frd* —4D **78**
Yew Tree Clo. *Shipl* —6K **61**
Yew Tree Ct. *Liv* —3J **135**
Yew Tree Cres. *B'frd* —4E **78**
Yew Tree Cft. *L'ft* —6E **110**
Yew Tree Dri. *Rothw* —1C **124**
Yew Tree Gro. *B'frd* —4E **78**
Yew Tree La. *All* —5H **77**
Yew Tree La. *Leeds* —6C **88**
Yew Tree Rd. *Hud* —7A **144**
Yew Trees. *S'wram* —4A **132**
Yew Trees Av. *N'wram* —4A **114**
York Av. *Hud* —7F **145**
York Cres. *Bgly* —2A **60**
York Dri. *Bat* —2H **137**
York Dri. *Heck* —2B **136**
York Ga. *Otley* —6G **27**
York Gro. *Bat* —2H **137**
York Ho. *B'frd* —5E **62**
(nr. Billing Vw.)
York Ho. *B'frd* —5E **62**
(off Fairhaven Grn.)
York Ho. *Ell* —2K **143**
(off Gog Hill)
York Ho. Far —3B **82**
(off South Dri.)
York Ho. *Sower B* —4A **130**
(off Beech Rd.)
York Pl. *Cleck* —7F **117**
York Pl. *Leeds* —5H **85** (6C **4**)
York Pl. *Weth* —3J **17**
York Rd. *Bat* —2G **137**
York Rd. *Bur W* —1B **26**
York Rd. *Dew* —7K **137**
York Rd. *Leeds & Pot* —5A **86**
(in three parts)
York Rd. *Weth* —3K **17**
York Rd. Ind. Est. *Weth* —3K **17**
Yorkshire Car Collection Museum.
—3A **40**
Yorkshire County Cricket. —1D **84**
Yorkshire Dri. *B'frd* —5C **98**
Yorkshire Way. *B'frd* —3H **97**
York St. *Bgly* —2A **60**
York St. *B'frd* —6E **78**
York St. *Brigh* —7G **133**
York St. *C'frd* —7E **126**
York St. *Hal* —2F **131**
York St. *Leeds* —6K **85** (7G **5**)
York St. *Q'bry* —5H **95**
York Ter. *Hal* —6F **113**
York Towers. *Leeds* —5C **86**
Young's Ct. *Aber* —6E **72**
Young St. *B'frd* —5F **79**

**Z**ealand St. *B'frd* —2F **99**
Zermatt Gro. *Leeds* —6J **67**
Zermatt Mt. *Leeds* —6J **67**
Zermatt St. *Leeds* —6K **67**
Zermatt Ter. *Leeds* —6K **67**
Zetland Pl. *Leeds* —2B **86**
Zion Clo. *Hud* —7B **144**
Zion St. *H Bri* —6A **110**
Zion St. *Oss* —7C **138**
Zoar St. *Morl* —3A **120**

# HOSPITALS, HEALTH CENTRES and HOSPICES
## covered by this atlas
### with their map square reference

N.B. Where Hospitals, Health Centres and Hospices are not named on the map,
the reference given is for the road in which they are situated.

AIREDALE GENERAL HOSPITAL —4D **20**
Skipton Rd., Steeton, Keighley,
West Yorks. BD20 6TD
Tel: (01535) 652511

Airedale Health Centre —7J **127**
The Square, Castleford,
West Yorks. WF10 3JJ
Tel: (01977) 465700

Allerton Health Centre —5B **78**
Wanstead Cres.,
Allerton, Bradford,
West Yorks. BD15 7PA
Tel: (01274) 548577

Ardenlea Hospice (Marie Curie Centre) —6A **12**
Queen's Dri., Ilkley,
West Yorks. LS29 9QR
Tel: (01943) 607505

Ardsley Health Centre —7H **121**
Bradford Rd.,
East Ardsley, Wakefield,
West Yorks. WF3 2DN
Tel: (0113) 2537627

Baildon Health Centre —1J **61**
Cliffe Av., Baildon, Shipley,
West Yorks. BD17 6NX
Tel: (01274) 581086

Barkerend Road Health Centre —5E **80**
Barkerend Rd., Bradford,
West Yorks. BD3 8QH
Tel: (01274) 661353

Batley Health Centre —3G **137**
130 Upper Commercial St., Batley,
West Yorks. WF17 5ED
Tel: (01924) 479033

Beeston Hill Health Centre —3G **103**
Beeston Rd., Leeds. LS11 8BS
Tel: (0113) 2709721

Bingley Health Centre —1K **59**
Myrtle Pl., Bingley,
West Yorks. BD16 2TL
Tel: (01274) 569131

BINGLEY HOSPITAL —1B **60**
Fernbank Dri., Bingley,
West Yorks. BD16 4HD
Tel: (01274) 563438

Birkenshaw Health Centre —1J **117**
Town St., Birkenshaw, Bradford,
West Yorks. BD11 2HX
Tel: (01274) 682374

BRADFORD ROYAL INFIRMARY —4E **78**
Duckworth La., Bradford,
West Yorks. BD9 6RJ
Tel: (01274) 542200

Bramhope Health Centre —1J **47**
Tredgold Cres., Bramhope,
Leeds. LS16 9BR
Tel: (0113) 2672664

Brighouse Health Centre —6H **133**
Lawson Rd., Brighouse,
West Yorks. HD6 1NY
Tel: (01484) 712515

Burmantofts Health Centre —4A **86** (4K **5**)
Cromwell Mt.,
Leeds. LS9 7TA
Tel: (0113) 2953330

Castleford Health Centre —7D **126**
Welbeck St., Castleford,
West Yorks. WF10 1HB
Tel: (01977) 465755

CHAPEL ALLERTON HOSPITAL —7K **67**
Chapeltown Rd.,
Leeds. LS7 4SA
Tel: (0113) 262 3404

Chapeltown Health Centre —2A **86**
Spencer Pl., Leeds. LS7 4BB
Tel: (0113) 2407000

Clayton Health Centre —2C **96**
Station Rd., Clayton, Bradford,
West Yorks. BD14 6JA
Tel: (01274) 882043

Cleckheaton Health Centre —1G **135**
Greenside, Cleckheaton,
West Yorks. BD19 5AP
Tel: (01274) 873501

COOKRIDGE HOSPITAL —2J **65**
Hospital La., Leeds. LS16 6QB
Tel: (0113) 267 3411

CORONATION HOSPITAL (ILKLEY) —6C **12**
Springs La., Ilkley,
West Yorks. LS29 8TG
Tel: (01943) 609666

Denholme Health Centre —5B **76**
1 Longhouse La., Denholme,
Bradford, West Yorks. BD13 4NQ
Tel: (01274) 832878

DEWSBURY & DISTRICT HOSPITAL —6E **136**
Healds Rd., Dewsbury,
West Yorks. WF13 4HS
Tel: (01924) 465105

Drighlington Health Centre —1C **118**
Station Rd., Drighlington, Bradford,
West Yorks. BD11 1JU
Tel: (0113) 2852115

Eccleshill Health Centre —6F **63**
Rillington Mead, Bradford,
West Yorks. BD10 0ED
Tel: (01274) 612121

Edmund Street Health Centre —7K **79** (6C **6**)
26 Edmund St., Bradford,
West Yorks. BD5 0BJ
Tel: (01274) 728421

ELLAND BUPA HOSPITAL —2A **144**
Elland La., Elland,
W. Yorks. HX5 9EB
Tel: (01422) 375577

Ellen Royde Health Centre —2K **143**
Westgate, Elland, West Yorks. HX5 0BB
Tel: (01422) 373647

Elms Mental Health Resource Centre, The —6K **97**
55 Odsal Rd., Bradford,
West Yorks. BD6 1PR
Tel: (01274) 693161

Fartown Health Centre —7H **145**
Spaines Rd., Huddersfield. HD2 2QA
Tel: (01484) 536981

Frank Swire Health Centre —4D **112**
Nursery La., Halifax,
West Yorks. HX3 5TE
Tel: (01422) 355626

Gildersome Health Centre —1H **119**
Finkle La., Morley,
Leeds. LS27 7HL
Tel: (0113) 2954030

HALIFAX GENERAL HOSPITAL —5G **131**
Huddersfield Rd., Halifax,
West Yorks. HX3 0PW
Tel: (01422) 357171

Haworth Road Health Centre —1D **78**
130 Haworth Rd., Bradford,
West Yorks. BD9 6LL
Tel: (01274) 491181

HIGH ROYDS HOSPITAL —1D **44**
Bradford Rd., Menston, Ilkley,
West Yorks. LS29 6AQ
Tel: (01943) 876151

Holmewood Health Centre —3G **99**
Holme Wood Rd., Bradford,
West Yorks. BD4 9EJ
Tel: (01274) 681103

Holt Park Health Centre —6K **47**
Holt Rd.,
Leeds. LS16 7QD
Tel: (0113) 2951855

Hunslet Health Centre —2A **104**
24 Church St., Hunslet,
Leeds. LS10 2PE
Tel: (0113) 2771811

IDA & ROBERT ARTHINGTON HOSPITAL —2K **65**
Hospital La.,
Leeds. LS16 6QA
Tel: (0113) 267 3411

Ilkley Health Centre —6C **12**
Springs La., Ilkley,
West Yorks. LS29 8TH
Tel: (01943) 608118

Keighley Health Centre —5K **39**
Oakworth Rd., Keighley,
West Yorks. BD21 1SA
Tel: (01535) 606111

Kensington Street Health Centre —5G **79**
Whitefield Pl., Bradford,
West Yorks. BD8 9LB
Tel: (01274) 495631

Kippax Health Centre —4B **108**
Moorgate Dri., Kippax,
Leeds. LS25 7QT
Tel: (0113) 2874427

Kirkstall Health Centre —1A **84**
15 Morris La.,
Leeds. LS5 3DB
Tel: (0113) 2951160

Laura Mitchell Health Centre —1G **131**
Great Albion St., Halifax,
West Yorks. HX1 1YR
Tel: (01422) 363541

LEEDS BUPA HOSPITAL —5C **68**
Roundhay Hall, Jackson Av.,
Leeds. LS8 1NT
Tel: (0113) 2693939

LEEDS CHEST CLINIC —5J **85**
74 New Briggate,
Leeds. LS1 6PH
Tel: (0113) 2951100

Leeds Dental Institute —4G **85**
Clarendon Way,
Leeds. LS2 9LU
Tel: (0113) 2440111

LEEDS GENERAL INFIRMARY —4H **85**
Great George St.,
Leeds. LS1 3EX
Tel: (0113) 243 2799

LEEDS ROAD HOSPITAL —6D **80**
Leeds Rd., Bradford,
West Yorks. BD3 9LH
Tel: (01274) 494194

Liversedge Health Centre —3K **135**
Valley Rd., Liversedge,
West Yorks. WF15 6DF
Tel: (01924) 408138

Luddenden Foot Health Centre —1F **129**
Kershaw Dri.,
Luddenden Foot,
Halifax, West Yorkshire. HX2 6PD
Tel: (01422) 882988

LYNFIELD MOUNT HOSPITAL —3D **78**
Heights La., Bradford,
West Yorks. BD9 6DP
Tel: (01274) 494194

# Hospitals, Health Centres and Hospices

MALHAM HOUSE DAY HOSPITAL —4G **85** (4A **4**)
25 Hyde Ter.,
Leeds. LS2 9LN
Tel: (0113) 2926716

Manningham Health Centre —4K **79**
Lumb La., Bradford,
West Yorks. BD8 7SY
Tel: (01274) 724298

Martin House Hospice —3E **36**
Grove Rd., Boston Spa, Wetherby,
West Yorks. LS23 6TX
Tel: (01937) 844836

Meanwood Health Centre —6F **67**
548 Meanwood Rd., Leeds. LS6 4JN
Tel: (0113) 2951350

METHLEY PARK HOSPITAL —4E **124**
Methley La., Methley,
Leeds. LS26 9HG
Tel: (01977) 518518

MID-YORKSHIRE NUFFIELD HOSPITAL, THE —4H **65**
Outwood La., Horsforth,
Leeds. LS18 4HP
Tel: (0113) 258 8756

Morley Health Centre —3A **120**
Corporation St., Morley,
Leeds. LS27 9NB
Tel: (0113) 2522051

Mytholmroyd Health Centre —6A **110**
Thrush Hill Rd., Hebden Bridge,
West Yorks. HX7 5AQ
Tel: (01422) 884199

New Cross Street Health Centre —3K **97**
New Cross St., Bradford,
West Yorks. BD5 7AW
Tel: (01274) 731006

New Wortley Health Centre —7E **84**
15 Green La., Leeds. LS12 1JE
Tel: (0113) 2310626

NORTHOWRAM HOSPITAL —3A **114**
Hall La., Halifax,
West Yorks. HX3 7SW
Tel: (01422) 201101

Odsal Health Centre —6K **97**
55 Odsal Rd., Bradford,
West Yorks. BD6 1PR
Tel: (01274) 674952

Oulton Health Centre —1A **124**
Quarry Hill, Woodlesford,
Leeds. LS26 8SZ
Tel: (0113) 2821149

Overgate Hospice —3H **143**
30 Hullen Edge Rd., Elland,
West Yorks. HX5 0QY
Tel: (01422) 379151

Park Road Medical Centre —1A **98**
Park Rd., Bradford,
West Yorks. BD5 0SG
Tel: (01274) 227575

Pudsey Health Centre —6C **82**
18 Mulberry St., Pudsey,
West Yorks. LS28 7XP
Tel: (0113) 2953200

Queensbury Health Centre —6H **95**
Russell Rd., Queensbury,
Bradford, West Yorks. BD13 2AG
Tel: (01274) 882531

Rastrick Health Centre —2F **145**
Chapel Cft., Brighouse,
West Yorks. HD6 3NA
Tel: (01484) 714688

Reevy Hill Health Centre —6E **96**
50 Reevy Rd. W., Bradford,
West Yorks. BD6 3LX
Tel: (01274) 679605

Rothwell Health Centre —2G **123**
Stone Brig La., Rothwell,
Leeds. LS26 0UE
Tel: (0113) 2820520

ROYAL HALIFAX INFIRMARY —3F **131**
Free School La., Halifax,
West Yorks. HX1 2YP
Tel: (01422) 357222

ST CATHERINES HOSPITAL —3J **79**
St Mary's Rd., Bradford,
West Yorks. BD8 7QG
Tel: (01274) 227599

St Gemma's Hospice —2K **67**
333 Harrogate Rd.,
Leeds. LS17 6QD
Tel: (0113) 269 3231

ST JAMES'S UNIVERSITY HOSPITAL —3B **86** (2K **5**)
Beckett St., Leeds. LS9 7TF
Tel: (0113) 2433144

St John's Health Centre —1E **130**
Lightowler Rd., Halifax,
West Yorks. HX1 5NB
Tel: (01422) 341611

ST LUKE'S HOSPITAL —2K **97**
Little Horton La., Bradford,
West Yorks. BD5 0NA
Tel: (01274) 734744

ST MARY'S HOSPITAL —5K **83**
Greenhill Rd.,
Leeds. LS12 3QE
Tel: (0113) 2790121

Saint Street Health Centre —2G **97**
Saint St., Bradford,
West Yorks. BD7 4AB
Tel: (01274) 521378

SEACROFT HOSPITAL —4J **87**
York Rd., Leeds. LS14 6UH
Tel: (0113) 2648164

Shelf Health Centre —1C **114**
Shelf Moor Rd., Halifax,
West Yorks. HX3 7PQ
Tel: (01274) 691159

Shipley Health Centre —5G **61**
Alexandra Rd., Shipley,
West Yorks. BD18 3EG
Tel: (01274) 595611

SHIPLEY HOSPITAL —5G **61**
90 Kirkgate, Shipley,
West Yorks. BD18 3LT
Tel: (01274) 773390

Steeton Health Centre —5E **20**
Chapel Rd.,
Steeton, Keighley,
West Yorks. BD20 6NU
Tel: (01535) 65244

STONEY RIDGE HOSPITAL —7C **60**
Stoney Ridge Rd., Bingley,
West Yorks. BD16 1UL
Tel: (01274) 495737

Sunny Bank Medical Centre —5J **115**
Town Ga.,
Wyke, Bradford,
West Yorks. BD12 9NG
Tel: (01274) 424111

Thornton Health Centre —7J **77**
Market St.,
Thornton, Bradford,
West Yorks. BD13 3EY
Tel: (01274) 833441

Vulcan Street Health Centre —5F **99**
Vulcan St., Bradford,
West Yorks. BD4 9QU
Tel: (01274) 682082

Westwood House —5C **96**
Cooper La., Bradford,
West Yorks. BD6 3NL
Tel: (01274) 882001

WHARFEDALE GENERAL HOSPITAL —7H **15**
Newall Carr Rd., Otley,
W. Yorks. LS21 2LY
Tel: (01943) 465522

Wheatfields Hospice —7E **66**
Grove Rd., Headingley,
Leeds. LS6 2AE
Tel: (0113) 278 7249

Wilsden Health Centre —7G **59**
Townfield, Wilsden, Bradford,
West Yorks. BD15 0HT
Tel: (01535) 273227

Woodhouse Health Centre —2H **85**
Woodhouse St.,
Leeds. LS6 2SF
Tel: (0113) 2951400

Woodside Health Centre —1G **115**
Eaglesfield Dri., Bradford,
West Yorks. BD6 2PR
Tel: (01274) 675113

Woodsley Road Health Centre —3F **85**
3 Woodsley Rd.,
Leeds. LS6 1SG
Tel: (0113) 2951240

Wrose Health Centre —7B **62**
King's Rd., Bradford,
West Yorks. BD2 1QG
Tel: (01274) 633711

Yeadon Health Centre —4K **45**
17 South Vw. Rd., Yeadon,
Leeds. LS19 7PS
Tel: (0113) 2954280

YORKSHIRE CLINIC, THE —5C **60**
Bradford Rd., Bingley,
West Yorks. BD16 1TW
Tel: (01274) 560311